D1074932

The Built Form of Western Cities

Frontispiece: M.R.G. Conzen

The Built Form of Western Cities

Essays for M. R. G. Conzen on the occasion of his eightieth birthday

Edited by T. R. Slater

Leicester University Press
(A division of Pinter Publishers)
Leicester and London

First published in Great Britain in 1990 by Leicester University Press
(a division of Pinter Publishers)

Editorial offices
Fielding Johnson Building, University of Leicester, University Road,
Leicester, LE1 7RH, England

Trade and other enquiries
25 Floral Street, London, WC2E 9DS, England

British Library Cataloguing in Publication Data
A CIP catalogue record for this book is available from the British Library.

ISBN 0-7185-1295-2

Library of Congress Cataloging in Publication Data
A CIP catalogue record is available from the Library of Congress

Filmset by Mayhew Typesetting, Bristol, England

Printed and bound in Great Britain by
Biddles Ltd, Guildford and King's Lynn

Contents

Contributors

Dr Michael Barke, BA, Ph.D., Principal Lecturer, School of Geography and Environmental Sciences, Newcastle upon Tyne Polytechnic, UK

C. James Bond, BA, FSA, MIFA, freelance landscape historian, formerly Department of Museum Services, Oxfordshire County Museum, UK

John Bradley, MA, Director of the Urban Archaeology Survey of Ireland, Dublin, Eire

Professor Emeritus Harold Carter, MA, D.Litt., formerly Gregynog Professor of Human Geography, Department of Geography, University College of Wales, Aberystwyth, UK

Professor Michael P. Conzen, MA, Ph.D., Professor of Geography and Chairman, Committee of Geographical Studies, University of Chicago, USA

Dr Mike Freeman, BA, Ph.D., Location Planning Manager, Granada TV and Video; formerly School of Geography, University of Birmingham, UK

Dr George Gordon, MA, Ph.D., Director of Centre for Academic Practice, University of Strathclyde, UK

Dr Robert Haswell, BA, M.Sc., Ph.D., Senior Lecturer, Department of Geography, University of Natal, Republic of South Africa

Dr Marek Koter, Dr, Dr (habil.), Dean of Faculty of Biology and Earth Sciences, Institute of Economic and Political Geography, University of Łódź, Poland

Dr Peter J. Larkham, BA, Ph.D., Research Fellow, School of Geography, University of Birmingham, UK

Professor Dr Elisabeth Lichtenberger, Dr, Dr (habil.), Institut für Geographie, Universität Wien, Austria

Professor Aidan McQuillan, BA, Ph.D., Associate Professor, Department of Geography, University of Toronto, Canada

Ivor Samuels, AA Dip., M.Sc., RIBA, MRTPI, Chairman, Joint Centre for Urban Design, Oxford Polytechnic, UK

Dr Terry R. Slater, BA, Ph.D., Lecturer, School of Geography, University of Birmingham, UK

Professor Joan Vilagrasa i Ibarz, Dr, Professor Titular, Department de Geografia i Historia de l'Estudi General de Lleida, University of Barcelona, Spain

Dr Busso von der Dollen, Dr, Dr (habil.), Secretary of German Castles Association, Marksburg, Federal Republic of Germany

Dr Jeremy W. R. Whitehand, BA, Ph.D., Reader, School of Geography, University of Birmingham, UK

Preface

Birthday *Festschriften* are not common in British academic circles. In central Europe, by contrast, such offerings by colleagues and students, especially on the retirement of a well-known professor, is a frequent occurrence. Eightieth birthday *Festschriften* are uncommon everywhere, simply because few scholars reach this advanced age and still fewer remain active researchers as does the man honoured here. One reason for the dearth of celebratory essay collections in Britain is that they are disliked by publishers. My first acknowledgement must therefore be to Peter Boulton, former editorial director of Leicester University Press, for agreeing so readily to publish this book, and to his successor, Alec McAulay, who has seen it through the press. I am grateful, too, to Professor Nicholas Brooks for his suggestion that I approach Leicester and for his encouragement thereafter.

The idea for this celebratory volume for M. R. G. Conzen's eightieth birthday first germinated only a month or two before the event in 1987 and it was recognized from the beginning that it would be a belated tribute. Potential contributors were circulated and asked to agree to a strict timetable for the production of their chapter so that the book might appear before the eighty-second birthday of its recipient. Everyone approached agreed readily and the first contributions appeared on time. As is often the case in collective works, however, others did not, for a variety of understandable reasons from busy academic schedules being stretched too far, to the intervention of translation difficulties. The patience of those who finished their chapters in good time has been much appreciated. The book will therefore appear in print just in time for the celebration of Conzen's eighty-third birthday, a little belated, but we hope that he will value it just as much and we assure him that it remains an affectionate tribute to the friendship that he has given us over the years.

It is perhaps unusual that a *Festschrift* should contain no contributions from former students and only one from a former colleague at the University of Newcastle (and even that link was for a very brief period). It is a reflection both of the limited academic interest in the study of urban form, and the processes which lead to those forms, in the English-speaking world when compared with studies of the social and economic aspects of towns, and of the way in which most British scholars interested in the subject have come to it via M. R. G. Conzen's writing in the first instance, and only subsequently have met the man who inspired the interest. This is in part, therefore, a volume by researchers who have taken up the academic challenges, concepts, problems and techniques laid down by Conzen in his papers and monographs and in part a volume by friends for a friend, rather than a tribute from students and colleagues.

The built form of western cities is a volume of original essays specially prepared by their authors for this book. They are written to form a coherent whole which, at the same time, reflects the main themes developed by M. R. G. Conzen in his own writing. Only one paper has appeared elsewhere, and that not in the English language. It is therefore a book intended to advance its subject as well as to honour one of the founding fathers of urban morphology. It is also a book with an international authorship and an international outlook, as befits the man whom it honours. That has produced its own problems and I am indebted to authors who produced chapters in English where it was not their native language and who then patiently endured my many questions and queries as terminology and interpretations where checked and rechecked. In this respect, I am grateful, too, to Jens Röhrkasten of the School of History at the University of Birmingham for his assistance with final queries about some of the contributions originally in German.

Urban morphology in Britain is now most strongly established at the University of Birmingham, where the Urban Morphology Research Group is part of the School of Geography. I am especially indebted to my colleagues in that research group, past and present, for their help and advice as editing proceeded. Jeremy Whitehand and Peter Larkham, in particular, have read and commented upon many of the chapters for me. Professor Gordon Cherry, as Head of the School of Geography, has allowed me to draw extensively upon the facilities of the School to complete this volume and I am most grateful. A great debt is owed to Jean Dowling who redrafted many of the illustrations, while others were completed by Kevin Burkhill, both with their customary good humour. Geoff Dowling, ARPS provided photographic services, and successive versions of most chapters were word-processed by Margaret Smith, Lynn Ford and most particularly by Claire Fothergill.

Given the international dimensions of this book, I must also acknowledge the considerable help in enlarging my horizons, and the hospitality, which has been given by many of the overseas contributors. Similarly, to Deryck Holdsworth, now at Pennsylvania State University, who encouraged the book in its early stages, and to Anngret Simms of the University College, Dublin, and Dietrich Denecke of the University of Göttingen, who have done so much to bring together German-language and English-language historical geographers. All three would wish to add their birthday good wishes to those of the other contributors.

Each of those contributors have their own stories of knowing the man whom this book honours; some of those stories helped in the creation of the film whose text is transcribed in chapter two, but editorial privilege allows me to tell of my own first meeting with M. R. G. Conzen. I was a raw young lecturer nearly twenty years ago, nervously giving my first paper to the Institute of British Geographers' Annual Conference. There was a good audience, a number of interested questions at the end of the paper, before an older man stood and gave his name – Conzen, Newcastle. I froze, unbelieving that I had been discussing morphological aspects of the Cotswold town of Cirencester with the great man sitting in the audience. However, he could not have been kinder in his comments and afterwards was both generous in his praise and genuine in his interest. Within a few minutes Professor M. R. G. Conzen had become 'Con', and a valued friendship and collaboration had begun. That interest in both the work and in the individual is his hallmark, and has been for all his long life. It is his friends and fellow-researchers who offer this book as a birthday tribute back to him.

Terry R. Slater
Midsummer's Day, 1989

Figures

Part I

Introduction

1 Urban morphology in 1990: developments in international co-operation

T. R. Slater

The most pressing need in urban morphological research is to strengthen inter-disciplinary co-operation in relevant subjects and thereby to create the widest geographical basis for comparison. Besides that inter-disciplinary co-operation, we also need international co-operation. In that way we can create an ultimately universal frame of reference for comparative study. And comparative study in subjects like geography, or history for that matter, is indispensable for the development and furtherance of conceptual thinking in these fields. You are the ideal researcher if in every individual case you can see both the individual as well as the general.

M. R. G. Conzen (Slater 1988)

Despite the relative paucity in the number of its academic practitioners urban morphology has received more than its fair share of overviews in the past decade, the most recent having been published in 1987 (Whitehand 1987). This introduction, therefore, will not needlessly repeat what others have already chronicled. Rather, it attempts to trace the developing international network of researchers who are trying to live up to Conzen's call for the development of comparative study in urban morphology in order to further conceptual thinking. In doing so, it tries to set the chapters which go to make up this volume in a broader context and to point their significance in the furthering of conceptual development in urban morphological research. The beginning of a new decade is an apposite moment to consider progress and to point the way forward.

It is a perhaps appropriate, given M. R. G. Conzen's Germanic origins and the early development of urban morphological approaches in the German-speaking world, that the beginnings of one strand of current international co-operation can be found in the two Anglo-German seminars in urban historical geography that took place in Germany and Britain in 1982 and 1983. They took the form of a peripatetic field seminar in both instances and the morphological development of the medieval city core (the *Altstadt*) was one of the principal themes addressed in both meetings. The papers presented at the seminars have recently been published (Denecke and Shaw 1988) and represent an important body of evidence as to the methodologies and interests of a group of scholars interested in furthering international comparisons. More particularly, the volume should enable a wider group of

English-speaking geographers and historians to become more familiar with some of the techniques and ideas which are current in the German-speaking realm.

A third conference was held in 1988, in Germany. It took as its theme 'genetic urban quarters in the context of urban expansion'. The theme was not a familiar one to the British and Irish participants and some time had to be spent on defining terms and gaining an understanding of how and why this was a significant research focus in central Europe. The conference sought to examine some of the nineteenth- and twentieth-century developments in the larger cities of central Germany. This has, indeed, become a major research focus in German historical geography over the past decade as scholars have begun to describe the built form and the forces generating the townscape of the modern city. There has been a particular interest in planning history (Fisch 1988), which has paralleled the similar development of such interests in Britain and North America, an interest in the changing functional structures of industrial cities (Heineberg 1987; Heineberg and De Lange 1988; Pinkwart 1987) and, quite recently, an interest in the idealistic rebuilding plans of the National Socialist era (Lafrenz 1987). The outstanding characteristic of almost all this work is that it is focused strongly upon particular places and, almost always, upon places near to, or in which, the researcher is employed. This results in part from the federal organization of modern Germany, including its higher education system. The strong regional basis, and relative lack of wider comparative analysis and model building, is particularly noticeable to researchers from the English-speaking realm.

Town-plan analysis

The Anglo-German conferences have enabled British participants to gain a much clearer understanding of the unbroken tradition of town-plan analysis and morphological research amongst central-European geographers and thereby to better appreciate the intellectual origins of M. R. G. Conzen's work in Britain (Whitehand 1981). These plan studies can be found to a greater or lesser extent for the towns in each major geographical region of central Europe, with the researches of staff and students in that region's one or more university departments and institutes at its heart. To take one example, in southern Lower Saxony researchers in Hannover and Göttingen have provided a corpus of studies of the development of the towns in that region from early in this century. Thus, in 1913, an experimental fascicule devoted to the town of Holzminden was published as part of a proposed *Niedersächsischer Städteatlas* by P. J. Meier, a historian based in Hannover. This began the first analytical town-plan atlas in Germany and was followed, in 1922, by a complete volume of plans at a much larger scale devoted to *Die Braunschweigischen Städte*, some fourteen towns being analysed.

In the inter-war years, urban studies in the University of Göttingen were being encouraged by Hans Dörries who published a book (1925) on the development of three of the largest towns in the vicinity, including Göttingen, before he moved to Münster. One of his students, Helmut Sauertig, took up the torch in a masterly study of the town of Duderstadt (Sauertig 1940). The careful mapping of the building fabric, building age and land use as a background to plan interpretation very clearly presages Conzen's work in post-war Britain, though the Duderstadt study lacks the conceptual richness which is the hallmark of Conzen's work. A similar study emanated from the Göttingen department in 1951 when Arnold Beuermann's analysis of Hann. Münden was published and, again, this is distinguished by the detailed plot by plot mapping of the built form of the town. Such detailed urban mapping continues through to the present, as Dietrich Denecke's work on Einbeck demonstrates (Denecke 1971).

Two further recent stimuli to urban studies in this region have been the major international exhibition *Stadt im Wandel* held in Braunschweig in 1985, for which two substantial catalogue volumes of the exhibits and two volumes of urban essays were published, many with a morphological theme (Meckseper 1985) and, secondly, the 'Historic Towns Atlas' project, directed from Münster, which included the city of Goslar in its second published volume (Stoob 1979). The atlas is a European project effected by national committees but, with characteristic thoroughness, the German contribution began earlier than most other national fascicules, has progressed further, and has provided the most detailed analysis of the towns studied, with the exception of the recently published first Italian fascicule (Bochii 1986). As well as the national volumes of the historic towns atlas, the Münster institute has also been responsible for a plan atlas of the historic towns in Westphalia (Stoob 1975) and for the publication of an urban history research monograph series, *Städteforschung*. Some of the ideas and methodologies devised by the Münster group have been taken up in other projects, including, for example, the Rhineland Palatinate town plan atlas (Wensky and Krötz 1972-82) and a recent study by Fahlbusch (1984) which interprets the town plan of Duderstadt in the same mode as the plan atlas.

Finally, the stimulus to urban history and plan analytical studies provided by urban archaeology over the last two decades has been as important in Germany as in Britain. Within the Lower Saxony region, for example, excavations in cities badly damaged by war-time bombing, which have been undertaken as reconstruction and redevelopment proceeds, have been crucial in revising and refining interpretations of the development of places such as Braunschweig (Rötting 1985) and Hildesheim (Reuther 1985). The most substantial series of excavations in this region have taken place in the Hanseatic town of Lübeck, however, where the long-term excavation programme (Fehring 1980; 1985) has also been accompanied by a parallel historical research project.

These types of study were, and indeed still are, being carried out in other central-European regions. The most sophisticated outcome is the two studies of Vienna, by Bobek and Lichtenberger (1966) and by Lichtenberger (1977), where such plan-analysis studies are fully integrated with other aspects of the development of the city concerned and are presented using sophisticated cartographical illustrations. As chapter 2 makes clear, in the inter-war period Bobek's work at the University of Berlin was very influential in developing some of these analytical methods and presentational techniques, and work in this tradition continues at Berlin on several scales of investigation from the individual small town, such as Charlotte Pape's recent study of Spandau (Pape 1984), to the city-wide investigation represented by the *Topographischer Atlas Berlin* (Pape and Freitag 1987), or Hofmeister's volume on the development of the city (Hofmeister *et al.* 1985; Elkins 1988). There are also a number of comparative studies of regional groups of towns, though these are less common than they should be. Perhaps the best known are the investigations of the towns of the Dukes of Zahringen in the upper Rhine valley and Switzerland (Metz 1961; Hofer 1963; Hager 1966).

In Britain, town-plan studies were largely neglected in the 1970s, despite the framework for further comparative analytical work which Conzen's studies of Alnwick and Newcastle provided. The few contributions that were made are detailed in the introduction to chapter 4. Archaeologists and historians have been equally tardy in using plan evidence, and slow to accept it as a valid form of evidence. One of the most prolific archaeological researchers has been Jeremy Haslam, who has used plan analytical techniques to propose models of development for Anglo-Saxon towns in Britain (Haslam 1984a; 1984b; 1988). Few other archaeologists have been prepared to take their studies of early towns within particular counties beyond the basic collection of plans found in 'implications of development' reports (for example, Aston and Leech 1977; Rodwell 1974). Similarly, the vast quantity of data provided in Keene's historical study of medieval Winchester is not conceptualised in plan analytic form, though it would be possible to use the material in this way. One of the few exceptions to this neglect of plan analysis is Bond's research on the plan of medieval Pershore which accompanied an archaeological report on the town (Bond 1977). Subsequently he has worked on the medieval towns of Oxfordshire (Bond 1986). Chapter 5 in this book is a development of this research concentrating on the growth of one medieval planned new town in that county. He brings to this work the techniques of metrological analysis developed by Slater in the 1980s (Slater 1981; 1987; see also chapter 4). Metrological analysis was also used in the studies of the Zahringian towns referred to above, and has proved an important tool in the analysis of medieval rural settlements in northern England (Sheppard 1976), the techniques ultimately deriving from historico-geographical studies of rural settlements in Scandinavia. Another recent example in an urban context, and by an archaeologist, is Spearman's study of the plot pattern of medieval Perth (Spearman 1988). This is of particular interest as it was inspired by the author reading Conzen's Alnwick study and trying to develop some of the ideas presented there to understand the development of this important Scottish town whilst being unaware of the wider corpus of urban morphological literature and ongoing research.

Bradley's studies of the plan development of Irish towns illuminate another link in the developing international network of researchers interested in using town-plan analysis to better understand the development of medieval towns. He is Director of the Urban Archaeology Survey of Ireland and a member of the informal 'Dublin Historic Settlement Group' based at University College, Dublin. There he meets regularly amongst others with Anngret Simms, who is, like Conzen, an emigré German, and who has strong research interests in both urban and rural settlement form. Her fellow researchers, including Bradley, have thereby been exposed to both the main strands of the German-language literature and, in the case of historians and archaeologists, to Conzen's work with which she is familiar. Her editing, with Howard Clarke, of two volumes of papers on urban origins in non-Roman Europe (Clarke and Simms 1985) has been of great significance in bringing to the English-speaking literature some of the details of important urban research from northern Europe originally published in other languages. Bradley's comparison of the built form of planned Anglo-Norman towns in Ireland appears in that volume, and his contribution to this book provides a parallel study of pre-Norman towns. Though not a full plan analytic study, it makes use of Conzen's concept of the plan unit to hypothesize a chronology in the early development of these towns to which archaeological evidence can be related. It was for the same reason that Spearman was inspired to undertake his Perth study. Simms has also been instrumental, with John Andrews, in establishing the *Irish Historic Towns Atlas* under the auspices of the Royal Irish Academy. The publication of the first three fasicules (Andrews, Simms and Davies 1986; 1988) make clear that the lessons of the German atlases have been absorbed and further developed to produce analytical maps of high quality.

The third chapter in the first section of this book illustrates the importance of comparative studies in advancing understanding of processes and contextual factors in the evolution of complex medieval town plans. Such comparative study is still at an early stage in Britain and, for example, it is not yet possible to posit even broad regional distinctions. However, using comparative studies of towns in the West Midlands region, Slater is able to suggest alternative interpretations for the evolution of plan elements in the town of Ludlow. This town has loomed large in Conzen's published work and has been the subject of intensive historical study by a local research group. It is a particularly good laboratory for the testing of conceptual ideas therefore, and further work is in progress on its medieval development, on townscape evolution, and on townscape management.

Industrial cities

Thus far, the discussion has concentrated on the links between the German and English-speaking realms but there are, of course, other international dimensions, In particular, other parts of northern and central Europe are rather more closely linked to, and more familiar with developments in, the German-speaking realm than the English. In Poland, for example, studies of urban form are widespread and demonstrate their familiarity with plan analytical methods. Archaeologists and historians are familiar with the *urbs/suburbium* model (Leciejewicz 1976; 1985), and architectural historians and conservationists are familiar with the techniques of mapping the built fabric of towns developed by Bobek (for example, Biranowska-Kurtz 1985). In contrast, few geographers have shown an interest in studies of urban form. What interest there was in the post-war years was centred on the University of Wrocław where Stefan Golachowski had a network of international contacts which enabled recent research results to be circulated there with relatively little delay. These links included ones with Scandinavia, where important work on the metrological analysis of field systems was underway; with Germany, and with Britain, where he was in contact with M. R. G. Conzen. Golachowski's work included contributions on the position and size of urban market places and on town field systems (Golachowski 1956; Golachowski and Szulc 1963). His work was taken up by Janusz Pudełko, who produced a number of very detailed comparative studies on the planning of medieval towns in Lower Silesia based on the careful metrological analysis of plans (Pudełko 1959; 1960). Golachowski's early death in 1965 deprived this incipient group of morphologists of their international contacts, but other studies followed from Pudełko and, more recently, by Zobolewicz (1975).

Marek Koter was a student of Golachowski at Wrocław and has maintained an interest in matters morphological while teaching in the Institute of Economic Geography at Łódź. His detailed studies of that city as it exploded into growth in the second half of the nineteenth century include consideration of the plan development, the effect of the underlying field systems on the development process and, most important, a careful consideration of the plot development cycle, the inspiration for which came from reading about Conzen's burgage-cycle concept in the Alnwick study. The essence of that work forms the substance of chapter 6. It is an important contribution, as it is the first study to utilize the burgage-cycle concept for a city developed in the industrial era. His findings that all aspects of the development cycle are equally applicable to this later type of development (Koter and Wiktorowska 1976) is important in widening the applicability of the concept beyond use in towns with a medieval core. Koter had had no encouragement or contact with like-minded scholars until comparatively recently when a visit to Britain included a chance meeting with the members of the Urban Morphology Research Group at Birmingham.

Subsequent exchange visits have encouraged him to continue his work in this field.

The comparison which can be made between the processes which Koter describes in industrial Łódź and the plan evolution described by Haswell in the colonial city of Pietermaritzburg, though not made explicit, are quite striking, and clearly there is much scope for comparative studies to be undertaken on the plan processes occurring in grid-planned cities, particularly regarding the development cycle of plots and plan evolution. Those comparisons also extend to North America where, again, little morphological work has thus far been undertaken despite the early work of Leighly (1928; 1939) on the form of Scandinavian towns and his taught courses on urban morphology in the 1930s (Miller 1988). American urban geography has always been more interested in the social and economic dimensions of city development than built form. However, recently there has been an increase in publication on townscape themes, many of them with an explicitly morphological interest.

Three reasons for this new interest can be deduced. First, the international CUKANZUS conferences of historical geographers in the English-speaking realm, which have been held alternately in Britain and North America through the past two decades, have encouraged contact and the appreciation of alternative approaches and methods, including the morphological. Secondly, there is the influence of individuals trained in Britain in universities with a tradition of such urban geography. David Ward, for example, was one of the first of a whole series of students from Leeds who undertook studies of nineteenth-century city development, using the West Riding woollen textile towns as exemplars, under the guidance of Glanville Jones. His study of Leeds (Ward 1962) was followed by work on Boston when he arrived in America (Ward 1966). Similarly, Deryck Holdsworth had been a student at Newcastle, and was taught by M. R. G. Conzen, before going to Canada where both initial (Holdsworth 1981; 1986), and recent research in association with *The Historical Atlas of Canada* has a clear focus on plan processes and where, again, comparisons could be made with Koter's work in Poland. To Europeans, American cities are symbolized as different by the image of the skyscraper and much work on the architecture, economics and symbolism of skyscrapers has been undertaken. The most overtly morphological has been Gad and Holdsworth's studies of the development of Toronto office buildings (1987a; 1987b) and Holdsworth has also written on that most ubiquitous of American city-centre land uses, the parking lot (Holdsworth 1987).

Michael P. Conzen is the son of M. R. G. Conzen. He graduated from the University of Cambridge and, when he began his research in North America, at Madison, he concentrated largely on economic aspects of nineteenth-century city development. Only in the last decade has he begun work on the processes underlying American city form (Conzen 1980; 1987) and chapter 7 is an introduction to his large-scale project comparing the morphology of two very different American cities, Boston and Omaha. The processes described in the development of Omaha again provoke comparison with Koter's work, but there are also differences brought about by the uncontrolled speculative land market. This chapter is important for the way in which it attempts to systematize some of the development processes in a grid-planned city and should provide the basis for more detailed comparative work elsewhere.

A number of other themes familiar in the European literature have been taken up by American scholars, including the history of planning, where the work of Reps has long been pre-eminent (Reps 1965; 1967; 1979). Reps's concern has been with reconstructing the original plat of colonial or frontier towns using cartographic evidence as his main source. It therefore differs from Michael Conzen's work as exemplified by chapter 7, where processes of development are followed much more explicitly through to the modern townscape. Another important recent American study, using maps as the basic source but concerned with underlying development processes in both the plan and in building forms, is Moudon's study of the evolution of a small area of San Francisco in the twentieth century (Mouden 1986). Moudon had had no contact with M. R. G. Conzen's work but her research has remarkably close parallels with his conceptual framework. As a planner, she had entered the study of urban form via the morphological work being undertaken by urban design practitioners which will be described later. Again, the parallels in her study area with Koter's description of Łódź are clear, with intensification of plot coverage and adaptation of both initial plan and building forms. Its concern with conceptual principles and generalities makes it of more than average relevance, and it might well be seen in retrospect as one of the most important contributions to urban morphology in the 1980s.

A final American theme given recent prominence is study of the suburbanization process, from a plan perspective (Hovinen 1985), as well as from social and economic viewpoints, together with studies of legislation and housing form (Power 1984), and of zoning legislation (Power 1989). Garrett Power is a member of the Law Faculty of the University of Maryland and, not surprisingly therefore, has had little contact with geographers generally or those interested in urban morphology specifically. However, his interest in the legal aspects of urban development provided contacts with the Planning History Group and through those contacts he has recently spent a sabbatical year at Birmingham researching comparative estate development policies in Birmingham and Baltimore and thereby interacting with the members of the Urban Morphology Research Group.

People and buildings

Three main themes can be discerned in research work which has attempted to integrate social and humanistic themes with the built fabric of towns and two scales of investigation can also be discerned. First, there are socio-topographical reconstructions of towns such as those which are perhaps most easily accessible through the work of Dietrich Denecke (1987; 1988) in Germany. The first example of this sort of building repopulation study occurs in the town-plan atlas of Lower Saxony already referred to (Meier 1933), where the pattern of householders in the town of Hannover is reconstructed as it was in 1435. Such work is also being undertaken in Poland and in Sweden, and the Scandinavian *Historic Towns Atlas* (Degn 1983; Ahlberg and Hall 1983; Tuxen 1987) contains comprehensive data for the cities of Ribe, Uppsala and Odense. In Britain, only Keene's work on Winchester (1986) is of equivalent detail and the tradition is unrepresented in this volume.

The second theme is what might be called the contextual. Serious attempts are made in these studies to understand the wider framework of society and national economy and their effects upon the built form of the city. Such work tends to be broad in scale, though concentration on one particular form element can be used to impose limits. Conzen's study of British towns in the industrial era (1978) is an example, and Lichtenberger's study of Vienna (1977) is perhaps the best known of such investigations. Chapter 11 exemplifies her approach in the context of housing development in that city. It is of interest that Lichtenberger does not see the form of central-European cities in the same way as Conzen. To her the application of the term 'middle-ring housing' to the areas of Vienna she describes, or indeed to the equivalent areas of Berlin or Munich or Warsaw, is inappropriate. To her, the formation, plan and built form, and the social differentiation of their residents, are so different as to constitute a very distinctive city type in the late nineteenth century and in the inter-war period which should not be described in the same ways as the British industrial city. In descriptive terms this is probably true and, clearly, there are different formative processes and contextual themes to be kept to the fore. However, in conceptual terms there are clear equivalents between the form of the central-European city and its British equivalent.

Gordon's chapter 10 says much the same for the Scottish city through the examples of Edinburgh and Glasgow. The Scottish city is a recognizably distinctive regional entity with form and plan complexes (again housing stands out) which are different to those in the rest of Britain. There are also distinctive contextual factors that affect the timing of particular developments but, overall, there are more similarities than differences when the scale of investigation is sufficiently generalized as Gordon, himself, recognizes. Clearly, housing is one of the most distinctive variants in the detailed form of industrial and modern cities. There is an extensive literature which examines housing form, its developmental history, the detailed and contextual factors which affect its built form, and which provides some cross-cultural comparisons. However, there are very few attempts as yet to provide broad-based conceptual frameworks for the study of housing in the industrial era. One noteworthy exception is Lawrence's work on housing in the French-speaking cantons of Switzerland (Lawrence 1986). The distinction between private and public space, both within tenement housing and in housing layouts, is a significant organizing principle, and more work at this methodological and conceptual level would refine explanations of both the distinctiveness of regional types and of individual cities.

The third approach is the investigation of the agents of change in the townscape. This was presaged twenty years ago in Harold Carter's exploratory study of the decision-makers behind the resort development of Llandudno (Carter 1970). Chapter 9 expands this idea, and Carter contends that this is a necessary reorientation of plan studies away from idiomatic form descriptions towards an examination of the processes of plan formation and transformation. He is critical, particularly, of historically layered texts where plans are seen as developing in chronologically distinct periods and where differences between periods are emphasized more than similarities. Few of the authors in this volume would disagree with Carter's premise and the whole thrust of urban morphological research undertaken in Britain since Conzen's publications in the early 1960s has been precisely in the direction of process studies within the conceptual framework which he provided. Land ownership, and the underlying pattern of rural field divisions which make up the morphological frame for urban development, were an early focus of attention in the British literature, particularly in investigations of nineteenth-century residential growth. The group of researchers at Leeds, beginning with David Ward, has already been referred to, and Beresford's (1988) magisterial study of the development of that same city in the eighteenth and early nineteenth centuries is a recent example in a similar genre, though by an economic historian.

The other major theme in studies of the agents of change in the townscape is represented by much of the work undertaken in the 1980s by the Urban Morphology Research Group at Birmingham. In the early 1980s the interest was in town centres. A series of linked projects examined the interaction between townscape and the people and processes responsible for townscape change in the twentieth century. This work was led by Jeremy Whitehand, whose own research concentrated on the towns of Northampton, a free-standing market town some 100 km. from London, and Watford, a town developed in the twentieth century on the outer fringes of London. The main source of evidence was the building plans deposited with the local authority for planning control purposes, and many hundreds of these were examined to extract information about the changes proposed and the architects, owners and specialists responsible for those changes (Whitehand and Whitehand 1984; Whitehand 1984). Mike Freeman undertook a parallel study of the development processes in the comparable towns of Aylesbury and Wembley (Freeman 1988). Chapter 12 brings the results of these two major investigations together so as to make statements of more general import about town-centre fabric change in twentieth-century Britain.

Another Birmingham graduate student, Ian Thompson, has extended one aspect of these studies back into the nineteenth century (Thompson 1987). The West Yorkshire town of Huddersfield has building control records going back to 1869, and these were utilized to study shop replacement and shop-front modification in the centre of that town between 1869 and 1939. He argues that shop facades were an important means by which new stylistic components were introduced into provincial town centres, and that many of the processes of change detailed by Freeman and Whitehand for the twentieth century were already under way by the last quarter of the nineteenth century.

Fringe belts

The transfer back to the German-speaking world of the conceptual ideas developed by Conzen in England in the 1950s and 1960s had not commenced before the late 1970s. One of the first examples of such a conceptual transfer, when the process eventually began to happen, was the paper that appeared in the first volume of the new German-language, multi-disciplinary journal *Siedlungsforschung*, and which is here translated as chapter 15 (Von der Dollen 1980). Von der Dollen was aware of Conzen's work and had met him and other English scholars on a visit to Britain seeking comparative material for his principal research interest in the field of conservation and townscape management. His paper was an important attempt to use the fringe-belt concept to understand the developmental history of medium-sized German towns. It is not, however, a straightforward transfer of the concept and care is taken to integrate other important themes in the German-speaking literature. To an English-speaking reader the chapter will be almost equally of value for its careful definition of the morphogenetic regions of medieval and early modern central-European towns in the context of the *urbs/suburbium* model (Ennen 1972). This is as unfamiliar to most English-speaking researchers as Conzen's concepts are to the German-speaking. One important difference which Von der Dollen's chapter points to in the development of central-European cities compared with those in Britain is the development of distinctive planned residential quarters from the mid nineteenth century onwards. In terms of his fringe-belt analysis, the model of successive fringe-belt generation posited by Conzen and by Whitehand (1967, 1975) continuing through to the present is, if not refuted by Von der Dollen, at least somewhat watered down in the suggestion that the current urbanization of the countryside has led to the cessation of fringe-belt formation.

In almost complete contrast, Vilagrasa's chapter attempts to broaden the fringe-belt concept to include particular kinds of housing development, namely the illegal and public-sector social housing, which were developed on the fringes of Spanish cities throughout the twentieth century. He argues that fringe-belts are characteristic of urban areas growing up at times of weak economic development and that, in the Mediterranean context, these types of housing are developed at the fringe at precisely these times. He also pays particular attention to the process of land development and the motives and actions of the agents of urban change to gain a clear understanding of the resultant town plan, thereby echoing Carter's call for further studies in this mode. Von der Dollen, too, emphasises a similar point with respect to the development of the inner fringe-belt of the medieval towns with which he was working. In terms of international comparison, the provision of evidence from the southern European context by Vilagrasa is an important addition to the literature. It is of interest to note that both Vilagrasa and Von der Dollen were initially inspired by Conzen's writing, developed their research on their own, and then came to Britain to meet him and other researchers in the field in order to further develop their ideas. Vilagrasa has recently begun a true comparative research project on city-centre redevelopment in two comparable towns in Britain and Spain.

In the English-speaking world research on fringe-belts has been dominated by the economic bid-rent model devised and refined by Whitehand through the 1970s and summarized recently by him (Whitehand 1988). It is in this tradition that Barke's study of the effects of urban size on fringe-belt formation is argued. Economic models, and the copious graphs and statistical tables that accompany them, may not have the immediate appeal of the maps, drawings and photographs that so often illustrate other types of morphological analysis. However, there is no doubt of their power of explanation and, as Barke suggests in his conclusion, some of the explanation of the differences in the environment, townscape and quality of life experienced in small towns compared with large is to be found in investigations such as that provided in this chapter. Hierarchical models and central-place theory have not yet been significantly integrated into explanations of the variations in the form of cities. This is true of both the Germanic literature, where Christaller's work was taken up with enthusiasm as an antidote to the unsatisfying morphographic analysis which had begun to dominate the urban research literature in the late 1930s and, even more so in the English-speaking world, where central-place theory became one of the foundation stones of the new model-building geography spearheaded by American urban geographers in the late 1950s and adopted enthusiastically elsewhere soon after. Barke's chapter is therefore an important corrective of this lack of integration. Further work is in progress by Slater on integrating hierarchical explanations into understanding medieval plan families in Britain.

Townscape management

The literature on urban conservation increases exponentially each year. It ranges from the description of individual schemes in particular towns to cross-national comparisons, and from simple evolutionary explanations of legislation (Dobby 1978) to complex understandings of culture and society (Lowenthal 1985). What is distinctively lacking is a wider theoretical or philosophical underpinning for the practicalities of conservation planning. Conzen's papers on townscape management (Whitehand 1981) are an exception to this neglect of theory but his ideas have not been further developed. Indeed, it is rare to find even a case study of a particular place which is refined by reference to plan classification. McQuillan's chapter 18 in this book is therefore unusual in that respect. It is unusual, too, in that it examines the conservation of the built form of colonial cities in a post-colonial era, comparing San Juan and Zanzibar. McQuillan is another case of an emigré European using his Irish academic training in a North American context. His writing reflects a broad experience in the practicalities of conservation consultancy work for a variety of planning authorities in many parts of the world.

Townscape management has been at the forefront of recent work by some members of the Urban Morphology Research Group at Birmingham. Larkham, in particular, has used the large-scale data-gathering techniques developed in Whitehand's studies of city-centre change, to examine built fabric change in conservation areas in British cities. Building control data provide an effective source for monitoring change but even such basic monitoring is neglected by most British planning authorities and few, if any, have positive and effective means of managing urban conservation areas. Larkham's chapter 16 surveys these problems in the light of Conzen's incomplete ideas for townscape management, using particular examples drawn from the small towns of the West Midlands.

Whitehand himself, together with a group of co-researchers, has also been developing ideas on townscape management. In this instance the focus of interest has been centred on change in upper-income housing areas developed in the inter-war or immediate post-1945 period. These areas are now being subjected to pressure for more intensive development because of their characteristic initial low densities with large houses and extensive gardens. Second-cycle development varies from small blocks of apartments, to estates of smaller houses on amalgamated plots. They can present problems of noise and overlooking for existing residents, and often produce a dramatically different townscape, but they can be extremely remunerative for those with plots suitable for development. Whitehand's chapter shows that British local authorities seldom have clear policies for dealing with such planning applications and their decisions are rarely affected by considerations of townscape continuity or appropriateness. There are comparisons to be made here with Moudon's work on San Francisco already referred to.

Similar changes are affecting cities in central Europe, but there the replacement of a large villa block by a block of modern apartments with similar massing provides more continuity in the townscape.

One of the problems in disseminating academic ideas on townscape management into the practical world of planning is their restriction at present to a relatively small group of academic geographers. The recent development of interest in what is called 'contextualism', by architects and planners who are concerned that modern replacement buildings should fit into their urban setting more acceptably than is often the case, demonstrates an interest in overall built form that could usefully bring the two groups together, but there is little sign of this happening so far. Contextualism is associated with the development of planning courses in urban design and one of the most prominent of these courses has been that developed at Oxford Polytechnic. It is of particular interest that urban morphological approaches are utilized in these courses but the ideas are not those of the Anglo-German school. Rather, ideas developed in Italy over the past forty years and extensively put into practice by Italian town planners and architects have been carefully examined. Thus far, there has been little translation of these ideas into other European language realms.

One of the principal exponents of this Italian school of planning morphologists was Gianfranco Caniggia. He taught and practised successively at Genoa, Florence and Rome so that theory and practice went hand in hand. The theory and terminology of this Italian school were derived from the earlier work of Muratori, and Malfroy has recently (1986) provided a detailed discussion of the work of this Muratorian school with parallel texts in French and German. The same volume also contains Caniggia's detailed analysis of the city of Florence using these principles. Samuels' chapter 19 in this volume provides one of the first discussions of this work to appear in English. It is particularly valuable as it shows the clear parallels between this Italian urban design morphology and Anglo-German academic approaches. Interaction between these two groups of urban morphologists should prove to be particularly fruitful and offers hope for the development of a practical, theoretically grounded approach to townscape management.

Urban morphology in the 1990s

This chapter has attempted to chronicle some of the developing international linkages between scholars who are interested in the built form of cities, the evolution of that built form, the processes which lead to particular built forms, and the management of historical townscapes to integrate past forms with present social and economic needs. This book is a further step towards developing those international links and bringing them to a wider audience. It remains to try to provide some pointers for research co-operation in the coming decade which might act as a checklist for audit at the end of the century.

Undoubtedly the two biggest challenges facing this community of scholars are, first, the integration of the two major schools of conceptual thought: on the one hand, the Anglo-German, historico-geographical group following the precepts developed by M. R. G. Conzen and, on the other, the Italian, architectural planning group following the precepts developed by Muratori and Caniggia. Secondly, there is the challenge of presenting these scholarly analyses in a way in which they can be utilized by those professionals, developers and public servants who have responsibility for managing the development of the townscape, as well as educating the public and politicians as to the significance of inherited townscapes.

Given the comparatively small number of researchers in the English-speaking world who are conversant with the complexities of even one of the two major schools of thought, and the continuing limitations of language barriers, it seems likely that the integration of the two academic schools of thought is likely to be a long-drawn-out process. Even between English- and German-speaking worlds, where recent progress in international co-operation has perhaps been strongest, only the very beginnings of a proper understanding of the scientific terminology of townscape processes and regionalization has begun to emerge. Some progress has also been made between German and Italian realms but there has been little co-operation as yet between Italian and English. The one major review of the conceptual writing on urban morphology, surveying the literature of both the geographical and the architectural groups and all three language realms, was published in French (Choay and Merlin 1986), thus further complicating the linguistic pot! None the less, some progress has been made in the 1980s and this must be expected to continue in the coming decade, particularly given the European Community's commitment to educational programmes with a Europe-wide dimension. The advent of an *Urban Morphology Newsletter* (Slater 1987–9) has also begun to bring workers in this research field into closer contact and to bring relevant projects quickly to notice.

European co-operation is important because of the variety of urban forms in this region and the very long history of the development of those forms. However, in many parts of the world it is the simpler, and more rapidly changing forms of the colonially-derived grid-plan city which is of greater significance and the continuance of the nascent North American interest in the processes and forms of this type of city development need to be nurtured and enhanced. The beginnings of a still wider international co-operation and comparison have also begun to bear fruit recently as Japanese historical geographers have made contact with their western counterparts. Despite the enormous cultural differences in these two realms there are many points of comparison between the development of complex western cities and equally complex and ancient oriental ones.

In terms of providing a practicable programme for the management of townscape change, urban morphology is perhaps even further from successful co-operation across the bounds of occupational specialism, at least in Britain, than it is in breaking the barriers of language and subject specialism. It is not so in the German-speaking world, and still less so is it true in Italy. The best strategy here would seem to be through co-operation with urban design practitioners who have a direct input into the planning profession. However, it also requires that an easily applicable method of urban survey and analysis be developed in conjunction with management techniques for all parts of the developing townscape. At present, relatively few planning authorities in Britain so much as monitor trends in the variety of development applications they receive in terms of their impact on the built form of the city. The programme for future action is therefore an onerous one for both pure and applied researchers. However, the city is one of the more significant of the physical manifestations of civilization's temporal advances and retreats, reflecting, perhaps more than anything else, the spirit of past societies and economies, polities and theologies for the present inhabitants, and as such it is worth taking some time and trouble both to understand it and to care for it.

References

Ahlberg, N. and Hall, T., 1983. 'Uppsala', *Scandinavian atlas of historic towns No. 4* (Odense).

Andrews, J. H., Simms, A. and Davies, K. M. (eds.), 1986–88. *Irish historic towns atlas No. 1, 2, 3* (Dublin).

Aston, M. and Leech, R., 1977. *Historic towns in Somerset.*

Beresford, M. W., 1988. *East End, West End: the face of Leeds during urbanisation 1684–1842* [Publications of the Thoresby Society, 131–2].

Beuerman, A., 1951. *Hann. Münden, das Lebenbild einer Stadt* [Niedersächsiches amt für landesplanung und statistik A1 *37*] (Hannover).

Bobek, H. and Lichtenberger, E., 1966. *Wien: Bauliche Gestalt und Entwicklung seit der Mitte des 19 Jahrhunderts* (Graz).

Bochii, F., 1986. 'Carpi', *Atlante Storico delle città Italiane No. 1* (Bologna).

Bond, J., 1986. 'The Oxford region in the Middle Ages', in *The archaeology of the Oxford region*, ed. G. Briggs, J. Cook and R. T. Rowley, 135–59.

Buranowska-Kurtz, A., 1985. 'Zabytkowy zespoł Drezdena w Świetle Najnowszych badań', *Kwartalnik Architektury i Urbanistyki, 30*: 27–50.

Carter, H., 1970. 'A decision making approach to town plan analysis: a case study of Llandudno', in *Urban essays: studies in the geography of Wales*, eds. H. Carter and W. K. D. Davies, 66–78.

Choay, F. and Merlin, P., 1986. *A propos de la morphologie urbaine, I rapport de synthese* (Paris).

Clarke, H. B. and Simms, A., 1985. *The comparative history of urban origins in non-Roman Europe* [Br. Archaeol. Reports, International Series, *255*].

Conzen, M. P., 1980. 'The morphology of nineteenth-century cities in the United States', in *Urbanization in the Americas: the background in comparative perspective,* ed. W. Borah (Ottawa) 119–41.

Conzen, M. P., 1987. 'The progress of American urbanism, 1860–1930', in *North America: the historical geography of a changing continent*, ed. R. D. Mitchell and P. A. Groves (Totowa) 360–72.

Conzen, M. R. G., 1978. 'The morphology of towns in Britain during the industrial era', in *Probleme des Städtewesens im industriellen Zeitalter*, ed. H. Jäger (Cologne) 1–48.

Degn, O., 1983. 'Ribe 1500–1950', *Scandinavian atlas of historic towns No. 3* (Odense).

Denecke, D. and Shaw, G., 1988. *Urban historical geography: recent progress in Britain and Germany*.

Dobby, A., 1978. *Conservation and planning*.

Dörries, H., 1925. *Die Städte im oberen Leinetal Göttingen, Northeim und Einbeck* (Göttingen).

Elkins, T. H., 1988. *Berlin: the spatial structure of a divided city*.

Ennen, E., 1972. *Die europäische Stadt des Mittelalters* (Göttingen).

Fahlbusch, F. B., 1984. 'Die Wachstumsphasen von Duderstadt bis zum übergang an Mainz 1334–66', in *Civitatum Communitas, Studienzum europäischen Städtewesen*, eds. H. Jäger, G. Petri and H. Quirin (Cologne) 194–212.

Fehring, G. P., 1980. 'Quellen, Methoden, Ziele und Problematik eines archäologisch-historischen Forschungsprojektes zur Hansestadt Lübeck', *Lübecker Schriften zur Archaeologie und Kulturgeschichte, 4*: 9–15.

Fehring, G. P., 1985. 'The archaeology of early Lübeck: the relation between the Slavic and German Settlement sites', in Clarke and Simms, *op. cit.*, 267–88.

Fisch, S., 1988. *Stadtplanung im 19. Jahrhundert* (Munich).

Freeman, M., 1988. 'Developers, architects and building styles: post-war redevelopment in two town centres', *Transactions, Institute of British Geographers, N.S. 13*: 131–47.

Gad, G. and Holdsworth, D., 1987a. 'Corporate capitalism and the emergence of the high-rise office building', *Urban Geography, 8*: 212–31.

Gad, G. and Holdsworth, D., 1987b. 'Looking inside the skyscraper: the measurement of building size and occupancy in Toronto office buildings, 1880–1950', *Urban History Review, 16*: 176–89.

Golachowski, S., 1956. 'Głos w dyskusji nad genezą rozplanowania średniowiecznego Wrocławia', *Kwartalnik Architektury i Urbanistyki, 1*: 67–78.

Golachowski, S. and Szulc, H., 1963. 'Rozłogi miejskie jako przedmiot badań historyczno-geograficznych', *Acta Universitatis Wratislaviensis, 9*: 37–53.

Hager, R., 1966. *The Zähringer new towns, a catalogue* (Thün).

Haslam, J., 1984a. 'The development and topography of Saxon Cambridge', *Proceedings of Cambridgeshire Antiquarian Society, 72*: 13–29.

Haslam, J., 1984b. 'The towns of Wiltshire', in *Anglo-Saxon towns in southern England*, ed. J. Haslam, 87–148.

Haslam, J., 1988. 'The Anglo-Saxon *burh* at *Wigingamere*', *Landscape History, 10*: 25–36.

Heineberg, H. (ed.), 1987. *Innerstädtische differenzierung und prozesse im 19. und 20 Jahrhundert* [Städteforschung. A/25] (Cologne).

Heineberg, H. and De Lange, N., 1988. 'The persistence and dynamics of office functions in West German cities since the late nineteenth century', in Denecke and Shaw, *op. cit.*, 211–35.

Hofer, P., 1963. 'Die Stadtgründungen des Mittelalters zwischen Genfersee und

Rhein', in *Flugbild der Schweizer Stadt*, eds. J. Boesch and P. Hofer (Bern) 85–102.

Hofmeister, B., Pochur, H-J., Pape, C. and Reindke, G. (eds.), 1985. *Berlin: Beitrage zur Geographie eines Grossstadtraumes* (Berlin).

Holdsworth, D. W., 1981. 'House and home in Vancouver: the emergence of a West Coast urban landscape, 1886–1929' (Ph.D. thesis, University of British Columbia).

Holdsworth, D. W., 1986. 'Cottages and castles for Vancouver home-seekers', *BC Studies, 69–70*: 11–32.

Holdsworth, D. W., 1987. 'Architectural expressions of the Canadian national state', *The Canadian Geographer, 30*: 167–71.

Hovinen, G. R., 1985. 'Suburbanization in Greater Philadelphia 1880–1941', *Journal of Historical Geography, 11*: 174–95.

Keene, D., 1986. *Survey of medieval Winchester.*

Koter, M. and Wiktorowska, D., 1976. 'Proces przemian morfologicznych Śródmieścia Łodzi (w granicach bytej kolonii Tkackiej) pod wptyem Ksztattowania się Ogólnomiesjskiego Centrum Ustugowego', *Acta Universitatis Lodziensis*, Ser II *7*: 41–88.

Lawrence, R., 1986. *Le seuil franchi: logement populaire et vie quotidienne en Suisse romande, 1860–1960* (Geneva).

Leciewicz, L., 1976. 'Early medieval sociotopographical transformations in West Slavonic urban settlements in the light of archaeology', *Acta Poloniae Historica, 34*: 7–28.

Leciewicz, L., 1985. 'Polish archaeology and the medieval history of Polish towns', in H. B. Clarke and A. Simms (eds.), *op. cit.*, 335–54.

Leighly, J., 1928. 'The towns of Mälardalen in Sweden: a study in urban morphology', *University of California Publications in Geography*, *3*: 1–134.

Leighly, J., 1939. 'The towns of medieval Livonia', *University of California publications in Geography*, *6*: 235–313.

Lichtenberger, E., 1977. *Die Wiener Altstadt: von der mittelalterlichen Bürgerstadt zur City* (Vienna).

Lowenthal, D., 1985. *The past is a foreign country.*

Malfroy, S., 1986. 'Introduction à la terminologie de l'école muratorienne avec une référence particulière aux ouvrages méthodologique de Gianfranco Caniggia', in *L'approche morphologique de la ville et du territoire*, S. Malfroy and G. Caniggia (Zurich) 18–260.

Meckseper, C. (ed.), 1985. *Stadt im Wandel, Kunst and Kultur des Bürgertums in Norddeutschland 1150–1650* (Stuttgart).

Meier, P. J. (ed.), 1922. *Niedersächsischer Städteatlas 1. Die Braunschweigischen Städte* (Hannover).

Metz, F., 1961. 'Die Zähringerstädte', in *Festschrift Friedrich Metz zum 70. Geburtstag* (Stuttgart).

Miller, D. H., 1988. 'John Leighly, 1895–1986', *Annals of the Association of American Geographers, 78*: 347–57.

Moudon, A. V., 1986. *Built for change: neighborhood architecture in San Francisco* (Cambridge, Mass.).

Pape, C., 1984. *Die Spandauer Altstadt* (Berlin).

Pape, C. and Freitag, U. (eds.), 1987. *Topographischer Atlas Berlin* (Berlin).

Pinkwart, W., 1987. 'Strukturmuster der Würzburger Innenstadt', in *Würzburg Stadtgeographische Forschungen*, eds. H. G. Wagner and W. Pinkwart [Würzburger Geographische Arbeiten, 68] 133–56.

Power, G., 1984. 'High society: the building height limitation on Baltimore's Mt. Vernon Place', *Maryland Historical Magazine, 70*: 197–219.

Power, G., 1989. 'The advent of zoning'. *Planning Perspectives, 4*: 1–13.

Pudełko, J., 1959. 'Rynki w planach miast Śląska', *Kwartalnik Architektury i Urbanistyki, 4*: 235–49.

Pudełko, J., 1960. 'Zagadnienie wielości i proporcji rynków w badaniach nad rozplanowaniem niektórych miast średniowiecznych', *Zeszyty Naukowe Politechnik Wrocławskiej*, 36: 25–45.

Reps, J. W., 1965. *The making of urban America: a history of city planning in the United States* (Princeton).

Reps, J. W., 1967. *Monumental Washington: the planning and development of the capital center* (Princeton).

Reps, J. W., 1979. *Cities of the American West: a history of frontier urban planning* (Princeton).

Reuther, H., 1985. 'Hildesheim als Kulturzentrum im 10. und 11. Jahrhundert', in C. Meckseper (ed.), *op. cit.*, 95–116.

Rodwell, K. (ed.), 1974. *Historic towns in Oxfordshire: a survey of the new county.*

Rötting, H., 1985. *Stadtarchäologie in Braunschweig* (Hameln).

Sauertig, H., 1940. *Stadtgeographie von Duderstadt* [Wirtschaftswissenschaftliche Gesellschaft zum Studium Niedersachsens, 55] (Oldenburg).

Sheppard, J., 1976. 'Medieval village planning in northern England: some evidence from Yorkshire', *Journal of Historical Geography*, 2: 3–20.

Slater, T. R., 1981. 'The analysis of burgage patterns in medieval towns', *Area, 13*: 211–16.

Slater, T. R., 1987. 'Ideal and reality in English episcopal medieval town planning', *Transactions, Institute of British Geographers, N.S. 12*: 191–203.

Slater, T. R., 1988. 'Conversations with Con', *Area, 20*: 200–3.

Slater, T. R. (ed.), 1987–9. *Urban Morphology Newsletter.*

Spearman, M., 1988. 'The medieval townscape of Perth', in *The Scottish medieval town*, eds. M. Lynch, M. Spearman and G. Stell, 42–59.

Stoob, H. (ed.), 1975. *Westfählischer Städteatlas I* (Dortmund).

Stoob, H. (ed.), 1979. *Deutscher Städteatlas II* (Dortmund).

Thompson, I. A., 1987. 'An investigation into the development of the building fabric of Huddersfield's CBD, 1869–1939' (Ph.D. thesis, University of Birmingham).

Tuxen, P., 1987. 'Stege 1500–1950', *Scandinavian Atlas of historic towns No. 5* (Odense).

Von der Dollen, B., 1980. 'Stadtrandphänomene in historisch-geographischer Sicht', *Siedlungsforschung, 1*: 15–37.

Ward, D., 1962. 'The pre-urban cadaster and the urban pattern of Leeds', *Annals of Association of American Geographers, 52*: 150–66.

Ward, D., 1966. 'The industrial revolution and the emergence of Boston's central business district', *Economic Geography, 42*: 152–71.

Wensky, M. and Krötz, W. (eds.), 1972–82. *Rheinischer Städteatlas* (Cologne).

Whitehand, J. W. R., 1967. 'Fringe belts: a neglected aspect of urban geography', *Transactions, Institute of British Geographers, 41*: 223–33.

Whitehand, J. W. R., 1975. 'Building activity and intensity of development at the urban fringe: the case of a London suburb in the nineteenth century', *Journal of Historical Geography, 1*: 211–24.

Whitehand, J. W. R. (ed.), 1981. *The urban landscape: historical development and management, papers by* M. R. G. *Conzen* [Institute of British Geographers, Special Publication, *13*].

Whitehand, J. W. R., 1984. 'Commercial townscapes in the making', *Journal of Historical Geography, 10*: 174–200.

Whitehand, J. W. R., 1987. 'Urban morphology', in *Historical geography progress and prospect*, ed. M. Pacione, 250–76.

Whitehand, J. W. R., 1988. 'Urban fringe belts: development of an idea', *Planning Perspectives, 3*: 47–58.

Whitehand, J. W. R. and Whitehand, S. M., 1984. 'The physical fabric of town centres: the agents of change', *Transactions, Institute of British Geographers, N.S. 9*: 231–47.

Zobolewicz, J., 1975. 'Rozplanowanie Starego Miasta w Toruniu, w swietle analizy metrologicznej', *Towarzstwo Miłonsników Torunia, Rocznik Toruńiski, 10*: 239–557.

2 Starting again: recollections of an urban morphologist

T. R. Slater

This chapter is an unusual one. It is not the review of an academic career which normally accompanies a *Festschrift*. Such a review, and an assessment of M. R. G. Conzen's academic work, has already been published by J. W. R. Whitehand (1981). Neither is it a full personal biography, though there is much biographical information; or a proper autobiography, though much of it uses Conzen's own words. Rather, the chapter seeks primarily to set down for a wider audience, and offer minimal interpretation of, large parts of a conversation video-recorded in November 1986, a few weeks before his eightieth birthday, between M. R. G. Conzen (Con, as he is known to his friends), myself, and J. W. R. Whitehand.

The inspiration for the recording came from Ann Buttimer's (1986) long-term project, *Explorations in Dialogue*, based at the University of Lund, and was modelled to conform to other tapes held in the project library. Some three hours of conversation was recorded in a single afternoon, after several days of preparatory talk between us, and this formed the basis for a final edited tape which plays for one hour. The edited tape can be borrowed from the Lund Library or copies can be purchased from Birmingham. The autobiographical words quoted in this chapter are taken from the original tapes, lightly edited where necessary to remove some conversational idioms, and partly rearranged to improve the narrative. Additional biographical information was obtained from further conversations, particularly over three happy days exploring the Welsh borders from Ludlow, with Con and Freda, his wife, in the summer of 1988. It is, in sum, part way to writing what Buttimer calls a 'life journey'.

It is only part way, because it is primarily concerned with the academic career path of its subject and the contexts and influences which affected that journey. It does not intrude more than necessary with those other aspects of any life journey – home and family. The filmed interview was shown at a session of the Institute of British Geographers conference in 1988 to an appreciative audience and their comments, together with those of the discussant, Anne Buttimer herself, have encouraged the further development of this material as a small contribution to the history of geography in the twentieth century, because, in part, that history is the combined life paths of all geographers.

Early years

M. R. G. Conzen was born in the Berlin suburb of Reinickendorf in January, 1907. He was the only child of German parents with strong practical and artistic skills. His grandfather was a porcelain painter of the highest quality who had been born in Köln but had moved first to Nürnberg, and then to a pottery in the Thuringian Forest near Coburg. At least two of his sons inherited artistic skills, one as an artist with a particular facility for pen and ink drawings, and Conzen's father who became a Classical sculptor. In his younger days Conzen's father travelled the country undertaking commissions for the aristocracy and gentry for busts, statues and decorative pieces but, after his marriage, he settled in Berlin and gained a more regular income by producing decorative sculpture for buildings and interior fitments such as marble ceiling roses, partly in Classical idiom, but also some *Jugendstil* (Art Nouveau) pieces. Some of his work survived the war-time destruction of Berlin.

At about the age of twelve, Conzen remembers, his father tried to interest him in stone carving but he was not a good teacher. However, Conzen recognizes the significance of this paternal artistic background on his later academic interests in that he inherited his father's 'propensity as a sculptor to see forms, shapes, colours, textures and so on. This, practised at first quite unconsciously, has stayed with me for life and is an obvious factor in my interest in the morphology of those things in the cultural landscape that have been my particular care.' Though his father failed to make a sculptor of him, his art master at school had more success and Conzen remembers being particularly inspired by the lessons on perspective. Practice was not as successful, however, as he began by trying to draw the school stairwell! Already, therefore, his family context was directing his interest towards the form of things.

During the poverty-stricken years of the First World War the family suffered great hardships as the building trade collapsed and builders reneged on their payments for his father's sculptures and fitments. They survived on what his mother earned as a skilled dressmaker providing garments for the aristocratic and professional classes of the city. By then they had moved to an apartment south of the city centre and, later, to the Halensee district near the woodland recreational areas further west. The constant fittings which his mother needed to have with her customers meant that the young Conzen often walked back from school not to home, but to the gentry houses where his mother was working. He thereby gained a knowledge of wide areas of the city suburbs. Another memory reflecting a developing interest in buildings is of a twelfth birthday present made by his father. This was a marionette theatre, modelled on the theatre at Delphi, complete with a proscenium of Classical columns and portico made in white hardwood, which was treasured for many years after.

Conzen remembers that, like many other children,

we were left hungry many a time in the last year of that war until Quaker meals came to the school. I got flat-footed as a result and I had a terrible gait. You could tell from way behind that I was flat-footed so, round about the age of twelve or thirteen, I decided I would get rid of it.

The war also led to some early journeys:

we began to be sent away in the summer, to the countryside, in order to recuperate and get sufficient food to eat. I remember being sent to East Prussia after Hindenberg had his great victory over the Russian Cossacks at Tannenberg and I was certainly very impressed as a boy of ten by the Masurian Lakes in the southern part of East Prussia.

There were frequent visits, too, especially after his father was called up for military service, to his grandfather's pottery in the Thuringian forest, which he remembers as an idyllic place. It was deep in the countryside and made everything from bathroom pieces to fine porcelain. His grandparents lived in the mill building and memories conjure up the sounds of mill machinery, running water, and the smells of the forest.

By the age of fourteen, Conzen was a member of one of the Free Youth Movements that were such a characteristic feature of the culture of the Weimar Republic. It provided the opportunity for seeing more of the countryside which he had grown to love, using maps, and for walking – to cure his 'gait'.

I was interested in maps from boyhood and, amongst my schoolfellows, I suppose I was practically the only one in the form who was knowledgeable with maps. I used them on all my hiking. Every weekend of the summer in some years we would be out in the countryside, mostly on our feet, camping or sleeping in the barn of a farmer overnight, getting up at 5.00 in the morning and we were off with our guitars, singing folk songs as we marched along. Quite naturally I connected everything that I saw with the interests that I was developing in geography. They were not specialized particularly – they were general, because the school encouraged us to see that in life it is best to look at all things around one, no matter how disparate they appear. It was absolutely marvellous for a shy boy who had been shut up from early childhood in a town.

This educational ideal of his school – to emphasize the connections between things; to view the world as a totality; to see the links between civilization and landscape – was not, of course, peculiar to that school but was part of the educational milieu of almost everyone growing up in central Europe at that time. The ideological clash with Modernism and the Berlin Bauhaus had begun but had not filtered down to secondary education. The developing interest in geography came, surprisingly, not from his teachers but from textbooks.

The teaching was so indifferent that during the few occasions when there were tests

I was dismal. I just hadn't done any of the work that I was expected to do and got low marks to the bitter end, whilst already knowing for at least three years that I would study geography at university. But the auxiliary text books we got to help us with the geography syllabus I found fascinating and, usually, when we got such a book, I was through it long before the rest of the class.

There was, however, a good history teacher who

brought a very vivid picture of a subject to which I might otherwise not have been attracted at all. All the more so because I never had a good head for dates and figures. At the time, I did not connect it with geography. However, there are many different things in human life and in human surroundings which will inevitably impinge on whatever specialisation in human geography one takes later – and history was a very powerful one.

Student days

When he began his studies in the Geographical Institute at the University of Berlin in 1926, Conzen was unaware that, fortuitously, he was entering one of the best departments of geography anywhere in the world at that time.

I went in Albrecht Penck's last year. He came from geology originally and built on the good start under Richthofen. Penck's lectures on geomorphology were absolutely irresistible; wonderfully fresh in delivery and in the amount of stuff he was able to put over – and, needless to say, without lecture notes.

Penck's lectures were often attended by as many as a thousand students, Conzen remembers, and he also heard Alfred Wegener lecturing on his revolutionary theories of Continental Drift.

Penck's teaching conformed to the organic world view that Conzen had already begun to absorb in his schooldays:

From the student's point of view, Penck built up a wonderful department in which a form of teaching was practised which was both characteristic of central European geography, but also peculiar to Penck. He was a man, like, much later, Wooldridge in England, for whom field observation was fundamental. When, long before my time as a student, Otto Schlüter had joined the department, he took a leaf out of his professor's book and insisted on field observations coming into human geography as well. I had been in the department in Berlin perhaps for six months or so when I discovered Schlüter in the literature. I realized that here was something that was not only imaginative but absolutely necessary in human geography. You can imagine that it suited my propensities; using your eyes to observe. It undoubtedly brought me into a morphological line, not exclusively at first, but very powerfully because this was my personal access to geography. [For a brief review of this work, see Whitehand 1981.]

Schlüter wrote some fundamental papers to do with the conceptual organization of geography as an organized field of knowledge. He took a leaf out of the physical geographers' early successes and progress in their systematic specialization and wanted the advantages of field observation to be used in cultural geography too. He was the founder of the whole school of *Kulturgeographie*. He had many, many Ph.D. students whose doctoral dissertations were published and so there was any amount of material available in the extremely good seminar library in Berlin and this, perhaps more than anything else, led me to settlement geography.

And so the pattern began to set. In terms of the trilogy of 'root metaphors' which Buttimer (forthcoming) uses to organize and interpret her academic life paths, the Conzen path of what she calls *Meaning* or vocational orientation, was already tending towards *logos*, towards research and intellectual inquiry. In terms of *Metaphor*, the poetic and artistic elements of his childhood education began to be substituted by Schlüter's scientific understanding and more rigorous analytical techniques and these were applied to both geomorphological problems, and, eventually, to settlements. The *Milieu*, or world view and contextual frame, adopted was not the organicism of Penck or, in Britain, of H. J. Fleure, and certainly not the mechanistic modernism of mathematical model-building in the way of Christaller. For Conzen it was the mosaic of the map and of forms, the sculptor's point of view, that held sway.

Herbert Louis, Penck's last graduate student, was another important early influence at Berlin and Conzen took note of his field teaching methods well before he got to know him personally:

He was a very good walker, very strong on his feet, and he would require from his students the same. Field excursions were not compulsory, they were voluntary, but they were so much sought after by students that there were always more applicants for an excursion than there were places. So I did a lot of solitary excursions on my own, with definite geographical tasks or subjects in mind, and in the meantime I had learned in the Youth Movement to become reasonably proficient in long-distance walking. I would go off on my own south-west of Berlin, right through the whole glacial series from terminal moraine through outwash plain, and so on, going out by the first train on Saturday morning and returning at about 11 p.m. on the Sunday, walking sometimes as far as 80 km., doing field observations as I went.

For one of these personal excursions, I remember, I went to Louis – because I was going to a well-known hiking area north of Berlin for several days – and asked him if he could suggest what I might usefully do in the area. He got a 1 : 25,000 topographical map out and asked me to look at it and said, 'What do you see on the map in terms of surface forms?' I said, 'Well, I see sickle-shaped hills there.' 'Do you know what they are?' 'I am afraid not.' 'Well,' he said, 'build yourself a clinometer from a protractor and a plumb weight and measure the slopes on either side of these hills at as many points as you feel are necessary; think about it, and see if you can make any sense of these slopes and how they behave as slopes as you measure one inclination after another.' Well, I wasn't a good enough geomorphologist to really make any sense of the measurements, but I did work very diligently, and I did think about it.

So it was settlement geography, not geomorphology, that became the main focus of interest, and it was the work of Schlüter's pupils at the University of Halle, particularly Geisler, which inspired it.

I very soon got hold of Geisler's book on the German town, *Die deutsche Stadt* [1924], and needless to say lapped up the morphology as fast as I could read. Indeed, much of my undergraduate work was undoubtedly very much conditioned by what I learned in that literature that emanated from Halle. So when I came to do my Diploma dissertation in geography, for preparation as a schoolteacher, I chose a subject in settlement geography and did a comparative study of some eleven towns on the River Havel in Brandenburg, which is the glacial country around Berlin. You will notice I said a *comparative* study, which was also something peculiarly central European.

Hans Bobek was the key figure here.

He must have been an assistant, I suppose, some kind of senior assistant, and he came to Berlin, I think, very soon after the rather fine doctoral dissertation that he had done on Innsbruck. He certainly helped me enormously, though he did not know about it until much later. There was an excursion he led, where we had to do field work in small groups, to the city of Brandenburg – a medieval city with large suburbs because it had industries. We were sent out by him to observe land use plot by plot, urban building types and that sort of thing. We used Geisler's classification of building types, I believe, and when we came back we had to map the individual work we had done onto an overall map for the department's manuscript map collection. In that way Dr Bobek gave me a particular impression of his ways of looking at towns and it was these methods that I took up for my own dissertation.

From refugee to planner

Dissertation completed in 1932, this diligent student was all set for a career in schoolteaching. But Hitler came to power and this first academic life fell to pieces.

I belonged to a free student organization that had moderate socialist leanings. The offices of our organization were raided by the SS, or the SA, I forget, and, as I came into the University one fine morning, the grapevine functioned and I was informed that all the membership records had been taken away. I went straight to the local police where I lived, got my passport to travel abroad for study purposes, wrote a letter to my future fiancée who was in London improving her English (and who, needless to say, was in the same student movement) telling her to stay in London and not to return on any account, then I hitch-hiked over two or three days to Hamburg. I got passage on a small boat from the Baltic, a Russian ship of all things, though I was far removed from Communism, and that brought me to Hays Wharf in London, where my fiancée was waiting. So there we were, refugees, no work permit, nothing, £10 in my pocket; enough for a fortnight, as the Immigration Officer said.

Conzen was already a good linguist; he had passed French, English and Latin in his school-leaving certificate and continued with his studies at University, so he could speak English well when he arrived in London. However, 'the first months were extremely hard. It was 1933, so unemployment was rife in Britain. I remember very distinctly groups of miners singing and begging in the street in London. But I did manage to teach Post Office girls German for their holidays.' He lodged where so many refugee generations before him had begun their new lives – in Bishopsgate, in London's East End, where East European and Soviet Jews predominated amongst 1930s immigrants. He kept sane, like so many other intellectual refugees before him, in the Reading Room of the British Museum, which he visited daily for six months. He also kept up his geographical studies by taking cheap Green-Line tickets out to the Chiltern Hills and Epping Forest at weekends to see anything that appeared interesting and to enjoy the countryside and fresh air.

He approached the International Student Service for help to complete his studies and gain a professional qualification but their adviser, 'a professor of geography, who was very interested in refugees', suggested that there was little hope of employment for a geography teacher in Britain as many such were already unemployed. The ISS suggested he might like to become a motor mechanic in Australia or New Zealand! Then, suddenly, the ISS asked him to come back to the office. Their adviser, who was H. J. Fleure, professor of geography at Manchester University, had written to say that there were openings in town and country planning. His colleague, R. A. Cordingley, professor of architecture, was just instituting the first Diploma course in England in town and country planning and Fleure suggested that Conzen might like to take this course. 'There were two students who entered and one of them was myself (the other was an architect). I said to the ISS, "If this planning is certain to get me a job, I will have to go." That took me to Manchester and opened up another professional field which I have found jolly useful.'

There was a chronic shortage of qualified town and country planners in the 1930s as new legislation began to demand the preparation of plans by local authorities. They commissioned this work from private planning consultancies, which architects quickly began to add to their more traditional services. Having gained his Diploma in the minimum two years, Conzen went immediately to work as an Assistant Chief Planner in the Cheshire firm of architects owned by one of the course lecturers, with a team of surveyors and an office of a dozen draughtswomen in his charge. He was responsible for dealing with the continuous stream of building applications for the county and was quickly appalled at the lack of any coherent conceptual organization in the planning system.

Hitler having been responsible for one change in the direction of Conzen's career also provided the impetus for the second – by starting the Second World War. As a result, he became an enemy alien overnight – an enemy alien, moreover, who was responsible for advising the Cheshire local authority on their civil defence procedures and the most suitable locations for air-raid shelters. The Chief Constable was apparently not amused! Conzen was arrested at 6 a.m. one morning but, after enquiries at the Home Office had revealed that his naturalization application of 1935 had at last been granted, he was released later the same day to the relief of Freda, by now his wife, who was already packing warm clothes for the internment camp. He remembers with gratitude the courtesy and consideration of the detectives at the police station.

He was free, therefore, but the planning work had to come to an end. Fleure came to the rescue once more by finding a temporary teaching post in a crammer school opposite the University geography department in Manchester for Conzen, and a secretarial post for Freda dealing with his Geographical Association business (Fleure was editor of *Geography*, the journal of the Association, and its Hon. Secretary). In the meantime the Manchester department was rapidly depleted as staff members were called up for war work, mostly with the Intelligence Service. Consequently, Fleure – 'was able to have the University engage me on a temporary basis because of these peculiar war-time circumstances. I took over the map library and did teaching in the cartography courses and gradually got into university teaching that way.' Eventually, he, too, was called up but the medical officer was not impressed and decided he would be of greatest service by remaining at the University.

On Fleure's advice, Conzen registered for an MA by thesis so as to be qualified for university teaching. He completed work on the historical geography of Chester that he had already begun during his town planning days and the thesis was successfully presented in 1942, the writing going on by day and fire-watching service at night. Conzen has a high opinion of Fleure. They got on well personally but he was not a strong influence on Conzen's work.

> He was not the type of person that exerted an active, strong influence from his side. He waited until students or colleagues responded to his general ways of thinking . . . I already had a strong intellectual basis, of course, that I had brought with me from Germany, but we understood each other very well . . . Fleure was very informal, very easy with his new staff member, and very soon we could often have conversations on aspects of cultural geography as he understood it. His approach influenced me in a very general way because he impressed me very much as an intellectual personality with a wide range of knowledge. He was very integrated, which appealed extremely to anyone coming from Germany with a German education where the emphasis *is* on integrating seemingly disparate things that in fact hang together. Fleure was such a man. He was in some ways, I suppose, almost like a polymath of the Renaissance.

For a decade Conzen's life path had been deflected from the foundations laid in Berlin in the late 1920s. His vocational orientation had had to be realigned from intellectual enquiry to the practicalities of planning in order to make a living. But it is noteworthy that the underlying curiosity to understand, to compare and organize conceptually kept breaking through: in the explorations of Chiltern countryside in the first months of exile; and in a paper written for the *Town Planning Review* in 1938 whose title reveals these interests to the full – 'Towards a systematic approach in planning science: geoproscopy'. The video record of this part of our conversation is particularly noteworthy, too. It reveals what Buttimer[1] called Conzen's 'theatrical distance' from events which must have been so traumatic at the time. Whatever wounds there were have been healed and his descriptions of events are full of humour and understated irony which is visible as much as verbal.

Back to geography

Conzen's MA resulted in a proper three-year contract from the University of Manchester and by the time these three years were up, the war had ended, the Conzens' son, Michael, had been born, and Fleure had retired. His successor chose not to continue the contract, 'so I applied to various places and I suppose my planning background, so recent and relatively short, must have appealed to Professor Daysh in Newcastle'. Within a week he had seen the town which was later to provide him with the material for his *magnum opus*, Alnwick, Northumberland.

> In the very first week that I arrived in Newcastle, Professor Daysh took me in his car over the whole of Northumberland in a lightning tour, just to help me get to know at least some part of the region in which I would spend my teaching life. We went up the Great North Road to Alnwick, but I had not nearly enough time. We went through Alnwick, I should say. As we came through the Hotspur Gate from the south, the streets divided and I said, 'By Jove, another one of these Anglian village greens that has become the market', and as we whizzed through leaving that central triangle to one side, I desperately looked back into Fenkle Street, and of course, I had got it for a future research programme!.

A moment of inspiration, which was magically captured in the video recording.

Conzen was stimulated to develop this initial inspiration almost by accident. Like many academics with a family to support, he took his share in school examining. The Durham examination board in the 1950s prided itself on being one of the few boards in the country to have a practical and oral examination in its geography syllabus. Conzen was allocated to examine the candidates at Alnwick Grammar School and thereby met the school's geography teacher, A. H. Robson, who was a keen local historian of the town. Expeditions out to explore the lanes and alleyways of the town followed and, eventually, he was invited to see the fine maps and plans in the archives of the Duke of Northumberland in Alnwick Castle, and the borough records in the Town Surveyor's Office.

The work on Alnwick was interrupted by an invitation from Daysh to participate in a planning study of the Yorkshire port town of Whitby. Conzen used the opportunity of his chapters on the history of the town to explore an idea which was fairly new in mid-1950s Britain – the idea of: 'appreciating the townscape as environment and therefore the relevant applications of geography in planning and conservation; studying to try to understand the historic character of the place and to to treat this historic character (which was very strong in Whitby) as an environmental asset which needs to be looked after.'

His own contribution was to provide a scholarly view of this historicity, to 'try to create a conceptual framework within which more study in depth of the townscape can proceed and from that principles of conservation can be evolved'. For Conzen, himself, the Whitby survey was also 'an opportunity to get published, so I was particularly keen that I shouldn't lose that. There was also the unusual opportunity of putting my work on polychrome maps of unusually large size, so for both these reasons Whitby pushed the work on Alnwick to one side.' The large-scale, multi-coloured maps found in the *Survey of Whitby* (Daysh 1958) are, indeed, an unusual attribute to a British academic study of a town and considerably ease the problems of presenting complex classifications of building form and chronology cartographically. This contrasts markedly with central Europe where such large-scale, polychrome maps have always been, and remain, an essential attribute of any urban geographical investigation.

The study of Alnwick was published in 1960. Simply as a geographical publishing event it, too, is remarkable in a British context. It took up a full volume of the Institute of British Geographers' *Transactions*; it contains a multiplicity of fold-out maps; those maps are printed in three colours, and the volume was reprinted in its entirety in 1969 with the addition of a glossary of technical terms. Its publication was a major editorial feat as Robert Steel,[1] the Institute's then editor, well remembers and was his final task as Hon. Editor. Looking back, he regards it as 'undoubtedly one of the outstanding research productions of the Institute' and it was 'widely, and favourably reviewed' (Steel 1984: 59). Steel's help and care is gratefully acknowledged by Conzen, as, too, is the interest and support of Lord Eustace Percy, the Rector of King's College, Newcastle in the 1950s, who was both generally accessible to his staff in a way unknown in today's universities, and who helped to secure grants to aid the publication of the Alnwick study, not least from the Duke of Northumberland. It was originally intended that it should be a university occasional publication and it was thanks to Steel that it reached a wider audience. In the interview we asked Conzen himself what he regarded as its significance:

Well, it is important because it has opened an avenue of thought and of ways of looking at the townscape which I do believe I have imported in a way. This goes right back to Otto Schlüter, although a lot had happened in the intervening half century and it is not a slavish repetition, therefore. It tries to promote organized intellectual work in this field along lines that see seemingly static townscape as something that has evolved and is evolving all the time. It tries to provide a conceptual framework for such studies by squeezing this individual case to the last drop for what it will give in conceptual contents as a basis for comparative study on a large scale. But that hasn't come yet.

Professor Conzen is quite clear as to why there have been no comparable studies of medieval towns such as Alnwick to similar levels of detail: 'it's far too much work for one person; you have to be dedicated; you have to be sure that this is something nobody else has yet done'. But, if comparative studies of whole towns have not yet been undertaken, several of the concepts developed in the Alnwick study have been taken further by other scholars, most fruitfully, the fringe-belt concept.

In this instance Conzen acknowledges the fundamental influence of Herbert Louis.

I think he was the first person to take a systematic, developmental, evolutionary approach to this geographical phenomenon. Being a born Berliner, like myself, he had there a grand example of a metropolitan agglomeration. With such a city it is extremely important to know how such a seemingly amorphous wen has grown physically through time. Did it grow gradually, bit by bit, without any particular principle in it, or did it go by leaps from one line to another? He was, I think, the first man to put this on paper for a very good example. I took this concept which, from my own experience, I could see was eminently real and did exist and, at the same time, was likely to be a pretty universal phenomenon therefore inviting, once again, comparative study, and refined the concepts that are grouped around the urban fringe-belt phenomenon. Louis's work was fundamental and it was only because he himself did not develop it further that I took the opportunity to add to our knowledge about several aspects of that concept.

Another important conceptual idea developed in the studies of Alnwick and central Newcastle was that of the burgage cycle. This is significant because it

has wide applications and it picks up an important developmental, evolutionary side of the townscape. In this case change in the details of plot pattern and change in the building fabric as a whole, as well as in terms of particular building types. That is, I suggest, a nearly universal principle that has come out of this work as far as medieval towns with burgage plots are concerned, though there are big regional differences depending on the size of the traditional medieval plot types. They are not the same over the whole of Europe. Round the North Sea we tend to have long strip plots; what I would call deep burgages. They don't occur everywhere in medieval Europe. So you have immediately one major point for future work; we must have comparative work on medieval plot types to find where the burgage cycle can get its full head because there are burgages long enough to provide for it.

One way in which comparative studies are often generated is, of course, through the work of graduate students. However, Conzen was what Adrian Randall[1] called a 'Master-class type of teacher'. He was best in a one-to-one situation with another person who empathized with his approach. Given the very different nature of Britain's education system at both secondary and tertiary level, compared with that in central Europe, most undergraduates found Conzen's style not to be student-friendly and, consequently, few graduate students were forthcoming. Still more was this so in the 1960s as statistically-based model building swept into fashion in Anglo-American geography. Also important in the lack of graduate students was a lack of sympathy and support from Professor Daysh, the Newcastle Head of Department, towards Conzen's work. This lack of empathy is an interesting example of the meeting of two completely different types of academic in Buttimer's organizational framework; the one, Conzen, oriented to research and conceptual thinking with an integrating world view, the other, Daysh, strongly practical, involved in problem solving in the public realm of regional planning, and with an event-oriented world view.

Besides the monographs on Alnwick and Newcastle, M. R. G. Conzen's best-known shorter paper is that presented to the first Urban History Group conference in 1966, which uses the Welsh *bastide* of Conwy and the Welsh-border town of Ludlow as its case studies (Conzen 1968). Ludlow in particular has generated a number of other plan studies in the past twenty years, including a continuing analysis by its local historical research group, and a second paper by Conzen himself in 1988. He got to know the town many years ago

when hiking and camping with my wife in the Welsh border. I fell in love with the townscape and knew that here was a key town. I had got a town plan and looking at it I found it immediately exciting. Knowing nothing about Ludlow, I could say, oh yes, here, stage one, the market; stage two, possibly this clearly-planned town that cannot be other than thirteenth century. There is a feature, Old Street – Corve Street, that looks ancient in general layout but is also full of houses, I wonder where that fits in time? The plan was so obviously composite and had such strong contrasts in its town plan that one had to investigate it. So I made sure that during my private teaching excursions, when I taught myself about English townscapes, that Ludlow was included . . . Like the other towns, I picked up what turned out to be key examples for furthering conceptual thinking about the townscape, at random, just as life went on.

And what does Conzen see as the most pressing need for the future in urban morphological research?

Oh, to strengthen inter-disciplinary and international co-operation in relevant subjects and thereby to create the widest basis for an ultimately universal frame of reference for comparative study. Comparative study in a subject like geography is indispensable for the development and furtherance of conceptual thinking. You are the ideal researcher if, in every individual case, you can see both the individual as well as the general.

Life continues to go on, happily and productively for Con and Freda in their home in Newcastle. He retired from the University of Newcastle in 1971, but research and comparative study have continued to occupy him. Besides visits back to the country of his birth, and to other European centres, he enjoyed a sabbatical visit to New Zealand, a golden wedding anniversary visit to the cities of North America, and two extended tours to Japan. The first, in 1971, was at the invitation of the Japanese government and it inspired a new interest in the comparative development of Japanese and European castle towns. Once a certain mastery of the Japanese language had been acquired, a second visit in 1980, at the time of the IGU conference in Tokyo, enabled him to collect material on the development of no fewer than sixty-two historical towns over a nine-week period. The analysis of this mass of, mainly cartographic, material continues to occupy him, and the paper comparing Japanese and European castle town might yet appear!

Acknowledgements

I am grateful to my colleagues J. W. R. Whitehand and P. J. Larkham, and to graduate students past and present, for help in the conversations leading up to the video-recording. A great debt is owed to Alan Duxbury who filmed and edited the recording, and to Anne Buttimer for her enthusiasm over the result and for sharing some of the text of her forthcoming book. Most of all I am grateful to M. R. G. Conzen for sharing a little of his life story with me.

Note

1 Quotations referenced under note 1 are derived from the discussion which followed the presentation of a shortened version of the video recording at the I. B. G. annual conference, Loughborough, 1988 (see Slater 1988).

References

Buttimer, A., 1986. 'Life experience as catalyst for cross-disciplinary communication', *DIA Paper No. 3* (Dept. of Social and Economic Geography, Lund).

Buttimer, A., forthcoming. *Humanism, geography, and life experience: exploring the history of geographic thought and practice.*

Conzen, M. R. G., 1938. 'Towards a systematic approach in planning science: geoproscopy', *Town Planning Review, 18*: 1–26.

Conzen, M. R. G., 1960. 'Alnwick, Northumberland: an essay in town-plan analysis', *Publications, Institute of British Geographers, 27.*

Conzen, M. R. G., 1968. 'The use of town plans in the study of urban history', in *The study of urban history*, ed. H. J. Dyos.

Geisler, W., 1924. *Die deutsche Stadt: ein Beitrag zur Morphologie der Kulturlandschaft* (Stuttgart).

Daysh, G. H. J. (ed.), 1958. *A survey of Whitby and the surrounding area.*

Louis, H., 1936. 'Die geographische Gliederung von Gross-Berlin', *Länderkundliche Forschung, Krebs-Festschrift*, 146–71.

Slater, T. R., 1988. 'Conversations with Con', *Area, 20*: 200–3.

Steel, R. W., 1984. *The Institute of British Geographers, the first fifty years.*

Whitehand, J. W. R. (ed.), 1981. *The urban landscape: historical development and management, papers by* M. *R.* G. *Conzen*, [I.B.G. Special Publication, No. 13].

Part II

Town-plan analysis (medieval towns)

3 The role of town-plan analysis in the study of the medieval Irish town

John Bradley

The medieval Irish town has been the subject of more scholarly attention during the past twenty-five years than at any time previously. In retrospect, two unconnected events can be seen to have stimulated this upsurge of interest. The first, in 1961, was the beginning of archaeological excavations in Dublin. These excavations, conducted initially by the Office of Public Works (1961–2), and subsequently by the National Museum of Ireland (1962–81), revealed the great wealth of archaeological data that lay entirely unsuspected below modern ground level. In particular the excavations at Wood Quay/Fishamble Street caught the public imagination and acted as a catalyst which initiated excavations in many of Ireland's smaller medieval towns. To date archaeological excavations have taken place in some thirty towns. The second stimulus was the publication of a comprehensive collection of Irish medieval borough charters in 1964 together with a thorough review of the information they contained about town life in medieval Ireland (MacNiocaill 1964). This encouraged the re-examination of town life in medieval Ireland from documentary sources, and it sparked off an interest in identifying those medieval boroughs whose charters did not survive. Indeed, in an inverse way, because of the emphasis subsequently placed on the chartered town, it can also be seen to have generated research into the unchartered 'monastic town'.

The increasing amount of research in the fields of archaeology, documentary history, and historical geography created the need for a forum in which scholars could keep in touch with relevant research in other disciplines. This prompted the formation of two interdisciplinary bodies which have contributed much to Irish urban studies, the Group for the Study of Irish Historic Settlement (1969) and the Dublin Historic Settlement Group (1975). The influx of primary archaeological data, the formulation of models of urban genesis, the fresh appraisal of documentary sources, and the increasing number of individual topographical studies, have all generated a climate of discussion which, if occasionally hot and heavy, has been extremely fruitful. The new awareness of the importance of urban research has led to the formal formation of two research bodies, the Irish Historic Towns Atlas, under the auspices of the Royal Irish Academy, and the Urban Archaeology Survey of Ireland, established by the Office of Public Works.

The sources for the study of the Irish medieval town are fourfold: documentary, cartographic, archaeological, and topographical. Very few towns have any significant body of documentary sources prior to 1600. Dublin and Kilkenny probably have the most extensive range of pre-1600 documentation but even in these towns there is nothing to compare with the range of information available for English towns such as Oxford and Winchester. The oldest town plans are of late sixteenth-century date, and almost all of these were prepared in conjunction with Elizabethan military campaigns. As a consequence their coverage of the country is very uneven, with good representation of the flashpoints in Munster and Ulster, but virtually nothing for the more peaceful areas of the east and south-east. The cartographic record of Carrickfergus, which has three Elizabethan, and eleven seventeenth-century maps, contrasts sharply with that of Kilkenny where the oldest town plan was prepared by Jean Rocque in 1757. In recent years archaeological research has become increasingly important as more and more towns are investigated (Bradley 1987). But the progress of archaeological investigation is slow and it will be many decades hence before it will be possible to propose theories of town growth based on archaeological data alone. In the meantime town-plan analysis remains the most significant means of investigating town origins and growth stages. The aim of this paper is to chart some of the progress made with town-plan analysis in the study of the Irish medieval town.

Three main phases of urban growth occurred in Ireland during the Middle Ages. The first is characterized by the monastic town, an essentially indigenous urban form. Elements of this urban phase are already evidenced by the seventh century, but it only reached fruition between the tenth and the twelfth centuries, probably because of the impact of Viking urban organization on native society. The second phase is represented by the Viking towns, established in Ireland during the mid to late ninth century. Five examples are known: Dublin, Wexford, Waterford, Cork and Limerick. Thirdly, there are the Anglo-Norman towns, founded during the late twelfth and thirteenth centuries, which are the best documented of all.

The monastic town

The monastic town forms the most controversial area of discussion in Irish urban studies at present (Doherty 1985; Clarke and Simms 1985; Graham 1987a, 1987b). The concept of indigenous urban sites is not a new one (Walsh 1922: 21; Green 1925: 259; MacNeill 1935: 40), but it is only in recent years that it has received critical attention. The basic thesis is that the fusion of secular and ecclesiastical power, together with a developing economic system based on redistribution, generated the conditions in which some of the larger monasteries became 'proto-urban sites'. This process is evident from the tenth century onwards but the origins of individual urban

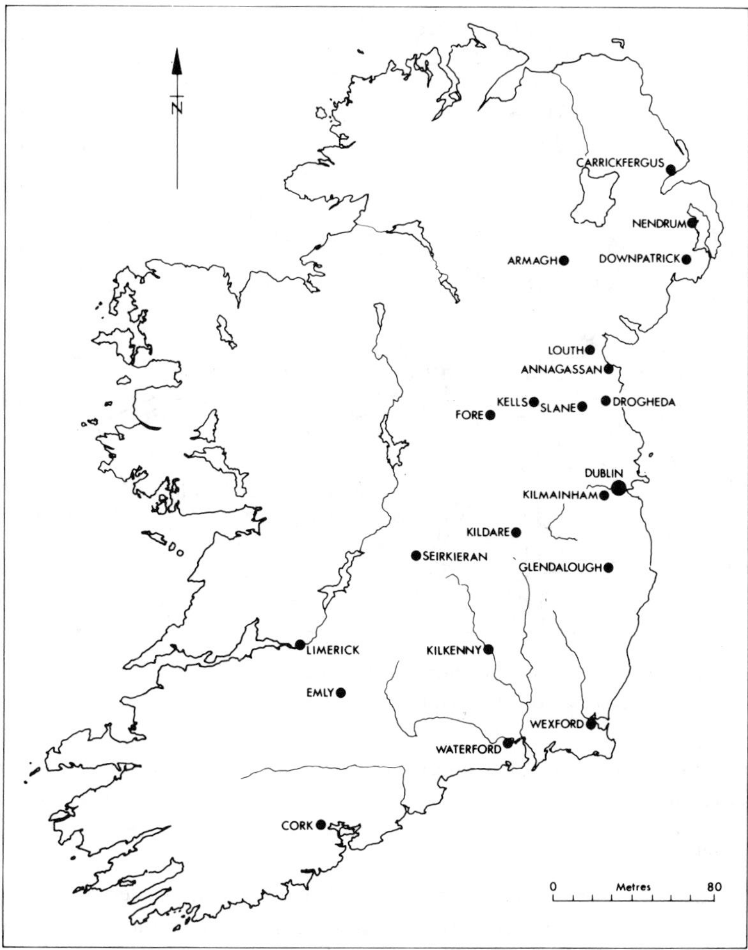

Figure 3.1 Location map of sites mentioned in the text

characteristics can be traced before this time. The exact number of monastic towns is not known but scholars are agreed that it was relatively small.

The study of early Irish monasteries has shown that a roughly circular or elliptical enclosure is one of their essential components. In today's built-up towns, the outline of these enclosures occasionally survives as a curvilinear or arcuate street pattern. In some instances it has proved possible to identify the location and approximate size of the monastic core by isolating the relict features and comparing their present course and alignment with that found on earlier maps and described in documents. The three monastic towns discussed below have all been the subject of fuller studies the results of which are utilized and summarized here. The similarities between the three sites

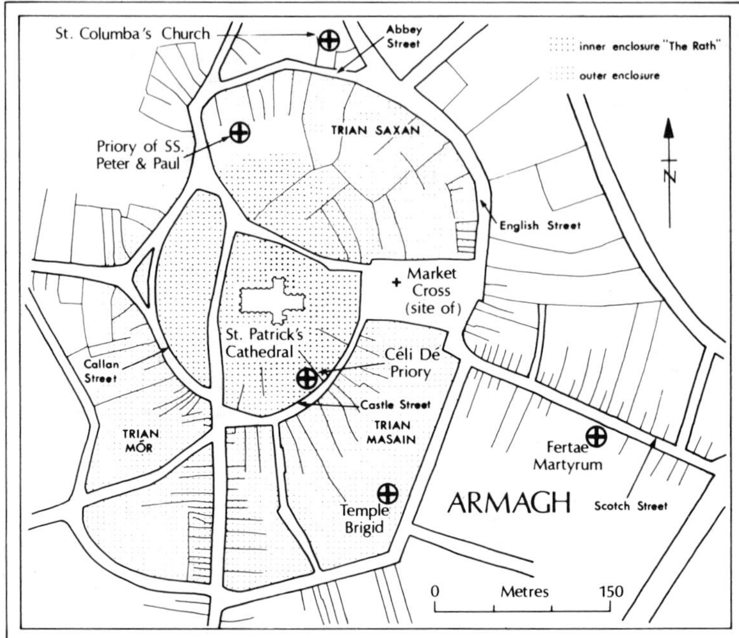

Figure 3.2 Plan of Armagh showing the position of the inner and outer enclosures. The plot pattern is based on Rocque's map of 1760

permit the formulation of a model for the topographical layout of the Irish monastic town.

(a) Armagh

Founded by St Patrick, Armagh (Fig. 3.2) has been the ecclesiastical capital of Ireland since the seventh century. According to the tradition recorded by Muirchú *c.*680, the first church was on the low ground at *Fertae Martyrum* (the martyr's burial-ground), and it was some time later before the ecclesiastics were granted the high ground, known as dorsum salicis ('the ridge of the willow'), on which the monastic capital was subsequently built (Bieler 1979: 191). Normally this would suggest a dual origin for the later 'monastic town' but examination of the topography and the later annalistic sources indicates that the hill summit became the focus for most subsequent development.

The summit is a terrace, about 250 m. across, known in numerous annals of the ninth to twelfth centuries as 'the Rath', a name which indicates that it was enclosed by a palisaded earthwork. The gate of this enclosure is mentioned on several occasions and within it were the principal ecclesiastical buildings. These comprised the *damhliac mór* (the principal church), two churches known as *damhliac an tsabhaill* and *damhliac na toe*, the *celí dé priory* (est. before 919), the library, abbot's house, a grove, a cemetery, and at least one round tower. The area outside this enclosure was divided into three precincts, known as *trians*. The *trian saxan* ('English precinct') was located to the north and north-east, where English Street still preserves its name. The *trian masain* ('middle precinct') lay on the south-east, and the *trian mór* ('large precinct') on the west (Reeves 1860: 19–20). Annalistic references of 1112, 1121 and 1166, indicate that these *trians* contained streets (*sreth*, literally 'row') and houses, which were probably lived in by students, craftsmen and functionaries. *Fertae martyrum* also remained in use and excavations have recovered the workshop evidence of a lignite jeweller, dating to the tenth/eleventh centuries.

The rath, the *trians*, and the sites of five churches outside the rath, can still be identified (Reeves 1860). The position of the rath is indicated on the west, south and east by the curving street pattern of Callan Street and Castle Street, while its location on the north-east is reflected in a curving property boundary. The *trians* formed part of a large outer enclosure, three sides of which are still delimited by streets but its exact western boundary is unclear. The approximate area of twelfth-century Armagh was 11·5 ha. (29 acres) but it is evident from excavations on the east side of Castle Street that parts of this area were not built up until the end of the Middle Ages (Lynn 1977: 278).

(b) Kells

Kells (Fig. 3.3) was established during the first decade of the ninth century on land given by Armagh to Columban monks fleeing the Viking raids on Iona. Like Armagh, traditions survive of the existence of an earlier fort, Dún Chuile Sibrille, but there is no tradition of a move onto the ridge from a site nearby. The importance of Kells increased during the ninth and tenth centuries after the removal there of St Columba's relics from Iona. Simms (1983) has examined Kells' urban functions between the ninth and twelfth centuries, and has shown that it was an administrative centre, a place of refuge and a storehouse for valuables, a major patron of art and craftsmanship, an educational centre, and it had a market-place which she tentatively located to the east of the monastic enclosure, where the market cross stands today.

The layout of Kells shows that the monastic enclosure measured about 360 m. east–west by 280 m. north–south, an area of roughly 9·5 ha. (22 acres). Its outline is preserved on the north and east by the line of Carrick, Castle and Cross Streets, on the west by Fair Green and on the south by the line of the town wall. The boundary is missing in the south-east quadrant where its line would have continued from the surviving piece of town wall towards Cross Street. The lack of definition in this quadrant may be due to an extension of the enclosure along Suffolk Street, a street name derived from *Siofoic*, an area of Kells mentioned on two occasions in the mid twelfth century (O'Donovan 1851, ii: 118–19; MacNiocaill 1961, v: 21; cf. Simmington 1960: 234–5; O'Connell 1960: 13). Simms (1983: 32–5) has

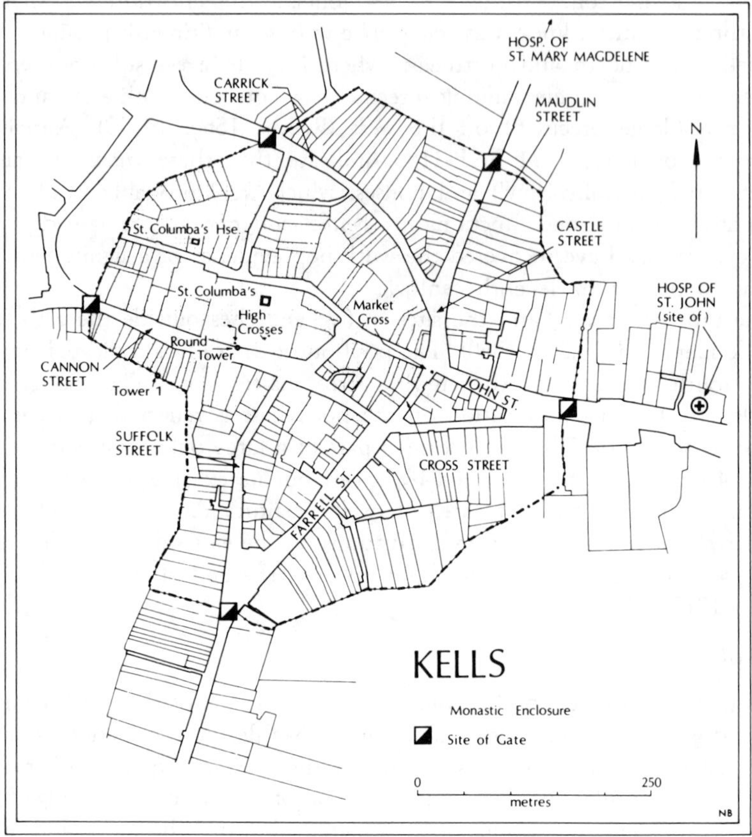

Figure 3.3 Plan of Kells showing the position of the monastic enclosure. The plot pattern is that of *c.*1910

suggested that there was an inner enclosure, isolating the principal church, round tower and high crosses in the manner of the rath at Armagh, but topographically it is not as clearly defined.

After the coming of the Normans the town was extended on the north, where Carrick and Maudlin Streets form a unit; and particularly on the east, along Castle Street, John Street and Kenlis Place; while to the south, Suffolk and Farrell Streets were further developed. The presence of a two-stage plot pattern on the east side of Farrell Street suggests that it may have been extended in two phases with the southernmost portion being incorporated perhaps as late as the seventeenth century.

(c) Kildare

Kildare (Fig. 3.4) is associated with St Brigid who is said to have founded the monastery during the early sixth century, but Brigid herself is a

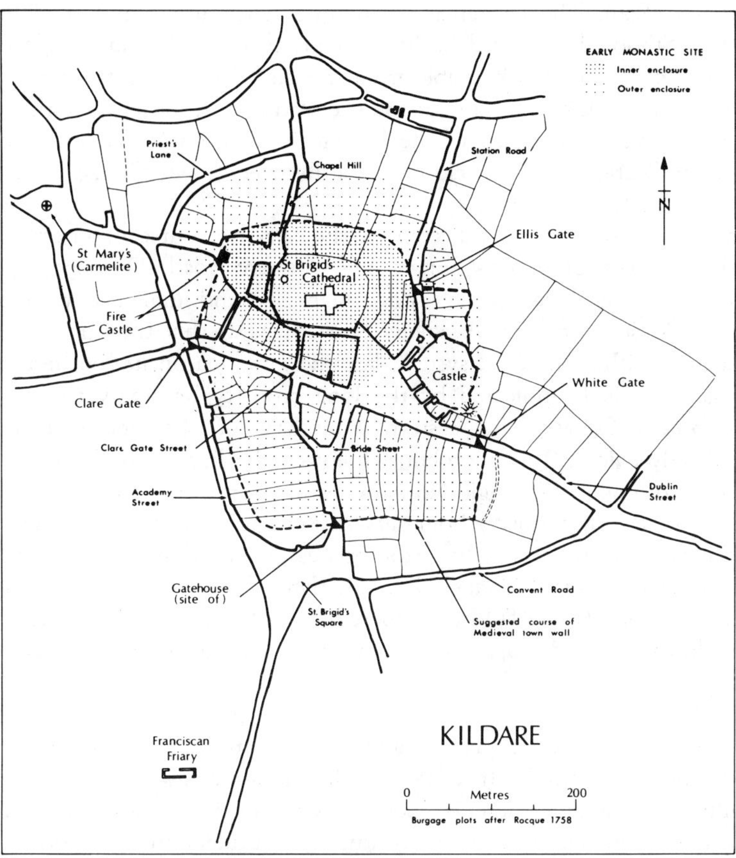

Figure 3.4 Plan of Kildare showing the suggested position of the inner and outer monastic enclosures. The plot pattern is based on Rocque's map of 1758

shadowy figure, and is quite possibly a Christianized version of a Celtic goddess, as Macalister (1919: 340–1) proposed. The site was associated until at least the twelfth century with a perpetual fire, tended by virgins, a feature which itself suggests a pre-Christian origin for this site (O'Meara 1982: 81–5; Doherty 1985: 61). The monastery was evidently sizeable by the mid seventh century when Cogitosus described it as 'a great metropolitan city', and its importance continued into the twelfth century as is shown by its episcopal status at the synods of Rath Bresaill and Kells. An eleventh-century source refers to the workshop of a comb-maker in 'the street of the stone steps' (Radner 1978: 165); additionally described as 'eastward running', it is quite likely to be the modern Claregate Street.

The street pattern of Kildare preserves a number of curvilinear features which are relict remains of pre-Norman enclosures, but despite a number of attempts at analysis no consensus has been arrived at on their exact course

(Andrews 1986). The existence of an inner enclosure is indicated by the bulge in Station Road, and its line is continued on the north side of the cathedral by a crop-mark visible from the air. Continuing the line of this curve, it crossed Church Lane at the site of the medieval Fire Castle, which seems to have formed part of the late-medieval defences. There is no self-evident indication of the enclosure's southern edge, but Claregate Street is the most likely boundary.

The outer enclosure is reflected in the curving course of Priest's Lane, Academy Street, St Brigid's Square and Convent Road. The topography of the north-west and west, which shows higher ground immediately inside the curve of Priest's Lane and Academy Street suggests that the original vallum lay slightly within the road system. For the same reason its southern boundary is most likely indicated by the long property boundary running east from Bridge Street. The eastern boundary of the enclosure is not immediately evident but it probably followed the line of the later medieval defences adjoining the Anglo-Norman castle. North of the castle, a map of 1757 shows a long property boundary running towards Station Road. From there it passed, probably behind the houses on Lourdesville, to the kink in the road at the foot of Chapel Hill. The date of the triangular market-place is unclear. Swan (1985: 86) has proposed an early Christian origin for it but as Andrews (1986: 3) suggests, it may be of seventeenth-century date.

(d) Comment

These three examples display a number of interesting similarities in their layout and development. In each case the monastic town was located on a prominent ridge and there is good evidence of site continuity with pre-Christian times. The element of continuity is evident in many other early church sites and, in so far as they would have been foci before the introduction of Christianity, it may help to explain the success and growth of some monasteries rather than others. Louth, Emly, Slane, Fore, Seirkieran, and Downpatrick, for example, were important monastic sites but each was also a centre of pre-Christian settlement and has evidence for ritual continuity.

At Armagh, like Cork (below) and Glendalough, there is evidence for the movement of the monastery, at a secondary stage, onto a summit or area of level ground, where there was room to build. Both Armagh and Kildare have topographical evidence for an inner sanctum, and at Kells its former existence has been suggested by Simms. The Armagh evidence clearly indicates that the inner enclosure contained the principal religious buildings, in a pattern which is also known from the small and remote monasteries of the western seaboard (Herity 1984). The outer enclosure at Armagh was divided into precincts, with rows of houses, lived in by craftsmen, students, and functionaries. The principal religious buildings also lay at the core of Kildare and Kells, and there is similar evidence from rural sites such as Nendrum, Co. Down (Lawlor 1925). The evidence for precincts with streets and houses is best documented at Armagh, and it provides the clearest model by which the occasional references to streets, houses and craftsmen, at other monastic towns, may be interpreted and visualized. Interestingly, there is no evidence from any of the monastic towns for a pre-Norman burgage pattern or for the careful regulation of properties which is evident in the Viking towns. This suggests that there was not only a different social organization, but also a significant difference in function between the monastic towns and their Viking counterparts.

The Viking town

The first Viking raid on Ireland occurred in 795 but it was not until the middle of the ninth century that the Vikings began to establish settlements. Dublin and Annagassan, the earliest of these, were founded in 841 but the physical form of both settlements is unclear. The term used to describe them in the annalistic entries is *longphort*, a word which indicates a fortress or enclosure associated with ships (Clarke and Simms 1985: 683). The site of the original Dublin *longphort* is unknown, but a coastal promontory fort remains at Annagassan, which was abandoned subsequent to 927. Here the remains consist of a D-shaped enclosure, measuring 73 by 34 m., defended by a bank and ditch on the landward approaches, and by a steep scarp on the seaward side. It is sited on a prominent ridge which affords commanding views across Dundalk Bay, and it overlooks a sheltered harbour in the estuary of the rivers Dee and Glyde. Wallace has suggested that these early *longphoirt* functioned as vicus/portus style settlements and it is possible that an area outside the enclosure may also have been occupied. In any event, Annagassan provides the best evidence for the characteristic features of the initial *longphort*: a prominent geographical location with easy access to the sea, a sheltered harbour and an enclosure delimited by defences. Similar settlements were established at Cork before 848, Waterford before 891, Limerick before 922, and, probably about this time, at Wexford.

Dublin, alone of the three Viking towns examined below, has been the subject of detailed town-plan analysis but I am taking the opportunity of summarizing the results of the analyses of Cork and Waterford which have been conducted by Andrew Halpin and myself, in advance of their fuller publication elsewhere. The comparative layout of the three Viking towns shows similarities which permit some general conclusions on the layout of the Viking town in Ireland and these are also important for understanding the nature of Scandinavian settlement in Ireland.

(a) Dublin

The location of the initial Viking *longphort* appears to have been to the east of the later medieval city, near Kilmainham-Islandbridge, where a cemetery of Viking burials dating to the ninth century was discovered over one hundred years ago (Coffey and Armstrong 1910). In 902 this settlement

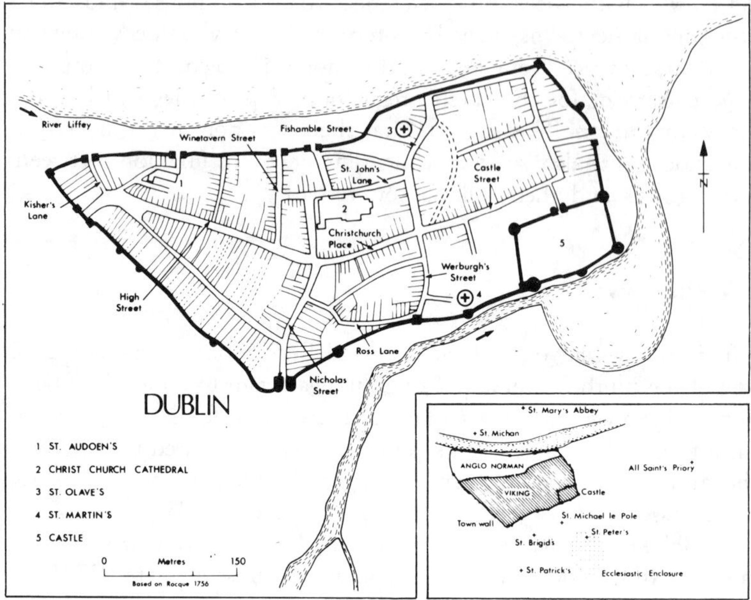

Figure 3.5 Plan of Viking Dublin. The plot pattern is based on Rocque's map of 1756. The street pattern, town walls, and the position of the river Liffey is based on Clarke (1978)

was captured by an Irish alliance and its destruction was so thorough that the site was abandoned. When the dispossessed Vikings returned in 917 they established themselves in a different location, on a spur overlooking the confluence of the rivers Liffey and Poddle in the vicinity of the present-day Christchurch cathedral (Fig. 3.5). The morphology of this new settlement has been the subject of important papers by Clarke (1977) and Simms (1979), but nothing is known about the layout of the earlier *longphort* and even its precise location is unclear.

Early Dublin's most dominant topographical feature was a long narrow ridge, some 15 m. high, running parallel to the river. It was a location that was easy to defend but the new site had a number of other important advantages. It had a sheltered haven at a point where the Liffey was not only broad but fordable; it was at the intersection of three major long-distance land routes, and it was also close to Dublin Bay. This combination of favourable geographical factors has prompted Clarke to suggest the existence of a pre-Viking settlement overlooking the ford, the *ath cliath* first mentioned in mid-seventh-century sources. In his analysis of Dublin's early topography he has also identified an ecclesiastical enclosure, coextensive with the medieval parish of St Peter, overlooking the *dubh linn* (black pool) from which the city derives its name. The outline of this enclosure is preserved in the modern street pattern, immediately south-east of the Viking town. Clarke has identified it with the otherwise mysterious ecclesiastical site of Dubh Linn, whose abbots' obits are noted in the seventh and eighth centuries. Both of these settlements, however, were rural in character and the beginnings of Dublin as a town rest clearly with the Vikings.

Simms' analysis of the first large-scale map of Dublin, prepared by Jean Rocque in 1756, has identified three plan units within the walled medieval town. The first unit is centred around the intersection of two routes, the east–west axis of Castle Street/Christ Church Place, and the north–south axis of Fishamble Street/Werburgh Street. The primacy of the east–west route is suggested by the fact that it hugs the northern edge of the ridge and avoids any alteration in street level. By contrast both Fishamble Street and Werburgh Street lead down steep slopes, and the marked bend in Fishamble Street probably arose in order to avoid a sharp break in slope. The boundary of this first plan unit on the north, east and south is indicated by the line of the town wall, while its western extent can be gauged from two features, the curving alignment of the former Ross Lane, on the south-west, and the excavated portion of the town's tenth-century rampart on the north-west. Archaeological support for this analysis comes from the excavations at Fishamble Street where the houses and plots were laid out in the early tenth century (Wallace 1984: 114–16), in contrast with the evidence from High Street and Winetavern Street where the earliest levels were dated to *c.*1010–1030 (Murray 1983: 43, 203).

Interestingly, two routes merge immediately outside the western entrance to Simms' first plan unit, the route leading to the ford, represented by High Street, and the route south, represented by Nicholas Street. High Street was evidently the more important of these two routeways because it forms the axis of the second plan unit, an extension of the original settlement to the west. The length of the High Street plots is irregular and Simms' suggestion that this may indicate piecemeal growth is supported by the archaeological evidence which has shown that the property boundaries did not stabilize until the mid eleventh century (Murray 1983: 43–9). The boundaries of this plan unit on the south, west and north coincide with the medieval town wall which dates from the late eleventh century. Thus the walled area of the Viking town would have comprised about 12 ha. Archaeological excavations at Dublin Castle in 1961–2 and in 1985–6 have revealed that its construction in 1204 caused the demolition of many Viking houses and the replanning of this area of the town.

In the light of this analysis it is interesting to note that the archaeological evidence suggests that the oldest parts of the Viking town, the first plan unit, were also the wealthiest (Murray 1983: 54–60). High Street, in contrast, was an area of large yards with small dwellings and workshops which probably supported an artisan population. Simms' third plan unit lies to the north of the other two, and is a more regularly laid-out area, north of Cook Street, which archaeological evidence indicates was reclaimed from the river Liffey during the early years of the thirteenth century.

Dublin is particularly fortunate in that the combination of archaeological research and town-plan analysis has successfully identified its earliest growth stages, but the most important result of the archaeological excavations is undoubtedly the evidence which they have provided for town layout. Excavation on the west side of Fishamble Street revealed ten plots, all of which were aligned to the modern street. The individual plots were trapezoidal with the broad end fronting onto the street, and they stretched back to the earthen embankment which defended the town. The property divisions were separated from their neighbours by a wooden fence, and these property boundaries continued in use throughout the tenth and eleventh centuries, indicating that the properties were 'the products of an ordered urbanised society in which property was respected and its regulation possibly controlled by the legal force of an urban authority' (Wallace 1984: 115). The presence of such a plot pattern has been suspected because of the reference in 989 to the imposition of a tax on every 'garth' (*garrdha*) in Dublin (O'Donovan 1851, ii: 722–5), but the regularity of its layout and the stability of the property boundaries themselves was not anticipated.

(b) Cork

The earliest settlement at Cork (Fig. 3.6) was a monastery dedicated to St Finbar or Bairre, founded in the sixth or early seventh century. The site had an added attraction for the Vikings, however, because its estuarine situation provided easy access to the sea. The monastery was located on a prominent ridge, offering a commanding view of the marshy estuary of the river Lee. The place-name 'St Finbar's Cave', later the site of the Augustinian foundation known as Gill Abbey, suggests that Cork, like Glendalough, may have been eremitical in origin, but the focus of the monastery subsequently moved eastwards to more open ground where there was room to build. The present cathedral occupies the site of its medieval and pre-Norman predecessors, and a round tower is known to have survived close to it until the seventeenth century (Barrow 1979: 71). The extent of the monastic enclosure is difficult to gauge, but both the form of the present churchyard and the curve of Barrack Street are tell-tale signs of the former existence of major curving boundaries, and a closer examination reveals its site. The street block bounded by Dean Street, Vicar Street and Barrack Street is divided longitudinally by a major plot boundary. This plot boundary is continued in the block immediately to the east towards the seventeenth-century Elizabeth Fort, where the curving alignment is preserved in Keyser's Hill. West of the cathedral, the former line is indicated by a long property boundary north of Gillabbey Street, while on the north the steep escarpment forms a natural boundary.

The foundation date of the Viking town is not recorded but it is known that there was a Viking settlement at Cork by 848 (O'Donovan 1851, ii: sub 848) and, by analogy with Dublin, it is likely that it was established a few years before. The nature of this ninth-century settlement, whether fortress,

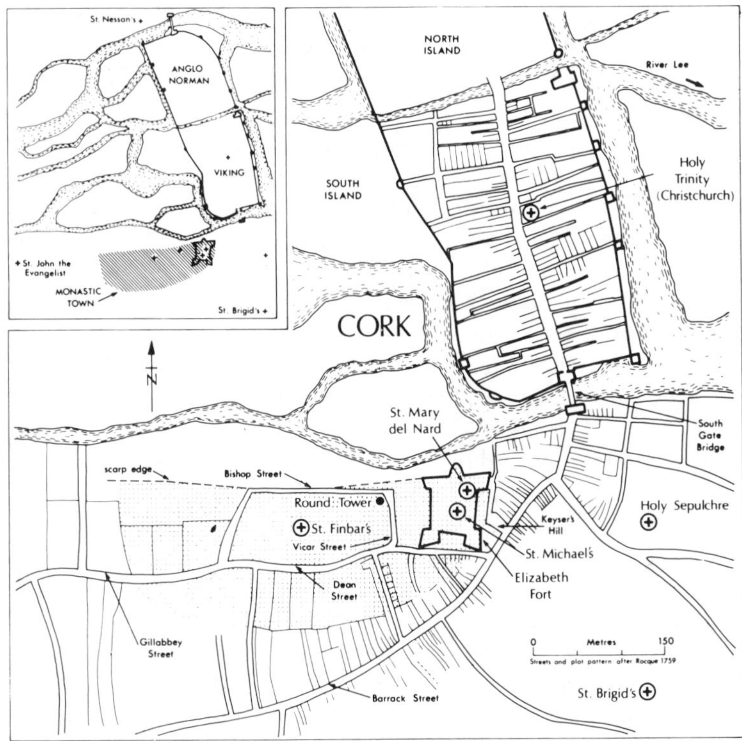

Figure 3.6 Plan of Cork showing the position of St Finbar's monastery and the Viking town. The plot pattern is based on Rocque's map of 1759

emporium or town, is unknown. An eleventh-century compilation, recounting an attack of 867, describes Cork as a *purt* (port), but this may be an anachronistic description, more appropriate to the eleventh century than to the ninth (Radner 1978: 125). Documentary information on the topography of Viking Cork is derived from a handful of Anglo-Norman charters, dating to between 1177 and 1185, the years immediately after their takeover of the city (Gilbert 1889: 202, 215; Brooks 1936: 322–5, 335–8).

These charters clearly indicate that the core of Viking Cork was on the island later known as South Island, which is overlooked by the monastic site of St Finbar (Candon 1985: 94–5). The fact that the Anglo-Normans had to besiege the city in 1177 in order to capture it, together with references to the gate and walls of Cork before 1182, suggest that the South Island was enclosed in Viking times (Gilbert 1889: 215; White 1936: 227). There was an unenclosed suburb on the south bank of the river (Jefferies 1985: 19), between South Gate Bridge, first referred to in 1163, and the monastic site of St Finbar.

South Island is laid out along one main street, running north–south, and is clearly a single plan unit. The parish church was dedicated to the Holy

Trinity (Christchurch), a dedication which is also found in the Viking towns of Dublin and Waterford. Five archaeological excavations have been conducted on the south island but in each case Viking period deposits have been absent. In the light of the documentary evidence, however, this must be interpreted as differential survival rather than indicating that South Island was unoccupied in Viking times. Most of the excavations have concentrated on the thirteenth-century town wall, at the edge of the settlement, on ground which may not have formed part of the Viking town. Only the excavations at Holy Trinity College have occurred near the street frontage but here the works associated with the construction of the college in 1482 possibly removed any earlier deposits.

The number of church sites at Cork by the middle of the twelfth century suggests a growing population. On the north side of the Lee was St Nessan's church (Candon 1985: 95–6), while one has the impression of a string of churches, reminiscent of twelfth-century Glendalough, along the south bank of the river. In addition to St Finbar's cathedral there was the Augustinian priory of Gill Abbey, founded before 1138, the church of the Holy Sepulchre, which existed before 1177 (Brooks 1936: 337–8), and most likely the churches of St Brigid, St Michael and St Mary del Nard, mentioned in a decretal letter of 1199. In the later Middle Ages the area immediately east of St Finbar's was known as 'the Fayth', a name derived from *faithche*, which is first mentioned in the twelfth-century Aislinge Meic Conglinne. Although usually translated as 'green' this was an area of peace in front of a dwelling, church or town (Doherty 1980: 83). At Dublin, for instance, the *faithche* lay outside the walls, to the west, and was the place where the *margad or oenach* was held (Doherty 1980: 83). It probably had a similar function in Cork. Indeed its existence raises the possibility that the settlement on the south bank of the Lee was on land belonging to the church and was perhaps a lay suburb associated with the monastery. Interestingly, in Anglo-Norman times this area formed part of the borough of Fayth, where it was under the jurisdiction of the bishop, and it did not lie within the borough of Cork.

(c) *Waterford*

The earliest clear indication of a Viking base at Waterford (Fig. 3.7) is an annalistic entry for 891, but reference to the 'fleet' of Waterford in 858 may indicate that the settlement was established during the mid ninth century. Unlike Dublin or Cork, however, there was no pre-Viking settlement although the site had obvious locational advantages. It was a prominent peninsular ridge overlooking the confluence of the Suir and the St John's river, easily defended on the landward side where there was only one approach route.

The most striking feature of the town's layout is its regularity, and three plan units are discernible. These consist of westward expansion from an eastern core. The east–west alignment of the Henrietta Street plots form a

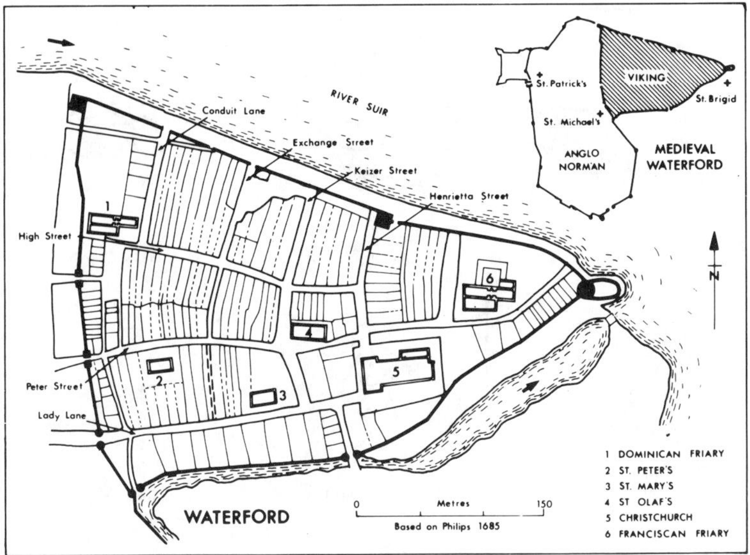

Figure 3.7 Plan of Viking Waterford. The street pattern and town defences are based on Phillips' map of 1685. The plot pattern is that of *c.*1840

clear break in the plot pattern to the east and west and one can only conclude that it marks a major boundary. Its exact significance is difficult to evaluate, however, because of the absence of a complementary plot pattern on either the east or west of the street block. The eastern tip of this plan unit, occupied from the thirteenth century by the Franciscan friary, was known until the seventeenth century as Dundory, a place-name which indicates its pre-Norman origin as a fort, presumably the Viking stronghold. The south-western portion of this plan unit is occupied by Christchurch Cathedral, indicating a clear topographical association between church and stronghold.

The second plan unit is the area between Henrietta Street and Exchange Street which has a curved northern line suggestive of a defensive boundary. The third unit is the area between Exchange Street and the medieval wall which was built just outside an eleventh/twelfth century rampart discovered during excavations at Lady Lane. The streets in both of these units are laid out in a rectilinear fashion and form a rough chequer pattern. Three major streets run east–west, High Street, Peter Street and Lady Lane, and these are cut by three narrower north–south running streets, represented today at the northern ends by Keizer Street, Exchange Street and Conduit Lane. The regularity of this plan pattern is unusual, and contrasts clearly with the simpler layout of both Dublin and Cork. Indeed it may be remarked that the layout of the Viking town is far more regular than that of the extension constructed to the west by the Anglo-Normans in the late twelfth/early

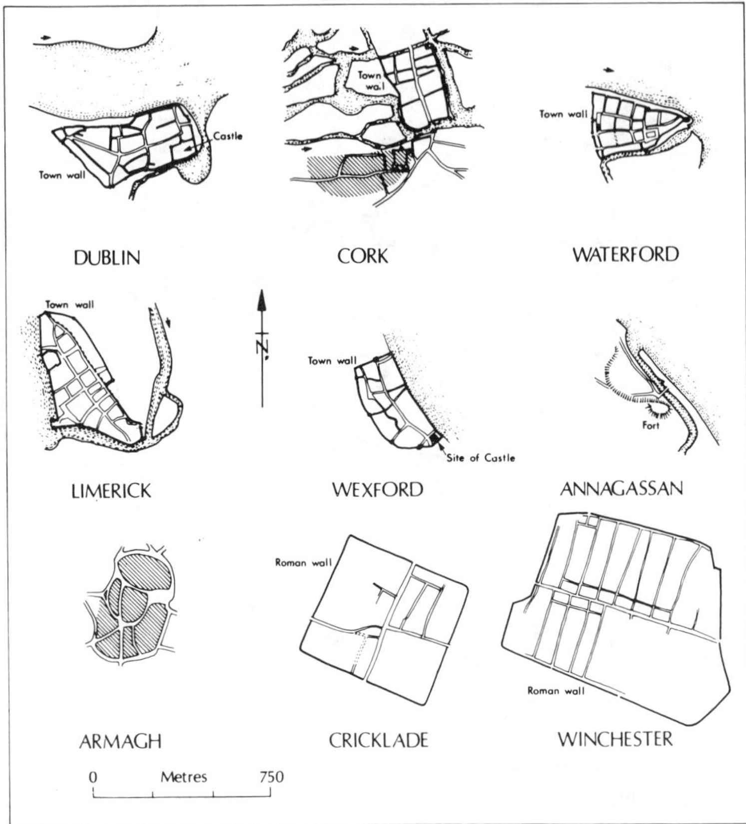

Figure 3.8 The relative size of the Irish Viking towns compared with the monastic town of Armagh and the late Saxon towns of Cricklade and Winchester

thirteenth century, a time when regular planning was more common. The street-plan of Viking Limerick (Fig. 3.8), aligned along two roughly parallel streets divided by cross streets, provides a close comparison, however, and indicates that the rectilinear layout of Waterford did not occur by accident.

The rectilinear layout of Viking Waterford finds a contemporary parallel in the plan-form of a number of late Anglo-Saxon towns, such as Winchester and Cricklade (Biddle and Hill 1971), and it may be that Waterford represents an extension of the rectilinear plan to Ireland. This provides an important indication of the route by which the Viking planned town concept was introduced to Ireland. Wallace (1981: 134) has suggested that the Vikings who fled to the Chester area from Dublin in 902 would have seen the burhs constructed in Mercia by Aethelred and Aethelflaed between 907 and 915. He has further proposed that these burhs inspired the organized layout of houses, property plots, streets and defences which characterized Dublin as it was re-established by the returning Vikings in

917, and he has argued that a rectilinear street pattern is missing at Dublin only because of the unsuitability of the topography. The Viking force which refounded Dublin actually landed at Waterford in 914, and the Annals note that they constructed a *longphort* there in that year (AFM). This was evidently something special because the same annals mention the arrival of other Viking settlers at Waterford in 912 without any allusion to structural works. The building of a *longphort* indicates the movement into Waterford in 914 of a sizeable population and this fact, together with the exposure of these Vikings to some of the planned towns of Anglo-Saxon England, suggests that the second and third plan units represents an expansion of the urban core after 914.

Peter Street running the entire length of the Viking settlement may well have been the main street of the Viking town. High Street, like its Dublin counterpart, follows the crest of the ridge overlooking the river. The 1088 reference to Waterford as a *dún*, indicates that by this time the settlement was enclosed by defences, and on analogy with other Viking towns it is probable that it was fortified during the tenth century. Excavations on the angle of the defences at Lady Lane revealed that they consisted of an earthen embankment with external fosse. The rampart was demolished towards the end of the twelfth century and spread over the fosse. Curiously no trace of the earthen defences was evident on the south, where the marshland perhaps afforded sufficient defence.

Apart from Christchurch cathedral, two other churches are known to have existed within the Viking town, St Peter's, where archaeological excavations uncovered the foundations of an apsidal church in 1987, and the church of St Olaf, whose cult in Ireland is exclusively Scandinavian. The presence of dedications outside the walled area to SS. Brigid, Michael and Patrick, who are frequently associated with pre-Norman dedications, may indicate that some form of suburb existed by the twelfth century. In this regard the discovery of house foundations built in the twelfth-century fill of the fosse at Lady Lane suggests that there was already pressure on building space within the town by this time.

(d) Comment

These three examples show that geographical factors were powerful arbiters influencing the Viking choice of town site. At Dublin and Waterford the town developed on a prominent ridge, overlooking a sheltered harbour, within easy reach of the sea, features which also characterize the Viking town of Wexford. At Cork, the prominent ridge was occupied by St Finbar's monastery, and the town developed instead, like Limerick, on an easily defended island fastness which had direct access to the sea. At Dublin and Cork the presence of existing settlements may have influenced the choice of site but there is no evidence for any pre-Viking settlement at Waterford or Limerick.

Dublin and Waterford developed in two major topographical stages. At

Dublin these phases belonged to the early tenth and early eleventh centuries respectively, while at Waterford they can be assigned to the mid ninth, and tenth centuries. Indeed Waterford is exceptional in that it is the only Viking town in which the position of the *longphort* can be tentatively identified. The development of Cork was more complex largely because of the prominent role of the earlier monastic site. South Island forms a single plan unit but an extra-mural suburb evidently developed between the island and the monastery.

Archaeological excavations in Dublin, Waterford and Wexford have provided clear evidence for the organized layout of houses, house-plots, and property boundaries and these show that the Scandinavians introduced the concept of the planned town to Ireland. The street pattern of Viking Waterford is particularly important in this respect. It is derived from the planned Anglo-Saxon towns of the late ninth and early tenth centuries and it indicates that the Viking town concept was derived from England. The Dublin excavations have also revealed that the eleventh century was a period of great prosperity and it is interesting to note that it also coincides with the *floruit* of the great monastic settlements whose growth at this time must be due in part to the impact of the Viking urban centres on Irish society.

Anglo-Norman

The coming of the Normans in 1169 was quickly followed by a major period of town foundation. Their initial urban activity consisted of expanding Viking centres and establishing towns at a number of monastic sites. New towns, such as Drogheda, were founded before the end of the twelfth century, however, and they were a common feature of the thirteenth.

The layout of the Anglo-Norman towns has been the subject of a recent study (Bradley 1985). This indicates that the predominant plan was linear single streets but examples of chequer plans also occur. Within the towns, the houses commonly appear to have had their gable towards the street and the burgage plots often stretched from the main street to the town wall. The market-place was in the main street of the linear towns and was occasionally embellished with a market cross. Most towns were enclosed by stone walls which consisted mainly of plain curtain wall except for the larger towns such as Dublin and Drogheda which tended to have many mural towers and gatehouses. The role of the manor is reflected in the number of towns which have seigneurial castles. Generally these are located outside or on the edge of the town. A characteristic feature is the presence of a single parish church in contrast to the pre-Norman towns, such as Dublin, which had a complex parish structure. The houses of the Dominicans and Franciscans are usually located outside the town or on the periphery. Suburbs are rare but in some instances 'Irishtowns' occur; these have been regarded as separate ethnic areas but the evidence from Kilkenny suggests that this was not the case.

Conclusion

When the principles established by Professor Conzen in his studies of Alnwick and Newcastle are applied to Ireland, where fewer documentary and cartographic sources survive, it can be seen that they provide a vital source of information on the origins, development and form of the medieval Irish town. The application of these principles to the study of all the towns in a particular phase of urban development or, as here, to a representative sample of towns in such a phase, reveals general patterns of urban layout characteristic of the particular phase in question. This provides otherwise unobtainable information on the concepts of urban design and layout found in Ireland at different times within the Middle Ages.

Acknowledgements

I am very grateful to Andrew Halpin for his assistance with a number of documentary references and particularly for his help with both Waterford and Cork. I owe a very special debt of gratitude to Dr Anngret Simms for discussing much of the content of this paper with me and for a series of most helpful comments which she made while it was still in a draft state. The accompanying line drawings are the work of Mr John Wallace to whom I also wish to offer my sincere thanks.

References

Andrews, J., 1986. *Kildare. Irish historic towns atlas: 1* (Dublin).

Barrow, G., 1979. *The round towers of Ireland* (Dublin).

Biddle, M. and Hill, D., 1971. 'Late Saxon planned towns', *Antiquaries. J., 51*: 70–85.

Bieler, L. (ed.), 1979. *The Patrician texts in the Book of Armagh* (Dublin).

Bradley, J., 1985. 'Planned Anglo-Norman towns in Ireland', in H. B. Clarke and A. Simms (eds.), *The comparative history of urban origins in non-Roman Europe*, [B.A.R. International Series *255*], 411–67.

Bradley, J., 1987. 'Recent archaeological research on the Irish town', in H. Jäger (ed.), *Stadtkernforschung* (Köln-Wien) 321–70.

Brooks, E. St-J., 1936. 'Unpublished charters relating to Ireland 1177–1182, from the archives of the city of Exeter', *Proceedings, Royal Irish Academy, 43* C: 313–66.

Candon, A., 1985. 'The Cork suburb of Dungarvan', *Journal of Cork Historical & Archaeological Society, 90*: 91–103.

Clarke, H. B., 1977. 'The topographical development of early medieval Dublin', *Journal of Royal Society Antiquaries Ireland, 107*: 29–51.

Clarke, H. B., 1978. *Dublin c.840 - c.1540: the medieval town in the modern city* (Dublin).

Clarke, H. B. and Simms A., 1985. 'Towards a comparative history of urban origins', in *idem* (eds.), *The comparative history of urban origins, op. cit.*, 669–714.

Coffey, G. and Armstrong, E. C. R., 1910. 'Scandinavian objects found at Islandbridge and Kilmainham', *Proceedings of Royal Irish Academy, 28* C, no. 5: 107–22.

Curtis, E., 1938. *A history of medieval Ireland*, 2nd ed. (Dublin).

Doherty, C., 1980. 'Exchange and trade in early medieval Ireland', *Journal of Royal Society Antiquaries Ireland, 110*: 67–89.

Doherty, C., 1985. 'The monastic town in early medieval Ireland', in H. B. Clarke and A. Simms (eds.), *The comparative history of urban origins, op. cit.*, 45–75.

Gilbert, J. (ed.), 1889. *Register of the abbey of St Thomas, Dublin* (London).

Graham, B., 1987a. 'Urban genesis in early medieval Ireland', *Journal of Historical Geography, 13* (1987): 3–16, 61–3.

Graham, B., 1987b. 'Urbanization in medieval Ireland ca. A.D. 900 to ca. A.D. 1300', *Journal of Urban History, 13*: 169–96.

Green, A. S., 1925. *A history of the Irish state to 1014*.

Herity, M., 1984. 'The layout of Irish early Christian monasteries', in P. Ní. Chathain and M. Richter (eds.), *Irland und Europa: die Kirche im Frümittelalter* (Stuttgart) 105–16.

Jefferies, H. A., 1985. 'The history and topography of Viking Cork', *Journal of Cork Historical & Archaeological Society*, 90: 14–25.

Lawlor, H. C., 1925. *The monastery of St Mochaoi of Nendrum* (Belfast).

Lynn, C., 1977. 'Recent archaeological excavations in Armagh city: an interim summary', *Seanchas Ardmhacha*, 8, no. 2: 275–80.

MacAirt, S (ed.), 1951. *The annals of Inisfallen* (Dublin).

Macalister, R. A. S., 1919. *Ireland in pre-Celtic times* (Dublin).

MacNeill, E., 1935. *Early Irish laws and institutions* (Dublin).

MacNiocaill, G., 1961. *Notitiae as Leabhar Cheanannais 1033–1161* (Dublin).

MacNiocaill, G., 1964. *Na Buirgéisí* (2 vols.) (Dublin).

Murray, H. A., 1983. *Viking and early medieval buildings in Dublin* [British Archaeological Reports, 119].

O'Connell, P., 1960. 'Kells: early and mediaeval', *Riocht na Midhe*, 2, no. 2: 8–22.

O'Donovan, J., 1851. *Annals of the kingdom of Ireland by the Four Masters* (6 vols.) (Dublin).

O'Meara, J. J., 1982. *The history and topography of Ireland by Giraldus Cambrensis* (Mountrath).

Radner, J. N. (ed.), 1978. *Fragmentary annals of Ireland* (Dublin).

Reeves, W., 1860. *The ancient churches of Armagh* (Lusk).

Simmington, R. C., 1960. 'Valuation of Kells, 1663, with note on map of Kells c.1655', *Analecta Hibernica, 22*: 231–68.

Simms, A., 1979. 'Medieval Dublin: a topographical analysis', *Irish Geography, 12*: 25–41.

Simms, A., 1983. 'Frühformen der mittelalterlichen Stadt in Irland', in W. Pinkwart (ed.), *Genetische Ansatze der Kulturlandschaftsforschung: Festschrift für Helmut Jäger* (Würzburg) 27–39.

Swan, D. L., 1985. 'Monastic proto-towns in early medieval Ireland: the evidence of aerial photography, plan analysis and survey', in H. B. Clarke and A. Simms (eds.), *The comparative history of urban origins, op. cit.*, 77–102.

Wallace, P. F., 1981. 'The origins of Dublin', in B. G. Scott (ed.), *Studies on Early Ireland* (Belfast) 129–43.

Wallace, P. F., 1984. 'A reappraisal of the archaeological significance of Wood Quay', in J. Bradley (ed.), *Viking Dublin exposed: the Wood Quay saga* (Dublin) 112–33.

Walsh, A., 1922. *Scandinavian relations with Ireland during the Viking period* (Dublin).

White, N. B. (ed.), 1936. *Irish monastic and episcopal deeds* (Dublin).

4 English medieval new towns with composite plans: evidence from the Midlands

T. R. Slater

Town-plan analysis has been comparatively little used in Britain by archaeologists, historians or historical geographers compared with an unbroken tradition of detailed analysis of town plans in the countries of central and eastern Europe. Despite M. R. G. Conzen's introduction of this tradition into the English-speaking literature, and its development with the publication of his seminal study of Alnwick (Conzen 1960), there have been almost no attempts to replicate detailed studies of this kind for other English towns (Whitehand 1981: 128). Conversely, the conceptual riches of the Alnwick study have remained almost unknown to researchers in Europe until comparatively recently. In Britain, there have been neither many comparative surveys of town plans of particular regions or periods (Whitehand and Alauddin 1969; Slater 1981 and Haslam 1984 are exceptions), or, until recently, many detailed expositions of particular towns for even one period of development using the methodology of Conzen (Bond 1977 and Spearman 1988 are amongst the few). However, since 1980, the present author has begun to remedy this latter situation with studies of a number of towns in their initial medieval phases of development. They include detailed analyses of Hedon, East Yorkshire (Slater 1984) and Lichfield, Staffordshire (Slater 1986), a comparative survey of episcopal medieval town-planning (Slater 1987), and studies of medieval burgage layouts based on metrological analysis (Slater 1981; 1988a). This research has taken much of its inspiration from what is perhaps Conzen's best-known shorter paper, contributed to the published proceeding of the first Urban History Conference at Leicester (Conzen 1968), though the metrological analysis of burgages clearly owes much to the only previous attempt to classify and analyse burgage dimensions, by Conzen (1960), in the Alnwick paper.

Progress in furthering both the understanding of medieval urban development processes and the classification of town plans depends on establishing a body of detailed case studies. This chapter is therefore intended to provide a further body of data on medieval town-planning in Britain which is both comparative in its own right, and also with these earlier studies, and which builds on the growing understanding of the way in which burgages in medieval towns were laid out, allocated and developed. In particular, it takes three planned medieval new towns in the West Midlands region which have composite town plans and examines the ideals, adaptations to existing development, and subsequent realities of plot division and building within those towns in order to demonstrate some of the the great variety of medieval urban development processes. Conzen's 1968 paper was concerned, in part, with the town of Ludlow, Shropshire, and he has recently provided a further consideration of the development of that particular town plan (Conzen 1988). This chapter, too, will use Ludlow as one of its case studies, both because of its appropriateness in the present context, because Conzen's work provides a base on which to build, and because Ludlow has a particularly fascinating town plan of considerable complexity, and a townscape of great renown (Clifton-Taylor 1978). The comparative case-study towns are close by Ludlow, in the valley of the River Severn, namely Bridgnorth and Bewdley and no detailed analysis of their plans has yet appeared in print.

Composite town plans

The recognition that the majority of English town plans are composite in nature, consisting of a number of discrete plan units which reflect the particular circumstances of their creative phase, is one of Conzen's more important contributions to our understanding of the nature of medieval towns in this country. This can be illustrated by the revolution wrought in the understanding of the development of Ludlow when Conzen's analysis is compared with that of Hope's fifty years earlier (Hope 1909), though historians have continued to make reference to Hope's outdated interpretation (Beresford 1967; Renn 1987). My own recent analysis of Lichfield's medieval development (Slater 1986) similarly recognized a considerable complexity of plan units in this town which had previously been recognized as a simple planned new town established in one phase (Taylor 1968; Gould 1976; Bassett 1980–1). However, little progress has been made in categorizing the variety of medieval plan units nationally, nor in providing a chronological framework for the evolution of plan types. Even in Ludlow, where extensive historical research has been undertaken (Lloyd 1979), as well as some archaeology (Klein and Roe 1988), there is uncertainty as to the precise chronology of the major recognized plan units, though Conzen's most recent interpretation has attempted to specify this more precisely (Conzen 1988).

Given the very long history of the central areas of the great majority of English towns, only archaeology and plan analysis are available as methods for elucidating the earliest phases of that development. The returns from archaeology are high, though often incomplete, but excavation is expensive of both money and labour. Few towns have other than extremely fragmentary historical records of their earliest developments even where this has been confined to the medieval period. Where their origins are derived from earlier periods, written evidence is even less likely. As a result town-plan analysis offers one of the few ways of appreciating these earliest phases of urban development, given an understanding of the limitations of the techniques involved. Unfortunately, in being taken up by some historians, and more particularly by archaeologists, these limitations have not always been appreciated. The efficacy of town-plan analysis in elucidating the early stages of urban development is well shown by the studies of Ludlow that have been published. Ludlow is an extremely well-documented town for a place of its size, but that documentation does not begin in detail until the mid thirteenth century, and does not become extensive until the early fifteenth century. By then, all the principal plan units of the historical town-centre had already been established and, indeed, had undergone some two centuries or more of intensive development with all its corollaries of plot metamorphosis and building fabric change. Such historical documentation as survives for the period before the early fifteenth century tells little of the phasing, ideals behind, or subsequent development of, the physical fabric of the town, as analysis of this historical documentation makes clear (Speight and Lloyd 1978).

The three towns which form the substance of this chapter bear close comparison and such comparison illuminates the processes and likely chronology of development in each town. Conzen has been at pains to explain the various units of the Ludlow plan in terms of an increasing sophistication of planning expertise and of contact with more advanced planning in other European countries (Conzen 1988). This may or may not be true. So little is known of the nature of medieval town-planning in Britain that it is impossible to say at present whether innovations were generated first in Britain or in mainland Europe. Certainly, our understanding of the English planning heritage has been revolutionized over the past two decades as the nature of late-Saxon town-planning has been made clear by archaeologists (Biddle and Hill 1971). It is no longer tenable to write of a lack of experience in the laying out of towns in the immediate post-Norman period; indeed, it has also been made clear that many of the largest late-Saxon towns, such as Norwich, Northampton and Hereford, were substantially extended in the half century following the Conquest (Carter 1983; Williams 1979; Shoesmith 1980, 1982). It may be more apposite, therefore, to seek explanation of the categories of plan types which may emerge when more detailed work has been undertaken, in terms of the status of landholders who founded particular new towns. The three towns under investigation here were all founded on the estates of high-status landholders who were important Marcher lords, and two of them, Bridgnorth and Bewdley, were held by the Crown for significant periods.

Three towns and their plans

Given Conzen's recent exposition of the Ludlow plan and its chronology (1988), relatively little need be said at this point to introduce that town. It is located on a strategically significant cliff-top site beside the River Teme, midway along the Welsh March. A substantial stone castle forms its pre-urban nucleus. An ancient, prehistoric, east–west route (Chitty 1963) and a ford on an important long-distance, north–south, medieval road helped generate economic links with the region around. Ludlow is not recorded as a settlement in 1086 (*contra* Renn 1987) but, by 1290, a burgage rental shows that all the existing elements of its complex plan, with its five major plan units, were in existence. Those plan units vary from the morphologically simple, single-street elements of High Street and Corve Street, to the complex Broad Street–Mill Street unit with its functionally differentiated rear service lanes. The town developed on the Stanton Lacy estate of the de Lacy family, principal landholders under the Montgomerys, Marcher Earls of Shrewsbury.

The Montgomerys also held extensive estates to the east, at Bridgnorth, a town of great strategic importance in the medieval period as it was one of only three bridging points on the central part of the River Severn. It is midway between Worcester and Shrewsbury, the only other bridge points, and a late-Saxon *burh* on the west bank provided an early central-place focus. Early Norman developments were concentrated further south, however, and on the east bank of the river, at Quatford, where a collegiate church, fortified house and incipient borough were founded in the late eleventh century (Mason 1957). Robert de Bellesme's rebellion against Henry I saw the removal of these institutions to the sandstone bluff at Bridgnorth which was more easily defensible. On Robert's defeat the place passed into the King's hands and developed rapidly as an important market town on a par with Ludlow. It has at least six major plan units which seem to have developed in quick succession, again as at Ludlow.

Bewdley is also established at a Severn crossing point, in this case a ford, where the road eastwards from Ludlow crosses the river. This road follows the important prehistoric routeway of the Clun-Clee ridgeway (Chitty 1963). Northwards, the Forests of Wyre and Morfe reached to Bridgnorth and provided plentiful resources for royal hunting. Consequently, on the south side of the routeway, a large area was enclosed as a deer park with a royal hunting lodge, Tickenhill, built near the river (Fig. 4.1). The Norman-French name of the town, 'Beau lieu', is not recorded before 1215 (Mawer, Stenton and Houghton 1927) and burgages are not recorded before 1367. Bewdley is usually characterized, therefore, as one of the last-founded of all the English medieval new towns. There are in fact two towns at Bewdley and the fourteenth-century new town, founded by the Countess of March, was a street borough along the road high on the hill between Forest and park (Fig. 4.1). A market charter was granted in 1446. The building of a

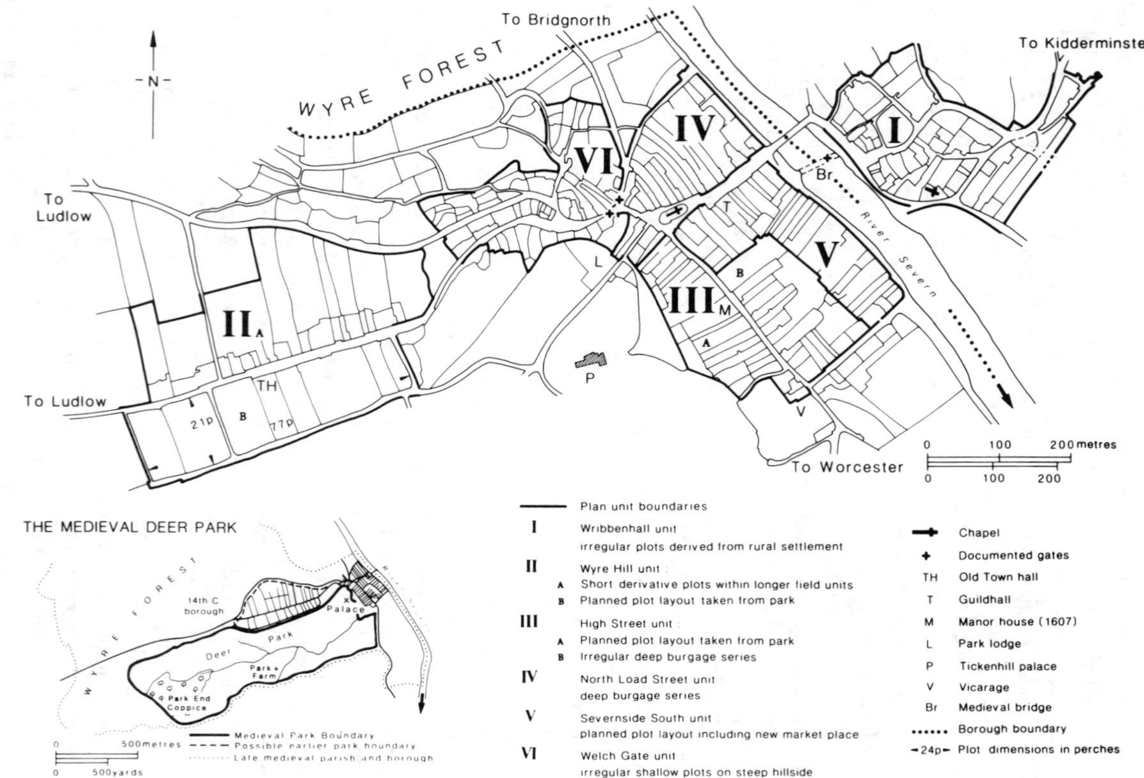

Figure 4.1 The plan-units of medieval Bewdley

new bridge over the Severn, in 1447, and a developing river trade moved the economic emphasis to the riverside and, by 1472, all the main streets of the modern town are recorded in documents. Again, however, this period of rapid development is characterized in the plan by six distinctive plan units which give substance to successive phases within this period. The manor was held by the Mortimer family, Earls of March, during the early phase of its development but, in 1425, it was inherited by Richard, Duke of York and, in 1461, was forfeit to the Crown. It gained a Charter of Incorporation from Edward IV in 1472.

The three towns have a number of comparable features; all are on routeways at a point where they cross a major river; all contain the residential building of their high-status lord, a castle in two cases and a palace in the third; all contain a variety of recognizable plan units, both planned and unplanned. Bewdley is smaller and later developed and has somewhat fewer points of comparison but Bridgnorth and Ludlow are very similar towns and their plans have a remarkable degree of coincidence; so much so that the question inevitably arises as to whether their respective surveyors were aware of developments in each town. This is leaping ahead, however; first it is necessary to examine the two unstudied plans in more detail.

(a) Bewdley

The town plan of Bewdley contains six principal plan units (Fig. 4.1). The most clearly planned is the burgages on the plateau top at Wyre Hill. It seems likely that this part of the town was deliberately established on land taken from within the bounds of the deer park by the Countess of March along a new, straight road which created a more direct, but steeper, descent to the Severn. The old road continued in use, utilizing a side valley to descend more gradually and, in the mid eighteenth century, was improved as the turnpike road and therefore regained its earlier primacy. The regular dimensions of the burgage series along the new road are still apparent and there was a rear service lane on the southern side (Fig. 4.1, IIA). One of the surviving timber-framed buildings is still known as 'the old town hall'. The second unit is the irregular group of plots on the east bank of the river called Wribbenhall (Fig. 4.1, I). This originally rural settlement is the oldest part of Bewdley as it is specified as one of the hamlets of the royal manor of Kidderminster in 1086. Thirdly, there is the High Street plan unit, not in this instance the most important street but, literally, the higher street. It runs south, parallel to the river, and the eastern burgage series is of irregular form (Fig. 4.1, IIIB). The western plot series abuts the deer park and is clearly planned, probably on land taken from the park (Fig. 4.1, IIIA). The northern side of Load Street, the broad, street market-place leading to the bridge, represents the fourth plan unit. The western end of the market-place contains the chapel of St Anne, the town church. The burgage series on either side are very different. Those on the northern side are extremely elongated with curving bounds running back to Dog Lane which may represent the line of an undocumented ditch linking the town gates with the river (Fig. 4.1, IV). Those on the southern side are much shorter and more regular and belong more properly with the fifth plan unit. Also notable is the deep setback in the frontages on this side of the road so as to increase the space available for market functions. The fifth plan unit, Severn-side South, is linked to these southern burgages of Load Street as the riverside plots are also very regular with a common back boundary (Fig. 4.1, V). It seems likely that at some stage this area contained by the rear of the High Street plots and Load Street was replanned, or planned anew, and laid out regularly. Finally, a series of very short plots, crammed between road and hillside, line each side of Welch Gate and represent a sixth plan unit. The town was gated by 1472 and there may have been a ditch to the south, along Lax Lane, as well as along Dog Lane, though there is no documentation.

(b) Bridgnorth

Bridgnorth, though a much larger town than Bewdley, can also be divided into six major plan units (Fig. 4.2), though two of them have distinctive subdivisions (Slater 1988b develops this analysis in more detail). The oldest contains both the site of the Anglo-Saxon promontory *burh* and the site of the later Norman castle. The northern neck of the promontory was marked by a substantial ditch, presumably of the *burh*, which is still evident in the townscape. The castle was very large, of double bailey form and the outer, northernmost, bailey provided the site for the incipient borough of Robert de Bellesme arranged along the parallel streets of the East and West Castle Street. This large unit might more properly be considered as two separate plan units therefore, despite its containment by the earlier *burh* ditch. East Castle Street was substantially rebuilt in the seventeenth century as one of the most fashionable streets of the town and its plots are of very different widths because of plot amalgamation (Fig. 4.2). It terminates in St Mary's collegiate church which also served as the castle chapel.

The second plan unit, perhaps of similarly early origin, is the eastern suburb, now called Low Town (Fig. 4.2). It has all the appearance of a typical suburban development along two streets at the approach to the bridge. However, it may well represent the medieval successor to a defined enclosure which, together with the bridge and the promontory *burh*, formed one unified defensive system designed to prevent Viking penetration up the Severn. Such a combination of elements is familiar from the early tenth century elsewhere in England (Hassall and Hill 1969: 191–4; Haslam 1984: 262–4). In later medieval times much of the area of this enclosure was given over to the Hospital of St John and Holy Trinity, founded before 1195. The road running along the east side of the narrow terrace of the Severn was diverted into the enclosure, presumably in Anglo-Saxon times, and medieval burgages are laid out along the two roads which lead to the bridge. It is consequently not a typical bridge-head suburb but should be regarded as a

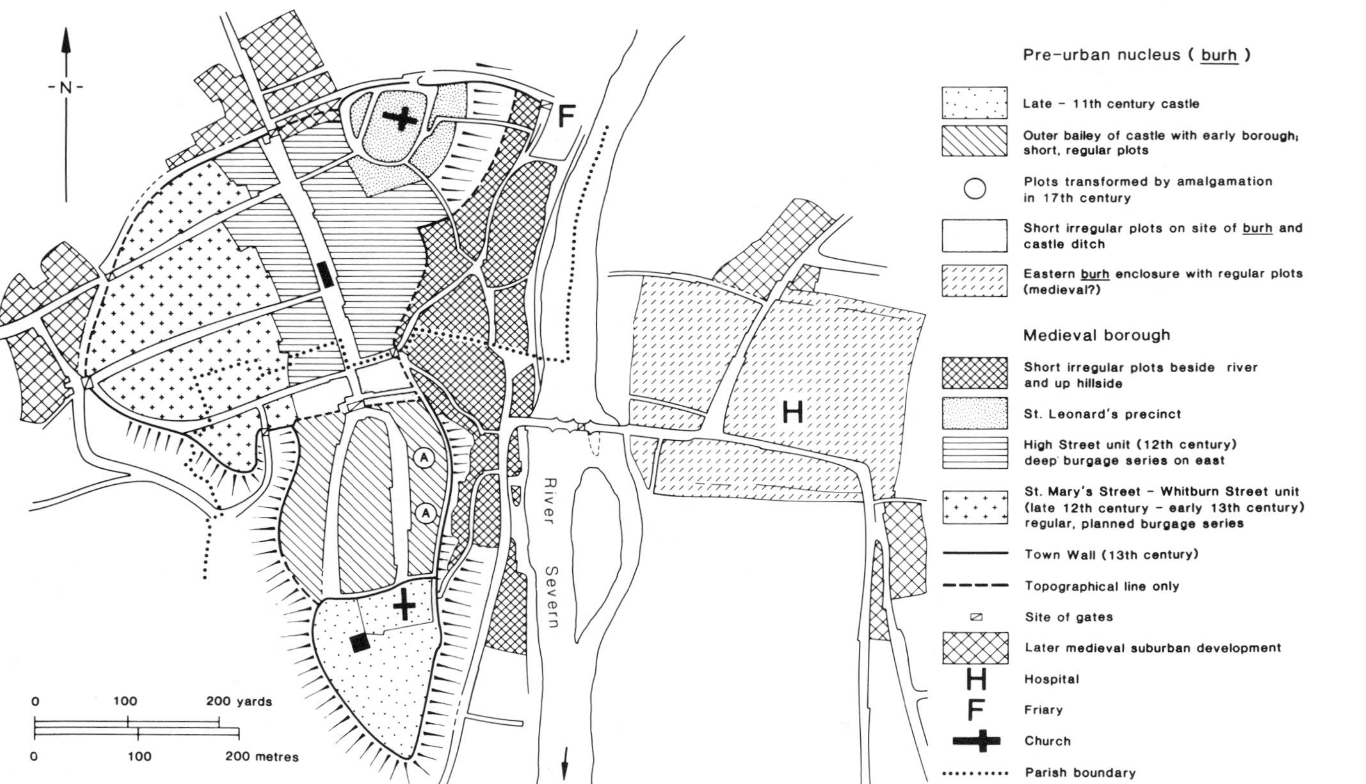

Figure 4.2 The plan-units of medieval Bridgnorth

properly urban unit which might well have had its own market space, since Mill Street widens appreciably at its junction with St John's Street (Fig. 4.2).

On the west bank of the Severn, climbing steeply up the slopes of the promontory, is an irregularly developed area of small plots and switchback lanes which forms the third plan unit. This area looks to the river and to Cartway (which formed the main entrance into Upper Town until the nineteenth century) for its livelihood. The area may already have been developing on the basis of river-borne goods before the medieval borough had been established, especially if the bridge was still in existence. Equally, however, it may have developed subsequent to the growth of the new borough. Linked with this plan unit is the circular enclosure of St Leonard's church and its associated buildings (Fig. 4.2). They form a miniature cathedral-close-like area at the northern end of the High Town but it is linked to the riverside area by a series of stepped lanes up the steep cliff.

The High Street forms the fifth plan unit and is remarkably similar to the Market Place unit in Ludlow. It is not quite as wide and therefore has not been subject to market colonization except for the town hall. High Street leads from the entrance gate of the castle and, though the regular width of the street gives an impression of careful planning, the plot pattern reveals that it developed by piecemeal development along its length from south to north as the town grew (Fig. 4.3). Since there was no planning of the plots they are of variable length on both sides of the road, those on the east being generally longer since they extend to the edge of the cliff top. Finally, grafted onto this High-Street unit, is the carefully-planned development of Whitburn Street, St Mary's Street and Listley Street at right angles to High Street. This, too, bears comparison with Ludlow in terms of its Broad Street–Mill Street unit. However, the Bridgnorth unit is not as sophisticated a piece of town-planning as it lacks the functionally differentiated service lanes between the main access roads. This plan unit, the High Street unit and St Leonard's, were surrounded with a ditch and town wall which linked with the defences of the castle. There are short suburban developments beyond the gates to the north, south and west, the latter gaining the name Little Brugg in medieval times. Other suburban features include St James's Hospital well to the south of Low Town, and a Franciscan friary beside the river below St Leonard's.

This outline of the town plans of Bewdley and Bridgnorth provide a base for more detailed analysis of a number of specific features which are of relevance to the interpretation of the Ludlow plan and which suggest that Conzen's interpretation requires modification in a number of respects.

Adaptation to existing development

Medieval surveyors commissioned to lay out new-planned areas within existing towns faced a number of problems. The most difficult to solve was

Figure 4.3 Planning processes in High Town, Bridgnorth

the fusing of the new area onto the old with the minimum of separation from, and disruption to, that older area. The provision of a plan which demanded a breakthrough street into the existing development presupposed an overarching authority which was not usually extant in medieval English towns. Most new developments therefore communicated with existing areas of the town via existing streets. Any rearrangement of existing burgages similarly required a centralized power structure and therefore existing plots were rarely interfered with. Unlike modern development processes, it was unusual in the extreme for a medieval surveyor to be able to impose an ideal plan upon a land surface that could be wiped clean of any existing features, whether natural or man-made. All medieval plans therefore have both an 'ideal' projection, which can usually be conceived as some geometrical figure, and which existed only in the mind of the surveyor, and an actuality – which was that ideal plan adapted by the surveyor to both the natural topography and to any existing features of the rural and sub-urban landscape. Even that actuality can be difficult to recover, however, since it may only have existed for a very brief period, if at all. Sometimes its existence was limited to a few pegs hammered into the ground a set distance apart over a period of a month or two (Slater 1987).

As with property sales in the industrial and modern periods, property allocation in medieval towns was often marked by the multiple purchase of plots by a single burgess with the aim of enhancing his income by the sub-letting of property. Once a burgess held three or four contiguous plots there was nothing to stop him departing from either the ideal, or the actual, plan devised by the surveyor within the outer boundary of his holding. This was especially so in the period before buildings were added to the street frontages but it could also be true of a later period. A series of contiguous medieval buildings could be demolished, or accidentally destroyed by fire, and redevelopment could be undertaken without regard to existing plot boundaries if those buildings and plots were all within a single holding. Documentation of these processes from the later medieval period are now available for some larger towns, and for some areas of Ludlow, but in most smaller towns such adaptation of the plot pattern is far less common than might be supposed. Even after major fires or war-time destruction, such as occurred in Bridgnorth in the Civil War period, towns were rebuilt within the existing framework of plots. This innate conservatism in town plans can be illustrated in both Bewdley and Bridgnorth for the phase of planned development in the medieval period.

One of the planned units at Bewdley is the plots that line the southern side of Load Street and the western side of Severn-side South (Fig. 4.1, V). Existing development to which they had to be adapted is represented by the plots lining the eastern side of High Street. These were, and are, of irregular length and the surveyor, rather than annex any of the longer plots, simply laid out a new, straight, rear boundary for his Severn-side South plots beyond the longest of the High Street plots and proceeded to lay out regular plots between this boundary and the new street (Fig. 4.1). The irregular piece of land without access which remained between the two plot series was annexed only slowly by one or two landowners from the High Street side, although a large area recently returned to the public realm to become a municipal garden. A similar process of grafting a new plot series onto an established one can be observed at Bridgnorth where the planned layout to the west of the High Town market-place was added to the irregular plot series which lined its western side. In this instance the new streets of the layout (Whitburn Street, St Mary's Street and Listley Street) provided access to the irregular intervening lands and they became plots in their own right (Fig. 4.3). The important point, however, is that the planned plot series of the side streets began with a straight line laid out beyond the irregular rear boundaries of the High Street plots, they did not annex land already occupied by those plot holders.

The addition of a planned unit to an irregular existing High Street layout is one of Conzen's hypotheses for the development and classification of the town plan of Ludlow, of course (Conzen 1968). However, it is noticeable that his hypothesis supposes that the irregular High Street plots have been largely absorbed by the plots laid out along the planned streets of the Mill Street–Broad Street unit. The comparative evidence from Bewdley and Bridgnorth suggests that such a process is unlikely and it becomes even more so when it is remembered that the High Street plots are supposedly amongst the first developed in Ludlow and the Mill Street–Broad Street plots amongst the last in Conzen's chronology. Long-established plots often with subsequent subdivisions and complex sub-ownership patterns, are much less likely to be absorbed by later-established, simply patterned plots especially when the former face onto the market-place, the prime social and economic focus of any medieval town. The implication of this reassessment is that either the High Street layout in Ludlow is later than the Mill Street–Broad Street layout or, more probably, that the two are contemporaneous and that Conzen has misinterpreted this part of the plan. If this is so, however, the whole morphogenetic developmental sequence in Ludlow has to be revised since the oldest and most recent medieval plan units are now being proposed as contemporary with each other. Further evidence might usefully be sought to uphold this revisionism, therefore, before proceeding along such a path.

The evidence of metrological analysis

The metrological analysis of medieval plot patterns using modern measurements of plot frontages has proved extremely fruitful in generating a more detailed understanding of the ways in which surveyors laid out new towns or parts of towns (Slater 1981; 1986). The techniques can be illustrated using an example from Ludlow where the pattern is particularly clear (Fig. 4.4). The plan shows the west side of Lower Broad Street, a contiguous plot series running from outside Broad Gate to the bridge. A continuous rear boundary encloses a block of plots which are very long (a breadth to length ratio of 1 : 16) though an intermediate transverse boundary midway along the length of many plots suggests that this extreme length is a result of the absorption of plots which once faced the southern continuation of Narrow Lane (Conzen 1988). However, the interest here is the width of the plots, not their length. Careful measurement of the modern house frontages are recorded in the third column of Figure 4.4, and then some of these measures are amalgamated where they lie between primary plot boundaries (those boundaries which run continuously from front to back of the plot without deviation) and the combinations are expressed in terms of statute perches (16·5 feet, 5·03 m.), the normal measure of medieval town planning in England (Slater 1981). The deviations from these statute measures are also recorded (Fig. 4.4, column 5). The interesting feature of this example is that the full plot series measures

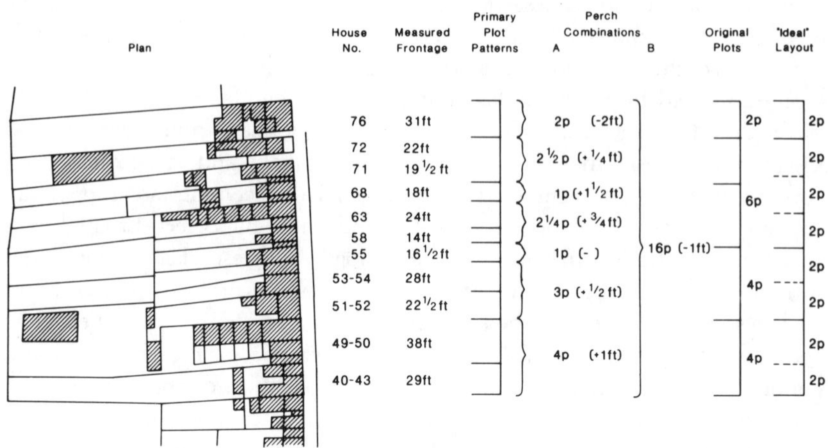

Figure 4.4 Metrological analysis of Lower Broad Street, Ludlow

exactly 16 perches, with an error of only one foot in 264. From these measures it is a short step, referring back to the pattern of primary boundaries, to suggest that there were originally four blocks of land ownership in this plot series, of 2, 6, 4 and 4 perches respectively from north to south. These blocks would then have been subdivided by the first landowners into smaller units which could be sublet, some of which accorded with statute perch measures and some of which did not. It also allows for speculation as to the 'ideal' layout in the mind of the surveyor when this area was first laid out for development since he would have been thinking in terms of regular plot dimensions, in this instance probably either two or four perches wide. Given that this was an area that was amongst the last to be laid out in the planned area of medieval Ludlow, and that it is known that a regularly recurring measure of burgage width elsewhere in the planned area was two perches (Speight and Lloyd 1978), this width seems the more probable. Conzen has noted elsewhere (1960) that this plot width is sufficient for a two-bay house parallel to the street frontage and it is not surprising, therefore, that most initial owners took up more than one burgage width if they hoped to sublet property to tenants.

These metrological techniques can be used to answer a number of other specific questions in the towns being studied. First, in Bewdley, analysis of the plots in the Wyre Hill plan unit confirms that this element of the town is a planned area and did not emerge from an area of earlier rural tofts. The plot series on the south side of Wyre Hill with its back lane and rectangular blocks of land has a depth of exactly 21 perches and the extant plot series as far as the end of Park Lane has a total length of 77 perches (Fig. 4.1, IIB). This suggests an individual plot width that would originally have been 3·5 perches wide giving 22 regularly-sized burgages. Unfortunately, none of the few surviving primary boundaries coincide with such a width, or with its multiples or divisions, probably because empty plots are far easier to rearrange than plots with buildings lining them, and, in this instance, metrological analysis can take us little further. There was a rapid decline of this part of Bewdley once the riverside settlement began to expand after the construction of the first bridge over the Severn in 1447. None the less, for a short period, these first recorded burgages were a profitable venture for the Countess of March.

A second example is the analysis of the plots in Low Town, Bridgnorth (Fig. 4.2). Again, the two series of plots lining the west side of Mill Street and the south side of St John's Street were carefully measured and when analysed both series prove to fit perfectly into a 16·5 foot, perch-based module showing that this area of the town was planned. In this instance five individual plots are just one perch wide, an unusually narrow plot width, suggesting either an above average degree of subdivision of original, larger plots, or unusually small plots from the beginning. Combination of plots within the primary boundary pattern shows that there is a recurring module of 3·5 perches and this is the more likely original size. There has therefore seemingly been an unusual degree of subdivision, either because of a great demand for burgage property (unlikely in this extensive town in an area so far from the principal economic focus in High Town) or in order to provide large numbers of cottage-sized properties. What is different in these divisions, again emphasizing the atypical nature of this suburban element of Bridgnorth, is that these subdivisions are burgage-like, with proper boundaries running the full length of the plot, rather than a pattern of groups of cottages sharing garden ground within an encompassing boundary.

The town plan of Bridgnorth also furnished an example of the possible unexpected complexity of metrological analysis. The most obviously planned area of the town is the parallel street system grafted onto the west side of High Street. The plot series lining each side of Whitburn, St Mary's, and Listley Streets have a clear geometric regularity with common rear boundaries and large numbers of primary boundaries which seem to the eye to be regularly spaced along parts of their length. Such clearly planned units of medieval towns should be easily analysed. In fact this plan unit proves to be unexpectedly complex. The two plot series lining St Mary's Street, for example, which are unaffected by the defences subsequently erected around this unit and which have been least affected by plot amalgamation and subdivision in the twentieth century (indeed, there has been little building replacement either), have proved unyielding to attempts to discern their original dimensions. The plots on the north side of the street are 12 perches deep and the series is 36 perches long in total but, though there are some perch-based combinations within this, there is no indication of the initial module despite the large number of surviving primary boundaries; similarly with the southern plot series. What is noticeable is the number of smaller plots on both sides of the street which are about 18·5 feet wide (eight in total) and the fact that multiples of this module recur between primary boundaries, particularly in the southern plot series. It is known that a variety of customary perch measures were in use in the countryside in England but, thus far, no example has been forthcoming of such customary measures being used in the planning of urban properties. It would be unusual, to say the least, to find such an example in a sophisticated piece of planning in a royal town like Bridgnorth and further analysis is called for before such a claim can be put forward with certainty; it is described here only to illustrate the complexity that can arise in seemingly simple metrological analyses.

An outline metrological analysis of Ludlow has already been published (Slater 1988a) but, as with Bridgnorth, there were many unresolved difficulties. Subsequent work has refined much of this interpretation and the pattern in Ludlow is much clearer so that it is now possible to suggest both the ideal plan of the Mill Street–Broad Street plan unit (to which should be added the High Street) and the early development processes. Taking the modern pattern of primary plot boundaries as the starting point (Fig. 4.5A), it is apparent that there are relatively few of them compared with Bridgnorth. This, in itself, suggests an active land market at some point in the past and, since the townscape is rich in buildings of the eighteenth century and earlier, in the distant past. Secondly, the irregularities in the boundaries of the street blocks are noticeable, with frequent indentations. These are probably to be explained as a necessary adjustment of the ideal plan as it was pegged out on the ground due to the steeply descending hillside on which it was located. Thirdly, the perch-based metrology of the plan is clear at the street block level of measurement (see below) but is much less so for the individual plots. There is little regularity discernible at the plot level.

Geometrical analysis

The relationship of these Ludlow plots to each other in terms of measurements can perhaps best be described in terms of relative proportions (Fig. 4.5B) because then some of the underlying regularity begins to emerge and it is possible to see some of the variety of ways in which initial landholders divided up their holdings. The reasons for the difficulties experienced in simple metrological analysis also become clear as it seems likely that these initial holdings may well have been quite large, amounting to half the street block in some instances. Though there are subsequent subdivisions into halves and thirds of these large blocks, there are also more complex proportional divisions, such as 4 : 5. This was particularly so where corner plots were involved with the possibility of development on two street frontages. This type of analysis is more properly termed geometrical rather than metrological and has been used to analyse the form of medieval

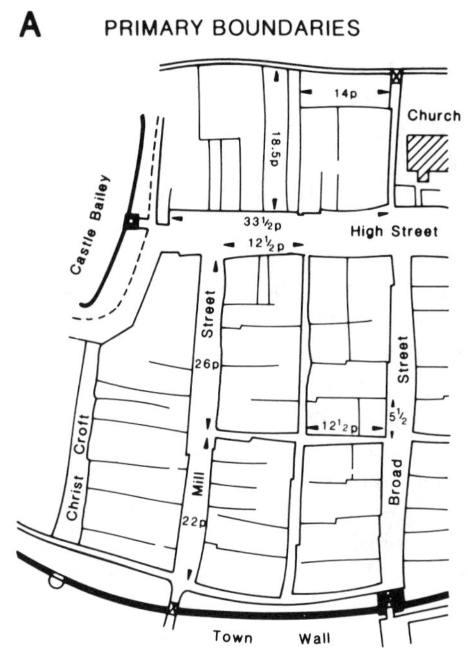

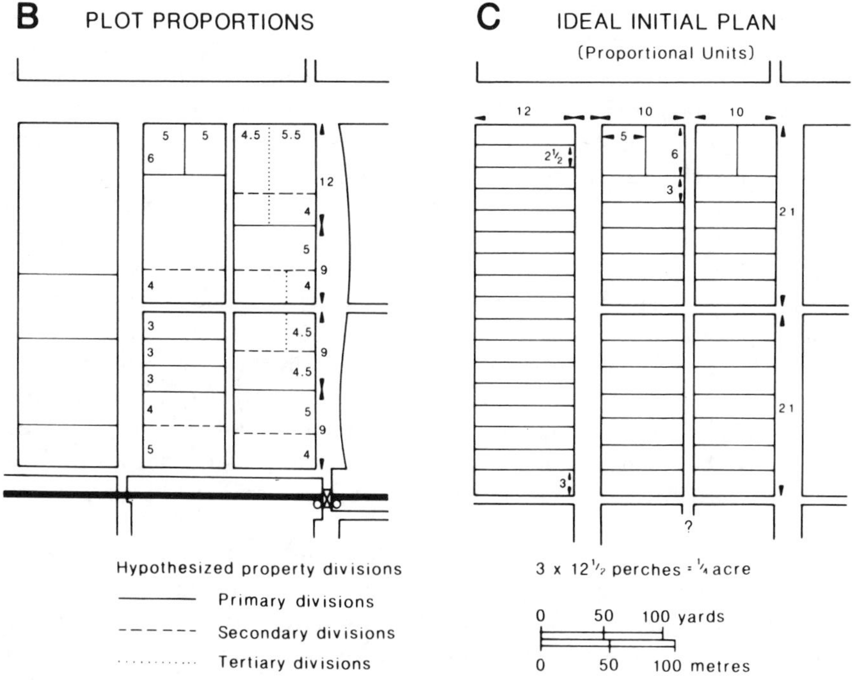

Figure 4.5 Geometrical analysis of Broad Street–Mill Street plan-unit, Ludlow

towns in Lower Silesia (Pudełko) 1964). What emerges from an analysis of this kind in Ludlow is a plot arrangement of great subtlety which matches the advanced nature of the overall plan of the Mill Street–Broad Street unit. Within this area there were originally three sizes of plots with length to breadth ratios of 6 : 5 (fronting the south side of High Street), 10 : 3 (on the east side of Mill Street and west side of Broad Street) and 12 : 2·5 (on the west side of Mill Street). They were therefore of different dimensions but of equal area (Fig. 4.5C). Consequently, initial burgage holders had the same quantity of land for their shilling rent. Translating these proportions in the ideal plan back into the perch-based measures of the actual ground layout, gives plots of 6·25 × 7·5 perches for the 6 : 5 proportioned plot, or just over a quarter of an acre (0·1 ha.), one of the most commonly recurring sizes of urban plots in medieval towns. Both in size of plot and in the variety of plot dimensions, this part of Ludlow bears close comparison with the planning of Lichfield in the mid twelfth century (Slater 1986), though the street-plan is very different.

The street block dimensions of the Mill Street–Broad Street unit are 12·5 × 26 perches for the blocks north of Bell Lane and 12·5 × 22 perches for the two southern blocks. This irregular geometry suggests some later disruption of the ideal plan and in this instance it may be that four perches of land, probably not yet built on, were removed from the southern street blocks to make way for the town wall. The planned cross lane which, with this adjustment, would have been outside the defences, was relocated inside the walls as Silk Mill Lane. However, the preparation for the construction of the walls implied by the 'Christ Croft' plot at the rear of the Mill Street plots (even though the walls were subsequently not aligned along this land (Conzen 1988)), implies that there should have been similar preparation made where the wall intersected Broad Street. Additional evidence that this might be the case is the fact that the full Lower Broad Street plot series on the west side of that street is also 22 perches long (Fig. 4.4). An alternative explanation, therefore, for the longer northern street blocks is that they deliberately contained more land for those plots which had frontages on the market-place as well as on Mill Street and Broad Street. It must be noticed in passing that many of the initial landowners in the two northern street blocks, nearer the economic focus of the town, subdivided their holdings not medially, as would usually be the case, but took advantage of the innovative back lanes to divide their holdings transversely (Fig. 4.5A). This is one reason why there are so few primary boundaries in this part of the plan.

Finally, it must be noticed that the plots on the north side of High Street are also laid out to precise perch-based dimensions; in this case they are 18·5 perches long and the plot series is a total of 33·5 perches along the frontage. This area, too, is therefore both clearly a planned layout, not an area of piecemeal development and, again, it is carefully integrated with the position of the town wall, itself dependent on the underlying topography along this part of the circuit. The impression that walls and plan unit were conceived at the same time is therefore strengthened.

To see what happens to a town plan where such planning is not integrated we must return to Bridgnorth. The superficial regularity and balance of the plan unit west of the market-place is exposed on closer examination to be an attempt to fit an 'ideal' defended town concept to an urban development which was already under way. The concept is a familiar one in the defence of high-medieval towns in continental Europe; a series of parallel streets are enclosed by an intra-mural street, walls, and a ditch which come to a point, marked by a heavily defended gate, at the central street. The result is like a castle bastion but on the scale of a whole town; additionally it minimizes the number of vulnerable gates while maximizing internal circulation. The plan was well suited to Bridgnorth High Town as this plan unit was laid out on fairly level land and the north and north-west were the most vulnerable parts of the town. Unfortunately, development of this plan unit had already extended well beyond the point along Whitburn Street where, ideally, the wall should have been curving to meet the gate in St Mary's Street. As a result, many established plots were truncated on the north side of Whitburn Street and some plot holders, in the area which was to become known as Little Brugg, found themselves outside the defensive circuit (Fig. 4.3). Despite this, the ideals of the plan were still compromised by the insertion of a gate at the point where the wall and ditch crossed Whitburn Street, as well as at the end of St Mary's Street. The intra-mural street between Whitburn and St Mary's Streets demanded by the ideal plan was probably never built and this area, with already poorly-endowed defensive capabilities, was left with two gates to defend (Fig. 4.3). The plan is an unusual one for Britain and almost certainly derives from the fact that Bridgnorth was held by the king, whose planners would certainly have been familiar with the most recent developments in town-planning in France and elsewhere in Europe.

Ludlow: a revised chronology

In its analysis of Ludlow this chapter has concentrated upon the most interesting of that town's plan units, the sophisticated Mill Street–Broad Street unit. Given the importance of Ludlow in Conzen's published work on both town-plan analysis and townscape conservation, it is apposite to summarize the conclusions of this analysis and to present a revised chronology for the morphogenetic evolution of the medieval plan of the town as a whole. First, it seems likely that Conzen, mindful of central European urban development, has given too much prominence to the castle as the pre-urban nucleus. Equally important was the long-distance north–south route which forded the Teme and followed the line of what was to become Old Street and Corve Street. It was this road that became the focus for the first elements of the town of Ludlow, not the High Street axis along the ridge. Dinham was developing at the same time, to the south of the castle, to house the people more concerned with servicing the castle but the early town grew up the slope from the ford, along the length of Old Street, and may already have been in existence in 1086 as one of the unspecified members of Stanton Lacy manor. It took its name from the *hlaw* (tumulus with Anglo-Saxon secondary burial) which marked the hilltop and which the church of St Lawrence had superseded, probably by the late eleventh century.

This settlement was expanded and made specifically urban with the laying out of the planned burgage series on each side of Corve Street down the hill north from the church. The (rectangular?) market-place was located at the east end of the church itself, on the top of the hill, and midway between the older tofts and crofts of Old Street and the new-planned burgage properties of Corve Street. Since 12 burgages at the northern end of Corve Street were granted to the Knights Hospitaller at Dinmore before 1186 and became a distinctive legal entity for the remainder of the medieval period, this part of the town must have been fully developed by the late twelfth century at latest. It was served by its own chapel of St Leonard and recent archaeological excavations have uncovered a substantial stone house with tiled floor on the west side of Corve Street which has been assigned to the twelfth century (Klein and Roe 1988). It was at this time too, that the castle was being enlarged and its gate realigned to face east along the ridge top towards the church and growing town (Renn 1987). In terms of defence this was the vulnerable side of the castle (surrounded as it was with steep slopes on its other three sides) and to fill this open space with a well-defended town must have been an attractive proposition both strategically and economically. At the same time, the rapid development of the ribbon-like town along the routeway must have led to demands for the improvement of the river crossing over the fast-flowing Teme. The provision of a bridge upstream from the existing ford was clearly one of those deliberately planned road diversions that are comparatively common in medieval England when manorial lords were anxious to divert traffic through new-planned market places for their own economic benefit (Beresford 1967). The new bridge and the laying out of Broad Street are necessarily complementary and, as Broad Street developed, Old Street may well have begun to decline. Broad Street was certainly developed before 1221, when St John's hospital was established at its southern extremity (Weyman 1909), and probably before 1216, when St Giles' leper hospital was founded in Ludford, on the other side of the bridge. Indeed, it may date to the turn of the century since work began on totally rebuilding the parish church in 1199 and the planned extension of the town would be a likely stimulus for such work. It may be that Broad Street was conceived, and began to be developed, before the rest of the plan between it and the castle, but it cannot have been many years before the sophisticated plan of High Street and Mill Street with the rear service lanes and the land reserved for the town walls (licenced in 1233) were pegged out and gradually sold off, development moving westwards and southwards away from the market-place. The market functions now found themselves with a much increased broad street space all the way from Bull Ring to castle gate and by 1270 the stalls in the new market-place were being recorded in the first surviving rental (Lloyd 1979). In 1283, the powerful Palmers' Guild built their guildhall on the western side of Mill Street, an indication, perhaps, that development of the new-planned town had nearly been completed and that only plots at its western extremity were still available. Metrological, geometrical and chronological evidence would therefore seem to support this revised interpretation of the development of the town plan of Ludlow.

Conclusions

M. R. G. Conzen has long advocated the necessity for comparative studies if the understanding of medieval plan development is to be advanced. He has suggested, too, that those comparisons need to be made on a European scale. In the past decade some progress has been made in both directions but research is still at an early stage. The complex, composite town plans of most English medieval towns of any size mean that the unravelling of the processes and chronology of their development has proceeded only slowly. However, though the number of detailed case studies is still small, some common threads are beginning to emerge and the processes of medieval property development and speculation, and of town-planning, are becoming clearer.

Comparative work has concentrated, thus far, on later medieval planned towns as a category and for this reason Conzen's study of Ludlow and Conwy acts as a standard against which new ideas can be tested and refined. At the same time, recent research reflects back to suggest revisions and reinterpretations of the plan development of Ludlow. The case studies used in this chapter are neighbouring towns of Ludlow existing in a generally similar social, cultural and economic milieu in the medieval period. They reflect a similar composite pattern of plan development to that analysed for Ludlow but the development of the techniques of metrological analysis of burgage series and the geometrical analysis of plan elements has suggested processes of development in these neighbouring towns which were most probably happening in Ludlow too.

None the less, although Bridgnorth in particular was a royal town with a population and level of economy somewhat higher than Ludlow, and with plan elements that reflect concurrent European practices, the still more advanced nature of the Ludlow Mill Street–Broad Street plan unit continues to stand out. Conzen has recently suggested (1988) that the continental influence in the Ludlow plan derives from Gascony and the close ties engendered by the wine trade between that region and the Severn basin. However, the chronology is not especially helpful to the argument (the Gascon bastide plans are of the 1260s) and, as he himself points out, none of Ludlow's neighbouring West Midland towns have such a developed plan unit with back lanes. Since both Bridgnorth and Bewdley are beside the Severn itself rather than on a tributary, as is Ludlow, it could reasonably be expected that such plan developments would take place in these towns too, especially given their royal lordship. However, it may be that the appropriate links with Gascony are not those of the Angevin royal house, but the de Lacy family themselves. Important a place though Ludlow was, much of the energy of the de Lacy family was concentrated in developing their rich Irish lands. As lords of Meath, the de Lacys had planned the town of Drogheda in the 1170s as their principal entrepôt and, in the thirteenth century, it was both a more important port than Dublin (Bradley 1985), and it had close links with the Gascon wine trade. The de Lacys may therefore have brought their new town-planning ideas to Ludlow from Gascony via Meath. Speculations such as these, and the further refinement of ideas on medieval plan development, will only be advanced by continuing comparative studies on a European scale.

Acknowledgements

I am grateful to James Bond for sharing some of his information on the development of Bewdley with me and to M. R. G. Conzen for friendly discussion in the streets of Ludlow.

References

Bassett, S. R., 1980–1. 'Medieval Lichfield: a topographical review', *Transactions, South Staffordshire Archaeological and Historical Society*, 22: 93–121.

Beresford, M. W., 1967. *New towns of the Middle Ages.*

Biddle, M. and Hill, D., 1971. 'Late Saxon planned towns', *Antiquaries Journal, 51*: 70–85.

Bond, C. J., 1977. 'The topography of Pershore', in Bond, C. J. and Hunt, A. M., 'Recent archaeological work in Pershore', *Vale of Evesham Historical Society Research Papers*, 6: 18–26.

Bradley, J., 1985. 'Planned Anglo-Norman towns in Ireland', in Clarke, H. B. and Simms, A. (eds.), *The comparative history of urban origins in non-Roman Europe* [BAR International Series, 255] 411–68.

Carter, A., 1983. 'The Anglo-Saxon origins of Norwich: the problems and approaches', *Anglo-Saxon England*, 7: 175–204.

Chitty, L. F., 1963. 'The Clum-Clee ridgeway: a prehistoric trackway across South Shropshire', in Foster, I. L. and Alcock, L. (eds.), *Culture and environment*, 171–92.

Clifton-Taylor, A., 1978. *Six English towns.*

Conzen, M. R. G., 1960. 'Alnwick, Northumberland: a study in town-plan analysis', *Publications, Institute of British Geographers, 27.*

Conzen, M. R. G., 1968. 'The use of town plans in the study of urban history', in Dyos, H. J. (ed.), *The study of urban history*, 113–30.

Conzen, M. R. G., 1988. 'Morphogenesis, morphological regions and secular human agency in the historic townscape, as exemplified by Ludlow', in Denecke, D. and Shaw, G. (eds.), *Urban historical geography: recent progress in Britain and Germany*, 253–72.

Gould, J., 1976. *Lichfield: archaeology and development.*

Haslam, J. (ed.), 1984. *Anglo-Saxon towns in southern England.*

Hassall, T. and Hill, D., 1969. 'Pont de l'Arche: Frankish influence on the West Saxon *burh?*', *Archaeological Journal, 127:* 188–95.

Hope, W. H. St J., 1909. 'The ancient topography of Ludlow', *Archaeologia, 61:* 383–9.

Klein, P. and Roe, A., 1988. *The Carmelite Friary Corve Street, Ludlow: its history and excavation* [Ludlow Research Paper No. 6].

Lloyd, D., 1979. *Broad Street, its houses and residents through eight centuries* [Ludlow Research Paper No. 3].

Mason, J. F. A., 1957. *The borough of Bridgnorth 1157–1957.*

Mawer, A., Stenton, F. M. and Houghton, F. T. S., 1927. *The place-names of Worcestershire* [English Place Name Society, IV].

Pudełko, J., 1964. 'Proba pomiarowej metody badania planow niektorych miast sredniowiecznych w oparciu o zagadnienie działki', *Kwartalnik Architektury i Urbanistyki, 9:* 71–92.

Renn, D., 1987. '"Chastel de Dynan": the first phases of Ludlow', in Kenyon, J. R. and Avent, R. (eds.), *Castles in Wales and the Marches: essays in honour of D. J. Cathcart King*, 55–74.

Shoesmith, R., 1980. *Excavation at Castle Green, Hereford city excavations I* [C.B.A. Research Report, 36].

Shoesmith, R., 1982. *Excavations on and close to the defences, Hereford city excavations II* [C.B.A. Research Report, 46].

Slater, T. R., 1981. 'The analysis of burgage patterns in medieval towns', *Area, 13:* 211–16.

Slater, T. R., 1985. 'Medieval new town and port: a plan-analysis of Hedon, East Yorkshire', *Yorkshire Archaeological Journal, 57:* 23–51.

Slater, T. R., 1986. 'The topography and planning of medieval Lichfield: a critique', *Transactions, South Staffordshire Archaeological and Historical Society, 16:* 11–35.

Slater, T. R., 1987. 'Ideal and reality in English episcopal medieval town planning', *Transactions, Institute of British Geographers, N.S.12:* 191–203.

Slater, T. R., 1988a. 'English medieval town planning', in Denecke, D. and Shaw, G. (eds.), *op. cit.*, 93–108.

Slater, T. R., 1988b. 'Medieval composite plan towns in England: evidence from Bridgnorth, Shropshire', *School of Geography, University of Birmingham Working Paper Series, 41.*

Speight, M. E. and Lloyd, D. J., 1978. *Ludlow houses and their residents* [Ludlow Research Papers, No. 1].

Spearman, M., 1988. 'The medieval townscape of Perth', in Lynch, M., Spearman, M. and Stell, G. (eds.), *The Scottish medieval town*, 42–59.

Weyman, H. T., 1909. 'Confirmation by Walter de Lacy of the Hospital of St John',

Transactions, Shropshire Archaeological Society, 3rd Ser. 4: xviii.
Whitehand, J. W. R., 1981. 'Conzenian ideas: extension and development', in Whitehand, J. W. R., (ed.), *The urban landscape: historical development and management, papers by* M. *R.* G. *Conzen* [Institute of British Geographers Special Publication, No. 13] 127–52.
Whitehand, J. W. R. and Alauddin, K., 1969. 'The town plans of Scotland: some preliminary considerations', *Scottish Geographical Magazine, 85*: 109–21.
Williams, J. H., 1979. *St Peter's Street, Northampton: excavations 1973–76.*

5 Central place and medieval new town: the origins of Thame, Oxfordshire

C. J. Bond

Towns have been described as 'the most complicated form of human settlement' (Dymond 1974: 141). Their social and physical complexity has compelled scholars interested in their origins and development to adopt approaches which have transcended disciplinary barriers. As a geographer, Professor Conzen has pioneered the analysis of town plans as a source of historical evidence (Conzen 1960, 1962, 1966; Whitehand 1981). Conversely, some historians have attempted the reconstruction of earlier town plans using documentary sources (Salter 1960, 1969; Urry 1967). Others have studied the urban fabric together with the documents to address wider questions of urban origins (Beresford 1967). Archaeologists, faced with the imminent destruction of much of their primary evidence, have carried out numerous surveys using both historical and topographical data to assess the implications of urban redevelopment (for the south Midlands of England, see Benson and Cook 1967; Fasham 1972; Miles and Fowler 1972; Simpson 1973; Rodwell 1975; Slater and Wilson 1977; Astill 1978; Leech 1981).

The need to reassess the origins, topographical development, status and function of individual towns, both large and small, has been a recurrent theme in many recent discussions. As an example, this chapter will examine the case of Thame, a small market town in the eastern part of Oxfordshire, England. Thame has been widely quoted as a classic example of a planned medieval new town (eg Beresford 1967: 477–8; Anderson 1970: 158–60; Airs *et al.* 1975; Aston and Bond 1976: 87–91; Beckinsale and Beckinsale 1980: 284–7), and has been the subject of several historical studies (Lupton 1860; Brown and Guest 1935; Guest *et al.* 1962; Clarke 1978). The aims here are first, to identify Thame's rank within the local settlement hierarchy; second, to assess its sphere of influence; third, to explore the origins of Thame's central-place functions and its character prior to its emergence as an episcopal planned borough after the late twelfth century; and, finally, to re-examine the evidence for the plantation of the new town, particularly by the use of the techniques of town-plan analysis pioneered by Conzen and developed further by Slater (1980, 1981).

The hierarchy of towns in the Oxford region

Various types of settlement hierarchy have been defined, reflecting different modes of social and economic organisation (Smith 1976; Hodges 1987). Since the early Middle Ages the settlement pattern of the Oxford region has included a well-stratified system of interlocking central places with competitive markets (Fig. 5.1), very much along the lines of Christaller's classic model (Baskin 1966; Haggett 1965: 121–5). By the early nineteenth century four distinct tiers of towns, places where central-place functions were concentrated, can be recognised within the region, standing out from the mass of rural villages. Oxford itself remained dominant as the regional capital, as it had been since the tenth century, with Reading emerging as a rival in the south-eastern extremity of the region. There were important secondary centres in Banbury, Abingdon, Newbury and Aylesbury, then a third tier of moderately prosperous market towns (including Thame) spaced at intervals of 15–20 km, and a fourth tier of smaller local market centres 8–15 km apart. Each fourth-tier centre might have 15–20 villages within its hinterland, but it did not have a monopoly on the provision of services for those villages, which would for some purposes have to look towards one or more of the higher-tier centres. A fifth tier of defunct market centres, places with urban aspirations in the Middle Ages which had lapsed long before the nineteenth century, can be recognised among the settlements now defined as villages.

Despite its stratified nature, this hierarchy was not inflexible or static, and both promotion and relegation were possible within it. Wallingford, for example, was on a par with Oxford in the late Saxon period, but had declined to the status of a third-tier centre by the fifteenth century. Several other third-tier towns, including Thame, are 'medieval new towns' which, by definition, might not be expected to take their place in the hierarchy until the twelfth or thirteenth century. Other promotions were abortive or short-lived; the acqusition of market or borough charters at places like Islip, Chinnor, Middleton Stoney and Stratton Audley, represented attempts to elevate those places into the fourth tier, but they soon reverted to their earlier village rank. Since 1900 more of the fourth-tier towns have dropped below the urban threshold (Bond 1980, 1986).

Thame and its hinterland

The sphere of influence of any one of these central places can be defined by a number of criteria, and one of the advantages of dealing with the medieval or post-medieval periods is that hinterlands defined by theoretical means can be compared with reality using documentary sources. The simplest theoretical device is the mesh of unweighted polygons which, in effect, identifies for every point on the ground its nearest town. Using the

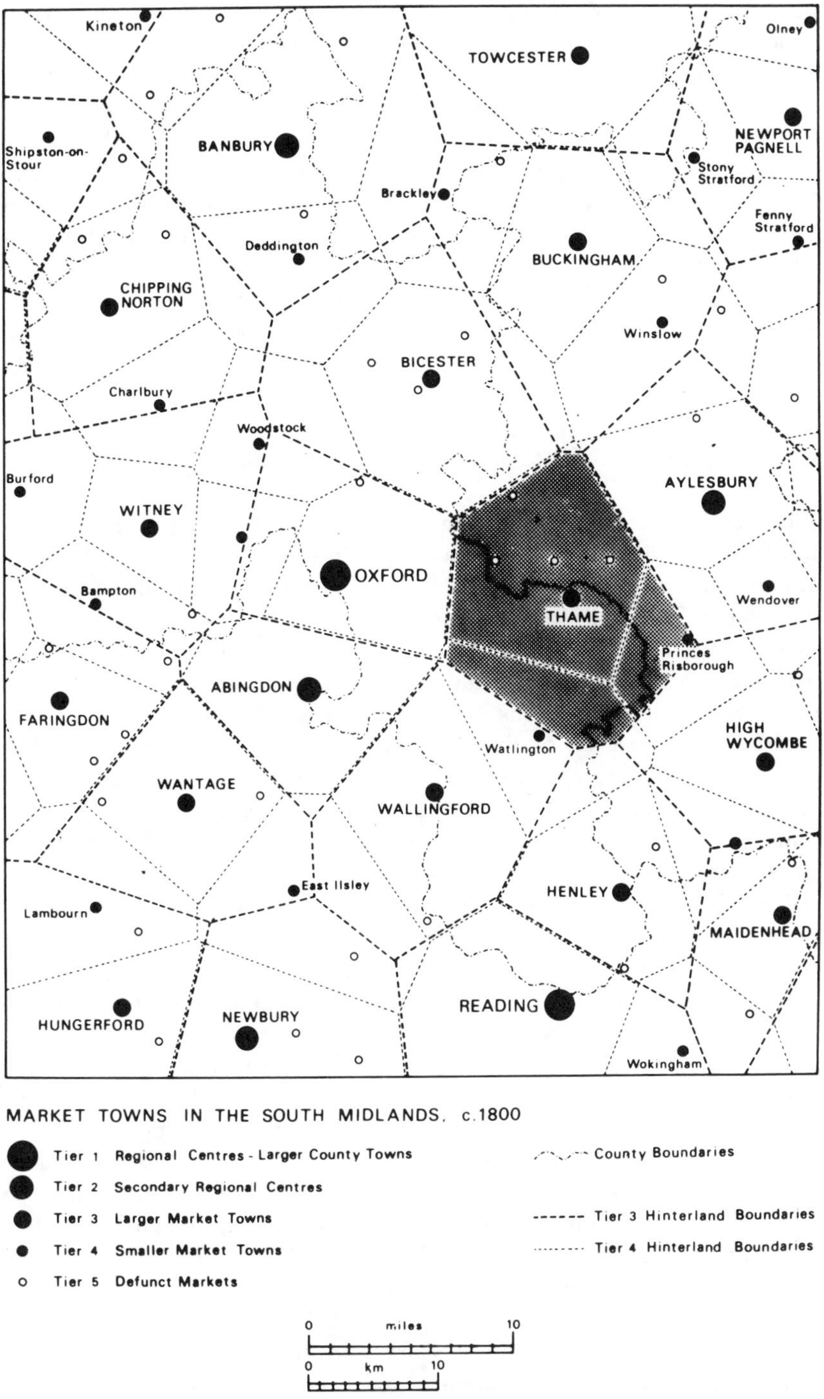

MARKET TOWNS IN THE SOUTH MIDLANDS, c.1800

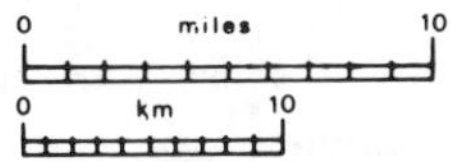

Figure 5.1 The urban hierarchy in part of the south Midlands, *c.*1800

particular example of Thame, the bounds of such a polygon erected for any period from the twelfth to the early nineteenth centuries lie between 5·3 km and 12·6 km distant from the town. The later eclipse of the fourth-tier centres of Watlington and Princes Risborough is reflected in the expansion of Thame's theoretical polygon southwards and eastwards over their former hinterlands (Fig. 5.1). Thame's real commercial hinterland can be assessed for the nineteenth century by the range from which market carts and carriers ran a regular service into its market. Its sphere of influence as an administrative centre is represented by the extent of its Poor Law Union or its County Court District. Although different criteria inevitably project slightly different areas, the general concordance between them is very striking (Fig. 5.2).

Central-place functions and the origins of Thame

What factors determined which particular places were going to emerge from the mass of agricultural settlements to attain this superior urban status? To answer this question it is necessary to look more closely at central-place functions. These fall into two major categories: first, the provision of services meeting the needs of the hinterland, such as market facilities whereby people living in the surrounding rural settlements can dispose of their own production surplus in exchange for goods which they are unable to produce themselves, or the industrial processing of hinterland products and their subsequent redistribution; and second, a variety of administrative, religious and sometimes military roles which were imposed by, or were under the ultimate control of, a more central authority based further up in the hierarchy.

For certain functions in the first category, especially marketing, the general spacing of centres was predetermined by the needs of traders and consumers. During the Middle Ages few places in Oxfordshire were more than 8–10 km from their nearest market, the maximum convenient distance for a man to cover on foot with goods for sale or goods purchased. Broadly comparable intervals between market centres have been noted elsewhere (Dickinson 1932; Coates 1965; Palliser and Pinnock 1971; Hodder and Orton 1976: 57–60). Other studies have pointed to more complex factors in the spacio-temporal distribution of markets, including the early emergence of periodic markets held on different days, which provided a cycle for itinerant traders within a relatively closely-spaced group of fourth- and fifth-tier centres (Fox 1973; Unwin 1981). Some evidence of a circuit network based on trader-requirements can be detected in the Vale of White Horse during the early Middle Ages (Bond 1986: 136), but over much of Oxfordshire the needs of the country-dweller were met by fewer, larger market towns; by the end of the Middle Ages, even after most of the fifth-tier markets had ceased, the average size of market hinterlands in Oxfordshire

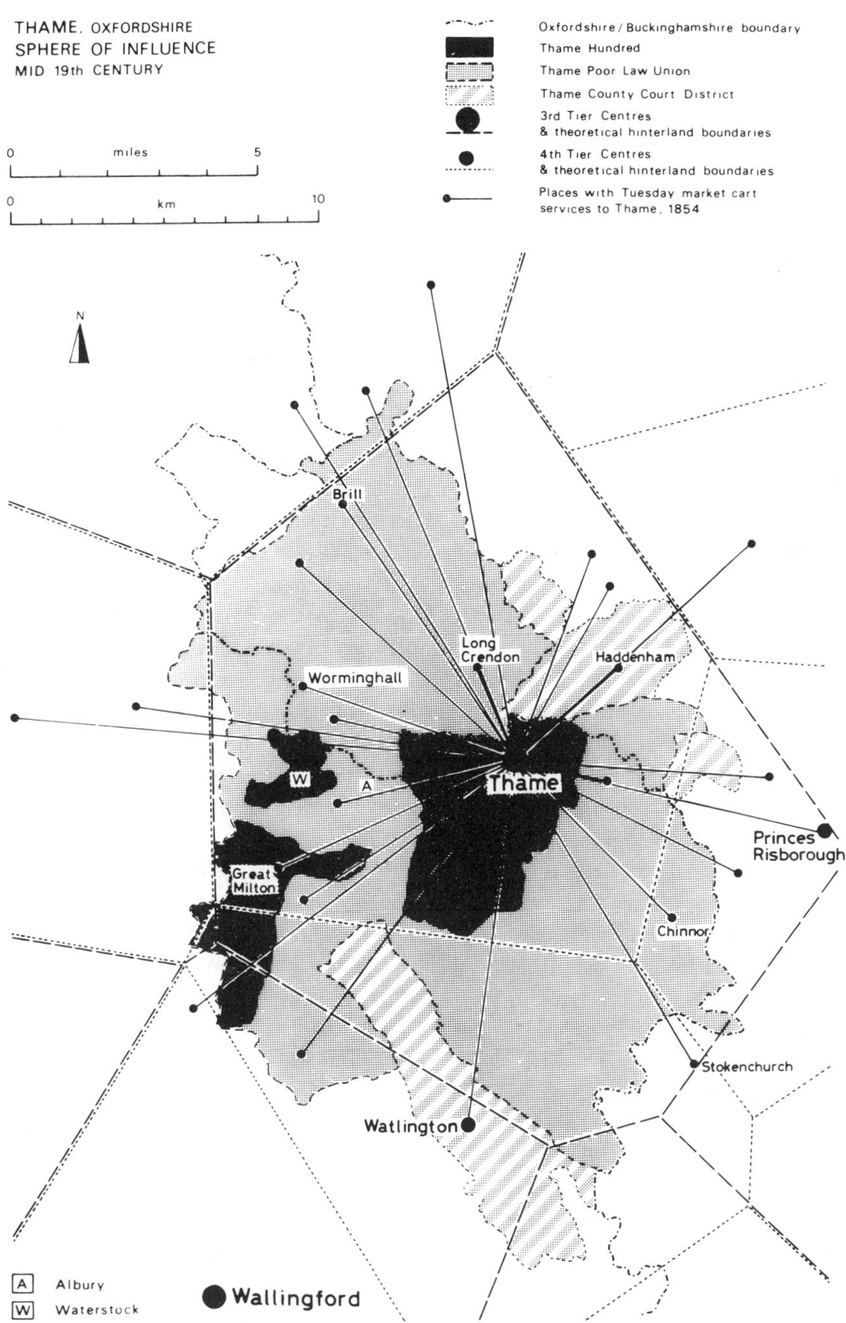

Figure 5.2 Spheres of influence of Thame, Oxfordshire in the mid-nineteenth century

was still less than the English average (Everitt 1967). This position remained almost unchanged into the nineteenth century, when improving transport facilities began to make this close-knit mesh an anachronism, and threatened the position of the smallest and weakest fourth-tier centres like Watlington (Bond 1980).

At a broad geographical level, the most favourable locations for markets are likely to be at the margins of two or more different regions specialising in different kinds of production, so that they can serve as points for the interchange of different commodities: local examples include Watlington, Princes Risborough and Wendover, in a line immediately below the Chiltern chalk scarp facing out over the flat claylands of the Thame valley. Accessibility is an important consideration for market centres, so they tend to develop in locations favourable for communications: Princes Risborough and Wendover are sited at the head of wind gaps through the Chilterns, while Thame and Aylesbury are located near crossing-points over the River Thame. The river was navigable until the eighteenth century, and Thame today is the focal point of no less than ten radiating roads. Where man-made features are concerned, however, there are always dangers of circular arguments – did the bridge or ford attract settlement to the site, or was the crossing-point constructed to improve access to the settlement? In the end it must be questioned whether as complex an organism as a town can ever develop spontaneously at a point of supposed geographical advantage, without deliberate encouragement and stimulation by some individual or institution in a position of power. Landownership and estate policy must now be seen as the key factor in initiating the emergence of towns, though their subsequent success or failure may be affected by a much wider range of factors.

For many centuries the functions of central places have been concentrated in settlements of the class which we refer to as towns, and up to this point the two terms have been used more or less interchangeably. However, this equation did not necessarily always apply. Just as hinterlands can be defined by a variety of criteria, central places could have a variety of functions, some of which could readily operate from outside the context of anything we would regard as a town. How can we identify central places in a pre-urban or proto-urban context?

In terms of territorial organization, it is now clear that before the ninth century in southern England certain large royal, episcopal or monastic estates were beginning to assume a special importance in the emergence of central places. A wide range of social and economic activities may be attached to an estate of this character, and it may develop several distinct foci, any of which may subsequently serve as pre-urban nuclei. The management of the estate and the consumption of its agricultural produce is likely to be conducted from an aristocratic residence or specialized precinct such as a palace or monastery. Arising out of this, such estates may contain a hundred meeting-place, reflecting a role as administrative and judicial centres. They may also become important ecclesiastical centres, containing a large and ancient minster church whose status is markedly superior to that of the surrounding rural parish churches. Some may acquire a strategic military role. Occasionally some may develop specialized craft or industrial functions. Any of these fields of activity will bring together numbers of military or religious personnel, bureaucrats and artisans, people who are not themselves primary producers, so there will be a need to import foodstuffs and other raw materials and establish a mechanism for the exchange of goods through markets and fairs (Haslam 1984; Hodges 1982, 1988).

As the example of the Ramsbury–Chisbury–Bedwyn group of settlements in Wiltshire shows, not all of these functions are necessarily important at the same time, or need to take place in exactly the same location (Aston and Bond 1976: 58–60, and discussed more fully in Haslam 1984: 94–102). Indeed, each function has certain specific locational desiderata which may be in conflict with the needs of others. The prime requirements of the commercial function are maximum accessibility, so market-places tend to be centrally sited, at meetings of routes, avoiding physical barriers; and, if the pre-existing route network was insufficient, roads might be diverted to improve access, as occurred in Thame in 1219. By contrast, the requirements of a religious rule or the wishes of a social elite to insulate themselves from the rest of the population may demand greater seclusion for those functions; and if there is a military component concerned with defence, then outright inaccessibility may be a positive advantage.

It is important to recognize that a wide range of central-place functions were already organized and operating before the period when many of our present towns first took shape; but that, because of the conflicting requirements of those functions, they could be segregated in different localities, rather than focussed in one place. The extent to which these activities subsequently become permanently concentrated in a single location is one of the criteria of urban success. To understand the origins of any town, we therefore need to explore its antecedents.

When we turn to the specific example of Thame, it appears at first sight to be an unpromising subject for such an investigation prior to the plantation of the medieval new town. The area is not especially well-endowed either with archaeological evidence or with early written sources such as pre-Conquest charters. However, some headway can be made by referring to some of the early central-place functions described above and testing the extent to which Thame accords with them.

(a) Thame as an ancient estate centre

'Thame' is an example of the topographical rather than the habitative class of place-names. The name of the estate is taken from that of the river, a Celtic or possibly pre-Celtic word, the meaning of which remains uncertain: Ekwall (1928: 390–1) doubted whether it was identical with the name 'Thames', which has connotations of darkness, but was unable to suggest any alternative etymology, and more recent scholarship has shed no further light on the problem. Gelling (1978: 126) has remarked that topographical names may be characteristic of areas of exceptionally early English settlement. Moreover, topographical names tend to be characteristic of places which were central to a great composite estate, and other examples have been noted elsewhere in the region, including Lambourn, Blewbury, Faringdon, Cuddesdon, Swalcliffe, and Cropredy (Gelling 1978: 123–5; Ford 1979: 152–5; Dickinson 1974).

In the Domesday survey Thame appears as a large sixty-hide manor held by the Bishop of Lincoln. It had previously belonged to the see of Dorchester, which had been transferred to Lincoln soon after 1072. The Anglo-Saxon Chronicle refers to the death at Thame in 971 of Oscetel, Archbishop of York and previously Bishop of Dorchester (Whitelock 1955: 207), perhaps implying that there was then some sort of episcopal residence there. A later tradition places this residence on the site of Thame Park, which was granted away by the Bishop of Lincoln in 1139 for the foundation of a Cistercian abbey (Brown and Guest 1935: 8).

The earliest documentary record of Thame occurs fortuitously in a charter of 672–4 granting lands in Surrey to Chertsey Abbey; this was confirmed by King Wulfhere of Mercia, who 'placed his hand on the altar in the residence which is called *Tamu* and subscribed with the sign of the Holy Cross with his own hand' (Whitelock 1955: no. 54, 440–1; Gelling 1979: no. 309, 148–9; Sawyer 1968: no. 1165, 343–4).

According to Stenton (1947: 432) Thame, together with the bishop's other demesne manors of Great Milton, Banbury, Cropredy and Dorchester, formed 'a great episcopal estate of immemorial antiquity'. It is not clear, however, when Thame was first acquired by the bishop. There is persuasive archaeological evidence for an early centre of West Saxon royal power north of the Thames around Dorchester and Cuddesdon (Dickinson 1974), and it is possible that Thame was one of several royal estates granted by King Cynegils after his baptism in 635 to endow the first West Saxon bishopric. Wulfhere's presence nearly forty years later may indicate that Thame had reverted to royal hands after the area had passed under Mercian control, in which case it must have been restored some time after 672–4 to the new Mercian bishopric of Dorchester, established after the removal of the West Saxon see to Winchester.

Thame thus conforms with one of the prerequisites for the emergence of a central place, probably royal and certainly episcopal ownership, with the likelihood of some sort of palace or episcopal residence somewhere in the vicinity.

(b) Thame as an ancient administrative centre

Thame was also the centre of a hundred, first recorded in detail in the Hundred Rolls of 1279, when it consisted of three detached, but not widely separated, parts: Thame itself (with its hamlets of Attington, Moreton and

North Weston) and Tetsworth; part of Great Milton (including Little Milton and Ascot); and Waterstock (Rot. Hundr. ii: 820–2). The same bounds endure on Bryant's map of 1823. The principal hundred courts met half-yearly in June and December at Harrington Hill on Milton Common, while three-weekly courts were held in Thame itself (Guest *et al.* 1962: 116). The courthouse, which stood immediately south of the church, was demolished in 1891 (Brown and Guest 1935: 13).

The origins of Thame hundred are unclear. Its boundaries significantly fail to respect the ancient parishes; the Thame portion excludes the chapelries of Sydenham and Towersey, and the Great Milton portion excludes the hamlets of Coombe and the two Chilworths; but there is no internal evidence for whether the parish or the hundred is the older unit.

Hundreds are very imperfectly rubricated in the Oxfordshire Domesday. The description of the Bishop of Lincoln's estates begins with his principal demesne manors of Dorchester, Thame, Great Milton, Banbury, Cropredy and Eynsham, the first of which is preceded by the sub-heading 'in Dorchester hundred', but the hundreds of Thame and Banbury find no mention. However, the Dorchester estate itself amounts to nearly a hundred hides, while Thame (sixty hides), with Great Milton (forty hides) and Banbury (fifty hides) with Cropredy (fifty hides) make up two more blocks of exactly a hundred hides each. The Bishop of Lincoln thus held a triple hundred in Oxfordshire which is reminiscent of the Bishop of Worcester's triple hundred of Oswaldslow in Worcestershire, and it has been suggested that such groupings were part of a reorganization carried out in the early tenth century, whereby each triple hundred was expected to provide the king with a ship for naval defence (John 1964: 113–26).

In Domesday Book the bishop's demesnes of Thame and Great Milton are described separately from the holdings of the knights or men-at-arms settled on his land (Table 5.1). Most of the holdings can be identified from the later history of the fees. The two tenants named William on Table 5.1 were probably the same person for, in the thirteenth century, the Quatremain holding consisted of three hides in North Weston and three-and-three-quarter hides at Ascot. The extra three virgates at Ascot take the overall total for the Great Milton estate to just over the forty hides attributed to it earlier in the Domesday text, but the excess is slight. The biggest uncertainty concerns the position of Waterstock. Sawold is said to have held five hides here from St Mary's of Lincoln, which had been held freely by Alwi in Edward the Confessor's time. If this entry is to be interpreted as a separate estate, it takes the total number of hides significantly over the hundred, and might suggest that Waterstock had been transferred to Thame from another hundred; but since Sawold was one of the bishop's knights holding four hides in an unnamed location in Thame, this may represent a duplicate entry despite the slight anomaly in the figures. Thus, although Thame hundred is not named in the Domesday survey, it was very probably already in being as an administrative or judicial unit before 1086.

Table 5.1 Hidage of Thame Hundred in 1086

Estate	*Locality of land*	*No. of tenant*	*No. of hides*
Thame	Thame	Bishop of Lincoln's demesne	37
Thame	Tetsworth	Robert	10
Thame	? Waterstock*	Sawold	4
Thame	North Weston	William	3
Thame	Attington & Moreton	Alured & companion	6
		Total no. of hides in Thame	60
Great Milton	Great Milton	Bishop of Lincoln's demesne	31
Great Milton	Ascot (d'Oilly fee)	Aluric	6
Great Milton	Ascot (Quatremain fee)	William	3.75
		Total no. of hides in Great Milton	40.75
Waterstock	Waterstock*	Sawold	5

* Possible duplicate entries

(c) Thame as an ancient ecclesiastical centre

The church of St Mary in Thame was entirely rebuilt in the 1230s by Bishop Robert Grosseteste. There are no visible remains of any earlier building on the site. Significantly, however, the present church is cruciform with a central tower. This plan-form is characteristic of ancient minsters elsewhere in Oxfordshire, for example at Bampton, where Saxon masonry survives, or Bicester, which retains a Saxon dedication to St Eadburg and clear evidence of a cruciform plan in the twelfth century. This association may persist despite comprehensive later reconstruction, for example at Witney, completely rebuilt in the first half of the thirteenth century, and St Kenelm's at Minster Lovell, rebuilt as late as the mid fifteenth century.

There is no mention of a church or priest in Thame in the Domesday record, but this has no particular significance. Oxfordshire fell within the commissioners' Circuit D, where churches were recorded haphazardly and in very limited numbers. A number of otherwise well-authenticated minsters in Oxfordshire similarly escape mention (Blair 1985).

One of the hallmarks of ancient minsters is the number of dependent chapelries which remained attached to the mother church later in the Middle Ages. Thame is still a large parish, and for many centuries it was the mother church for Tetsworth, Sydenham and Towersey. Tetsworth church was wholly rebuilt in 1855, but its predecessor is said to have had a north-western quoin of Anglo-Saxon long and short work (Lee 1883). Two grants to Thame Abbey in *c.*1199–1200 were witnessed by the *presbyter* or *persona* of Tetsworth (Thame Cart. ii: 107, 111), which may imply that it was for a time independent, but it was certainly a chapelry of Thame by the thirteenth century. In 1146 Thame church was given to Lincoln cathedral and formed into a prebend, which became one of the richest in the diocese (Lee 1883). The livings of Thame, Towersey, Sydenham and Tetsworth were not divided into separate vicarages until 1841 (Lupton 1860: 100).

(d) Thame as an ancient market centre

The origins of Thame's market are unknown. In 1215 King John granted to the Bishop of Lincoln a general right to hold markets and fairs in his manors, and when Henry III confirmed this grant Thame was specifically mentioned (Cal. Chart R. 1226–57: 33). There is, however, an earlier record in the time of Bishop Walter de Coutances (1183–4), when the market is said to be well-established and held by prescriptive right. The holding of a market by ancient custom may well antedate the formal creation of the new town.

Later on, Thame successfully resisted several challenges to its local pre-eminence. When the Prior of Rochester set up a Thursday market at Haddenham in 1294, Bishop John Dalderby successfully petitioned the king for its suppression because of the prejudice to his Tuesday market at Thame (Cal. Chart R. 1257–1300: 461; Lupton 1860: 9; Guest *et al.* 1962: 179). Other markets established within Thame's hinterland at Long Crendon (1218), Worminghall (1304) and Brill (by 1317) were similarly abortive (V.C.H. Bucks. iv: 16, 42, 127).

Thame thus possesses several key characteristics which suggest that it was more than an ordinary rural settlement and had some significance as a central place long before the plantation of the new town in the Middle Ages. While its environs have not been subjected to particularly intensive archaeological investigation, the antiquity of settlement is attested by several chance finds of Iron Age and Romano-British material, with a particular concentration immediately south-east of the town (Oxon. Sites and Monuments Record, Woodstock, PRNs 985–6, 988, 11212–3). Too much should not be made of this particular site while its nature and extent remain undefined; however, the basic needs of marketing in the Roman period were perhaps not very different from those of the Middle Ages, and it is therefore of some interest that evidence for quite sizeable Roman settlements has recently emerged in or very close to several other Oxfordshire market towns, notably Abingdon, Chipping Norton and Bicester. The only significant central-place function not represented in Thame itself is the military one; this role might have been filled by Albury, a small hilltop hamlet 5 km. to the west. This name is almost certainly 'Old *burh*, or fortified place', and the church there has a dedication to St Helen, which has clear associations with significant Roman and Saxon centres elsewhere in Oxfordshire at Abingdon and Benson (Lambrick 1968; Bond 1985: 109; for the significance of St Helen dedications generally see Jones 1986). While Albury lies just outside the parish and hundred of Thame, it is none the less centrally placed with respect to the three detached parts of the hundred.

Town-plan analysis

Thame's single main street, taking the form of a spacious cigar-shaped market-place lined with burgage tenements, has been described as a typical example of medieval town-planning, with the church standing aloof a short distance away in the centre of the older village (Fig. 5.3). The new town appears to have been founded by the Bishop of Lincoln shortly before 1219, and a survey of *c.*1230 lists sixty-three burgages laid out over former open-field strips originally each of one acre, for which a standard shilling ground rent was charged (Queen's Coll., Oxford: MS 366 fol. 23b, 25). Some writers have, with some justification, preferred to regard Thame as a planned extension to an older settlement rather than a wholly new plantation (Beckinsale 1968), but the basic concept of the new borough as a single entity has gained general acceptance. Yet, as Conzen (1966) has demonstrated at Conwy and Ludlow, more detailed plan analysis of a superficially simple layout may reveal evidence of a much more complex development involving several stages of growth.

The plan of any settlement is a product of the disposition of public, institutional and private space, built and unbuilt areas, and the boundaries between them. Public space may be defined as those unbuilt areas over which all people have unrestricted rights of passage at any time – main street, side streets, and back lanes, including areas such as street market-places which may from time to time be reserved for special functions. Institutional space is land or buildings controlled by particular groups within the community and reserved for special purposes, to which the public have limited access – administrative buildings such as town hall or guildhall, ecclesiastical precincts, commercial premises and defensive components. The extent of land given over to communal or institutional uses reflects the rank of any given settlement within the hierarchy. Private space comprises land and buildings reserved for the exclusive occupancy of individuals or families. In towns possessing basic privileges of self-government the typical unit of private space is the burgage tenement, defined in legal terms as a property unencumbered with manorial services which could be bought, sold or bequeathed freely without reference to any manorial authority. As an urban land parcel it tends to have a characteristic shape, with the main dwelling at the street front and a long and relatively narrow strip behind, usually more or less at right-angles to the street, containing an open yard or garden and frequently also ranges of outbuildings used for storage, workshops or further domestic accommodation. Burgage tenements normally occur in blocks defined by main and side streets, with the tail of the tenements forming a continuous line, often followed by a back lane.

The extent and disposition of any of these components can change with time. Market-places may become infilled with institutional or private buildings, streets may be blocked off by individuals or institutions with the necessary power, new areas of buildings and tenements may be laid out and

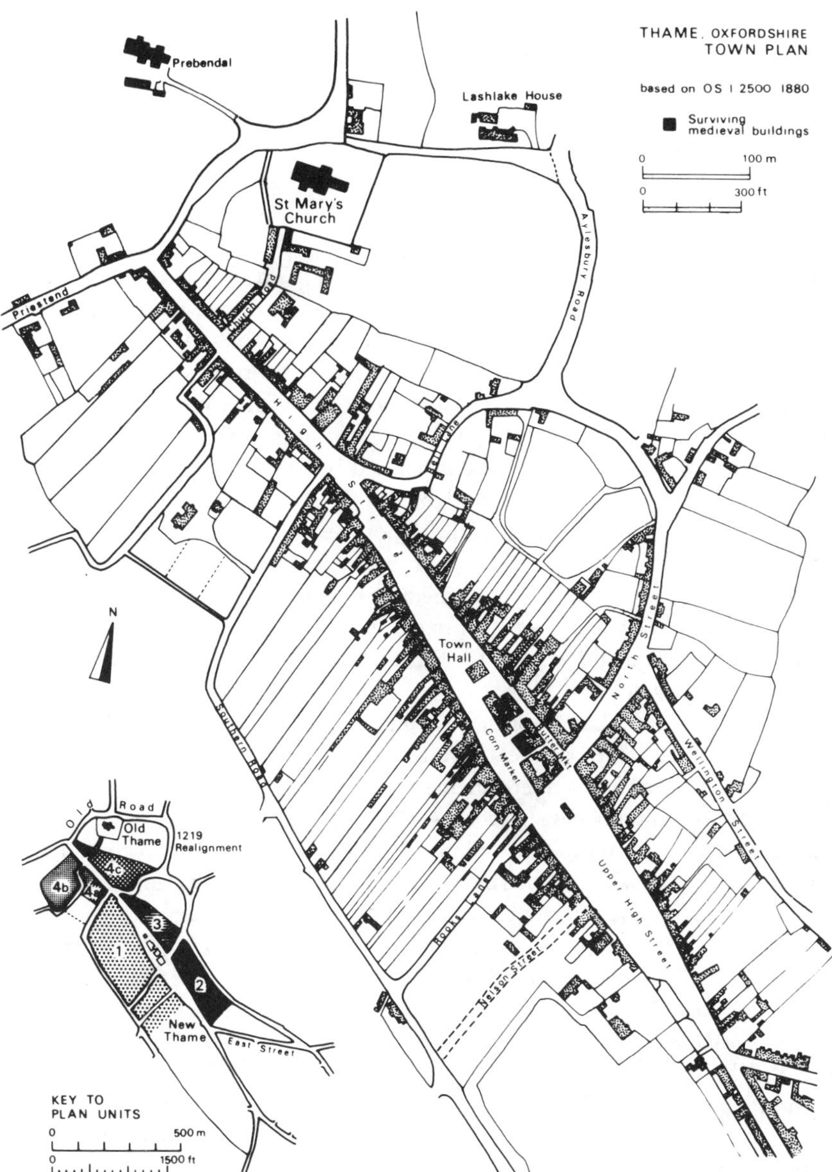

Figure 5.3 The plan and plan-units of medieval Thame

old ones abandoned. However, the assumption of a fundamental stability in the arrangement of plan components is the basis of the morphological approach. The belief is that changes usually take place on a piecemeal basis within a framework of constraints provided by neighbouring property boundaries, and that only in exceptional cases of wholesale replanning on a very large scale can all such constraints be overridden and eliminated.

If the principles of town-plan analysis are applied in Thame, many interesting points emerge, and there is only space for a brief summary here. First, the long-recognized and fundamental distinction between the pre-urban settlement around the church (Old Thame) and the new borough (New Thame) is readily confirmed (Fig. 5.3). It is evident that the post-Conquest main street and burgage plots of the bishop's new town have cut through an earlier curvilinear pattern comprising at least one oval enclosure, and possibly two conjoined enclosures in figure-of-eight formation, both outlined by streets. The more compact of these is defined by the conspicuous loop of Bell Lane, part of Aylesbury Road and North Street. This loop is cut by the continuous tail of the tenements on the north-eastern side of the High Street and Butter Market, and if it ever was a complete circuit, as is suggested, the remainder is lost beneath the medieval new town; though, perhaps significantly, the Corn Market frontages by the Spread Eagle Hotel undergo a slight change of angle very close to the point where the circuit is likely to have come through.

The curve of Bell Lane appears to bite a concave arc out of the south-eastern flank of a larger and less regular loop of streets enclosing the church, the north-western High Street tenements and a large open space. Documentary evidence initially suggests that this second loop may be a wholly fortuitous conjunction of roads of quite different date and origin. The original course of the old Oxford–Aylesbury road, which followed the southern flank of the Thame Valley, is probably represented by the lane from Lashlake passing north of the churchyard, and then by the modern road on to Priestend. In 1219, the Bishop of Lincoln acquired permission to divert the Oxford-Aylesbury road from Lashlake into the centre of his new town (Rot. Litt. Claus. i, 402), and that part of the Aylesbury Road between Lashlake House and Bell Lane is probably the product of that licence. The new route then seems to have followed the pre-existing curve of the North Street loop in order to break through to the market-place; the wedge-shaped southern section of this street has its western side aligned upon the earlier loop and its eastern side upon the new burgage plots of plan unit 2, for which see below. However, what happened in 1219 may merely have been the upgrading of one road and the downgrading of the other, and the position of the church within this second enclosure suggests that it cannot be dismissed as a feature of the pre-urban topography.

Katherine Barker has suggested that similar ovoid outlines in certain small towns in Wessex may preserve the circuits of ancient ecclesiastical precincts (Barker 1980; 1982), and although this view did not initially attract strong support (Hinton 1981; Keene 1984), more recent work has again underlined not only the frequent occurrence of both single and double curvilinear enclosures in association with minsters but also the significance of minsters as pre-urban nuclei (Blair 1988: 35–6, 48–50). If the larger and apparently secondary enclosure containing the church represents the minster precinct, could the Bell Street–North Street loop conceivably represent the perimeter of the postulated Anglo-Saxon royal or episcopal residence? The potential morphological influence of long-extinct enclosures can be demonstrated elsewhere, for example from an estate map of Lower Heyford (Oxon.) made for Corpus Christi College in 1606, which shows the fossilised outline of a neolithic henge still respected by the open-field strips.

The main axis of the bishop's new town is the High Street. This broadens out into a cigar-shaped central market-place which, by its size, was designed to accommodate considerable quantities of livestock. Although never entirely specialized, Thame had a particular reputation as a cattle market in the sixteenth and seventeenth centuries (Guest *et al.* 1962: 182–3; Everitt 1967: 492). The market street is bisected by island blocks of infill, the north-eastern side being known as Butter Market and the wider south-western side as Corn Market. The Hundred Rolls record that in 1221 Bishop Hugh de Welles had built a block of at least six houses in the king's highway in Thame, 100 feet in length, to augment his rents, and that between 1251 and 1279 later bishops had erected eighteen stalls in the market-place, the encroachments still being augmented from year to year (Rot. Hundr. ii: 31, 37). There are later references to 'le shop rew' with stalls (1345) and 'le Bocher rew' (1377). Among the surviving encroachments is the Bird Cage, a fifteenth-century timber building with older cellars, probably identical with the 'tenement called the cage' which belonged to the town's guild in 1529, and was perhaps originally the bishops' prison (Guest *et al.* 1962: 115, 165, 179).

Even a superficial examination indicates that the layout of New Thame is not quite as simple as has sometimes been implied. It can be subdivided into four distinct plan units, each possessing some internal uniformity of pattern, but distinctly different from its neighbours. (For the sake of simplicity in the following descriptions the main road, which in reality is aligned from north-west to south-east, will be treated as if it runs from west to east with the lower end of the town towards the church and Priestend in the west and the upper end towards the Chinnor road in the east.)

(1) The southern side, from the Southern Road junction eastwards through Cornmarket to beyond the junction of Nelson Street (a nineteenth-century intrusion), is the most obviously planned area, with a series of parallel plot boundaries extending from the main road frontage to the back lane, a length of 210–230 yards (192–210 m.). The general grain of the plots is not perpendicular to the street front, but angled at about 67 degrees at the lower end, increasing because of the street's curvature to about 80 degrees in Upper High Street. This alignment was probably dictated by the orientation of the underlying open-field strips. The pattern of long tenements ceases east of

Nelson Street, but the back lane continues to the Stokenchurch road, supporting the view that the burgages were fitted into pre-existing land parcels. The upper end of this plan unit was either never settled, or has subsequently been abandoned.

(2) On the north side, from the fork of East Street to no. 1 Upper High Street, the plot boundaries are less regular and much shorter, only 110 yards (101 m.) in length, and aligned at about 68–75 degrees to the street frontage. Although East Street is itself another nineteenth-century intrusion, it does none the less join the main street at a significant plot boundary on the eastern edge of the older built-up frontages (Enclosure map, 1826, Oxon. C.R.O. bk. 56). Wellington Street, formerly Pound Lane, runs parallel with the main street and provides rear access to this plot series; but its divergent easterly course suggests that it belongs to a pre-urban road network and is not a true back lane contemporary with the planned burgages.

(3) On the north side from no. 12 Butter Market westwards to no. 85 High Street the tenements span the North Street–Bell Lane loop. There is no back lane, though the line of Wellington Street is projected along a continuous rear boundary. The tenements in this block are aligned at about 75 degrees to the frontage, decreasing in length westwards as their tail alignment converge upon the High Street–Bell Lane junction, where the final wedge of buildings perhaps represents encroachment over a former junction green.

(4) West of this point the High Street changes direction slightly and is more uniform in width. The building frontages are not continuous, and the tenements are distinctly broader than in the market-place area. Several subunits can be distinguished:

(a) On the south side from no. 27 to no. 35 High Street the plot lengths are only 80–100 yards (73–91 m.), and even allowing for possible curtailment by the National School in 1838 they can never have exceeded 180–200 yards (165–183 m.); they are angled at 77 degrees to the street front.

(b) From no. 36 to no. 52 plot boundaries are longer, 200–230 yards (183–210 m.), with a rather less regular tail alignment, orientated at 85 to 90 degrees to the street. The westernmost frontages on the southern side of High Street up to the Oxford Road have no significant linear plot developments to the rear.

(c) On the north side of the lower High Street (nos. 54 to 84) the plots are short and generally irregular, though there are signs of a former continuous rear boundary from the north end of Bell Lane intersecting Church Lane at the point where it changes direction.

One of the characteristics of medieval planned boroughs is a tendency towards uniform burgage sizes; the documentation for acre-sized plots in New Thame has already been mentioned. Correspondingly, variations in standard burgage dimensions in different parts of a town may provide evidence for different stages of growth. In 1984–5 some 164 building frontages on the main street of Thame were measured, with the intention of ascertaining (i) whether any vestiges of the original standard plot sizes survived in the modern street frontages, (ii) whether, on this basis, it would be possible to reconstruct the pattern of tenements laid out at the beginning of the thirteenth century and (iii) whether the separate plan units identified above displayed any significant variations in their frontage widths.

It soon became clear that in Thame the orientation of the burgages in relation to the street creates special difficulties, since the accommodation of rectangular buildings into the angled plots must inevitably have caused some interference with their frontages, a problem likely to be exacerbated by successive rebuildings. Ideally, measurements should have been taken deeper behind the street fronts, where the plot widths would be less modified, but access was not uniformly available. Although the measurements were originally taken to the nearest six inches, for the purposes of initial analysis they were grouped into two-foot bands (Fig. 5.4). The resulting histograms emphasized the separate character of plan unit 4, where plot-widths were fairly broadly and evenly spread on either side of a peak of 23–25 feet, and supported the view that this part of the town was laid out within a different framework. By contrast the sum of the 114 plots within plan units 1–3 revealed a significant clumping of frontages around the one perch (16½ feet or 5·03 m.) and two perch marks: thirteen properties had widths within a foot either way of two statute perches, eight properties lay within the same range of a single perch and three further properties lay equally close to a width of three or four perches. If the margin of error is increased to two feet, nearly 40 per cent of all the properties measured in plan units 1–3 equate with the statute perch or a whole multiple of it. These results are unlikely to be a matter of chance, and imply that this dimension was a significant factor in the planning of those parts of Thame laid out over former open fields, which has persisted through to the present day. The prevalence of the perch unit has also been detected in Burford (notes by Martin Foreman in Oxfordshire Sites and Monuments Record, Woodstock), and in various towns in Devon, Warwickshire and Worcestershire (Slater 1981).

The best hope of reconstructing the pattern of the original thirteenth-century burgages rests in plan unit 1. Since the documentary evidence implies plots of one acre and the average plot length in this part of the town is a fraction over one statute furlong (660 feet or 201 m.), their original standard width should be around four statute perches (66 feet). Any preponderance of regular fractions of this width would, therefore, be significant. At least seventeen of the tenement boundaries extend backwards in a continuous line through the full depth of the plot, though sometimes interrupted along the front building line for reasons already indicated. The analysis of the frontages as regular fractions of the putative original four-perch width is presented on Figure 5.5. Unfortunately neither of the two side roads provide a satisfactory starting-point for this exercise; Southern Road comes in at an angle slightly more acute than that of the general grain of the plots, while Rooks Lane may be an intrusion; the count therefore

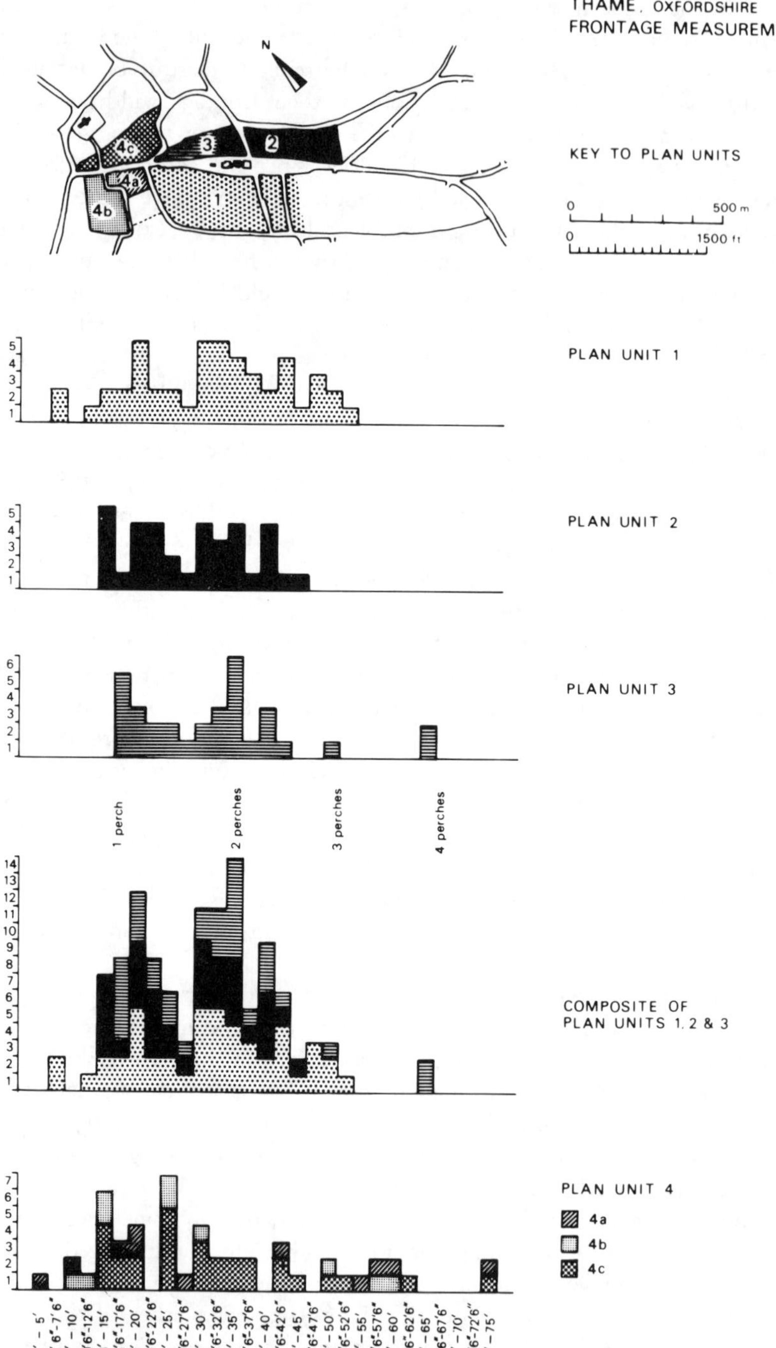

Figure 5.4 Plot frontage measurements in Thame

THAME, OXFORDSHIRE
FRONTAGE ANALYSIS OF PLAN-UNIT 1
(HIGH STREET SOUTH / CORN MARKET)

Frontages as proportion of 4-perch units (± 3 ft)	Frontage Measurements	Properties
		ROOKS LANE
	40′ 6″	**Black Horse Hotel**, former Fleur de Lys
½	35′	former White Horse
¾	48′	Lloyds Bank
¼	16′	
1	18′	
	46′ 6″	**Spread Eagle Hotel**, former Oxford Arms
½	31′	no 18 Corn Market
1⅓	20′	no 19
	20′	no 20
	13′ 6″	
	34′	**Abingdon Arms**, former Chequers
⅓	22′	
	31′	
	30′ 6″	former Fighting Cocks
1⅔	23′ 6″	
	47′	
	38′ 6″	Boots
½	31′ 6″	Tesco
1¼	36′ 6″	Co-Op.
	35′	no 8 High Street
	8′	Passageway
1	24′	no 9
	40′ 6″	no 10
¾	51′	nos 11-12
1¼	20′ 6″	no 13
	16′	no 14
	38′ 6″	no 15
	12′	Passageway
½	28′ 6″	no 16
¾	46′	**Adelaide House**
½	34′	**Thame Gazette**
⅓	20′	**Bay Tree**, former Seven Stars
⅔	41′	no 21
	7′	Passageway
½	30′	Lancastrian Cottage
1	37′ 6″	Starbank House
	29′	no 24
¼	14′ 6″	no 25
	40′ 6″	**Rising Sun**
		SOUTHERN ROAD

Tenement boundaries continuing through to back lane

Figure 5.5 Metrological analysis of plan-unit 1, Thame

excludes the corner properties, the Rising Sun and the Black Horse. For the remainder, if a latitude of three feet either way is allowed (and most of the measurements fall well within that margin), all but a couple of the measured properties can either be linked directly, or grouped together to link, with multiples of quarters or thirds of the four-perch unit.

How, then, were the original uniform four-perch plots broken up, and at what period did this occur? Archaeological evidence is non-existent: the only excavation in the town centre to date, at no. 6b High Street, revealed virtually no stratification, with the foundations of the eighteenth-century house overlying amorphous rubble containing late medieval pottery which lay directly on the natural (Hinton 1974). The survey of *c.*1230 shows the majority of burgesses still holding one burgage apiece, but there are occasional rents both for multiple holdings and for half-burgages, suggesting that the processes of amalgamation and subdivision were already beginning. By the third quarter of the thirteenth century subdivision was much further advanced: many burgages had several houses built on them, and there are frequent transactions involving half- or quarter-acre burgage plots (Guest *et al.* 1962: 179). The evidence from surviving medieval houses is slight: of the three known cruck-framed buildings in the town, two are aligned parallel to the street, but Lancastrian Cottage (no. 22 High Street) stands gable-end to the front, suggesting that the plot frontage was already restricted at the time of its construction. To follow the break-up of the original pattern in detail depends on an exceptional survival of property records, such as exists for Winchester or Wells (Keene 1985; Scrase 1989). At Thame there may be potential in the numerous later thirteenth-century charters preserved at Rousham, but these have yet to receive detailed scrutiny.

Conclusion

The need for a multi-disciplinary approach to the study of urban origins and development has been stressed, but the archaeological, architectural and documentary records are all in their various ways fragmented and incomplete. The type of morphological analysis pioneered by Conzen still offers the best hope of progress in the hundreds of small towns like Thame which are never likely to rank as priorities for archaeological investigation.

No town can be understood when divorced from its context, and it is necessary to look at the surrounding landscape for several reasons. The factors governing the spacing between neighbouring towns also affect both the potential and the limits of their success. Competition between neighbouring centres with respect to functions such as marketing creates a dynamic relationship, in which some towns prosper at the expense of others, and their hinterlands correspondingly undergo enlargement or contraction at different periods. As each town ascends or descends within the settlement hierarchy, its size and urban fabric are correspondingly affected. The local context of early estates and their ownership is a major factor in selecting which places would emerge to achieve urban status; and in the case of Thame, ostensibly a classic medieval new town, there are clear signs that it was beginning to develop a significant local administrative and ecclesiastical pre-eminence well before the Norman Conquest.

This background becomes significant when we attempt to analyse the town plan. Even the layout of a comparatively small town like Thame can reveal unexpected complexities and multiple phases of development. The somewhat isolated church has for long been rationalized as a pre-urban nucleus, but the potential significance of the loops of streets to its south-east has only become fully appreciated as work on other minster centres has produced parallels. Examination of the burgage pattern suggests that the concept of a single-period new town plantation is itself simplistic, and that several distinct phases of growth are represented which interrupt the pre-urban curvilinear road pattern. It has been suggested elsewhere that the building of the prebendal house for the prebend of Lincoln Cathedral established in 1146 may have produced an early phase of planned growth in the Priestend liberty at the west end of the town (Bond 1986: 137), and the separate character of the Lower High Street plots (plan unit 4) suggests that they may belong to this development. Even in the centre of the bishop's new town the northern and southern sides of the main street are quite different in character; while the shape and size of the long regular plots to the south (plan unit 1) accords with the documentary indications of a planned expansion over open-field strips after the beginning of the thirteenth century, the arrangement of shorter, more irregular burgages to the north suggests that there might already have been some occupation on this side which was incorporated into the plan. Measurement of burgage frontages in the bishop's new town has revealed some indications of the underlying perch standard which has been found in other English towns. Finally there are indications in the empty frontages at the east end of the marketplace that the original design was over-ambitious, and though New Thame was a successful plantation, it did not entirely measure up to the aspirations of its episcopal founders.

Acknowledgments

I would like to thank the American students of the Oxford/Berkeley Summer Schools of 1984 and 1985 for their cheerfulness, enthusiasm and hard work while measuring the plot frontages in Thame, and the inhabitants of the town for their interest and forbearance during this operation. My wife, Tina, gave much assistance with the subsequent arithmetic. I am also grateful to Terry Slater for his most helpful editorial comments, which have considerably improved the first draft of this paper.

References

Printed sources

Cal. Chart. R., *Calendar of Charter Rolls* (1903–).

Rot. Hundr., *Rotuli Hundredorum temp. Hen. III & Edw. I*, ed. W. Illingworth (2 vols., 1812, 1818).

Rot. Litt. Claus., *Rotuli Litterarum Clausarum* (2 vols., 1833, 1844).

Thame Cart., *The Thame Cartulary*, ed. H. E. Salter (2 vols., 1947–8).

Secondary works

Airs, M., Rodwell, K. and Turner, H., 1975. 'Thame', in Rodwell, K. (ed.), 1975: 147–9.

Anderson, J. R. L., 1970. *The Upper Thames.*

Astill, G., 1978. *Historic towns in Berkshire: an archaeological appraisal.*

Aston, M. and Bond, C. J., 1976. *The landscape of towns.*

Barker, K., 1980. 'The early Christian topography of Sherborne', *Antiquity, 54:* 229–31.

Barker, K., 1982. 'The early history of Sherborne', in S. M. Pearce (ed.), *The early Church in western Britain and Ireland* [British Archaeological Reports, 102] 77–116.

Baskin, C. W., 1966. *Central places in southern Germany* (New Jersey) – translation of Christaller, W., 1935. *Die Zentralen Orte in Suddeutschland* (Jena).

Beckinsale, R. P., 1968. 'Urbanization in England to AD 1420', in *Urbanization and its problems*, ed. R. P. Beckinsale and J. M. Houston, 1–46.

Beckinsale, R. P. and Beckinsale, M., 1980. *The English heartland.*

Benson, D. and Cook, J. M., 1967. *City of Oxford redevelopment: archaeological implications.*

Beresford, M. W., 1967. *New towns of the Middle Ages.*

Blair, J., 1985. 'Secular minster churches in Domesday Book', in *Domesday Book: a reassessment*, ed. P. H. Sawyer, 104–42.

Blair, J., 1988. 'Minster churches in the landscape', in *Anglo-Saxon settlements*, ed. D. Hooke, 35–58.

Bond, C. J., 1980. 'The small towns of Oxfordshire in the nineteenth century', in *The Oxford region*, ed. R. T. Rowley, 55–79.

Bond, C. J., 1985. 'Medieval Oxfordshire villages and their topography: a preliminary discussion', in *Medieval villages: a review of current work*, ed. D. Hooke, 101–24.

Bond, C. J., 1986. 'The Oxford region in the Middle Ages', in *The archaeology of the Oxford region*, ed. G. Briggs, J. Cook and R. T. Rowley, 135–59.

Brown, J. H. and Guest, H. W., 1935. *A history of Thame.*

Clarke, G., 1978. *The book of Thame.*

Coates, B. E., 1965. 'The origin and distribution of markets and fairs in medieval Derbyshire', *Derbyshire Archaeological Journal, 85:* 92–111.

Conzen, M. R. G., 1960. 'Alnwick, Northumberland: a study in town-plan analysis', *Publications of Institute of British Geographers, 27.*

Conzen, M. R. G., 1962. 'The plan analysis of an English city centre', in *Proceedings of the IGU symposium in urban geography, Lund, 1960*, ed. K. Norborg (Lund), 383–414.

Conzen, M. R. G., 1966. 'Historical townscapes in Britain: a problem in applied geography', in *Northern geographical essays in honour of G. H. J. Daysh*, ed. J. W. House, 56–78.

Dickinson, R. E., 1932. 'The distribution and functions of the smaller urban settlements of East Anglia', *Geography*, *17*: 19–31.

Dickinson, T. M., 1974. *Cuddesdon and Dorchester-on-Thames: two early Saxon 'princely' sites in Wessex* [British Archaeological Reports, 1].

Dymond, D., 1974. *Archaeology and history: a plea for reconciliation.*

Ekwall, E., 1928. *English river-names.*

Everitt, A., 1967. 'The marketing of agricultural produce', in *The agrarian history of England and Wales, Vol. IV, 1500–1640*, ed. J. Thirsk, 466–592.

Fasham, P. J., 1972. 'The archaeological implications of redevelopment in Banbury', *Cake & Cockhorse, summer 1972*: 49–56.

Ford, W. J., 1979. 'Some settlement patterns in the central region of the Warwickshire Avon', in *English medieval settlement*, ed. P. H. Sawyer, 143–63.

Fox, H. S. A., 1973. 'Going to town in thirteenth century England', in *Man made the land*, ed. A. R. H. Baker and J. B. Harley, 69–78.

Gelling, M., 1978. *Signposts to the past: place-names and the history of England.*

Gelling, M., 1979. *The early charters of the Thames valley.*

Guest, W., Lobel, M. and Jenkins, H., 1962. 'Thame', in *V.C.H.*, *Oxfordshire*, *VII*: 160–219.

Haggett, P., 1965. *Locational analysis in human geography.*

Haslam, J. (ed.), 1984. *Anglo-Saxon towns in southern England.*

Hinton, D. A., 1974. 'Thame, Oxon', *Oxoniensia*, *39*: 100.

Hinton, D. A., 1981. 'The topography of Sherborne – early Christian?', *Antiquity*, *55*: 222–3.

Hodder, I. and Orton, C., 1976. *Spatial analysis in archaeology.*

Hodges, R., 1982. *Dark Age economics: the origins of towns and trade, AD 600–1000.*

Hodges, R., 1987. 'Spatial models, anthropology and archaeology', in *Landscape and culture: geographical and archaeological perspectives*, ed. J. M. Wagstaff, 118–33.

Hodges, R., 1988. *Primitive and peasant market.*

John, E., 1964. *Land tenure in early England: a discussion of some problems.*

Jones, G., 1986. 'Holy wells and the cult of St Helen', *Landscape History*, *8*: 59–75.

Keene, D., 1985. *Survey of medieval Winchester* [Winchester Studies, 2].

Keene, L., 1984. 'The towns of Dorset', in Haslam, J. (ed.), 1984: 203–48.

Lambrick, G., 1968. 'The foundation traditions of the abbey', in M. Biddle, G. Lambrick and J. N. L. Myres, 'The early history of Abingdon, Berkshire, and its abbey', *Medieval Archaeology*, *12*: 26–34.

Lee, F. G., 1883. *The history, description and antiquities of the prebendal church of the Blessed Virgin Mary of Thame.*

Leech, R., 1981. *Historic towns in Gloucestershire.*

Lupton, H., 1860. *The history of Thame and its hamlets, including the abbey of Thame, prebend, free school &c.*

Miles, D. and Fowler, P. J., 1972. *Tewkesbury: the archaeological implications of development.*

Palliser, D. M. and Pinnock, A. C., 1971. 'The markets of medieval Staffordshire', *North Staffordshire Journal of Field Studies*, *11*: 49–63.

Rodwell, K. (ed.), 1975. *Historic towns in Oxfordshire: a survey of the new county.*

Salter, H. E., 1960, 1969. *Survey of Oxford* [ed. W. A. Pantin, Oxford Historical Society, new series, *14*, *20*].

Sawyer, P. H., 1968. *Anglo-Saxon charters: an annotated list and bibliography* [Royal Historical Society Guide & Handbooks, 8].

Scrase, A., 1989. 'Development and change in burgage plots – the example of Wells', *Journal of Historical Geography, 15*: 349–65.

Simpson, C., 1973. *Wallingford: the archaeological implications of development.*

Slater, T. R., 1980. *The analysis of burgages in medieval towns* [Dept. of Geography, Univ. of Birmingham, Working Paper 4].

Slater, T. R., 1981. 'The analysis of burgage patterns in medieval towns', *Area, 13*: 211–16.

Slater, T. R. and Wilson, C., 1977. *Archaeology and development in Stratford-upon-Avon.*

Smith, C. A., 1976. 'Exchange systems and the spatial distributions of elites: the organisation of stratification in agrarian societies', in *Regional Analysis, 2*: 309–74.

Stenton, F. M., 1947. *Anglo-Saxon England* (2nd edn.).

Unwin, T., 1981. 'Rural marketing in medieval Nottinghamshire', *Journal of Historical Geography, 7.3*: 231–51.

Urry, W., 1967. *Canterbury under the Angevin Kings.*

V.C.H., various dates. *Victoria History of the Counties of England.*

Whitehand, J. W. R. (ed.), 1981. *The urban landscape: historical development and management* [Institute of British Geographers, special publication 13].

Whitelock, D. (ed.), 1955. *English historical documents, c.500–1042.*

Part III

Town-plan analysis (industrial cities)

6 The morphological evolution of a nineteenth-century city centre: Łódź, Poland, 1825–1973

Marek Koter

The development of M. R. G. Conzen's many valuable concepts in his classic papers on Alnwick (Conzen 1960) and Newcastle upon Tyne (Conzen 1962) has varied considerably in the extent to which they have been taken up by other geographers. Clearly, the fringe-belt concept has met with the most immediate response (Whitehand 1967; 1972; Barke 1974), and the variability of medieval plot size and shape has more recently been explored by Slater (1981; 1987). Little attention has thus far been accorded to the concept of the burgage cycle of development on the long narrow plots of medieval 'old town' areas, other than passing reference to its validity. The idea of an urban building plot undergoing processes of change through time whereby an increasing proportion of the area of the plot is covered by buildings as it becomes enmeshed in the built fabric of the town has an equal reasonableness for plots other than medieval burgages, of course. It is one of the aims of this chapter to explore Conzen's ideas about the burgage cycle in the context of nineteenth-century urban building plots and thereby to extend its usefulness and applicability.

The development of an industrial city

The case study chosen for the detailed town-plan analysis necessary to test the burgage-cycle concept in this new context is Łódź. Łódź, the second most populous city of Poland, is a good example of a town which underwent explosive physical growth during the period of industrialization. It developed rapidly from a population of only some 500 persons in 1820, to more than 300,000 at the end of the nineteenth century, near 600,000 in 1914, and to almost 900,000 at present. The first nucleus of the settlement, an episcopally-owned village, had been established at the beginning of the fourteenth century. It evolved gradually into a small town, gaining its town charter in 1423, but it never developed into a real town in the social and economic sense of the word; there was no castle or monastery which could support a weak urban economy, and the surrounding woodland area was too thinly settled and too poor to create real urban functions. Before 1800 Łódź had never had more than 100 houses, all of them wooden and, until the third decade of the nineteenth century, it led a semi-rural life with agriculture as its main function and very limited craft and trade as complementary ones.

The real development of Łódź began in the 1820s when the government of the autonomous Kingdom of Poland ('Congress Poland') started to effect its programme to industrialize the country. Łódź, which was now a state-owned town (it was secularized in 1794), together with several surrounding towns, was chosen as a centre for the newly-created textile industry. It soon became the main textile industrial centre in Poland and, by the end of the nineteenth century, probably the biggest textile centre in the whole of Europe. Łódź is a splendid example of a new-planned and homogeneous industrial town entirely built by the government over a short timespan (Koter 1970). The Kingdom of Poland's government created the new industrial town in every detail. It laid out an urban pattern for the whole area and built the first manufactories as well as hundreds of identical houses for handicraft workers brought in from abroad – from Great Poland and Silesia (then under Prussian occupation), as well as from Moravia, Saxony and other German countries. The aim was to build in Łódź a complete complex of all the traditional branches of the textile industry as it then was, largely unmechanized and based upon water power. Eventually the town consisted of four different functional units: namely a cloth colony, a number of linen spinners' colonies, a linen and cotton weavers' colony, and a zone of linen and cotton manufacturers (Fig. 6.1).

The cloth colony, called New Town (Nowe Miasto), was built in 1823 southwards of the medieval old town (Stare Miasto), which thereby found itself in a marginal situation, its fields surrounding the new colonies on their western side. The New Town had a very regular layout with an octagonal market-place in the centre and drapers' gardens separately to the east of the built-up area (Fig. 6.1). The linen and cotton industrial settlement, called Łodka, was built in 1824–8 southwards of the New Town. It consisted of an elongated series of new colonies with linen spinners located in back streets, a linen and cotton weavers' colony along the main road, and a zone of so-called 'hydro-manufacturing properties', with fulling mill, bleach works, cotton mill, dyers' works, printing works and some other manufacturers situated along the valley of the River Jasien. The linen spinners' colonies consisted of numerous very large, elongated plots (1·68 ha. in area) similar to rural fields because they had an obligation to plant flax for themselves. The weavers' colony consisted of much smaller plots though they were still substantial (0·56 ha. in area) and, again, elongated (Fig. 6.1).

This logical and functional layout of the new industrial town had an essential weakness however, namely, the lack of a common town-centre for the urban area as a whole. All three fundamental parts of early nineteenth century Łódź, the Old Town, the New Town and the linen and cotton

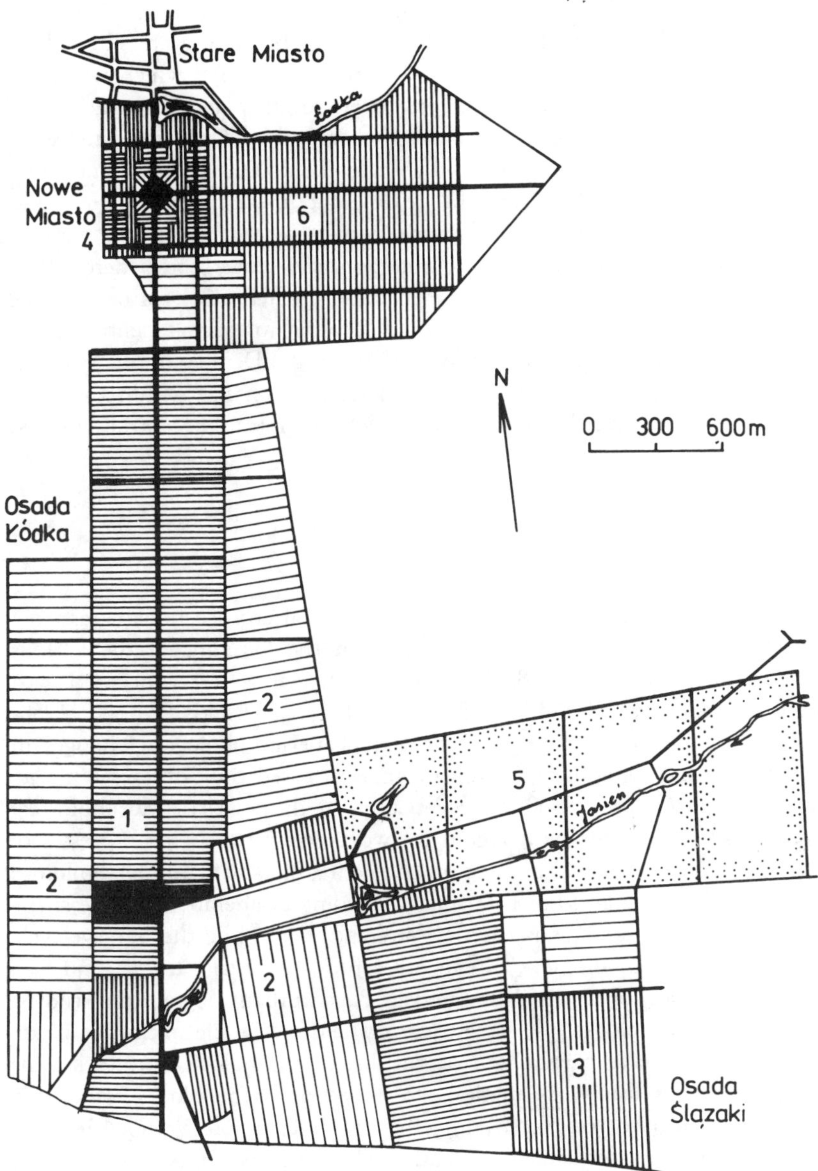

Figure 6.1 Functional plan-units of Łódź, 1827: 1. linen and cotton weavers' colony; 2–3. linen spinners' colonies; 4. cloth colony; 5. hydro-manufacturing properties; 6. drapers' gardens

plots of Łodka, had their own market-places and, until the mid nineteenth century, were developed separately (Koter 1984). But they were situated on the same urban axis – the 3 km.-long Piotrkowska street, which was both the only street that joined all the three parts together and the main traffic thoroughfare of Łódź. So, when in the second half of the nineteenth century, population increased rapidly (to some 35,000 in 1860 and then from 50,000 to 100,000 during the 1870s), and the new urban trade and service functions developed, it became necessary to integrate the various parts of the town by creating a common city-centre somewhere along Piotrkowska street. It was the weavers' colony, situated exactly in the middle of the urban area, that was the obvious location for such a centre and it began to evolve spontaneously into a substitute CBD. It is the aim of this chapter to analyse the processes of morphological change within the plots of this former weavers' colony as it developed into the central business district.

Methodology

The process has been analysed in seven temporal cross-sections at approximately twenty-year intervals beginning with the founding of the various colonies in the years 1824–8. The subsequent analyses are concerned with the following years: 1853, 1877, 1894/1897, 1917, 1937 and 1973. The 1950s have been omitted as there were no significant morphological changes in this period. Cartographical town-plan analysis based on Conzen's burgage-cycle method (Conzen 1960) has been used in the analysis. Morphological changes were examined with regard to two processes: first, the processes of adaptive change, that is the filling up of existing plots with various buildings and secondly, the transformative changes leading to alterations in the shape of the original plots. This is the first attempt at adapting the burgage-cycle concept to research on new, nineteenth-century industrial towns, and also the first adoption of Conzen's method in Polish urban geographical studies.

Original urban blocks (the street quarters laid out at the institutive phase of the colony) have been taken as the basic morphological units in this work. All the statistical calculations are based on urban blocks comprising from sixteen to eighteen plots. Altogether, some 227 plots, grouped in fourteen urban blocks, were analysed, marked with uneven numbers on the west side of Piotrkowska street and even ones on its east side. In cases where original blocks had been divided into two by the laying out of a new street, the calculations refer both to the area of the former blocks (numbered 1, 2, 3, etc.) and also to the new ones (numbered 1a, 1b, 2a, 2b, etc.). Calculations concerning single plots have been given only to illustrate extreme differences in building coverage and transformative changes within different blocks.

The institutive phase (1821–1827)

During the institutive phase, regular urban blocks had been founded on both sides of Piotrkowska street using modules of the so-called 'new-Polish measure'. In the case of the eight northern blocks a linear 5-'pret' module was used (including multiples or halves; 1 pret = 4·32 m.). This meant that a normal plot was 5 prets wide (21·6 m.) and 67·5 prets long (291·6 m.) with an area of 6307 m^2, somewhat larger than one 'morga' of the new-Polish measure (1 morga = 300 sq. prets = 5,598 m^2). A typical full block consisted of sixteen plots and had overall measurements of 80 prets width and 67·5 prets length (345·6 m. × 291·6 m.), with an area of 18 morgas (10·0912 ha.). In the case of the six southern blocks a 'one morga module' was chosen. This meant that a typical block of the same dimensions as previously, consisted of 18 one-morga plots. But in order to attain this area the plots had to be of a smaller width than 5 prets, namely 19·2 m.

At the beginning of this phase, houses were built by the government for immigrant weaver-colonists from abroad (Ginsbert 1962). The first of them were constructed in 1825 in the south-eastern part of the colony. They were small, partly made of brick, partly timber-framed or wooden houses with dimensions of 24·5 × 11·4 'łokiec' (this means elbow) of the new-Polish measure (that is 14·1 m. × 6·3 m. × 2·3 m.) and a building coverage of some 90 m^2. It was quickly appreciated that the houses were too small for weavers' purposes so the next series, built in 1826, were larger with dimensions of 26·5 × 14 × 5 łokiecs (17·9 m. × 8 m. × 2·9 m.) and 123 m^2 in terms of building coverage. These were detached, one-storey houses with steep, tiled roofs, facing to the main street and situated at the front of the plots. They functioned as both a dwelling house and a work place and consisted of weaver's workshop, two rooms, a kitchen and a scullery, and a linen and cotton storeroom in a garret upstairs.

The houses and backyards occupied only some one-eighth of the plots' area with vegetable gardens or orchards behind them. There were fields for potatoes and cereals backing up to the ends of the plots and, beyond the back streets, spinners' colonies were laid out (Fig. 6.1). Free access had been kept to the plots from Piotrkowska street and from the back lanes. There were no houses along the sides of the plots adjacent to the side-streets.

The government ceased constructing houses itself after 1827 and put the later colonists under an obligation to build their houses themselves. However, this had to accord to a standardized scheme and the government gave them both credit and a supply of building materials. After the defeat of the Polish insurrection against Russia in 1830–1, when the Kingdom of Poland lost its autonomy, this aid came to an end and during the next few years the Łódź textile industry passed through an economic depression. Consequently, many of the new colonists were not able to build their houses. Instead, they constructed temporary dwellings at the rear of their plots along the back streets. The front parts of the plots were kept free in order to build their permanent houses there later on. As late as 1835, the mayor of Łódź notified a higher authority that on many plots in the weavers' colony there existed only 'back houses' while plot frontages 'were covered with grass'. There were even plots entirely without buildings, put under corn, and sometimes with windmills on them (Rynkowska 1970). The continuous building frontages along Piotrkowska street were probably not completed until as late as the 1840s. The institutive phase of the weavers' colony therefore, should probably be prolonged until that period, and certainly until the end of the 1830s.

Building coverage for this phase averaged probably from 2 to 4 per cent of the plots' area. The plan of the main front houses covered only from 1·6 per cent to 2·2 per cent of the plots' area (90 to 123 m^2), and additional buildings such as wood-houses, garden sheds, hen-coops, lavatories, etc. could give another 1·5 per cent to 2 per cent of the coverage. Only on those plots which had been built up first with 'back houses', and subsequently completed with front ones, did the building coverage exceed this.

Cross-section two: 1853

For the next cross-section, in the 1850s, proper cartographic materials are lacking. Unfortunately, the only town plan from that period, drawn by Flatt in 1853, gives a very generalized picture of the town (Fig. 6.2). It shows only that morphological changes within the weavers' colony had not been much advanced. The only changes which can be seen are along side-streets. In the original scheme of the colony these streets were not intended to be built up. Even their names: Pusta, Boczna, Zielona, Przejazd, Dzielna (Empty Street, Side Street, Green Street, Passing Street, Division Street) expressed their lesser importance. From other sources it is known that some of them figured only on the map and that for a long time there was no real reason to lay them out in the terrain (Rynkowska 1970). From the middle of the nineteenth century, these 'empty streets' began to be built up by a new category of building connected with the service sector. There appeared also new types of derivative plots which came into existence as a consequence of the crossways division of the original long plots adjacent to the side streets. They were subdivided first into two or four small plots, some 146 m. or 73 m. in width and 21·6 or 19·2 m. deep, according to the width of the two categories of the original plots. Later, the subdivision of these plots was to be developed much further.

The process of subdivision of the side-street plots started first in the central, eastern part of the colony. It was probably provoked by the creation of the so-called 'New Quarter'. This was of multi-functional character, and had been laid out in 1840 in a gap between the New Town's gardens and the manufacturing zone, to the east of the weavers' and spinners' colonies. It was an area where the result of centripetal forces – from the Old and the

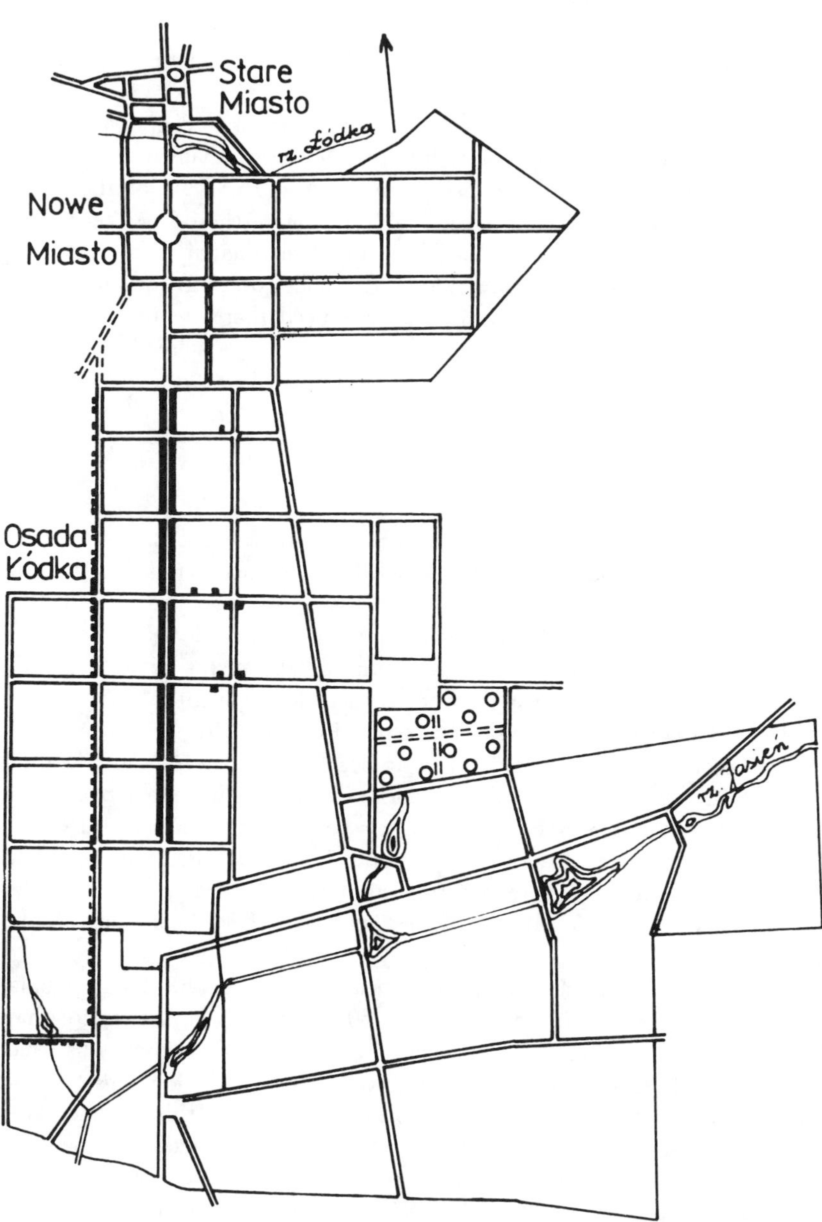

Figure 6.2 Łódź after Flatt's map of 1853

New Town from the north, the industrial zone and marginal spinners' colonies from the south and south-east, and from the New Quarter from the east – met and integrated with each other. Thus, within the north-eastern blocks of the weavers' colony, the very beginning of the substitute Łódź city centre, can be recognized in the middle of the nineteenth century (Koter and Wiktorowska 1976).

The calculations of building coverage in 1835 cannot be precise because of the lack of detailed maps. It is inferred, however, that the increase of building coverage was still inconsiderable, and at the scale of the entire weavers' colony the ratio reached probably not more than 5 per cent, with some 10 per cent coverage within the individual original plots along the side-streets which had been subdivided into smaller ones. In the majority of urban blocks the institutive phase was prolonged therefore to the second cross-section, but in a few blocks a repletive phase had already begun.

Cross-section three; 1877

The third cross-section is derived from Micinski's map of 1887 (Fig. 6.3A) and shows a radical change when compared with the 1850s. It illustrates both a continuing additive process, which had developed considerably, and a transformative one, which was no less dynamic and caused a modification of the shape of almost half the original plots. Between the second and the third cross-sections, and particularly in the 1860s, events of fundamental importance had taken place for the further development of Łódź as a whole, and for the former weavers' colony in particular.

Three background events should be indicated: first, the peasants' enfranchisement in 1864 had caused an enormous influx of cheap labour from rural areas to the Łódź textile industry; secondly, the construction of the railway which connected the town with both home and foreign markets and imparted a new dynamism to its economic life; and thirdly, the Civil War in the USA in 1861–5 which caused a shortage of raw materials on the European cotton markets.

The first two events caused an unparalleled increase of the town's population from some 35,000 in 1860 to about 50,000 in 1872 and to more than 100,000 in 1876. This resulted in building operations on an enormous scale. Tenement and terraced houses and industrial and service buildings were all constructed in large numbers. As a consequence of the third event, most of the individual weavers and spinners failed, and many small- and medium-sized textile enterprises went bankrupt, too. However, a few individuals were rich enough to wait till the depression ended, owned their properties outright and subsequently became very powerful. This third event therefore changed Łódź from a handicraft and manufacturing town into an industrial one in the full sense of the word. It caused an extreme concentration both of industrial capital and industrial land. The whole original

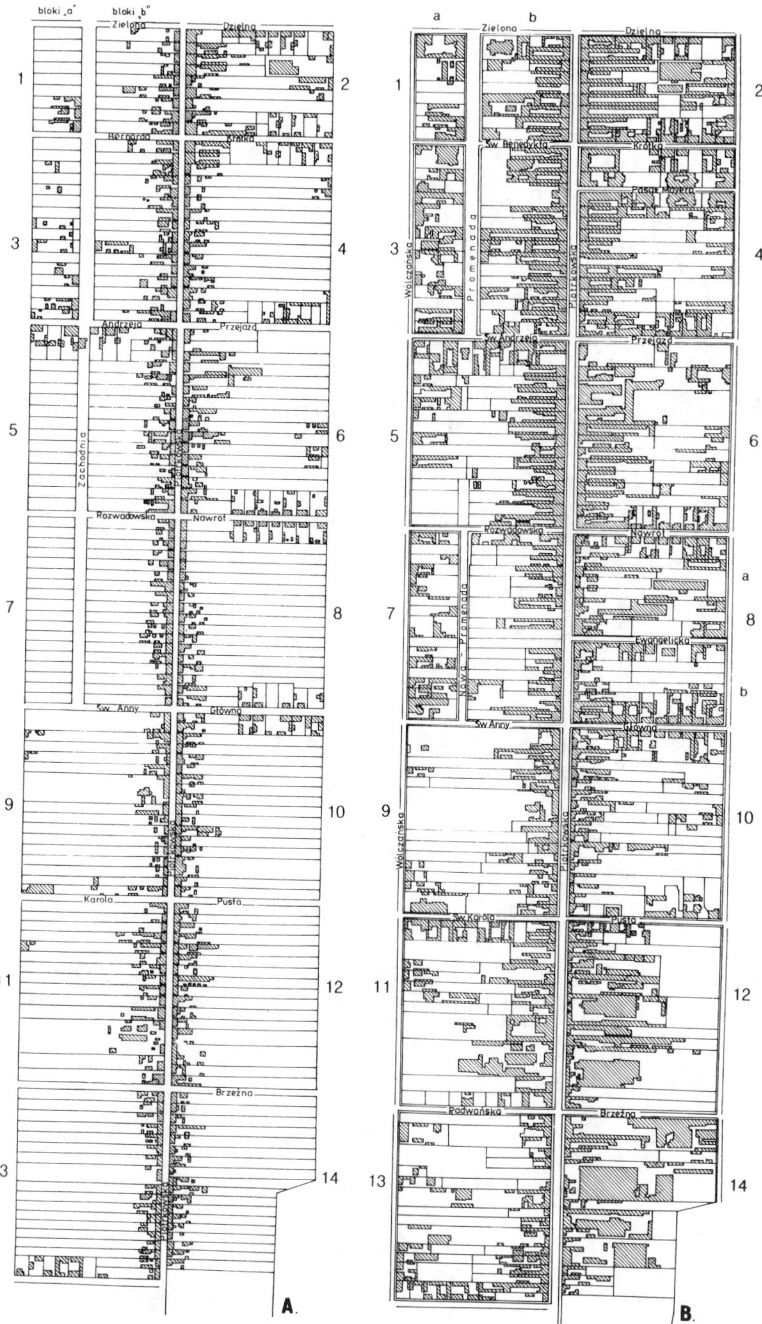

Figure 6.3 A, Weavers' colony after Micinski's map of 1877; **B,** Weavers' colc after Starzynski's map of 1891/97

Table 6.1 The degree of the repletion and transformation of blocks in 1877

No. of block	*Additive-repletive process*					*Transformative process*					
	Ratio of building coverage in %			*Number of untransformed original/parent/plots*		*Number of parent plots being transformed/number of derivative plots after transformation*					
	Of entire block	*Of individual plots*				*Joint/after joining*	*Divided/after division*	*Cut by new street/after cutting*	*Derivative cut plots*		
		Minimum	*Maximum*	*At the start*	*At the moment*				*Untransformed*	*Joint/after joining*	*Divided/after division*
1	11·5	4·5	20·0	9	—	—	—	9/18			
1a	8·0	0·0	25·8	—	—	—	—	9	9	—	—
1b	15·7	7·9	30·4	—	—	—	—	9	9	—	—
3	13·9	8·1	31·4	16	—	—	—	16/32			
3a	12·1	0·0	33·0	—	—	—	—	16	16	—	—
3b	19·1	4·3	39·5	—	—	—	—	16	14	2/1	—
5	9·5	3·0	30·5	16	—	—	—	16/32			
5a	5·2	0·0	37·9	—	—	—	—	16	13	—	3/3
5b	13·2	5·1	21·5	—	—	—	—	16	13	—	3/5
7	5·8	3·6	7·3	18	—	—	—	18/36			
7a	0·0	0·0	0·0	—	—	—	—	18	18	—	—
7b	9·6	6·1	12·2	—	—	—	—	18	18	—	—
9	8·0	3·1	33·2	18	12	5/2	1/2	—	—	—	—
11	7·8	4·6	13·7	18	11	7/3	—	—	—	—	—
13	7·3	1·7	26·1	19	15	2/1	2/8	—	—	—	—
1–13	x	x	x	114	38	14/6	3/10	59/118	110	2/1	6/8

Table 6.1 contd.

No. of block	*Additive-repletive process*					*Transformative process*					
	Ratio of building coverage in %			*Number of untransformed original/parent/plots*		*Number of parent plots being transformed/number of derivative plots after transformation*					
	Of entire block	*Of individual plots*				*Joint/after joining*	*Divided/after division*	*Cut by new street/after cutting*	*Derivative cut plots*		
		Minimum	*Maximum*	*At the start*	*At the moment*				*Untransformed*	*Joint/after joining*	*Divided/after division*
2	23·9	4·5	43·2	9	3	—	6/20	—	—	—	—
4	12·4	5·1	43·8	16	12	—	4/17	—	—	—	—
6	11·5	2·2	25·4	16	12	—	4/12	—	—	—	—
8	7·6	3·4	20·3	18	13	—	5/17	—	—	—	—
10	8·6	3·7	33·5	18	14	2/1	2/7	—	—	—	—
12	7·6	3·4	14·4	18	14	4/2	—	—	—	—	—
14	5·9	2·2	11·0	18	18	—	—	—	—	—	—
2–14	x	x	x	113	86	6/3	21/73	—	—	—	—
Total	x	x	x	227	124	20/9	24/83	59/118	110	2/1	6/8

industrial zone, for example, some 3 km. long and from 300 m. to 900 m. wide, was owned by only three factory owners. One of them, Carl Scheibler, owned about 80 per cent of this area, or one-sixth of the total town area. Thus, when the raw material depression came to an end, an urgent demand for alternative industrial grounds was generated in order to build new textile works.

All these circumstances brought about large scale morphological changes within the former weavers' colony. A demand for thousands of new dwellings caused an increase in the building coverage of plots and transverse subdivision of the original plots and large urban blocks. On the other hand, the demand for new industrial ground caused, simultaneously, the opposite process in the southern part of the colony. Here new textile firms tended to locate near the main industrial zone, and purchased two, sometimes three, former weavers' plots, amalgamating them in order to build new factories.

The character and scale of the morphological changes within the area being examined is shown in Figure 6.3A and in Table 6.1. The calculations concerning additive–repletive processes on the one hand and transformative ones on the other, have been drawn up separately. In order to emphasize the different conditions of the eastern and western blocks of strips each of them has been summed separately, as too has the northern (subdivided into smaller blocks) and southern (undivided) parts of the western strip.

Both map and table show that the repletive process, although much accelerated, did not reach substantial proportions in the 1870s. The building coverage on all of the original blocks (except the north-eastern one, where it amounted to 23·9 per cent), was still only between 5·8 per cent and 13·9 per cent. It must be remembered, however, that the original very large weavers' plots were not designed for urban purposes as they were both very elongated and faced to only one side of the block. One cannot compare them with typical medieval burgages, which were generally much smaller (Slater 1981), with elongations of 1 : 6 to 1 : 7 (here plots are 1 : 13·5 to 1 : 15).

There were distinct difference between the various parts of the former colony with regard to the development of additive and transformative processes too. The intensity of both processes had been increasing generally from southern to northern blocks and from western to eastern ones, with its climax in the north-eastern block beside the railway station. These differences resulted from various forces.

To the west of the developing town there was little that could introduce any dynamism likely to promote morphological change into the western blocks since there were only agricultural fields and the semi-rural spinners' colony on that side. Consequently building coverage was lowest in this area, especially in south-western blocks where it reached only 7·3–8 per cent. Within those blocks only six new plots had been created in the side streets and almost three-quarters of the plots kept their original dimensions (see Table 6.1). On the other hand, the low building coverage allowed a new breakthrough street, Zachodnia, (Western Street or Promenade) to be laid out across the north-western blocks (Orłowski 1984). It lay parallel to the main Piotrkowska street, at right angles to the original plots, and therefore divided blocks 1–7 into pairs of smaller blocks (1a, 1b . . . 7a, 7b). The plots within these new blocks kept their original breadth but with an elongation of only 1 : 4 in the 'a' blocks and some 1 : 7·5 in the 'b' blocks. They were thereby much better adapted for urban purposes.

From the south, plots were affected by the impact of industrial development as factories sought new localities outside the water-power sites along the River Jasien, which were still occupied by Carl Scheibler's industrial estate. This quest led to the amalgamation of groups of original plots. Within blocks 9–14 it is possible to recognize eight such examples. However, this was just the start of the process of industrial expansion into the former weavers' colony and the building coverage remained quite limited (5·9–8·9 per cent).

The strongest external impact was from the north-eastern side. Here, the influence of the siting of the railway station caused the neighbouring north-eastern blocks of the colony to become economically the most attractive part of the city. Within a brief period after the railways had been built, the best hotels, theatres, restaurants, cafés, confectioners and shops were established there. It also became the most attractive residential area for the upper and upper-middle classes. Thus, the building coverage was densest in this region (11·5–23·9 per cent of the total area of blocks 2–6). Similarly, transformative processes such as the subdivision of plots and the creation of small transverse plots along the side streets with subsequent backward absorption, also took place here on a greater scale than elsewhere. These processes also affected neighbouring north-western blocks where building density reached 9·5–13·9 per cent. Clearly, then, it was during this period that the nucleus of the common city centre within block 1–4, or perhaps 1–6, started to be formed. In general, the transformative processes were much more advanced during this period than the repletive ones. Some 101 original plots, that is 44·5 per cent of the total, had been more or less transformed; 59 of them were transversely cut by a new street, 22 were joined and 30 were subdivided (see Fig. 6.3A and Table 6.1).

Cross-section four: 1894–1897

The great industrial development of Łódź, that had commenced in the mid 1860s, grew stronger and stronger during the next decades. It was accompanied by an enormous increase in the population from some 50,000 in 1872, to 314,000 in 1897. Such rapid economic and demographic growth inevitably had morphological consequences for the city. The two decades between the third and fourth cross-sections were strongly marked as the period of the greatest

Table 6.2 The degree of the repletion and transformation of blocks in 1894/1897

No. of block	*Additive-repletive process*					*Transformative process*					
	Ratio of building coverage in %			*Number of untrans-formed original/parent/plots*		*Number of parent plots being transformed/number of derivative plots after transformation*					
	Of entire block	*Of individual plots*				*Joint/after joining*	*Divided/after division*	*Cut by new street/after cutting*	*Derivative cut plots*		
		Minimum	*Maximum*	*At the start*	*At the moment*				*Untrans-formed*	*Joint/after joining*	*Divided/after division*
1	34·1	13·8	49·5	9	—	—	—	9/18			
1a	37·3	0·0	62·5	—	—	—	—	9	5	4/2	—
1b	41·4	21·4	62·4	—	—	—	—	9	4	—	5/8
3	34·7	12·7	55·0	16	—	—	—	16/32			
3a	37·2	0·0	78·2	—	—	—	—	16	9	6/3	1/1
3b	39·0	19·0	66·7	—	—	—	—	16	6	2/1	8/13
5	27·0	12·3	51·2	16	—	—	—	16/32			
5a	22·0	0·0	60·9	—	—	—	—	16	9	4/2	3/3
5b	29·7	20·0	56·0	—	—	—	—	16	9	—	7/15
7	23·9	0·0	53·4	18	—	—	—	18/36			
7a	30·1	0·0	60·0	—	—	—	—	18	8	2/1	8/11
7b	24·2	0·0	56·2	—	—	—	—	18	10	2/1	6/9
9	16·4	8·6	45·0	18	5	5/2	8/13	—	—	—	—
11	25·3	6·4	63·6	18	1	8/3	9/27	—	—	—	—
13	18·5	2·9	52·4	19	3	4/2	12/22	—	—	—	—
1–13	x	x	x	114	9	17/7	29/62	59/118	60	20/10	38/50

Table 6.2 contd.

No. of block	*Additive-repletive process*					*Transformative process*					
	Ratio of building coverage in %			*Number of untransformed original/parent/plots*		*Number of parent plots being transformed/number of derivative plots after transformation*					
	Of entire block	*Of individual plots*							*Derivative cut plots*		
		Minimum	*Maximum*	*At the start*	*At the moment*	*Joint/after joining*	*Divided/after division*	*Cut by new street/after cutting*	*Untransformed*	*Joint/after joining*	*Divided/after division*
2	43·8	21·0	69·0	9	—	—	9/27	—	—	—	—
4	32·7	14·9	64·5	16	1	—	14/36	1/0	—	—	—
4a	41·4	39·6	44·4	3	—	—	3/8	—	—	—	—
4b	31·1	14·6	64·5	12	1	—	11/28	—	—	—	—
6	29·4	11·6	53·9	16	1	5/1	10/23	—	—	—	—
8	34·0	4·7	68·0	18	—	—	17/47	1/0	—	—	—
8a	34·4	22·5	49·1	9·5	—	—	9·5/22	—	—	—	—
8b	36·2	4·7	68·0	7·5	—	—	7·5/25	—	—	—	—
10	18·0	6·0	49·3	18	2	3/1	13/28	—	—	—	—
12	27·6	9·2	49·4	18	4	7/2	7/10	—	—	—	—
14	35·9	6·3	58·9	18	1	12/4	5/7	—	—	—	—
2–14	x	x	x	113	9	27/8	75/241	2/0	—	—	—
Total	x	x	x	227	18	44/15	104/303	61/118	60	20/10	38/60

morphological changes, both additive and transformative, in the whole history of industrial Łódź.

While the building coverage of the whole weavers' colony grew during the half-century between 1827 and 1877 only from 2 per cent to 9·5 per cent, by 1897 it had reached 27·6 per cent. It remained more dense in the eastern street blocks (18·0–43·8 per cent) than in western ones (16·4–34·7 per cent), but within the smaller secondary blocks 'a' and 'b' amounted to between 22 and 41·4 per cent. On the other hand, the differences between northern and southern blocks had been much reduced (see Table 6.2), mainly because of the spread of the big industrial plants with their amalgamation of three or four original plots, especially within blocks 14, 12 and 11 (Fig. 6.3B). As a result, the building coverage of the fringe 14th block grew sixfold during these twenty years.

Two additional side-streets were laid out within blocks 4 and 8. However, they did not cut the plots transversely, as in the western blocks, but ran parallel to them so that it was possible to create only a few new plots facing those streets. In the first case, the street (called Mayer's Passage) was constructed by the former manufacturer Mayer who transferred his factory to the fringe of the city and converted the old factory buildings into the huge Grand Hotel. Nearby, in the centre of his three-plot-wide area he laid out the passage and built several substantial villas for the richest members of society (Augustyniak 1977). The passage remained private and closed to public access until 1905. In the other case, the new street (Evangelical Street) was laid out just in front of the Lutheran church. The rest of the plots used for the street were amalgamated with their neighbours which allowed wider side-street plots to be created and for them to be filled with better tenement houses.

The building activity that started in the 1870s and became most dynamic in the 1890s did not result simply in an increase in the number of the houses but also in qualitative changes in their size and constructional standard, as well as building replacement. This was especially so with regard to the front houses. Replacing the small wooden or timber-framed weavers' houses, many multi-storeyed tenement houses were built. In the middle of the 1870s brick houses composed only one-third of the total number of houses in the city but, by the mid 1890s, they constituted some three-quarters of the total (Rynkowska 1970). The building transformation proceeded in two phases. During the first, which began in the 1870s, the new, higher, brick houses were built mainly as outbuildings. They were raised beyond the small wooden front houses, on one or both sides of the plot, with a narrow courtyard between them. During the second phase, in the early 1890s, those small front houses were replaced by new, large tenement houses. In those cases where medium-sized houses already existed, an adaptative replacement was undertaken. It consisted of enlargement and the building of additional storeys. The process of repletive absorption taking in adjoining front houses can be observed, too. Finally, supplementary side and back houses were constructed further back long the length of the plots.

The process of the horizontal and vertical intensification of building developed in different ways according to the value of land. The price of land was highest in the northern part of the former colony, especially along Piotrkowska street. A square łokiec (0·33 m^2) of land there at the end of the nineteenth century cost as much as a whole morga (5,598 m^2) in the 1830s! In the southern part, the prices of land were much lower and the quality of houses changed according the the land value. While the northern part of Piotrkowska street was closely built up with multi-storeyed houses, many one-storeyed buildings (including thirty original weavers' houses) still remained in the southern part.

The northern part of the colony, namely blocks 1–6, became the most presentable part of Łódź in the 1880s and 1890s: a real centre for a great city. First-class hotels, banks, the most elegant shops and stores, theatres and cafés were all situated there. It was also the area of the biggest and most expensive tenement houses where the flats cost almost twice as much as similar ones in the southern sector of Piotrkowska street. In the front houses of Piotrkowska street, Promenade and some side streets, there lived the elite of the city manufacturers, bankers, doctors, lawyers, engineers and rich businessmen. The architecture of these buildings was generally eclectic, mostly neo-Classical and neo-Baroque, and at the end of the nineteenth century there appeared also some houses in the new Art Nouveau style (Popławska 1976).

But beyond the magnificent, pompous front houses there existed a quite different world of ugly outbuildings with sub-standard dwellings for the working classes. The prices of the building plots were so high here that owners tried to build them up to as great a density as possible. Social factors played no role in this period, so, in extreme cases, landowners built high tenement buildings on both sides of a plot, then a transverse house, then two more rows of buildings along the sides of a plot and a back-house at the rear. The enclosed double 'well-courtyards', were dark, badly ventilated, and without any tree or grass. The coexistence of tenement houses with warehouses, stores and factories made living conditions within such yards extremely hard and unhealthy (Ginsbert 1962).

It was not until the end of the nineteenth century that the city council forbade the construction of new factories within the city centre. Some effort had been made to remove existing factories, at least from Piotrkowska street, but many of them still remained. In some cases the manufacturers themselves decided to convert their factory buildings to other functions as Mayer did, for example. This was mainly for economic reasons because of the increase of land values, especially after 1898, when the first electric tramway line was established along Piotrkowska.

As a result of all these processes, transformative changes to the plan also took place on an enormous scale during this period (Table 6.2). While, in

Table 6.3 The degree of the repletion and transformation of blocks in 1917

No. of block	*Additive-repletive process*					*Transformative process*					
	Ratio of building coverage in %			*Number of untransformed original/parent/plots*		*Number of parent plots being transformed/number of derivative plots after transformation*					
	Of entire block	*Of individual plots*				*Joint/after joining*	*Divided/after division*	*Cut by new street/after cutting*	*Derivative cut plots*		
		Minimum	*Maximum*	*At the start*	*At the moment*				*Untransformed*	*Joint/after joining*	*Divided/after division*
1	38·1	17·4	54·8	9	—	—	—	9/18			
1a	40·9	0·0	79·2	—	—	—	—	9	5	4/2	—
1b	48·3	24·9	65·4	—	—	—	—	9	4	—	5/10
3	38·5	21·3	66·8	16	—	—	—	16/32			
3a	41·7	0·0	84·3	—	—	—	—	16	6	7/3	3/5
3b	44·1	17·1	72·0	—	—	—	—	16	5	—	11/17
5	28·2	15·8	51·9	16	—	—	—	16/32			
5a	28·7	0·0	62·6	—	—	—	—	16	12	—	4/5
5b	39·7	21·8	61·4	—	—	—	—	16	8	—	8/17
7	29·7	8·3	60·3	18	—	—	—	18/36			
7a	36·9	0·0	80·8	—	—	—	—	18	11	2/1	5/7
7b	30·6	7·3	56·4	—	—	—	—	18	9	6/3	3/6
9	19·5	8·6	47·8	18	3	5/2	10/20	—	—	—	—
11	28·4	7·2	63·6	18	1	8/3	9/27	—	—	—	—
13	20·7	3·1	48·3	19	4	5/2	11/21	—	—	—	—
1–13	x	x	x	114	7	18/7	30/68	59/118	60	19/9	39/67

Table 6.3 contd.

No. of block	*Additive-repletive process*					*Transformative process*					
	Ratio of building coverage in %			*Number of untrans-formed original/parent/plots*		*Number of parent plots being transformed/number of derivative plots after transformation*					
	Of entire block	*Of individual plots*				*Joint/after joining*	*Divided/after division*	*Cut by new street/after cutting*	*Derivative cut plots*		
		Minimum	*Maximum*	*At the start*	*At the moment*				*Untrans-formed*	*Joint/after joining*	*Divided/after division*
2	51·6	28·6	69·0	9	—	—	9/29	—	—	—	—
4	35·2	24·3	64·5	16	1	—	14/41	1/0	—	—	—
4a	42·5	40·2	44·9	3	—	—	3/12	—	—	—	—
4b	35·7	24·3	64·5	12	1	—	11/29	—	—	—	—
6	34·1	10·0	60·5	16	1	4/1	11/25	—	—	—	—
8	37·9	9·0	68·0	18	—	2/1	15/44	1/0	—	—	—
8a	41·8	24·4	64·5	9·5	—	2/1	7·5/18	—	—	—	—
8b	37·2	9·0	68·0	7·5	—	—	7·5/26	—	—	—	—
10	27·9	6·2	70·1	18	3	3/1	12/32	—	—	—	—
12	33·6	16·4	65·2	18	2	9/2	7/19	—	—	—	—
14	42·9	11·8	58·9	18	—	15/5	3/4	—	—	—	—
2–14	x	x	x	113	7	33/10	71/194	2/0	—	—	—
Total	x	x	x	227	14	51/17	101/262	61/118	60	19/9	39/67

1877, 124 original plots (54·6 per cent of their initial number) still existed, in 1897, only eighteen of them remained. Almost half of the secondary short plots within uneven blocks 'a' and 'b' had been changed by then, too, although they were a more adequate size for urban development purposes. The total number of derivative plots had grown by 1897 to exactly 400.

There were different forms to the morphological transformations of these plots. Apart from the simple joining or transverse division of the original plots, some new types of combination appeared for the first time: the merger of a plot with the front or tail of an adjoining one, for example. More common, however, were examples of broad short plots created from the tails, or occasionally the front parts, of two neighbouring plots. This happened when commercial and industrial premises, already occupying individual plot tails, spread over adjoining plots in a process of repletive absorption. Elsewhere, there is an example of three plots being amalgamated and afterwards being divided lengthwise to form two wider ones. There were also odd examples of plots being amalgamated with the front part of the plot on one side and with the rear part of the plot on the other to give a 'z'-shaped holding. In the side streets investors tended to merge two or three plots and then divide them transversely into small plots facing the streets. There are also examples of individual side-street plots being extended backwards absorbing land crossways from neighbouring holdings. There were a few other untypical combinations which it is very difficult to classify and so the statistical tables specify only the classical forms of morphological plot transformation.

Cross-section five: 1917

All of the processes mentioned above were continued during the first decades of the twentieth century. But in neither the early twentieth century nor in the following periods was the dynamism of morphological change – additive, repletive and transformative – so strong as it had been during the last quarter of the nineteenth century. It is for this reason that so much space has been devoted to the third and fourth cross-sections and why remaining periods will be treated more concisely.

Between the fourth and the fifth cross-sections the rate of morphological change in the former colony slowed down for economic, social and political reasons. In 1897, and again in 1900–1, economic and building depressions occurred in Łódź, followed, in 1905–8, by bloody revolution. It was not a good time to buy land or to build houses and factories (Kulesza 1984). Economic prosperity and a building boom appeared for a short time in 1909, but the outbreak of the First World War in 1914, and German occupation, interrupted it once more.

As a result, the ratio of the building coverage of the whole area investigated within the original blocks grew during that twenty years only from 27·6 per cent to 31·2 per cent (Table 6.3). The increase of new buildings was relatively greater in the southern blocks than in the northern ones as a result of extensions to industrial plants (Fig. 6.4A). On the other hand, the disproportions in the building coverage between western and eastern blocks increased slightly. The transformative changes were of even less importance and the indexes of the original plots, and of the derivative ones, in 1897 and 1917, were almost the same (Table 6.3).

Cross-section six: 1937

In the inter-war period the dynamism of all morphological changes was again maintained only at a low level, though slightly higher than in the previous period. It was caused by the economic difficulties of the newly-independent state of Poland, and of Łódź itself, but also reflected the fact that the morphological structure of the area under discussion became ripe for redevelopment and in many blocks reached the climax phase of its development.

From the very beginning of independence, Łódź struggled with many economic difficulties. During the war the city lost many inhabitants and the textile industry was not only plundered but, to make things worse, it also lost its traditional eastern Russian and Chinese markets. The war with Soviet Russia (1920–2), and general economic depression following the Great Crash of 1929, were unpropitious for city development, too. As a result the main factor that created the city – industry – was much weakened from its former dynamism; many textile firms had to be closed down or to reduce their production (Ginsbert 1962).

The fact that the city did develop, however, was thanks to the acquisition of new functions – administrative, military, religious and commercial. From 1922, Łódź became successively the centre of regional administration; of a newly-created Catholic diocese; of a military district, and gained other regional public institutions such as new banks, hospitals and secondary schools, besides social infrastructure such as libraries and theatres and some cultural institutions. However, the cultural function was still rather weak and, for example, the city (which reached 672,000 inhabitants in 1939) still had no university. Łódź was also the seat of a number of consulates, international industrial trusts and agencies for textile staff and the raw-materials trade.

Most of these institutions were situated in the centre of the city, especially in the part which had become the CBD. The majority of them used existing houses and premises, but in some instances new buildings were built for their own particular purposes. Within the area examined some new banks, the bishop's palace and a theological seminary, the headquarters building of the telephone authority and a YMCA were built. There appeared also many multi-storeyed luxurious tenement houses for senior civil servants and other

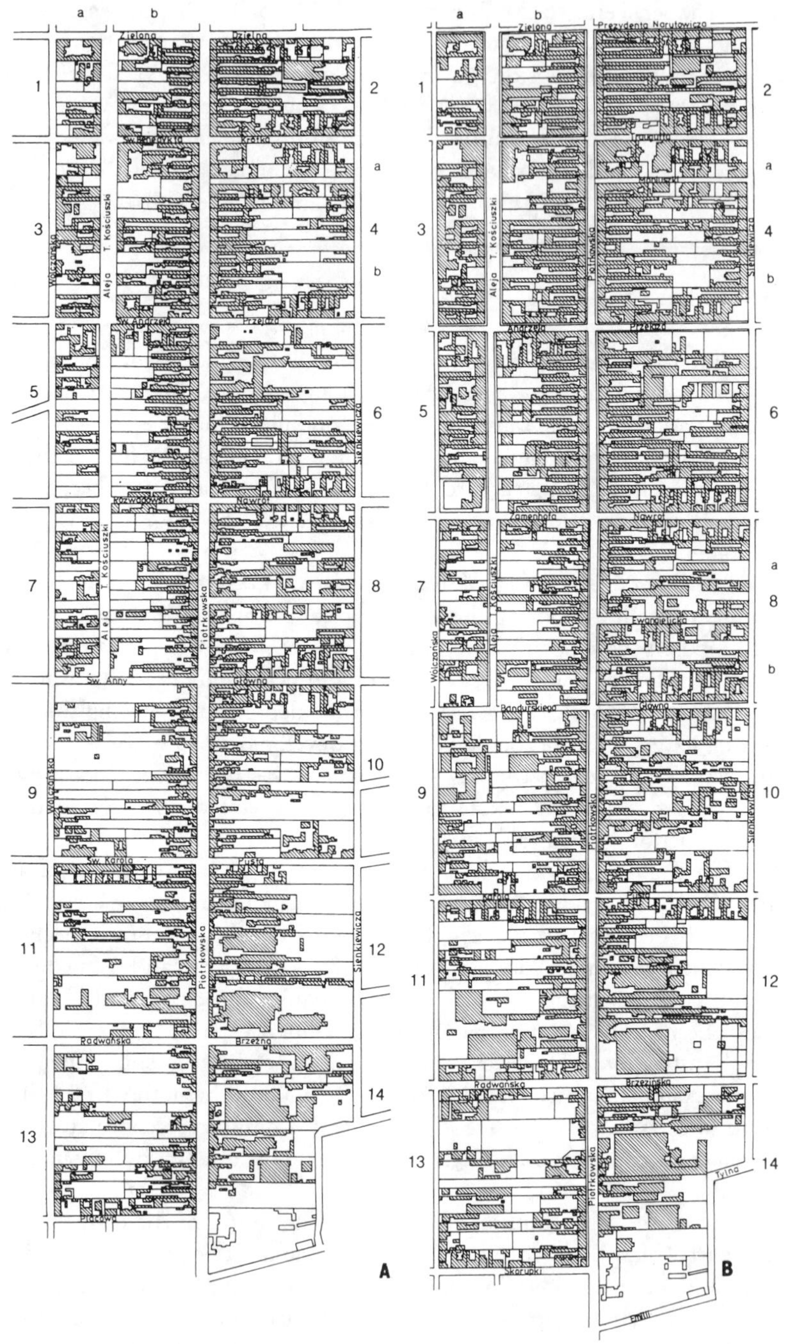

Figure 6.4 A, Former weavers' colony after Fasinski's map of 1917; **B**, Former weavers' colony after official map from 1937

white-collar workers as well as for professionals such as businessmen, doctors and lawyers (Fig. 6.4B). They were built mainly from the middle of the 1930s (after the Depression was over) in the new Modern style (Popławska 1984), mostly along the Promenade (by then called Kosciuszki Avenue), the middle part of Piotrkowska street and neighbouring side-streets which had been less built up in previous periods.

Eventually, the differences between western and eastern blocks were reduced and the total building coverage of the former colony grew from 31·9 per cent in 1917 to 39·2 per cent in 1937 (Table 6.4). Within the limits of the individual blocks, especially the north-eastern ones, it reached 47–49 per cent and in the extreme case of the second block – as much as 60 per cent. In the case of one of the individual original 'parent' plots, by then divided, an extreme value of 92·5 per cent was reached. These were the highest rates of building coverage recorded. Thus, it can be said that by the date of the sixth cross-section the former colony as a whole, as well as the majority of its blocks, except for the four south-western ones, had reached the climax phase of the additive–repletive process of development (Fig. 6.4B).

None the less, transformative changes were still very limited in 1937 (Jaworski and Walczak 1984). As before, they led to the creation of a greater number of derivative plots by the division of the remaining original plots or of previously amalgamated ones. The number of undivided plots fell from fourteen in 1917 to eight in 1937, and the number of amalgamated original plots from seventeen to eleven (Table 6.4). In the second case this was an effect of the economic depression and the bankruptcy of some industrial firms which had to sell their land for other purposes. The demand for new building plots influenced the further subdivision of the already divided plots not only in 'normal' blocks but also in the shorter ones. As a result the number of plots grew from 417 in 1917 to 441 in 1937. The fact that during the twenty years between the third and fourth and the sixth cross-sections (1877–97) the number of plots grew by sixty-five (from 335 to 400) and during the forty years between the fourth and the sixth cross-sections only by forty-one plots, signifies that the pattern of the former weavers' colony had reached its morphological maturity and a relative stability.

Cross-section seven: 1973

The economic boom of the late 1930s was brought to an end by the Second World War. Although the centre of Łódź did not suffer damage at all, the consequences of the war were felt for a long time. As a result of the catastrophic damage to Warsaw, Łódź had to play the role of the capital of Poland for some years and therefore had to accommodate many central institutions and thousands of homeless people. It was not a time for urban reconstruction, for all buildings, even sub-standard ones, were needed as there was no money to construct new ones.

Table 6.4 The degree of the repletion and transformation of blocks in 1937

No. of block	*Additive-repletive process*					*Transformative process*					
	Ratio of building coverage in %			*Number of untransformed original/parent/plots*		*Number of parent plots being transformed/number of derivative plots after transformation*					
	Of entire block	*Of individual plots*				*Joint/after joining*	*Divided/after division*	*Cut by new street/after cutting*	*Derivative cut plots*		
		Minimum	Maximum	*At the start*	*At the moment*				*Untransformed*	*Joint/after joining*	*Divided/after division*
1	40·6	21·6	62·1	9	—	—	—	9/18			
1a	43·7	0·0	86·7	—	—	—	—	9	3	6/3	—
1b	48·5	26·7	64·8	—	—	—	—	9	2	—	7/15
3	45·7	28·7	77·2	16	—	—	—	16/32			
3a	60·2	32·8	71·0	—	—	—	—	16	4	6/3	6/9
3b	44·2	24·7	72·0	—	—	—	—	16	4	—	12/20
5	42·5	25·1	79·4	16	—	—	—	16/32			
5a	48·3	20·8	81·7	—	—	—	—	16	6	3/1	7/8
5b	46·5	32·4	97·1	—	—	—	—	16	8	—	8/16
7	31·6	15·1	64·8	18	—	—	—	18/36			
7a	36·9	1·6	80·8	—	—	—	—	18	9	4/2	5/9
7b	48·0	13·3	69·5	—	—	—	—	18	7	2/1	9/12
9	35·0	20·5	49·1	18	—	2/1	16/18	—	—	—	—
11	38·1	7·2	62·0	18	1	4/1	13/32	—	—	—	—
13	24·5	0·0	49·5	19	2	—	17/34	—	—	—	—
1–13	x	x	x	114	3	6/2	46/84	59/118	43	21/10	54/89

Table 6.4 contd.

No. of block	*Additive-repletive process*					*Transformative process*					
	Ratio of building coverage in %			*Number of untransformed original/parent/plots*		*Number of parent plots being transformed/number of derivative plots after transformation*					
	Of entire block	*Of individual plots*				*Joint/after joining*	*Divided/after division*	*Cut by new street/after cutting*	*Derivative cut plots*		
		Minimum	*Maximum*	*At the start*	*At the moment*				*Untransformed*	*Joint/after joining*	*Divided/after division*
2	60·0	49·0	73·3	9	1	—	8/27	—	—	—	—
4	49·0	31·7	92·5	16	1	—	14/41	1/0	—	—	—
4a	58·9	54·7	64·3	3	—	—	3/12	—	—	—	—
4b	51·2	31·7	92·5	12	1	—	11/29	—	—	—	—
6	48·0	21·8	78·0	16	—	—	16/35	—	—	—	—
8	46·8	24·4	89·9	18	—	—	17/45	1/0	—	—	—
8a	49·7	24·4	89·3	9·5	—	—	9·5/22	—	—	—	—
8b	49·6	23·6	82·8	7·5	—	—	7·5/25	—	—	—	—
10	34·4	6·2	81·0	18	1	4/2	13/30	—	—	—	—
12	33·6	13·0	56·0	18	2	11/3	5/12	—	—	—	—
14	37·2	11·8	66·7	18	—	14/4	4/5	—	—	—	—
2–14	x	x	x	113	5	29/9	77/195	2/0	—	—	—
Total	x	x	x	227	8	35/11	123/279	61/118	43	21/10	54/89

The first inconspicuous morphological changes did not appear in the area being examined until the end of the 1950s. An attempt was made then to improve traffic flow at the most congested points of the city centre. Thus, many corner houses were removed to make easier access to or from side-streets and to create parking places or lawns. The biggest parking lot, complete with a petrol filling station, was built on the corner of the sixth block. Next, Kosciuszki Avenue was extended across block 9 (Fig 6.5). This represented a significant improvement for it augmented the street-system and created new street frontages. A big Party Office and some commercial enterprises were built there. In another part of the centre, a tall TV building was built in block 2 – the first skyscraper in Łódź. Later, within the plots where the larger gardens had existed, or where the building coverage was less dense, some new passages for pedestrians were created, most of them in the western blocks. Two were laid out across block 19, two others in blocks 7b and one in 3b. In the eastern part of the centre the only new passage was laid across block 6. In block 3 parts of three adjoining plots were joined in order to create a larger square (Fig. 6.5).

The great transformation of the city centre did not begin until the early 1970s and was the result of a new plan for the reconstruction of the centre. This provides: (i) for shaping the main core of the central business district within blocks 1–8, with many high buildings of different institutions; (ii) for the creation of a central housing area within blocks 9–14, with several 16- to 24-storey apartment houses; (iii) for the reconstruction of the street-system, with special reference to the further extension of Kosciuszki Avenue and to the construction of a main west–east city route by the considerable broadening of Głowna and Mickiewicza streets.

By the beginning of the 1970s, therefore, it can be said that the recessive phase of the plot cycle had commenced in several blocks of the area examined (Table 6.5). It was manifested in the demolition of many buildings and the obliteration of plots in preparation for redevelopment. The extensive areas of urban fallow appeared first within blocks 7–10 and completely removed the former pattern of plots. In their place, there arose free-standing, high buildings, unconstrained by the limits of former plots and with free access from all sides.

The 1973 cross-section brought to an end a particular stage of morphological change in the centre of Łódź which was based on the concept of the plot cycle. In earlier cross-sections the number, size and shape of plots could change, but the principle of the division of the urban area into series of plots remained invariable. From the moment, however, when this traditional principle was broken in the individual blocks, a new stage in the morphological processes at work commenced, and that requires new methods of investigation, too.

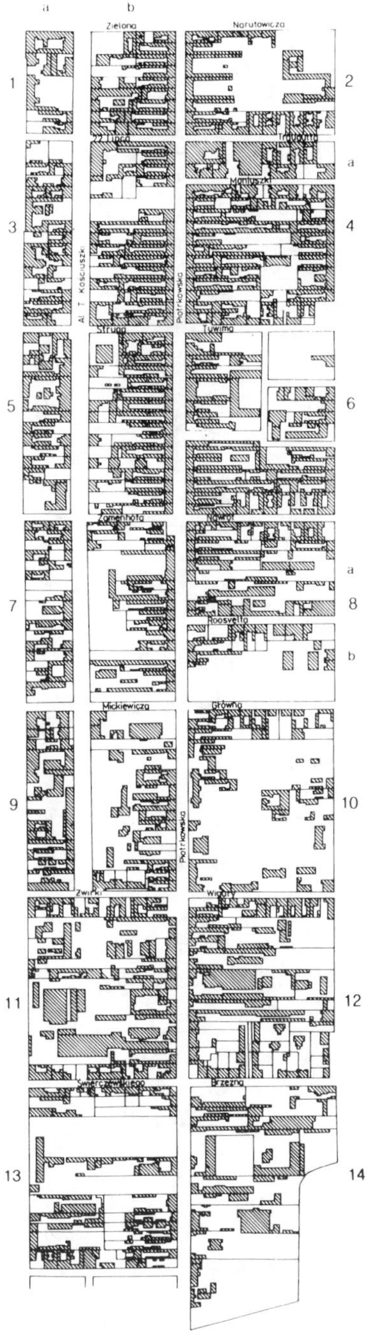

Figure 6.5 Former weavers' colony after official map of 1973

Table 6.5 The degree of the repletion and transformation of blocks in 1973

No. of block	*Additive-repletive process*					*Transformative process*					
	Ratio of building coverage in %			*Number of untransformed original/parent/plots*		*Number of parent plots being transformed/number of derivative plots after transformation*					
	Of entire block	*Of individual plots*				*Joint/after joining*	*Divided/after division*	*Cut by new street/after cutting*	*Derivative cut plots*		
		Minimum	*Maximum*	*At the start*	*At the moment*				*Untransformed*	*Joint/after joining*	*Divided/after division*
1	45·4	27·8	62·1	9	—	—	—	9/18			
1a	44·8	16·7	89·2	—	—	—	—	9	2	5/2	2/2
1b	53·7	26·7	64·8	—	—	—	—	9	1	—	8/17
3	42·2	15·9	64·9	16	—	—	—	16/32			
3a	51·9	19·2	79·2	—	—	—	—	16	5	2/1	9/11
3b	43·4	10·5	79·5	—	—	—	—	16	4	—	12/20
5	38·1	22·4	58·4	16	—	—	—	16/32			
5a	48·7	21·7	70·8	—	—	—	—	16	5	6/2	5/8
5b	45·5	27·6	74·2	—	—	—	—	16	6	—	10/19
7	32·4	11·9	50·8	18	—	—	—	18/36			
7a	41·1	0·0	62·5	—	—	—	—	18	6	2/1	10/13
7b	33·2	0·0	61·9	—	—	—	—	18	2	—	16/12
9	37·5	13·6	56·7	18	—	—	—	18/36			
9a	54·4	21·6	63·3	—	—	—	—	18	3	2/1	13/10
9b	36·4	15·0	56·0	—	—	—	—	18	—	3/1	15/11
11	41·2	17·3	62·9	18	—	5/1	13/25	—	—	—	—
13	27·6	0·0	63·8	19	—	8/1	11/30	—	—	—	—
1–13	x	x	x	114	—	3/2	24/55	77/154	34	20/8	100/123

Table 6.5 contd.

No. of block	*Additive-repletive process*					*Transformative process*					
	Ratio of building coverage in %			*Number of untransformed original/parent/plots*		*Number of parent plots being transformed/number of derivative plots after transformation*					
	Of entire block	*Of individual plots*				*Joint/after joining*	*Divided/after division*	*Cut by new street/after cutting*	*Derivative cut plots*		
		Minimum	Maximum	*At the start*	*At the moment*				*Untransformed*	*Joint/after joining*	*Divided/after division*
2	39·0	18·2	73·3	9	—	—	9/14	—	—	—	—
4	50·2	40·3	91·5	16	—	—	15/41	1/0	—	—	—
4a	58·7	54·6	64·3	3	—	—	3/10	—	—	—	—
4b	55·9	40·3	91·5	12	—	—	12/31	—	—	—	—
6	37·5	19·4	69·1	16	—	—	16/29	—	—	—	—
8	30·8	0·0	89·3	18	—	—	17/30	1/0	—	—	—
8a	41·8	19·2	89·3	9·5	—	—	9·5/20	—	—	—	—
8b	21·8	0·0	57·3	7·5	—	—	7·5/10	—	—	—	—
10	21·8	7·5	62·5	18	—	—	18/14	—	—	—	—
12	32·9	19·3	56·0	18	1	2/1	15/37	—	—	—	—
14	26·5	12·7	54·3	18	—	9/3	9/10	—	—	—	—
2–14	x	x	x	113	1	11/4	99/175	2/0	—	—	—
Total	x	x	x	227	1	24/6	123/230	79/154	34	20/8	100/123

Conclusions

This study has shown that the institutive phase of the plot cycle in central Łódź began in 1827 and lasted until the date of the second cross-section (1853). The repletive phase, which commenced in the 1860s, lasted right through to the date of the sixth cross-section (1937), but reached the culminating point of its activity in the period of the fourth cross-section (1894–7). Before World War II, the repletive phase passed into the climax phase of development and that lasted until the 1960s. In the next decade a slow process of pulling down buildings was observed, indicating the beginning of the recessive phase of the cycle. In some blocks a total demolition of buildings quickly followed and an urban fallow period occurred on those sites so that the cycle had effectively been completed. Soon afterwards, the institutive phase of a succeeding cycle, connected with the new morphological forms not based on the concept of the plot system, commenced there.

The course of the plot cycle was not uniform in all street blocks. It depended on their locality within the territorial structure of the city. The most dynamic additive changes occurred in the north-eastern blocks located in the vicinity of the railway station where the CBD developed. The slowest changes were observed in the south-western blocks which, for a long time, had only a semi-urban character. Figure 6.6 shows this growth in the building coverage both within the previous weavers' colony as a whole (A), as well as within individual street blocks (B) in all seven cross-sectional periods.

This study has suggested a wider application of Conzen's concept of morphological change with reference to additive–repletive processes. It should be noted, however, that each particular town has its own individual values characteristic for each phase of the cycle. They depend on the size and elongation of the plots, their institutional or functional purpose, and locality within the town. In the case of long burgages in the centre of Newcastle, for example, with an elongation of about 5 : 1, the following values of building coverage are given by Conzen (1962):

Institutive phase	10–30 per cent
Repletive phase	30–70 per cent
Climax phase	70–100 per cent

On the considerably bigger plots of the Łódź weavers' colony, with an elongation of over 13 : 1, these values were much lower and amounted to 2–5 per cent, 5–35 per cent and 35–60 per cent respectively. The case of transformative processes is different. It has been stated that types of transformed plots may vary in different towns according to the dimensions and proportions of parent plots. In the case of the Łódź weavers' colony they are shown in Table 6.6.

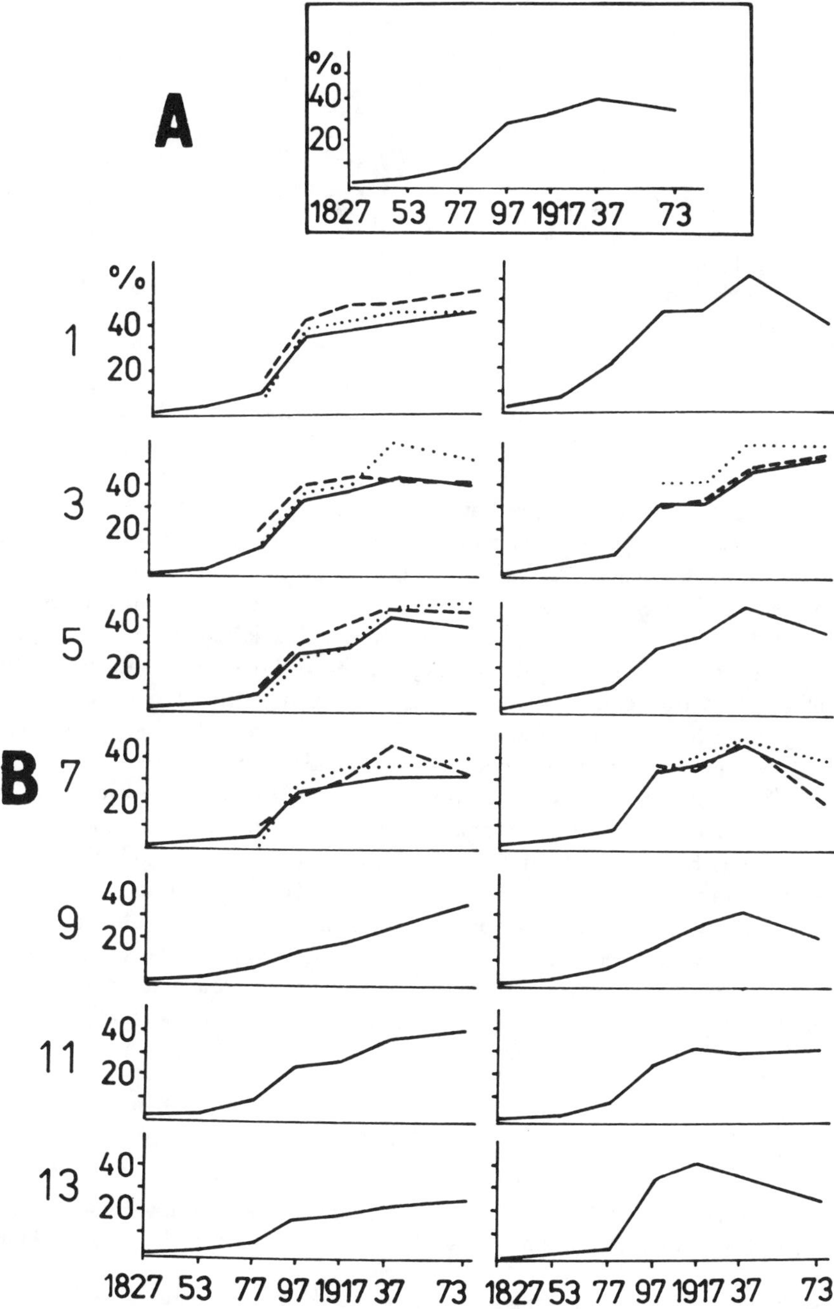

Figure 6.6 Morphological changes of former weavers' colony by street blocks: additive processes

Table 6.6 Transformative changes in the plots of the former weavers' colony and their derivative forms (in numbers)

	1827	1853	1877	1897	1917	1937	1973
Original plots	227	221	124	18	14	8	1
Derivative plots created by:							
Division of original plots	—	13	83	240	252	280	230
Combination of original plots	—	—	9	15	17	11	6
Cutting through by new streets:							
Untransformed	—	—	110	60	60	43	34
Divided	—	—	8	58	65	89	123
Joint	—	—	1	9	9	10	8
Total number of actual plots	227	234	335	400	417	441	402

Although Conzen suggests that there are no evident, observable relationships between the process of additive–repletive changes and transformative ones, this study has suggested that such a relationship may exist. In the case of the Łódź weavers' colony, these processes proceeded more or less in parallel to each other. The institutive phase, that lasted up to the second cross-section (1853) was also the stage of the orthomorphic pattern in the plots. Then the repletive phase was accompanied by the hypometamorphic stage until the sixth cross-section (1937). Even the periods of most dynamic change were convergent for both processes and occurred between the third and fourth cross-sections (1877 and 1897). Similarly, the recessive phase of the additive process that became visible during the seventh cross-section (1973) has been accompanied by the metamorphic stage of transformative plot change. It seems then that Conzen's concept of orthomorphic, hypometamorphic and metamorphic stages of transformative change might also be of wider application as they can be identified in the development of different plan units, yet the symptoms of the approach of these stages, as well as the criteria of their distinguishing characteristics, may, in each case, be greatly individualized.

References

Augustyniak, M., 1977. 'Pasaż Meyera w Łodzi. Z dziejów dziewietnastowiecznej zabudowy miasta' (Meyer's passage in Łódź. From the nineteenth-century building of a city), *Kwartalnik Architektury i Urbanistyki*, 22.1: 53–70.

Barke, M., 1974. 'The changing urban fringe of Falkirk: some morphological implications of urban growth', *Scottish Geographical Magazine*, 90: 85–97.

Conzen, M. R. G., 1960. 'Alnwick, Northumberland. A study in town-plan analysis', *Publications, Institute of British Geographers*, 27.

Conzen, M. R. G., 1962. 'The plan analysis of an English city centre', in K. Norberg (ed.), *Proceedings of the IGU symposium in urban geography, Lund 1960* [Lund Studies in Geography, B, *24*].

Ginsbert, A., 1962. Łódź. Studium monograficzne (Łódź, a monograph study) (Łódź).

Jaworski, H., Walczak, W., 1984. 'Planowanie przestrzenne w procesie rozwoju Łodzi w latach 1918–1939' (Territorial planning in the process of the development of Łódź 1918–1939), *Miscelanea* Łódzkie, 1.

Johnson, J. H. and Pooley, C. G. (eds.), 1982. *The structure of nineteenth century cities.*

Koter, M., 1970. *Geneza układu przestrzennego Łodzi przemysłowej* (Origin of the spatial pattern of industrial Łódź) (Warszawa).

Koter, M. and Wiktoroswka, D., 1976. 'Proces przemian morfologicznych śródmieścia Łodzi (w granicach byłej kolonii tkackiej) pod wpływem kształtowania sie ogólnomiejskiego centrum usługowego' (The process of morphological change in Łódź centre [within the limits of the former weavers' colony] as influenced by the development of the central business district), *Acta Universitatis Lodziensis*, (ser. II) 7.

Koter, M., 1984. 'Rozwój układu miejskiego Łodzi wczesnoprzemysłowej' (The development of the urban lay-out of early industrial Łódź), *Miscelanea Łódzkie*, No. 1.

Kulesza, M., 1984. 'Procesy polityczne, gospodarcze i kulturalne a urbanistyczny rozwój Łodzi' (Political, economic and cultural processes and the urban development of Łódź), *Miscelanea Łódzkie*, No. 1.

Orłowski, T. H., 1984. 'Elementy planowania urbanistycznego Łodzi w latach 1860–1914' (Elements of the urban planning of Łódź, 1860–1914), *Miscelanea Łódzkie*, No. 1.

Popławska, I., 1976. 'Architektura przemysłowa Łodzi w XIX wieku' (The industrial architecture of Łódź in the 19th century), *Studia i Materiały do Teorii i Historii Architektury i Urbanistyki, 11*, (Warszawa).

Popławska, I., 1984. 'Architektura Łodzi w dwudziestoleciu miedzywojennym' (The architecture of Łódź in the inter-war period), *Kwartalnik Architektury i Urbanistyki, 29.*

Rynkowska, A., 1970. *Ulica Piotrkowska* (Piotrkowska Street) (Łódź).

Slater, T. R., 1981. 'The analysis of burgage patterns in medieval towns', *Area, 13*: 211–16.

Slater, T. R., 1987. 'Ideal and reality in English episcopal medieval town planning', *Transactions, Institute of British Geographers, N.S.12*: 191–203.

Whitehand, J. W. R., 1967. 'Fringe belts: a neglected aspect of urban geography', *Transactions, Institute of British Geographers, 41*: 223–33.

Whitehand, J. W. R. and Whitehand, S. M., 1983. 'The study of physical change in town centres: research procedures and types of change', *Transactions, Institute of British Geographers, N.S.8*: 483–507.

Whitehand, J. W. R., 1984. *Rebuilding town centres: developers, architects and styles* [University of Birmingham, Department of Geography, Occasional Publication No. 19].

7 Town-plan analysis in an American setting: cadastral processes in Boston and Omaha, 1630–1930

*Michael P. Conzen**

Urban communities express the tenor and quality of their past and present life in the external appearance of their habitat. During the course of history the townscape is created and transformed by its 'local urban society'. In historic towns it is the result of secular processes of morphological change, actuated by that society during many centuries in response to successive changes in its social, political, economic and cultural requirements within a wider historical and regional context.

(M. R. G. Conzen 1988: 253)

In a global setting, the comparative morphology of American cities is measured by the generosity with which space has traditionally been appropriated, the short useful life that land parcels and buildings seem to possess, and the long-standing pervasiveness of individual over communal choice in shaping the built environment (Wissink 1962: 287–97; Hofmeister 1971: ch. 3; Vance 1977: 354–60, 373, 393). In contrast to urban centres in other highly developed regions, especially Europe, American cities display dynamic morphologies that, in gross volume of turnover and rapidity of change, make up for what they lack in the longevity of their historical development. To any student of the urban process, this makes the morphological analysis of American cities a challenge: if change comes quickly, how well can the individual factors be isolated and measured, and how significant are patterns inherited from the past in shaping new conditions? All too often the analytical response has been to answer these questions from a functionalist perspective, assuming that the dead hand of the past has no role in the present and that most urban spatial patterns can be explained by social and economic processes operating now (Conzen, M. P. 1978). The expansiveness of new residential and other land-use districts, together with the frequent renewal of structures in the urban core, have confirmed for many observers the sufficiency of a view fixed upon the ubiquity and success of the new simply replacing the old.

* The research that underlies this study was supported by a research grant from the Geography and Regional Science Program of the U.S. National Science Foundation (Grant No. SES-8025062).

No urban culture, however, remakes its cities overnight. Even the most dynamic urban places in the United States reveal everywhere the influence of antecedent conditions, of investment, of ownership, and of prior decisions about design that have etched the urban space with boundaries and masses that profoundly condition the course of change. And even in the land where individualism has so long been favoured, the stamp of public authority is felt in various ways throughout the cityscape. The claim that urban form is merely the incidental outcome of social interactions has led to a serious misreading of the power of physical structures to mediate and constrain subsequent action in the organization of cities. American city form then, no less than its European and other counterparts, requires an active, morphogenetic approach to its study (Gordon 1984; Whitehand 1987; *idem*. 1988, provide reviews of modern work in urban morphogenesis. For cross-cultural comparisons see Holzner 1967; Hofmeister 1982).

The American urban landscape has traditionally drawn interest from architectural historians, planners, landscape architects, and especially geographers; and to a lesser degree, economists and historians. No perspective, however, has brought a balanced focus to its subject. There are questions concerning the exact content of the urban landscape, the scale at which it is best viewed, the degree of historicity that should be examined, and the role that perception and thought about the cityscape should play in explaining urban morphogenesis (Ley 1988). In geographical writing there has been much concern with 'urban form', usually pitched at the level of the overall shape and direction of urban expansion in the light of general population growth, transport improvements and social trends, but little of this has paid attention to the deeper ways in which the urban landscape in its specificity has evolved at more intricate scales (Bourne *et al.* 1973). If we accept that the townscape comprises three directly accessible components – town plan, building types, and urban land use (Conzen, M. R. G. 1962) – much more attention has traditionally been given in America to patterns of land-use evolution than to building and rebuilding processes, and even less attention has been accorded to the development of the ground plan of cities (Conzen, M. P. 1980).[1] Without a better grasp of the changing pattern of land division and tenure over time, however, geographers cannot hope to achieve a more balanced understanding of the ways in which building fabric and urban circulation continue to be affected by past decisions regarding land assignment and planning, and how all these aspects influence the relationship between functional needs and inherited fabric (Vance 1971).

Morphological study

If urban form connotes a very general conception of the physical structure of cities – at least as used in American geographical literature – it may be useful to consider urban morphology as a term referring more precisely to the particular character of the urban landscape: the detailed interplay of land subdivision, buildings and their combined patterns of use. This distinction has a longer history of acceptance in European, and specifically British, geography than in American. Systematic morphological analysis of United States cities has been a largely understudied field for geographers. With relatively few exceptions, it has been left to architectural historians, landscape architects, and planners to explore and measure the visible forms of the city in America and speculate on their origins, and consequently more is known about building styles and park systems than about changing land-use morphology and the spatial structure of land tenure (for example, Tunnard and Reed 1955; Mumford 1961: chs. 14–18; Reps 1965; Fitch 1966; Chadwick 1966; Condit 1968; Banz 1970; Schuyler 1987). Most urban geographers have followed functional interests (for example, Mayer and Hayes 1983; Berry and Kasarda 1977; Pred 1966); only recently have cultural geographers taken on the city, and then largely through an interest in current forms and new visual elements (for example, Ford 1980; Foote 1983; exceptions are Vance 1977; Lewis 1976 and Relph 1987). Historical geographers too have followed a functional approach in the social and economic development of cities (Ward 1971; Goheen 1970; Olson 1979).

As a result, our view of evolving American urban structure is shaped overwhelmingly by the market theory of urban rent and 1920s' theories of urban social geometry (Alonso 1964; Berry and Kasarda 1977). Missing in these interpretations of the relationship between urban residents and their man-made environment is any consideration of the inescapable dynamics of physical city form. For example, neglect of explanatory models to account for the specific cultural characteristics of land division and building stock implies that these components of the city's geography are to be assumed as given. But for all the malleability of the urban fabric in response to functional change, land-ownership patterns and building development represent a colossal urban investment, historically layered through time, too powerful by their presence to be merely passive and incidental outcomes of a mechanical rent theory operating smoothly upon a featureless plain. Nor can the urban polity, divided by preference and prejudice and stimulated by unequal income distribution, simply define and redefine the social geography of the city without reference to the cumulative character of the inherited urban fabric as capitalized, designed, and valorized by earlier generations (for an antidote to this outlook, see Lampard 1977; Suttles 1984).

These considerations may seem self-evident, but they reflect the state of American urban morphology today and the context in which formulating concepts and examining cases must proceed. Because the ground plan of American cities has been far less examined than their land use and building patterns, this study attempts a contribution towards filling the gap and is concerned with reconstructing some trends in land development in two American cities from their founding up to the period of the early twentieth century, when formal planning controls began to appear on a large scale.

The ultimate purpose is to ascertain the extent and types of influence that cadastral practices (that is, modes of land subdivision) have exerted on the process of city-building in the United States. These universal practices have carved up and otherwise moulded urban space into an intricate and variably-changing pattern of individual property parcels, building coverage, streets, blocks, and open spaces devoted to a variety of special purposes, which represent the fundamental preparation of urban space for all manner of occupation.

Cadastral processes in American cities

The general theme developed here is that pre-World War I cadastral processes, that is, land-parcel and building-pattern transformations, in reconciling the inertia of prior investment and physical durability with the dynamism of needed functional change, provide independent evidence of the search for a kind of rational urban order in a strongly privatistic, *laissez-faire* era. Cadastral developments also illustrate a delicate shift over time towards a stronger element of public control under the severe pressures of urban growth. Whilst most pre-twentieth-century changes in cadastral practices fell far short of later and more uniform planning principles, they reflect significant innovation and experiment, both the successes and failures of which understandably guided the thinking of the first modern planners.

It is hard to find a conceptual framework within which to place evolving cadastral patterns in American cities. There has been considerable interest in the origins of particular plan configurations, and James Vance has offered a skeletal scheme for classifying early American town plans according to their European morphological heritage (Vance 1982). He suggests that the Spanish towns created according to the *Laws of the Indies*, and French and English towns with medieval bastidal plans succeeded, in effect, in securing the perimeter of the American colonies through the late eighteenth century, but had no future as plan types beyond that. Nor did the medieval organic plans, such as those of early Boston and Dutch New York, have a future when faced with the competition of the 'speculator's town', the Philadelphia grid plan modelled on 'London rebuilt'. This open, democratic cadastre proved so adaptable that it spread along mercantile alignments throughout the interior of the English colonies and westward across the new nation.

The urban planning historian John Reps has been by far the most preoccupied with the ground plans of American cities, but in his extensive treatment of early plans of cities he has been content to focus largely upon initial morphology and the decision-making that underlaid it (Reps 1965; 1979). He has been loath to generalize about broad processes except to counter the Turnerian view that western cities were post-frontier and unplanned but, notwithstanding this, some implicit conclusions can be drawn from his work to provide the skeleton of a 'Repsian thesis' about American urban morphology.

For Reps, it is the *initial* plan that matters in the morphological history of a city, and he also stresses that nearly all American town plans were speculative in their origins. Related to this is the almost universal use of the grid-iron principle for urban planning throughout the town-founding period. Grids offered simplicity in land surveying, recording, and subsequent ownership transfer. One might add that they also maintained a remarkable neutrality towards the presumptive issues of where specific types of urban function should be sited. Few urban plans had locations within them designated and designed for particular functions. Furthermore, grids favoured a fundamental democracy in property market participation. This did not mean that individual wealth could not appropriate considerable urban property, but rather that the basic initial geometry of land parcels bespoke a simple egalitarianism that invited easy entry into the urban land market. Finally, Reps calls attention to the relative infrequency of public amenities provided for in initial town plans, particularly open space in the form of squares and parks, and relief from the monotony of the grid in the form of Baroque-style diagonal and radial street systems. He emphasizes that such amenities tended to decline over time to virtually nil in most western town foundations by the end of the nineteenth century. Such trends he ascribes seemingly to the increased dominance of speculative town origins coupled with a lack of imagination on the part of their opportunistic founders. Despite such broad-scale cadastral tedium, Reps has proven indefatigable in chronicling the endless minor variety in early plan elements that was produced with so limited a *morphological vocabulary*. Others have sought to extend such study by conceptualizing the platting or subdivision phase of plan development in terms of design evolution in relation to location within urban areas (Burns 1977), and in the light of the social and institutional processes necessary for their development (Kramer 1976; Hovinen 1985). A recent study of North Dakota towns, for example, shows a systematic learning sequence by which major railway companies in the nineteenth century evolved suitable town plans for their new urban creations across the prairies and plains of the interior (Hudson 1985).

Reps has chosen to focus by and large on the *institutive phase*[2] of urban plan development and thus inevitably overlooks the problems of subsequent adjustment as the rapidly evolving functional structure of towns placed constant pressure on the urban plan. Even when considering towns at later stages of growth, it is their plan accretions (or *plat additions* in American parlance)[3] that primarily interest him. A partial exception is afforded by his study of Washington (Reps 1967) but, even here, his concern is with the role of periodic formal plans dealing with civic aspirations for new levels of order in this governmental centre, and not with the vernacular changes to lot lines, streets, and building coverage that actually occurred over time. In fact, he implies a planning vocabulary so limited that his only implicit explanation of the coming of major planning theory and controls is as a response to extreme spatial disorder. His study of initial plan designs and their instigators simply gives no adequate idea of the experiments made and experience developed in co-ordinating urban change over time and modernizing the urban ground plan inherited from earlier times (likewise Sears 1979). Yet it is this concern for subsequent plan modifications, large and small, that is needed to cast light on the efficacy of plan types and cadastral practices of various periods and their role in hastening or delaying public reforms and physical improvements.

When concern shifts to the *transformative phase* of American town-plan development, there is far less systematic literature upon which to draw. For one thing the distinction between institutive and transformative development is often blurred in comparison with European practice because buildings did not necessarily spring up immediately and contiguously in newly-established subdivisions. For example, some lots might acquire second structures at street front or at the rear while neighbouring lots remained yet unoccupied; some lots have undergone redevelopment before all lots in the vicinity have been built upon. Thus, even at a fairly mature urban stage, single blocks or groups of blocks in some neighbourhoods might evidence colonization, repletion, and redevelopment at the same time (Bailey 1982; Moudon 1986: 46–7, 51–6, 97–100, 139–44). Nevertheless, transformative processes can be recognized quite clearly (Conzen, M. P. 1980: 136–40), and include lot and building repletion; the ubiquitous American phenomenon of *replatting*[4] – whether merely to increase development densities by creating smaller, more tightly-packed building lots or to augment that with increased access streets; and redevelopment, from lot level to whole blocks and districts (Gad and Holdsworth 1988), including arterial *breakthrough streets* and comprehensive redevelopment.

A comparison of two cases

The best way of developing a keener appreciation of the historical complexity of plan development is through a series of case studies of individual cities representing different regional and historical contexts of growth. Changes in plan evolution and adaptation can be considered in detail in the light of functional changes and locational factors. This study does not go that far, but seeks to present an overview of specific land development patterns in Boston and Omaha up to 1917. These two cities were chosen because they represent almost polar extremes in American urban morphogenesis. Boston, founded in 1630, was a regional capital nearly three centuries old by World War I. As a type it represented a mature, East Coast, industrialized port-city of three-quarters of a million people that had also created the most irregular, complex ground-plan of any American city; an irregularity, moreover, which had developed from earliest times and which was thus likely to have offered the most scope for, but resistance to, modern planning concepts. In contrast, Omaha, founded in 1854 on the empty bank of the

Missouri River, sprang up as the eastern terminus of the transcontinental Union Pacific Railroad and, on the basis of the wholesale trade, gained 100,000 inhabitants in thirty-seven short years, adding 72,000 people in the decade of the 1880s alone. This genuine boom town sprawled across the rolling prairies newly gridded by the Federal Land Survey system, and offers an illustration of urban grid-plan development almost unparalleled for its expansiveness, rapidity, and potential malleability. Boston is the star representative of Vance's 'medieval organic' type of initial plan morphology planted in America, whereas Omaha represents a late western example of his 'London rebuilt' speculator's town plan.

This study focuses on the cartographic record of these two cities as a source of evidence of cadastral imposition and change over long periods of time. Difficulties with source materials severely hindered data collection and analysis. Detailed, large-scale maps of these cities exist for a number of useful dates, but variations in exact scale, planimetric quality, content, and cartographic symbolism due to differing purpose, sponsorship, and technical reproduction standards have made direct comparability difficult to achieve. The observations made here are based on: 1) fire insurance and real estate atlas maps for Boston and Omaha in 1917, 1887, and 1874 (scale between 1 : 1,200 and 1 : 4,800) (Library of Congress 1981); 2) a detailed urban plan of Boston, 1852 (scale *c.* 1 : 2,800) (Slatter and Callam 1852); 3) an extraordinary series of deed-based cartographic reconstructions of central Boston as it appeared in 1633, 1648, 1676, and 1798 by Samuel C. Clough,[5] created between 1895 and 1927 (scales between 1 : 1,200 and 1 : 2,400); and 4) various other contemporary street maps of the two cities (Boston Engineering Dept. 1903). Evidence from registry of deeds records, municipal and commercial reports, newspapers, and selected biographical research would represent a further stage of analysis, leading to a clearer picture of Boston and Omaha land development patterns, but remains beyond the scope of this chapter. Therefore, the following study offers a broad overview of the chief characteristics of land development practices followed in the two cities and the consequences they had for the future morphology of each metropolis.

Morphological periods

Both cities fall into morphological periods determined more by regional settlement experience than by national chronology alone (for a general periodization see Conzen, M. P. 1980: 140). Boston's early start as a North American urban centre and its singularity as the *only* large city in the nation with a large, complex non-grid core plan put it in a category by itself. Its first morphogenetic phase stretched from early-seventeenth-century founding until about 1795, by which time the town's population and economy had recovered from the severe effects of British occupation and blockade during the Revolution. Thereafter, a period of sustained growth within peninsula limitations extended until about mid-century, after which a third period of grand suburban mainland expansion and central area replanning brought the city up to the First World War. The initial period, though long in duration, will be covered in summary fashion in order to concentrate on nineteenth-century processes comparable to and contrasting with those in Omaha.

Morphologically, Omaha's growth from 1854 to 1917 falls into a single, uniform period that spanned two major depressions but saw little resulting differentiation in either cadastral practices or preferred building styles. It can be compared directly with later-nineteenth-century changes in Boston's cadastral evolution, though without the weight of the past as a factor.

(a) Boston

Boston was founded in 1630 with no grand urban vision in mind. While it quickly emerged as the seat of the Massachusetts Bay colony, in form it was a simple farm village with a good harbour. At what point it became precisely 'urban' is less important here than that the pre-urban nucleus consisted of a small collection of settlers' homesteads clustered very loosely around the meeting of several agricultural lanes near the centre of a hilly peninsula in the Bay with some shipping docks nearby (Whitehill 1968: 8–9). In the first half-century of existence, Boston grew steadily to a size of about 4,500 inhabitants, and this growth was accommodated simply through early ribbon development of homestead lots along the proliferating agricultural lanes, and by lateral subdivision of inner-village homestead lots (Fig. 7.1a). Homestead lots were frequently set off from surrounding fields in what might be termed European-style pseudo-burgage series along major streets. Ribbon colonization and lot partitioning raised the density of central housing to the level where individual residences sometimes came close to touching eaves and where some loose infilling of homestead lots was beginning along newly-established orthogonal access lanes that would eventually become part of the town's major street system. These inner village lanes and the extended arterial roads that gave access to the far-flung fields of individual land grants distributed between hill, marsh, and shoreline, developed principally along property boundaries which comfortably followed topographical controls. Hence, within the first half-century the *morphological frame* for central Boston's basic street pattern was all but fixed. It consisted of a major spine leading from the isthmus connecting the mainland in the south to the town green-turned-market-place, from which radiated three subsidiary axes northward to the Town Dock and the North End, westward to the New Field and Trimount, and eastward to the Fort Hill area (Fig. 7.1a).

More than a century later, Boston's morphology had changed remarkably although along conservative lines. While population rose quickly to about 18,000 as early as 1710, and stood around that level through most of the

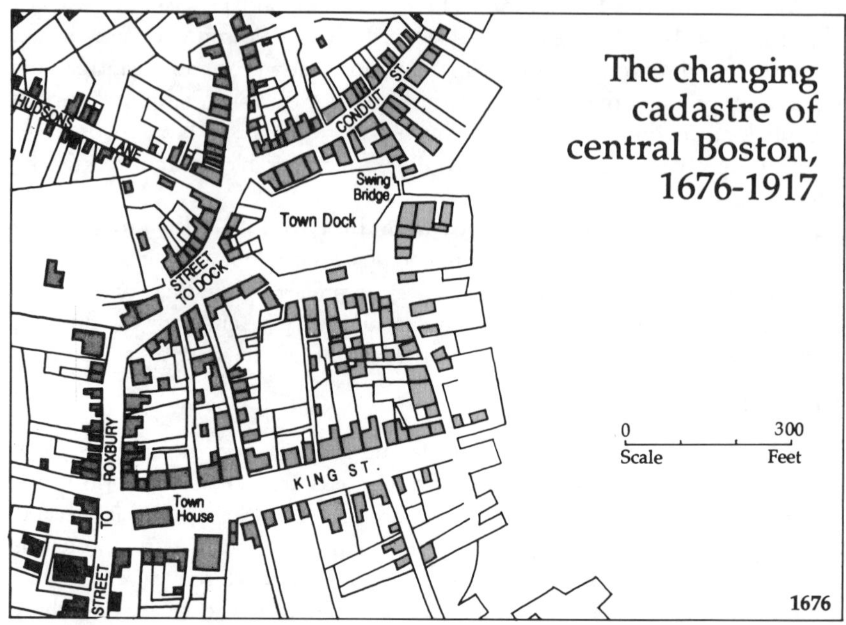
The changing cadastre of central Boston, 1676-1917
HUDSONS LANE
CONDUIT ST.
Swing Bridge
Town Dock
STREET TO DOCK
ROXBURY
KING ST.
Town House
TO
STREET
0
300
Scale
Feet
1676

1798
UNION ST.
No data
ANN ST.
WINGS LANE
Town Dock
Veg. Mkt.
Faneuil Hall
DOCK SQ.
Ch.
MARKET SQ
CORNHILL
MERCHANTS ROW
LONG WHARF
STATE ST.
U.S. Branch Bank
Old State House
KILBY ST.
P.O.
Ch.
MPC

Figure 7.1 The changing cadastre of central Boston 1676–1917

eighteenth century, it took a long time for the ground plan and building stock to reflect this growth. By 1798, however, the street system had added many new cross-connecting streets that developed out of earlier country lanes and property lines (Fig. 7.1b). Building densities associated earlier only with the Town Dock and Market areas were now reached throughout such districts as the North End, reflecting not only increased residential development but also a significant rise in the number of meeting houses, schools and other public buildings, taverns and, along the wharf-front, a steady increase in dock facilities and warehouses. In the town centre, homesteads had largely given way to commercial buildings, many built of brick and stone, set in a warren-like irregular network of alleys for easy cartage that had largely obliterated former land-grant boundaries (Hales 1814). In the newly-dense districts further away, land parcels were so fragmented that the street system had created blocks of narrow, quasi-rectangular plots with an average street-front-to-length ratio of 1 : 3. These, while often subdivisions of earlier, larger homestead lots, represented old and new freehold property on which there was little backyard development as such to be found, but the frequent emergence of side lanes multiplied public access.

Boston's position of commercial prominence in North America continued into the nineteenth century and ensured increased trade and industry which stimulated heavy immigration, both from the hinterland and abroad. The Shawmut Peninsula site had by then filled up with urban settlement and further growth meant either breaking out of the confines of the old high-tide shoreline or yet-higher development densities. Both processes occurred. Between 1798 and 1852 central Boston witnessed intense building repletion as backyards filled up with new housing, manufacturing facilities, and storage buildings (Fig. 7.1c). Blocks in 1798 rarely exceeded 15 per cent building coverage of ground space but, by 1852, in the North End common densities reached 75–80 per cent. Most of this increasing density occurred in ground cover rather than an increase in building height, with averages in 1867 still between two and three storeys in the North End (Sanborn map 1867). At the same time, tidal marshes in the coves of the peninsula proved too attractive to leave undeveloped and major land-fill projects and wharf extensions expanded available land near the commercial centre. Indeed, the intensification of business activities between the wharves and the former symbolic centre of town (the old state house at the head of State Street) led to the first significant case of commercial redevelopment: the Quincy Market complex, including the nearby Customs House.[6] Similar land-filling in neighbouring coves around the peninsula came just in time to accommodate the new railway terminals and associated wholesale facilities. The new transport medium, successful in reaching so close to the heart of the city's commercial centre, further solidified commercial centrality and therefore high land values, leading to dense development and redevelopment on what was by mid-century an overcrowded peninsula.

By century's end, the process of central-area *densification* was further advanced. Repletion had long ago engrossed all remaining land within street blocks, so replacement that involved lot amalgamation and increased building bulk was the dominant form of change (Fig. 7.1d). Throughout the core, but particularly in the vicinity of State Street – which by 1917 had clearly emerged as the spine of Boston's financial district (Ward 1966) – whole street blocks were redeveloped with single, large structures (e.g. the State Street exchange). Also, the intensified commercial activity clogged the circulation system so that in desperation a number of breakthrough streets were sanctioned by city government (e.g., an extension of Washington Street north of Dock Square, Devonshire Street south of Dock Square, and a new diagonal street leading north-westward from Faneuil Hall).

Away from the business core, a small district centred on Hanover and Salem Streets in the North End vividly documents the detailed sequence of cadastral change there during the two morphological periods of the nineteenth century (Fig. 7.2). By 1852, one-third of the buildings that existed in the sample area in 1798 had been replaced by new and somewhat larger structures on the same site. At the same time, however, the total count of buildings had been trebled largely through backyard repletion, or infilling, and comprehensive redevelopment. Building repletion was by far the most important single process in this period because it was the least costly form of change. Comprehensive redevelopment occurred either to insert public institutions, such as a school, into the crowding district, or at the boundary zone between the old solid land area and the new land-fill to the south-west, where a new street grid needed to make some accommodation with old lanes running down to the tidal flats from Salem Street. In this half-century, about half the colonial property boundaries disappeared under the intense building and rebuilding of the period.

Change in the district from 1852 to 1917 was of a different order. The overall ground density increased only modestly – there was little further proportion of horizontal space left to appropriate – and infilling virtually died out, but individual building replacements (usually tenements) and comprehensive redevelopments (both public and private) accounted for substantial new change. What emerges from these trends is a pattern of early densification within essentially colonial property constraints and a traditional building scale. This gave way under the pressures of neighbouring land-fill operations, institutional provision for schools and churches, and the advent of large tenement development to a pattern of partial street rationalization and a significant increase in building bulk (Fig. 7.2). Seen at a larger scale, the North End during this later period was essentially transformed from a two- to three-storey, to a four- to five-storey district. This change occurred when it did only because backyard land was no longer available for easy building colonization, and because immigrant housing needs close to central-business-district (CBD) employment opportunities made expensive redevelopment profitable. The cadastral significance of these changes lies in the heavy reinvestments made in inner-district residential fabric within a now-archaic,

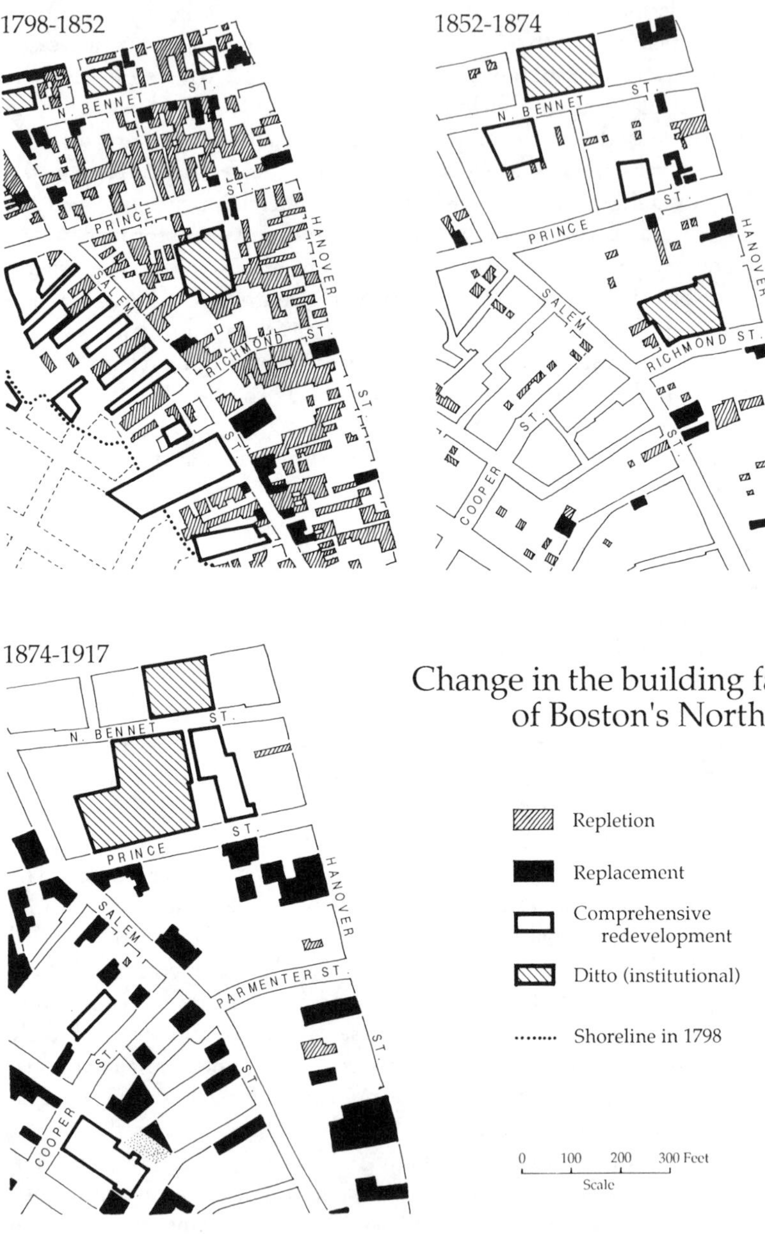

Figure 7.2 Change in the building fabric of Boston's North End

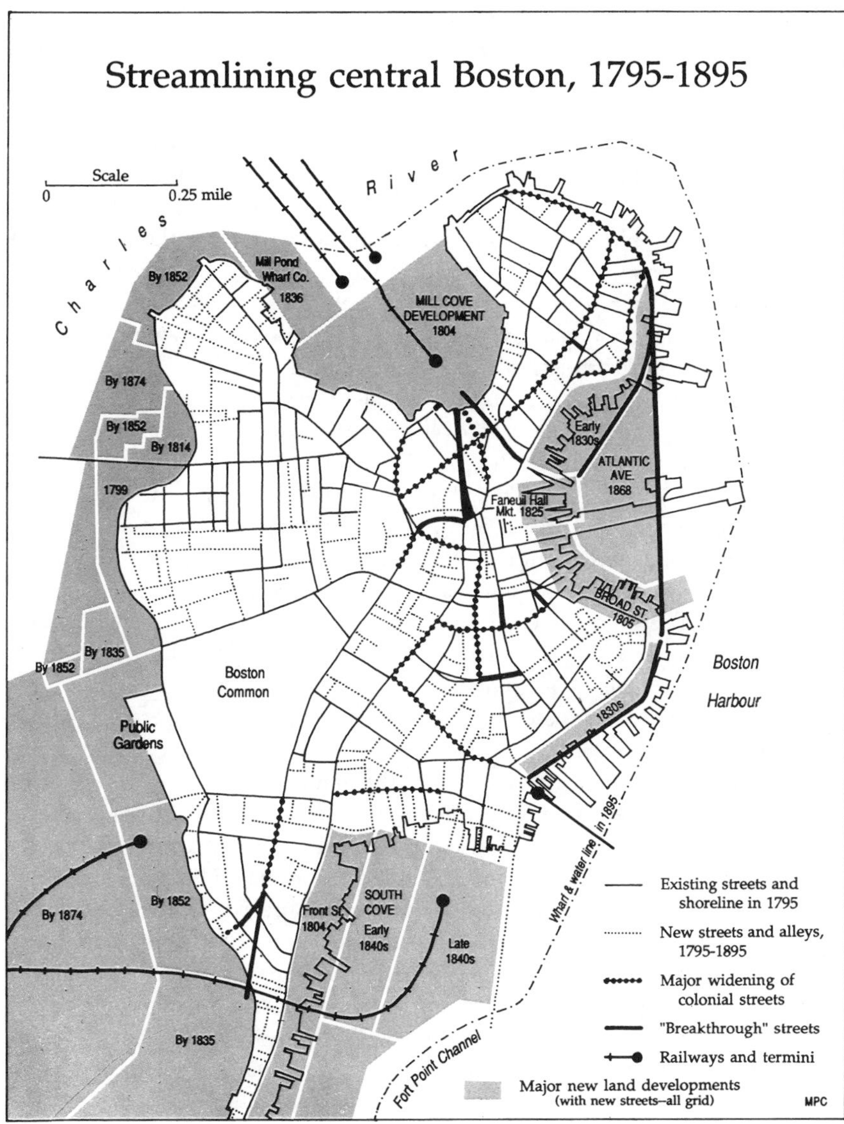

Figure 7.3 Streamlining central Boston, 1795–1895

narrow, property layout ill-suited to high-density living and lacking proper sanitary facilities. Vast capital was poured into building up a district to new densities without public powers to insist on sufficient light, air, water and sewerage, and without private power sufficient to rationalize the district's layout beyond narrow property lines. The district gained national attention at century's end through the writing of Progressive reformer Robert Woods on the slum housing conditions (Woods 1902).

Urban growth in Boston burst the confines of the Shawmut Peninsula during the course of the nineteenth century through extensive land-fill operations and far-out suburbanization tied to the centre by commuter railways and horse-car services. Changes in the central district can be summarized for the core area as a whole (Fig. 7.3). New land on the old urban fringe extended both residential areas to the west, and old fringe-belts on the north, east and south of the CBD. These new districts invariably sported grid street-plans which jarred more or less severely with the informal network of colonial streets. As traffic increased in the CBD and better access was needed along major arterials, as well as between traffic concentrations such as the new railway stations, an extensive programme of street widening and breakthrough streets where none had existed before helped rationalize somewhat the over-used colonial-era street system. The great fire of 1872 forced some street improvements, too, but little in the way of radical street reorganization (Rosen 1986).

The morphology of Boston's suburban expansion during the nineteenth century hinges on three cardinal characteristics. First, suburban developments occurred within a morphological frame composed essentially of the routeways of colonial and early national age criss-crossing the rural zone between Boston and neighbouring town centres (Fig. 7.4). This divided the countryside into a lattice of irregularly sized and shaped polygons that presented no compelling alignments, cardinal or otherwise, to which new subdivisions could or should adhere. Consequently, the pattern by which this frame was filled in was fragmented and disorderly. Secondly, early subdivision developments appeared on the landscape in a scattered, non-contiguous fashion, overrunning the countryside without immediate saturation. This can be tied to the positioning of stations along newly-established suburban railway lines at distances optimal for steam rail service (Conzen, M. P. 1987). Only later was a closer mesh encouraged by the appearance of streetcar lines (Warner 1962). And, thirdly, suburban subdivision plans followed the changing dictates of fashionable design, given the evolution of suburban ideology and the specifications chosen to appeal to different income groups. This does not show up well at the scale of Figure 7.4, but is reflected in different street and lot widths, boulevard development, and, ultimately, the appearance of curvilinear street layouts.

Boston's early cadastral development had been organic; from small, informal, democratic origins that anticipated neither the future dimensions of building forms and traffic, nor the inertia of early cadastral geometry. By the early twentieth century, however, the vocabulary of street, block and lot patterns, and building arrangement had been greatly enlarged. The private land market provided easy access to suitably-sized building lots throughout the seventeenth to mid-nineteenth centuries without great investments. As buildings grew larger in height and ground coverage, developers engaged in increasingly expensive land assembly through lot amalgamation, but always within given street lines. As a variety of major public institutions became

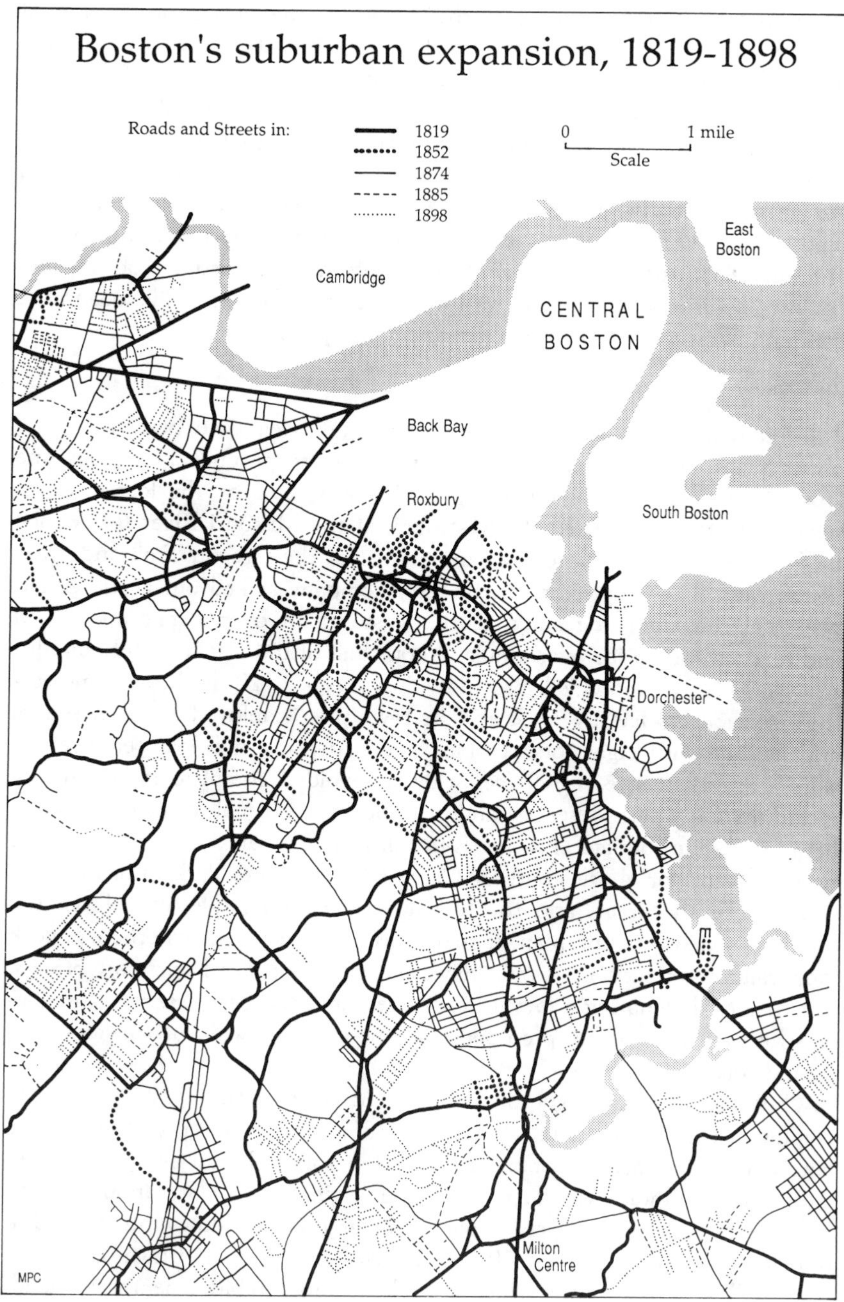

Figure 7.4 Boston's suburban expansion, 1819–1898

commonplace in the townscape, the power of the public purse inserted schools and other facilities needing significant land into dense neighbourhoods with, in Boston, a minimum of disruption. Powers of eminent domain had to be developed and extended to accomplish necessary street widenings, regrading, and actual realignments, though the latter were kept to an absolute minimum. In all, the dictionary of cadastral forms had grown substantially in this old city, and it presented a considerable repository of *ad hoc* planning experience in the era before modern planning, and offered, in theory, a variety of object lessons in cadastral problems and potential solutions for residents and would-be town-founders alike out in the booming West – had they any attention to spare.

(b) Omaha

The founders of Omaha, of course, had other models than Boston to draw on for planning inspiration and, in fact, set out to produce a very opposite kind of city. The site of Omaha (Fig. 7.5) was fixed by the location of a steam ferry that connected the west bank of the Missouri River to Council Bluffs, Iowa, one of the great staging points for the Oregon Trail and other points west. The proprietors of the ferry company staked out a grid street-plan that ran along the banks of the Missouri for over a mile and a half and reached inland for over a mile. About half of the plat was laid out with city blocks fully subdivided into individual lots – 1,320 in all, each measuring a spacious 66 feet by 132 feet. The town plan employed a strictly square grid module with eight lots per block (at a density of 5 lots per acre) set within a grid of streets 100 feet wide. It avoided complete monotony by including four park reserves and a wider than usual ceremonial street between Capitol Square and the river. All lots faced onto east–west running streets except for those abutting Capitol Square, the 'Park', north/south-running Tenth Street, and the lots directly fronting the river. From the internal evidence of the plan, if there was an anticipated hypothetical peak land value intersection it would have lain at Tenth and Davenport Streets. But besides designating a few through street and the park reserves, the plan is strikingly neutral in presupposing where the town's urban functions should locate.

While the new town got off to a decent start in the 1850s, it was the coming of the Union Pacific Railroad in 1867 that precipitated a speculative land boom of immense proportions. City lots sold well and many times over and, notwithstanding the large size of the original town plat, landowners on its outer fringes were moved to plat their large landholdings into city additions and subdivisions. By 1870 such activity extended the fringe of the city zone well into the countryside. It took a considerable time for all landowners in a particular sector of the city to get around to platting their land, however. In the meantime, ideas changed as to suitable lot size and street orientations, and there were, of course, no limitations on parcel size in the pre-urban land transfer process (for a useful discussion of the Omaha

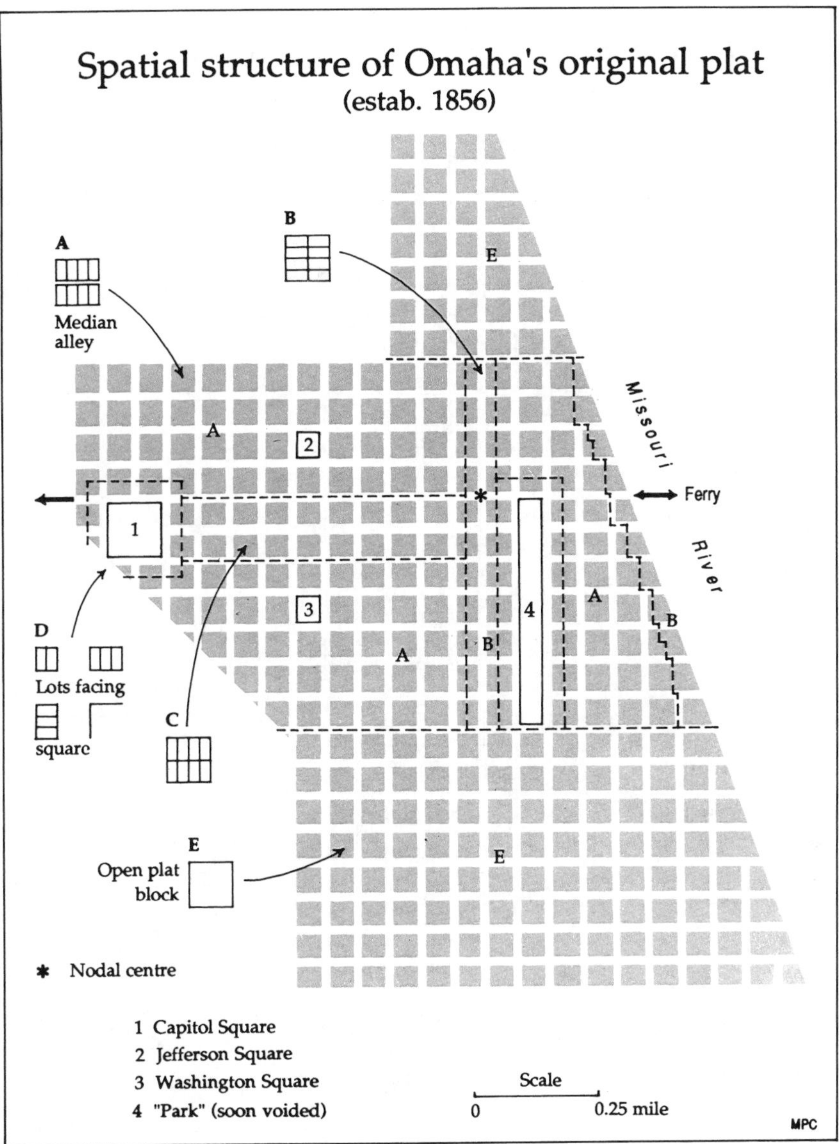

Figure 7.5 Spatial structure of Omaha's original plat, 1856

housing market 1880–1920, see Chudacoff 1972: 111–29).

What resulted was an extraordinary patchwork quilt of plat additions of various sizes and often differing internal design, for the most part bound together only by their common moorings within the Federal Land Survey system (Fig. 7.6). It would be a mistake to draw premature conclusions about the implied chaos of such a pattern, but there is no question that

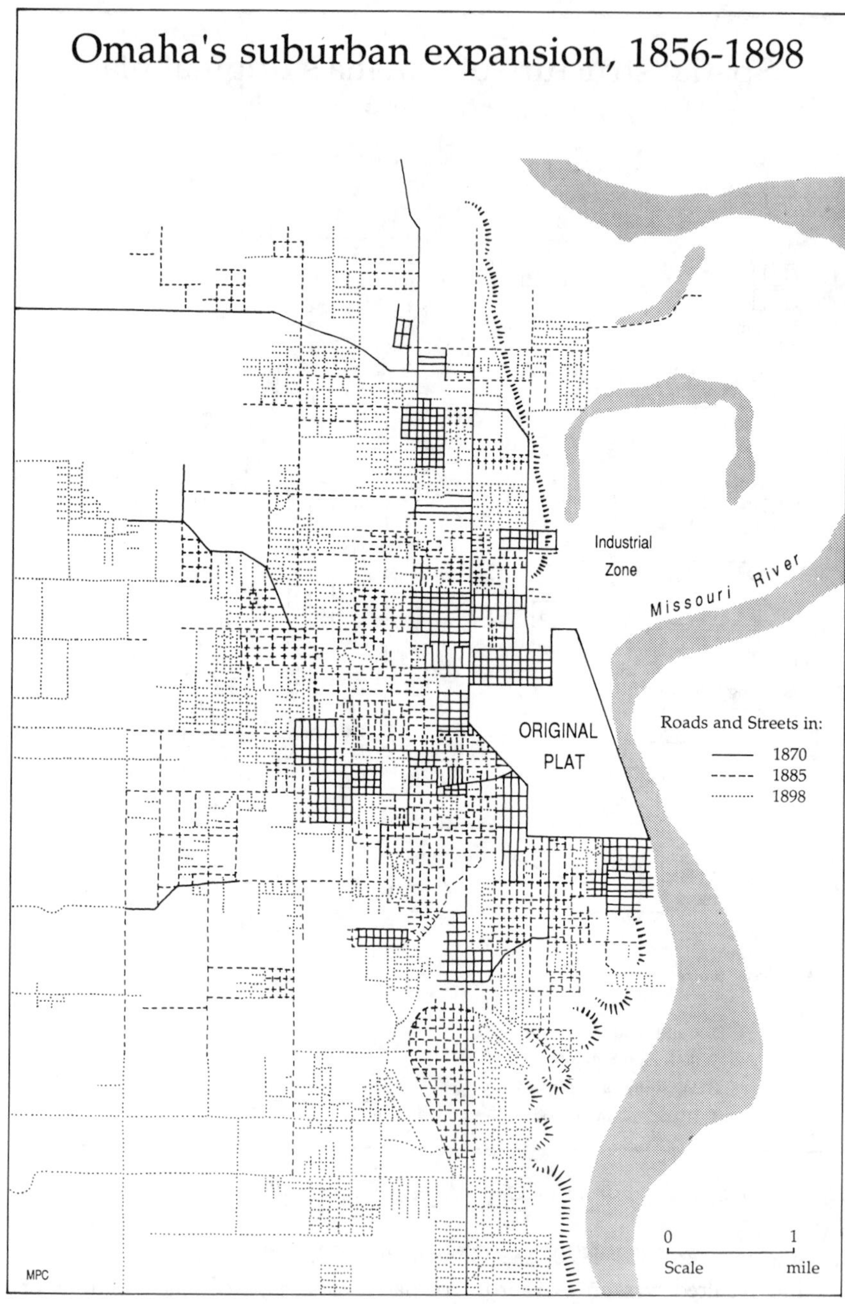

Figure 7.6 Omaha's suburban expansion, 1856–1898

Figure 7.7 Evolved cadastral pattern of western Omaha, 1918

some cadastral practices favoured an upper-class clientele and others a lower order. *Closed plats*, in which streets, blocks, and lots were all demarcated, began early simply to replicate the original city plat on a smaller territorial scale. Soon, however, differences appeared in lot size, block orientation, front footage, alley provision, and diversity of lot sizes (Fig. 7.7). This reflected several factors: an experimentation with dimensions to match the right combination of size, location, price, and presumably clientele; an adjustment to changing perceptions about the socio-residential possibilities of particular localities; and, especially when lot densities increased for no other apparent reason, greed.

More fateful, however, were the *open plats* in which street blocks were left unsubdivided or streets were themselves mostly absent. Such plats created, in effect, medium-sized estates that were held vacant for speculative purposes or acquired the owner's often substantial residence. These estate units were invariably sold off eventually for further subdivision, and the results of such a process, prolonged and fragmented, were to complicate vastly the urban cadastre with consequences for efficient mobility and access, rationality of layout, and service provision.

Open and closed plats appeared in the peri-urban landscape at the individual whim of a multitude of landowners of diverse occupation, background, and real estate expertise. In Omaha they produced an extraordinary scattering of urban lots of different character (Fig. 7.7). This dispersion, together with the complete independence of land sales from house construction, not to mention utility provision such as sewers, water service, etc., produced an enormous reservoir of urban home sites that discouraged progressive, orderly, residential development, and placed much of the burden of defining or anticipating correctly the social tone of new neighbourhoods squarely upon the shoulders of the buyer. Any negative conclusions, however, must be tempered by the impressive contrast that Omaha's overall low living densities made with conditions in central and near-suburban Boston during the same period.

If Omaha's residential accretions seemed low density and disorderly, how did the development of central Omaha appear in the light of its generous original plan and lack of historical forms to inhibit change? In cadastral terms, central Omaha evolved quickly, efficiently, and with great functional flexibility. Two of the four reserved public spaces fell victim to public shortsightedness and entrepreneurial gain, including the large seven-block park reserve, which was simply too close to the meeting ground of the railways and the warehouses to survive. The street system proved more than adequate, so that the only changes needed after half a century were a few minor breakthrough streets to connect the original city plat with adjoining subdivisions, two viaducts to carry traffic over railway tracks to districts south of the CBD, and some selected street narrowings where solid residential development obviated the need in that technological era for major traffic arteries.

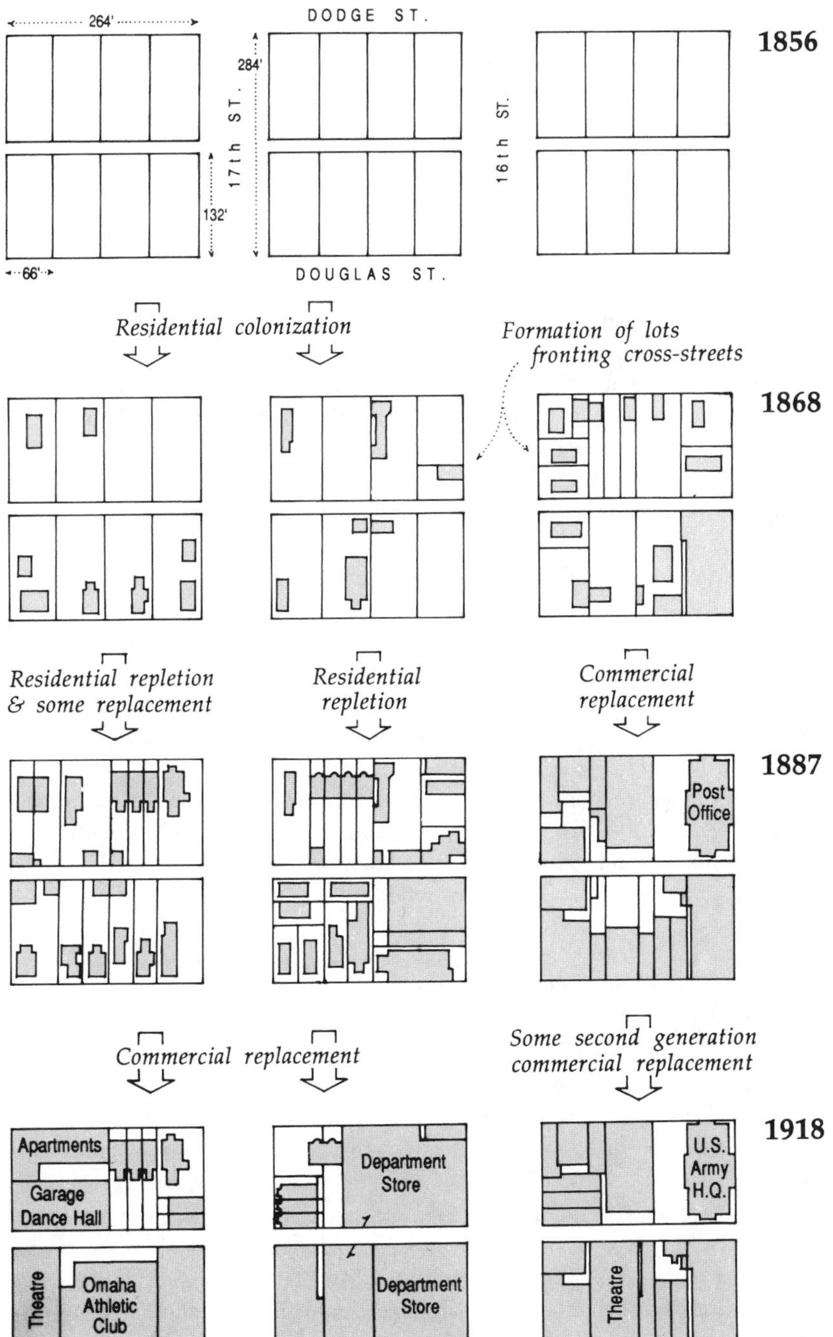

Figure 7.8 Lot and building evolution of blocks 106–8, central Omaha, 1856–1918

Plot and building evolution in central Omaha was exceptionally simple (Fig. 7.8). There was a very high degree of lot partitioning that reflected residential and business needs much more modest than the original lot size set forth. Secondly, there was a particular pattern of partitioning of block-end lots to create increased individual lot frontages on north–south streets, given that the original plan made practically no provision for this. In developing major arterial streets out of the CBD, especially connecting with the railway depots, and in intensifying the spatial structure of the CBD itself, this process showed how easily an early shortcoming could be remedied.

As a result of simple lot changes and generous street access, the manner in which central Omaha's building stock evolved illustrates again the effects of abundant space and few artificial controls on market forces (Fig. 7.9). The CBD expanded greatly between 1867 and 1917, and was able to accomplish this with a minimum of internal building: it simply leapfrogged to blocks with vacant lots or a few residences, generally of wooden construction, that were easily supplanted (Fig. 7.8). Clearly the original plan's gentle prediction of the future location of the CBD centre was off by four to six blocks. Residential changes near the CBD showed great scatter in the patterns of house colonization, repletion, and replacement, but the latter – usually representing the construction of apartment buildings – did concentrate somewhat towards the advancing commercial/institutional edge of the CBD. The Missouri River served as a *fixation line* for plan and land-use developments in central Omaha. River wharf activity on the low-lying floodplain attracted the railway and an extensive fringe-belt emerged along the river-front and to the south of the city centre. Between 1887 and 1918 slender zones of residences and assorted other development between the fringe-belt and the CBD succumbed to the pressures of both, resulting in CBD expansion and fringe-belt consolidation, especially marked to the north, east, and south of the commercial core.

Formative processes in the American urban cadastre

What can be learned from the processes and patterns of cadastral evolution and practice in Boston and Omaha before 1930? Five immediate findings stand out. First, generous early land parcel dimensions created urban 'shells' too large for current needs, so internal subdivision was great, widespread, and varied in type. However, in ownership terms this provided a relatively orderly, hierarchical sequence for speculative transfer. In fast-growing cities, the shell could be grown into with fewer wrenching adjustments to be made. Boston's irregular, colonial street and land parcel pattern was not problematical until commercial pressure, immigration, and a transport revolution rendered it inefficient for circulation purposes. Omaha's generous grid and smaller CBD development obviated the need for major changes (or proved resistant to them) well into the automobile era.

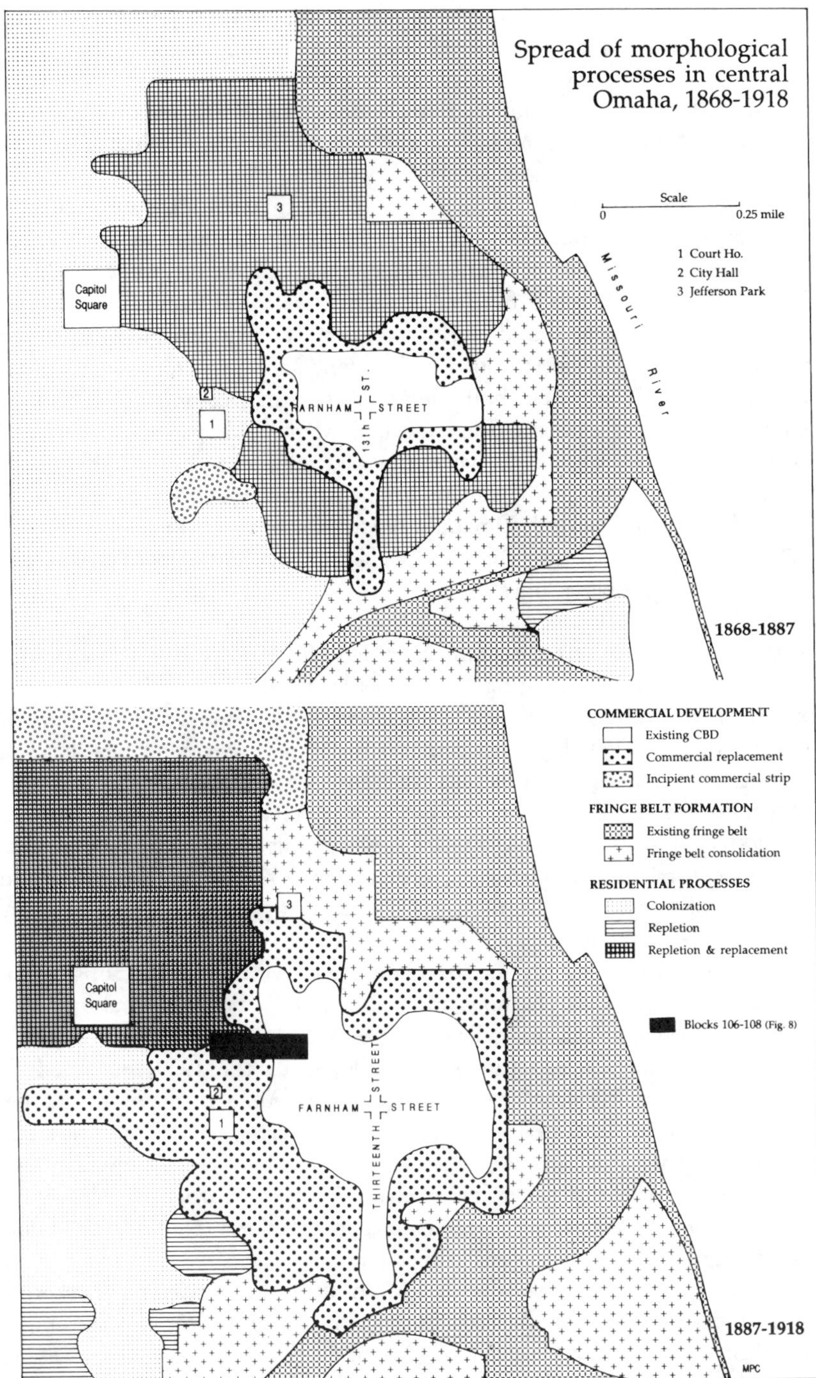

Figure 7.9 Spread of morphological processes in central Omaha, 1868–1918

Secondly, the divorce of land sales from building development resulted in vast overplatting and a scattered and far-from-homogeneous urban grid pattern. Individualism in real estate designs, market behaviour, and minimum regulations created cadastral idiosyncrasies that were adjusted to by means of either later replats or other modifications, or higher costs of service provision and access.

Thirdly, commercial evolution of the CBD induced strong pressures in neighbouring residential areas, resulting in sustained repletion and replacement, especially in Boston. The different site characteristics of Omaha's CBD allowed much more freedom for cheaper spatial expansion.

Fourthly, nineteenth- and early twentieth-century streamlining of the urban core brought forth both public and private efforts at cadastral rationalization. The worst bottlenecks of Boston's colonial street system required powers of eminent domain which were used sparingly by modern comparison. In Omaha, only when the grid grew chaotic enough to cease being a proper grid was adjustment deemed necessary. Private streamlining, as in the case of central Omaha's north–south street lot reorientations, generally functioned only when the cadastre was neutral enough to allow change within property lines.

And fifthly, the plan vocabulary of both cities expanded greatly over time. Boston adopted grid street systems in its land-fill zones and out in suburban areas before also adopting curvilinear streets. Omaha landowners experimented endlessly with grid characteristics and moved away from the confines of the original plat to respond to (as well as create) new land-use patterns and social geographies in different parts of the city.

Morphogenetic changes in Boston and Omaha as reflected in their ground-plan history reinforce the tremendous importance of site characteristics in constricting or dispersing growth, with results for the timing, for example, of public intervention. Differences in historical founding and length of development clearly set the two cities apart, but mid- to late-nineteenth-century suburban developments witnessed a considerable convergence of physical planning practice, except that Boston's suburbs grew in the framework of colonial village centres and rural connecting roads. The types of cadastral patterns that had developed by the 1920s indicated the increased need to regulate growth in ways other than through the market, and intervention became more common in cases where morphological limitations either prevented private solutions, or where private interests were unwilling to respond to public needs. From a European perspective, American urban cadastral characteristics may appear to have developed wasteful predispositions toward dispersion and diversity, but this can be viewed alternatively as a broad indication of democratic experiment in urban forms under different resource conditions. The advent of formal planning in American cities such as Boston and Omaha in the 1920s and 1930s was not so much an admission of past failures – as much commentary in American planning history would claim – but rather a move to codify prior experience collectively acquired but less collectively practised. Formal urban planning controls and design preferences did not spring freshly minted from the wave of Progressive-era reform. The advent of the now-familiar tools of city planning in terms of physical design and public intervention after 1914 was evolutionary, not revolutionary, and so were their consequences for the malleable form of American cities.

Notes

1 The terms *town plan*, *urban cadastre* and *ground plan*, all in use in the scholarly literature, mean in the context of this study essentially the same thing.

2 Usage of technical terms relating to morphological features and processes in this study follows that current in British literature on the subject, except when American differences require locally valid terminology. For definitions of terms used in British work, see Conzen, M. R. G. (1969).

3 The *plat* is the common American term for a new urban ground plan additional to a city, consisting of a more or less comprehensive *street system* giving access to individual ownership *lots* (plots) grouped in *blocks*. Plats are also referred to in legal records as *additions*, or *subdivisions*.

4 The *replat* or *resubdivision* of an existing plat or subdivision implements a new lot pattern, almost invariably at a higher density than before.

5 Manuscript maps in the Clough Collection, Massachusetts Historical Society, Boston. These maps are planimetrically correct maps prepared at a scale 1″ : 50′ which show all property lines and buildings for the respective dates. They were derived from the city's official street base maps (of the period *c.*1900–20), incorporating streetlines backdated from reports of street changes to the Record Commissioners and other records of the City Engineer's office, and containing lot and building lines derived from data abstracted from the Suffolk (County) Registry of Deeds (76 vols.), Town (of Boston) Records, Suffolk Probate Office Records, and other sources. A fuller description of their method of construction is given in *Publications of the Colonial Society of Massachusetts, Volume 21. Transactions 1919* (Boston 1920), 251–4. Clough, an electric utility company head draughtsman, made compilation of these large maps a lifetime hobby. It is testimony to his precision that the 'fit' between his maps and the modern Boston Redevelopment Authority property maps based on aerial photography, when reduced to common scale, is extremely close. Many segments of modern property lines fall exactly along the line of property lines shown in his 1648 map, for example, when superimposed. This map series is, to the present author's knowledge, simply unique among the historical cartographic resources of America's major cities, and is a tribute to a rare form of dedicated – but extraordinarily systematic, and hence useful – antiquarianism. Figure 1a and 1b are simplified redrawings of portions of his maps of 1676 and 1798.

6 Quincy Market, named after the mayor who authorized it in 1825, consists of a long central market building, placed directly to the east of famed Faneuil Hall, and flanked north and south by two buildings of 'stores', see Whitehall (1968: 96–7).

References

Alonso, W., 1964. *Location and land use: towards a theory of land rent* (Cambridge, Ma.).

Bailey, B. R., 1986. *Main Street northeastern Oregon: the founding and development of small towns* (Portland).

Banz, G., 1970. *Elements of urban form* (New York).

Berry, B. J. L. and Kasarda, J. D., 1977. *Contemporary urban ecology* (New York).

Boston City Engineering Department, 1903. *List of maps of Boston published between 1600 and 1903, copies of which are to be found in the possession of the city of Boston or other collections of the same* (Boston).

Bourne, L. S. *et al.* (eds.), 1973. *The form of cities in central Canada: selected papers* (Toronto).

Burns, E. K., 1977. 'Subdivision activity on the San Francisco peninsula: 1860–1970', *Yearbook of the Association of Pacific Coast Geographers, 39*: 17–32.

Chadwick, G. F., 1966. *The park and the town: public landscapes in the nineteenth and twentieth centuries* (New York).

Chudacoff, H. P., 1972. *Mobile Americans: residential and social mobility in Omaha 1880–1920* (New York).

Condit, C. W., 1968. *American building: materials and techniques from the beginning of the colonial settlement to the present* (Chicago).

Conzen, M. P., 1978. 'Analytical approaches to the urban landscape', in *Dimensions of human geography: essays on some familiar and neglected themes*, ed. K. W. Butzer [University of Chicago, Department of Geography Research Paper No. 186] 128–65.

Conzen, M. P., 1980. 'The morphology of nineteenth-century cities in the United States', in *Urbanization in the Americas: the background in comparative perspective*, ed. W. Borah *et al.* (Ottawa) 119–41.

Conzen, M. P., 1987. 'The progress of American urbanism, 1860–1930', in *North America: the historical geography of a changing continent*, ed. R. D. Mitchell and P. A. Groves (Totowa) 360–72.

Conzen, M. R. G., 1962. 'The plan analysis of an English city centre', in *Proceedings of the IGU Symposium in urban geography Lund 1960*, ed. K. Norborg [Lund Studies in Geography, Series B, 24] 383–414.

Conzen, M. R. G., 1969. 'Alnwick, Northumberland: a study in town-plan analysis', *Publications, Institute of British Geographers, 27*, (2nd edn.) glossary, 123–31.

Conzen, M. R. G., 1988. 'Morphogenesis, morphological regions and secular human agency in the historic townscape, as exemplified by Ludlow', in *Urban historical geography: recent progress in Britain and Germany*, ed. D. Denecke and G. Shaw, 253–72.

Fitch, J. M., 1966. *American building: the historical forces that shaped it* (New York).

Foote, K. E., 1983. *Color in public spaces: toward a communication-based theory of the urban built environment* [University of Chicago, Department of Geography Research Paper No. 205].

Ford, L. R., 1980. 'Historic districts and urban design', *Environmental Review, 4*: 20–6.

Gad, G. and Holdsworth, D. W., 1988. 'Streetscape and society: the changing built environment of King Street, Toronto', in *Patterns of the past: interpreting Ontario's history*, ed. R. Hall *et al.* (Toronto) 174–205.

Goheen, P. G., 1970. *Victorian Toronto, 1850–1900: pattern and process of growth* [University of Chicago, Department of Geography Research Paper No. 127].
Gordon, G., 1984. 'The shaping of urban morphology', *Urban history yearbook*, 1–10.
Hales, J. G., 1814. *Map of Boston* (Boston).
Hofmeister, B., 1971. *Stadt und Kulturraum Anglo-Amerika* (Braunschweig).
Hofmeister, B., 1982. 'Die Stadtstruktur im interkulturellen Vergleich', *Geographische Rundschau, 34*: 482–8.
Holzner, L., 1967. 'World regions in urban geography', *Annals of the Association of American Geographers, 57*: 704–12.
Hovinen, G. R., 1985. 'Suburbanization in greater Philadelphia, 1880–1914', *Journal of Historical Geography, 11*: 174–94.
Hudson, C., 1985. *Plains country towns* (Minneapolis).
Kramer, C. E., 1976. 'The origins of the subdivision process in Louisville, 1772–1932', in *An introduction to the Louisville region: selected essays*, ed. D. E. Bierman [Association of American Geographers, 76th Annual Meeting Handbook] (Washington, D.C.) 25–38.
Lampard, E. E., 1977. 'Some aspects of urban social structure and morphology in the historical development of cities in the United States', *Cahiers Bruxellois: Revue d'Histoire Urbaine, 22*: 73–115.
Lewis, P. F., 1976. *New Orleans: the making of an urban landscape* (Cambridge, Ma.).
Ley, D., 1988. 'From urban structure to urban landscape', *Urban Geography, 9*: 95–105.
Library of Congress, 1981. *Fire insurance maps in the Library of Congress: plans of North American cities and towns produced by the Sanborn Map Company* (Washington, D.C.).
Mayer, H. M. and Hayes, C. R., 1983. *Land uses in American cities* (Champaign).
Moudon, A. V., 1986. *Built for change: neighborhood architecture in San Francisco* (Cambridge, Ma.).
Mumford, L., 1961. *The city in history: its origins, its transformations, and its prospects* (New York).
Olson, S., 1979. 'Baltimore imitates the spider', *Annals of the Association of American Geographers, 69*: 557–74.
Pred, A. R., 1966. *The spatial dynamics of U.S. urban-industrial growth, 1800–1914* (Cambridge, Ma.).
Relph, E. C., 1987. *The modern urban landscape* (Baltimore).
Reps, J. W., 1965. *The making of urban America: a history of city planning in the United States* (Princeton).
Reps, J. W., 1967. *Monumental Washington: the planning and development of the capital center* (Princeton).
Reps, J. W., 1979. *Cities of the American West: a history of frontier urban planning* (Princeton).
Rosen, C., 1986. *The limits of power: great fires and the process of city growth in America.*
Schulyer, D., 1986. *The new urban landscape: the redefinition of city form in nineteenth-century America* (Baltimore).
Sears, J. N., 1979. *The first one hundred years of town planning in Georgia* (Atlanta).
Slatter. J. and Callan, B., 1852. *Map of the city of Boston, Massts. 1852* (New York and Boston).

Suttles, G. D., 1984. 'The cumulative texture of local urban culture', *American Journal of Sociology*, *90*: 283–304.

Tunnard, C. and Reed, H. H., 1955. *American skyline: the growth and form of our cities and towns* (Boston).

Vance, J. E., 1971. 'Land assignment practices in the pre-capitalist, capitalist, and postcapitalist city', *Economic Geography*, *47*: 101–20.

Vance, J. E., 1977. *This scene of man: the role and structure of the city in the geography of Western civilization* (New York).

Vance, J. E., 1982. 'The American urban geography: the old world strongly influenced the new', in *Cities: the forces that shaped them*, ed. L. Taylor (New York).

Ward, D., 1966. 'The industrial revolution and the emergence of Boston's central business district', *Economic Geography*, *42*: 152–71.

Ward, D., 1971. *Cities and immigrants: a geography of change in nineteenth-century America* (New York).

Warner, S. B., 1962. *Streetcar suburbs: the process of growth in Boston, 1870–1900* (Cambridge).

Whitehand, J. W. R., 1987. 'Urban morphology', in *Historical geography: progress and prospect*, ed. M. Pacione, 250–76.

Whitehand, J. W. R., 1988. 'Recent developments in urban morphology', in D. Denecke and G. Shaw (eds.), *op. cit.*.

Whitehill, W. M., 1968. *Boston: a topographical history* (Cambridge, Ma.).

Wissink, G. A., 1962. *American cities in perspective, with special reference to the development of their fringe areas* (Assen.).

Woods, R. (ed.), 1902. *Americans in process: a settlement study* (Boston and New York).

8 The making and remaking of Pietermaritzburg: the past, present and future morphology of a South African city

Robert F. Haswell

Many cities pass through phases in which the ideology of the dominant group(s) is given visible expression in the townscape. South African cities are no exception, yet research on either their general or their specific morphological characteristics has been limited and sporadic, and academic rather than applied (Davies 1963; Christopher 1983; 1987). Even the assertion that 'many southern African towns within the orbit of former British domination exhibit similar features of layout' (Whittington 1970: 26) remains largely untested. In the case of Pietermaritzburg, Natal, South Africa, three main city-making phases - Dutch Voortrekker dorp, British colonial capital and Afrikaner apartheid city – can be clearly identified. The purpose of this chapter is to document both the specific and more general morphological characteristics of these phases in order to produce guidelines for a 'new' Pietermaritzburg – a South African city which openly and proudly proclaims its multi-ethnic heritage and composition.

Dutch Voortrekker dorp

The nucleated settlements established during Dutch rule of the Cape (1652–1806), and during the nineteenth century in the interior of South Africa by the *Voortrekkers* (Dutch pioneers), constituted a close-knit family of places (Fig. 8.1). They represented the ecclesiastical nodes within a dispersed farmstead settlement fabric. The lengthy *nagmaal* (quarterly communion services) encouraged older people to take up sizeable and irrigated *erwe* (plots) in close proximity to the church. Despite this organic origin these settlements were characterized by regularity. A single row of Cape-Dutch houses, built alongside a canal and tree-lined street which led to the church, constituted the essential morphology and, because the occupants all engaged in agriculture in their extensive backyards, these settlements are more accurately described as *dorps* (nucleated agricultural settlements), rather than

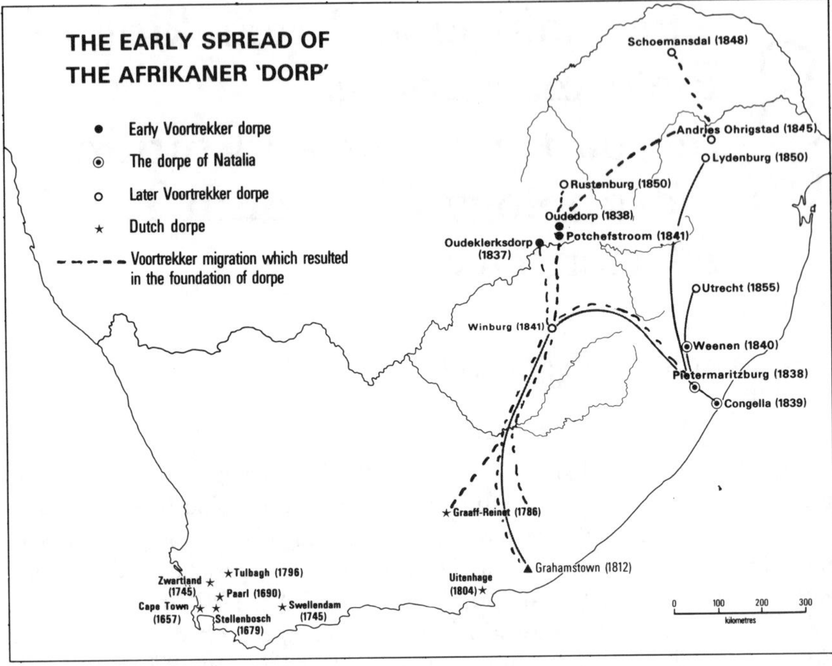

Figure 8.1 The early spread of the Afrikaner 'dorp'

towns, which owe their existence to commercial and/or administrative functions. The *dorp* streetscape can surely be traced back to Holland, where the 'tenet that the street should be regarded as a single architectural composition' was widely adhered to in the making of Dutch towns (Burke 1956: 71).

Such single street *dorps* grew into fully-fledged *dorps* by the laying out of additional streets parallel to the original *Kerkstraat* (Church Street). Consequently each *erf* extended from street-to-street and, in many of the Cape *dorps*, were one morgen (2,11654 acres or 8,568 m^2) in area. This *dorp* image and plan formed part of the cultural baggage hauled along by the Voortrekkers.

Pietermaritzburg was laid out in 1838 to accommodate several hundred prospective *erf* owners, and although Voortrekker hegemony over Natal was shortlived, an almost indelible Dutch Voortrekker imprint, in the form of a rectangular grid, is still readily apparent (Fig. 8.2). Indeed, the choice of site – an irrigable spur, streetnames – *Kerk*, *Langmarkt* (Longmarket), Burger (Citizen), Loop (Walk) and Boom (Tree), as well as the peripherally located inter-denominational cemetery – are further diagnostic morphological relics of the modern city's *dorp* origins. In the case of Pietermaritzburg the street-to-street *erwe* measured 450 feet by 150 feet (6,271 m^2), and the stipulation that every dwelling must be built in a single line at street's edge ensured

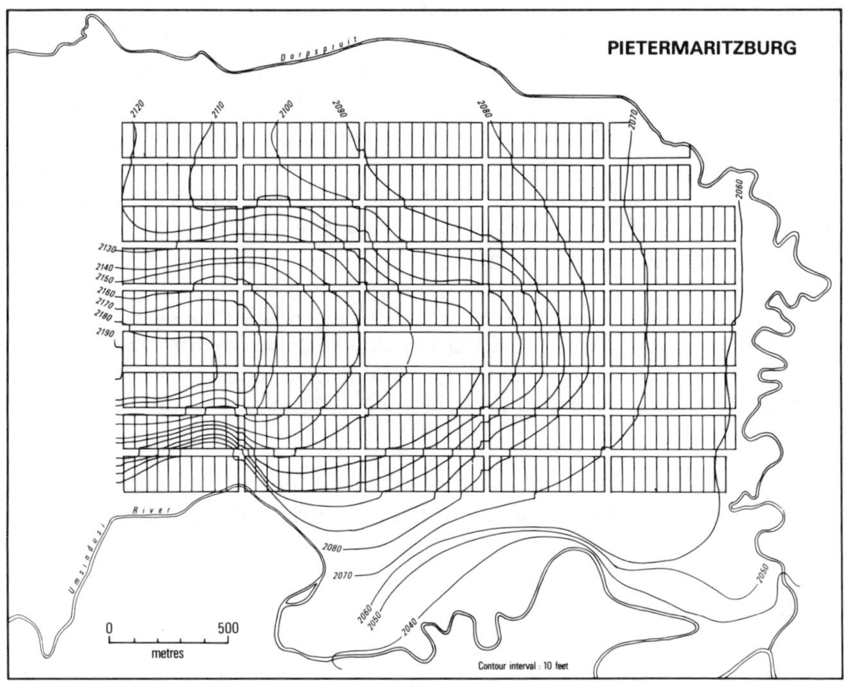

Figure 8.2 The site and plan of Voortekker Piertermaritzburg

Figure 8.3 View of Pietermaritzburg *c.*1848 (Natal Museum)

that the settlement was a fitting member of the Dutch Voortrekker *dorp* family (Fig. 8.3). Another characteristic of the Dutch Voortrekker *dorp* is the initial absence of cross-streets. In Pietermaritzburg such streets were only named late in 1844, in order to prevent the influx of British settlers from entirely changing the character of the *dorp* (South African Archival Records, Natal No. 1 1958: 237). The street-to-street extent of individual properties and a preference for houses to face each other across streets, resulted in rows of houses only along every alternate street.

In 1851, an English visitor after strolling around the *dorp* declared:

> Its streets were really at right angles, its simple whitewashed houses exhibited few architectural vagaries. Neatness and Dutch cleanliness was perhaps the prevailing characteristic, and yet we could not fail at once to observe that the selection of the spot and the original design had been the work of no mean prentices of their craft (Barter 1852: 22).

Clearly the Voortrekkers inherited a penchant for town planning, as well as an ability to read the lay of the land for irrigation purposes.

British colonial capital

The British annexation of Natal in 1845, an influx of British settlers in the early 1850s, and the establishment of Pietermaritzburg as the capital of the Colony of Natal in 1856, were to result in considerable changes to the *dorp's* morphology.

The large Voortrekker *erwe* enabled African domestic servants to be inconspicuously housed in backyard shelters, but already, in 1848 – a century before the coming to power of the present South African government – sixty-five Europeans complained about alleged continuous and unpunished robbery by Africans (*Natal Witness*, January 1848). In response, Surveyor-General Stanger expressed the view that each town should have a portion of its Town Lands appropriated for the use of Africans engaged in daily labour in those towns. In 1854 it was reported that Africans were squatting on Town Lands and, in the following year, the Town Council resolved that a portion of the Town Lands be set aside for an African village (Town Council Meeting, 11 September 1855). The Council's intentions were described thus: 'they aim not, at least in this instance, at the straightening of city obliquities, but the rearing of a Model Village, where native good manners may find encouragement' (*Natal Chronicle*, 17 October 1855). Repeated attempts to find a site for such a village were met by stern opposition from white ratepayers, and it was not until separate townships for Blacks became enforceable in terms of the Native (Urban Areas) Act of 1923 that the much-discussed 'Native Model Village' was established. The chosen site, to the east of the city, was on a floodplain, adjacent to the refuse dump and sewage works, and therefore undesirable to Europeans. In order to

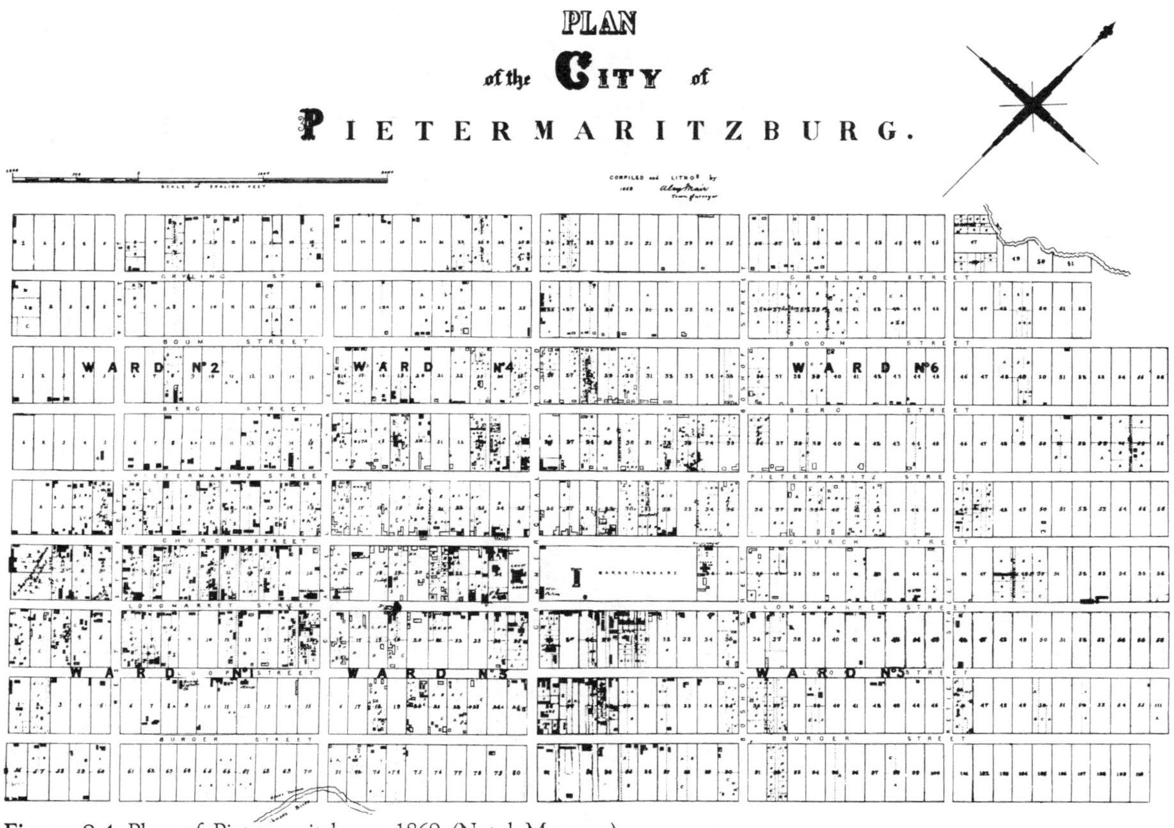

PLAN of the CITY of PIETERMARITZBURG.

Figure 8.4 Plan of Pietermaritzburg, 1869 (Natal Museum)

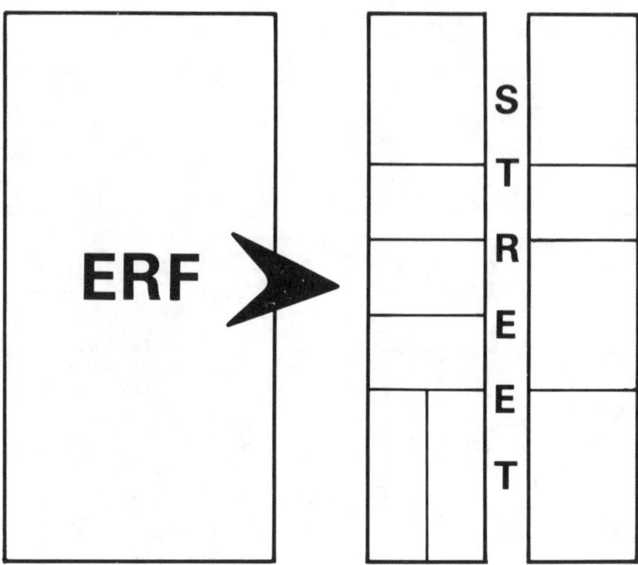

Figure 8.5 The subdivision of an agricultural erf (450 × 150 ft) into a narrow street lined by small residential properties

secure its own labour needs the Town Council had erected barracks for Blacks in 1877, and hostels in 1914. In this manner Blacks were tolerated and accommodated in embryonic colonial Pietermaritzburg but Indians, who were imported to the colony from the 1860s, as intended labour for the sugar industry, could not be so readily put in their place.

The initial Indian settlers were thus ex-indentured labourers, and were predominantly Hindi- or Tamil-speaking Hindus. Pietermaritzburg's large and irrigated *erwe*, many still unoccupied in the 1870s (Fig. 8.4), were well-suited to these Indian agriculturalists, and to a market-gardening economy producing both European and Indian vegetables and fruit. By the 1890s, the eastern or lower sector of the grid contained a Hindu enclave comprising temples, gabled houses and stores, barracks and a distinctive vegetation complex. The 1869 plan (Fig. 8.4) also reveals that the town's predominantly British population had begun to subdivide the large *erwe* by narrow streets and smaller plots more suited to commercial and residential, rather than agricultural, requirements (Fig. 8.5). Such one-block streets increased circulation within the town's highly rectangular grid, and facilitated the appearance of lanes lined by English cottages built on properties just large enough to allow for flower gardens (Fig. 8.6).

In the 1880s, Moslem Indians who had come to Natal of their own free will began to set up shop in Pietermaritzburg. Unlike the indentured labourers, they were entitled to own land and had the means to do so. They called themselves 'Arabs', possibly to dissociate themselves from the

Figure 8.6 Shepstone Street, Pietermaritzburg, 1987: one of the many cottage-lined streets of the colonial era

ex-indentured class, and soon came to be regarded as the coming evil by the British shopkeepers. A young barrister, Mohandas Gandhi, was brought to South Africa in 1893 by some 'Arabian' merchants, and he elaborated on the growing antagonism felt by the Europeans towards Indians:

> The white traders were alarmed. While they first welcomed the Indian labourers, they had not reckoned with their business skill. They might be tolerated as independent agriculturalists, but their competition in trade could not be brooked. This sowed the seed of antagonism to Indians. Many other factors contributed to its growth. Our different ways of living, our simplicity, our contentment with small gains, our indifference to the laws of hygiene and sanitation, our slowness in keeping our surroundings clean and tidy, and our stinginess in keeping our houses in good repair – all these, combined with differences in religion, contributed to fan the flame of antagonism (Narayan 1927: 231).

In Pietermaritzburg 'Arab' merchants focused their activities mainly in two lucrative trading areas: the vicinity of the Town Hall (Fig. 8.7) and the upper Church Street area. An 1894 visitor to the city described the view from atop the Town Hall as follows:

> From the four turret windows we obtained magnificent birdseye views in different directions. Just below us was the market square, crowded with wagons . . . In the

Figure 8.7 An Arabian merchant and a European chemist cheek-by-jowl alongside the Pietermaritzburg City Hall. The flags on the clock tower celebrate the relief of Mafeking in May 1900 (Town Clerk's Office, Pietermaritzburg)

opposite direction stretched a long narrow street, with crowds of Indians and Kaffirs constantly passing. It was called Commercial Road, our guide said, but Arab-street would have been a more suitable name, for most of the low, dark shops seemed occupied by Indian traders, dressed in flowing robes (Thomas 1894: 12).

The 'Arab' stores along Commercial Road were small shops, whereas in upper Church Street several more imposing two-storey buildings, housing shops on the ground floor and residences above, made their appearance by the 1890s. Amod Bayat, for example, imported builders from India to

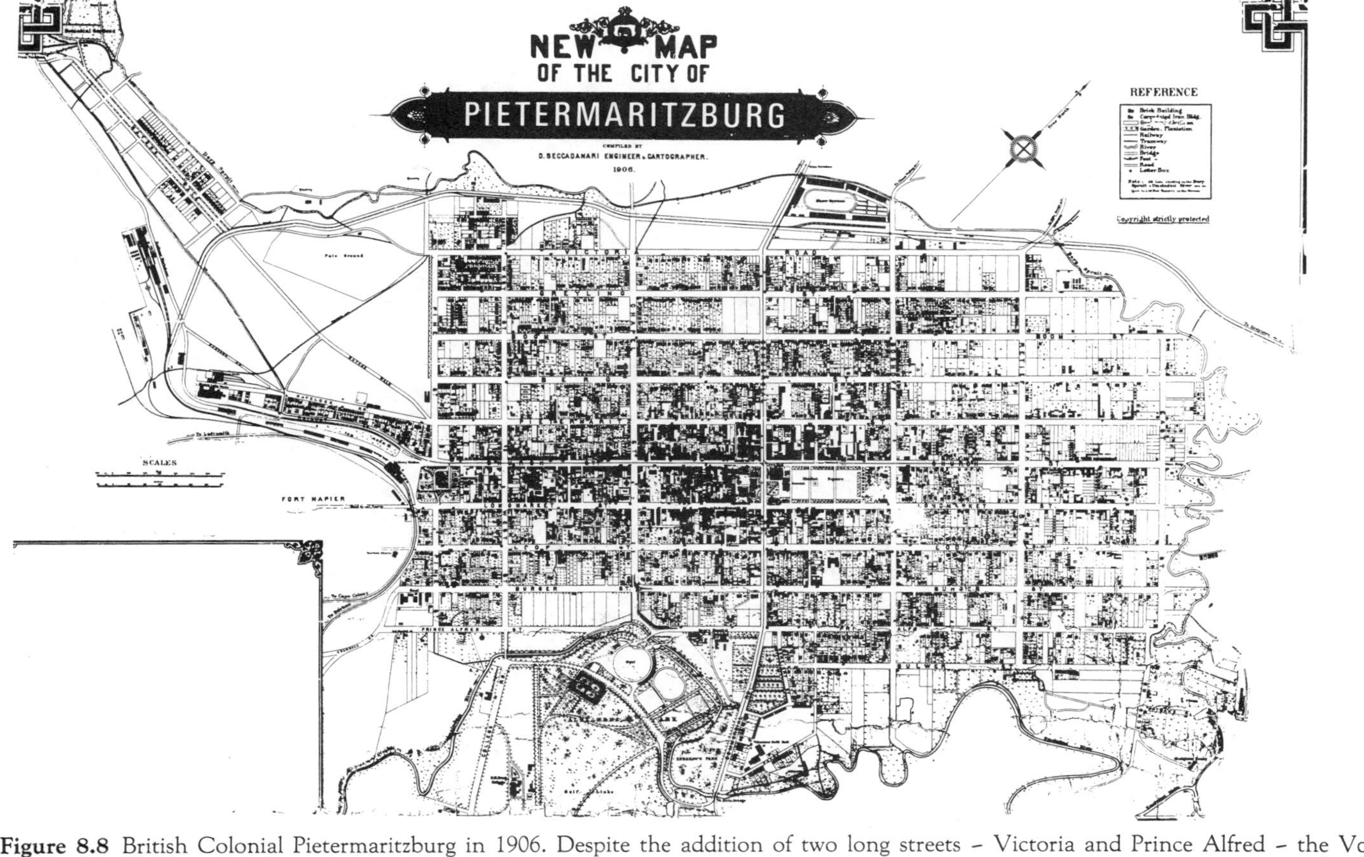

Figure 8.8 British Colonial Pietermaritzburg in 1906. Despite the addition of two long streets – Victoria and Prince Alfred – the Voortrekker grid remains largely intact. Alexandra Park, on the southern perimeter, containing formal gardens, cricket oval and golf links is accessible via a tramway, as is the Botanical Gardens to the west.

construct his fine store and a well-concealed mosque. A *Madressa* (school), and other stores and houses are diagnostic features of a *Jama'at* (Moslem community). The proximity of this area to the homes of many of the capital's leading White officials and citizens and, after the construction of the railway station in the 1890s at the head of Church Street, to the passing Black trade, resulted in an increasing Moslem congregation in this area. Thus, by 1906, central Pietermaritzburg had been intensively developed and occupied for trade and residential purposes by several ethnic groups (Fig. 8.8). Depending upon the scale and the index employed to measure the level of segregation, one could describe it as a partially integrated city, but at the neighbourhood scale a high degree of ethnic congregation was apparent. Thus, although Pietermaritzburg's layout was distinctive, the city's social geography at the turn of the twentieth century was typically colonial. It has been asserted that: 'European colonial practice, be it French in Dakar, Belgian in Elisabethville (now Lubumbashi), or British in Nairobi, revealed a similar pattern. The South African city is still a member, and definitely not the most extremely regimented or segregated member, of a large set of new, imperial-era urban centers' (Western 1986: 251).

Pietermaritzburg's colonial milieu and ambience was further enhanced by the almost complete British rebuild of the *dorp*. British settlers soon found the Voortrekker cottages to be 'slimly built and inconveniently small for persons who come to them with English notions and habits. Every succeeding year, however, presents unmistakable instances of amendment in this particular' (Mann 1859: 147). A 'Maritzburg (the English abbreviation of the town's name) vernacular, based on English traditions, and strongly influenced by prevailing late-nineteenth-century styles, particularly Gothic Revival, developed. Local deposits of red clay were used to produce bricks and tiles which weathered to softer, pinker tones, and were widely used for many public buildings – a cathedral, banks, public baths, a railway station, schools and a town hall. Patterned-cast-lead and ornate iron verandah railings were imported to put the finishing touches to many private and public buildings. As befitted a colonial capital, Pietermaritzburg was graced by a classical parliament building, complete with a white marble statue of Queen Victoria, which soon faced a grand post office (Fig. 8.9). Not surprisingly, therefore, the German geographer Siegfried Passarge, who visited the city in the early years of the present century, described it as follows: 'The bright streets and green squares, the gardens of the villa suburbs, and the state buildings such as the Parliament, town hall, schools, churches and the theatre, make a friendly and thoroughly European impression' (Passarge 1908: 321 editor's trans.). In both architectural and social terms therefore, Pietermaritzburg was, by the first decade of the twentieth century, decidedly colonial. The almost complete remoulding of the land use and architectural components of the *dorp*-scape, while the Voortrekker grid survived essentially intact, is another striking affirmation of the Conzen dictum that street-plans are the most resilient of townscape components.

Figure 8.9 The Natal Parliament Buildings, *c.*1902 (Natal Museum)

Afrikaner apartheid city

Although the seeds of commercial and residential segregation, and indeed separation, can be traced back to the advent of Responsible Government for Natal in 1893, and their subsequent legislative refinement in the 1920s and 1940s, it was not until the coming to power of the present South African government that a systematic policy of racial and spatial separation was imposed (Davies 1981). In order to achieve the 'ideal' apartheid city in the case of Pietermaritzburg (Fig. 8.10), some 9,000 people, 75 per cent of whom were Indian, were obliged to move into racially exclusive sectors. The Black, Indian and Coloured residential areas are now dominated by box-like, low-cost housing schemes located at a considerable distance from the areas of employment. In effect such people have been largely cast out of the White cities (Western 1981). Furthermore, until recently, these so-called non-White areas were planned as purely residential, with limited commercial, community and recreational facilities. By contrast, the White suburbs with their swimming pools and manicured gardens, golf courses and country clubs, are brazenly affluent (Fig. 8.11).

Now, after nearly forty years of social and spatial engineering, significant amendments, as distinct from wholesale repeal, of the Group Areas Act, have either been promulgated or are the subject of parliamentary reports. In 1986, for instance, all land zoned for business purposes in central

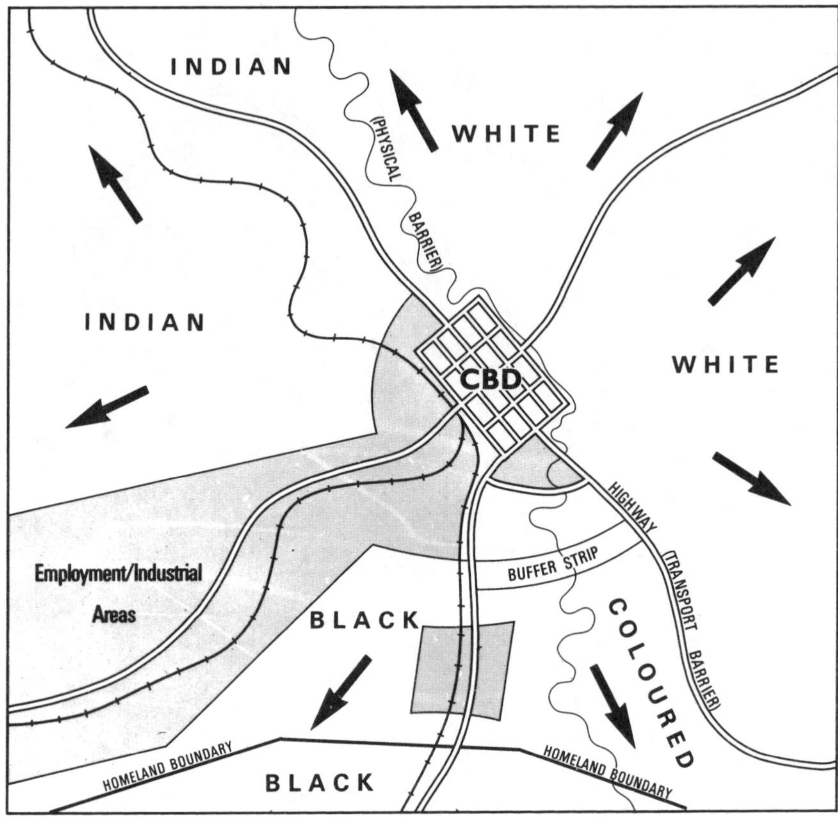

Figure 8.10 The 'ideal' Apartheid city, featuring racially homogeneous sectors separated by physical or man-made barriers, such as buffer strips

Pietermaritzburg was declared to be a Free Trade Area. Within such areas the members of any race may engage in trade, but may not take up residence. There are already distinct signs that Indian traders will soon once again dominate the upper Church Street area, and make their presence felt in the former White CBD. With respect to trade patterns, history seems set to largely repeat itself and, even if all racial residential restrictions were lifted, tomorrow's South African city may well look much like yesterday's – particularly the 1940s' forerunner. Given that income correlates with race to such a high level in South Africa, only a modest number of Blacks, Coloureds and Indians could afford to move into existing White suburban areas. However, in the case of inner-city residential areas the recent emergence of grey, or mixed, areas in defiance of the Group Areas Act is surely a portent of one of the consequences of the repeal of the Act. Any commitment to social justice in cities such as Pietermaritzburg dictates therefore that active, positive steps be taken to redesign the city.

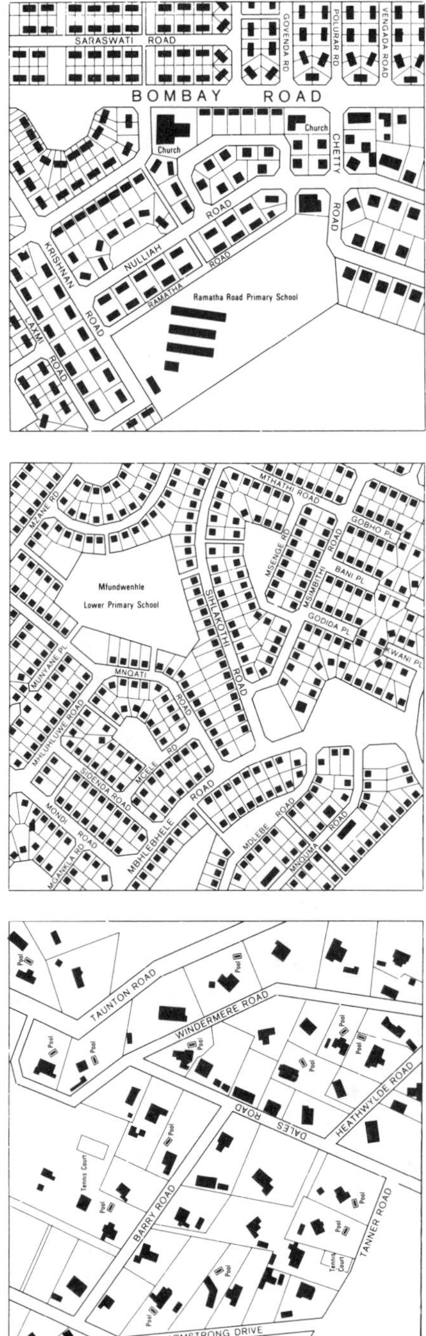

Figure 8.11 Contrasting layouts in (from top to bottom) an Indian, a black and a white residential area of Pietermaritzburg

Towards a 'new' Pietermaritzburg

The post-apartheid city in Natal is likely to experience a concerted effort on the part of the lower income groups to occupy land closer to their place of work. In Pietermaritzburg such centripetal residential migration will be strengthened by the fact that, whereas there is a chronic under-supply of housing units in the Black, Indian and Coloured sectors of the city, the White sector has a surplus of housing standing empty. Clearly, therefore, such housing backlogs have to be met before all owners and would-be owners can find their place in the housing market. But if the challenge of meeting the demand for housing is met by simply building more low-cost housing even further from the city centre, the inverse logic of the apartheid city – those who can least afford it live furthest from their place of employment – will remain and will bedevil the attempts of such people to move up the housing ladder. The vacant buffer strips – one of the few positive relics of the apartheid era – provide the opportunity to make available affordable accommodation in terms of both housing and transportation costs. Concomitantly, White suburban plots can be subdivided to provide additional building plots and, in central Pietermaritzburg, the city's Voortrekker legacy (in the form of deep properties) has bequeathed planners largely empty mid-blocks. Appropriate and environmentally sensitive infill housing in these areas could also make a major contribution to the city's housing needs.

Pietermaritzburg is an internationally significant repository of Victorian architecture, and the city has embarked on an innovative conservation programme. Clearly, however, such conservation activities can no longer be élitist or ethnocentric. Voortrekker, Victorian, Indian and African contributions to the built environment have to be afforded equal footing. The central city possesses distinctively African, Moslem, British, Colonial, Voortrekker and Hindu enclaves. Each of these areas can be upgraded and linked to encourage commercial, social and cultural interaction. Europeans play chess, Africans play *umlabalaba* (Nine Men's Morris). A public place containing a juxtaposition of tables and chairs for each type of game could stimulate cultural cross-pollination. There must be few cities in the world where such diversity can be so readily experienced, and this could be developed to encourage tourism, informal trading and respect for traditional customs, costumes and food – to name but three culture traits. What better place than Pietermaritzburg to establish an African–Indian market-place? White statues need Indian and African counterfoils, and what better place than Pietermaritzburg – where East meets West meets Africa – for a townscape feature, be it statue or fountain, which symbolizes just how enriched the lives of everyone have become as a result of this meeting and borrowing of cultures? Many of the colonial edifices are not simply architectural masterpieces, but were the setting for stirring debates, memorable speeches and significant trials – they need to, and readily can, take on broader historical and symbolic import by expanding the biased view of their significance. Men such as Mohandas Ghandhi and Alan Paton walked the streets of Pietermaritzburg, and were deeply moved by the experience, and went on to champion social justice and mutual respect for ethnic diversity. Perhaps that larger and deeper meaning of the townscape can positively shape the minds of men in the new South Africa.

References

Barter, C., 1852. *Dorp and Veld.*

Burke, G. L., 1956. *The making of Dutch towns.*

Christopher, A. J., 1983. 'From Flint to Soweto: reflections on the colonial origins of the Apartheid city', *Area, 15*: 145–9.

Christopher, A. J., 1987. 'Race and residence in colonial Port Elizabeth', *South African Geographical Journal*, 69: 3–20.

Davies, R. J., 1963. 'The growth of the Durban metropolitan area' *South African Geographical Journal, 45*: 15–43.

Davies, R. J., 1981. 'The spatial formation of the South African city', *Geojournal, 2*: 59–72.

Mann, R. J., 1859. *The colony of Natal.*

Narayan, S., 1927. *The selected works of Mahatma Ghandi* (Ahmedabad).

Passarge, S., 1908. *Südafrica: Eine Landes-, Volks- und Wirschaftskunde* (Leipzig).

South African Archival Records, Natal No. 1, 1958. *Notule van die Natalse Volksraad 1838–1845* (Cape Town).

Thomas, E. N., 1894. *How thankful we should be, comments on Natal* (Cape Town).

Western, J., 1981. *Outcast Cape Town* (Minneapolis).

Western, J., 1986. 'South African cities: a social geography', *Journal of Geography*, 85: 249–55.

Whittington, G., 1970. 'Towards urban development in Swaziland', *Erdkunde, 24*: 26–39.

Part IV

Processes, people and buildings

9 Parallelism and disjunction: a study in the internal structure of Welsh towns

Harold Carter

It has long been accepted that the towns of Wales are the products of two dominant, but markedly contrasted, phases of genesis (Carter 1963). The first was the period of the Anglo-Norman occupation beginning in the late eleventh century and culminating with the Edwardian conquest in 1284, although towns such as Beaumaris and Caerphilly were founded subsequently. During that period an array of castle-towns or *bastides* was created which formed the basic layer in the Welsh city system. The second was the industrial phase beginning in the 1750s and lasting until the end of the nineteenth century. It resulted in the development of a series of metallurgical and coal-mining settlements which both greatly extended and modified the existing system of towns. *A priori*, it would seem that there can be little in common between the plan-forms of these two sets of towns created in response to such different circumstances and totally contrasted in function. However, it is possible to contend that, rather than complete disjunction, there are parallels, even in observed form, suggesting that there are general processes in the formation of town plan which can be abstracted and which should become the analytical basis, in spite of the obvious contrasts in mode and period of formation and in function. Even further, perhaps an attempt is necessary to reorientate plan studies, which have long been lodged in the traditional geographic basis of form description explained in idiomatic terms, towards the character of other areas of urban investigation where emphasis is on process and where the possibilities of generality can be explored.

In seeking the more universal characteristics of process it is necessary to revive the concept of the formation of town plan as based on decision-making (Carter 1970). Any layout is the consequence of decisions usually, though not necessarily, consciously made. Foremost amongst those decisions is that of the allocation of land either to owners or to renters, for if the settlement is to function effectively then land must be provided for settlers. Street layout follows, or is an integral part of that process; seldom is the first decision made in the abstract for some desirable geometrical shape. It is, of course, necessary to exempt from that statement towns laid out for some symbolic purpose, sacred or secular. Thus the radial-concentric schemes of Renaissance and Baroque towns were related to the first and overriding demand for the symbolic representation of political and social power. But even the exception confirms the generalization for in those cases, too, one has to call in the nature of the decision-making process in explanation.

In many cases the decisions to be made were not unconstrained, for two inhibiting circumstances derive from the pre-existing settlement and the physical nature of the terrain. Pre-existing settlement is the least confining of conditions for, given an effective concentration of power, be it individual or municipal, it can simply be removed. Comprehensive redevelopment has by no means been limited to modern times. To establish the parallelism between the two genetic phases which this study seeks to maintain, it is appropriate to begin by considering episodes in the growth of Caernarfon, one of the classic Welsh *bastides*, and Merthyr Tydfil, the major town of the early industrial period in Wales.

When Edward I undertook the construction of the new castle town at Caernarfon he was not working with an open and unsettled site (Carter 1969). The Earl of Chester, during the initial phase of conquest, had built a motte and bailey structure which, by 1115, was in the possession of the Welsh. The castle became a royal residence and the centre for the administration of Gwynedd, and the town became a small trading centre. By 1277 Edward had decided to undertake the final solution of his Welsh problems. As part of the second phase the castle and town of Caernarfon were constructed, work beginning immediately after occupation in 1283. The site chosen was that of the earlier development and the old motte lay in the centre of the upper ward of the new castle. A new moat was excavated between the castle and the town (Fig. 9.1). But if the old defensive structure was incorporated in the new layout, the Welsh town was not, for it was simply removed so that the formal plan of the new town could be achieved. The old bailey was cleared and transformed into the large market-place outside the defences of the castle and the town. There was certainly accommodation to the site, which will be considered later; there was an element of adaptation to the earlier defences; but there was no attempt to relate the new town plan to the existing settlement which was just removed, a symbol of the power of the occupying forces.

A similar process can be identified at Merthyr Tydfil, for it, too, was effectively a new town. What existed was exploited or removed. The iron-masters, in the process of developing their works, bought up whole farms and leased land from others. In the former case, the farmhouses were used initially by the iron-masters themselves but, after those entrepreneurs had built their own mansions, the farmhouses were let to managers and agents. Much of the remaining land, and most of the leased land, especially the higher rough grazings, was used to tip spoil from the furnaces and mines. And, as the works and the spoil heaps advanced, so earlier settlement which happened to be in the way was removed. 'The old houses at Tranch Bach had to be vacated as tipping operations took place' (Pedler 1930: 115) (Fig. 9.2). Or again, 'In High Street, Dowlais . . . there used to be a row of

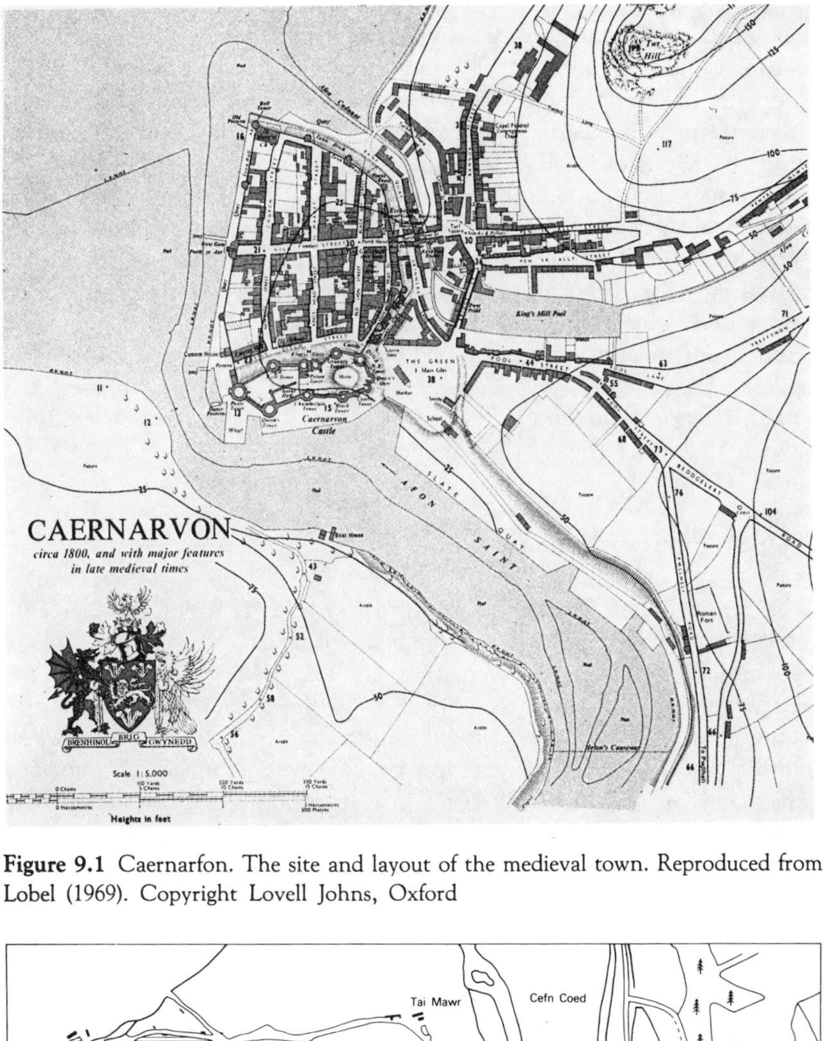

Figure 9.1 Caernarfon. The site and layout of the medieval town. Reproduced from Lobel (1969). Copyright Lovell Johns, Oxford

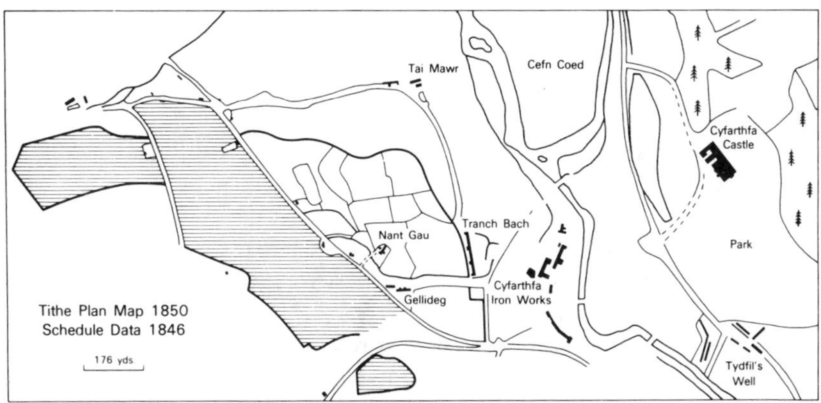

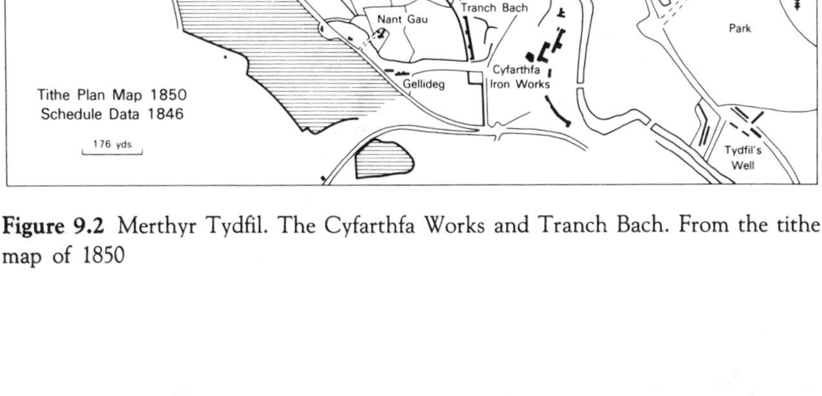

Figure 9.2 Merthyr Tydfil. The Cyfarthfa Works and Tranch Bach. From the tithe map of 1850

cottages called Forge Row . . . To make room for the works they were demolished about thirty years ago' (Davies n.d.), that is, about 1860.

There is no suggestion of any similarity of plan consequent upon the actions in Caernarfon and Merthyr which have been described, but from the viewpoint of procedures and processes there is much in common. Power lay in the hands of small but dominant immigrant groups who, therefore, had the means to dispose of any pre-existing settlement from areas which were part of their development schemes. That power and those processes are central to the analysis of town plan. In such a direction the future of plan analysis must lie, rather than in the ever-more-detailed study of shapes on the ground which nevertheless refuse to take up objective statistical measurement (Carter 1976: 18–19). After this brief identification of a similarity between the very different towns of the two genetic phases, it is appropriate to move forward to develop more fundamental associations between the plan-forms of the two periods.

The plan forms of *bastide* towns

In his seminal work on the *bastide* town in England, Wales and Gascony, Beresford developed a series of chapters dealing with different aspects (Beresford 1967). These are successively, profit or *nouvum forum*, site or *beau lieu*, content or *beau regard*, security or *bonne garde*, and finally the town's liberties as *ville franche*. In undertaking an analysis of the plans of the Welsh *bastides* these aspects can be appropriately deployed although in a modified order, for they are no less than a set of decision-making conditions. The immediate and overriding need on a miliary frontier was security and, of necessity, along with that went choice of site. Once the prime defensive demands were met then the settlements were intended to develop their associated role, that of market centre firmly locking economic control of the hinterland onto new towns and making them eventually commercially viable, that is profitable. In order to attract settlers both to provide a garrison and to ensure the market function, as well as to provide a basis for cultural transformation, liberties were offered and the content so ordered as to make land available; that is, a system of land allocation was imperative. The application of all these conditions can be illustrated with reference to Caernarfon, although the evidence to demonstrate the way in which decisions were made is inevitably very limited.

The priority of security is emphasized at Caernarfon by the massive castle which, in turn, derived the maximum possible protection from the site. There is no evidence as to how sites were chosen. Certainly there was a compromise between local defensive needs and general regional accessibility. Presumably the prior use for a motte and bailey structure, the use of the site by the Welsh, and the proximity of the decayed Roman fort of Segontium all played a part. Sea access, to ensure supply in time of siege, demanded a coastal location and, given that constraint, then the low peninsula on the Menai Straits formed by the rivers Saint and Cadnant was eminently suitable (Fig. 9.1). A moat constructed around the castle reinforced the natural protection. Immediately the site was chosen the physical conditions exerted a controlling influence upon the layout of the new town. The walls which enclosed the peninsula were adapted to its shape and took the form of a half-circle with the diameter along the Menai shore, the circumference being defined by the course of the rivers. Because of this site-determined shape it was impossible to divide the intra-mural area into a true rectangular pattern – the simplest means of organizing the content and providing standard parcels of land for allocation. A close approximation was, however, achieved by the creation of eight blocks, the central four being rigidly rectangular whilst the two blocks to the west were slightly smaller, and the two to the east were shaped to meet the form imposed by the semi-circular wall. These blocks were broken into two groups of four to the north and south of the main east–west street, High Street, which was a major traffic street linking the East Gate (Porth Mawr) with the West Gate (Porth yr Aur). The other streets which broke the blocks north to south were solely access streets and the breaks in the walls to which they lead are modern.

Unfortunately the decision-making process can only be inferred but the scheme was probably dominated by two factors. The one was the limitations imposed by the peninsular form, but the other was the paramount need to deploy an effective number of burgages within the walls and of a size acceptable to settlers. As early as 1911, E. A. Lewis maintained that there was a standard-sized burgage in these North Wales towns, measuring 80 feet by 60. But he also commented on the variations which occurred (Lewis 1911: 63). Beresford notes the 12½ *virgae* at Winchelsea (Beresford 1967: 18–19) and these, translated into modern measurements, give a plot of 40 feet by 85, which is nearer to the burgages at Beaumaris. Nevertheless, whilst there was clearly no rigid plot size, there seems to have been some general acceptance of the sorts of dimensions which were acceptable. But they had to be fitted into the land available as decreed by site conditions. If the size suggested by Lewis is fitted regularly into the plan of Caernarfon then it is possible to generate some seventy burgages. Between 1298, the date of the first rental, and 1356, the number of actual burgages varied between sixty-one and sixty-three.

There is no direct evidence as to how the decision to lay out Caernarfon was arrived at but inferences can be made from the plan itself, together with the documented details of the assembly of the work force for its building (Taylor 1974: vi). These suggest a primarily local, empirical approach in which a general familiarity with the *bastide* form was adapted to the exigencies of the local conditions. This can be supported by examining some other examples of towns founded at the same period.

Flint has the only truly rectangular plan amongst the Welsh *bastides* and

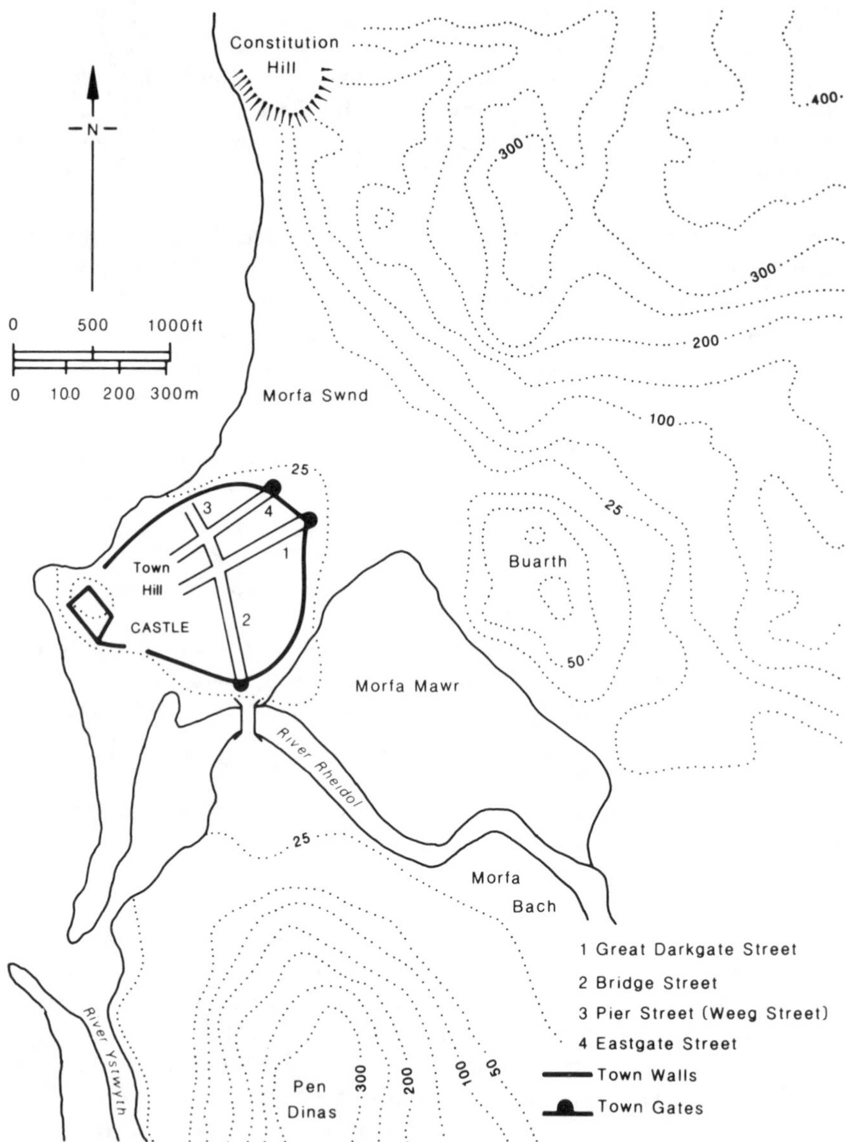

Figure 9.3a The site of Aberystwyth

it was also the only town built on an open and level site, on the banks of the Dee estuary. It is difficult to reconstruct the pattern of burgage plots. From what can be derived from a nineteenth-century map they seem to have been 40 feet by 100. But even under these most favourable of conditions the town was far from a true grid.

Aberystwyth, founded in 1277 during Edward's first campaign, was, like

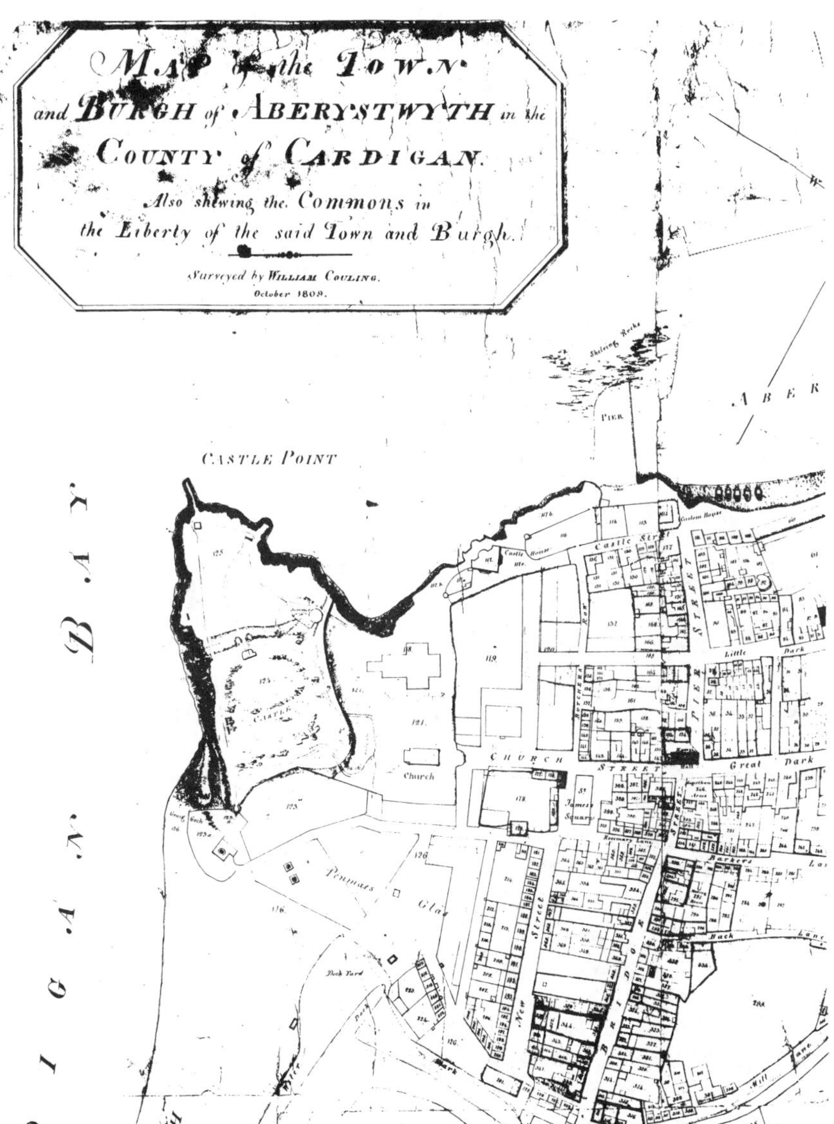

Figure 9.3b Part of the town in 1809 as shown on the map by William Couling

Caernarfon, built upon a peninsular site (Fig. 9.3a). It was again a coastal location, but, in this instance, a low, rounded hill which was isolated by the sea to the west, marshland to the north and east, and the river Rheidol to the south. These elements which provided protection – sea, river and land liable to flooding – necessarily limited settlement to the low hill, and accordingly the town walls, in place by 1280, were adapted to its shape.

The semicircle at Caernarfon became a full circle at Aberystwyth. Again, there is no evidence as to how the layout was decided but it took what can be regarded as the simplest, direct *ad hoc* solution. The town was set out in the form of two crossing streets, the cross within the circle. There seems to have been one minor street, Little Darkgate Street now Eastgate Street, which led to a small gate giving access to the storm beach. It was probably the simplest way in which the contents, the land holdings, could be fitted in.

As in most other cases in Wales the earliest map which gives adequate internal detail of any value dates to the early nineteenth century (Fig. 9.3b). The part reproduced shows the greater part of the walled town with the two main streets, by that date called Bridge Street–Pier Street and Great Darkgate Street–Church Street, forming the cross. Little Darkgate Street can also be identified, but New Street had only been laid out in 1793, on common land, to which designation most of the unallocated land of the medieval town had been assigned. In spite of considerable modification, the pattern of the burgages can still be identified. Lewis noted that the 80 by 60 feet lots at Caernarfon had apparently been carefully measured and departures recorded. At Aberystwyth it is difficult to identify that size or, indeed, the 80 by 40 feet of Beaumaris. The width at the street seems to be about 40 feet, but the length is much greater, extending to 100 feet. Again, the conclusion seems to be that each case was taken locally by itself, although against a general background of what was appropriate. *Ad hoc* forms and plots were set up and structures established in relation to local conditions.

The above conclusion can be reinforced if still more drastic modification of the peninsular form is considered and in an earlier baronial, rather than royal, context. Pembroke was built about 1138, by Gilbert de Clare, to whom it was granted by Henry I (Soulsby 1983: 214). It was sited on an elongated, steep-sided peninsula of limestone, bounded to the north and south by small streams or pills, as they are called locally. There was only one possible form it could take, that of a single main street along the ridge. There was also only one way in which the burgages could be arrayed, that of two series on either side of the single street and extending to the bounding town wall which followed the outline of the peninsula and giving what is usually called a herring-bone pattern (Fig. 9.4). Under such circumstances the burgages were narrow, though still near 40 feet, but very much longer, extending to some 200 feet. Decisions were again local and adapted to local circumstances.

There is one further aspect of the layout of these towns which has to be added. Such settlements became an immediate attraction to elements of the indigenous population who could benefit from association with the town even if they could not hold land within it. About the walls an extra-mural grouping of cottages came into being, unplanned, though usually in the form of an extension along lines of communication. Characteristically, it was located outside the main gate of the town. Such developments can be

Figure 9.4 Pembroke in 1908

clearly identified at Caernarfon (Fig. 9.1) and Aberystwyth, where it grew to the south of the river Rheidol and across from the gate at the bridge. Unplanned groupings of meaner cottages were therefore often found in those towns which experienced some growth after foundation.

At this point it is useful to summarize the sorts of processes which created the plans which have been examined even if it has not been possible to isolate the actual decision-making sequence. An incoming, colonizing group, in response to the demands for security and economic dominance, created towns. The internal organization of these towns was dominated by the prime operational element, the castle, and the layout of the lands granted to the settlers was locally adapted to the site predicated by the castle. The settlers were the necessary basis for both garrison and economic development. Little else was of great importance. The church was always of minor significance, often fitted in to some corner of the plan. However, areas of unregulated settlement came about as the towns grew, creating a contrast between intra-mural regularity and extra-mural irregularity of form.

The plan forms of industrial towns

At this point the apparently abrupt switch to the industrial period can be made. It is a jump of some seven hundred years and one apparently involving complete disjunction as far as town plan is concerned. But immediate parallels appear. The predatory Norman barons and the exploiting industrial entrepreneurs have much in common. In consequence, discussion of this later period can revolve about the controls set out by Beresford for the medieval era of town foundation. Profit was the obvious imperative, even if it was to be derived from the exploitation of point resources rather than the collection of rents and tolls. Site was, of course, an equally dominant demand, not for defence, it is true, but for least-cost access to raw materials and the power sources needed to work them. In the first phase of industrialization the location of iron works was as nearly controlled by physical geography and geology as the locations of medieval castles. The locations of coal mines even more so. In the early stages of development, as indeed was true of the castle towns, settlement simply clung to the operative core. But later the content, as with the later *bastides* of Edward I, was dictated by the need to attract population. As an incentive, the provision of shelter was undertaken giving rise to formal geometrical layouts; if Aberystwyth was a cross, then Pentrebach, in the south of Merthyr Tydfil, was a triangle (Lowe 1977). The medieval need for security has no parallel in these industrial towns nor, initially, has the provision of liberties. Even so, out of the agglomeration of workers arose the demand for rights of self-government which were the foundation of municipal reform. The royal or baronial castle town and the company town were expressions of the same need, and their forms the result of similar decision-making sequences.

The industrial entrepreneurs, like the castle builders, were constrained by the exigencies of site. The two critical elements in the iron industry which developed after 1750 were the outcrop of the Lower Coal Measures which gave easy surface access to the coal and clay ironstone. Water was also essential, both for power and for scouring. The result was that the first iron-works 'were located precisely where the rivers began to cross the coal seams. They were thus most favourably situated for exploiting to the full the main catchment areas of the rivers and the most accessible iron and coal measures' (Davies 1948: 32). On setting up their works the iron-masters faced the same problem as the medieval town founders: they needed to attract settlers to an area. Although there was no problem of security there was most certainly an absence of manpower. Money wages replaced land grants but, even so, the bare conditions for living had to be provided. The description of Aberamman by the Commissioners of Inquiry into the State of Education in Wales of 1847 is immediately reminiscent of the description of the assembly of workmen by Edward I to build his castle towns. 'To judge of the rapidity of the building here there were in the hamlet today 80 masons at work and 50 carpenters. There are also several rows of cottages where foundations have been commenced within the last few weeks' (Report of the Commissioners 1847, Appendix: 332).

As with the medieval towns a number of examples can be taken in illustration. The iron-masters clearly could not rely on haphazard development about a point of attraction any more than the castle builders. They therefore undertook the construction of urban villages, though the numbers housed were comparable to the earlier towns. Figures 9.5a and 9.5b are derived from the tithe map and a public health map of Merthyr both of the same date. Figure 9.5b is a detail of Georgetown, the general location of which is shown on Figure 9.5a. The Crawshay family had first become associated with the Cyfarthfa works but, in 1801, a site was developed at Ynysfach. Georgetown, named after the second son of William Crawshay I (that he was called 'the first' is not without significance), was built to house workers at Ynysfach. Unfortunately, as with the castle towns, there seems little documentary detail as to its inception and planning. But a good deal can be inferred from its form. Its outline was dominated by the availability of building land which was in the possession of the Crawshays. To the east was the river Taff, the Glamorganshire Canal, and the tramroad which led from the Ynysfach works to the Cyfarthfa stonehouses and the canal. There was also the parish road. Immediately to the south was the small stream, Cwmpantbach, and the Ynysfach works itself, whilst to the north were extensive spoil heaps built up from the Cyfarthfa works on land belonging to the Crawshays. To the west was land belonging to Lord Dynevor. Here, then, was an area of unused land, unwanted for industrial purposes and hardly ideally suited for building since it sloped steeply from the river. Within the confined area, and in spite of the steep slope, the layout was unmistakably rectangular. It was based on two main streets: one, George

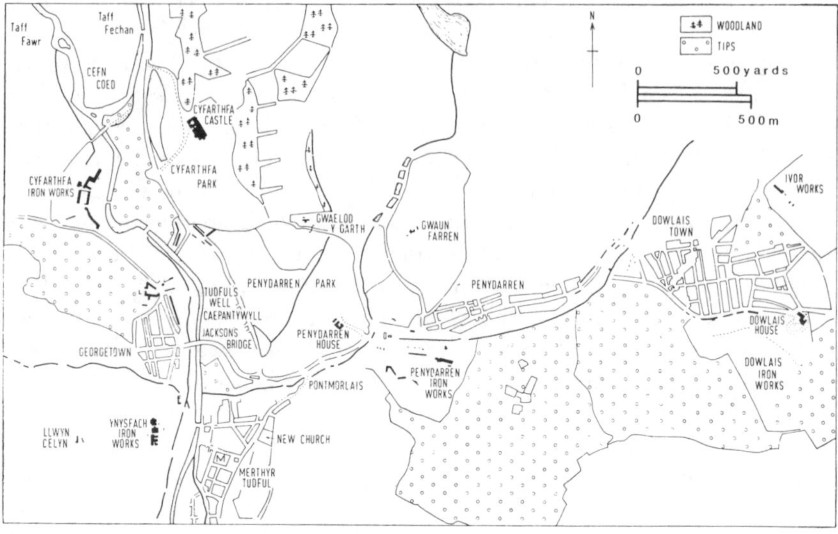

Figure 9.5a Georgetown, Merthyr Tydfil. General location from the tithe map of 1850. Note the same type of geometrical layout in Dowlais which was built for the Dowlais Works

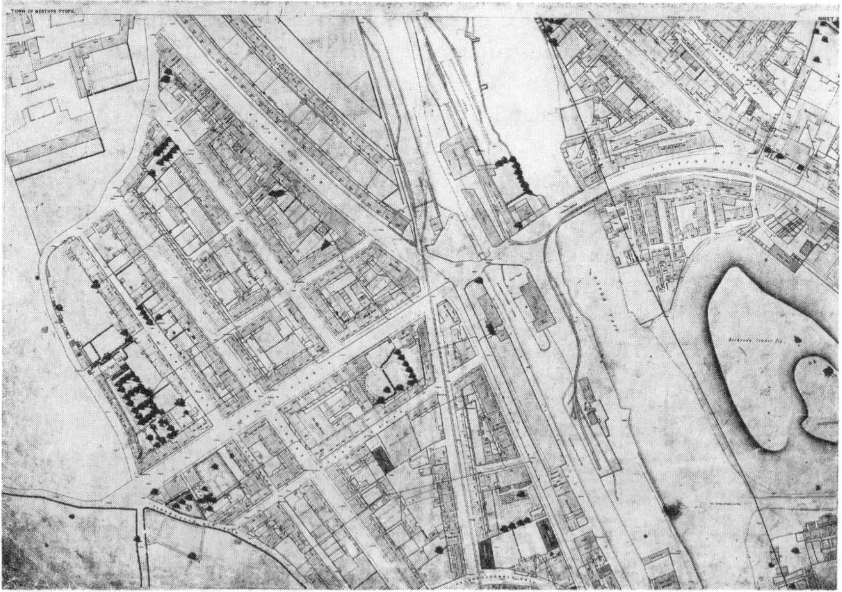

Figure 9.5b Georgetown from the 1 : 500 Public Health map of 1851

Street running up the slope and another, John Street, across the slope. The shape of the tract of land available did not allow an absolutely symmetrical plan, but Iron Lane to the north across the slope increased the regularity of the layout. Lot size varied, but there were two distinctly larger plots, one of which in 1851 was occupied by a doctor. Superficially, on the map, this could easily be taken for a medieval planned town. Indeed, it has an arrangement not unlike that at Aberystwyth.

Perhaps the most significant testimony of the conjuncture of medieval and industrial need is provided by Flint (Fig. 9.6). During the late eighteenth and early nineteenth centuries, Flint was caught in the general upsurge of industry on the North Wales coalfield. It became a port for the export of coal and a centre for the smelting of lead and silver and the manufacture of associated by-products, especially chemicals. A large, though loosely-constructed, industrial area grew to the north of the town. After destruction at the time of the Glyndŵr rising the town had not recovered and the Speed plan of 1610 shows it as almost rural in aspect. Now, terraces of workers' cottages were put up along the lines of the *bastide* preserving its outline, though splitting the burgages. The perceptions of Sample Lewis in his 'Topographical Dictionary' of 1833 are revealing. 'The buildings are notwithstanding very inferior in appearance to what might be expected from the regularity with which the streets are disposed . . .' (Lewis 1833). To him regularity apparently meant superiority in quality, whereas across Wales that was manifestly not so. The mean industrial cottages – 'the town possesses few recommendations as a place of residence' – fitted without any problem at all into the pre-existing rectangular pattern, for that pattern was closely akin to many being created by industry in Wales. The sole difference was the subdivision of burgages which elsewhere remained partially (but only partially, for there was subdivision as well as amalgamation) in their medieval form.

A study by Jeffery R. Davies of the construction of a small settlement in the Rhondda valley during the later coal-mining-dominated phase of industrial development makes it possible to examine the processes of plan development more closely.

Davies's review is based on letters between Thomas Joseph, a colliery owner, and John Randall, who was the agent of the Countess of Dunraven. The Countess owned the land in question which was situated towards the head of the Rhondda Fawr. The letters are preserved in the Dunraven Manuscripts in the National Library of Wales. Joseph wished to attract workers to what was, at the time, a remote area and his first intention was to establish something very like a model village, though Davies emphasizes that he never used that term. Joseph's first proposal was essentially in the nature of such a model village and included houses of different quality graded into first, second and third classes. Disagreement arose, however, with the Dunraven estate over the size of the individual plots and the associated rents. On May 12, 1857, Randall wrote in a letter commenting on Joseph's plan:

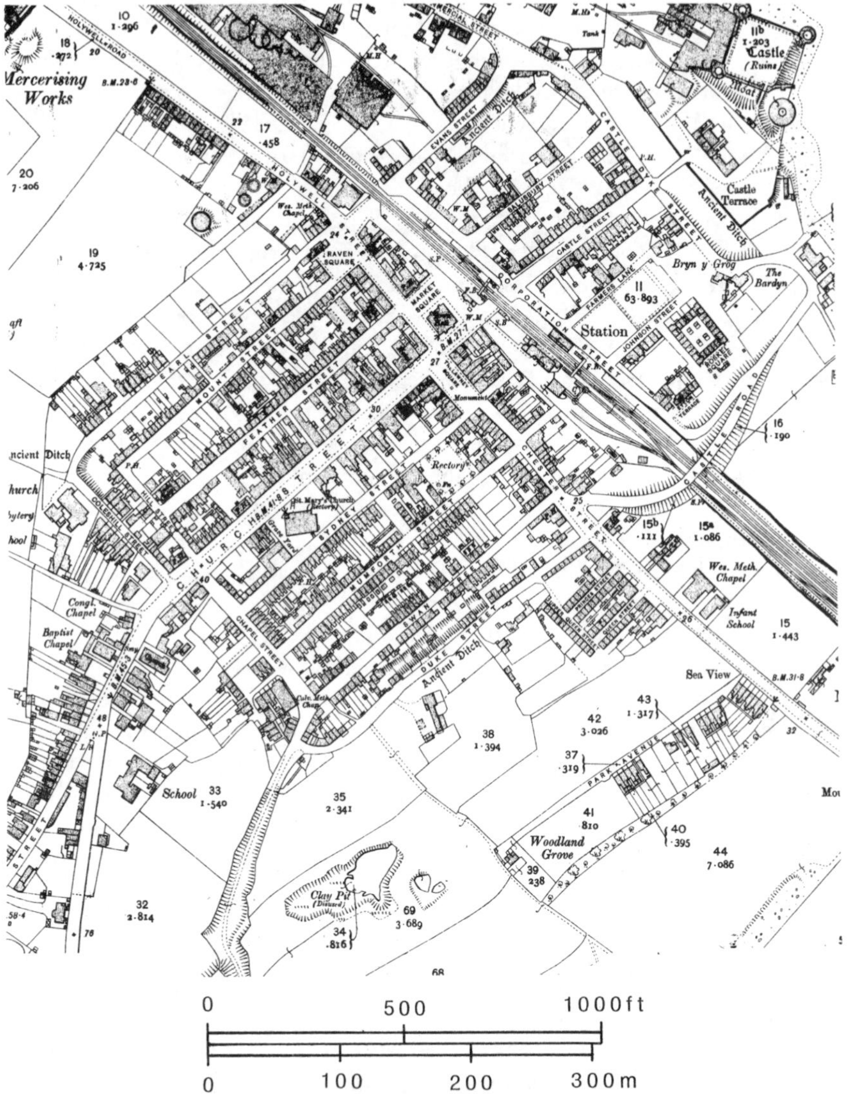

Figure 9.6 Flint in 1912. Note that some of the burgages seem not to have been divided, especially along the main street, Church Street

If I am correct in my admeasurement from your plan a cottage and garden will not be more than four perches of ground, this seems to me too little as it will crowd the people too much and their gardens will be so small that they will not be much use as gardens . . . The terms wd be 60 years at 1*d* per square yard ground rent' (Davies 1976: 58).

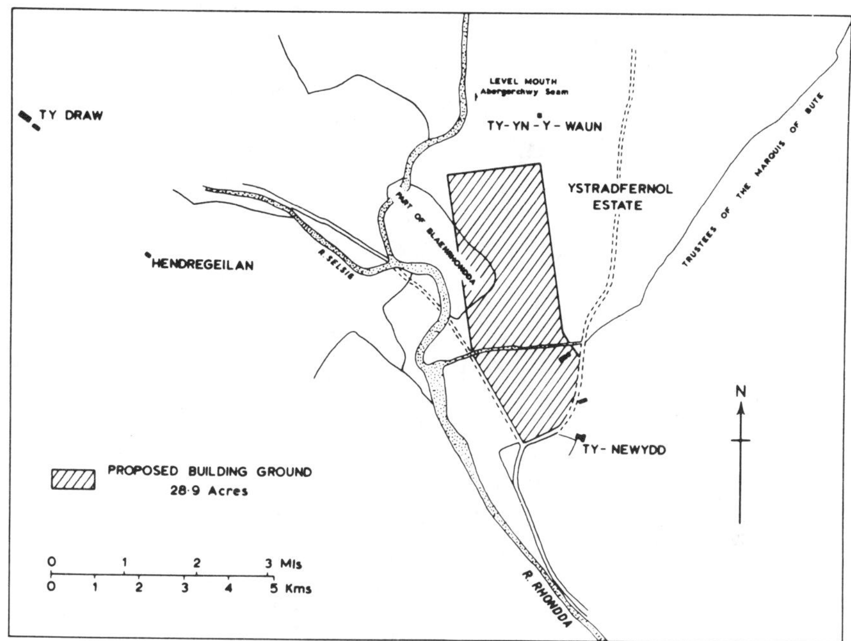

Figure 9.7 Tynewydd; the second proposed site for the village (after J. R. Davies)

Joseph responded, 'I fear that you will have no applications for building ground at "Bryn Wyndham" . . . if you will attach such a large allotment of land to each cottage as it would take two calendar months to pay the ground rent each year' (Davies 1976: 59). Joseph went on to write, 'Should you sadly insist upon your view of the case on this point, as I am sadly in want of cottages, I would have no alternative but to recommend the parties at once to apply for building land on the Bute estate . . .' (Davies 1976: 60). Apparently Joseph did achieve some compromise, indicated in a later letter, but he then continued, 'It will be necessary to change the building site from the place which I first suggested to another equally suitable, so as not to interfere prejudicially with the working of the mines etc.' This second choice, shown on Figure 9.7, was 'on Ystradfernol farm at the boundary of that farm with the Bute-owned Tynewydd farm, and in the fork of the parish road' (Davies 1976: 61).

There are three aspects of this development which are worthy of note. The first is that Joseph did take site factors into account when demarcating the residential area noting that 'it lies well has good aspect and good approaches to it'. That, however, was most certainly secondary to the needs of mining and profit as the reason – 'so as not to interfere prejudicially with the working of the mines' – in the quotation above makes clear. The same order of priorities is revealed in the switch to the second site – 'it will not be required by me for sinking upon, or as tipping ground'. The third aspect

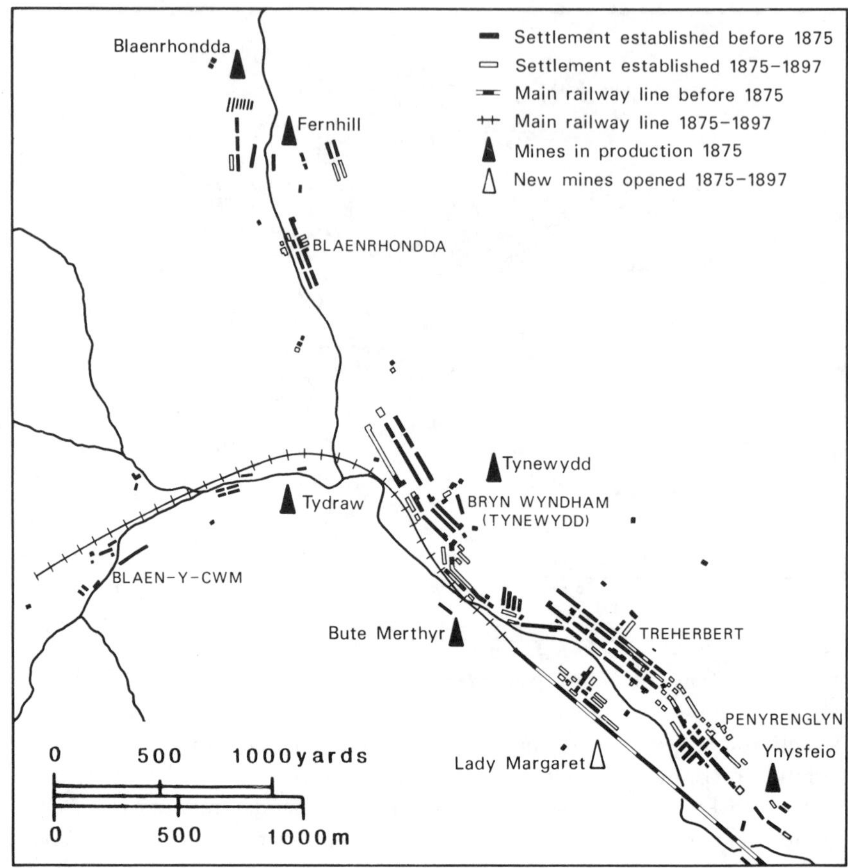

Figure 9.8 Settlement development at the head of the Rhondda Fawr (after P. N. Jones)

is concerned with the relation between the settlement and the coal mine (Fig. 9.8). It would seem that Tynewydd, as the settlement became called, was developed in relation to Tynewydd colliery, but that was not so for Joseph's interests were in Tydraw to the north-west.

Figure 9.8 is a reproduction of P. N. Jones's interpretation of settlement growth at the head of the Rhondda Fawr (Jones 1969: 78). It shows Tynewydd as a simple series of parallel terraces. But Davies's analysis of the correspondence between developer and land agent reveals the lengthy decision-making process which must have been characteristic of many at the time. The first priority was a site which was related to, but which was in no way likely to interfere with, the mining operation, either directly or in the disposal of waste. Only then was a settlement site chosen, with individual plots of a size commensurate with the ability of the house-occupiers to pay. At a time, and in an area, lacking any sophistication in

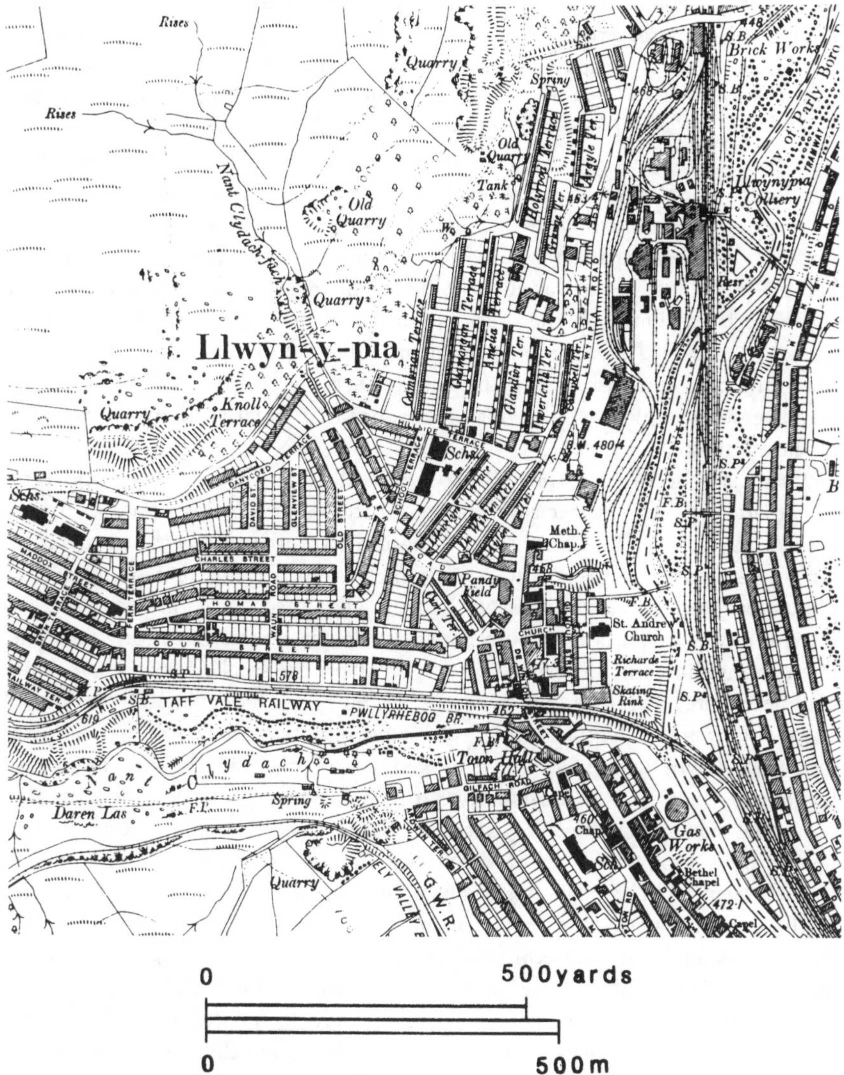

Figure 9.9 The terraces at Llwynpia. The area referred to in the text lies immediately to the east of the name Llwyn-y-pia

urban planning and design, the simplest arrangement was parallel lines of houses with crossing access streets. It would not be over fanciful to envisage the same discussions going on some seven hundred years earlier as to the siting of a castle town, the priority of defensive needs, and the nature of the land allocation.

The general outcome in the industrial period is again admirably illustrated by Treherbert, where the name commemorates 'the family name of the earls of Pembroke, whose estates the Butes had inherited' (Davies 1981: 220). It is absolutely characteristic of the layout of the coalfield settlements, though the houses were regarded as being of a better quality than many. Figure 9.9 shows the so-called 'Scotch houses' at Llwynpia, also in the Rhondda Fawr. J. B. Lowe writes of them that they 'were built from about 1865 onwards in connection with Archibald Hoad's Llwyn-y-pia Colliery'. Part of a development of more than 200 houses, often simply called 'The Terraces', they are a classic example of the parallel row layout in its final form. Each house faces westward across the Rhondda valley. In front is its garden, behind is an access path about two and half metres wide at its maximum; a vehicle road climbs up the hillside, cutting across the ends of the terraces. This is a standard pattern of adaptation to site. It is of interest to observe that the plot dimensions within the terraces were some 35 feet by 95, measurements which would not have appeared greatly unusual within a medieval town.

Within this section on the industrial period there will have been apparent clear parallels with the decision-making processes of the first phase of urban genesis in Wales. The core of the situation in both cases was the need to attract settlers or workers into areas which were peripheral, remote, thinly populated and lacking an urban base. That need was mostly met by providing lots or plots for house construction, or houses built for rent. The main motivation in that provision was to allow the smallest amount of land commensurate with the achievement of purpose. Plot dimensions varied even amongst the *bastides* and, as has been noted, many of the plots in industrial towns would not have looked out of place in the *bastide* towns. In general there was little difference in the length of plot but those in the industrial towns designed to accommodate terraced houses were usually nearer to half-plots in the castle towns. The processes of design in both periods seem to have been essentially pragmatic, fixed at the time in relation to the overriding needs of the operational core, castle, factory or mine, and the site available. In consequence, the eventual layouts are not fundamentally dissimilar, although the contrasted nature of the buildings sometimes disguises that fact. Where the two became directly related as at Flint, the earlier form was translated into the latter without any difficulty whatsoever.

It is possible to pursue the parallelism still further. It was noted that one of the distinctive features of the castle town was the development of extramural, irregular groupings of cottages, mainly occupied by what can be termed 'hangers-on' who sought to gain what they could from the activities of the towns. A similar process can be identified in the industrial towns where unskilled immigrants created distinctive areas of irregular housing of the lowest quality. In Merthyr two areas, one to the north and one to the south of the town-centre, came into being. The one to the north, an area called 'China', was described as made up of 'mere huts of stone – low, confined, ill-lighted and unventilated; they are built without pretensions to regularity and form a maze of courts and tortuous lanes . . .' (Morning

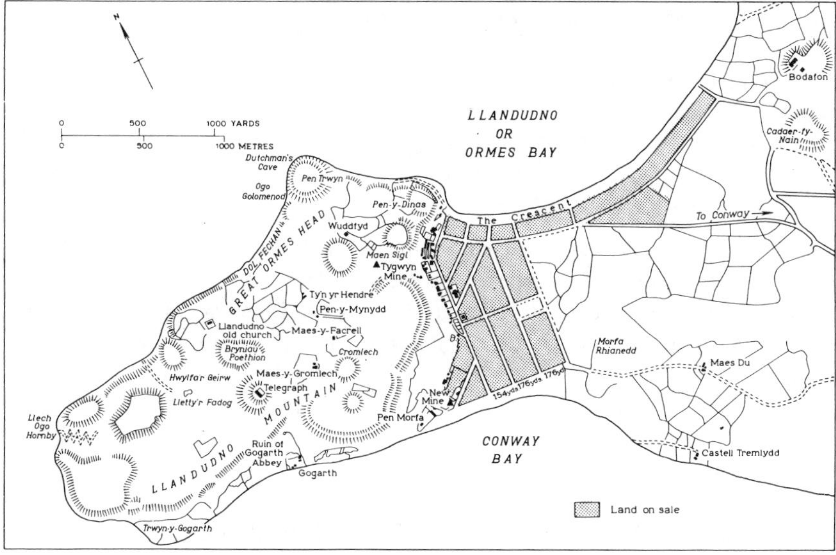

Figure 9.10 Llandudno. The plan of the sale of land in 1849

Chronicle 1850: 5). There is a distinct element of comparability in the reaction of sanitary reformers to these areas towards the end of the century. Even at Aberystwyth, following a petition, a survey was carried out under the Public Health Act. The ensuing report constantly refers to the condition of Fountain Court in Trefechan, the old extra-mural settlement: 'In Fountain Court there is not a house that has a privy . . . Every one of the 12 houses in Fountain Court is a common lodging house.' That any comparison can be made between a *bastide* transformed into a seaside resort and an industrial town is in itself significant.

One final example can be added which is not directly related to the two genetic phases. Llandudno was created in the middle of the nineteenth century to be a seaside resort and to capitalize on the demand which was being generated in the growing areas of north-west England and north Wales. The developer was Lord Mostyn who exploited the consolidation of the Gloddaeth estate after the enclosure awards. Building lots were offered for sale in 1849 within a carefully-constructed plan (Fig. 9.10). There were three elements in the town as it appeared in the mid 1850s. The first was the pre-existing village of Llandudno which extended along the eastern edge of the Great Orme; the second was a clear grid which had been established on the flat marshland, at the foot of the Orme, which had been drained; the third was 'The Crescent', the sea front, which curved along Llandudno Bay. The scheme was completely conventional and unimaginative. It was again a pragmatic adaptation to site carried out in the most elementary way.

True, there was a clear intention to avoid industrial squalor in constructional terms. The 'Tourist's Guide' of 1849 wrote,

> Great care has been taken to provide salutary restrictions, without making them extremely irksome, and to classify the whole locality, one neighbourhood for large houses and another for a smaller description . . . With a view to provide for the health and comfort for all who may visit or settle in the district the . . . code of building regulation has been prepared.

The various regulations were again standard in form, effectively introducing covenants to control the type of building – 'No courts of houses will be permitted to be erected for habitation' – and to maintain land and property values. But again the basic layout and plot pattern was unexceptional.

Conclusions

At the outset of the essay the notion of a complete disjunction between the two major phases of town genesis in Wales was set out. The implication had always been that since these periods were historically separated by some seven hundred years, and were related to entirely different functional characteristics, then the towns created during them must be morphologically dissimilar. The conventional historical approach, assigning towns to particular phases, which forms the basic organization of every book on town plan, has demanded that the sets of towns be treated separately. The intention of this essay is to challenge that approach. An attempt has been made to demonstrate that all these towns have much in common, or at least can be subject to a common treatment which is not historically bound. Layout is the consequence of a common sequence of decisions. In some cases it is true that location and site are chosen in relation to a preconceived plan. But such instances are relatively few. In other cases there is an overriding symbolism, as in the radial-concentric scheme of Renaissance princes. But setting those aside, the underlying processes in the formation of town plan are universal. Operating within the constraints of site, the dimensions of plot size, the demands generated by traffic roads and access roads and on-the-spot pragmatism, all lead to comparable solutions whatever the period. Analysis of the forms themselves is therefore of limited value. That view is supported by the very limited progress made in the detailed measurement of plans as graphs and, indeed, the considerable reservations expressed as to its value. Townscape is a completely different issue, dominated as it is by buildings of contrasted historical styles. But the approach to layout must surely become ahistorical, released from the conventional pigeon-holes of the standard periods. In this way it would be more linked to much of contemporary geographical analysis which sees its aim in the discovery of process rather than in the local description and interpretation of pattern. There still remains a study of town plan to be written based on characterizing processes rather than historical periods.

References

Beresford, M., 1967. *New towns of the Middle Ages: town plantation in England, Wales and Gascony.*

Carter, H., 1965. *The towns of Wales: a study in urban geography.*

Carter, H., 1969. 'Caernarfon', in M. D. Lobel (ed.), *Historic towns*, Vol. 1.

Carter, H., 1970. 'A decision making approach to town plan analysis: a case study of Llandudno', in H. Carter and W. K. D. Davies (eds.), *Urban essays: studies in the geography of Wales*, 66–78.

Carter, H., 1976. 'The town in its setting: the geographical approach', in M. W. Barley (ed.), *The plans and topography of medieval towns in England and Wales* [C.B.A. Research Report No. 14].

Davies, C., 1948. 'The development of industry and settlement in the region from Merthyr Tydfil to Abergavenny 1740–1840', (MA thesis, University of Wales).

Davies, J., 1981. *Cardiff and the Marquesses of Bute.*

Davies, J. H., n.d. 'The history of Dowlais'. Ms. Merthyr Library.

Davies, J. R., 1976. '"Bryn Wyndham" village, upper Rhondda Fawr', *Morgannwg*, *20:* 53–65.

Jones, P. H., 1969. 'Colliery settlement in the South Wales coalfield 1850 to 1926', *University of Hull, Occasional Papers in Geography* No. 14.

Lewis, E. A., 1911. *The medieval boroughs of Snowdonia.*

Lewis, S., 1833. *Topographical dictionary of Wales.*

Llandudno, 1849. *The tourists guide to the romantic beaches, bays and other objects of interest at the fashionable watering place of Llandudno and the Great Orme's Head.*

Lowe, J. B., 1977. *Welsh industrial workers housing 1775–1875.*

Morning Chronicle, 1850. 'Labour and the poor. The mining and manufacturing district of South Wales', *Letters to the Morning Chronicle.*

Pedler, F. J., 1930. *The history of the hamlet of Gellideg.*

Royal Commission, 1847. *Report of the Royal Commissioners of Inquiry into the State of Education in Wales.*

Soulsby, I., 1983. *The towns of medieval Wales.*

Taylor, A., 1867. Report of inquiry at Aberystwyth under the Sanitary Act (P.R.O. MH.13. Box 2).

Taylor, J. A., 1974. *The Kings Works in Wales.* Reprinted from J. A. Taylor, 1963. *The history of the Kings Works.*

10 The morphological development of Scottish cities from Georgian to modern times

George Gordon

Introduction

'The term Scottish City is used with some caution. It will be argued that a distinctive species does exist but it must also be recognized that the Scottish City has been variously affected by experiences, developments, innovations and forces from furth of Scotland' (Gordon 1985: 1). Two factors have contributed to the distinctiveness of Scottish cities: the preservation of a separate legal system and more tenuously, the influence of Scottish culture and cultural traditions.

The verticality of the townscapes of the pre-industrial and industrial city in Scotland echoed European traditions rather those those of neighbouring England. Overbuilding on gardens and infilling of backlands were, of course common practices throughout Britain as urban growth accelerated in the late and post-medieval period when many cities were still constrained by walls. Inevitably an intensification of use of space fostered increasing verticality of townscapes. In many ways it was during the subsequent phase of explosive growth of the burgeoning cities of the Victorian era that the distinctiveness of the townscape of Scottish cities crystallized.

> Characteristically, four-storey Scottish tenements were built in stone. Frontages of dressed stone and rear construction of rough courses of stone rubble were virtually universal. Brickwork was sparingly used, usually only for external stair towers, interior and gable walls, though after the withdrawal of the brick tax in 1850 and with the development of factory-produced bricks and increasing pressure on adjacent quarry resources, brickwork did assume a greater importance in the second half of Victoria's reign. (Rodger 1986: 154)

Additionally, the building standards introduced in Scotland in the second half of the nineteenth century differed significantly from those in England and Wales. In Scottish houses the main walls were thicker and main timbers more substantial. Supplying water in tenements was more problematic than in two-storey terraced buildings but, in Scotland, there was the further complication of more demanding strictures about the physical separation of waste pipes from sources of clean water.

Worsdall (1979: 14–15) has outlined an explanation for the peculiar place of the tenement in Scottish townscapes which involves a quintessential marriage of legal tradition, the economics of urban development, and custom and practice in the building industry. At the root of the argument is the Scottish practice of feuing land (Rodger 1979: 78–9; 1986: 172–3), whereby the seller of undeveloped land not only received a lump sum at the moment of sale but also an annual feu-duty in perpetuity. (The system ended in 1974, although many unredeemed feus remain in existence.) In effect the feudal superior (seller of the land) obtained some recompense against future increases in the value of land through the fixed feu-duty. There were obvious attractions to feudal superiors in maximizing the potential income from feu duties. The construction of tenements was an attractive proposition for, whilst the feu-duty for each small flat was modest, the total could represent a considerable return in relation to the size of the plot.

The persistence of the tenement tradition is illustrated by the reversion to a modified form of single or double tenement blocks in place of the flatted villa as Scottish local authorities sought to address the issues raised in the mid 1930s of growing housing lists, a perceived need for more intensive development and the encouragement of higher subsidies to tackle the problems of older districts of slums. Nor was the renaissance of the tenemental style temporary. Thousands of tenement-style blocks were constructed by Scottish local authorities in the 1950s and 1960s as the cities grappled with the post-war backlog of demand for housing.

It should not be assumed that the thesis for a degree of distinctiveness in the morphological development of Scottish cities rests solely on the tenement form, or indeed on the greyness and solidity of the stone-built townscapes. The argument is more broadly based. The separate legal system of Scots Law provides a unique institutional framework, with private and public transactions, urban development and government legislation guided by its rulings, practices and precedents.

Nor should other sources of distinctiveness be underestimated. The fires of Scottish culture may burn with varying intensity but they are always present to some degree. There may have been few truly Scottish architectural styles in the last two centuries but one of the most creative of Scottish architects, artists and designers, Charles Rennie Mackintosh, wrote of one phase in a paper on Scotch Baronial Architecture (Mackintosh 1891). That style offered an outlet for national romanticism (Walker 1985), adding formal and symbolic significance to many nineteenth-century public buildings, office blocks, hotels, mansions and tenements.

The evolution of planning in Scotland has also experienced elements of cultural distinctiveness. In an exposition of the evolution of Scottish town-planning, Rodger (1983) records the crucial role of Dean of Guild Courts up to the nineteenth century, in relation to building control. From the mid nineteenth century, the Burgh Police (Scotland) Act 1862, and subsequent supplementary legislation by individual burghs, introduced strict building controls and codes (Rodger 1986: 185). An unwanted consequence of these actions was that the legislation caused building costs in Scottish cities in the late Victorian period to greatly exceed those in English cities. This situation contributed to the early-twentieth-century crisis of housing supply for the working class in Scottish cities.

Two further points related to town-planning can be used to extend the argument. Scottish planners, like other professionals, can operate on various spatial scales and seek various goals. Patrick Geddes and his son-in-law, Frank Mears, provide interesting illustrations of the point. Both were deeply committed to Scotland and to the revival of the fortunes of the nation. Geddes' anti-metropolitan views were coloured by a fervent love of Scotland and, in particular, of Edinburgh. Geddes longed for a rebirth of Scotland as a great power in European culture and of Edinburgh as a true capital of the Scottish nation (Cuthbert 1986). Yet Geddes, a visionary figure in the founding of town-planning as a discipline, spent much of his time abroad. He was not acclaimed during his lifetime as a famous son of Scotland and, arguably, did his most successful planning in Scotland on comparatively small projects in Edinburgh, and in plans for small burghs such as St Andrews. In contrast, though Mears assisted Geddes on plans for Jerusalem, he spent most of his working life in Scotland, largely eschewing the philosophy of the leading English figures in the blossoming profession of town-planning. Through his professional work in many small burghs and, later, on major surveys and plans, but primarily through his membership of influential committees in the 1930s and 1940s and through his many years of teaching planning students at Edinburgh College of Art, Mears exerted a much greater influence upon planning in Scotland than his father-in-law had done. Moreover, Mears deliberately sought to provide Scottish responses to Scottish problems (Purves 1988).

In the field of politics, important distinctive features have also contributed to these broader contextual factors. The composition of political parties, at the national, and more particularly at the local, level has often exercised considerable influence as Keating (1988) has recently recorded in the context of Glasgow. Another illustration of these important contextual differences is the fact that the reform of local government in the 1970s resulted in Scotland adopting a different organizational system from that favoured in England and Wales. In Scotland, a basic two-tier structure was introduced of macro-units (regions), composed of meso-units (districts). Each tier was allocated particular functions. Thus planning, transport, education and social work are regional functions whilst housing, conservation, leisure facilities and cleansing services are the responsibility of the districts.

The vicissitudes of the Scottish economy constitute another set of contextual factors. Whilst the sequential successes of the tobacco, cotton, iron, and steel industries fuelled industrialization and urbanization in Scotland

(Gordon 1983), especially in the Central Lowlands, the temporal and spatial patterns were uneven, as were the socio-economic consequences. For example, below-average wages, by British standards, were an important contributory factor to nineteenth-century industrial growth in Scotland (Rodger 1986: 170). Though advantageous for the industrialist, for the workers the situation adversely affected the amount of disposable income available for expenditure on housing. Coupled with comparatively high levels of broken time in certain occupations, escalating housing costs in the late-Victorian period and the prevalence of renting residences on fixed leases (commonly annual), many families adopted a risk-minimumization strategy, determining their housing needs with reference to some sense of security about ability to pay rent (Rodger 1986). These factors also impinged upon the increasing spatial segregation, as the Victorian era progressed, of the 'aristocracy of labour', separating the skilled working class from the unskilled working class (Gray 1976).

This introduction has focused upon a Scottish dimension to contextual factors but it is acknowledged that there are limits to that argument. Scotland is not an independent socio-economic system. Scottish cities are subject to national and international economic pressures and forces and, increasingly, to the policies and legislative decisions of central government sitting in Westminster. None the less, notwithstanding the existence of national policies and guidelines and equivalent macro-trends in the diffusion of innovations and the shaping of attitudes and tastes or the impact of economic cycles, there remains considerable scope for local interpretations and actions. The remainder of this chapter examines these issues in the context of morphological development, with particular reference to the cities of Edinburgh and Glasgow.

A temporal sequence

Various terms have been advanced to categorize the timespan of this study. The period under survey is commonly seen as capturing the urban transition from the pre-capitalist to the industrial or Victorian city, which is then succeeded by the modern city. Structurally, this chapter is concerned with what has been described as the Transitional City, the Victorian City, and the Modern City (Knox 1987: 11). However, the timing of the transformations are complex and it is often simpler to assemble the evidence into chronological sequences. Thus, when analysing long-term changes in the form of the city centre, Whitehand (1978) used the following architectural periods: Victorian, 1840–94; Edwardian, 1895–1918; inter-war, 1919–45; post-war, 1946–69. A different set of time units could be advocated if the emphasis was placed upon planning of the environment. For instance Knox (1987) posits the following trilogy: private paternalism, 1840–70; public paternalism, 1870–1910; professionalized paternalism, 1910–45.

This chapter is concerned with all of the issues underpinning these typologies. With the caveat that the primary purpose is ease of description and analysis rather than rigorous classification, a broad threefold sequence is therefore adopted, namely: the Georgian city 1760–1830; the Victorian city 1831–1914; the Modern city 1915–88.

The Georgian city: 1760–1830

(a) Edinburgh

The Golden Age of Edinburgh has been generally defined as the period from the 1760s to the 1830s. It was a period when Edinburgh's reputation soared as a centre of learning, a centre of jurisprúdence and a centre of the arts. At the beginning of this golden age the competition for a new town heralded the dawn of sophistication; towards its conclusion, from the 1830s on, a galaxy of neo-Greek monuments was rising on Edinburgh's own Acropolis, the Calton Hill, to symbolise a new found conviction of the Scottish capital's role as *The Athens of the North*. (Skinner 1976: 56)

The Age of Enlightenment in Edinburgh was also a period of significant urban extension and morphological transformation as new geometric districts of stone-built terraces were constructed, primarily to the north of the medieval 'herringbone' city astride the hog-backed castle ridge. Henceforth, this morphological dichotomy was captured in the descriptive spatial terms of the Old Town and the New Town.

Youngson (1966: xii), the seminal chronicler of *The Making of Classical Edinburgh*, has suggested that two circumstances favoured the planners and builders of the New Town. First, the Scottish system of feuing land, and specifically the details which could be written into the feu charter, meant that landowners could seek to plan large areas in a unified way, yet leave the actual development to individual purchasers and a multitude of small builders. Secondly, in architecture the forms of Greece and Rome became fashionable, and in town-planning there was agreement that proper planning should seek to create well-proportioned geometric layouts set in a park-like landscape.

Supportive as these factors may have been, it would be unwise to overstate their importance. Evidence suggests that widespread effective use of the feu charter as a planning device post-dated the commencement of the New Town. Similarly the mid-eighteenth-century proposals to found the New Town of Edinburgh met with stiff parliamentary opposition from Midlothian landed interests and not a little cynicism from contemporary commentators in Edinburgh. The external climate may have been opportune, and the enthusiasm of influential champions such as Provost Drummond ensured that the local administrative machinery backed the plans, but success was by no means guaranteed. The hesitant start to the project is well-documented, as is the fact that the crucial local by-laws, which secured the detailed attainment of Craig's plan, were not enacted until the 1780s.

By the end of the eighteenth century it became apparent that the venture was a success and owners of adjoining land were encouraged to sponsor similar developments in that style. By far the most substantial properties were erected on the lands of the Earl of Moray, to the north and north-west of the western extremity of the original New Town. However, the largest areal extension was located immediately north of the New Town. A western extension developed beyond Queensferry Street but the building of an extensive eastern district, crowned by terraces flanking Calton Hill, was not completed. Instead, in the early Victorian era industrial and lower-quality residential properties were built on the lower slopes of the planned eastern district.

It was in these extensions to the New Town that the full potential of the feu charter as a planning device was realized. Youngson (1966: 208–11) recorded fifteen principal clauses of a contract, dated 1806, for the lands of the northern extension, between the City of Edinburgh, the Governors of George Heriot's Hospital (a charitable school) and three architects of Edinburgh and two Writers to the Signet (solicitors). The first three clauses were:

First — The houses in Heriot Row and at the west end of Abercromby Place to be two storeys plus a basement or sunk storey, not to rise more than 33 feet above street level, except for the projecting houses which are to be limited to 51 feet.

Second — The houses in Dublin Street, Howe Street, India Street, Pitt Street and other streets running north from Abercromby Place and Heriot Row shall not overtop the projecting houses mentioned in the first clause.

Third — The houses in Drummond Place, Great King Street, Royal Circus, etc. shall not exceed 46 feet except for the projecting houses; in Northumberland Street they shall not exceed 33 feet. Also the roofs of all the houses in the different streets, Rows, Squares, etc. shall not exceed one third of its [*sic*] breadth, i.e. there were to be no high-pitched roofs.

The whole northern extension was developed under these legal structures, to a street-plan of Sibbald and Reid, by a multiplicity of builders for an almost equivalent number of clients: an impressive testimony of the potential for control in the feu charter when conditions were favourable.

Contemporaneously with the launching of the New Town project, two squares, Brown Square and George Square, were constructed to the south of the Old Town. The larger, George Square, was the more important and, indeed, is classed by Youngson (1966: 68) as 'the first truly modern house-building project in Edinburgh, and the first true square'. It enjoyed a period of fashionable success before being eclipsed by the sheer magnitude of the northern districts. Nor were the new developments confined to these locations. Smaller and less prestigious districts were erected at peripheral locations such as Stockbridge (on the estate of Sir Henry Raeburn, beside the Water of Leith) and at Lauriston (beside Heriot's Hospital).

Just as the development of the New Town was assisted by the construction of the North Bridge across the valley now occupied by Princes Street Gardens and Waverley Station, so extension southward from the Old Town was facilitated by the bridging of the Cowgate valley by South Bridge and by George IV Bridge. Inevitably these bridgeworks and their breakthrough streets had an important impact upon the morphology of some of the most populous parts of the Old Town. Industrial premises, markets and residences, and substantial parts of several closes and wynds, were removed to make way for these viaducts.

New embryonic industrial and working-class areas were emerging in the late-Georgian period such as the district of Fountainbridge, which adjoined the eastern terminus of the Union Canal at Port Hopetoun, and the area known as the South Side which was situated to the south and south-east of the Old College of Edinburgh University.

Several major new public buildings were erected in the Georgian period. In the Old Town, the most significant were the Royal Exchange which, in 1811, became the City Chambers, and St Cecilia's Hall at the Cowgate end of Niddry's Wynd. Notable amongst the new public buildings in the New Town were Register House, at the eastern end of Princes Street, and the Assembly Rooms and Physicians' Hall in George Street. Towards the close of the period the new High School was built on the southern flank of Calton Hill. The foundation stone of the Old College of Edinburgh University was laid in 1789 although the southern side of the new quadrangle was not redeveloped until the end of the Georgian phase (Daiches 1980: 225).

There were some modest additions to the residential stock of the Old Town, notably in the less-intensively-developed former independent ecclesiastical burgh of Canongate but the general cumulative trends in the Old Town were towards declining social status and, with increasing numbers of inhabitants, additional congestion and pressures upon an inadequate and insufficient supply of houses. Given that the Old Town also continued to perform the roles of the principal market area and industrial district, the scale of the problem was considerable. In the Canongate the tails of some of the narrow rectangular plots remained undeveloped but there were few vacant spaces accessible from the closes and wynds off the Lawnmarket and High Street.

Urban extension in the Georgian period swept aside the established medieval fixation line of the city walls. Much of the land to the north of the Old Town was converted from agricultural to urban use, although some unattractive and poorly organized urban-oriented functions did occupy the area subsequently bounded by Market Street, Princes Street and the North Bridge. To the south of the Old Town, expansion incorporated industrial and trading districts which had developed at extra-mural sites such as Bristo and Causewayside, in addition to extensive tracts of land devoted primarily to agricultural purposes.

(b) Glasgow

The Georgian phase of urban growth in Scotland was facilitated and promoted by a long-term improvement in the Scottish economy. This process originated in the seventeenth century but accelerated rapidly with the restoration of the political stability after the defeat of the 1745 Jacobite rebellion. Scotland may not have become reconciled to the Union but merchants were seizing on the opportunities offered by the expanded trading markets available to them, industry was growing and agricultural output increasing.

In many ways, the growth of Glasgow provided a striking testimony to the long-term upswing in the emerging urban-industrial economy of the nation. The narrow linear north-east to south-west alignment of the medieval burgh along the axis of High Street was transformed in the eighteenth century. A few additions were built on the eastern flank but the overwhelming focus of growth was towards the west. Although a few streets were laid out in the 1720s, the principal phase of extension dated from the 1750s. Gibb (1983: 73) found that there were strong similarities and contrasts in the approaches and experiences of public and private developers. Among the similarities were the use of the services of land surveyors, particularly one surveyor, James Barrie, to lay out the plots; preferences for the type of building to be erected and, frequently, a lengthy delay in attracting purchasers. Gibb identified the degree of rigour in the enforcement of specific building regulations and limitations on land use as the principal basis of contrast, with the private sector favouring less stringent measures than those adopted by the Council. As he noted, it is difficult to attribute precisely the respective contribution to this slowness of development of stringent regulations and temporal lack of demand for new plots. However, the experience in Glasgow may have caused the Council in Edinburgh to defer the imposition of strict conditions about the development of plots in the New Town until the project had been initiated. Certainly the evidence from Glasgow substantiates the thesis that Scottish cities experienced the diffusion of an innovation in the 1750s: namely, the laying out of broad new streets, essentially on grid plan – the difference in precise timing between Glasgow and Edinburgh being explained by the political opposition which the latter encountered from Midlothian interests.

In addition to a minor variation in timing, there was a more significant temporal and structural difference in the morphological outcomes of the new initiatives in the two cities. Because Glasgow was growing rapidly as a trading centre, one component of demand for plots in the new western suburb of the city came from industrialists and merchants seeking commercial premises. The coming of the Age of Cotton (Gibb 1983: 82–110; Gordon 1983) sharpened this process to such an extent that, by the 1820s, over 270 firms, of which four-fifths were involved in the textile industry, had invaded the streets between George Street and Argyle Street which had been laid out in the early Georgian period for select residential development (Gibb 1983: 93–4).

To the north of the repleted burgages of the old medieval core, new industrial developments arose around the terminus of the Monklands Canal and the Hamiltonhill basin of the Forth and Clyde Canal. To the east of the city, weaving districts emerged in the first half of the nineteenth century at Calton and Bridgeton. A third industrial zone flanked the Clyde in the vicinity of Broomielaw. Progressively this zone extended westwards on both sides of the river. Thus Glasgow acquired extensive areas of industrial premises, warehouses and workshops on a scale, and at a pace, far exceeding that experienced in Edinburgh (Gibb 1983: 91).

Yet, while industry spearheaded growth in certain quarters, the amount of select residential expansion was substantial. The release of large acreages previously held in trust or as private estates, which were at, or close to, the urban edge, facilitated this process. The development of the large Blythswood estate, crowned by Glasgow's most elegant Georgian setting, Blythswood Square, occurred towards the close of the period (1823–37) but between 1779 and 1815 forty-eight new streets were constructed on the north side of the Clyde (Gibb 1983: 95).

Adams has asserted that the

> important contribution of Georgian town planners to urban Scotland was their ability to look at problems in spatial terms. Once burghs had broken out of their medieval bounds, large areas of single land use appeared. At first upper-class residential suburbs were built, but these were often taken over by the central business district while the displaced residents had to renew their exclusive environment elsewhere. As transport systems improved, the whole process inevitably extended outwards, a process which accelerated with the rise of the industrial town. (Adams 1978: 85)

In essence, this description captured the basic ingredients of morphological change in the Georgian era, although, as has been illustrated, the detailed process was more complex. Hague has extended the argument with specific reference to Edinburgh's New Town which he attributed to the practice of a class which owned land and controlled finance and benefited most directly from the project. None the less, the New Town provided subsequent generations of planners with 'an inspiring definition of an idealized set of relationships between local politics, the market and the professional planner, an idealization proved in the most appealing way in practice by results on the ground' (Hague 1984: 135–7).

The Victorian city: 1831–1914

If the Georgian period was characterized by the growth of planned, select suburbs and the breaching of the medieval bounds of the burghs, what trends distinguished the Victorian period? A major force was the development of the railways and, later in the period, urban tramways. Intense competition between different railway companies led to a multiplicity of lines, sidings, depots and stations, effectively leading to a submergence of conscious town-planning (Hague 1984: 137). Yet, while the morphological impact of the railways was considerable, some measure of planning control was retained, both formally and, from the 1860s onwards, in practice. Indeed, the Improvement Acts of the 1860s and 1870s represented renewed attempts at formal planning but, in these instances, involved the redevelopment of overcrowded slums rather than the construction of select suburbs on greenfield sites. To that extent the proposals embodied in the various mid-Victorian Improvement Acts can reasonably be described as constituting a step towards socially-conscious planning. More generally, there were many attempts in the second half of the century, private and public, to address the issue of environmental problems in older, congested residential–industrial districts and to attend to the question of the quality and, subsequently, quantity of housing for the majority of urban residents.

There were also elements of continuity and change in relation to townscapes. The former was illustrated by the fact that some of the largest terraced dwellings were erected during the Victorian era at locations such as Park Circus in Glasgow and Drumsheugh Gardens in Edinburgh, whilst the latter found expression in the increasing popularity of the stone-built villa as a middle-class suburban residence and the predominance of the tenement in working-class districts. If spatial segregation of social classes was a characteristic feature of the transformation from the pre-capitalist to capitalist city, it can be argued that, thereafter, the process was furthered with an increasing fineness of social shadings (Gordon 1979).

It was during this period, too, that central business districts began to emerge as shops, offices, hotels and clubs occupied large Georgian terraced properties or as such properties were demolished and customized Victorian edifices erected in replacement. The High Streets of both Edinburgh and Glasgow ceased to be the principal shopping and business thoroughfares as Princes Street in Edinburgh, and Buchanan Street, Argyle Street and Sauchiehall Street in Glasgow, acquired new functional attributes.

There were also changes to the geography of industrial location in the cities. New firms sought sites suited to the current transport technology and the changing basis of production, whilst existing firms relocated in relation to these factors. In the case of service industries a major factor was the changing distribution of the urban population and, in particular, the relocation of the central business district. These processes were not uniquely Scottish but they were shaped by local, as well as national, contextual factors and the precise morphological outcomes often displayed a peculiarly Scottish component, most readily identified by distinctive building materials and forms.

(a) Transport developments and industry

The morphological impact of developments in transportation were several and varied. To a considerable degree, the differences were dependent upon the form of transportation. Thus the construction of docks in the Victorian era had a significant impact upon the urban form of the harbour at Leith and of particular riverside locations in Glasgow, such as at Partick and Govan. Associated service and industrial developments reinforced the distinctiveness of these marine-orientated townscapes. By contrast, the impact of the railways was more ubiquitous, often sectionalizing cities into districts or making boundaries between different uses of land. Equally, focal points in the railway network and concentrations of lines almost invariably became associated with industrial zones. Another dimension of the facilitating role of railways was illustrated by the way in which the construction of the suburban railway networks in Edinburgh and Glasgow in the last quarter of the nineteenth century initiated, fostered, or furthered, the extension of a number of middle-class suburbs and suburban villages such as at Corstorphine and Colinton in Edinburgh. Commonly, the suburban villa was the dominant dwelling type although in many cases there were higher density components, either terraced dwellings or high-quality tenements near the station, such as beside Trinity Station in northern Edinburgh, for example.

The introduction of the tramway system towards the close of the century facilitated urban commuting. Again there were various morphological consequences. The fact that the tramlines were laid along the streets of the cities had implications for road-building and design, and for traffic congestion. In many suburban districts it also produced a situation where tenements were constructed flanking the streets acting as routes for the tramways whilst villas or terraces were built at adjacent accessible, but more secluded, locations. Towards the end of the period, the various modes of urban transportation, including the water-buses, or cluthas, on the Clyde, played an increasingly important role in the functional life of the expanded Victorian city, not only conveying suburban residents to the city centre to work and shop, but also transporting workers to major industrial activities at peripheral sites.

Industry had a lesser presence in, and impact upon, Edinburgh than in Glasgow. The capital city was primarily the home of the professions although it was also the location of a number of skilled trades such as printing and publishing, and of several manufacturing industries, most notably brewing, distilling, rubber-making and some aspects of engineering. By comparison Victorian Glasgow had a virtual cornucopia of industry; textiles, tobacco manufacturing, iron founding, steel-making, shipbuilding, railway locomotive engineering and numerous aspects of marine and other branches of light and heavy engineering. Inevitably, therefore, industrial growth had a more widespread morphological influence in Glasgow, especially in the several major industrial districts which emerged during this period.

(b) The central business district

Notwithstanding the importance of industry to the physical and economic growth of Glasgow, the city also developed a large and flourishing supporting office sector which contributed significantly to the extension and alteration of the central business district during the Victorian period. Whitehand (1978), in a study of changes in the form of the city centre in Glasgow, found that Victorian redevelopment, which he dated between 1840 and 1894, was dominated by the shop and the warehouse. By comparison, in the ensuing Edwardian period (1895–1918) it was the warehouse, office and institutional areas which experienced the greatest amount of morphological change. In the Victorian phase with the exception of bank buildings, most offices occupied previous terraced residences. It was the main shopping streets which were the sites of large-scale redevelopment as specialized buildings designed as shops became increasingly fashionable. Whitehand found this phenomenon to be most apparent in Union Street, Jamaica Street, the southern portion of Buchanan Street, and the eastern section of Sauchiehall Street, all of which had only been occupied by commercial functions for a comparatively short period of time. Although considerable redevelopment also occurred in Argyle Street, it was on a lesser scale than in the streets listed above, a fact which may have been associated with the relatively extensive changes in that street in the Georgian period.

During the Edwardian period there was a marked boom in office building in central Glasgow, creating many of the distinctive properties which remain in use today. In part, the boom reflected the satisfaction of demand which may have built up during the economic depression of the 1880s. A structural shift in employment towards white-collar occupations doubtless contributed to the buoyancy of demand. Additionally, architectural and engineering innovations, most notably multi-storey office blocks and lifts, produced a new species of high density commercial building which introduced a distinctive component into the townscapes of the heart of the city.

Functional invasion and redevelopment also affected central Edinburgh. Princes Street, in particular, experienced considerable change with the construction of new shops, offices, clubs and hotels. New retail premises were erected in South Bridge and it was during this period that retailing became the dominant ground-floor use in many of the properties flanking the principal thoroughfares leading from the commercial core. Some towering Edwardian office blocks were built in the New Town and in adjoining districts but there was also a plentiful supply of elegant, readily-adapted, centrally-located large Georgian and Victorian terraced houses.

Both cities acquired sizeable new central land uses such as the major railway stations (four in Glasgow, two in Edinburgh) and, in the case of Glasgow, the massive Victorian edifice of the City Chambers which occupied the whole of the eastern frontage of George Square. Such redevelopment not only involved new buildings but, in many instances, changes to the pattern of building plots. In the case of the alterations enacted under the Improvement Acts in both cities, it also entailed alterations to the layout of the streets.

(c) Improvement Acts and housing

Largely as a result of the horrendous accounts of environmental conditions described by Dr Henry Littlejohn, Edinburgh's first Medical Officer of Health (Hague 1984: 145), the Town Council, in 1865, decided to take action and redevelop some of the more congested districts of the Old Town. Provost Chambers supported his own proposals, which modified a number of the morphological changes suggested by Littlejohn. One feature of the Provost's plan was the creation of improved access by the construction of new thoroughfares which transgressed the traditional alignment of the medieval burgage plots. The plans were put out to consultation and several professional, philanthropic and vested interest bodies supported the scheme. Opposition came from the ratepayers, particularly those in the New Town, who expressed concern about the potential cost of social reform. Parliament passed the Improvement Act in 1867, authorizing the Council to clear thirty-four areas, to develop new streets and widen existing ones, and to develop the remaining cleared land. No obligation was placed on the Council to rebuild housing, although it was given limited powers to find accommodation for families evicted by the process (Hague 1984: 148).

The final proposals, and the actual scheme, were strongly influenced by a concern for civic pride, although the original catalyst, the Littlejohn Report, had highlighted environmental and social issues. None the less, the work carried out under the Act affected several parts of the older central districts. One focus of attention was the eastern section of the High Street. Here St Mary's Wynd and Blackfriars Wynd were enlarged into wider modern streets, whilst on the northern flank of the hog-backed ridge a new diagonal street, Jeffrey Street, was constructed. Additional new streets which had been planned for this congested part of the Old Town were not developed but all of the new planned streets in other older districts did materialize. To the south of the Old Town, perhaps the most substantial changes were associated with the construction of Chambers Street, linking George IV Bridge to South Bridge. The plan for this area set the land aside for 'a superior class of buildings to those hitherto contemplated' (*The Builder* 1878). 'The main users were to be a government department (the Department of Science and Art, for a Museum of Industry), Edinburgh University, and the Watt Institute and School of Arts. Thus, what had originally appeared to be an exercise in sanitary reform was in fact an expensive scheme for improving traffic movement and catering for institutional space requirements' (Hague 1984: 149).

Slightly further to the south, new thoroughfares were also constructed at Marshall Street, Davie Street and Simon Street, and on the western flank of Lauriston ridge access was improved by demolishing seventy-five houses in Lady Lawson Wynd to produce the greatly widened Lady Lawson Street. Later, Patrick Geddes condemned the work of the Improvement Act as a process of dehousing. There was a net loss of houses in the redevelopment. Additionally, higher rents were charged for flats in the new tenements, putting them beyond the means of most of the displaced families and effectively contributing to an early form of gentrification.

The process in Edinburgh was, of course, not unique, save in relation to details. In Glasgow, in a similar manner, the 1866 Improvement Act led to extensive demolition of old tenements and the construction of thirty-nine new streets and numerous shops, warehouses and residences. As in Edinburgh, there was a succession of Improvement Acts in the mid and late Victorian period. In contrast to the particular pressures and interests affecting the plans in Edinburgh, in Glasgow it was the demand of the railway companies for access to central sites which profoundly influenced detailed redevelopment proposals, for example, around Glasgow Cross and also near the original site of Glasgow University in the High Street, although the primary outcomes were similar: population displacement, increased rents; widened streets; new commercial properties. Later, the Improvement Trust was involved in the redevelopment at other locations such as Gorbals village (Robb 1983) and in limited attempts to stimulate the construction of working-class housing on greenfield sites at Overnewton and Oatlands (Gibb 1983: 143).

Considerable changes affected the residential geography of the two cities during the Victorian period. Many large, centrally-located, Georgian terraced properties were subdivided into flats or converted to commercial uses. Extensive new suburbs were built with villas as the dominant dwelling type, although the terraced house never went out of fashion entirely and regained a measure of popularity towards the end of the century, perhaps in response to the rapid escalation in land prices. Legislation introduced minimal standards for housing and prompted a standardized design response in terms of 'basic' room and kitchen and two-apartment tenement flats. Apart from the work under the Improvement Acts, there were various attempts – philanthropic, private initiative and municipal – to construct 'improved' housing. One substantial example of the private initiative category was the product of the Edinburgh Co-operative Building Company. Over a period of more than thirty years the company built more than two thousand flats on various inner suburban sites within walking distances of industrial districts (Gordon 1984). Typically these flats were in narrow, two-storey stone-built blocks in which the lower flat was entered from one street and the upper flat from the adjacent row. Each flat had a tiny garden and the properties, which attracted skilled tradesmen and people in similar secure employment, were sold by installment (Gordon 1983). These properties provide an illustration of the complex residential morphology which was created over several decades. Each residential district was the product of the interaction of specific factors, influences and forces and normally each could be identified clearly, even if, on occasion, the distinguishing features were minor aspects of layout, architectural style or materials.

(d) The urban fringe

For much of the nineteenth century urban growth was limited to the immediate vicinity of the existing city, although that restriction was broken by the construction of the suburban railway routes. One consequence of the general trend was the fact that the Victorian urban fringe consisted of intrusive uses such as institutions and, latterly, recreational space, set amidst the predominant spread of city-orientated farms. This situation was particularly evident around Edinburgh (Strachan 1969) where the environs, not surprisingly, experienced a lesser degree of direct urbanization and industrialization than in Glasgow, set, as the latter was, at the heart of the burgeoning Clydeside conurbation. Within the cities some open spaces managed to resist the pressure for development in order to provide centrally-located recreational space such as Glasgow Green and The Meadows in Edinburgh.

The construction of substantial institutional buildings was a feature of the Victorian era. Whilst it was possible to create these by rebuilding on a developed site via an Improvement Scheme, as in the case of the Royal Scottish Museum in Edinburgh, there were obvious attractions in favour of the adoption of an undeveloped, or sparsely developed, site. An example of the latter process affected the Lauriston district in Edinburgh with the development of hospitals, schools and the Medical School of the University.

Cumulatively, the Victorian period produced a larger, more segregated and, in many ways, a more complex city. Whilst the processes described above were not peculiar to Scottish cities, the specific expressions in space and time were not only distinctive, but there were also important inter-city differences. By the close of the Victorian period, pre-Victorian Edinburgh accounted for less than a quarter of the urban area of the capital. At the start of the era, the social topography could justly be divided into Old Town and New Town but a third dimension had been added – suburban Edinburgh. The transformation in Glasgow was, if anything, more extensive. Such was the scale of expansion and growth that Glasgow at the dawn of the twentieth century vied for the title of Second City of the Empire.

The modern city: 1915–88

Knox has commented that, 'like cities of earlier times, the modern city can be seen as the product of changing economic organisation, reflecting the social relationships inherent to these changes, moulded by the prevailing means of transport, and continually reshaped by the public policies (or lack of them) and personal life-styles which stem from the dominant spirit of the age' (Knox 1987). In fact, these ingredients have varied significantly at different periods since 1914. Much of the energy of planners has been devoted to coping with the environmental aftermath (physical, social and economic) of the nineteenth century. Many new factors exercised important influences, not least new forms of transport which freed production from earlier locational constraints whilst simultaneously affording the possibility of a dramatic improvement in levels of personal mobility for a growing proportion of the population. Professional planning has established the guidelines for most of the physical and spatial changes which have affected the modern city, although the extent of control and the precise direction of policy have not been constant. Cumulatively, the morphological consequences of the processes of development, renewal, adaptation and conservation have been substantial.

Both cities have grown considerably in area since 1914 although much of the physical extension took place prior to 1945. Thereafter the prevailing philosophy has been one of urban containment through the mechanism of the preservation of a green belt around the effective limits of the inter-war city. Whilst collective action was predominant in the 1950s, 1960s and 1970s, it has been less important, or certainly has taken a modified form, in the 1980s. Some forms of collective action occurred in the inter-war years, most notably in connection with the newly-acquired role of local authorities as the primary, virtual sole, supplier of new housing for renting. Soon the sector also accepted the task of rehousing families displaced by redevelopment. The scale of change was most marked in Glasgow where the proportion of the total housing stock accounted for by this sector grew from around 2 per cent to over sixty per cent in the span of six decades.

(a) Housing

In both Edinburgh and Glasgow, after 1918, the local authority estate came into being. Initially this consisted of flatted villas in gardened suburbs but by the mid 1930s the modern version of the tenement block regained dominance. The 1960s heralded the age of the tower block. The 1970s witnessed greater diversification of house type whilst, subsequently, new peripheral construction in this sector virtually ceased as the emphasis shifted in the late 1970s towards rehabilitation, or selective renewal, of inner-city, Victorian tenement districts.

National and local governments played important roles in the development of this sector of housing supply. The former established the legislative parameters, willed the means, set the priorities and offered specific advice about suitable locations for development and designs of buildings (Gordon 1984). The latter translated these measures into action. It has been demonstrated (Butt 1983) that important variations occurred in the detailed responses by local authorities, indicating that decision-making at that level was influenced by local factors, perceptions, traditions and attitudes. None the less, some common trends can be discerned, most notably the construction of large tracts of local authority housing, frequently, after the mid 1930s, in a somewhat utilitarian style. Typical examples of such local authority estates are the districts of Easterhouse, Castlemilk and Drumchapel in Glasgow and Craigmillar, Pilton and Wester Hailes in Edinburgh.

Growth occurred in a cyclical and spatially differential manner in the privately-occupied sector. During the inter-war years there were periods of standstill and of frenzied activity in this sector in Scottish cities. Cheap money and modest prices stimulated the market for bungalows in the 1930s to such an extent that one of the major building firms, MacTaggart and Mickel, managed to sell 134 bungalows within twenty-four hours in 1930 (McKean 1987). Substantial bungalow districts were constructed, normally consisting of a very small range in styles of design and variations in layout. An important difference between the two cities was that a considerable proportion of bungalow construction occurred in surrounding suburban communities rather than within the boundaries of Glasgow whereas, in the capital, development primarily took place within the legal confines of the burgh.

In the second half of the 1930s a further distinctive component was added in the form of estates of flatted villas for renting at a fixed sum over a set term. The development of these gardened suburbs resulted from government pressure upon local authorities to extend the range of available suburban housing options, in order to stimulate house-building, promote the private sector and introduce an additional means of reducing large, and growing, lists of families awaiting rehousing from older districts. When the set term expired, the occupants of these houses had restricted inheritable rights of transfer of rented occupancy. Thereafter the rights to the property reverted to the developer who offered the houses for sale. Now the majority of these flatted villas are owner-occupied.

(b) City-centre change

It is tempting to dismiss many of the products of twentieth-century architecture but that would be both sweeping and unjust. The period has attracted considerable criticism such as the view that Edwardian grandeur was replaced by 'something mechanical and charmless' to be followed in turn by 'the naked bogey of modern architecture' (McWilliams 1975: 176–7). Classicism dominated in the prestige buildings of the inter-war years although there were many interesting examples of Art Deco: in Glasgow,

> two of the best-known being Montague Burton's premises at the corner of Argyle Street and Buchanan Street (designed by a Leeds architect, Harry Wilson) and James Templeton and Company's colourful factory extension facing Glasgow Green (George Boswell, 1936) but Glasgow Art Deco mainly consisted of cafés, pubs, restaurants and shops – consumer Art Deco which did much to brighten up the Depression-stricken city. (McKenna 1985)

There were also modest attempts, in the late 1930s, to rediscover a more distinctly Scottish style, a phase fostered by the Saltire Society and by the work of Frank Mears and others.

Modernism was offered the opportunity of a promotional showground with the decision to hold the 1938 Empire Exhibition in Glasgow at Bellahouston Park. The Empire Exhibition was, of course, primarily intended to project a positive view of the Scottish economy and provide a boost to the Depression-bruised morale of industrial Scotland. Amongst the initiatives introduced in the mid 1930s was the construction of industrial estates such as Hillington, intended to attract modern light industries to new, spacious, single-storey buildings at suburban locations. This formal, and largely successful, response to the ills debilitating the Scottish industrial economy was greatly extended in the post-war period. In terms of spatial trends, the initiative merely recognized, organized and fostered an existing process, namely the decentralization and dispersion of industrial locations in cities. Abandonment of substantial centrally-located industrial sites was relatively rare in the inter-war period but it became increasingly characteristic of urban change in the 1960s, 1970s and 1980s.

Whitehand (1978) observed that economic conditions in the inter-war period in Glasgow (and it could be argued also in Edinburgh) permitted separate investigation of the effects of innovation from those of economic growth. He argued that particularly important innovations, causing redevelopment of central sites, were department and variety stores and cinemas. Whitehand found that the adoption of retailing innovations was localized within the city centre in existing shopping areas but the construction of customized cinemas involved a greater variety of locations and functional displacement. New uses such as bus stations, garages, car showrooms and telephone exchanges caused redevelopment, often at sites near the periphery of the city centre but, in general, there were comparatively low rates of central development in the inter-war period (Sim 1982: 18).

(c) Planning

Reference was made earlier to the important role played by planning in the post-war years, in shaping, controlling and guiding both the policies and details of urban change. Major planning surveys, such as the Clyde Valley Plan, and those for Central and South East Scotland, and for Edinburgh, commissioned during the Second World War, along with national planning legislation enacted in the immediate post-war years, established the climate for most of the collective action in the ensuing three decades. Not every recommendation in the plans was adopted or implemented. Moreover many proposals were reshaped in detail in the light of changing circumstances, perception, practices and preferences. None the less, these differing plans and the major pieces of planning legislation had a powerful impact upon the direction and nature of subsequent urban development and redevelopment. Central tenets of the new age were the redevelopment of poor quality residential environments, the creation of orderly patterns of non-conflicting land use, the creation of attractive new environments and the containment and organization of urban growth.

Both cities were affected by these policies, even though the detailed outcomes differed significantly, because of differences in the scale of inherited problems, in local politics and traditions and in the subsequent influence of economic, social and spatial forces.

In Glasgow, the primary focus of change in the immediate post-war years was the provision of new houses near the periphery of the city and the policy of arranging the overspill of population both to the New Towns and to other urban settlements. However, an integral part of the strategy was the clearance and redevelopment of the older congested central districts. In the 1950s Glasgow declared twenty-nine comprehensive development areas. In fact, the redevelopment process only occurred in some of these areas but in them, morphological change was extensive as townscapes were demolished and new urban landscapes constructed. Whilst many of the problems promoting these changes were shared by Edinburgh, the latter did not implement a policy of widespread comprehensive redevelopment. Substantial clearance occurred in a section of the South Side and in Central Leith but, with these exceptions, renewal in the capital, both planned and effected, was at a more modest spatial scale.

Suburbanization and decentralization continued to affect other land uses. To varying degrees industry, retailing, wholesaling, warehousing, services, institutions and recreation progressively succumbed to these pressures. Innovations played a role in the form of phenomena such as planned suburban shopping centres, self-service supermarkets and stores, garden centres and riding schools. Peripheral sites offered more space (normally at lower unit costs), greater ease in adopting new layouts and reduced congestion.

(d) Conservation and redevelopment

Notwithstanding these trends, the pressure upon the city centre, and the need for change, has increased. To a considerable degree it has been caused by the growing importance of the service sector in the urban and national economy. Edinburgh, in particular, has gained from these trends which have fostered substantial growth of the office sector and also of tourist-related activities. Further invasion and conversion of central properties has occurred in response to these trends but there has also been new development. In relation to offices, much of the recent constructional activity has been situated around the periphery of the New Town and Old Town Conservation Areas but the apparent success of a speculative venture near the western edge may herald more sustained development of similar locations.

Significantly, the conservation policy in both cities attaches considerable importance to morphology, normally seeking to restrict further damage to the pattern of plots, limit conversion of use and exercise detailed control over proposals to alter almost any aspect of the external appearance of buildings. With a combined total of more than forty conservation areas these measures affect substantial sections of the historic townscapes of Edinburgh and Glasgow.

Perhaps inevitably, changes have altered historic townscapes. Alterations to facade, both minor and major, have taken place, including changes to a number of properties in conservation areas. Redevelopment has produced sharp discontinuities. An example of the later process has been the demolition of large Victorian villas in areas such as Grange or Merchiston in Edinburgh with replacement by blocks of high-quality flats.

Substantial changes have taken place in several parts of the city centre in Glasgow. There has been considerable redevelopment in the principal shopping streets with the construction of new stores and new shopping centres, replacing outdated uses such as department stores, cinemas and theatres. The site of St Enoch's Station and Hotel has been cleared and a new shopping centre, incorporating office and other uses, is nearing completion. On the northern periphery an extensive educational and institutional zone has been created. The Princes Square shopping centre has been developed off Buchanan Street, whilst on the western flank, several new office blocks and hotels have been built. Indeed, the period since around 1960 has been characterized by the extent both of detailed and of large-scale morphological change.

In Edinburgh corresponding changes have affected the central area including the construction of the St James shopping centre, hotel and office complex at the eastern flank of the New Town, Waverley Market has been converted into a shopping centre, Rose Street has been invaded by shops and other services activities and the abandoned railway goods yard at Lothian Road used as the site for a major hotel.

Attempts to preserve a green zone around the cities have suffered setbacks. Commonly, major incursions arise from planning appeals, inquiries, and the ultimate authorization by the Secretary of State. Whilst such powers are used sparingly, several of the intrusions have been substantial: for example, in Edinburgh, the local authority housing at Wester Hailes, the Riccarton campus of Heriot-Watt University and Edinburgh Airport. These decisions, combined with the inherent attractiveness of sites on the western periphery of the city with good access to transport routes, suggest that further development of the preserved fringe-belt is likely. The policy of urban containment inevitably increased the value of remaining undeveloped sites. Development was not impeded in a period of buoyant demand but the exact character and form was affected. Generally, these pressures led to higher density or higher-value outcomes than might otherwise have occurred.

Recently there has been a marked revival of centripetal forces, most notably in Glasgow. The fortunes of the declining Merchant City have been revived through the conversion of warehouses and other commercial buildings to modernized residences, the construction of new houses on cleared sites and the attraction of supporting and complementary services. Similarly, riverside locations have experienced revived fortunes with the infilling of docks and the demolition of sheds to make way for the Scottish Exhibition Centre, new housing and, temporarily, the site for the Garden Festival. Now pressures are mounting for office and industrial development on neighbouring portions of the south side of the Clyde.

In Edinburgh, similar processes of gentrification, economic revival and urban renewal have affected parts of the Old Town. In the New Town districts, basement (or garden) flats have enjoyed a new lease of life (partly due to the availability of improvement grants) and mews properties have been converted to residential use, whilst riverside locations in Leith have been affected by similar developments to those in equivalent locations in Glasgow. In aggregate both cities have experienced modest, but growing, counter-centrifugal processes within the last twenty years.

For much of this century the dominant processes have favoured outward expansion and the decentralization of existing activities, often involving the destruction, or neglect, of older centrally-located townscapes. That process advanced further in Glasgow than in Edinburgh but even in the former a reversal of fortunes intervened before much of the historic morphology was destroyed. Both cities retain substantial morphological components, or partial townscapes, dating from the Georgian and Victorian eras. Many changes have affected both cities in the modern era, yet they remain places of architectural interest and economic importance, of considerable centrality despite decentralization, with a complex morphology stemming from the detailed interplay of the inertial forces of inheritance and the modern pressures for change. The explosion of collective action through planning in the post-war era was biased in favour of change; more recently, the emphasis has shifted with conservation of townscape and of other morphological components and the rehabilitation of buildings receiving wider professional and economic support. Further swings of the pendulum may occur in the future but it is unlikely to revert to the planning ethos of the 1950s.

Conclusion

Elsewhere, the author has advocated the articulation and testing of a conceptual framework for urban morphology which could accommodate the various approaches to the subject (Gordon 1984), notably the Conzenian tradition (Whitehand 1981; 1987), Whitehand's innovation – constructional activity – townscape interactions (Whitehand 1977), and studies which emphasize decision-making (Carter 1970; Gordon 1981).

This chapter was not designed to develop fresh theories or new conceptual insights. Instead it has sought to examine the varying spatial and temporal influences of processes and agents of morphological change in the context of Scottish cities. A wide-ranging analysis has been adopted to accommodate strands from various analytical traditions in an attempt to extend the treatment of complex inter-relationships of factors and causative forces. Most studies seek a dominating, though not exclusive, organizational force or process. That would have been inappropriate in the present context but an important ingredient of the analysis has been the discussion of the changing influences of three levels of spatial scale: Scottish; British and international; local or city-specific. Given the multi-functional nature of morphological change it was perhaps unlikely that definitive answers could be provided in respect of the precise weighting of each component in every situation. Instead, the goal of the chapter has been to provide a discussion of these relationships and an airing of the thesis that a distinctive, if elusive, Scottish dimension played a significant part in the story.

Scotland is more than a region of the United Kingdom. It was for many centuries an independent country, it has a distinct cultural tradition, it retains many separate institutions (e.g. the Scottish legal system and the Church of Scotland) and separate Scottish orders (as well as branches) of many professions. Collectively, these agents and forces introduce an additional component which, it is argued, must be addressed if the student of urban form is to achieve a rounded understanding of the morphology of Scottish cities.

References

Adams, I. H., 1978. *The making of urban Scotland.*

Builder, The, 1878. *36*: 1004.

Butt, J., 1983. 'Working class housing in Scottish cities 1900–1950', in *Scottish urban history*, eds. G. Gordon and B. Dicks, 233–67.

Carter, H., 1970. 'A decision-making approach to town plan analysis: a case study of Llandudno', in *Urban essays: studies in the geography of Wales*, eds. H. Carter and W. K. Davies, 66–77.

Cuthbert, M., 1986. 'The concept of province and metropolis in British town planning', in *Regional cities of the UK: 1890–1980*, ed. G. Gordon, 233–42.

Daiches, D., 1980. *Edinburgh.*

Gibb, A., 1983. *Glasgow – the making of a city.*

Gordon, G., 1979. 'The status areas of early to mid-Victorian Edinburgh', *Transactions, Institute of British Geographers, N.S.4*: 168–91.

Gordon, G., 1981. 'The historico-geographic explanation of urban morphology: a discussion of some Scottish evidence', *Scottish Geographical Magazine, 97*: 16–26.

Gordon, G., 1983a. 'Industrial development, c.1750–1980', in *An historical geography of Scotland*, ed. G. Whittington and I. D. Whyte, 165–90.

Gordon, G., 1983b. 'The status areas of Edinburgh in 1914', in Gordon and Dicks (eds.), *op. cit.*, 168–96.

Gordon, G., 1984. 'The shaping of urban morphology', *Urban History Yearbook*, 1–10.

Gordon, G. (ed.), 1985. *Perspectives of the Scottish city.*

Gray, R. Q., 1976. *The labour aristocracy in Victorian Edinburgh.*

Hague, C., 1984. *The development of planning thought.*

Keating, M., 1988. *The city that refused to die.*

Knox, P., 1987. *Urban social geography.*

Mackintosh, C. R., 1891. 'Scotch baronial architecture', Hunterian Museum Archive, F (c).

McKean, C., 1987. *The Scottish thirties.*

McKenna, R., 1985. *Glasgow Art Deco.*

McWilliams, C., 1975. *Scottish townscape.*

Purves, G., 1988. 'The life and work of Sir Frank Mears', (Ph.D. thesis, Heriot-Watt University).

Robb, J., 1983. 'Suburb and slum in Gorbals', in Gordon and Dicks (eds.), *op. cit.*, 130–67.

Rodger, R., 1979. 'The law and urban change', *Urban History Yearbook*: 77–91.

Rodger, R., 1983. 'The evolution of Scottish planning', in Gordon and Dicks (eds.), *op. cit.*, 71–91.

Rodger, R., 1986. 'The Victorian building industry and the housing of the Scottish working class', in *Building the industrial city*, ed. M. Doughty, 152–206.

Sim, D., 1982. *Change in the city centre.*

Skinner, B. C., 1979. 'Edinburgh 1750–1850: Georgian city', in *Looking at Lothian*, ed. J. B. Barclay, 56.

Strachan, A. J., 1969. 'The rural urban fringe of Edinburgh: 1850–1967' (Ph.D. thesis, Edinburgh University).

Walker, F., 1985. 'National romanticism and the architecture of the city', in Gordon (ed.), *op. cit.*, 125–59.

Wannop, U., 1986. 'Glasgow/Clydeside: a century of metropolitan evolution', in *Regional cities of the UK*, ed. G. Gordon, 83–98.

Whitehand, J. W. R., 1977. 'The basis of an historico-geographic theory of urban form', *Transactions, Institute of British Geographers, N.S.2*: 400–16.

Whitehand, J. W. R., 1978. 'Long term changes in the form of the city centre: the case of redevelopment', *Geografiska Annaler, 60B*: 79–96.

Whitehand, J. W. R., 1981. 'Background to the urban morphogenetic tradition', in *The urban landscape: historical development and management, papers by* M. R. G. *Conzen*, ed. J. W. R. Whitehand [Institute of British Geographers, Special Publication, 13], 1–24.

Whitehand, J. W. R., 1987. 'M. R. G. Conzen and the intellectual parentage of urban morphology', *Planning History Bulletin*, 9: 35–41.

Wordsall, F., 1979. *The tenement, a way of life.*

Youngson, A. J. 1966. *The making of Classical Edinburgh.*

11 Municipal housing in Vienna between the wars

Elisabeth Lichtenberger

The status of social housing programmes in the various urban regions of the world varies widely according to the prevailing political systems and traditions of residential building. Taken to extremes, the range of possibilities stretches from the social housing programme of the United States federal government to the housing programmes of the state capitalist systems. In the latter case the housing forms part of the social infrastructure, financed out of internal revenue and fulfilling a function of social integration, that is, a redistributive function. In the first case, the USA, the intention is to provide programmes of help for the poorest of the poor. The strict and regularly-checked income limits determine eligibility for this housing, ensuring that the more enterprising and upwardly-mobile population groups are filtered out so that, in general, only economically marginal groups and a variety of anti-social elements remain. The legal requirement that the construction costs for this housing may not exceed 50 per cent of comparable costs in the private housing construction sector is an important aggravating factor in the undesirability and the social and physical problems of this type of housing.

In this broad field of widely varying socio-political and architectural solutions, the municipal housing programme of the Vienna City Council between the two world wars occupies a special place. This chapter presents a summary of the author's research on Vienna's municipal housing for this period based on surveys of all the construction plans, of official planning publications and internal communications within the council, and of field survey. The bibliography at the end of the chapter provides a wider setting for this research in the context of municipal housing provision in the German-speaking world.

The political and socio-economic background

The development of Vienna in the inter-war period was overshadowed by the fall of the Austro-Hungarian Empire. After the Treaty of St Germain, Vienna changed from the capital of an empire of 50 million people, the largest country after Russia in pre-war Europe, to the 'swollen head' of a small country with not quite seven million inhabitants. This capital, with its varied historical, national, cultural and economic relationships, was a sort of foreign object in the Austrian political landscape now dominated by the aspirations of small settlements; furthermore, the ideals and political dominance of the social-democratic Vienna City Council were rejected by the largely conservative Austrian population.

The consequences of the breakdown of the old social and economic order can scarcely be imagined by those who did not experience the events. The general impoverishment of Vienna's population affected not only the nobility, whose estates were now located in the succession states, nor just those with financial and investment interests in those same lands, but also large numbers of the bourgeoisie – civil servants and army officers who returned to Vienna from the far-flung reaches of the empire without any means of supporting themselves. Unemployment was extremely high: in 1934 more than 25 per cent of the working population were unemployed, and among industrial workers the figure had reached 37 per cent. The majority of the tertiary sector was bankrupt as a result of the loss of Vienna's role as a financial, administrative and commercial centre. Furthermore, the effects of the Depression were greatly intensified in a city whose industrial sector specialized in the production of sophisticated consumer goods. Given this background, it is difficult to understand how a housing shortage could arise in a city whose population catchment area had been drastically reduced by the new political division and whose population, following the return of substantial numbers of non-German-speaking nationals to the succession states, had fallen from 2,275,000 in 1915 to 1,842,000 in 1919 and stood at 1,874,000 in 1934.

An understanding of the reasons for this housing shortage, and of the housing requirements in Vienna between the wars, leads directly to more general questions about the urban housing requirements of any society during industrialization and in the post-industrial period. The development of such housing requirements can generally be described as passing through a series of partly overlapping stages with varying parameters. These stages are: first, a period of general population growth; secondly, a reduction in the size of households, and consequently an increase in the number of households; and thirdly, rising expectations concerning living-space. The situation in Vienna between the two world wars corresponded to the second stage.

A comparison between the structure of households in Vienna in the inter-war period and that prevailing during the *Gründerzeit* (the period of rapid population growth and economic development in the late-nineteenth and early-twentieth centuries), reveals the following differences:

- a reduction in the number of persons not belonging to the family;
- a reduction in the number of servants;
- a reduction in the number of commercial and industrial employees

(apprentices, etc.) living in employers' households;
a reduction in the number of children.

These factors led to a decrease in the average size of households from 4·3 in 1910 to only 3·0 in 1934. A correspondingly large increase in the number of households, from 479,000 (1910) to 631,000 (1934), resulted in a substantial housing shortage and provided the impetus for the new building activity of this period. Additionally, the numerous children of the *Gründerzeit*-period immigrants to Vienna created new households in the 'marriage boom' of the post-war years, making further heavy demands on the housing market. Finally, the impoverishment of the upper and middle classes resulted in a greatly reduced demand for large, and even for middle-sized, apartments. At the same time, the expectations of new, young households were essentially based on traditional patterns of housing, which included a predominance of small apartments. This point is particularly relevant in that it played a decisive role in determining the nature of subsequent council building activity.

The collapse of the capitalist housing market

In order to protect the families of serving soldiers, practically all countries involved in the First World War introduced legal protection for tenants, generally in the form of rent restriction and limitation of the landlord's right to give notice to quit. The first such regulation in Austria was introduced in 1917. At the same time a housing department was established to enable the council to gain a picture of the number, size and occupation levels of the existing housing. While other European countries gradually repealed these tenant protection regulations in the course of the inter-war years, Austria's temporary measure became permanent. The Vienna housing market in particular was fundamentally affected.

The *Wohnungsanforderungsgesetz* (Housing Control Act) was passed in 1919. It empowered local councils to dispose of vacated apartments with more than three rooms. More than 44,000 apartments, representing some 8 per cent of the then housing stock in Vienna, had been allocated in this way by 1925, using an extremely complicated points system.

The regulations protecting tenants were converted into an Act of Parliament in 1922 – the *Mieterschutzgesetz* (Protection of Tenants Act). This new law severely limited the right of landlords to give notice, and froze all rents at a level of 150 times the rent paid in August 1914. Given the massive inflation prevailing at this time (before the currency reform of 1924, when the schilling was introduced, the krone had plummeted to 1/14,400 of its value at the end of the war), rent subsequently played no more than a nominal role in the composition of the family budget. The introduction of this *Mieterschutzgesetz* represented a complete about-face from the principles and structure of the *laissez-faire* housing market of the *Gründerzeit*. Two consequences followed: first, the construction of tenement houses was one of the chief economic activities of bourgeois circles during the *Gründerzeit* period, owing to the excellent financial return. The income so produced was sufficient to enable around half of all house-owners to live comfortably. Reinvestment in repairs and maintenance went without saying, since the amount of rental they could charge depended on the condition of the house. As a result of the *Mieterschutzgesetz* the building of private tenement houses became completely unprofitable, existing houses ceased to produce any meaningful return, and necessary repairs remained unattended to. Secondly, tenants had been extremely mobile during the *Gründerzeit*. In the years immediately preceding the First World War practically one third, and in working-class districts around a half, of all tenants moved flats every year. After the *Mieterschutzgesetz* the housing market became petrified, with the annual mobility rate dropping below 2 per cent.

This immobilization of the population led to further consequences; in particular, there was an increase in commuting, since a change in workplace or occupation no longer implied a change in the place of residence as well. The widespread *Gründerzeit* custom of walking to work was replaced by the use of public transport. Similarly, changes in the size of the family no longer led to a change of apartment. The effect of this on the internal spatial organization of the city was to prevent any tendency towards widespread social segregation. In large and middle-sized apartments the impoverished members of the nobility and middle class could be found, often supporting themselves by sub-letting now that their apartments were too large for the changed social and economic conditions. On the other hand, it ceased to be necessary for ordinary people (as it had been during the *Gründerzeit*) at least partly to cover the cost of their rent through sub-letting or taking in *Bettgeher* (persons who rented a bed rather than a whole room). In this way the sub-letting of apartments changed from being characteristic of the working-class districts of the city to characterizing the middle-class districts. Finally, as a result of the freezing of rent levels, a custom of demanding 'key-money' from incoming tenants rapidly developed as a form of capitalization of the rental. Landlord, property manager and lessor all participated in the system which, although illegal, rapidly became institutionalized.

The land, tax and housing policies of the council

The elimination of private capital necessitated the financing of new housing construction out of public funds. The social democrats, who soon gained control of the city council after the introduction of universal suffrage in 1908, made social housing provision the first plank of their programme, taking precedence over all other investment areas. This concentration on housing construction, to the exclusion of everything else, was only possible owing to the extensive provision of technical service infrastructure, both in the nineteenth century, and particularly under Mayor Lueger. His municipal socialism in the immediate pre-war period had seen the construction of a system of water mains, sewers, gas and electricity supply systems. The social infrastructure (schools, hospitals, etc.) was also extensively developed. The housing construction policy of the municipal administration cannot, however, be seen simply in isolation. Rather it was part of a policy package which was summarized by the catchwords 'a new land policy – a new tax system – a new housing policy'.

This is not the place for a general discussion of the history of the land policies of the Vienna city council. However, the decisive change in policy can be pinpointed as occurring in 1912. The council then decided that no more council land should be sold off, and that the council should instead pursue a policy of increasing the amount of land in its possession. Ever since, this new policy has been energetically pursued, and land was purchased from the impoverished landed classes such as religious foundations, the landed gentry, and industrial entrepreneurs. By 1926, the land in the possession of the city council amounted to 6,689 ha., around one quarter of metropolitan area at that time.

Another important factor in the development of new settlements on the city periphery was the simultaneous introduction of a right to build, such as that which played a major role in the English-speaking world. Public bodies were thereby empowered to lease building land to private interests on long-term leaseholds which could not be terminated by the lessor. The prospective developer obtained the right, against payment of a previously determined rental, to develop the land, to raise mortgages, and to will or sell the land which, on the expiry of the lease, after anything from thirty to eighty years, subsequently reverted to the owner against compensation.

In the light of these changes in housing and infrastructure policies, the existing finance and taxation system proved unworkable. Even in 1913 the council had derived some 45–50 per cent of its revenue from the rent tax levied on house owners; a further 20 per cent from taxes on municipal services such as water, gas and electricity supplies; 11–12 per cent from consumer taxes on the sale of meat and various other products; and only 15 per cent from trade and income taxes. A basic change in financial policy therefore proved to be necessary. The resulting system has passed into history as the 'Breitner tax system', named after its inventor. Two new taxes were introduced: the residential building tax, levied on tenants, and the payroll tax, levied on employers. Around 40 per cent of the cost of the housing construction programme was covered out of the proceeds of these taxes; the remainder was financed out of general revenue. During the inter-war years the council devoted some 25–30 per cent of its budget to housing construction, a proportion that has never since been equalled.

With the introduction of the residential building tax in 1923 came a period of intensive building activity. In the same year the council approved

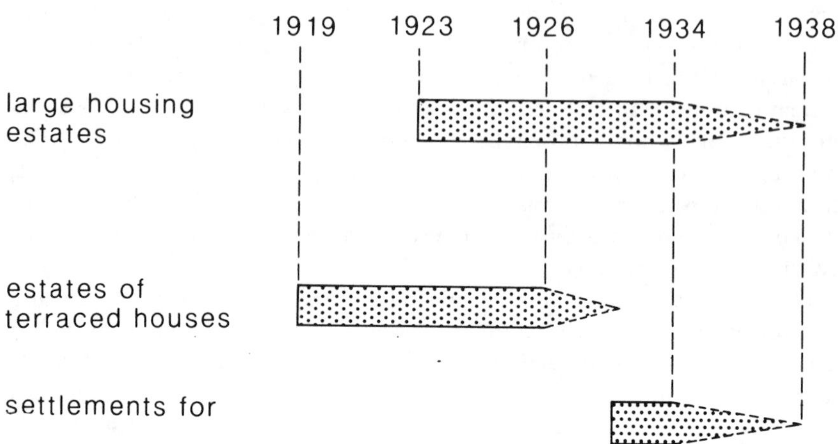

Figure 11.1 Timescale and categories of council building activity in Vienna

a five-year programme for the construction of 25,000 flats. By 1934 the council had built a total of 63,070 flats, of which 54,150 were in multi-storey buildings and 5,917 in garden estates. This very respectable achievement nevertheless failed to equal the extent of housing construction in the late *Gründerzeit*. In the period between the wars a total of around 91,200 flats were built in the Vienna metropolitan area, representing an average of less than 5,000 per year. The only year in which the average of the *Gründerzeit* years was reached was 1926, when 10,000 units were built. Council building represented 70 per cent of the total housing construction.

The time-scale, location and major categories of the council's building activity are shown on Figure 11.1. It can be seen that the terrace-house estates, financed by the building societies, dominated the period immediately after the war until 1923 when this co-operative housing movement was taken over by the council. By the end of the twenties building activity on the urban periphery had almost ceased by comparison with that to be found in the already densely-settled city areas. Not until the thirties did the peripheral area again experience a similar, though much more land-intensive, style of building. Then, following German examples, settlements were built on sufficiently large lots for small-scale market-gardening and the keeping of small livestock. It can thus be seen that municipal housing construction in the inter-war years went from the one extreme of large housing estates in densely-built city areas, to the other extreme of relatively spacious settlements on the then undeveloped areas on the outskirts of the city.

Apartment-house estates

There is a long tradition of large courtyard houses in Vienna. They provide

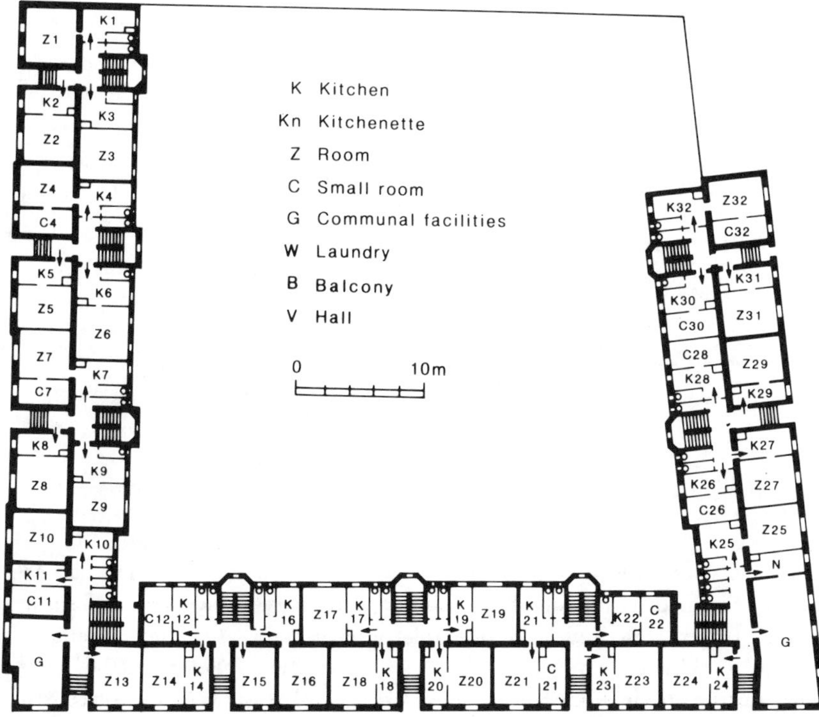

Figure 11.2 *Lobmeyerhof* of the Emperor Franz-Josef I Jubilee Foundation, Vienna

a nearly perfect example for the application of the cultural and historical theory of the handing-down of cultural traditions to increasingly lower social classes. The tradition began with courtyard houses of the eighteenth century. These occupied the sites of the former dairy yards which had supplied the city with milk. The landlords were large religious foundations, the tenants senior and middle-ranking civil servants working in the newly-established bureaucracy of the absolutist state. During the *Gründerzeit*, Vienna, in contrast to other cities, lacked developers with the necessary financial means to build apartment courts, and the construction of large courtyard houses was restricted to a handful of examples. Only towards the end of the *Gründerzeit*, in 1898, did a sufficiently well-capitalized institution come into being. This was the Emperor Franz-Josef I Jubilee Foundation for People's Housing and Welfare Facilities, founded at the instigation of upper- and upper-middle-class social reformers.

The choice of location, the dimensions and the fabric of the buildings which this organization erected anticipated the council housing of the inter-war period in many ways. The 'Lobmeyerhof', a large courtyard house built in the 16th district of Vienna (since demolished), provides a good example (Fig. 11.2). Around a central courtyard containing a children's playground

Table 11.1 Council housing constructed 1919–38, classified by the number of flats per development (including settlements on the periphery)

Number of flats per development	Number of developments
Up to 50	121
51–100	78
101–200	93
201–500	59
501–1000	13
1001 and more	7
Total	371

and lawns were situated 480 flats on sixteen staircases. The small flats were mostly planned as independent units with their own lavatory and running water. This represented a considerable improvement over the 'Bassena' flats in the working-class tenement houses during the *Gründerzeit* (the bassena was the tap in the corridor from which the inhabitants had to fetch their water). The provision of communal facilities – bathrooms, a laundry, a lecture-hall and library, a doctor's surgery – and the improved equipment of the flats themselves, all provided a model for subsequent council housing.

This link between the council housing of the inter-war years and the courtyard-house tradition must be particularly stressed, since the 'average' tenement house in Vienna during the *Gründerzeit* was of comparatively modest dimensions compared to those in other European cities with more than a million inhabitants, particularly Berlin. In Vienna, such houses rarely contained more than fifty apartments in the inner districts, nor more than twenty in the outer districts. Table 11.1 shows that council housing followed a quite different pattern.

The largest of these estates clearly approached the concept of 'neighbourhood', as propagated by the English garden-city movement. Of the seven housing estates containing more than a thousand flats, the 'Sandleitenhof' in Ottakring (1,587 flats) and the 'Karl Marx-Hof' in Heiligenstadt (1,325 flats) are worthy of particular mention (Fig. 11.3). In town plan terms these enormous developments could no longer be accommodated in the grid-like street layout stemming from the *Gründerzeit*, and such an integration was not sought. The buildings did, however, still respect the height levels established at that time. On the other hand, the wide facades blocked off cross-streets and the alignments formed a border between the edge of the densely-built city area and the outskirts of the metropolitan area. In the

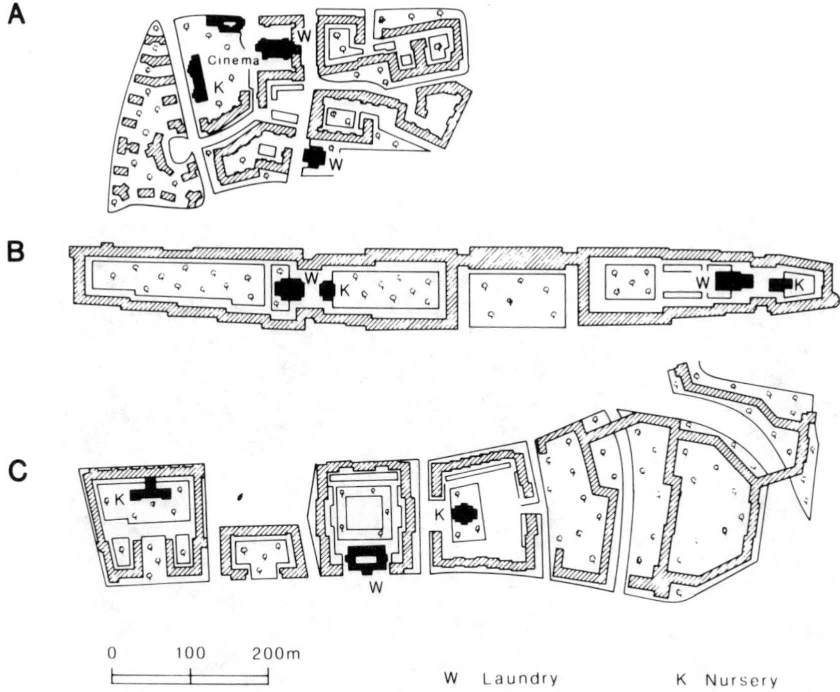

Figure 11.3 The development of the plans of municipal superblocks during the inter-war period. (A. Sandleitenhof B. Karl Marx-Hof C. Washington Hof)

final analysis, this was the symbolic expression in bricks and mortar of a political consciousness of power that took its dimensions from the public buildings of the imperial capital. The commonly-employed description of these buildings as 'residential citadels' is both architecturally and politically justified, as can be seen from the fact that they were widely used as social-democratic strongholds in the civil war of 1934.

The ground-plans of these housing estates developed in three stages (Fig. 11.3). The first developments were related to the street- courtyards of the late *Gründerzeit* (e.g. Sandleitenhof (Fig 11.4); later came the linking of various sections in the style of terraced housing around large inner courtyards (e.g. Karl Marx-Hof) and finally groups of buildings separated by lawns, in a way which anticipated the decline of terraced house construction after the Second World War.

In spite of the frequent independence and individuality of the ground-plans and elevations of these estates, there was no genuine functional separation with respect to the provision of shops and services in the council estates of this period. This did not become common until after 1945. The economically-determined policy of the inter-war years of building on empty sites in the developed areas of the city meant that the inhabitants of council

Figure 11.4 Air view of the Sandleitenhof, Ottakring, Vienna

houses generally had no difficulty in making use of the existing shops and services in the long-established districts of the city. The provision of social-infrastructure facilities was modelled on that of the earlier Jubilee Foundation apartment courtyard houses of the *Gründerzeit*.

It was precisely this provision of social facilities which was internationally praised and imitated. The size of the flats, on the other hand, attracted both contemporary and later criticism. However, this criticism was only partly justified in the light of the socio-economic background to the housing requirements of the period previously described.

Data show that flatlets were built almost exclusively until 1927, of which 75 per cent had a floor area of 38 m^2 (entrance hall, WC, kitchen + living room, bedroom) and 25 per cent a floor area of 45–48 m^2 (with a second bedroom). Only as a result of the spirited criticism voiced at the international urban planning congress in 1926 did the council decide to build somewhat larger flats. Three types were subsequently employed (Fig. 11.5):

40 m^2, kitchen, entrance hall, WC, bedroom;
49 m^2, kitchen, entrance hall, WC, bedroom, living room;
57 m^2, kitchen, entrance hall, WC, living room, two small bedrooms.

Nevertheless, the proportion of small flats in the subsequent building programmes was still 74·6 per cent of the total, so that no significant improvement in Vienna's housing structure was effected, and the predominance of small units was perpetuated.

The practice of building on vacant land in the developed areas of the city as the predominant location policy has already been mentioned (Fig 11.6). In this way the council resumed the construction activity of the *Gründerzeit* which had been interrupted by the First World War. This policy of location on vacant sites enabled the cost of new technical and social infrastructure to be minimized. Public buildings such as schools and hospitals were already to be found within easy reach of the council houses, and existing public transport facilities remained sufficient in most cases. An important source of land was real estate that had been acquired by speculators at the turn of the century and which was now offered for sale at low prices, thanks to the changed economic situation. Generally, the council housing was built on previously undeveloped land – waste land, agricultural land used during the lean war years, market gardens and storage yards. Only rarely were older, lower buildings demolished.

The council generally respected existing regulations concerning the heights of buildings, although areas were sometimes rezoned to permit taller buildings. The overall effect of the council's housing programme was to increase building density on the margins of the built-up area. On the other hand the permitted density, which had reached 60 per cent in the early twenties, was reduced to 30 per cent by the new building regulations introduced in 1929.

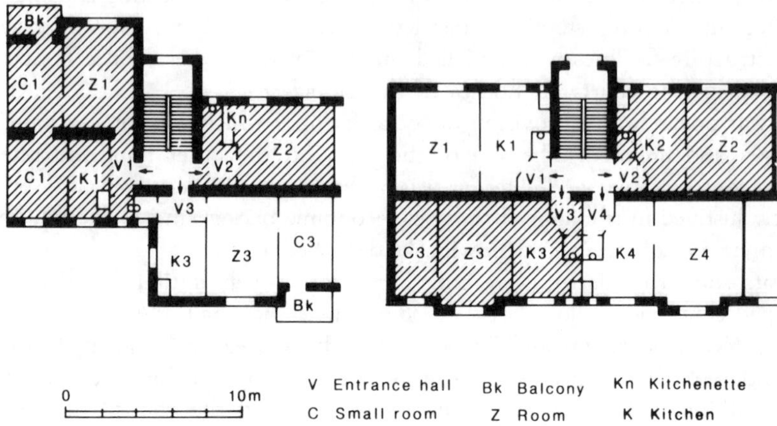

Figure 11.5 Apartment types in municipal housing in the inter-war period

The new council developments were not equally distributed around the periphery of the city, but were concentrated in the working-class districts of the *Gründerzeit*. They are therefore contiguous with the much-quoted 'strangling ring' of small flats in the exterior districts. The spatial segregation of the *Gründerzeit*, and the socio-spatial gradation from the centre to the periphery, remained largely unchanged by the council's building activity. In this respect council policy concerning housing location was very different to that pursued after the Second World War. Housing was then frequently located according to electoral considerations, in particular in middle-class districts where conservative voters were in the majority.

The council housing was intended to meet the housing requirements of the lower classes and, more particularly, of newly-established households within these groups. They thus possessed a demographic function. This generation of new households was, however, the group that had most drastically reduced the number of children per family, as a reaction to the economic depression of the inter-war years. In the 1930s the birth rate in Vienna dropped to a low of 5·5 per thousand, causing demographers to predict a 'dying city'. Because of this, the otherwise customary practice in social housing of giving precedence to large families was of only limited applicability in the inter-war years in Vienna. This was just as well since the immobilisation of the housing market had begun to affect council housing too, a council flat came to be part of its occupier's inheritance in the same way as with the *Gründerzeit* flats. It was, therefore, not possible for the council to achieve an internal redistribution in order to benefit large families.

The hygienic improvements in the flats of the inter-war years appear modest by present standards, but were nevertheless a considerable improvement over the standards prevailing in the working-class housing of the

Figure 11.6 Municipal row housing built at medium density in the inter-war period, Hietzing, Vienna

Gründerzeit. This meant that the flats appeared attractive and desirable to large sections of the population. The stigma of discrimination which social housing often bears in other countries has never developed in Vienna. The selection criteria for the assignment of council flats were in no way restricted to criteria of economic marginality, but in fact became extremely complicated. It must also be emphasized, although it was never expressly stated, that the city council expected applicants for council housing to sympathize with the social-democratic party and to possess the right of domicile in Vienna.

From all this there emerged a very specific population structure in the council housing of the inter-war years. The spectrum included young couples, small families, skilled workers and clerical employees, all supporters of the social-democratic party. Immigrants and criminal elements were very uncommon, in marked contrast to the social housing of New York and Philadelphia.

Peripheral settlements

New planned settlements were also established on the fringes of the area of *Gründerzeit* land speculation. Here, agricultural villages in the environs of the city had already slipped into a state of crisis during the *Gründerzeit* period and large industrial firms had purchased land to provide them with reserves. By means of linking up with existing developed areas (suburbs and villages), the majority of these settlements were directly linked to the already-developed body of the city. The existence of two principal types of settlement, namely terraced houses for families, and settlements providing for some market gardening and keeping small livestock, has already been mentioned.

The terraced-house estates were not originally built by the council, but by co-operative societies right after the First World War, as a self-help measure by people looking for a home. They were inspired by the example of the English garden-city movement. The individual societies contained similar occupational and social groups such as craftsmen or clerical employees. However, many obstacles stood in the way of the development of a co-operative settlement movement from the very beginning. These included the multitude of societies; the lack of effective organization (in particular the lack of officials possessing the necessary technical and administrative skills); the lack of a satisfactory legal framework (e.g. building regulations deficient of pertinent specifications), and difficulties in the purchasing and financing of land.

The strong support for this movement from the experts attending the international urban planning congress in 1926 persuaded the council to take over the development of these settlements themselves, or in some cases to entrust it to the trustee-company GESIBA. All the larger terraced-housing

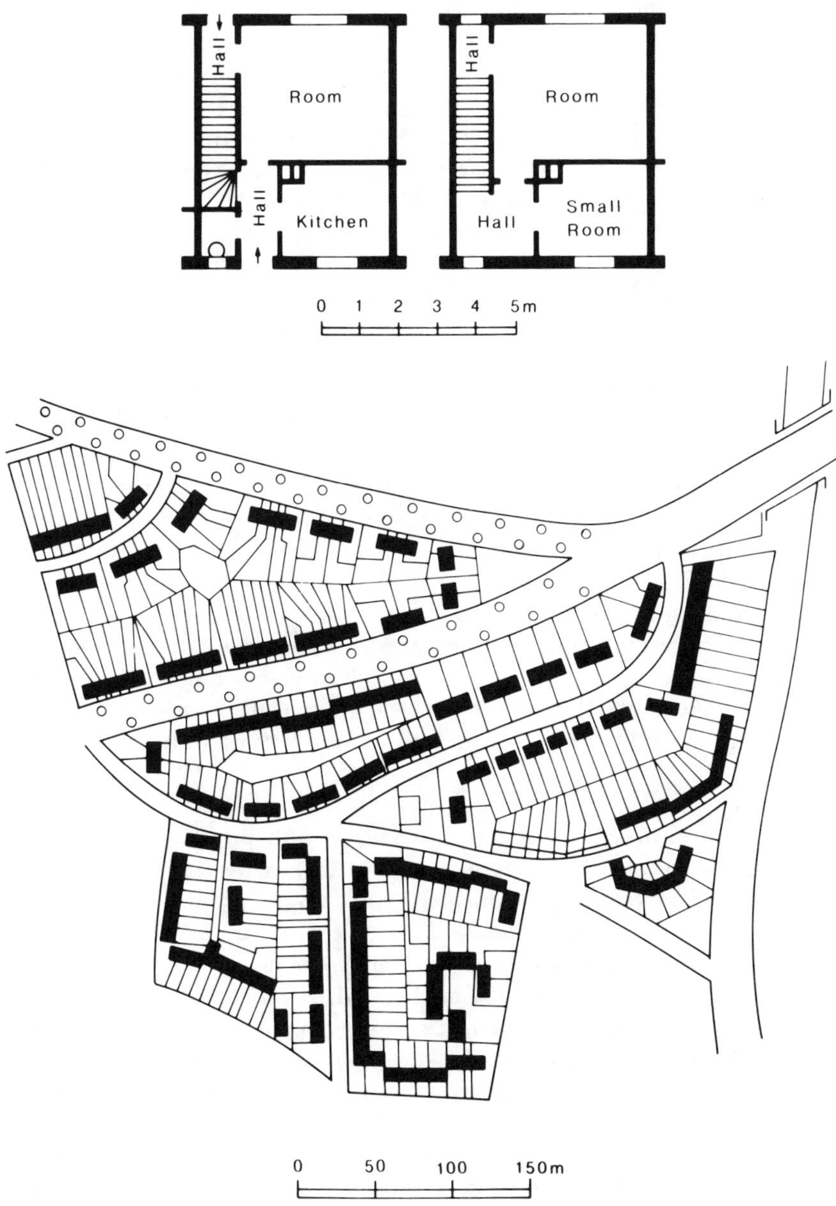

Figure 11.7 a, Plan of low terraced houses in the inter-war period. **b,** Layout of the Flötzersteig and Antaeus estates

estates of the inter-war period were built by either co-operative societies possessing the right to develop council land and receiving substantial financial support from the council (118·3 hectares were developed in this way), or by the council itself.

These terraced houses represented something of a novelty with respect to the Vienna building regulations. For the first time houses were permitted to be built of lightweight construction, with wooden staircases, with cellars not extending under the whole house and having a headroom of only 2·2 m. (Fig. 11.7a). The pattern for these houses was clearly provided by the terraced houses of Britain. Special regulations for the size of the plots also came into force, similar to those governing allotment gardens (200 m^2) (Fig. 11.7b).

If one attempts to pursue the similarities between these terraced-housing estates and those of the country from which the idea originated, however, one comes across marked dissimilarities. First, the participation of the residents themselves in the building of the estate commonly compensated for the lack of capital. Secondly, owing to organizational difficulties and failing means, it often proved impossible for ambitious developments to be completed. The result was a variety of transitional forms consisting of mixtures of terraced houses, allotment gardens, summer shelters and temporary homes. Thirdly, social infrastructure facilities and shops were not always included at the planning stage and were sometimes not developed even at a later stage. Finally, the size of the settlements varied from large settlements with hundreds of units to modest estates with only a dozen houses.

An impression of the type of ground-plan and layout employed can be gained from Figures 11.7a and b. In common with British terraced council housing, the majority of terraced houses in Vienna were also two-storeyed, the frontages containing two, or rarely three, windows and with a built-area of 30–40 m^2 and a corresponding floor-space of 60–80 m^2. The sheds and byres, today often converted to garages, are a reminder of the time of partial self-sufficiency through the yield of the gardens and the domestic animals.

The settlements for part-time market gardening, built by the council and by GESIBA in the thirties, were based on a fundamentally different concept to that of the terraced-housing settlements. They were an attempt to reduce the effects of unemployment by the creation of minute-scale, intensive agricultural units in the immediate vicinity of the city, where there was a good market for the products of market gardens and the raising of small animals. Large areas of land were developed in this way.

By 1937, 1,407 lots covering a total of 267 hectares were in existence, all in the north-east of the city (Fig. 11.8). The largest settlement was the Grossfeldsiedlung north of Leopoldau with 324 2,500 m^2-lots. The residents were entitled to build on their lots; they had to contribute 3,400 working hours and 500 schillings in cash. A loan for 4,500 schillings was guaranteed by the federal government and the city council. The semi-detached houses

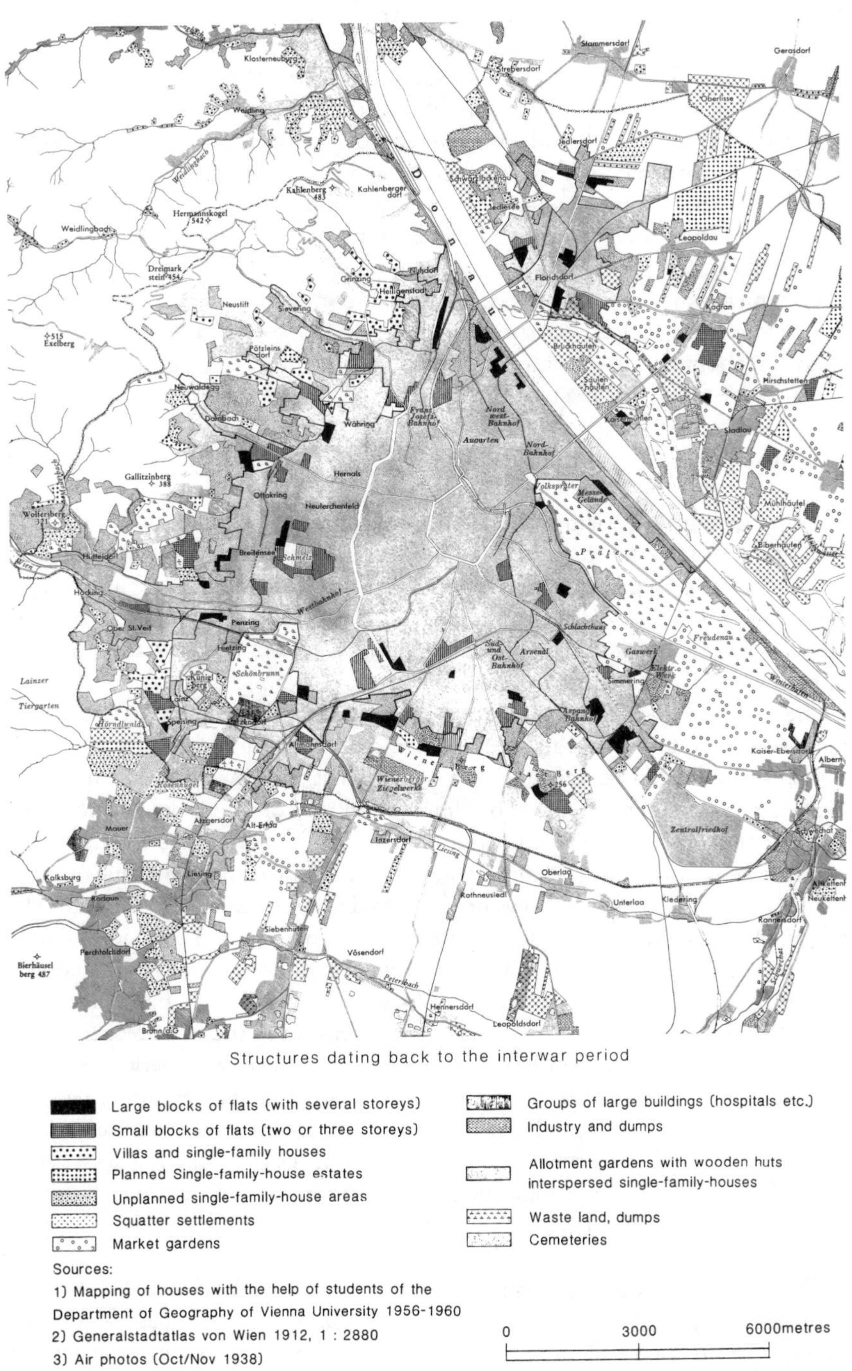

Figure 11.8 Inter-war residential plan elements in Vienna

were considerably smaller than the terraced houses, consisting only of entrance hall, living room + kitchen and bedroom and having a floor area of 28–30 m^2. The provision of a social infrastructure was not planned. Shops to meet the everyday needs of the residents only developed later.

In the prosperity and full employment of the post-Second World War years these settlements rapidly degenerated to a kind of slum on the outskirts of the city, particularly because the land was under-utilized and ill-cared-for. The council decided after long discussion to replace the Grossfeldsiedlung by a large housing estate with the same name. This development, the largest single example of urban expansion in Vienna since the Second World War, consisted of high-rise blocks, a consequence of the council's adoption of pre-cast construction.

Conclusions

Building activity in Vienna in the period between the wards was directed towards meeting the quantitative housing requirements created by the increase in the number of households and the reduction in their average size. The retention of the structure of small flats stemming from the *Gründerzeit*, but hygienically better-equipped, was thus seen by the population in general as an improvement.

The residents of council housing cannot be described simply as marginal socio-economic groups, as is generally the case with social housing in other capitalist countries. To move into a council flat was the ambition of wide sections of the population. The immobilization of the Vienna housing market and the development of a pseudo-ownership of apartments, the consequences of the *Mieterschutzgesetz*, also affected council housing. Once they were in occupation, households stayed in the same flat through all stages of the family life cycle. Consequently, there was the same marked over-representation of old people and single-person households characteristic of much of the *Gründerzeit* housing. However, the council has made the necessary investment in repairs and maintenance over the past decades and today the low rents thus ensure that flats in houses from this period are still sought after. To ameliorate the undeniably cramped living conditions, many people have acquired second homes in the last decade as a response to the prevailing housing structure in Vienna and the lack of open spaces. The amalgamation of flats, a significant practice in *Gründerzeit* housing, presents complications in council housing and has to date not been practised by the council.

The settlements on the periphery of the city have developed in various ways according to the attractiveness of their situation and the ease of access. Today, the pronounced traditional east–west division in the inter-war socio-spatial structure of Vienna makes itself apparent again in this respect. The terraced-house settlements in the west of the city, on the borders of the

Vienna Woods, are mostly occupied by members of the middle classes, while those in the east, across the Danube, are predominantly lower-class in character (Fig. 11.8). The subsequent development of the part-time market gardening settlements has already been discussed with reference to the Grossfeldsiedlung. A basic role in the development of all the peripheral settlements is played by the administration and duration of the right to build, and by the possibilities of converting property from collective to individual ownership. The contemporary influx of foreign workers has so far been denied the right to occupy council housing. The result is the diversion of these people into the housing of the *Gründerzeit*.

The most important legacy for the present can be seen to be the location policy followed for council housing in the inter-war years: namely, of building predominantly on vacant sites in the built-up area and thus the linking of new development to the existing structure of the city. This policy, largely dictated by the economic crisis and widespread poverty of the inter-war years, meant that Vienna was spared the problem of inter-war satellite estates or towns which no longer meet present-day standards and expectations.

Acknowledgements

I am grateful to J. Godfrey of Vienna for translating the initial draft of this chapter into English.

Selected literature

Anon, 1910. *Die Kaiser Franz Josefs I. Jubiläums-Stiftung für Volkswohnungen und Wohlfahrtseinrichtungen* (Wien).

Anon, n.d. 'Vorber ichte für den internationalen Wohnungs- und Städtebaukongreß in Wien 1926'.

Anon, 1924. *Die genossenschaftlichen Einrichtungen* (Wien).

Anon, 1926–28. 'Das neue Wien', *Städtewerk* (Wien).

Anon, 1928. *Der Baugenossenschaftskongreß, veranstaltet vom Zentralverband der gemeinnützigen Bauvereinigungen Österreichs* (Wien).

Anon, 1931. *10 Jahre Gesiba* (Wien).

Anon, 1931. *20 Jahre gemeinnützige allgemeine Bau-, Wohn- und Siedlungsgenossenschaft in Wien* (Wien).

Anon, 1937. *Wien im Aufbau. Wohnungs- und Siedlungswesen, städtischer Grundbesitz* (Wien).

Anon, 1939. 'Die Leistungen der Wiener Stadtrandsiedlungen', *Zeitschrift für Wohnungswesen, 37*.

Anon, 1950. *Wohlfahrtsstaat Wien. 30 Jahre Bundesland Wien (1920–1950)* (Wien).

Bittner, J., 1926. *Die Neubauten der Stadt Wien* (Wien).

Bundesministerium für soziale Verwaltung (ed.), 1953. *30 Jahre Bundes-Wohn- und Siedlungsfonds* (Wien).

Czeike, F., 1959. *Wirtschafts- und Sozialpolitik der Gemeinde Wien* (Wien).
Danneberg, R., 1930. *Das neue Wien* (Wien).
Hautmann H. and R., 1980. *Die Gemeindebauten des Roten Wien 1919–1934* (Wien).
Holzbauer, W., 1973. 'Die Wiener Gemeindebauten der Ersten Republik', *Zeitgeschichte* (Salzburg), *1*: 10–12.
Honay, K., 1926. *Die Wohnungspolitik der Gemeinde Wien* (Wien).
Jehly, E., 1930. *10 Jahre rotes Wien* (Wien).
Kodré, H., 1964. 'Die Entwicklung des Wiener Sozialen Wohnungsbaues in den Jahren 1919–1938', *Der Aufbau* (Wien), *19*: 343–50.
Kunze, H., 1969. 'Kommunaler Wohnungsbau in Wien der zwanziger Jahre', *Bauwelt* (Berlin), *60*: 44–9.
Kurrent, F. and Spalt, J., 1970. 'L'evolution historique de l'architecture en Autriche depuis le début du siècle jusgu'aux années 50', *L'Architecture D'Aujourd'hui* (Paris), *151*: 2–9.
Mahr, A., 1933. *Die Stadtrandsiedlung* (Wien).
Pawlik, H., 1937. *Das Kleinwohnungshaus* (Wien).
Rauchberg, H., 1897. *Die Kaiser Franz Josefs I. Jubiläums-Stiftung* (Wien).
Rosenblum, S., 1935. 'Die sozialpolitischen Maßnahmen der Gemeinde Wien', *Berner wirtschaftswissenschaftliche Abhandlungen 11*.
Ross, Th., 1950. 'Der moderne Städtebau und die Wiener Wohnungs- und Siedlungsanlagen zwischen beiden Weltkriegen', Dissertation, Universität Wien.
Schlandt, J. and Ungers, O. M., 1978. 'The Vienna Superblocks', *Oppositions* (Cambridge, Mass. - London), *13*: 83–111.
Schneider, J., 1937. 'Die Bodenpolitik der Gemeinde Wien seit 50 Jahren', *Die Wohnung, 12*.
Wondrazka, W., 1936. *Die Kommunalpolitik Wiens von 1919 bis 1934* (Wien).

12 Commercial building development: the agents of change

Mike Freeman

Introduction

In view of the importance of the townscape in the human environment, it is perhaps strange that geographers have remained so detached from detailed examination of its built form. The clearly defined basis provided by M. R. G. Conzen (1960, 1962) over a quarter of a century ago, in which the urban landscape was divided into three elements – the town plan, land use, and the building fabric – makes this detachment the more surprising. Although studies of the physical fabric of settlements appeared in the geographical literature as early as the 1890s (e.g. Schlüter 1899a,b), most of the research has been restricted to the post-war period. Few attempts have been made in the English-speaking countries, however, to follow the early precedent set by Conzen (1958) of detailed investigation of the townscape's fabric at the scale of the individual plot and within a morphogenetic framework. Only in Germany has the challenge been taken up (e.g. Möller 1959; Bobek and Lichtenberger 1966; Sabelberg 1983).

There are signs in both Britain and North America that there is now a resurgence of interest in urban morphology (Conzen, M. P. 1978: 135; Whitehand 1984a: 98) and in an historico-geographical approach to the urban fabric (e.g. Bastian 1980; Jakle 1983; Mattson 1983). Despite this resurgence, however, and despite the obvious link between the building fabric and the individuals, firms and organizations responsible for its adaptation and renewal, there remains little systematic examination of the relationships between the two. Of the studies that have taken place, most have tended to concentrate on a particular group of agents or to provide a biographical account of a particular individual or firm. Furthermore, little of this work has been undertaken by geographers. Dyos (1968), for example, examined the building industry and the role of building firms in the development of Victorian London. Aspinall (1982), pursuing the Victorian building theme, analysed the residential building industry of nineteenth-century Sheffield. Others have adopted a more particularistic approach. Hobhouse (1971) investigated the role of a single master builder, Thomas Cubitt, in the urban development of early- and mid-nineteenth-century London, and Nash (1975) has examined the work of the Victorian architect

A. E. Cogswell in Portsmouth. Unfortunately, although such studies are important to the advance of knowledge and our understanding of townscape change, they provide insights into only one of the many actors engaged in the process of building development. An important step forward, however, has been made by Trowell (1985) in his detailed investigation of landowners, developers and architects in speculative suburban housing in Leeds between 1838 and 1914.

Sources

A major reason for the dearth of systematic analysis of the agents adapting and renewing the townscape has been widespread ignorance of the sources available to identify them. In Britain, however, there exists a readily available data source that enables the date, nature and location of changes to the building fabric to be ascertained and the agents responsible for the changes to be identified. This source is the building plan applications submitted to local authorities in accordance with the administration of local bye-laws to ensure certain minimum standards of construction. These applications should not be confused with planning applications, which were an additional statutory requirement under the 1947 Town and Country Planning Act. Whether the fabric change involves the comprehensive redevelopment of numerous individual sites, the extension of an existing building, the refurbishment of a facade or the modification of a drainage pattern, a building plan application must be submitted for the approval of the local authority. Only after this approval has been granted can the change be implemented. Although differences exist between local authorities in the information contained in each application, it is usually possible to identify most of the information pertaining to the nature and agents of each fabric change. This includes:

i) the date of plan submission;
ii) the site of the proposed change;
iii) a description of the change and architect's drawings, including block plans and elevations;
iv) the decision of the local authority and the date of that decision;
v) the name and address of most of the agents engaged in the fabric change. This usually includes the initiator (often referred to in the plans as 'the applicant'), the architect, builder, engineering consultant, and specialist contractors;
vi) miscellaneous details, including the extent of new floorspace, the cost of the work and correspondence between the local authority and the agents.

Where information is missing, such as the address or profession of a particular firm, it is often possible to rectify this by recourse to other

Figure 12.1 Location of study towns

sources, such as professional trade directories, local newspapers and photographic archives, or by personal communication and correspondence with firms or local authorities. More detailed accounts of the content, availability, limitations and uses of building plan applications can be found in Aspinall and Whitehand (1980), Rodger (1981) and Freeman (1986a).

Research framework

Current research within the Urban Morphology Research Group at Birmingham is employing local authority building plan applications to examine the nature of building fabric change and the agents responsible for them (initiators, architects, builders, consultants and specialist contractors) in selected town centres in south-east England. Early work focused on the commercial cores of Northampton, a medium-sized county market town some 100 km. north-west of London, and Watford, a dormitory settlement 25 km. north-west of London, between 1918 and 1980 (Fig. 12.1) (Whitehand 1983, 1984b, 1984c, 1984d; Whitehand and Whitehand 1983, 1984). Later work made an extensive analysis of commercial building change between 1935 and 1983 in the town centres of Aylesbury, a free-standing county market town 56 km. north-west of London, and Wembley, a suburban centre 12 km. north-west of London (Freeman 1986a, 1986b, 1987, 1988). Other work examined the firms erecting new buildings in the town centre of Epsom, a dormitory settlement 25 km. south-west of London (Callis 1986). Related research using local authority planning applications has analysed the nature and agents of change in selected commercial and residential conservation areas in the English Midlands (Larkham 1986a, 1986b, 1986c, 1988a). By following broadly similar research procedures and adopting the Conzenian tradition of detailed study of the townscape at the scale of the individual building plot and within a morphogenetic framework, a comprehensive series of interrelated studies is being developed. Sufficient projects have now been completed for general statements regarding the agents engaged in the adaptation and renewal of the commercial building fabric to be made.

Research findings

(a) The provenance of firms

One of the most important findings to emerge from the research thus far, and which is consistent throughout each study, is the displacement over time of local initiators, architects and builders by non-local firms (Fig. 12.2). This finding is of greater significance when it is realized that in many cases the local agents are small firms or individuals and are being replaced by large companies, often with national spheres of influence and large financial resources. The timing and extent of the displacement, however, varies between study centres. It occurs earliest in the suburban and dormitory settlements close to London, where the influence of metropolitan firms is great. In the free-standing county market towns of Aylesbury and Northampton, the greater distance from London and the greater age and self-sufficiency of the settlements have encouraged the development of locally-based firms and organizations. Some of these were highly active in property development during the inter-war years and played important roles in shaping the built form of the towns. In Northampton, for example, a small, local nineteenth-century builder, Richard Cleaver, expanded to become a limited company and one of the major owners and developers of property in the town during the 1920s and 1930s. In Aylesbury, some local firms have continued to play a prominent role in adapting and renewing the urban fabric to the present day.

Two points are worthy of note about the firms from outside the study

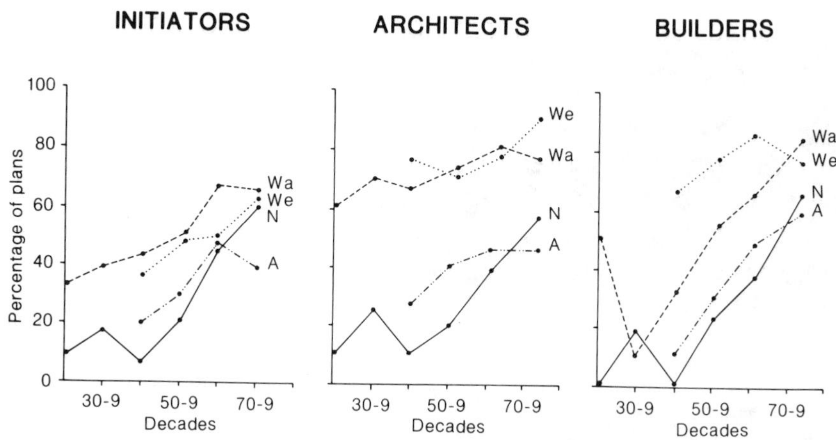

Figure 12.2 Proportion of initiators, architects and builders submitting building plans in Aylesbury, Northampton, Watford and Wembley from outside the study towns

towns who are displacing those of local provenance. First, there is the entry of the national retail and service chains during the inter-war and early post-war years. Supported by the greater availability of finance through their flotation on the Stock Exchange, these firms expanded from their traditional trading centres to towns all over the country. Since many had distinctive house styles and possessed their own architects' departments or had standing relationships with particular firms, buildings and shop fascias of similar appearance were replicated in numerous town and city centres, often with little regard to traditional townscapes. Marks & Spencer, the largest of the retail chains and a public company since 1926, built or rebuilt 211 stores between 1926 and 1939 (Rees 1973), a large number of which used neo-Georgian styles (Fig. 12.3a). Similarly Montague Burton, the largest of the men's fashion retailers, and a public company since 1920, undertook a massive building programme between the wars and peppered the country with shops in its own house style (Redmayne 1950) (Fig. 12.3b).

The second point concerns the growth in the activity of property companies. Encouraged by the widespread destruction of property during the war and the abolition in 1953–4 of the national restrictions on building activity imposed during the war (Whitehouse 1964: 13–22), property companies quickly gained a prominent position in the development industry. In 1939, only thirty-five property companies were quoted on the London Stock Exchange. By 1958, this had increased to 111 and within a further six years to 183. In the study towns, these agents undertook an increasing volume of building activity from the 1950s onwards and by the 1970s they were responsible for the majority of the redevelopments taking place in those towns. Of the eighteen buildings erected in the centre of Aylesbury between

Figure 12.3 Inter-war national retail chain buildings. **a.** Aylesbury: designed in 1939 by Dugdale & Ruhemann, London for Marks & Spencer Ltd., London; **b.** Wolverhampton: designed in 1932 by H. Wilson, Leeds for Montague Burton Ltd., Leeds

1979 and 1986, for example, all but two were developed by property companies.

The evidence suggests that the displacement of local firms over time by non-local firms and, in particular, the large-scale entry of national concerns into the local property market, has left its imprint on the townscape. It seems inescapable that the building forms created in the townscape by local firms and individuals, often with restricted commercial spheres of influence, will be different from those created by external firms, many with national fields of operation, corporate images and huge financial resources. Traditional-sized building plots, for example, were often too small for the efficient operation of the national retail chains and the speculative activities of property companies. These firms were interested in economies of scale, and quickly found that these could best be achieved by amalgamating plots. The impact of this process, however, has varied between town centres. It has been greatest in the historic county towns of Aylesbury and Northampton, where new developments have replaced a rich assemblage of eighteenth- and nineteenth-century buildings, many accommodated on plots 10 m. or less in width (Conzen's (1960) 'standard' burgage width). This is particularly well shown in Figures 12.4a, b and 12.5a, b. In Wembley, and the dormitory settlements of Epsom and Watford, the existence of numerous shopping parades erected just before and after the First World War has

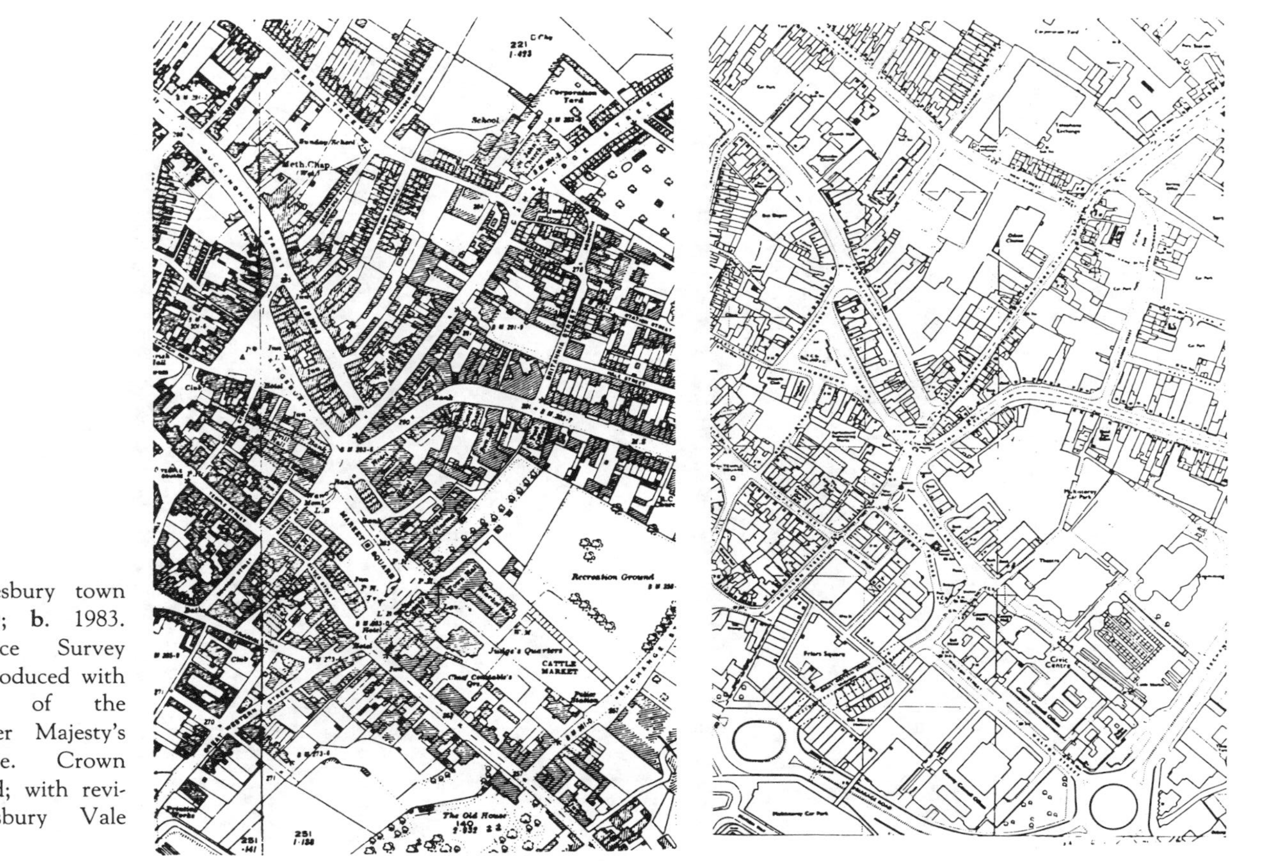

Figure 12.4 Aylesbury town centre: **a**. *c*.1930; **b**. 1983. Source: Ordnance Survey 1 : 2500 plans reproduced with the permission of the Controller of Her Majesty's Stationery Office. Crown Copyright reserved; with revisions by Aylesbury Vale District Council

Figure 12.5 Aylesbury: west side of Market Square. **a.** 1963; **b.** following development of Friars Square shopping centre, designed 1964 by B. Engle & Partners, London for Aylesbury Borough Council and Aylesbury and Hammerson Property & Investment Trust, London

tended to mitigate the visual impact of further plot amalgamations undertaken later by property companies and the national retail and service chains.

Evidence also suggests that external firms erected buildings of greater height than local firms. In the study centres, buildings had traditionally

Figure 12.6 Office blocks in concrete and glass. **a.** Aylesbury: designed in 1963 by E. S. Boyer & Partners, London for Rivoli Investments Ltd., London; **b.** Wembley: designed in 1963 by R. Spratley & Partners, London for Regents Park Land Co. Ltd., London

seldom exceeded three storeys. This was changed by the influx of property companies erecting speculative office blocks and attempting to maximize plot ratios within the constraints of local authority planning policies (Fig. 12.6a). Office blocks of four or five storeys have become a common feature since the 1960s, although their visual impact has largely been confined to the periphery of commercial areas where the majority of major office developments take place.

External firms have further disrupted the traditional townscape by their use of cladding materials out of harmony with those already existing. In the town centres studied, brick has been the traditional building material since the eighteenth century, a position broken only in Aylesbury by the occasional building faced with stucco, and in Northampton by a sizeable proportion of buildings clad or built in stone. During the 1950s and 1960s, however, concrete and glass became widely used, with property companies playing a pivotal role in the introduction and widespread adoption of these materials (Fig. 12.6b). These observations suggest that non-local firms are less imbued with a 'sense of place' than local firms, many of which are of small size, often family-run and with a long period of association with a particular town. In addition, since the tendency for local firms to engage other local firms has declined, the extent to which agents initiating and designing fabric changes possess a 'sense of place' is still further reduced.

Figure 12.7 Buildings with sub-divided facades. **a**. Aylesbury: designed in 1979 by Hubbard Ford & Partners, Bristol for Shellwin Ltd., Bourne End; **b**. Aylesbury: designed in 1983 by Hobbs, Corbey & Associates, Milton Keynes for Rycote Property Co. Ltd., Aylesbury

The influence of national companies on the townscape, however, has not been consistently detrimental. Larkham (1988b) reports on the case of the national supermarket chain J. Sainsbury which, despite a strong corporate identity with regard to interior design and its company logo, has offered different design solutions to different local environments in the construction of its supermarkets. There is also evidence of a reaction to one of the many criticisms often held against buildings erected by corporate organizations, namely the excessive length of their frontages. Although the economics of redevelopment continue to necessitate the amalgamation of traditional building plots, the sub-division of a facade to give a building an external appearance of traditional scale, often independently of its internal divisions, is a reaction against this. This is evident in a number of buildings erected in the centres of Aylesbury and Northampton since the late 1970s (Fig. 12.7a, b).

Concentration of building plan applications

The displacement of local firms by national companies that are undertaking fabric changes all over the country implies that building activity may be concentrating in the hands of a smaller number of firms at a national level. It has long been recognized that manufacturing industry has become increasingly concentrated in the hands of fewer firms (Blair 1972; Hart and Clarke

1980). Research suggests that this may also be occurring nationally within the property development industry. Barras (1979a: 56), for example, notes that the phase of takeovers and mergers amongst property companies during the late 1960s and early 1970s has led to the concentration of activity amongst a small number of leviathans, with portfolios amounting to hundreds of millions of pounds. Thus, while in 1960 the ten largest property companies owned 20 per cent of the assets of the sector, by 1970 this had risen to almost 50 per cent (Barras 1979b: 41). It perhaps comes as no surprise, therefore, to learn that half of the shopping precincts of over 5,600 m^2 in size in Britain that were completed between 1965 and 1978 were initiated by only four development companies (Hillier Parker Research 1979: 33).

At the scale of the individual town centre, however, the picture appears to be more complex. Data for the centres of Northampton and Watford during the periods 1920–39 and 1960–79 would seem to indicate that activity is, in fact, becoming more dispersed at the local level (Fig. 12.8). The fact that the large national owners of property (such as the national retail and service chains and the property companies) are responsible for a significant amount of building activity at a national level but are characterized by a wide geographical spread of property ownership over the country as a whole and are displacing local firms, some of which have played an active role in fabric change, may be crucial in this respect. This argument also holds for architects and builders, many of whom are engaged on buildings all over the country. Although amongst builders no clear picture emerges in Aylesbury and Wembley (Fig. 12.8), there is an increased dispersion amongst architects in both towns during the periods 1940–59 and 1960–79. It is perhaps not wholly coincidental that there is evidence of a greater diversity of architectural styles amongst buildings erected in individual town centres since the early 1970s. Amongst initiators, however, activity is slightly more concentrated in the 1960–79 period than in the 1940–59 period (Fig. 12.8). Admittedly, the difference from Northampton may arise from the different study periods and the fact that the 1940–59 period is in many ways an atypical one due to the effects of the Second World War. It appears that part of the explanation, however, may lie in the provenance of the firms undertaking the changes. Although Whitehand (1983: 324) notes in the case of Northampton and Watford that 'the displacement of local firms by external, frequently national, ones has on balance dispersed rather than concentrated activity', it appears that in Aylesbury, and to a lesser extent in Wembley, the continued importance of a handful of local firms has tended to concentrate activity. In Northampton, there was an absence in the 1960–79 period of any prolific local owners or architects comparable to those that were so active in the 1920–39 period.

Unfortunately, it is often difficult to identify relationships between different firms engaged on a particular building development from the building plan records. For example, it is often the case that firms with

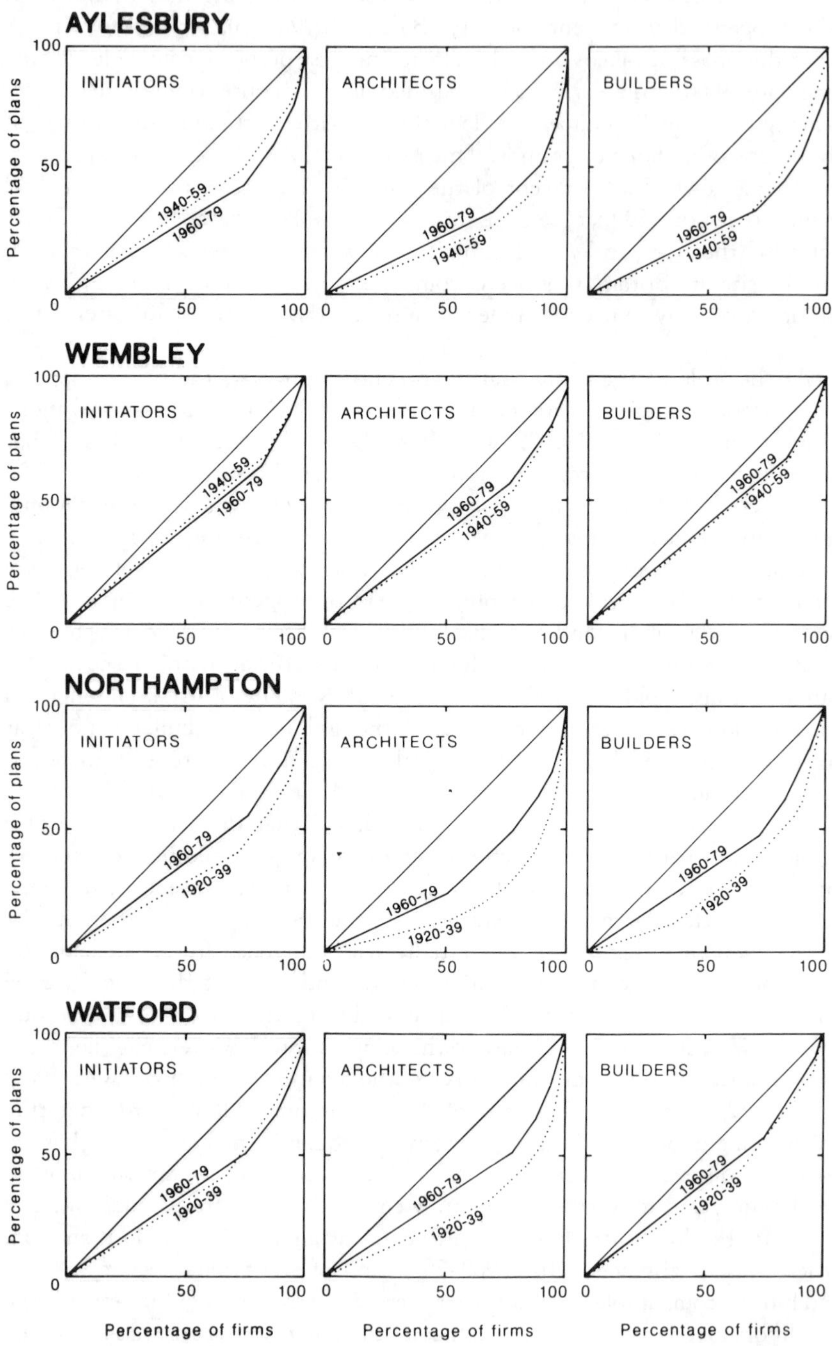

Figure 12.8 Degree of concentration of building activity in sample towns

different names and seemingly independent of one another are, in fact, part of the same corporate structure. The level of concentration amongst the agents adapting and renewing the urban fabric, therefore, may be greater than revealed by the building plan records alone. The Burton Group, for example, comprises a whole range of High Street retail outlets including Debenhams, Top Man, Top Shop, Peter Robinson and Dorothy Perkins, as well as Burton themselves. Further, many of the national retail and service chains maintain their own architects' departments, a practice in which Boots the Chemist had been a forerunner before the First World War and which was subsequently adopted by many of the banks and national retail and service chains during the 1920s and 1930s.

Both the initiation and the design of a development may thus be undertaken by the same firm. This has repercussions for the level of concentration, since a trend develops towards vertical, as well as horizontal, concentration. In some cases, this vertical concentration may be quite discrete. In Aylesbury, Audley Properties Ltd of London initiated a mixed retail-office redevelopment on the edge of the town centre in 1971. It was designed by a Reading-based group of architects, Barton-Willmore Partnership, and built by Bovis Construction Ltd. Recourse to other sources, however, revealed that Audley Properties and Bovis Construction are both part of the Bovis Property Group which, in turn, is owned by the P & O conglomerate which has extensive interests in property and shipping. In this case, therefore, both the initiation and construction of the development were undertaken by sections of the same corporate group. During the periods 1940–59 and 1960–79 in Aylesbury, there was an increase from 7 per cent to 9 per cent in the proportion of plans emanating from firms undertaking the dual role of initiator and builder. In Wembley, there was a slight fall from 5 per cent to 4 per cent. In the case of firms performing the dual role of initiator and architect, there was a rise from 13 per cent to 24 per cent in Aylesbury and from 12 per cent to 16 per cent in Wembley.

This evidence of vertical concentration in the initiation and design of building developments, however, must be viewed in the context of the greater diversity of firms engaged in the building process generally. Although specialist contractors, supplying materials and specialist services, have a long history, redevelopments today are so large-scale that a plethora of such firms may be required. These firms supply everything, often on a subcontract basis, from facing bricks, roof tiles or concrete to undertaking the plumbing or electrical work or the installation of air-conditioning and ventilation systems, elevators or fire escapes.

Similarly, the structural complexities of modern building have led to the growth of a specialist engineering function to act on a consultancy basis to the architect or builder. This function is a relatively recent phenomenon and it is rare for building plan records to record the engagement of such firms before the 1960s, although this is partly the result of the fact that local authorities are under not obligation to do so.

Spatial and contractual relationships

The agents undertaking building fabric changes are often intimately related in a spatial and contractual sense. Of all the agents of change the initiators and architects are the most closely related. Their dominating role in the decision-making process is confirmed by the fact that builders, consultants and specialist contractors each have higher spatial associations with initiators and architects than between themselves (Fig. 12.9). Spatially, 61 per cent of the architects in Aylesbury and 42 per cent in Wembley were located in the same town as the initiator. Differences in the geographical location of the two towns, however, are reflected in the fact that in Aylesbury, this relationship is largely accounted for by local architects being associated with local initiators, and in Wembley by London architects being associated with London initiators. These findings are consistent with evidence from the free-standing town of Northampton and the dormitory settlement of Watford. They have implications for the townscape.

Since it is the initiator and the architect that have the greatest impact upon the townscape, the extent to which these two agents are associated with each other on a local or non-local basis assumes particular importance. In Wembley, although the majority of initiators and architects engaged on the same plan are still local to each other, they are not local to the study town. In Aylesbury, by contrast, initiators and architects with a common location are still generally locally based. The spatial divorce of agents from the study towns is thus far greater in the case of Wembley. This is reinforced when the locations of architects engaged by local and non-local initiators are examined. In Aylesbury, the town's free-standing character has encouraged the survival of a number of active local architects. This is reflected in the fact that local firms account for 80 per cent of those architects engaged by a local initiator. In Wembley, the corresponding figure was only 34 per cent. Further, while one-quarter of all architects in Aylesbury commissioned by a non-local initiator came from the town itself, in Wembley the comparative figure was only 9 per cent. These observations assume importance given that there is evidence that the character of buildings erected in the townscape may differ according to whether they are locally or non-locally initiated and designed. This relates, in particular, to the scale of building, facade materials and architectural style. The extent to which agents are likely to be imbued with a 'sense of place' is therefore much greater in free-standing towns such as Aylesbury. There, a considerable concentration of decision-making remains in local hands, both on the part of initiators and architects individually, and in their engagement together on the same plan.

The agents of change are also intimately related in a contractual sense, and it is common for 'standing relationships' to be formed whereby the same architect, builder or consultant is engaged by the same initiator on a number of plans. In some cases this relationship can extend over many years

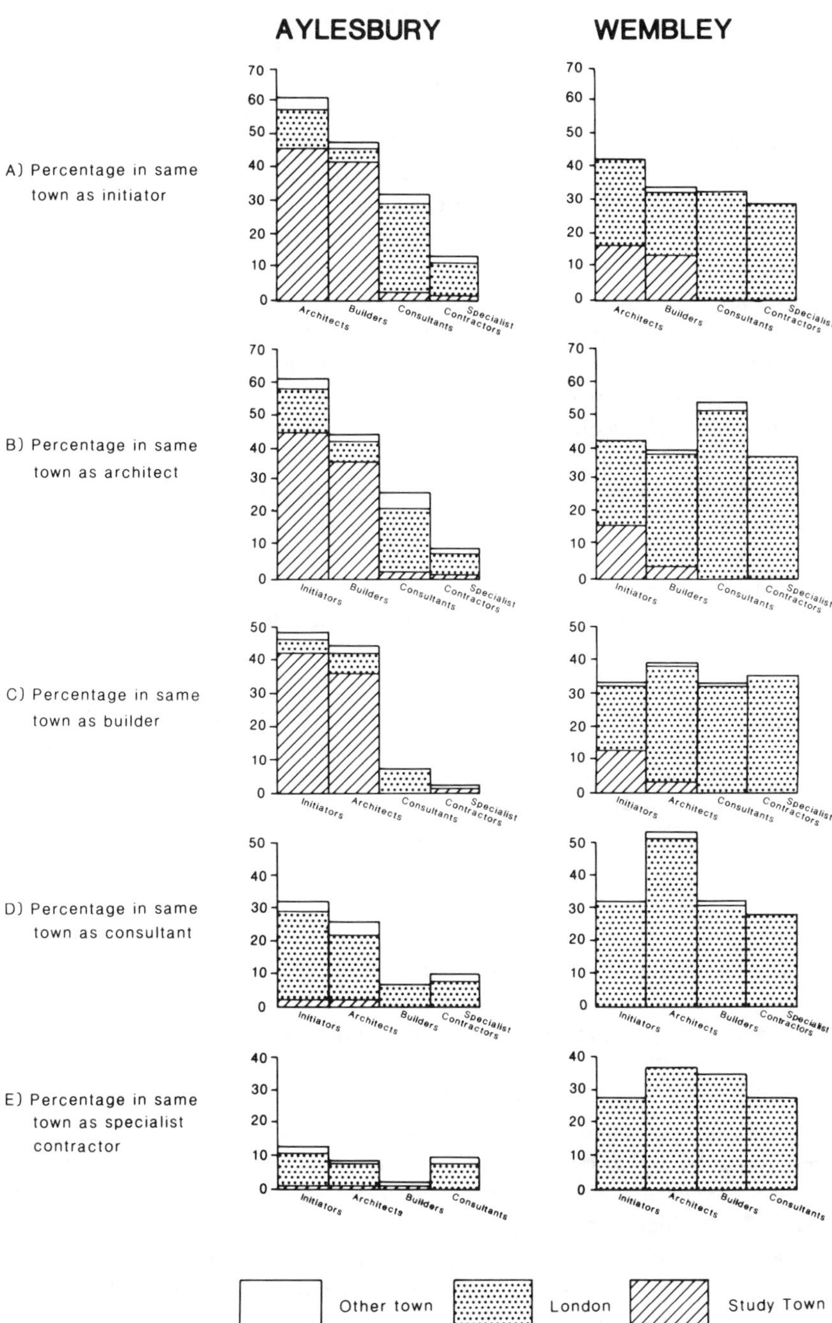

Figure 12.9 Locational relationships between firms engaged on the same plan in Aylesbury and Wembley, 1935–1983

and, in the case of national companies, on a national scale. During the sudden growth of the Leeds-based men's clothing retailer Montague Burton, during the inter-war years, the company engaged the Leeds architectural practice of H. Wilson for the design of many of its new buildings. Evidence suggests that Wilson later became Burton's own in-house architect. The results of the relationship are visible in town and city centres all over the country. Burton buildings erected before the Second World War show a marked similarity in appearance with strong use of Neo-Georgian styles. Following the 1925 *Paris Exposition des Arts Decoratifs*, Art Deco motifs were incorporated into many new buildings.

The example of Marks & Spencer, the biggest High Street retailer in the UK by market capitalization, is particularly interesting. Despite having its own architects' department, Marks & Spencer has pursued a policy of engaging external architects to design its new buildings. During the 1930s and 1940s, A. E. Batzer of London was commissioned to design new stores, including those in Aylesbury and Northampton. In Wembley the London, and later Guildford, practice of Lewis & Hickey were engaged for all post-war alterations including the new store built in 1958. In Aylesbury, Northampton and Watford, Monro & Partners of Watford were engaged during the 1960s and 1970s. These standing relationships also extend to the construction stage, although here Marks & Spencer has engaged a single firm, Bovis Construction Ltd, for over forty years (Ministry of Public Building and Works 1970; Rees 1973). The standing relationships between Marks & Spencer and its several architects, and with Bovis, also exist in the case of engineering consultants and specialist contractors. The Midland Bank provides another example of a national company engaging the same agent on a number of plans over a period of many years. In this case it was the architectural firm Whinney, Son & Austen-Hall. The relationship can trace its antecedence back to the last century when T. B. Whinney, founder of the practice in 1884, met Sir Edward Holden who was then expanding the Midland Bank. The implications of this relationship are clearly reflected in townscapes in many parts of the country, each of which has a Midland Bank building in a similar Neo-Classical style (Figs. 12.10a, b).

Speculative and owner-occupied developers

The displacement of local firms by external, frequently national, ones has been matched by a transition from a predominance of development by owner-occupiers to one in which speculative agents have gained ascendancy. Although speculative building has a long history in Britain (Chalklin 1974) and speculative ventures by private individuals were fairly common in the 1920s and 1930s, its relative incidence in the town centres of Aylesbury, Northampton and Wembley has increased dramatically in the post-war period, although not in central Watford. This growth has been associated with the vigorous activity of property companies and, more recently, insurance companies and pension funds. The engagement of the latter two

Figure 12.10 Neo-Classical bank buildings. **a.** Watford: designed in 1907 by Whinney, Son & Austen-Hall, London for Midland Bank Ltd., London; **b.** Aylesbury: designed in 1926 by Whinney, Son & Austen-Hall, London for Midland Bank Ltd., London

agents in speculative building development arose largely from the events of 1973–4. The world oil crisis and the raising of British interest rates led to the collapse of many of the property companies then actively engaged in widespread property development since they were supported by large-scale loans. It was the insurance companies and pension funds which, looking for sources of investment for their huge reserves of capital, bailed out the property companies. In many cases they took on the mantle of property developers themselves (*The Economist* 1978).

Although this direct involvement of financial institutions in the development process appears to be restricted to the more grandiose developments, and largely to the big cities, there is evidence that it has filtered through to the provincial towns. In most cases, however, the role of financial institutions is essentially a passive one of providing funding. In Aylesbury, for example, the Abbey National Pension Fund and the British Airways Pension Fund both acted as funding agents in redevelopment schemes. During the mid 1980s, there was some evidence of another major shift within the property sector away from the financial institutions and back towards the development companies (Branson 1987). Partly because of disenchantment with yields and partly because of better returns from other areas, especially equities, institutions began cutting back on their funding of property development. Some, such as the Norwich Union – a joint developer of Birmingham's Bull Ring Shopping Centre during the 1960s –

continued to be active agents in the property market, but the implications of the multi-million-pound rights issues from some of the property companies, and their buying of institutional property, were clear to see. Since the stock market collapse in October 1987, however, insurance companies and pension funds have once again been focusing investment in the property sector. In the last quarter of 1987, their purchases of property showed a ten-year high (*Estates Gazette* 1988a).

There are more concerted signs, however, of another shift in the speculative property market towards direct development by retailers themselves, who have traditionally only been engaged in development for owner-occupation. The Burton Group, for example, acquired Pengap Estates, a privately-owned property company, in 1987 to add to its existing property development business, Burton Property Trust. Burton are now engaged in speculative shopping centre developments in Coventry, Darlington, Dartford, Newport, Redhill and Scarborough (Management Horizons 1987). The Dixons Group, which comprises over 1,000 electrical and photographic shops, and the rapidly-growing Next Group, which owns a diverse range of over 1,000 newsagents and fashion shops, have also formed their own property development companies. More recently, J. Sainsbury has announced that it is teaming up with London & Edinburgh Trust to exploit the supermarket chain's property portfolio (*Estates Gazette* 1988b) and Woolworths has launched a wholly-owned subsidiary, Chartwell Land, to tap its £800m property assets. This makes Chartwell Land the tenth largest property company in the UK (*Chartered Surveyor Weekly* 1988).

The increase in speculative building development has a number of implications for the townscape. First, in terms of the timing of activity, it would seem that speculative development is more sensitive to economic downturns than building for owner-occupation (Whitehand 1981). Certainly in the centres of Aylesbury, Northampton and Wembley, there was a high incidence of speculative activity in the years preceding the property crisis of 1973–4, a hiatus between 1974 and 1976 and a subsequent growth from 1979 with the return to power of a Conservative government. Secondly, it has been suggested in building generally, that 'fashions in speculative markets tended to follow those in the bespoke market at a distance' (Bowley 1966: 390). Since a speculative developer aims to let or sell his development upon completion, the primary aim is to produce a building that is pleasing to as many potential clients as possible. This involves creating a building that is economically and functionally efficient; time and money will rarely be spent on lavish architecture. Owners-occupiers, in contrast, erecting tailor-made buildings for their own use, can afford to give more care and attention to aesthetics and to be stylistically innovative without offending clients (Booker and Lycett-Green 1973: 144). However, the evidence in the town centres studied has provided inconsistent results about the contrasting attitudes of speculators and owner-occupiers. While evidence from Northampton and

Watford would seem to lend support to the conservative image of the speculator, there is little evidence of this in Aylesbury, Wembley or Epsom. Indeed, Neo-Georgian styles, which had passed out of the mainstream of architectural fashion by the Second World War, were still used into the 1950s and 1960s by both owner-occupiers and speculators alike. Further, the introduction of Post-Modern styles during the late 1960s and 1970s was largely undertaken by both groups of developers in Aylesbury and mainly by speculators in Epsom and Wembley. Thirdly, the increase in speculative development seems to have had implications of a spatial nature. Although there is no evidence of any difference in the intra-urban distribution of redevelopments undertaken by owner-occupiers and speculators in the centres of Northampton and Watford, there is a tendency in Aylesbury and Wembley for owner-occupied redevelopments to cluster in the core of the commercial area and for speculative redevelopment to be dispersed over the entire central area, with many redevelopments occurring on the commercial periphery. This peripheral distribution in Aylesbury and Wembley seems to have been encouraged by two primary factors. First, since the majority of speculative redevelopments have been for offices, often with associated car-parking, land requirements have best been satisfied by vacant or non-commercial land-use sites on the edge of the town centre. In Aylesbury, the construction of an inner ring road during the 1960s led to a large number of extensive vacant plots of land on the commercial periphery. In Wembley, the former British Empire Exhibition grounds, on the eastern extremity of the town centre, have provided large-scale sites for redevelopment. Secondly, the centrifugal pattern has been consolidated by local authority planning policies which have explicitly prevented non-retail functions being accommodated in the commercial core. The large number of speculative office developments in both towns since the 1960s have, therefore, been directed to the edge of the commercial core.

Conclusions

The study of the agents adapting and renewing the urban fabric sheds light upon the complex web of relationships that lie behind physical changes in the townscape. To afford a more complex understanding, greater attention needs to be devoted to the study of individual firms, their history, internal structure, decision-making process and their movements within and between centres. To this end, the internal records of individual corporate bodies will become an increasingly important primary source. The work already undertaken on the agents of change provides a firm base from which such an approach can be adopted.

Perhaps the most striking of the observations to arise from the research is the displacement over time of local firms by non-local ones and the large-scale entry into local property markets of national companies. The geographical location of centres, particularly in relation to London, and their position in the urban hierarchy, are important in determining the timing of this displacement. Epsom, Watford and Wembley, for example, strategically placed in London's suburban ring, were obvious proving grounds for property companies during the early post-war years, most of which were operating nationally for the first time. The activity of national firms, often with corporate structures, readily-available capital, and distinctive house-styles, left its imprint on traditional townscapes. Building heights and frontages increased and new cladding materials and architectural styles were introduced. In free-standing centres some distance from the metropolis, local firms, invested with a stronger sense of place, to some extent mitigated the visual impact of change. The displacement of local firms by national companies has led to changes in the concentration of activity. In Northampton and Watford evidence suggests that building plans have become spread amongst a greater number of firms over time. This was supported in Aylesbury and Wembley in the case of architects and has been matched nationally by evidence of a greater diversity of architectural styles over the last two decades. Amongst initiators in Aylesbury and Wembley, however, the continued importance of a handful of local firms has tended to concentrate activity. Unfortunately, all the linkages between firms are not always revealed by the building plan records. Agents engaged on ostensibly independent developments may, in fact, be closely associated with one another and part of the same corporate structure. Property development, may, therefore, be more concentrated than the evidence from the study towns suggests.

The dominant decision-making role of initiators and architects is confirmed by the close spatial association between these two agents and the fact that builders, consultants and specialist contractors each had greater associations with initiators and architects than between themselves. The geographical position of the town, however, is a prominent factor determining the character of association. In the free-standing study towns, agents with a common location are largely locally based. In the suburban and dormitory settlements close to the metropolis, agents with common location are invariably concentrated in London. Thus, although firms engaged on the same plan are still local to each other, there is a spatial divorce of agents from the town where the change is occurring. There is thereby a reduction in the sense of place. This is further consolidated by many of the standing relationships between firms, a large number of which are between national firms with distinctive house styles and corporate fascias and logos.

The supplanting of local firms in property development by non-local ones has been matched by a significant increase in the activity of speculative developers. In inter-war townscapes private individuals were at the forefront of this activity but during the post-war years they have given way to development by property companies, and, more recently, by financial institutions and retailers themselves. Although evidence supports the theory that speculative development is more sensitive to economic downturns than that for owner-occupation, there are inconsistent results as to the conservative image of the speculator and to the spatial implications of speculative activity.

The agents of change, in performing their role in the adaptation and renewal of the townscape, should not be studied in isolation. First, they cannot be readily disentangled from changes that were taking place at the national level. The growth in speculative redevelopment during the post-war years, for example, should be seen in context of the character of the property market following the Second World War and the revocation in 1953–4 of the national restrictions on building activity. Similarly, the large-scale entry of national retail companies into local property markets needs to be seen in relation to the post-war growth in consumer spending and changes in the character of retailing generally. Secondly, townscape change is strongly influenced by historical legacies. These include the existing morphological frame, the existence of conservation areas and listed buildings, the nature and pattern of land ownership, and the extent of development activity by local firms with strong associations with a particular place. The latter two factors, for example, were of primary importance in delaying the supplanting of local firms by external ones in Aylesbury relative to Wembley.

Although the research summarized here clearly has its antecedence in the Conzenian tradition, it departs from it in the attention that it gives to the agents of change. This departure is an important one in that it enables the forms created in the townscape to be related to the characteristics of such significant decision-makers as building owners and architects. Since the building fabric and the agents responsible for its adaptation and renewal are intimately related, a genuine understanding of the way in which our townscapes have developed can only be achieved if the two are studied together as Carter (1970) noted two decades ago. Such work will go a long way towards forming the basis for a proper organizational framework for urban morphology in which the agents of change are assigned a position alongside the role of bid rents, building cycles, innovation and diffusion.

References

Aspinall, P. J., 1982. 'The internal structure of the house-building industry in nineteenth century cities', in Johnson J. H., and Pooley, C. G., (eds.), *The structure of nineteenth-century cities*, 75–105.

Aspinall, P. J. and Whitehand, J. W. R., 1980. 'Building plans: a major source for urban studies', *Area 12*: 199–203.

Barras, R., 1979a. 'The development cycle in the City of London', *Research Series 36*, Centre for Environmental Studies, London.

Barras, R., 1979b. 'The returns from office development and investment', *Research Series 35*, Centre for Environmental Studies, London.

Bastian, R. W., 1980. 'Storefront remodelling in small Mid-Western cities, 1890–1940, *Pioneer Society America Transactions*, *1*: 1–14.

Blair, J. M., 1972. *Economic concentration: structure, behaviour and public policy.*

Bobek, H. and Lichtenberger, E., 1966. *Wein: Bauliche Gestalt und Entwicklung seit der Mitte des 19, Jahrhunderts* (Graz).

Booker, C. and Lycett-Green, G., 1973. *Goodbye London – an illustrated guide to threatened buildings.*

Bowley, M., 1966. *The British building industry: four studies in response and resistance to change.*

Branson, C., 1987. 'Development companies move in', *Chartered Surveyor Weekly*, 2 April: 1.

Carter, H., 1970. 'A decision-making approach to town-plan analysis: a case study of Llandudno', in Carter, H. and Davies, W. K. D., (eds.), *Urban essays: studies in the geography of Wales*, 66–88.

Callis, S. E., 1986. 'Redevelopment in Epsom commercial centre, 1898–1984: a spatial analysis of agents and architectural styles' (unpublished B.Sc. dissertation, University of Birmingham).

Chalklin, C. W., 1974. *The provincial towns of Georgian England: a case study of the building process, 1740–1820.*

Chartered Surveyor Weekly, 1988. 'Woolies unveils a spring surprise', 21 April: 13.

Conzen, M. P., 1978. 'Historical geography: changing spatial structure and social patterns of western cities', in Butzer, K. W. (ed.), *Dimensions of human geography: essays on some familiar and neglected themes*, Research Paper 186, Department of Geography, University of Chicago, 128–165.

Conzen, M. R. G., 1958. 'The growth and character of Whitby', in Daysh, G. H. J. (ed.), *A survey of Whitby and the surrounding area*, 49–89.

Conzen, M. R. G., 1960. 'Alnwick, Northumberland: a study in town-plan analysis', *Publications, Institute of British Geographers, 27.*

Conzen, M. R. G., 1962. 'The plan analysis of an English city centre', in Norborg, K. (ed.), *Proceedings of the I.G.U. symposium in Urban Geography, Lund 1960*, 383–414.

Dyos, H. J., 1968. 'The speculative builders and developers of Victorian London', *Victorian Studies*, *11*: 641–90.

Economist, The, 1978. 'Property Survey', 10 June: 3–38.

Estates Gazette, 1988a. 'Buying Power', 2 April: 7.

Estates Gazette, 1988b. 'Sainsbury checks out LET', 2 April: 7.

Freeman, M., 1986a. 'The nature and agents of central-area change: a case study of Aylesbury and Wembley town centres, 1935–1983' (unpublished Ph.D. thesis, University of Birmingham).

Freeman, M., 1986b. 'Town-centre redevelopment: architectural styles and the roles of developers and architects'. *Occasional Publication 20*, Department of Geography, University of Birmingham.

Freeman, M., 1987. 'Commercial redevelopment: concentration or dispersal?', *Area*, *19*: 123–9.

Freeman, M., 1988. 'Developers, architects and building styles: post-war redevelopment in two town centres', *Transactions, Institute of British Geographers*, N.S. *13*: 131–47.

Geisler, W., 1924. *Die Deutsche Stadt: Ein Beitrag Zur Morphologie Der Kulturlandschaft* (Stuttgart).

Hart, P. E. and Clarke, R., 1980. *Concentration in British industry.*
Hillier Parker Research, 1979. *British Shopping developments.*
Hobhouse, H., 1971. *Thomas Cubitt: master builder.*
Jackle, J. A., 1983. 'Twentieth century revival architecture and the gentry', *Journal of Cultural Geography*, 4: 28–43.
Larkham, P. J., 1986a. 'Conservation, planning and morphology in West Midlands conservation areas, 1968–1985' (unpublished Ph.D. thesis, University of Birmingham).
Larkham, P. J., 1986b. 'The agents of urban change: a case study of the agents involved in changes to the built fabric in West Midlands conservation areas', *Occasional Publication 21*, Department of Geography, University of Birmingham.
Larkham, P. J., 1986c. 'The role of estate agents in the development process: a wider perspective', *Land Development Studies*, 3: 181–9.
Larkham, P. J., 1988a. 'Changing conservation areas in the English Midlands: evidence from local planning records', *Urban Geography*, 9: 445–65.
Larkham, P. J., 1988b. 'The style of superstores: the response of J. Sainsbury PLC to a planning problem', *International Journal of Retailing*, 3: 44–59.
Management Horizons, 1987. *Retail International*, April: 17–18.
Mattson, R., 1983. 'Store front remodelling on Main Street', *Journal of Cultural Geography*, 3: 41–55.
Ministry of Public Building & Works, 1970. *The building process: a case study of Marks & Spencer Limited.*
Möller, I., 1959. 'Die Entwicklung eines Hamburger Gebietes von der Agrar-zur Groszstadtlandschaft: mit einem Beitrag zur Methode der Städtishen Aufrissanalyse', *Hamburger Geographische Studien 10*, Institut für Geographie und Wirtschaftsgeographie de Universität Hamburg.
Nash, A., 1975. *A. E. Cogswell: architect within a Victorian city.*
Redmayne, R. (ed.), 1950. *Ideals in industry.*
Rees, G., 1973. *St. Michael: a history of Marks & Spencer.*
Rodger, R. G., 1981. 'Sources and methods of urban studies: the contribution of building records', *Area*, 13: 315–21.
Sabelberg, E., 1983. 'The persistence of palazzi and intra-urban structures in Tuscany and Sicily', *Journal of Historical Geography*, 9: 247–64.
Schlüter, O., 1899a. 'Über den Grundriss der Städte', *Zeitschrift der Geselischaft für Erdkunde zu Berlin*, 34: 446–62.
Schlüter, O., 1899b. 'Bermerkungen zur Siedlungsgeographie', *Geographische Zeitschrift*, 5: 65–84.
Trowell, F., 1985. 'Speculative housing development in the suburb of Headingley, Leeds, 1838–1914', *Publications of the Thoresby Society*, 59: 50–118.
Whitehand, J. W. R., 1981. 'Fluctuations in the land-use composition of urban development during the industrial era', *Erdkunde*, 35: 129–40.
Whitehand, J. W. R., 1983. 'Renewing the local CBD: more hands at work than you thought?', *Area*, 15: 323–6.
Whitehand, J. W. R., 1984a. 'Urban Geography: the internal structure of cities', *Progress in Human Geography*, 8: 95–104.
Whitehand, J. W. R., 1984b. 'Commercial townscapes in the making', *Journal of Historical Geography*, 10: 174–200.
Whitehand, J. W. R., 1984c. 'Architecture of commercial redevelopment in post-war Britain', *Journal of Cultural Geography*, 4: 41–55.

Whitehand, J. W. R., 1984d. 'Rebuilding town centres: developers, architects and styles', *Occasional Publication 19*, Department of Geography, University of Birmingham.

Whitehand, J. W. R. and Whitehand, S. M., 1983. 'The study of physical change in town centres: research procedures and types of change', *Transactions, Institute of British Geographers, N.S.* 8: 483–507.

Whitehand, J. W. R., and Whitehand S. M., 1984. 'The physical fabric of town centres: the agents of change', *Transactions, Institute of British Geographers, N.S.* 9: 231–47.

Whitehouse, B. P., 1964. *Partners in property.*

Part V

Fringe belts

13 Morphogenesis, fringe-belts and urban size: an exploratory essay

Michael Barke

Introduction

Unlike many other terms commonly used by students of urban morphology, the term 'fringe-belt' may be found in the recently published major reference work *The Dictionary of Human Geography* (Johnson *et al.* 1981). Such omissions may be a reflection of editorial predilections but other reasons may be found in the continuing underdevelopment of morphological studies in British urban geography. In this context it is worth noting that the publication of probably the two most seminal works in British urban morphology (Conzen 1960, 1962) coincided with what contemporaries were pleased to call the 'conceptual revolution' in geography. The essentially inductive approaches and traditions of urban morphology found little sympathy with those anxious to '. . . make geography more scientific, and . . . develop a body of theory' (Burton 1963). Inevitably, the more readily quantifiable aspects of urban geography attracted the attention of research workers. Two decades later it is possible to take a more balanced view of the content of urban geography, and the growing interest of disciplines such as history and archaeology in morphological studies should act as a catalyst for a revival of interest amongst urban geographers. Perhaps the greatest need of all is for a geographical text book on urban morphology that is accessible in terms of price, language and concepts to a generation of undergraduates.

Despite the limited and uneven level of interest in urban morphology shown by British urban geographers, a number of ideas, terms and concepts have found their way into more general use and text-book recognition (Carter 1972) and one of the most significant of these is the fringe-belt concept. Recent research on fringe-belts has been summarized by Whitehand (1981a) and the same author has recently reviewed the history and ramifications of the concept (Whitehand, 1988). The present essay will therefore include only a brief outline of the fringe-belt idea and will then proceed to its central theme which is concerned with the issue of how urban size may influence some of the basic processes of morphogenesis and especially the formation and subsequent modifications of fringe-belts. Some of the possible effects of urban size will be introduced in an essentially deductive way and a range of empirical evidence will then be examined. Despite the latter it is stressed that this chapter is written in an exploratory spirit. The intention is to draw attention to some of the possible implications of urban size within the rather narrow context of the fringe-belt concept. It is not intended to present any unified theory of urban size and urban morphology.

The fringe-belt concept

A fringe-belt has been defined (Conzen 1969, 125) as:–

> a belt-like zone originating from the temporarily stationary or very slowly advancing fringe of a town and composed of a characteristic mixture of land-use units initially seeking peripheral location. Significant changes in the whole civilizational context of a town's development such as fluctuations in population and economic development or repeated intensification in the introduction of all kinds of innovations causes intermittent deceleration or standstill in the outward growth of a town as well as marked changes in the admixture of new land-use types at the town fringe. In towns with a long history the geographical result emerging gradually from the dynamics is often a system of successive, broadly, concentric fringe-belts more or less separated by other, usually residential integuments.

Of major significance in the formation of a fringe-belt is the existence of a fixation line, defined (Conzen op. cit.) as:–

> the site of a strong, often protective linear feature such as a town wall marking the traditional stationary fringe of an ancient town. During subsequent growth it causes the topographical fixation of a consequent ring system of streets as the backbone of an incipient Inner Fringe-Belt and as the dividing line between its intramural and extramural.

Conzen saw the fringe-belt concept as a way of introducing order into the complexity and variety of urban evolution. It is probably true to say that his concern was less with fringe-belts *per se* and more with their significance for the entire morphological evolution of a whole town of considerable antiquity. Conzen's approach has been termed by Openshaw (1973) the 'medieval fringe-belt model' to distinguish it from other variants of the same theme.

One such variant was identified in a major addition to the literature on fringe-belts in Whitehand's (1972a) paper which adopted a deductive approach based upon neo-classical urban economics. Thünian analysis was used to construct a model of the process of conversion of land from rural to urban use. Two major types of urban development, housing and institutions, were considered, the latter being representative of many typical fringe-belt land-uses. Zones of residential accretion were, of course, associated with booms in house-building when land values were relatively high. In periods of house-building slump, characterized by somewhat lower land values, institutional land-uses tended to be able to compete more effectively and colonize the existing urban fringe to form a fringe-belt.

Ostensibly, it would appear that the two major approaches to fringe-belt formation are complementary – Conzen's primary concern being with successive phases in the evolution of the town plan and its constituent elements, and Whitehand's major interest lying with the built environment and land use. Whitehand's house-building slump period may, on the face of it be equated with the existence of a fixation line in Conzen's 'medieval fringe-belt model'. However, the chronologies of the two approaches are far from similar (Sutcliffe 1983). It is certainly not the case that each trough in the building cycle is associated with the formation of one fringe-belt. Neither does the term fringe-belt as identified by Conzen relate to a feature resulting from longer historical periods than those encapsulated within the building cycles identified in the industrial era. Furthermore, the true fringe-belt almost certainly requires the existence of a fixation line such as a town wall or some physical feature to introduce a major discontinuity to urban expansion.

Nevertheless, Whitehand's approach, using bid-rent theory, has isolated a most important morphological process. It is argued that increasing distance from the urban core diminished the utility of sites for residential use more quickly than for miscellaneous institutional uses. The costs of accessibility for housing are high per unit area but tend to be relatively lower per unit area for institutions. This produces a steeper bid-rent curve for housing, compared to institutions, with distance from the city centre. However, this only describes the situation in a housing boom. In a slump period the shortage of available capital is likely to have a greater impact upon house-building than upon institutions. Site development costs for the latter tend to be lower per unit area than for house builders. Table 13.1 gives some indication of this factor and illustrates the major difference between residential development and fringe-belt-type land uses in the contribution of land costs to total costs. It is clear that institutions are much more likely to be more sensitive to changes in the price of land than are residential developers. Consequently, when land prices are depressed, as in a slump period, institutions may be able to acquire sites which normally would have been acquired by house builders.

Further empirical verification of this process on a national scale can be seen in Figure 13.1. The cost of residential building land (indexed to 1900 prices) is compared to house building activity and an index of building costs (Mitchell and Deane 1962; Mitchell and Jones 1971). The generally positive relationship between building activity and land prices is confirmed. However, the index of building costs behaves quite differently and in a house building slump there is little or no commensurate fall in building costs. Although presented at a highly aggregated national level, these relationships are suggestive of cyclical fluctuations in morphological and land use development. A slump period clearly favours less intensive types of development in which building costs are a lower proportion of overall costs – that is, the institutional type of development. In boom periods, such land

Table 13.1 Urban development: land and capital costs per 10,000 population (1967 prices)

a) Housing

Population density per acre	Building costs (£m)	Site area (acres)	Development costs (£m)	Land* cost (£m)	Total (£m)	Land cost as % of total cost
30	9·52	333	1·11	0·67	11·30	5·9
37	9·73	270	0·97	0·54	11·24	4·8
50	10·47	200	0·76	0·40	11·63	3·4
75	11·95	133	0·50	0·27	12·72	2·1
100	14·54	100	0·42	0·20	15·16	1·3

b) Miscellaneous development

Category	Building costs (£000)	Site area (acres)	Development costs (£000)	Land* cost (£000)	Total (£000)	Land cost as % of total cost
Golf courses	3	10	7	20	30	66·7
Parks and public gardens	3	7	9	14	26	53·8
Stadium, hall swimming baths	90	3	4	6	100	6·0
Playing field	6	37	24	74	104	71·1
Total	102	57	44	114	260	43·8

* At £2,000 an acre. But note that in reality this would vary between uses. For example, golf clubs would on average pay less per acre than housebuilders.

Source: Stone (1973) 114–19

uses are less likely to be able to afford the inflated land values that prevail. On this highly aggregated national scale, therefore, there appears to be considerable empirical evidence for the morphological and land-use implications of the building cycle. Whether such cycles automatically lead to the formation of fringe-belts in individual towns is a rather more contentious issue.

The implications of the fringe-belt concept for the study of urban morphological change extend further. So far, the changes subsequent to the encapsulation of a former fringe area within the totality of the built-up area of a town have been ignored. Clearly, in such circumstances the relative location of the fringe-belt is changed and this is likely to induce long-term change in land-use competition. With such encapsulation, a variety of possibilities present themselves (Fig. 13.2). Although the original use may survive, bid-rent theory would suggest that many such sites will fall to bids for residential development. However, in order to justify the occupation of

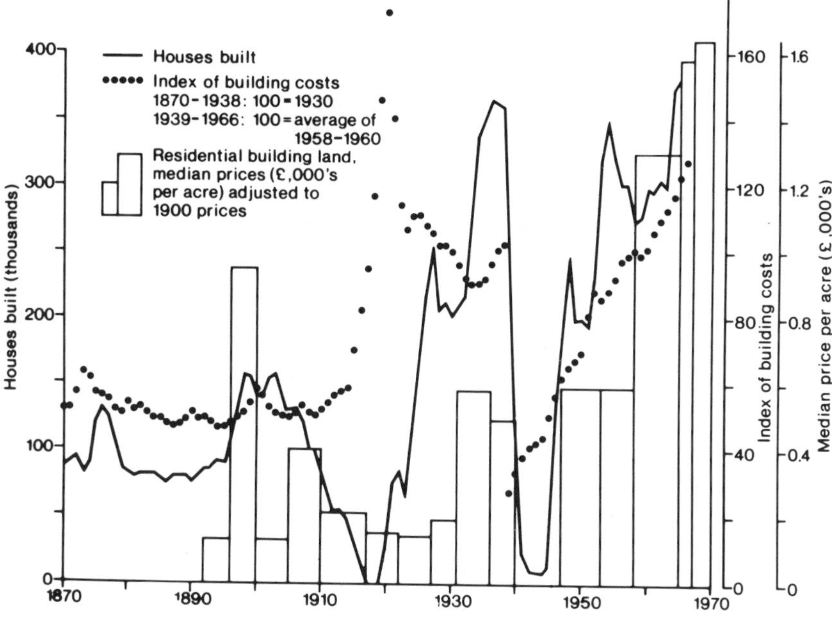

Figure 13.1 House-building, building costs and residential building land prices, 1870–1970. Source: Mitchell and Deane (1962), Mitchell and Deane (1971) and Vallis (1972)

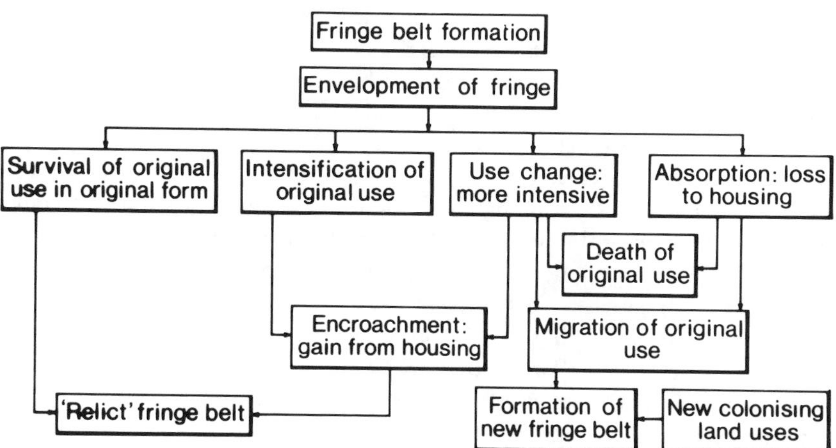

Figure 13.2 Possible outcomes for fringe-belt land use with envelopment by urban growth. Source: Barke (1982)

a now relatively more central and accessible site the fringe-belt land use may utilize it more intensively, thus steepening the gradient of its bid-rent for its own site. Whitehand (1972b) has pointed out that it is unlikely that the bid-rent curve of housing will steepen as much as a number of institutions. As the latter almost certainly initially utilized a smaller fraction of the total site than the former, the potential for additional capital investment is much greater. If this takes place, then the institutional land use will tend to experience a relatively larger increase in accessibility costs per unit area than housing. Such uses may therefore remain, or even expand, as distinctive morphological zones embedded within the built-up area of a town. However, not all land uses are capable of intensifying site utilization in this way and, for many, migration to the new urban fringe may be the only alternative to total extinction. Such moves may clearly lead to the development of a new morphological zone on or beyond the current urban fringe. Thus, the fringe-belt concept may be extended to give some insights into the processes of morphological and land-use change. The concept, introduced into British urban geography by Conzen, has proved to be an extremely fertile one, extending far beyond the mere identification of a static morphological feature into a theoretical exposition of fundamental morphogenetic processes. As such, the possibilities for extension are considerable. The remainder of this chapter is concerned with one such extension.

The implications of urban size

Despite the fact that questions of scale and hierarchy have long dominated urban geography there are surprisingly few published papers which are explicitly concerned with the implications of urban size. This is surely a major omission, for the possibility that urban size influences morphogenetic processes is an issue not just of academic interest but also one of considerable practical relevance.

Deductive reasoning would seem to suggest that the very factor of size itself is likely to have modifying effects upon urban processes. First, it could be argued that accessibility costs in the small town are likely to be much less significant than in the large city. There are two reasons for this. In the small town it may well be feasible to walk to a large proportion of the desired destinations, and there is also the simple fact that because lesser distances are involved than in the large city the cost of transport is likely to be reduced. Therefore, we may hypothesize that in the small town the gradient of transport costs from core to periphery will be shallower than in the large city. Secondly, it is, of course, conventional to plot accessibility costs in relation to distance from the town or city centre. The justification for this is often expressed in terms of commuting costs to the urban core, the latter representing, in effect, the mean centre of gravity of employment. The validity of such an assumption in the small town may be questioned, especially in those towns with a low proportion of service employment. In such cases the significance of the centre in employment terms is likely to be limited and therefore commuting journeys (although not necessarily all other journeys) and costs will be less than in a large city. There is ample empirical evidence to support this view. Stone (1973), for example, found that travelling costs per head were 22 per cent lower in urban areas of 50,000 population than in those of 100,000 and almost 50 per cent higher in cities of 250,000. The net result is that a shallower bid-rent gradient for housing would be expected in the small town compared to the large city.

A further contribution to the argument may be found in considering the actual cost of sites for residential development at the periphery of the city in comparison with those at the periphery of the small town. Two further reasons may be advanced in support of the view that there are likely to be substantial differences relating to urban size. Urban economists have recently drawn attention to the significance of future expectations of urban growth for land costs (Ottensmann 1977). Briefly, the argument is that in a city where the future expectations of urban growth are high, there will be a greater tendency to withhold land from current development, thus forcing up the price and the density of use on the land that is developed in the current period. It seems logical to argue that in an aggregate historical sense (for example, Britain in the nineteenth and early twentieth centuries), the future expectations of urban growth in large urban areas would be higher than in the majority of smaller towns. Therefore, the price of land at the periphery of the large city seems likely to have been forced up much more than in the small town. The main effect would be to ensure that in the large city land development of all kinds will tend to take place in a more intensive manner than in the small town. This tendency would be especially marked in a boom period and therefore the significance of the building cycle on the intensity of development would be more pronounced in the large city than in the small town.

A second factor concerning the cost of land relates to the relative size of sites used for residential development in the large city compared to those in the small town. On average, sites in the former will tend to be larger than those in the latter. For example, Rodger (1986) has shown that the scale of building projects in Scottish burghs increased with urban size. In this context, the work of Vallis (1972) on long-term trends in urban land and building prices is of considerable interest. Data are presented on the price of land for residential development and the price of residential building plots. The latter relates to land sold on a foot-frontage basis and usually consists either of a single building plot or a plot sold with a degree of infrastructure, such as roads and services, provided. With such plots '. . . there is a more direct relationship to the demand for houses at any given time', (op. cit.: 1211). Residential land, sold per acre, is more likely to be virgin land which, due to proximity to an urban area, has become suitable – in the eyes of developers – for residential development. In many such areas, the price per acre will be considerably influenced by 'hope' value, that is, there will be a strong speculative element. It can be contended that the latter is much more likely in the large city and its vicinity than in the small town. By definition, the actual potential for speculation in the latter will be limited. Smaller size is almost certain to mean greater ease of prediction of overall future demands. In periods of rapidly rising land prices speculative activity increases (McAuslan 1972) and it is unlikely that such a tendency would be as pronounced in a small town as in a large city. Sheer size is bound to mean uncertainty and seems likely to fuel a greater degree of speculation. Vallis (1972) has shown that the price per acre of land for residential development is considerably more volatile than the price of residential building plots. In the slump period immediately before the First World War (1910–16), the price of residential development land per acre fell by 47·5 per cent in real terms from the 1905–9 level, whereas the price level of residential building plots was exactly maintained. Similarly, in the 1936–9 period the real price per acre of residential development land fell by 15·5 per cent from its 1931–5 level, but that of residential plots increased by 97 per cent. If it is accepted that the latter does bear a more direct relationship to the actual demand for houses at any given time, and that such sites will tend to constitute a higher proportion of the total building sites in the small town compared to the large city because of the higher proportion of speculative land (i.e. not divided into residential plots) in the latter, then it follows that we may expect proportionally rather more residential development during a national building trough in the small town rather than in larger urban areas. Further arguments on the significance of urban size may be suggested. It is certainly the case that for most of the nineteenth century there was a greater speculative element involved in the building of working-class housing than middle-class dwellings (Rodger 1979). Greater susceptibility to unemployment, short-time working and casualization of work amongst manual workers would all affect the potential rents affordable (Gauldie 1974) and therefore the security and consistency of rental income available. Furthermore, it is arguable that, because of their economic structure, large industrial cities were likely to contain a higher proportion of working-class residents than many smaller places. For example, Phillips and Walton (1975) have shown for nineteenth-century England that, with the exception of London, individual wealth tended to be concentrated in smaller towns. Similarly, it has been shown (Cameron 1980) for the mid twentieth century that the major conurbations contain a larger proportion of manual workers than smaller places. If these differences in population composition exist then the suggestion that there is a '. . . tendency for the building of higher-class houses to diminish less than that of the working-class houses during slumps in house-building' (Whitehand 1981b: 135) is of considerable interest. Widely scattered and fragmentary evidence tends to support such a view if not conclusively prove it (Beresford 1971; Long 1940; Rodger 1976, 1979, 1986; Whitehand 1981b). Analysis of some additional evidence from Liverpool for the period 1838–66 (Lewis 1965) shows that the proportion of highest valued houses (over £35) being built, although consistently low, is relatively constant and fluctuates less than the building of houses in the lowest two categories of value (less than £25). From this reasoning and, admittedly, limited evidence we may tentatively suggest that house-building in the small town may be somewhat less susceptible to booms and slumps in national building activity than is the case in the large city.

So far, the arguments have been concerned exclusively with house-building activity and it has been suggested that the bid-rent gradient for this land use is likely to vary with urban size and that the susceptibility to booms and slumps in residential development will also vary with size. The fringe-belt concept, however, is concerned with low accessibility-cost land uses such as institutions. If we turn our attention to these, then different arguments apply which may be summmarized briefly. It seems unlikely that the reasoning outlined in this section will apply to many institutions. As already noted, accessibility costs are of lesser significance for such land uses, whether they be in the large city or small town. For this reason alone, few significant differences with urban size in the bid-rent gradient for such land uses should be anticipated. It may also be argued that susceptibility to the overall building cycle is unlikely to vary for institutions between urban areas of different sizes. Whether in the small town or the large city, the majority of institutions seem less likely than house-builders to be affected by the general shortage of capital that characterizes a housing slump. The social demand for such development remains and many are publicly financed. Barras and Ferguson (1985: 1381) have recently noted that public-sector non-residential building derives 'less from business cycle effects than from autonomous policy factors' and Barras (1987) has asserted that public investment programmes in institutional buildings such as schools and hospitals are subject to much less extreme shifts in government policy than is the housing programme. Systematic variation in institutional development which may be attributed to building-cycle effects in settlements of difference sizes would seem unlikely.

Figure 13.3a is an attempt to summarize much of the argument in a graphic manner. The distances AB and AC represent, for both the small town and the large city, the maximum theoretical distance to which any bid-rent is possible for residential and institutional development respectively: in other words, where bid-rent levels reach zero. In reality, of course, the actual distances involved would be much greater for the city than the small town. Figure 13.3 simply shows the *relative* gradients with distance from the existing urban fringe. Following the arguments above, the bid-rent curve for housing in the small town is shallower than for housing in the large city, but the bid-rent curve for institutional land use is approximately the same. The main implication to be drawn from Figure 13.3a is that, even in a housing boom, it is possible for institutions in the small town to out-bid residential development for sites relatively nearer to the edge of the existing

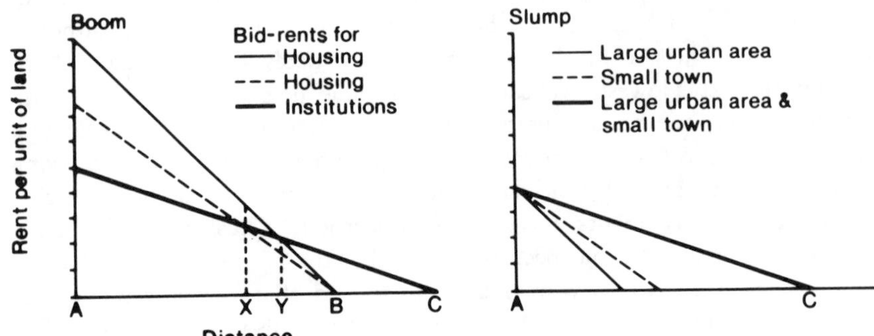

Figure 13.3 Hypothetical relationships between bid-rent and distance from the edge of the built-up area in small towns and larger urban areas, **a** *left* during a house boom, **b** *right* during a house slump

built-up area than is the case in the large city. At distance zone AX in the large city, residential development is still successfully out-bidding institutional land use but in the small town the probabilities of sites falling to one or other of these two land use categories is approximately the same. Not until distance zone AY is reached in the large city, that is, relatively much further from the edge of the existing built-up area, would parity in bid-rents be experienced.

Figure 13.3b shows the situation in a housing slump. Once again it must be stressed that the distance zones on the horizontal axis are relative. The institutional bid-rent curve slides down the rent axis, but only a little. The housing bid-rent curve slides down much further, so much so that only at the very edge of the built-up area is there approximately equal competition for sites between the two uses. The gradients remain as in Figure 13.3a as it is assumed that, for both land-use categories, transport costs remain a constant proportion of total cost (Whitehand 1972a). The significance of the hypothesized shallower bid-rent curve for housing in the small town compared to that in a larger urban area should be immediately obvious from Figure 13.3b. Bids for housing in the small town are possible over a relatively (although, not, of course, absolutely) greater distance from the present edge of the built-up area than is the case in the large city. Although for both sizes of settlement the housing curve is below the institutional curve, the relative probabilities of some sites falling to housing development on the fringe of the small town during a slump period seem to be greater than in the large city. Put another way, the impact of booms and slumps in the overall building cycle seems likely to be somewhat less in the small town that in the large city.

Some empirical evidence

Having outlined some of the basic ideas which support the view that there may be significant modifications to morphogenetic processes resulting from urban size, it remains to test these empirically. The modifications proposed imply that during a housing boom residential development in the small town will tend to colonize the urban fringe but that such a tendency will be less pronounced than in the large city. The principal reason for this is the shallower bid-rent gradient for residential development in the small town compared to the large city. It may well be possible, therefore, for institutional land use to compete more effectively with housing for proximal sites in the small town *even during a housing boom.* In a housing slump a similar situation will obtain, although considerably less land will be developed overall, but it is postulated that a higher proportion of residential development will take place in the slump phase in a small town than in a larger urban area. In other words, housing development will constitute a more constant proportion of overall urban development in the small town than in the large city.

This proposition and its implications may be tested at the level of the individual settlement. Previous research by the author (Barke 1974; 1976) has produced data which allow an examination of the impact of building cycles on the temporal pattern of the evolution of residential and institutional land use in the small town of Falkirk, central Scotland.

The variations in the ratio of institutional development to residential development in Falkirk for eight time periods over the period 1851–1961 are shown in Figure 13.4. To facilitate comparison, the methodology used by Whitehand (1972a) in north-west Glasgow has been followed as closely as possible. Throughout this section, comparison will be made with what is termed the 'Whitehand model' and visual comparison may be made with the graphs included in his 1972 paper.

The 1851–71 period in Falkirk produced a relative slump in house-building but the pattern of development clearly does not conform to the Whitehand model of slump conditions. Residential development is more significant than would be expected in all distance zones. In fact, the relationship is almost the opposite of what one would anticipate from the Whitehand model. Residential development constituted the only form of development at some of the more distant sites, even in this slump period. This is, of course, entirely consistent with the view that in small towns accessibility costs for housing are of lesser significance that in large urban areas. Also in the 1851–71 period, there is some limited support for the idea that, in the small town, institutions may be able to compete relatively more successfully for proximal sites. However, a word of caution is necessary at this stage. The absolute amount of development of all kinds in this period is rather low and chance factors may therefore be significant. It is unfortunate but inevitable that the amount of development taking place in the

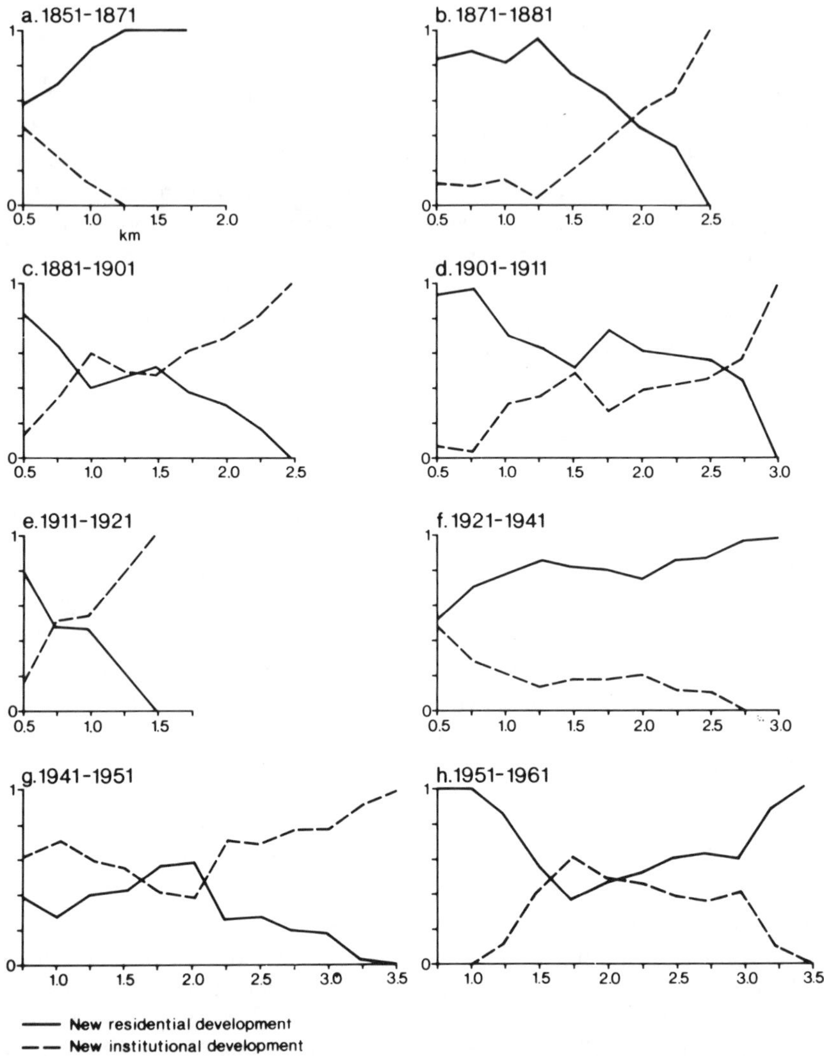

Figure 13.4 Ratio of residential to institutional development with distance from edge of built-up area in 1851: Falkirk, 1851–1961. (Conversion from rural land use only.) Running means of three zones

small town in all periods is likely to be less than a larger urban area, thus making direct comparison difficult.

In contrast to the previous period, the 1871–81 pattern conforms much more closely to the anticipated boom pattern of development. Residential development predominates to a distance of two kilometres from the edge of the built-up area at it was in 1851. However, the linearity of the relationship is not as great as one would have expected from the Whitehand model and there is a minority of institutional development taking place on proximal sites.

The 1881–1901 period covers a slump in the local building cycle. Once again, the decline in residential development with distance is not quite as linear as one would expect, some development taking place on relatively more distant sites. Institutions are competing relatively more successfully for sites at or near the edge of the built-up area to a more marked degree than in the previous boom period.

In the 1901–11 boom period, although the ratio of institutional development does not exceed that of residential development until the 2·5 km. zone, institutional development is successfully maintaining a presence in some relatively proximal sites, for example in the 1·0 to 1·5 km. zone. The subsequent slump (1911–21) appears to conform well with the expected model of rapid distance decay in residential development and a corresponding increase in institutions. However, in this period, as in 1851–71, the total amount of development was rather limited.

The 1921–41 period is of particular interest as it suggests that the modifications of urban size, already established for the nineteenth century, continued even in the changed social and economic conditions of the twentieth century. The by now familiar feature of institutional land uses competing more effectively for proximal sites than one would expect from the Whitehand model is readily apparent. Furthermore, instead of showing a linear decline with distance, the proportion of residential development actually increases up to the 3 km. distance zone. This supports the view that accessibility costs in the small town are less significant than in a larger settlement, although it is worth noting that this period saw the adoption of public transport on a significant scale (Lawson 1975) and this undoubtedly helped to open up some more distant sites for residential development.

The 1941–51 pattern again fails to conform precisely with the Whitehand model of a slump period. In particular, residential development is more significant than one would expect, especially in the intermediate zones. Finally, the pattern in the 1951–61 boom fails to show the anticipated linear trend. The curves from the edge of the built-up area as far as the 1·75 km. zone conform to the expected pattern but then housing picks up again, adding further support to the thesis that in a small town residential development at some distance from the existing built-up area is a feasible proposition.

At a very general level there is some similarity between the patterns in Figure 13.4 and those in north-west Glasgow, but the principal conclusion must be that the response to booms and slumps is by no means as clear-cut in the small town. Two qualifications of the Whitehand model appear to be that, in the small town, institutional land use can compete more successfully for proximal sites and that there tends to be relatively greater proportions of residential development on more distant sites. Both features are, of

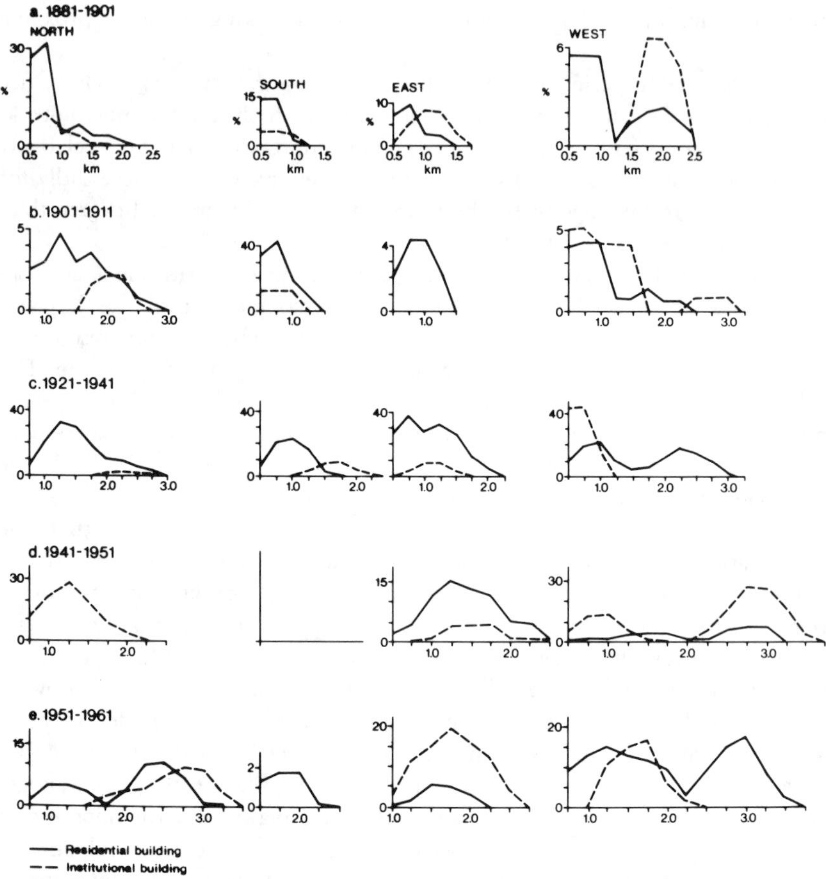

Figure 13.5 Falkirk: new housing and institutional developments (as a percentage of available land) by sectors and distance from edge of built-up area in 1851. Running means of three zones

course, entirely consistent with the hypothesis advanced earlier.

However, one obvious problem with the analysis so far is that the diagrams show in Figure 13.4 are aggregate ratio curves for the whole circumference of the town of Falkirk. It is quite feasible that the edge of the built-up area can be at different distances in different sectors. In the north-west Glasgow study sectoral orientation was obviously a constant factor. Distortions may be introduced by examining development for the entire circumference of a town when such development may have a sectoral bias. Consequently, Figure 13.5 disaggregates the Falkirk data into four sectors and shows that in some cases there has indeed been sectoral bias in development. For example, the peaking of institutional development in the 0·5 km. zone in the 1921–41 period is limited to the western sector only. Close scrutiny of the sequence of graphs will reveal similar if less extreme features for other periods. This disaggregation by sector leads to a further problem in analysis. It has already been noted that small size implies less development overall and therefore makes comparison with larger places on a uniform basis difficult. Disaggregating the data by sector compounds the difficulty of such comparison. In any one sector there may be insufficient development within one time period to warrant the construction of a graph. Figure 13.5 therefore includes only those time periods and sectors where a meaningful amount of data was available.

With these reservations in mind we can examine the time periods for which sufficient data are available and assess the extent to which they support the Whitehand model and the small-town modifications proposed earlier. It should be noted that Figure 13.5 shows the proportion of available land in a particular zone in a particular sector that underwent development, not the relative proportions of residential and institutional development as shown in Figure 13.4.

Two general observations may be made from the examination of the disaggregated graphs. The Whitehand model stressed that, during a slump, development of all kinds would tend to be concentrated at the immediate edge of the built-up area and tend to be more widely dispersed during a boom. This feature does not appear to be so marked in the small town, whether the data are examined in aggregate form (Fig. 13.4) or by sectoral orientation (Fig. 13.5). Although there is clearly less development overall during a housing slump, that which does take place is still spatially quite extensive, colonizing some quite distant sites. Once again, this is consistent with the notion of a shallower bid-rent gradient in the small town. Secondly, it is clear that various forms of institutional land-use can successfully compete for sites adjacent to the edge of the built-up area – for example, in the west sector in 1901–11, 1921–41 and 1941–51, the north sector in 1941–51 and the east in 1951–61. Yet again, this is consistent with the suggestion that accessibility costs for residential development are of reduced significance in the small town and therefore relatively cheaper sites further out may be sought, leaving some proximal sites for other uses.

So far, concentration has been solely upon the conversion of agricultural land to residential or institutional use. A most interesting field for morphological research is concerned with the changes subsequent to such areas being incorporated within the built-up area (Fig. 13.2). Applying the reasoning of simple neo-classical land-use economics, it might be hypothesized that during a housing boom low accessibility-cost land uses such as institutions, once they are embedded within the built-up area, would be vulnerable to the bids of a high accessibility-cost use such as housing and that the former might be expected to be replaced by the latter. However, work on such modification (Whitehand 1972b) has suggested that many institutions, instead of proving vulnerable to bids from a high accessibility-cost land use such as housing, successfully increase their bid-

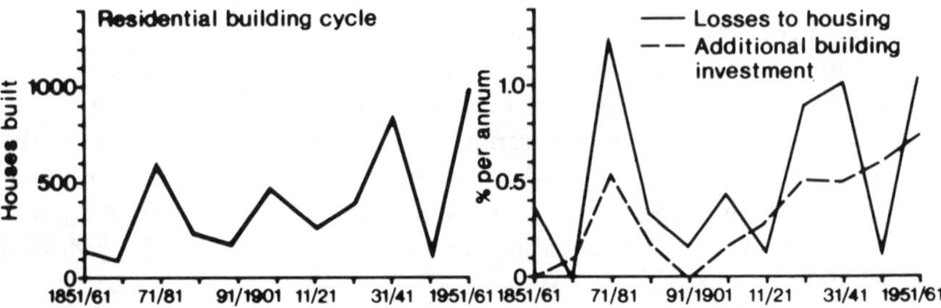

Figure 13.6 Falkirk: proportion of fringe-belt sites incurring losses to housing and undertaking additional building investment, 1851–1961

rents for their own and even adjacent sites. 'These increases were related to the tendency for more capital to be invested over time in institutional sites than in housing sites and for the strength of the linkages between institutions and the urban area to increase as they became well established . . .' (Whitehand 1981a: 136). However, not all extensive fringe-belt land uses are capable of such a strategy and during the passage of a housing boom there is likely to be some redevelopment of fringe-belt sites for housing (Whitehand 1972).

If the role of accessibility costs is limited in the small town in the way that has been argued earlier in this chapter, then it should follow that there will be relatively less pressure on land for redevelopment of all kinds once it is incorporated within the built-up area. There is some scattered empirical support for such a hypothesis. For example, Slater (1978) has drawn attention to the greater longevity of survival of villas in small country towns. In Falkirk it was not until comparatively late that many sites in the inner areas were coming under pressure for modification. Figure 13.6 shows that during the housing boom of the 1870s a minority of inner sites were redeveloped for housing but that it was not until the twentieth century, and especially after 1921, that this feature became more widespread. A fruitful area for further research would therefore seem to be concerned with the length of time that a plot remains in its original use. Does this vary significantly between the small town and the large city?

However, the main concern lies with the relative differences in the bid-rent curves of residential and institutional uses once they have been incorporated within the built-up area. If there was a marked difference between these two in the small town, as there appears to be in a large city, then it would be anticipated that the most central, accessible sites in institutional use would be the most vulnerable to redevelopment for housing. As a town grows in physical size then accessibility costs may be expected to increase in importance and therefore extensive land uses on relatively central sites may be highly vulnerable to bids by residential developers. Furthermore, such a process would be expected to be especially pronounced during a

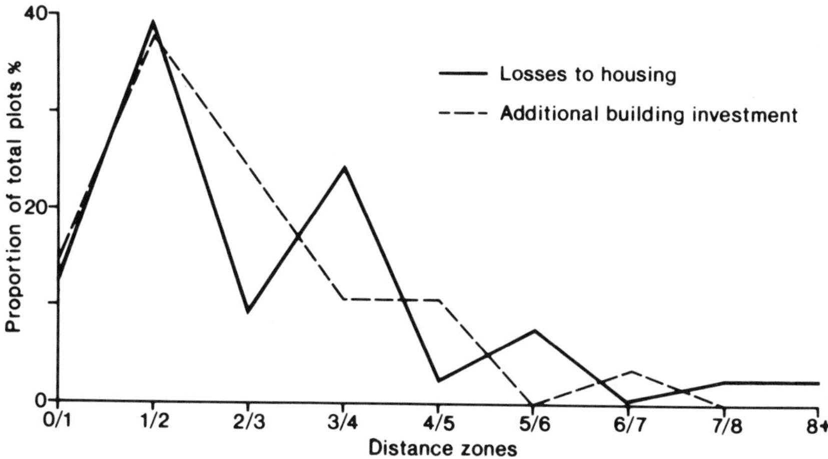

Figure 13.7 Falkirk 1851–1961: proportion of fringe-belt sites incurring losses to housing and undertaking building investment by distance zones from edge of built up area in 1851

housing boom. Yet, it has been argued throughout this chapter that, in the small town, there is less difference between the two bid-rent curves and the significance of booms and slumps in this morphogenetic process is somewhat reduced. Examination of the histories of former fringe-belt sites in Falkirk, once they have been incorporated into the built-up area, allows some analysis of the fringe-belt modification process in the small town (Fig. 13.6). The result is consistent with the reasoning in suggesting that the overall losses to residential development are limited. However, such losses do tend to occur in boom periods, for example 1871–81 and 1931–41. It is equally noteworthy that a significant proportion of such sites are also likely to experience additional building investment by institutional land uses in the same boom period. The temporal process of morphogenesis is by no means as clear as postulated in the Whitehand model and the difference between the booms and slumps are not as marked as in north-west Glasgow (Whitehand 1972b).

Figure 13.7 shows the losses to housing and additional building investment for the entire period by distance zones from the town centre. It is the case that the central, more accessible sites are more likely to fall to bids by residential developers but this is by no means an exclusive phenomenon. In several cases additional building investment (that is, by institutions) is equally important. Although this feature could be a product of a steepening bid-rent gradient for some institutions over time, it is also consistent with the concept of limited difference between the bid-rent gradients for both residential and institutional land uses in the small town.

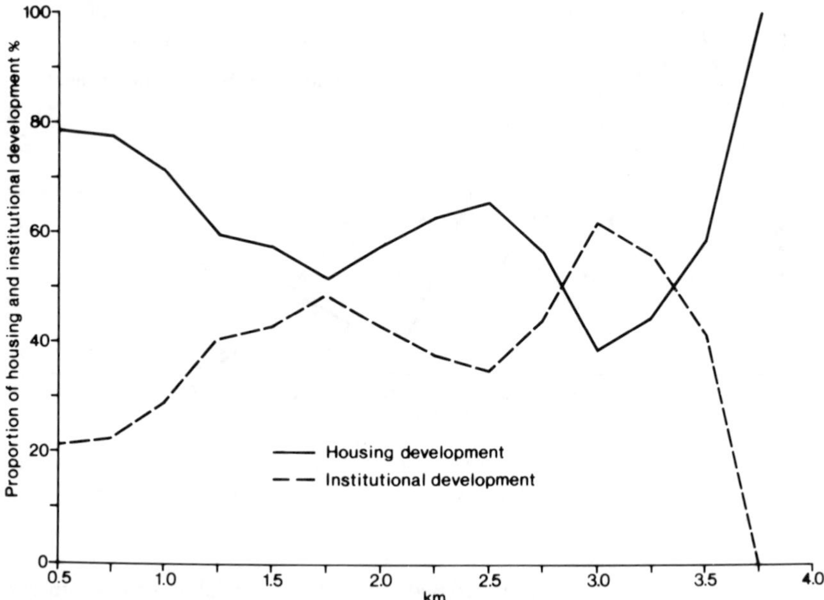

Figure 13.8 Falkirk: relative proportions of residential and institutional development by distance zones, 1851–1961. (Conversion from rural land uses only.) Three zone running means

Conclusion

The general tenor of much of the above discussion has been to suggest that, in the small town, there is a degree of indeterminacy between residential and institutional bid-rents. As the fringe-belt model developed by Whitehand depends so much on the different behaviour of these two, it may be thought that this essay has sought to undermine the fringe-belt concept as applied to a small town. This would be especially ironic as the concept was introduced into British urban geography by Conzen through the medium of the the small town of Alnwick. It is not the author's intention in any way to deny the existence of fringe-belts in small towns. Indeed, a full account of Falkirk's fringe-belts is in print (Barke 1974) and Figure 13.8 clearly suggests that at least two may be recognized during the industrial era in Falkirk. These, in fact, correspond to the intermediate and outer fringe-belts of the town, the formation of the inner fringe-belt taking place earlier than the study period 1851-1961. Yet, if the deductive reasoning presented earlier has any validity, the basic question remains as to why fringe-belts should form in a small town like Falkirk. Should a haphazard scattering of low density, miscellaneous institutional development not be expected?

The answer to this apparent dilemma is to be found in the work of both Conzen and Whitehand. The latter (Whitehand 1988) has recognized that the formation of a fringe-belt may require more than the reduction of house-building in a building-cycle trough. Other features, especially the presence of Conzen's complementary concept of the fixation line or 'changes in the whole civilizational context of a town's development' (Conzen 1969: 125), are necessary for the formation of a fringe-belt as a distinctive, relatively continuous morphological feature. However, if these conditions are present in the small town then the bid-rent mechanisms suggested here would lead to a greater degree of perpetuation of the fringe-belt than in the large city for it would be less subject to disturbance over time by competing land uses.

It must be acknowledged that the modifications to morphogenetic processes suggested here for small towns relate to differences of degree rather than differences of kind. This does not diminish their significance. The morphological outcomes of the processes discussed relate to issues which extend far beyond the mere formation and subsequent modification of fringe-belts. They lead into considerations of land-use composition (Champion 1972), density (Best and Rogers 1973) and environmental contrasts in towns of different sizes and, ultimately, into questions of the quality of life of inhabitants. There is an almost universal consensus amongst the more reflective of writers on urban affairs that the morphological and environmental characteristics of small towns are fundamental contributors to quality of life (Chamberlin 1983; Clifton-Taylor 1978; Hoskins 1949) and, interestingly enough, this forms a prominent theme in Conzen's later work (1966, 1975).

References

Barke, M., 1974. 'The changing urban fringe of Falkirk: some morphological implications of urban growth', *Scottish Geographical Magazine*, 90: 85–97.

Barke, M., 1976. 'Land use succession: a factor in fringe-belt modification', *Area*, 8: 303–6.

Barke, M., 1982. 'Beyond the urban growth map: suggestions for more analytical work in urban morphology', *Teaching Geography* 7: 111–15.

Barras, R., 1987. 'Technical change and the urban development cycle', *Urban Studies*, *24*: 5–30

Barras, R. and Ferguson, D., 1985. 'Spectral analysis of building cycles in Britain', *Environment and Planning, A*, *17*: 1369–91.

Beresford, M. W., 1971. 'The back-to-back house in Leeds, 1787–1937', in *The history of working-class housing*, ed. S. D. Chapman, 93–132.

Best, R. H. and Rogers, A. W., 1973. *The urban countryside.*

Burton, I., 1963. 'The quantitative revolution and theoretical geography', *The Canadian Geographer*, 7: 151–62.

Cameron, G. C., 1980. *The future of the British conurbations.*

Carter, H., 1972. *The study of urban geography.*

Chamberlin, R., 1983. *The English country town.*

Champion, A. G., 1972. Variation in urban densities between towns of England and Wales', *Research Papers, 1*, School of Geography, University of Oxford.

Clifton-Taylor, A., 1978. *Six English Towns.*

Conzen, M. R. G., 1960. 'Alnwick, Northumberland: a study in town-plan analysis', *Publications, Institute of British Geographers, 27.*

Conzen, M. R. G., 1962. 'The plan analysis of an English city centre' in *Proceedings of the IGU symposium in Urban Geography Lund 1960*, ed. K. Norborg, (Lund) 383–414.

Conzen, M. R. G., 1966. 'Historical townscapes in Britain: a problem in applied geography', in *Northern geographical essays in honour of G. H. J. Daysh*, ed. J. W. House, 56–78.

Conzen, M. R. G., 1969. 'Glossary of technical terms' in 'Alnwick, Northumberland: a study in town-plan analysis', *Publications, Institute of British Geographers, 27* (2nd ed.) 123–31.

Conzen, M. R. G., 1975. 'Geography and townscape conservation', in Anglo-German symposium in Applied Geography, Giessen-Würzburg-München, 1973, *Giessener Geographische Schriften*, 95–102.

Gauldie, E., 1974. *Cruel habitations: a history of working-class housing, 1780–1918.*

Hoskins, W. G., 1949. *Midland England.*

Johnston, R. J., Gregory, D., Haggett, P., Smith, D. M., and Stoddart, D. R., 1981. *The dictionary of human geography.*

Lawson, L., 1975. *A history of Falkirk.*

Lewis, J. P., 1965. *Building cycles and Britain's growth.*

Long, C. D., 1940. *Building cycles and the theory of investment* (Princeton).

McAuslan, J, 1972. 'Residential land prices', *Estates Gazette, 222*: 294–5.

Mitchell, B. R., and Deane, P., 1962. *Abstract of British historical statistics.*

Mitchell, B. R., and Jones, H. G., 1971. *Second abstract of British historical statistics.*

Openshaw, S., 1973. 'A theory of the morphological and functional development of the townscape in an historical context', *Seminar Papers, 24*, University of Newcastle upon Tyne, Department of Geography.

Ottensmann, J. R., 1977. 'Urban sprawl, land values and the density of development', *Land Economics, 53*: 389–400.

Phillips, A. D. M., and Walton, J. R., 1975. 'The distribution of personal wealth in English towns in the mid-nineteenth century', *Transactions, Institute of British Geographers, 64*: 35–48.

Rodger, R. G., 1976. 'Scottish urban housebuilding 1870–1914' (unpublished Ph.D. thesis, University of Edinburgh).

Rodger, R. G., 1979. 'Speculative builders and the structure of the Scottish building industry, 1860–1914', *Business History, 21*: 226–46.

Rodger, R. G., 1986. 'The Victorian building industry and the housing of the Scottish working class', in *Building the industrial city*, ed. M. Doughty, 151–206.

Slater, T. R., 1978. 'Family, society and the ornamental villa on the fringes of English country towns', *Journal of Historical Geography, 4*: 129–44.

Stone, P. A., 1973. *The structure, size and costs of urban settlements.*

Sutcliffe, A., 1983. 'Review of *The Urban Landscape: Historical Development and Management*', *Journal of Historical Geography*, 9: 77–9.

Vallis, E. A., 1972. 'Urban land and building prices', *Estates Gazette, 222*: 1015–19.

Whitehand, J. W. R., 1972a. 'Building cycles and the spatial pattern of urban growth', *Transactions, Institute of British Geographers*, 56: 39–55.

Whitehand, J. W. R., 1972b. 'Urban-rent theory, time series and morphogenesis: an example of eclecticism in geographical research', *Area*, 4: 215–22.

Whitehand, J. W. R., 1981a. *The urban landscape: historical development and management.*

Whitehand, J. W. R., 1981b. 'Fluctuations in the land-use composition of urban development during the industrial era', *Erdkunde*, 36: 129–40.

Whitehand, J. W. R., 1988. 'Urban fringe belts: development of an idea', *Planning Perspectives*, 3: 47–58.

14 The fringe-belt concept in a Spanish context: the case of Lleida

Joan Vilagrasa

This study is an analysis of the processes involved in the conversion of peripheral land into the urban built-up area. It focuses on the impact of construction in Lleida, a medium-sized Catalan town, at different stages of its recent history. Far from being a simple empirical investigation, it seeks to contribute general theories useful for the historical understanding of city plans and, more specifically, for understanding the forms of urban growth on the peripheries of Spanish cities since the Civil War. To this end, the Conzenian concept of the fringe-belt and ideas concerning building cycles are employed. In contrast to most English works on the subject, the link between the two concepts is seen to lie not only in land-use analysis but also in understanding the processes affecting urban land development and analysing the social agents involved.[1]

Fringe-belts, building cycles and agents of change

The fringe-belt concept, already used in 1936 in the study of Berlin (Louis 1936), was formulated for morphological analysis by M. R. G. Conzen in his research on the evolution of the town plans of Alnwick (Conzen 1960) and Newcastle upon Tyne (Conzen 1962). In this work, fringe belts comprise new elements in the urban plan that appear at times of little economic development and low population growth. According to Conzen these elements are predominantly low-density land uses. He suggests that for cities with long histories, morphological periods and stages of city growth can be related to a series of historical fringe belts. In the settlement plan, each fringe – however subsequently changed – is succeeded by an area of more intensive land use, originating in times of economic and demographic expansion.

Whitehand contributed to the consolidation of the fringe belt as an analytical concept for morphological research by linking it with building cycles and land-rent theory (Whitehand 1972a, 1972b, 1974). He states that the formation of fringe belts coincides with periods of stagnation in house building when peripheral land is cheap. Conversely, periods of growth in construction coincide with increases in land prices. At times of building recession and low land prices, the urban periphery tends to be colonized by institutional and extensive land users. In building booms, land use is mainly residential and of an intensive nature. This relationship is explained by the theory of land rent, which suggest a greater capacity to purchase land for residential development during booms and the greater competitiveness of institutional land uses, compared with residential ones, during slumps owing to a reduced effective demand for housing.

Whitehand's conceptualization, while establishing a strict separation between institutional and residential land uses, also seems to imply a direct relationship between urban population growth and increased construction. On the other hand, he suggests only a single homogeneous housing market governed by supply and demand, without distinguishing between different sectors of either urban population or housing. In more recent publications Whitehand has enriched these parameters by drawing attention to the decision-making processes of institutions and property owners (Whitehand 1977). He also notes the differing behaviour of a variety of land developers, and the role of housing and urban legislation (Whitehand 1981), though he has not applied these ideas in fringe-belt studies.

This chapter incorporates some of these points developed by Whitehand. Here, institutional behaviour, the strategies of property owners, the characteristics of land developers and the legislation governing housing, as well as urban policy in general, are all vital in understanding the newly built-up areas of the urban periphery. Furthermore, the incorporation of these elements into the analysis of fringe belts makes the theory more flexible and adaptable to different historical contexts.

The analytical framework proposed here examines four different aspects. First, it is shown that, in general, correlations can be established between demographic growth and building development, but in some specific examples these do not necessarily coincide. The congruency or discrepancy between the two factors is the key to the historical understanding of the characteristics of the housing market and the supply of housing; moreover, to a large extent it influences institutional activity and housing policy.

Secondly, the framework assumes a heterogeneous housing market. Divisions are made on the basis of differences in the suppliers of residential development – rather than on the basis of differences in the ability to pay for certain types of housing – which presuppose differing forms, layouts, locations and accessibilities.

Thirdly, the analytical concept of the fringe belt is incorporated. In summary, the idea of fringe-belt formation at times of economic stagnation or slight growth is accepted and equated with periods of slump in the building cycle. The most appropriate definition of a fringe belt is taken to be that used by Conzen in the glossary of technical terms in the 1969 edition of his study of Alnwick: 'A belt-like zone originating from the temporarily stationary or very slowly advancing fringe of a town and composed of a characteristic mixture of land-use units initially seeking peripheral locations' (Conzen 1969: 125). This suggests that the periphery-seeking land uses could be diverse and that, under some circumstances, they may also include residential ones.

Finally, analysis is undertaken of both the characteristics of the housing market and the strategies employed by land owners, housing developers and institutions. This reformulation incorporates into fringe-belt theory the study of the agents who induce urban change. This provides a more rigorous study of the processes of land development and of the interests and influential factors which guide the different agents involved in the urbanization of rural land. The following analysis of the characteristics of Spanish post-Civil-War urban growth, and the empirical study of the peripheral areas emerging in Lleida at three stages of building recession, shows contrasts with the earlier framework of Conzen and Whitehand.

The post-Civil-War Spanish experience

A short review of Spanish post-Civil-War urban growth will allow the elucidation of this scheme of analysis. First, it is important to note a discrepancy between urban population growth and the increase in dwellings built during the first twenty years after the war. Although it was in the 1960s that the greatest population increase in cities took place, the 1940s and, even more so, the 1950s were marked by an important population migration from the country to the cities. While from 1940 to 1960 the overall population of Spain grew by 17 per cent, that of cities with over thirty thousand inhabitants grew by 52 per cent. However, the arrival of immigrants in large- and medium-sized cities was not met by an adequate supply of housing. In 1958 the housing deficit in these cities was calculated at more than a million units (Alcala 1960).

Capel has noted how, as a result of the lack of housing, illegal housing, or self-built dwellings on rural land[2], became common on the urban fringes in the post-war period (Capel 1975). They were normally located outside the influence of urban planning and built by residents with substandard materials and without building plan permits. A number of empirical studies have shown the importance of this type of suburb in the development of the periphery of many Spanish cities (Busquets 1976; Canosa *et al.* 1985; Garcia 1981; Habsburgo 1983).

The lack of a sufficient supply in the orthodox housing market not only brought about examples of illegal housing on the peripheries of cities, but also encouraged another segment of the housing market to adopt similar locational parameters. This was public social housing, hitherto of negligible importance. A study of social housing in Barcelona (Ferrer 1974) shows clearly the relationship between the low price of land and the decision of the public administration to locate new housing areas for migrants on the outskirts of the city. Studies of this particular phenomenon in the Madrid

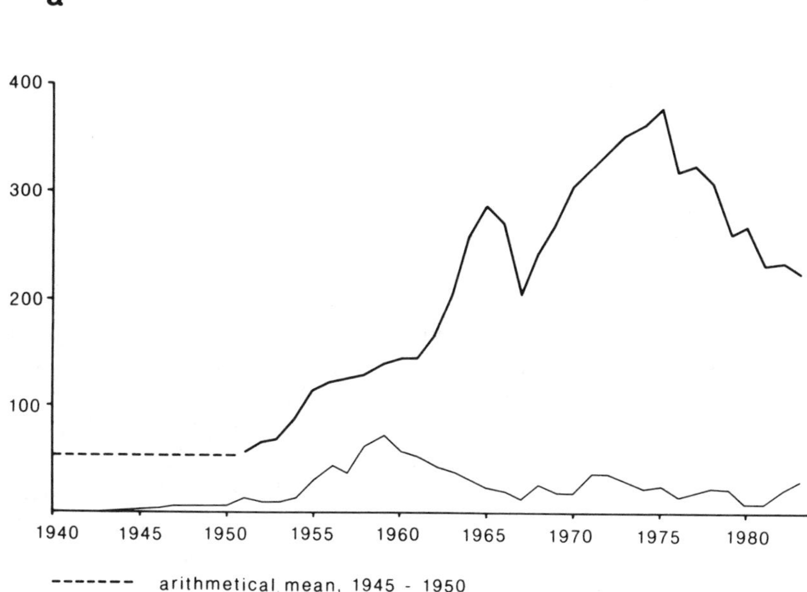

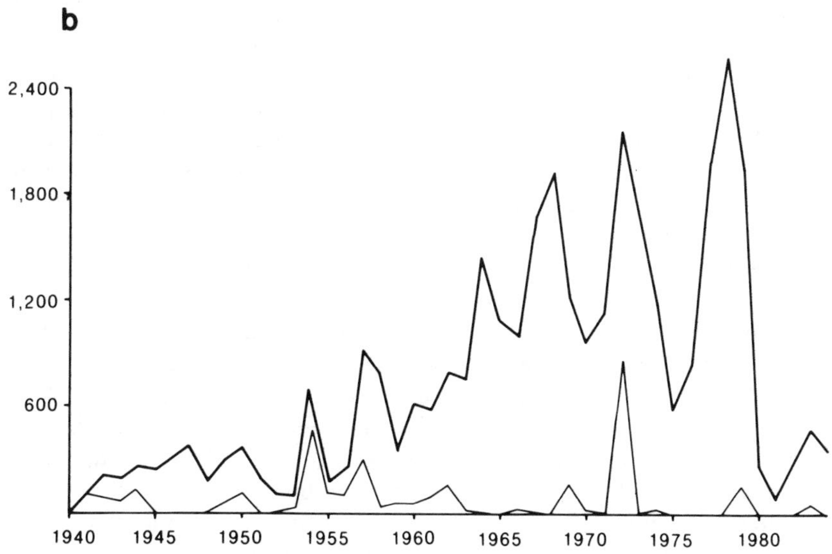

Figure 14.1 a, Building cycles in Spain, 1941–1983; all housing and social housing. **b,** Building cycles in Lleida, 1940–1984; all housing and social housing

area (Valenzuela 1974; Moya 1983) suggest similar decision-making processes.

The building cycle for the whole country, in terms of the number of dwellings built year by year, is shown in Figure 14.1a. The main curve demonstrates the growth stage of the cycle in the 1960s and part of the 1970s. However, it can be seen that it is not reflected by the curve representing the evolution of public housing development, which reached its highest point during the 1950s, when, overall, it accounted for over one-third of houses built, and,in some years it accounted for more than 50 per cent of the total.

The economic slump between 1940 and the end of the 1950s is characterized by the weakness of the private housing sector, which faced two basic difficulties. On the one hand, there was the state housing policy, whose main effect was to freeze housing rents (Rent Act 1946); on the other, there was the scarcity and expense of building materials which adversely affected a very fragmented economic sector which had very few companies with a large economic potential and financial capacity (Tamames 1970: 236). Hence the importance of direct construction by public bodies and of illegal housing. It is impossible to quantify the latter owing to its omission from official statistics.

In this context, the post-Civil-War creation of peripheral fringe belts does not just relate to the development of non-housing urban land use by institutions. It also relates, to a significant extent, to residential land use created outside the orthodox housing market, which was the predominant type of housing built during these years. This new housing can be explained by the mismatch between demand and supply, and especially by the locational characteristics of the land that was offered to lower income groups. In many cases illegal housing and social housing had an importance out of proportion to the volume built. They formed discontinuous areas of urban space which were separated from the main built-up area but which later influenced its growth.

The expansionist phase in the building cycle coincided with a substantial change in the forms of housing development. This was induced by a new housing policy. On the one hand, direct construction on the part of the public administration decreased considerably; on the other, illegal housing began to be integrated into the official system through legalization, though this was a much slower process and varied substantially from city to city. Housing development was, from the 1960s onwards, predominantly carried out by private initiative, a circumstance brought about by favourable legislation. Among other measures, important subsidies and fiscal levy reductions were offered to property developers (Subsidized Housing Act 1957). These allowed a large amount of family, enterprise and financial capital to be moved into the construction sector. This shaped the new development companies of the 1960s and 1970s; a poorly-studied sector and one which is very significant in understanding the processes of economic growth at the time. It had characteristics similar to the Italian property development sector between 1950 and 1967 (Secchi 1974).

The minor recession that occurred in housing construction between 1965 and 1967 is a clear sign of the relationship that exists between housing policy and private development. In these years the qualifications for housing subsidy were considerably tightened, an action that affected the total number of housing units constructed since it induced a withdrawal of private developers.

From 1975 the downswing in the building cycle began. This coincided, after the first democratic local elections in 1979, with considerable institutional activity, especially by councils. Thus, Bohigas has entitled his work defending urban municipal policy in Barcelona 'The *reconstruction* of the city', (Bohigas 1985). This 'reconstruction' entailed much organizational activity in the city after a long period of *laissez-faire* under the previous political regime. In fact, it is not difficult to see how, today, institutions and, in particular, local councils are the main urban land developers in Spanish cities (Tarrago 1985). Thus, in several Spanish cities new fringe belts are being created in which official and semi-official organizations are defining residential and non-residential land-use patterns.

Although this interpretation of the processes of recent urbanization in Spanish cities can be adapted to the basic scheme of fringe-belt development, it raises questions about some of its central concepts. Fundamentally, the main problem is the coincidence between the creation of non-residential land uses and the outward growth of the built-up area, since it can be seen that residential uses played an important role in the formation of the periphery during building slumps. Moreover, it is difficult to reconcile the construction of illegal and social housing with the classical theory of a housing market ruled by a supply–demand equilibrium, owing to the inverse relationship observed between such construction and house-building in general. In many cities recent municipal activity has been orientated towards greater control of the land market and has influenced the free housing market. Furthermore, municipal land has been successively given over to residential and non-residential uses.

What is emphasized here is the need to focus attention on the form of land development, on the agents that carry out development and on the conditions and contingencies that guide the decision-making process, rather than on the present and past uses of land. This focus allows elaboration of mechanistic views about land and the housing market. It brings into view different types of developments for differentiated segments of the housing market, each of which functions with its own logic and must be examined in its own time period to be understood.

Peripheral space in Lleida

It is now possible to show the utility of this newly-defined fringe-belt concept by applying it to a specific example: the development of the layout of the Catalan town of Lleida in north-east Spain. To this end, three different phases in the urban history of the town which have given rise to different fringe belts have been chosen. Their study allows for a greater understanding of some of the more relevant parameters of the present urban structure and an ability to place them in their historical context.

(a) The town wall as a fixation line

Although this work focuses on urban growth since the Civil War, it begins, as an initial analysis and counterpart, with a brief analysis of the creation of the contemporary town space. In Lleida, this began in the 1860s with the occurrence of the characteristic phenomena of nineteenth-century Spanish urban growth: the arrival of the railway (1860), royal permission to knock down the city walls (1861) and the first plan for urbanization outside the city walls (1865).

A plan of 1910 (Fig. 14.2), shows institutional land uses originating before 1860 together with those created after the start of the city wall demolition. Their abundance suggest that the creation of fringe belts is due to non-residential developments. The appearance of these land uses is not always the same through time. Some pre-date the demolition of the city walls and are found within them. Others, also situated within the walled city, were built at a later date, as were all extra-mural developments. There are also those built at a very much later date, suggesting that in some cases the existence of the fringe belt has served to attract further institutional land uses, a process for which Conzen's work would provide support (Conzen 1960, 1962).

Temporal and social identification of these spaces (Lladonosa, 1961–71) indicates that the main period of fringe-belt formation was the years from the demolition of the city wall until the first decade of the twentieth century, with ecclesiastical, as well as council and central government properties as key attractions. On the other hand, the first third of the twentieth century can be described as a period of housing accretion, important for the colonization of extra-mural space by residential land uses.

In this picture of expansion from 1860 to 1936, the classical fringe-belt concept is shown to be correct in its focus upon the differentiation between institutional and residential land uses as a key to interpretation. Two features condition the assimilation of institutional development with non-residential uses in this period. The first is the fact that, historically, a public tradition of social housing appears at a later date and, appearing later still, is the now common guiding and conditioning of city growth on publicly-owned land by urban public policy.

The second characteristic is, from an historical perspective, perhaps more

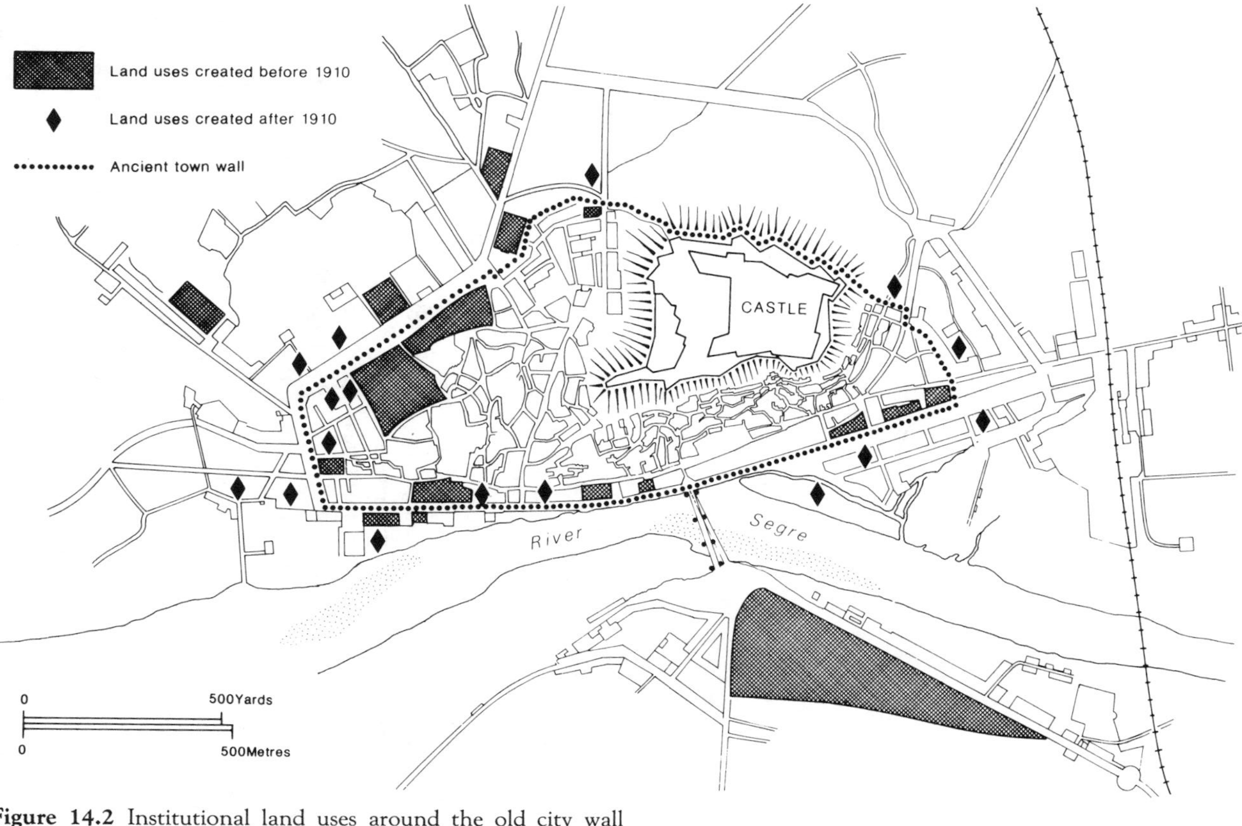

Figure 14.2 Institutional land uses around the old city wall

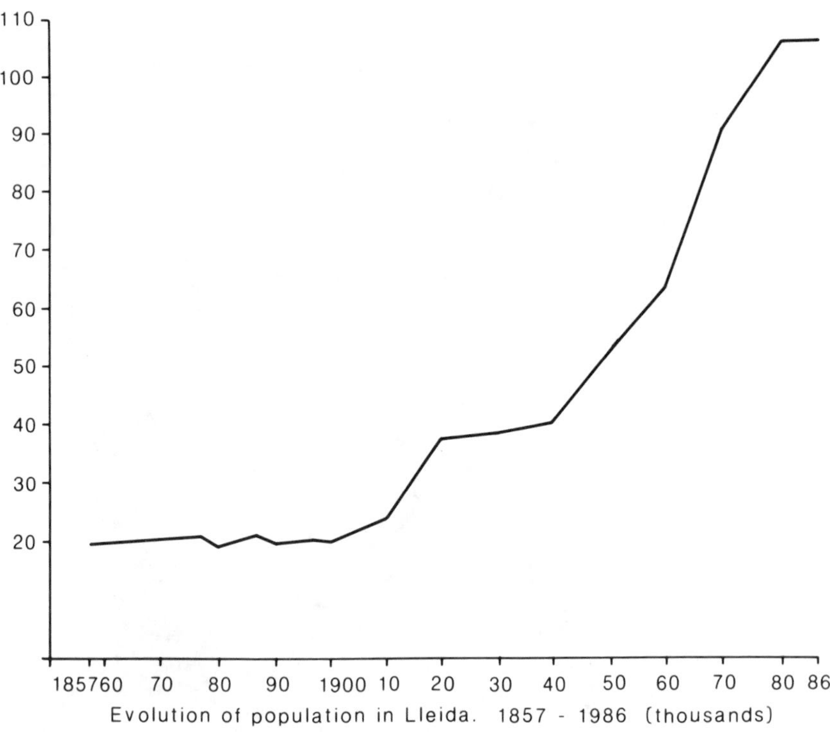

Figure 14.3 Population of Lleida, 1857–1986

significant. This is the congruence between, on the one hand, demographic stagnation and institutional colonization of the fringe, and, on the other, between population growth and increased residential land uses. In fact, the growth of the population of Lleida between 1860 and 1986 closely approximates to the classical proposition previously outlined, in that the stage of fringe-belt formation coincides with a slump phase and that of residential expansion with one of demographic growth (Fig. 14.3). Thus, from 1860 to 1900 the urban population increased from 19,557 to 21,432: fewer than two thousand inhabitants in a forty year period. Significant population growth occurred between 1910 (24,531) and 1930 (38,868) and continued until the Civil War, when the town had more than 40,000 inhabitants (Lladonosa 1981).

We only have estimates relating to the building cycle during this period, though it should be pointed out that 2,200 houses were counted in 1847 (Madoz 1847) against 2,232 houses in 1910 (Monzon 1933). The latter source counted 2,344 houses in 1920, signifying minimal growth, and 3,388 in 1930, of which 1,489 were located outside the old city walls. According to these figures the 1920s was a decade of major expansion, continuing into the 1930s, until interrupted by the outbreak of the Civil War in 1936. It can thus be concluded that there is a positive relationship between the creation of these fringe belts and demographic and building slumps. This, coupled with the absence of institutional housing and land policies, supports the classical proposition based mainly on the study of land use.

(b) Institutional housing and the housing market: 1939–1979

The building cycle in Lleida from 1936 to the early 1980s (Fig. 14.1b), despite its more pronounced oscillations, is comparable with that for Spain as a whole, especially in the timing of the cycle: a slump phase from 1940 until the late 1950s; a growth phase during the 1960s and 1970s; a recession phase from 1980 onwards. The relationship between public and private development is also comparable, the former being more important during the 1950s than during the expansionist phase.

Post-Civil-War peripheral expansion up to the late 1950s is shown in Figure 14.4, which also distinguishes different land uses. There are varied institutional uses: schools, military barracks, prison, hospitals, and wholesale livestock and agricultural markets. In all these cases there was a common element in the locational decision-making processes. The town council bought or exchanged land that was either directly developed or given to other official development bodies. These plots are located in areas not considered favourable to other competitive land uses due to their poor accessibility to the urban nucleus or their topographical disadvantages. All of them were distant from the built-up area, and their development was encouraged by the low prices of such peripheral land. The growth of population in Lleida (Figure 14.3) shows how the 1960s were the years of greatest increase, but it is important to note that this trend began in the early 1940s. The arrival of rural emigrants caused a serious housing shortage. This shortfall was calculated at more than two thousand units in 1953 (Saurina 1953) and rose to five thousand units four years later (Sanchis 1957).

The most conclusive evidence of the housing shortage and the absence of a supply capable of resolving the accommodation problems facing the less affluent sector of the population was, however, the appearance between 1945 and 1955 of three areas of illegal housing. The style of these developments was similar to that found in other Spanish towns: namely, the subdivision of rural land into small building plots in defiance of urban planning legislation. In all three cases in Lleida, the sites selected were far from the town – in fact the most distant of all such subsequent post-Civil-War developments – and on unirrigated land of low agricultural potential. This fact explains the willingness of landowners to divide such low-value land into small building plots.

The construction of public social housing was another typical trait in the housing market after the Civil War. From 1939 onwards, official and semi-official bodies have been responsible for 10 per cent of all housing constructed. But, between 1940 and 1960, public-sector housing construction reached its peak. It accounted for one fifth of housing constructed in the 1950s and more than one third in the 1950s. In the suburbs it assumes even

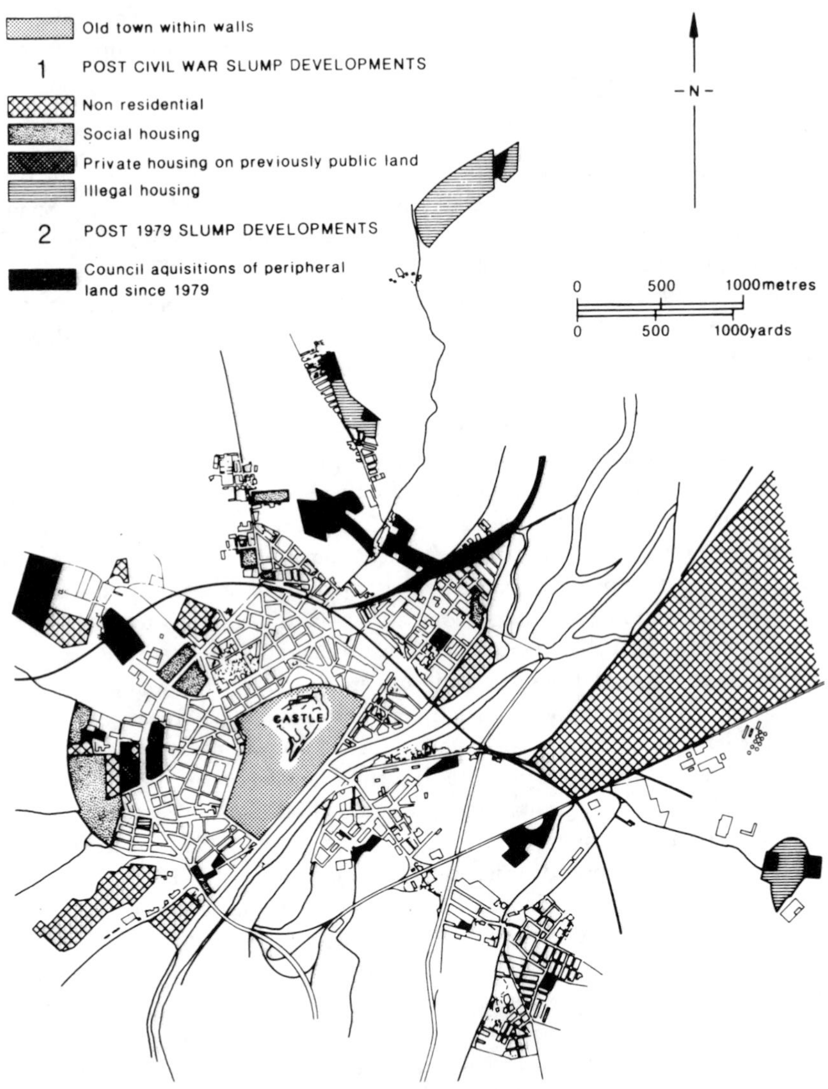

Figure 14.4 Post-Civil War peripheral development in Lleida

greater importance – not only through its numerical impact, but because it created new nodes from which later suburban growth undertaken by private developers would diffuse. The private house-building cycle in the six suburbs in which the main public developments took place is shown in Figure 14.5. Housing built by the administration has been separately identified on the graphs. It can be observed how, with one exception, the first social housing development preceded the establishment of all other residential types. The private house-building cycle began later, basically filling in empty space

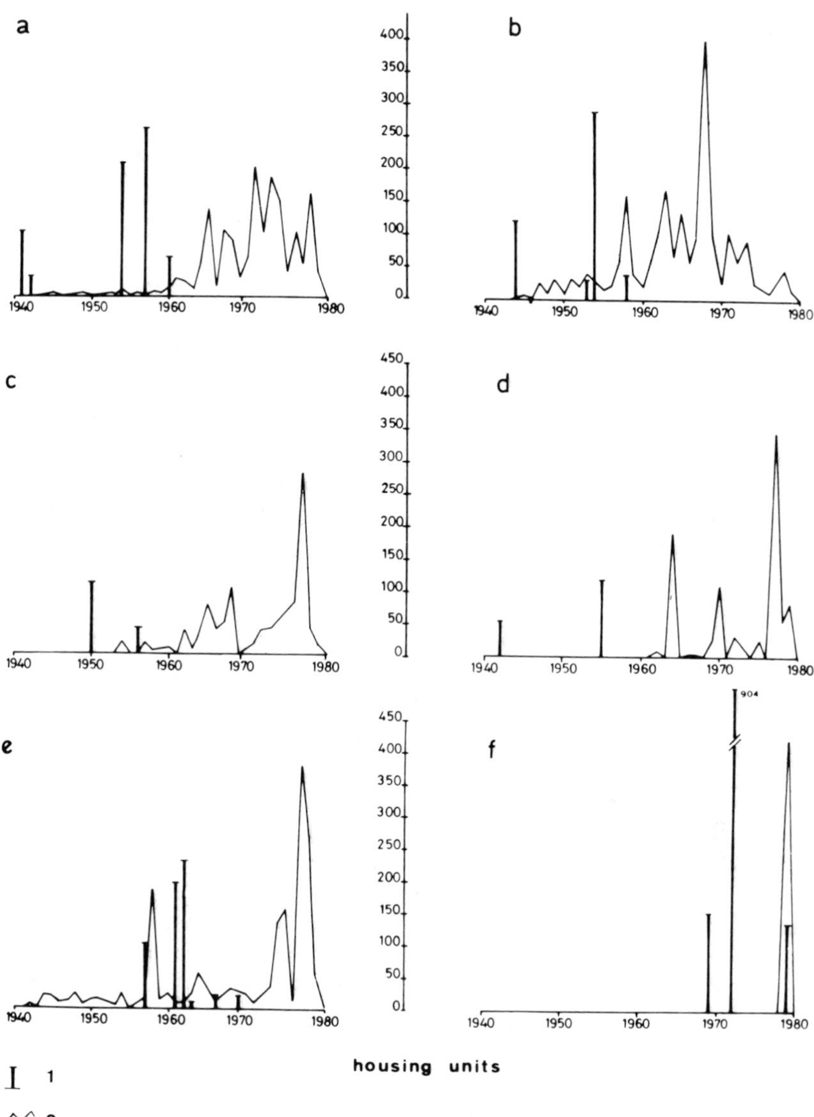

Figure 14.5 Social housing and private development in six Lleida suburbs, 1940–1980. 1. Social Housing 2. Private development cycle

within suburbs and the land between individual suburbs and the main built-up area. The exception (bottom left) is not an important one, for, although private development occurred before public development, it was small-scale and the more intensive private development took place after the official intervention.

Municipal management played a major role in the location of public social housing in the majority of cases. Construction was always the responsibility of official and semi-official bodies of central government, though, with one exception it was the local council which bought the land and gave it to these bodies. This is significant if one takes into account the circumstances governing development prior to 1957, since initial development in four suburbs took place on land classified as rural in the urban plans at the time. It can therefore, paradoxically, be considered 'public' and 'illegal' housing at the same time. Again, this situation can be explained by the low price of such land.

In 1957, coinciding with the new law on housing subsidies, a new town plan was approved which greatly extended the area designated for urban land uses. Basically, previously created areas of social housing and their surroundings were classified as urban land legally open to high-density development. At the same time illegal housing was also legalized. It is in this climate that the property boom of the 1960s and 1970s took place. The areas of social and illegal housing created during the slump acted as the main diffusive sources for subsequent urbanization.

The new fringe belt of the 1980s

The down-turn in the building cycle, which for Spain as a whole began in 1975, started in Lleida in 1980 with constructional activity dwindling to levels equal to, or lower than, those found in the period immediately after the Civil War. Moreover, social public housing development is now low in comparison with the past. Demographic growth began to decelerate during the last five years of the 1970s, reaching its lowest post-Civil-War level in the first five years of the 1980s. Different hypotheses on population growth indicate slight increases over the coming years (Servei d'Urbanisme de la Paeria 1983). Coinciding with this deceleration in demographic growth and with a crises in the development sector, a political change (the first general and democratic elections of 1977 and 1979 respectively) also implied a new direction for urban management. This was helped by a new plan for urban management approved in 1979 which, as one of its principal objectives, sought to unify the new suburbs created in the early 1940s with the central nucleus of the city. Present municipal action in these areas is actively shaping the new fringe belts. This has been defined as 'a tactical option of urban planning' (Llop 1984) and consists of municipal acquisition of substantive quantities of peripheral land (Figure 14.4). Today the council is the principal owner of vacant urban land within the city. Its ownership strengthens its ability to control urban organization and design, as well as regulating the land market. This has discouraged the speculative operations so typical in the past.

This, then, is a third situation which can be labelled fringe-belt creation, meeting some of the basic characteristics observed in the earlier cases but differing from them in its internal logic. As in other cases there is a slump in the building cycle and institutional action plays a key role in the formation of new fringes. The difference is that during the creation of the fringe around the ancient city wall there was a congruence between fringe-belt fixation and institutional land uses. Later, during the post-Civil-War period, residential uses were added defining a new fringe which resulted from new trends in the housing market; at present, though it is possible to find some similar land uses, general council policy, management and strategy are keys to understanding the process.

Conclusion

Some of the elements underlying the development of land peripheral to Lleida in three troughs in the building cycle are sketched in Table 14.1. Some similarities between slumps can be recognized, but there are differences related to the historical contexts in which particular slumps occur.

This study suggests that there are two features common to building slumps. The first, deriving from the crisis in the building and housing sectors, is the lack of competitiveness of the private sector with the public which allows institutions a greater capacity for acquiring peripheral land. The second characteristic is that of the persistence of one of the driving forces behind institutional action on the urban fringe: namely, the adjustment of deficits in infrastructural services and equipment bequeathed from previous times. Hence the three periods of recession studied follow periods of residential growth characterized by a lack of institutional and public infrastructure. City growth outside the existing city walls began in the 1860s following two centuries in which, both in Lleida and in Spanish cities generally, growth had been taking place by increased density of settlement within the established town boundaries. Thus it was not strange that Church, town council and State, searching for sufficient funds to satisfy their requirements, should acquire and build on fringe land. In a similar way, the motivation after the Civil War was to take advantage of the period of reconstruction in order to expand existing public building and to create new units. In this context the urban periphery offered abundant vacant land at low prices. From 1979 onwards, the driving force has been that of making good building deficits created in a period between 1960 and the end of the 1970s – a period of great population growth and housing impact, yet lacking urban order and the provision of collective services. The characteristics of differentiation over time derive from different climates in the housing

Table 14.1 Three slump periods in Lleida

Period	*Demographic evolution*	*Building cycle*	*Forces promoting development*	*Decision-making factors*	*Agents*	*Land uses*
1860–1910	Stationary	Slump	Lack of institutional and public infrastructure	Low land prices	Church	Non-residential
				Lack of competitiveness from the private sector	Council Central government	
1939–1960	Expanding	Slump	Lack of institutional and public infrastructure	Low land prices	Council	Non-residential
			Lack of cheap housing	Lack of competitiveness from the private sector	Central government	Public social housing
				Public social housing policy	Rural land owners	Illegal housing
				Urbanistic permissibility		
From 1979	Stationary	Slump	Lack of institutional and public infrastructure	Low land prices	Council	Non-residential
				Lack of competitiveness from the private sector		Public social housing
			Investment to cover future needs	Urban control		Privately developed housing

market and from different urban policy strategies on the part of the state and councils.

On the first point, it is important to emphasize the unique nature of the post-Civil-War period. Since 1940, the coincidence of population growth and increase of housing demand with the inability of the private building sector to offer sufficient housing units at low prices, gave rise to the appearance of unorthodox segments in the market: illegal housing and public social housing. But to understand the appearance of the new housing nuclei it is not enough to analyse only the demand–supply imbalance. The second feature of historical differentiation, that of urban policies, is a key here. The fall in supply is, in great part, explained by the freeze imposed by the 1946 Rent Act. Although there were some precedents, one can only really talk of social housing policies after the Civil War when the State decided that the way to put an end to the housing problem was by direct construction of cheap dwellings. A major characteristic of urban policies was their permissiveness, especially on the part of local councils which allowed the sale of rural land and the subsequent development of illegal housing. Nowadays urban fringe areas of illegal housing constitute relict morphologies which are as much evidence of the period of *laissez-faire* as the failure of the social housing policy that the state sought to promote.

At times of house-building boom the interaction between the housing market and urban policy once again became a key explanatory factor. At such times, the state began to offer a subsidy to private developers to build housing to satisfy the demand from low wage-earners as a substitute for its own construction of social housing (Subsidized Housing Act 1957). A permissive attitude towards the creation of illegal housing was replaced by legal controls over it. Finally, new aids to urban development appeared; the state housing subsidy, which originally favoured the construction of cheap housing, became more and more extensive in its application, spreading to other sectors of the market and even, at times, extending to high-class housing and second homes. In parallel, local councils made frequent changes in land-use regulations which led to extensive speculative operations and, in part, explains the high density of urban areas created at this time.

The first period of recession studied also shows urban policy as a key to historical differentiation. It is characterized not only by sectoral policies or legislation referred to in the urban or housing plan. There is also an overall urban policy carried out by the council of the city. It takes advantage of the withdrawal of the private building sector in order to improve existing collective services, and at the same time, to control future urban growth. It achieves this by acquiring large areas of urban land which may be used to cover present shortages in infrastructure and collective services and to control the market for land. It is then able to provide for social housing when and where necessary and to sell to private enterprise where and when housing demand advises such action. A strategy of unified urban management is therefore creating current fringe belts: a unified strategy that will produce diversified land uses.

One of the important contributions of studies of fringe belts has been to show the significance of the areas growing up at times of weak urban growth. They are important for their contribution to the analysis of the overall structure of the city. Fringe belts create morphological elements which influence later urban development in phases of growth. The use of the cyclic approach and in particular, of building cycles has provided a route for further progress in the study of fringe belts (Whitehand 1987). This chapter opts for a broad characterization of the fringe-belt concept that, combined with the study of building cycles, focuses interest on the agents of urban change. This is done by considering the motives for action on urban fringe land and the decision-making factors affecting land-use type and location. In general, changes in the condition of land and housing markets and urban policies have been shown as keys to understanding the process. What has been demonstrated is the importance of focusing on the process of land development – from land acquisition to building. This is fundamental if the genesis of land-use is to be understood.

Acknowledgements

I should like to thank Malcolm J. Hayes and Leslie H. Marillier who initially translated the Castilian original into English, and the editor, Terry Slater, and Jeremy Whitehand for further work on improving the English text.

Notes

1 The empirical work on which this study is based has been discussed in detail in two previous studies. One is about urban policies and the agents of change in Lleida between 1939 and 1979 (Vilagrasa, forthcoming). The other is the first integration in Spanish geography of the concepts of fringe belts and building cycles (Vilagrasa 1986) and is a detailed study of the different periods of building recession experienced in Lleida since 1860.

2 Illegal housing is a common phenomenon in slowly developing countries and has been seen throughout Mediterranean Europe during the twentieth century, particularly in the middle decades. Its basic characteristics are: (i) illegal construction carried out on rural land near urban nuclei undertaken by the occupants themselves; (ii) serious deficiencies in urban infrastructure, collective services and accessibility to the urban centre; (iii) absorption into the built-up city over time, unlike in Latin American and other Third World shanty towns. The buildings which initially are small and precarious are turned into family housing and improved. The settlement, with time, becomes *legalized* and incorporated into the official urban plan. The characteristics of this type of settlement have been studied

in Spain (Sola-Morales 1974) and Portugal (Williams 1981).

References

Alcala, F., 1960. 'El problema de la vivienda en Espana', *Documentacion Social*, 8–9: 5–24.

Bohigas, O., 1985. *Reconstruccio de Barcelona* (Barcelona).

Busquets, J., 1976. *La Urbanizacion Marginal en Barcelona* (3 vols) (Barcelona).

Canosa, E. and Rodriguez, I., 1985. 'Urbanizacion marginal en la periferia noreste de Madrid', *Ciudad y Territorio*, 66: 11–41.

Capel, H., 1975. *Capitalismo y Morfologia Urbana en Espana* (Barcelona).

Conzen, M. R. G., 1960. 'Alnwick, Northumberland: a study in town-plan analysis', *Publications, Institute of British Geographers*, 27.

Conzen, M. R. G., 1962. 'The plan analysis of an English city centre' in *Proceedings of the IGU Symposium in Urban Geography Lund 1960*, ed. K. Norborg (Lund) 383–414.

Conzen, M. R. G., 1969. *Alnwick, Northumberland: a study in town-plan analysis* (2nd ed.), glossary of technical terms.

Ferrer, A., 1974. *Los Poligonos de Viviendas en la Comarca de Barcelona* (2 vols.) (Barcelona).

Garcia, L. M., 1981. *Sta. Cruz de Tenerife: La Formacion de la Ciudad Marginal* (Sta. Cruz de Tenerife).

Habsburgo, A., 1983. *Propiedad y Espacio en Castelldefels* (Barcelona).

Lladonosa, J., 1961–78. *Las Calles y Plazas de Lerida a traves de su Historia* (5 vols.) (Lleida).

Lladonosa, J., 1981. *Historia de la Ciutat de Lleida* (Lleida).

Llop, J. M., 1984. 'La actuacion en suelo urbano. Una opcion tactica del planeamiento', *Ciudad y Territorio*, 59–60: 157–67.

Louis, H., 1936. 'Die Geographische gliederung von Gross-Berlin' in *Länderkundliche Forschung: Krebs-Festschrift*, eds. H. Louis and W. Panzer (Stuggart) 146–71.

Madoz, P., 1847. *Diccionario Geografico, Estadistico, Historico de Espana y sus Posesiones de Ultramar* (16 vols.) (Madrid).

Monzon, P., 1933. *De com Lleida Creix, Prospera y Progressa, 1920–1930* (Lleida).

Moya, L., 1983. *Barrios de Promocion Oficial. Madrid 1939–1976* (Madrid).

Sanchis, J. A., 1957. 'J. A. Sanchis, arquitecto de la O.S.H.', *Tarea*, 85: 12–14.

Saurina, E., 1953. 'El problema de la vivienda en Lerida', *Tarea*, 34: 17–19.

Secchi, B., 1974. 'Il settore edilizio e fondiario in un processo di svoluppo economico' in *Lo Spreco Edilizio*, ed. F. Indovina (Padova), 37–87.

Servei d'Urbanisme de la Paeria, 1983. *Informe sobre els Criteris de Revisio del Programa i les Normes Complementaries del P.G.M.* (Lleida).

Sola-Morales, M., 1974. 'La urbanizacion marginal y la formacion de plusvalia del suelo', *Papers. Revista de Sociologia*, 3: 365–80.

Tamames, R., 1970. *Introduccion a la Economia Espanola* (Madrid).

Tarrago, M., 1985. 'Cambio de signo en la olitica urbana? Reflexiones sobre la influencia de la crisis economica sobre el urbanismo actual', in *Urbanismo e Historia Urbana en el Mundo Hispanico*, ed. A. Bonet (Madrid) I, 139–46.

Valenzuela, M., 1974. 'Iniciativa oficial y crecimiento urbano en Madrid (1939–1973)', *Estudios Geograficos*, 137: 593–655.

Vilagrasa, J., 1986. 'Una aproximacio morfogenetica al creixement urba. El cas de la Lleida contemporania'. *Bio-Bis*, *10*: 23–36.

Vilagrasa, J., forthcoming. *Creixement Urba i Politica Urbana a Lleida, 1939–1979* (Barcelona).

Whitehand, J. W. R., 1972a. 'Building cycles and the spatial pattern of urban form', *Transactions, Institute of British Geographers*, *56*: 39–55.

Whitehand, J. W. R., 1972b. 'Urban-rent theory, time series and morphogenesis: an example of eclecticism in geographical research', *Area*, *4*: 215–22.

Whitehand, J. W. R., 1974. 'The changing nature of the urban fringe, a time perspective' in *Suburban growth: geographical processes at the edge of Western Cities*, ed. J. H. Johnson, 31–52.

Whitehand, J. W. R., 1977. 'The basis for an historico-geographical theory of urban form', *Transactions, Institute of British Geographers*, *N.S. 2*: 400–16.

Whitehand, J. W. R., 1981. 'Fluctuations in the land use composition of urban development during the industrial era', *Erdkunde*, *35*: 129–40.

Whitehand, J. W. R., 1987. 'Urban morphology' in *Historical geography: progress and prospects*, ed. M. Pacione, 250–76.

Williams, A. M, 1981. 'Bairros clandestinos: illegal housing in Portugal', *Geografische Tijdschrift*, *15*: 24–34.

15 An historico-geographical perspective on urban fringe-belt phenomena

Busso von der Dollen

Introduction

The concept of the urban fringe-belt (as a geographical phenomenon) was first introduced in 1936 by Herbert Louis in his paper entitled 'The geographical development of Greater Berlin'. Louis attributed the recognition of these urban phenomena to his functional–morphological method of observation. He emphasized that this approach would not have led to a satisfactory result without a genetic component. Louis's early essay was subsequently taken up, further developed and applied more precisely through the use of English examples by the Anglo-German M. R. G. Conzen after he was forced to leave Berlin in 1933 for political reasons (Conzen 1960, 1978; Whitehand 1981). His findings should afford a framework for research and study on more highly-developed settlements which until now have only been researched and understood by the narrative–descriptive historical method. The methodological question posed by this chapter is as follows: can the genetic-functional approach to urban fringe-belt analysis contribute to a better understanding and exposition of processes of transformation in urban areas? To this end, this chapter will attempt a temporal transect through central-European urban development, the argument being supported by the use of a limited number of case studies.

The process of urban fringe-belt development in the industrial age

The urban fringe-belt is not identical with the urban accretionary integument of a stage of development. Rather, it is a zone in which elements have coalesced having been pushed to the edge of the urban area as a result of inner restructuring and differentiation. If, at a time of boom and demographic growth, the town experiences physical expansion then these fringe zones are leap-frogged by new residential areas and remain as fossils of earlier development processes. Periodic growth spurts in the urban entity effect the change from old town (*Altstadt*), to urban fringe-belt, to new residential areas, in a way which is comparable to the growth rings of a tree trunk. Successive fringe belts may form in subsequent quiet or recessionary periods.

Whitehand (1967) undertook one of the first analyses which pointed to the mutual dependence of urban fringe-belt and urban development. The city is the result of centripetal, and the urban fringe-belt of centrifugal, forces. Urban functions either develop in a particular area or force their way into it. This is the law of the city centre which, as a result of its history, is firmly demarcated and prescribes intensive land-uses. Accordingly, Whitehand ascribed a relative stability to the inner city. It will be suggested, however, that this stability is actually of only brief duration relative to the overall development of a city. In contrast, the available space at the urban fringe allows extensive usage which leads to continued expansion, but even this is limited by the overall development of the city.

(a) Urban fringe-belt elements

What are urban fringe-belt elements? First, such elements consist not only of unimportant functions pushed out from the centre – the fact that Baroque palaces (*Residenz*) are located primarily in the urban fringe-belt is clear evidence of this. Such palaces are found in Ansbach, Bayreuth, Bonn, Darmstadt, Koblenz, Mainz, Munich, Münster, Nancy, Saarbrücken, Stuttgart, Trier, Weimar, Vienna and Würzburg, to name only the most obvious. Such a fringe location was dictated from the outset by the spacious building requirements of that era and the philosophy which sought to join town and country in a new cosmos. The predecessors of these palaces, the castles, are also frequently found in fringe-belts for reasons which are both tactical/political and defensive. Room at the fringe is also available for other administrative and public buildings, such as government buildings, the armoury and barracks, as well as for new transportation structures, the railways in particular. Functions with substantial space requirements such as cemeteries, parks, sports fields (Whitehand 1981) and new relief roads can also be accommodated at the fringe. It can be seen from these examples that the edge of the built-up area is 'transformed into a zone of increased urban life' (Louis 1936: 2), a phrase which is not used in a pejorative sense, even if the fringe acquires functions like waste disposal and shows the scars of providing the materials for increased constructional activity, such as stone quarries and gravel pits. Structurally, the urban fringe-belt is characterized by large, irregularly-shaped parcels of land and large buildings. In some sectors, areas of random villa-type development occur while in other zones temporary buildings and poor, welfare housing are found interspersed with more specific fringe-belt uses. The pre-industrial-age suburb (*Vorstadt*) is one of the oldest types of urban fringe-belt phenomena.

(b) Transformative processes

At an earlier point reference was made to 'fossil fringe-belts'; however, no urban zone remains fully intact in the growth and transformation phases that a city experiences. It was Conzen who once more grasped the dynamics of the situation: the innermost fringe-belt is formed during a long, pre-industrial fixation phase. It is topographically oriented to the town fortifications and is consequently particularly resilient. With the beginning of industrialization it moves into a phase of expansion characterized by:

1 An accumulation of varied urban fringe elements which results in consolidation and expansion;
2 Intensification and infill of plots with additional buildings;
3 A succession of different urban fringe elements on the same parcel of land;
4 Consolidation of the belt with spatial ordering and separation of the variety of functions into a sectoral pattern.

According to Conzen (1960), a final phase of development is reached when urban fringe-belt expansion is brought to a halt as it becomes hemmed in by other urban accretionary integuments. At this stage of development, new functions seeking a central-city location as a result of growth in the town through economic specialization and sectoral expansion (such as a university, secondary schools, administrative buildings, hospitals, and cultural activities) look first to the town centre for a location but find that space is only available on the edge of the city centre (*Altstadt*). Once this occurs, the urban fringe-belt loses much of its former character, usually to the advantage of the city. It becomes the space for additional city-centre functions, though individual elements often keep their traditional form for a long time.

(c) Other aspects of fringe settlement

The incorporation of new residential functions, such as villa quarters, into the definition of fringe-belts leads to a lack of clarity in the term since late-nineteenth-century planning regulations established quarters for 'open country house building'. What, for example, is the difference between an urban accretionary integument and an assortment of functions (including residential) which form a belt? Local government building ordinances catered for the expansion of a city in regard to both form and scale. There was space for new building and, normally, an official plan. In contrast, the urban fringe-belt is characterized by spontaneity, not planning, and is typified by the singular relocation of individual functions from the centre to the periphery. Decisions on users, reasons for removal, and space requirements are here made at the lowest, individual, level, whereas city expansion requires a legal act. The difference is also a question of quantity. Disparate residential development along arterial routes remains a characteristic of the urban fringe-belt until it is systematically integrated into the urban entity – a process which only results from a substantial growth spurt brought about by, and steered by, planned decision-making. Naturally, urban fringe elements can be established in settlements in the surrounding countryside of an expanding town regardless of whether these settlements are of an urban or rural character. Such a process is a significant element in the development of an urbanized village (*Vorort*) (von der Dollen 1978) which transforms the shape of the whole settlement. The suburb becomes part of the urban fringe-belt but the undisturbed village is not an urban fringe element (Carter 1980: 322), rather, it is a rural settlement in a specific geographical situation.

The make-up of the urban fringe-belt is generally characterized by a nexus of land uses in parcels of land which vary both in area and in shape. It is by no means a 'geographical no-man's land' (Carter 1980: 332). An unequivocal classification as either urban fringe-belt or urban expansion, as in the example of the Vienna *Ringstrasse* region (Lichtenberger 1970), will not always be possible. It is therefore usually necessary to understand the overall process of urban topographical development so as to establish that the processes are congruent with normal urban fringe-belt formation.

Stages of urban transformation and development at the urban fringe

Conzen has noted that the integration of former inner fringe-belts into the city is one of the many transformative processes which may be detected in urban development. The quantitative growth in both population and in the overall built-up area creates a new quality in the total settlement. This can be demonstrated by means of a summary temporal transect which bears reference to the overall context. The author, let it be stressed, sees this approach to be a basis for discussion and not an absolute credo. He is aware that any attempt either to generalize or to schematize historical reality can cause misunderstanding. Contrary examples can always be found for every phase dealt with. However, given the wealth of source material involved, it would seem sensible to order the multiplicity of settlement processes and their effects on the geographical substance of the city.

(a) The Middle Ages

From the outset, the historical course of urbanization is taken to be understood. Discussion will be limited, therefore, to explanation of the overall view of the stages of urban transformation and to evidence relating to the particular problem. The early phases in the development of towns in central and north-western Europe is characterized by a topographical/legal dualism (Rietschel 1897; Ennen 1953: 121 ff.). Briefly, Rietschel states that the *suburbium*, a settlement of free-traders and merchants, grows up (given a favourable geographical location) in the early Middle Ages beside, or in the vicinity of, a seigneurially-organized fortified settlement core (*urbs*) which might have been an episcopal *civitas*, a religious institution or a secular fortress. This develops further according to its functional mix (Schlesinger 1969: 11 ff.) either as a *Wik* trading centre for long-distance merchants, as a local market, or as a castle market-town. The inhabitants organize their relations on a co-operative basis. The process of melding with the seigneurial core with its civic/constitutional rights, then takes place over a long period of time.

This last process can be understood more clearly from a topographical viewpoint. The formerly open *suburbium* is, at some point, enclosed by walls which join it to the already fortified core. Edith Ennen (1953: 121 ff.), in agreement with earlier research, has highlighted this fusion of pre-urban core (*urbs*) and *suburbium* as a constituent trait of central-European urbanization. It is a process which stretches over many centuries. Very few important towns in the high Middle Ages had carried out this walling process before the year 1000 AD (Regensburg 917 AD, Köln 947 AD are exceptions). Others were walled only in the second half of the twelfth century (including important towns such as Erfurt, Aachen, Antwerp and Hamburg), and smaller towns often not until the thirteenth century. Bonn's murage grant was given in 1244, for example (Ennen 1953). The crucial epochs for medieval town formation are extended and do not conform with the normal periodization of history, but this cannot be avoided.

Schlesinger dealt with the terminological clarification of these processes during the course of a seminar held by the Working Group for Research into south-west German Urban History (*Arbeitskreis für Sudwestdeutsche Stadtgeschichtsforschung*) in 1967. He called the settlement which arose from the topographical–legal duality an 'early town', (*Frühstadt*) (Schlesinger 1969: 13). Urban life unfolded in such places in the sense used by Bobek. Such a settlement possessed the endogenous ability to locate urban elements on its periphery. The growth of a *suburbium* is, in contrast, largely an exogenous process. This differentiation between endogenous and exogenous processes facilitates a greater understanding of the situation during later stages, even when clear-cut differentiation is not always possible (Table 15.1). The size and importance of a town is, of course, of considerable relevance here. The construction of the fortifications is generally an exogenous process dictated and financed by the overlord, though there are a few examples of towns which financed expensive fortifications from their own resources (such as Bremen and Lübeck), or which built walls as part of an urban expansion policy (again, Bremen). It would, at the very least, be confusing to portray this centrifugal development of the *Frühstadt* early town as simply pre-urban development. It is rather a matter of a temporal analogy with the process of urban fringe-belt development, mentioned above, resulting from processes of inner differentiation. Nothing demonstrates this better than the peripheral annexation of market places for which space was not available within the early town. The practical/technical necessity of moving certain industries out of the densely-populated settlement demanded the development of new quarters, whether

Table 15.1 Stages of transformation of the town and growth phenomena on the town fringe

1 *Epoch*	2 *Process of change*	3 *Exogenous/ endogenous*	4 *Fringe-belt elements, plan and built form*	5 *Forms of integration with the extended town*	6 *Planned/unplanned*	7 *Outcome (new types of settlement)*
Early Middle Ages (large towns)	Mixing of pre-urban core (*civitas*, founding church, castle), and *suburbium*	Exog.	Linear, single street layout, aligned on course of trunk roads	Merger into urban settlement; external fortification, walling (Köln 947)	Beginning unplanned, realization without planning control	Early town (*Frühstadt*)
High Middle Ages (early phases of town development)	(service plots with craftwork and local trade; *wik*, market)					
High Middle Ages (heyday of town development)	Merger of early town and *Vorstadt*; quantitative and qualitative growth on the basis of inner processes of differentation	Endog.	New urban functions irregular, activity-specific according to geogr. & topogr. position, concentric for new buildings transferred to periphery for new functions; around churches and monasteries small agglomerations of formerly rural nature	Topographical irregularities e.g. decentralization of market, walling of newly expanded settlements, final second walling (Köln 1180–*c*.1300)	Planned, unplanned	Old town or corporate town (*Altstadt* or *Rechtstadt*)
Late Middle Ages/Early Modern (later time of town formation)	Stagnation (losses of population from mid 14th century); intramural fringe formation (rarely extramural)	Endog.	Irregular, variable dimensions	Remains as fringe-belt element	Unplanned (partly planned)	Genuine town fringe phenomena
	Vorstädte rarely	Endog.	Linear on arterial roads	Remains extramural	Unplanned	
	Apparent formation of *Vorstadt* through function loss and reagrarianization	Endog.	Single street plan on arterial roads, agrarian built form	None	Planned	Agrarianization of total settlement

Table 15.1 contd.

1 *Epoch*	2 *Process of change*	3 *Exogenous/ endogenous*	4 *Fringe-belt elements, plan and built form*	5 *Forms of integration with the extended town*	6 *Planned/unplanned*	7 *Outcome (new types of settlement)*
Age of Absolutism (Early Modern)	Building of fortress with inner consolidation	Exog. Rarely endog.	Clearly delineated zones (defences, etc.); new military elements and function intramural; emergency accommodation under the arches of the town wall (cheap housing for soldiers etc.)	Physical destruction of old fringe elements; transfer of functions within the walls and integration or consolidation outwards (gardens) filling up	Planned Advent of market economy features Communal assent (unplanned)	Fortress town (*Festungsstadt*)
	Development of *Residenz* — and *Hauptstadt* functions	Exog.		None	Unplanned	Capital/palace town (*Haupt-* and *Residenzstadt*)
	Suspension of fortification	Exog.	Renewed separation of fringe-belt elements	Demolition of fortifications; possibility of town expansion	Planned	Open town
	First trends towards centrifugal differentiation	Exog.	Depots for mass goods; cemetery, gardens; completion of palaces in fringe positions, opening to the landscape, avenues, green areas Vauxhall		Unplanned	Open town
	Town expansion ("*Neustadt*")	Exog.	Expansion of the area, geometric design, standardized cross-sections, more space	Joining up through breaks in the wall and movement of defence works	Planned	Topographical dualism

Table 15.1 contd.

1 *Epoch*	2 *Process of change*	3 *Exogenous/ endogenous*	4 *Fringe-belt elements, plan and built form*	5 *Forms of integration with the extended town*	6 *Planned/unplanned*	7 *Outcome (new types of settlement)*
Modern times/industrial age (particularly in 2nd half of 19th century)	Industrialization and technical innovation	Endog.	Industrial building (large constructions) on large plots, in a distribution area or agglomerations	Several possibilities	1st half 19th c.: within the walls, market hall, police station	1st half 19th c.: town differentiating with fringing at the edges
	Heavy population growth and greater mobility	Exog.				
	New means of transport, new construction, for urban infrastructure	Endog.	Transport installations cause clusters of fringe elements or linear structure	a) Functionally and physically integrated	Extramural planning as police give street protection	
	Origins of city formation	Endog.	Administrative officials; institutions (university, schools)	b) Physically integrated		
	Suburban creation		Communal provisions	c) Functionally & physically as "foreign body" d) As agglomeration of independent quarters	2nd half 19th c.: establishment of terrace buildings; building inspectors' ordinances; zone construction not relating to function	2nd half 19th c.: modern town with dispersed patterns (on the way to conurbation)
	Incorporation of villages		Care of sick; military installations; green areas (parks, cemeteries) in the 1st half of 19th c. as dispersed developments on old road system			

Table 15.1 contd.

1 *Epoch*	2 *Process of change*	3 *Exogenous/ endogenous*	4 *Fringe-belt elements, plan and built form*	5 *Forms of integration with the extended town*	6 *Planned/unplanned*	7 *Outcome (new types of settlement)*
	Movement of industry to edge of town		2nd half of 19th c. opening up of space for expansion and closed areas; open construction; circular ring growth		Planned town extension (controlled by function)	
Modern 20th c.	Personal transport	Endog.	Strengthened traffic infrastructures for private transport forms, new fringe to town	New areas of town development	Planned town development	Urban region and conurbation with trend for total integration
	Growing tertiary sector	Endog.				
	City consolidation	Endog.	Inner urban fringe belt to the city	Space with former fringe element traits in expansion area; urbanized zone and fringe zone merge	Regional planning	
	Urbanization of entire space and of town/country gradient Communal styles	Both		Substitution of physically characterized fringe zones in favour of sub-urban fringe zones; all-encompassing urbanization		
	War damage and reconstruction					
	Fringe and outward migration of industry					

this resulted from their need for a more suitable location or as a result of their nuisance value. Such areas may be laid out in a planned fashion or else they may crystallize onto the old settlement in an unco-ordinated manner. Noxious trades included smiths and salt makers, because of the fire risk; tanners, because of the foul-smelling soaking pits (see the example of Leipzig in Czok (1979: 12)); and weavers, because of their need for bleaching greens. All these traders tended to be moved to the fringe. Planitz (1954: 193) mentions several towns where market places established at the edge of an early town ended up in the later medieval town centre because of the planning of new town quarters (for example, Heilbronn, Merseburg and Herford amongst others). On the other hand there are towns which deliberately planned new market places in the town centre, such as Bautzen and Nürnberg. The topographical situation of the town walls dictated the term *Vorstadt* ('suburb') for the new part of the town (the terminology of the sources is quite decisive on this). In this instance, however, the term should not be adopted because it fulfils the criteria of expansion and should therefore be recognised as part of the town's endogenous expansionary processes at work.

The *Vorstadt* is a closed agglomeration of urban functions which, in both legal and social status, is below the level of the *Frühstadt* town and is characterized physically by dilapidated ribbon development radiating along arterial routes from the town gates. This type of urban settlement differentiates itself in its overall form from urban fringe elements, and the latter phenomenon has been attributed much less attention than the suburb in recent literature (for *Vorstädte* suburbs see Blaschke 1970; Czok 1979; Kuhn 1971: 47 ff.).

Many of these early fringe elements and agglomerations were contained within the second, more complete, walling of a town and so look like established medieval elements. Schlesinger terms this the *Altstadt* ('old town') or, with reference to Gdansk and Glauchauer, *Rechtstadt* ('chartered town') for it is only at this stage of urban development that a town is granted full legal status (Schlesinger 1969: 14). Usually, sufficient space was enclosed within the second town wall circuit to cope with growth up to the inaugural phases of industrialization. This is true both for medium-sized towns such as Bonn and Koblenz, and for large cities such as Köln where, of 405 ha. within the walls in 1815, 117, or more than a quarter, were still in agricultural usage (Stoob 1979). Only in a few instances did a town have sufficient economic dynamism to create extra-mural suburbs; one example is the suburb in front of the Severin and Eigelstein Gates in Köln (Blaritz 1954: 219).

The *Neustadt* ('new town') of the Middle Ages is to be distinguished from the *Vorstadt* suburb. *Neustadt* refers to a foundation (fully developed in terms of its economy, plan, built form and legal status) established in the immediate vicinity of an older town (Brandenburg and Neustadt Brandenburg for example). It is a phenomenon found particularly in the new settlement land (*Ostsiedlung*) to the east of the Elbe. The *Neustadt* may be recognized externally as such by its own walls. The term 'double-town' (*Dopplestadt*) is advanced for this type of settlement, even when more than one pair of developments are located together as at Königsberg in East Prussia. Planitz (1954: 217) observes that a *Neustadt* can grow out of a fringe settlement and in one way or another they influenced the edge of the *Altstadt*.

Pre-urban settlement could sometimes remain outside the walls of high-medieval chartered towns and take on a suburban character; the Weimar Jakobvorstadt is an example (see also Czok 1979: 13). Genetically they are to be differentiated from the *Vorstadt* suburb, even though they may approach it in terms of their functional characteristics, and in their relationship to the chartered town they are to be ranked as urban fringe-belt phenomena.

The 'town village' (*Stadtdorf*) of the eastern settlement region (*Ostsiedlung*), which is also termed suburb (*Vorstadt*) in the medieval sources, is another form of settlement at the edge of the town (Kuhn 1971). A *Stadtdorf* is not an urbanized village but a rural settlement founded contemporaneously with a town and usually located in the immediate vicinity of the town walls or near a gate. The farms are part of the overall urban-rural territory which also includes jointly-used common land. The town and the village are mutually protected, perform services jointly for the overlord, whilst taxes and military service are furnished in common. Usually the village is within the parish of the town church. Only a few of these 'town-villages' possess distinctive names; normally they simply reflect the relationship with the town.

A single example will exemplify some of these characteristics of the relationship between towns and urban fringe elements. The topographical/legal dualism of early urban development cannot be gleaned from the town plan of Koblenz. The late-Roman *castrum*, which subsequently incorporated a Merovingian royal court and later survived Norman assaults intact, was transferred in AD 1018 to Fiskus, Archbishop of Trier. The walled area offered not only sufficient space for initial settlement but also enough of that space free from flooding for additional developments as in the classical model of *urbs* and *suburbium*. However, what this settlement was like at Koblenz is far from clear. Several large buildings of C.1180 attest to inner urban consolidation in the *Frühstadt* and there were expansionary trends. Figure 15.1 illustrates the high-medieval urban fringe elements (established before the building of the outer town walls in 1276) laid onto Fritz Michel's (1963) plan of the town. As is to be expected, these consists mainly of monasteries and nunneries (Benedictine nuns 1143, Franciscans 1236, Dominicans 1233), several 'Begine' convents (1211, 1276) founded on the site of the knights' houses (*Ritterhöfe*); as well as monastic town houses (*Klosterhöfe*), and a hospital.

The foundation church (*Stiftskirche*) of St Kastor, whose Romanesque building was dedicated in AD 536 in the presence of Ludwig the Pious, has

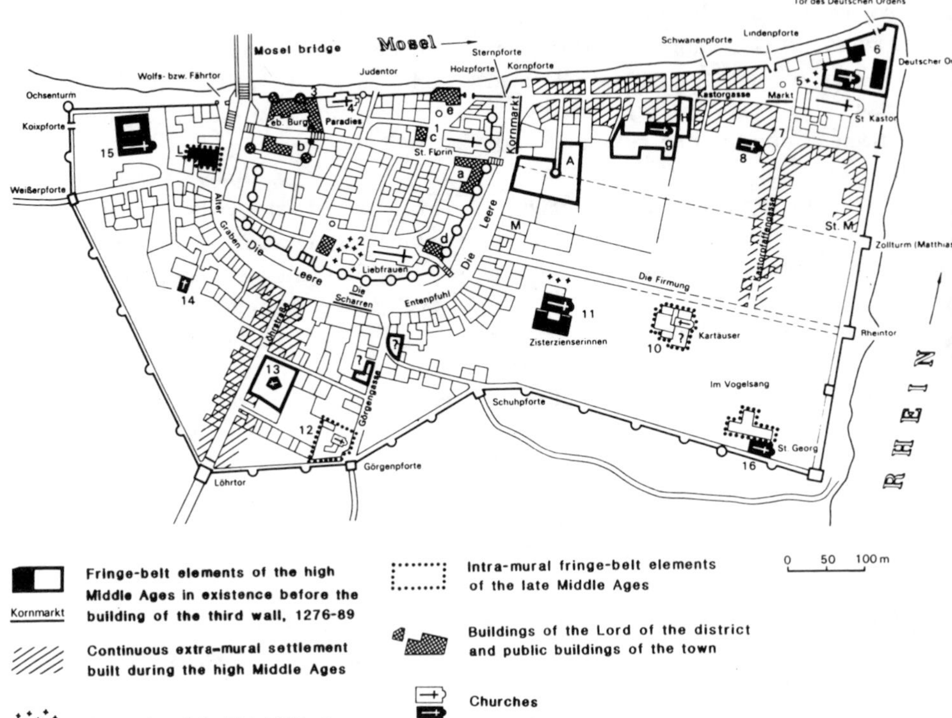

Figure 15.1 Koblenz in the Middle Ages; fringe-belt elements.

I. Churches and chapels: 1. foundation church (*Stiftskirche*) St Florin with chapels of SS. Martin and Catherine; 2. Our Lady's parish church with chapels of SS. Michael and Andrew and its cemetery; 3. Castle chapel (in Eck tower); 4. All Saints chapel; 5. Parish church of St Kastor with St Michael's chapel at entrance to its cemetery; 6. church of Teutonic Knights with its oratory; 7. chapel of dean of St Kastor's; 8. chapel given to the Teutonic Knights by the widow Pazza (later the Leyden family *Hof*); 9. Franciscan monastery church (later Jesuit church); 10. Carthusian chapel in Vogelsang; 11. Cistercian convent church (later Jesuit church); 12. Dominican nuns church of St Martin in Görgengasse; 13. Augustinian convent church of St Barbara in Löhrstrasse; 14. Dominican convent church of St Katherine in Weissergasse; 15. Dominican convent church on the Mosel; 16. Franciscan convent church of St George in Vogelsang.

II. Buldings of the ruling prince (Landesherren) and the town: a. old royal palace, later the bishop's palace; b. archbishop's castle; c. archbishop's hay house; d. town guild-hall; e. former market and town hall.

III. Courtyard houses (Höfe) of monasteries beyond the town: A. *Hof* of Cistercian abbey at Altenberg; H. *Hof* of Cistercian abbey at Himmerod (Rosenhof); L. Laacher *Hof* of Benedictine abbey at Maria Laach beside Mosel Bridge; St. M. *Hof* of Benedictine abbey of St Matthew at Trier on the Rhine bank; M. *Hof* of Cistercian abbey of Marienstatt in the Kornpfortstrasse been deliberately omitted by the author. It was the ancient parish church of the Society of the Mark and is therefore not an urban fringe element since the *castrum* or *castellum* called Koblenz was at that stage not yet a town. In this area, still described in the eighteenth century as *Unterstadt* ('lower town'), two linear roadside settlements came into being which contrast with the contemporary nodal urban fringe elements described above. The settlement in the Kastorpfaffengasse consists entirely of canonical houses as the name suggests. It was socially homogeneous and therefore not a *Vorstadt* suburb in the proper sense of the definition, whereas the Kastorgasse exhibited *Vorstadt* suburb characteristics – namely a mixed social structure – even before the wall construction of 1250 (Michel 1963: 16). The Franciscan monastery was founded there in 1236. Sydow (1969: 108) has discussed, with many examples, the location of such mendicant orders in marginal and deprived urban areas which acted as a magnet for both migrants generally and the poorer social groups in particular. Hospitals, which had originally been founded near the episcopal church were, by the late twelfth century, relocated at the edge of the town (Sydow 1969: 112). In Koblenz, for example, the hospital was relocated beyond the wall in 1239, in Löhrstrasse (Fig. 15.2 no. 13). It was not until 1706 that it moved further towards the periphery, to Vogelsang, the original buildings being converted into an Augustinian monastery. The hospital found a new home in the old Georgian monastery (founded 1143, later Franciscan). With hindsight it is clear that it became a fringe-belt element of the Baroque fortress until the work of defortification and urban restoration made another relocation necessary (not in fact carried through) to the former Dominican nunnery. Thus, at the end of the eighteenth century, it still lay within the intramural urban fringe-belt. After the secularization of religious property it found a place in the buildings of the Franciscan convent (Michael 1964; Michel 1954; Michel 1937).

Certain trends can already be deduced from these examples of the relocation of this one particular function. Hospitals moved from the early centre to the periphery in order to serve and support the sick and needy at the town entrances. It is conceivable that their location characterizes a contemporary peak in the growth of the Löhrstrasse *Vorstadt* suburb which even after the construction of the second wall in 1276–89, was described as 'vicus que itur Bopardiam extra leram' in 1298 and 1319 (Michel 1963: 35). The term *vicus*, as examples from other towns show (Dietz 1962–3: 569, 629; Ennen 195: 321), does not mean 'village' (*Dorf*) or 'trading settlement' (*Wik*) but a street or lane which exhibits a certain social and physical uniformity. The fact that this suburb had already extended beyond the hospital by the time of the wall's construction necessitated the extension of the wall alignment itself (Fig. 15.1).

With this event, the preconditions for the integration of this urban fringe-belt settlement were also provided. A hospital could no longer be tolerated on one of the city's main streets, especially once its functions began to

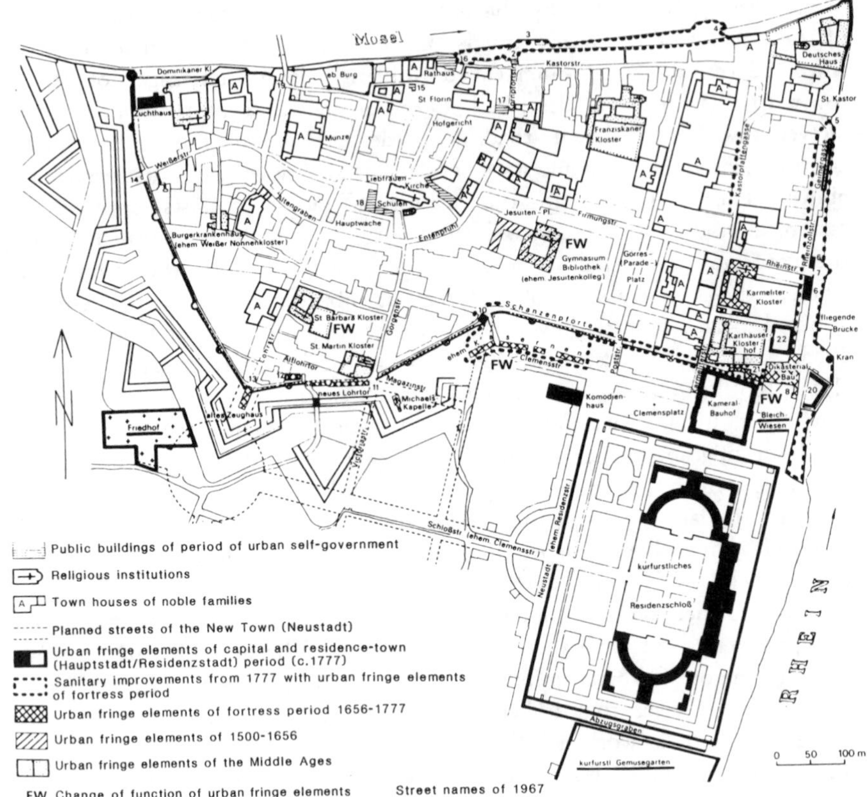

Figure 15.2 Koblenz: the ducal city at the end of the Prince-Elector's epoch (c.1792); fringe belt elements

concentrate on the care of the sick in early modern times; it was therefore relocated to the fringe, which was experiencing significantly more rapid change in the modern period. The conservation of the building fabric is one characteristic of an age of limited mobility and relatively scarce material supplies. As a rule, buildings continued to be reused, with a certain amount of renovation or rehabilitation when deemed necessary.

The later medieval period in towns was characterized by falling population and a stagnation of topographical development. This raises the question of whether the countryside began to impinge upon the town in this period and how intramural fringe-formation is structured. This has to be differentiated from the reagrarianization of small towns whose urban life did not survive the loss of a major function (palace, fortress, administrative seat) and was no longer sufficiently dynamic to continue as an economically self-sufficient entity. Within the walls there was no longer enough space for new agricultural buildings, and so rural farms were established outside the walls. Owing to their purely agrarian nature they did not possess the townscape characteristics of a *Vorstadt* suburb despite often exhibiting the plan characteristics (Raisch 1969).

(b) The early modern period

It is clear from the outset that the new functions imposed on towns by the absolutist ducal state such as the defensive fortress, capital (*Haupstadt*) or palace (*Residenzstadt*) were to have a considerable restructuring effect. First, the bastion fortifications, which were adopted also by a few of the free Imperial cities (*Reichstadt*), abruptly limited the amount of available space within the town. In addition, age-old fringe-belt elements were sacrificed in the construction of deep ditches and substantial earthworks. Most such fringe functions were relocated to the inner part of the belt finding accommodation in buildings old and new and consolidating the built fabric. Otherwise they migrated to surrounding villages or to terrain outside the defensive ring (von der Dollen 1978a: 71 ff.). The large areas of open land between the medieval and the bastion walls were developed for military and civic purposes including the magazine, barracks and a military church as well as functions connected with the *Haupt-* or *Residenz*-town (see below the equivalent Marstal area in Bonn). The medieval walls became superfluous and were leased by the city to provide emergency housing for the needy in the arches. Elsewhere, in Bonn for example, houses were built for soldiers and their families which bore the name *Kaserne* (barracks) but which are very different from modern buildings of that kind, both functionally and in their built form.

The wall towers were likewise adapted for new uses. In Koblenz (Fig. 15.2) they were used to house NCOs, the prison (with later additions), a seminary (later to become a church court house) the arsenal (in the Lohr gate courtyard) and, in one instance, as a water tower for the castle and *Neustadt*. Later, the bastion defences were breached in order to create room to facilitate the city's new role as regional capital and *Residenzstadt*. In Louis's sense, the new palace (*Residenz*) belongs to the urban fringe belt. The palace garden, the vegetable garden, the theatre and the drainage canal of the *Neustadt* are associated functions. The city's expansion after 1786 however, does not fit in to the classification of an urban fringe element proposed here, even though, in the case of Koblenz, this is related to the development of the palace (von der Dollen 1979). This *Neustadt* area is a planned urban expansion resulting from a sovereign act.

Land for the Assembly building (*Kameralbauhof*), a *Haupstadt* function, was made available in the area cleared of bastion fortifications. This building also had urban structural functions in that it formed the architectural focus of Clemensplatz which, until the Assembly building was completed, was an ill-formed square. A large old building in a fringe position on the bank of the Rhine was used to house the central administration. This was formerly a bastion housing a seminary and an orphanage which, at the time of fortification, was classified as an urban fringe element. The barrack buildings in Clemensstrasse changed their function and were used to house the poor. The planning efforts of the Court building office (*Hofbauampt*) aimed to eliminate any fringe functions which might have disturbed the aesthetic setting and social exclusivity of the new part of the town in the environs of the palace. This included the small gardens, sheds and slipways along the banks of the Moselle and Rhine. This process is an example of the renewal policies of the enlightened despotism of the absolutist period (von der Dollen 1978b). Many medieval urban fringe elements did, however, survive, sometimes adopting new functions.

The locational choices for the town houses (*Adelshöfe*) of the nobility have still to be examined. The cores of many of these mansions were first established at the settlement fringe; however, thereafter, locational inertia led to site expansion which, in densely built-up areas, was at the expense of neighbouring buildings. This occurred particularly when people began to value spacious plots with gardens in early modern times. Naturally, however, the palaces and mansions of the nobility were also attracted to existing large plots which were available in the intramural urban fringe belt.

Typical of the age is the establishment of new graveyards in extra-mural locations for health reasons. Such measures normally resulted from the will of the ruler and planning actions by his officials. They reflect the absolutist conception of the state and its polity with its all-embracing concern, and control, of the welfare of its inhabitants. It is too modernistic a thought to assume that the eighteenth-century city already presented the possibility of unrestrained development and the formation of new urban fringe-belts. The Koblenz *Neustadt*, for example, could not remain without bounds – it was protected by a pallisade fence which, although functionally inadequate, was supposed to incorporate the functions of policing and excise collection. In fact the medieval walls continued to fulfil policing and fiscal tasks right up until the mid nineteenth century. They were only finally abolished by the Prussians in 1873 (Gesetzessammlung Preussen 1873: 222) with the removal of the flour and butcher's taxes, which had been traditionally collected at the city gates. The civic and social preconditions for the creation of an area governed independently of the city or surrounding countryside which could facilitate the further development of urban settlements into their environs, was a phenomenon of the nineteenth century. Only then did the regional, spatial concept of the community displace the corporate, and reform take place (Matzerath 1978: 68).

The industrial age

The process of urban fringe-belt developments in the industrial age has already been broached briefly in the introduction in connection with the development of the conceptual background. The processes of urban restructuring are well known. Any analysis of nineteenth-century town plans in search of urban fringe elements must highlight the difference between the first half of the century and the stormy developments in the latter half (up until the First World War). Careful scrutiny and intimate local knowledge is required to uncover the disintegrating urban fringe-belt at the beginning of the century and in 1900. By then the modern town begins to be encountered with its expansive growth and concentric planning such as that initiated by Stübben, the Cologne town planner (Burgess 1925: Carter/Vetter 1980: 206).

New transport systems, the railways in particular, were of major significance. Their infrastructure took up large plots of land where functionally necessary and the network of tracks influenced the location of industrial development and of municipal utilities, a linear distribution pattern growing up within the total plan along railway lines and waterways. Government administrative buildings, institutions, hospitals, military complexes and parks become widely dispersed throughout the urban area resulting in an overall ring-shaped arrangement around the *Altstadt*.

If an individual city's town plans are examined during its development stages with reference to urban fringe elements, then a variety of distribution patterns emerge as can be seen, for example, in a medium-sized city such as Bonn (Fig. 15.3). The left-hand column of Table 15.2 corresponds to the situation at the end of the ducal period, which is very similar to the situation already portrayed in Koblenz. Intra- and extramural elements are grouped under (a) whereas the elements under (b) generally belong to the inner urban area beyond the defences. Individual uses are distributed throughout a broad area which we can term the contact zone (after Schöller 1953: 175). Persistence and development on the old square are shown in bold figures; movement and locational change in normal print. New urban fringe belt elements have been added at every stage of development. It can be seen that in the vicinity of the fortifications the urban fringe-belt elements which originated in the eighteenth century had been reduced by two thirds in 1865 and to two (15 per cent) by 1913 (Table 15.2a); all the remainder had disappeared completely or had been substantially reduced. The urban fringe elements in the contact zone were more resistant, with more than half surviving until the First World War and all elements which were new in 1865 survived until 1914. These elements are to be seen on Fig. 15.3b clustered around the Weber-, Dyroff- and Tilmannstrassen as well as in a more dispersed pattern along arterial routes such as the Popplesdorfer Allee and Koblenzer Strasse. Apart from Weberstrasse, there were still no new through streets in the middle of the nineteenth century; new building continued to use the existing road network.

Half a century later new residential blocks, as well as most of the publicity-owned fringe-belt elements, were integrated into the zone of expansion. Four alternatives were possible at this point (see Table 15.1 col. 5):

(a) functional and built form integration, i.e. the buildings and function fit into a locality and are not disruptive;
(b) built form integration (a hospital in villa style, for example);

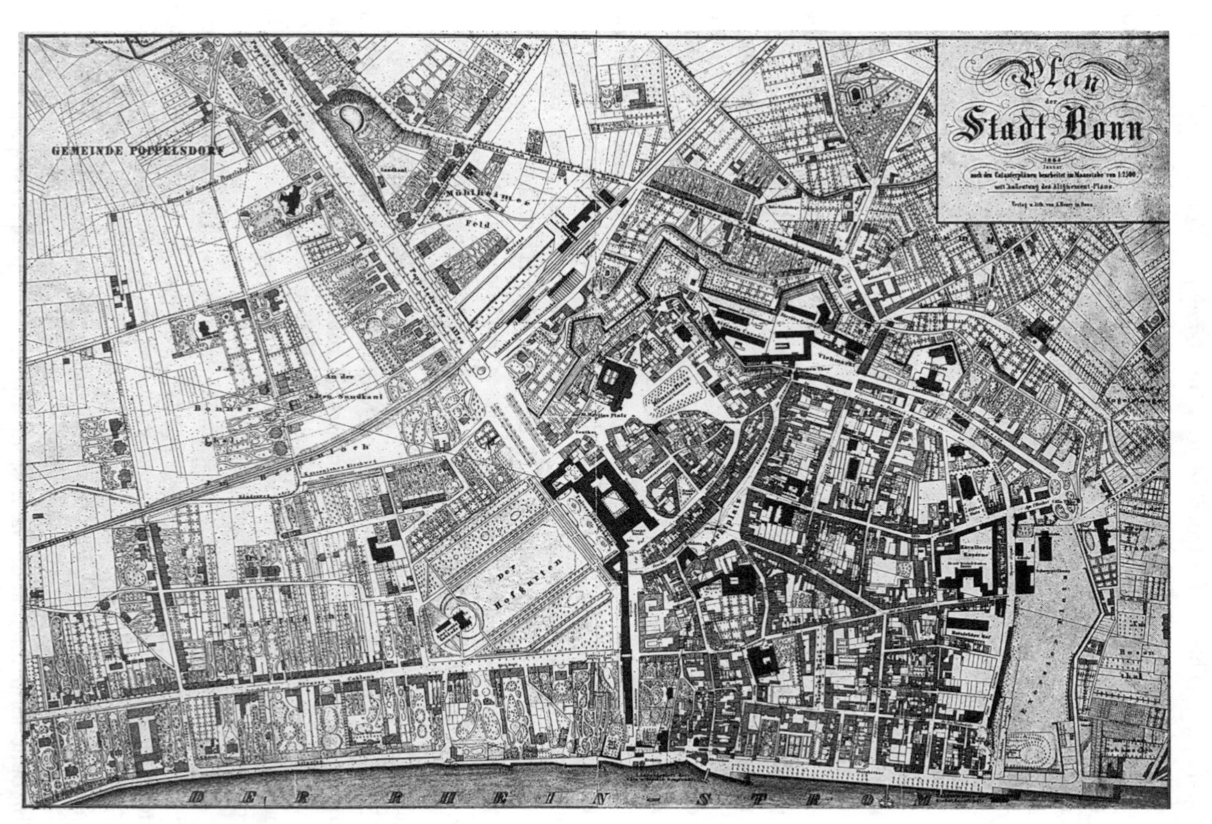
Plan
der
Stadt Bonn
Januar
nach den Catasterplänen bearbeitet im Maasstabe von 1:2500
mit Andeutung des Alignement-Plans
GEMEINDE POPPELSDORF
Poppelsdorfer Allee
Mühlheimer Feld
Der Hofgarten
DER RHEIN-STROM

Figure 15.3 Bonn: development of extramural fringe-belt elements from *c*.1820–1865. **a** *Left*, topographical plan of Bonn and Poppelsdorf by Bernhard Hundeshagen 1 : 3600; *c*.1819. Source: Stadtarchiv Bonn Bb 60. **b** *Right*, plan of town of Bonn, 1865 by A. Henry 1 : 2500. Source: Stadtarchiv Bonn

Table 15.2 Persistence and change in fringe-belt elements of nineteenth-century Bonn

c.1800	1865	1913
(a) *Near the fortifications*		
opened up defences	diminished	diminished
castle	**changed function**	**retained**
palace garden	**retained**	**retained area**
observatory	removed to fringe	—
barracks	**retained**	removed to fringe
bleachfields	diminished	removed
anatomy building	removed to fringe	—
garden houses (Belvedere)	diminished	removed
windmill	**retained**	removed
small almshouses in town walls	diminished	removed
parade ground	**enlarged/renewed**	removed to fringe
botanical garden	removed to fringe	—
materials depots	diminished	removed to fringe
ferry	—	—
	New uses	
	theatre	**retained/integrated in new area**
	new streets (town)	**retained/integrated in new area/new function**
	railway (reception and office buildings)	**enlarged/retained**
	courts	**enlarged/integrated in new area**
	detention building	**enlarged**
	mayor's office	**enlarged**

Table 15.2 contd.

c.1800	1865	1913
(b) *distributed in the contact zone*		
garden houses	diminished	removed
palace avenues	**retained**	**retained/integrated**
bleachfields	diminished	removed
industrial activities ('factories')	**enlarged/renewed**	reduced/removed to fringe
supply depots	**enlarged/renewed**	removed
quarries/sandpits, brickworks	diminished	removed to fringe
individual farms	diminished	**integrated/to fringe**
cemetery	**enlarged/renewed**	**retained/integrated/to fringe**
villas (which follow the Elector's castles)	**enlarged/renewed**	**retained/integrated/to fringe**
tree nursery	**retained**	**retained/integrated/to fringe**
excursion destinations (e.g. Vauxhall)	**enlarged/renewed**	**retained/integrated/to fringe**
watermills	**retained**	removed
highways	**retained**	**integrated in new area**
	New uses	
	residences; closely built-up forms, dispersed sites	**retained/integrated in new area**
	residences; closely built-up forms, inner sites	**retained/integrated in new area**
	county museum	**enlarged/integrated in new area**

Table 15.2 contd.

c.1800	1865	1913
	hospitals	**enlarged/integrated in new area**
	hotels	**enlarged/integrated in new area**
	church	**enlarged/integrated in new area**
	observatory	**retained/integrated in new area**
	Scientific institute of university in Poppelsdorf	**enlarged**
	Botanical gardens in Poppelsdorf	**retained/integrated**
	factories	**enlarged/integrated**
	cemetary in Poppelsdorf	**enlarged**
	[still no new access streets (except Webrstr.) new linear building along old roads]	[new streets to the opened up suburban areas]
		new:
		town museum
		two prisons
		town 'forward culture' school
		orphanages
		barracks
		administration
		(c) *New fringe elements, not yet integrated*
		old people's home (Wilhelm Augusta)
		parks department
		barracks

Table 15.2 contd.

c.1800	1865	1913
		schools
		salvation and nurse institution
		provincial health building
		sports grounds
		secondary boarding school
		north cemetery
		goods stations
		tram depots
		exercise place
		factories
		gas works
		slaughterhouse
		hospitals
		town hall
		waterworks
		parks

(c) functional and built form intrusiveness (a factory in a residential area, for example);
(d) self-contained agglomeration (a university, for example).

A new fringe belt was formed during the *Gründerzeit* or Wilhelmine period (the period under Kaiser William II in the late 1860s) (Table 15.2c) and the growth and consolidation of urban fringe-belt elements followed in a concentric pattern. It is quite evident that older, eighteenth-century, urban fringe-belt elements could not satisfy the requirements of the industrial age and new capital investment from the mid-nineteenth century onwards proved to be remarkably persistent, surviving for the most part until the destruction of the Second World War. A new stage in the city's development began thereafter, in which the advent of private motor transport resulted in a major restructuring of the inner-urban road network, the blurring of the difference between town and country, and acceleration of the growth of new city regions (Boustedt 1952: 1970) and of conurbations. The urbanization of the total habitable area no longer allows the formation of urban fringe elements and a genetic approach is therefore necessary to explain fossilized relics.

Until now, the effect of both parish and city boundaries on the urban community has not been broached. This is not particularly important for either the Middle Ages or the early modern period since the town was, for the most part, insufficiently dynamic to absorb neighbouring rural settlements or to create new boundaries, though political and politico-economic considerations in the creation of urban territories were another matter. Even here, however, the process of incorporation followed late on in the scale of integration in the relatively few instances where urbanization occurred in surrounding settlements (Von der Dollen 1978a). Conversely, many villages which existed within the town boundaries from the Middle Ages kept their agrarian character until the beginning of the twentieth century (such as the example of Rheindorf and Dransdorf in Bonn).

Mazerath (1978: 75), in a decadal overview of the period 1850–1918, demonstrated that it was not until a third phase, between 1885 and 1918, that incorporations increased. On the basis of an examination of eighty-five towns with 1910 populations over 50,000, 90 per cent of incorporations were in this later period. A detailed study would be necessary to clarify how, to what extent, and where, fiscal conditions were responsible for the location of industry within a town, or for its relocation outside city boundaries, and as to how such boundaries affected the outermost parts of the urban fringe belt. In general, it seems likely that complex factors influence the location of both industry and urban fringe-belt elements, as the example of Berlin industrial firms moving to the fringe from the Oranienburger Tor, across the Moabit, to the area on the far-side of the Ringbahn after 1980 demonstrates (Hofmeister 1981).

Conclusions

This chapter has attempted to place urban fringe-belt phenomena within the overall context of central-European urban development by means of a restricted temporal transect. Medium-sized towns where local knowledge played an important role were chosen as case studies. The method does not concern itself with inductive approaches but more with an attempt to fathom to what extent regularities more perceptible in large cities can be recognized and illustrated in the development of medium-sized towns. Urban fringe-belt phenomena are fundamentally associated with the processes of growth in the town – a factor which helps to explain the occasional blurring of the concept. It is in the nature of a fringe belt that it owes its existence to a permanent state of flux. Urban fringe-belt elements are too heterogeneous in their function, plan and built form to be understood as *a priori* zones. Their inception tends to follow a set order and they are dominated by nodal groupings which can be differentiated from spatially-planned urban extensions. The concepts of Louis and Conzen have proved to be applicable to towns of the later early modern and industrial ages and to be capable of differentiating urban levels of the early medieval *Frühstadt* from those of the high medieval *Altstadt* in a precise methodological fashion and certainly more precisely than existing approaches with their terminologically imprecise views of *Vorstadt* formation. Conzen's demonstration of the persistence of the inner urban fringe belt was, as expected, confirmed more clearly for the medieval and the early modern periods than for the nineteenth century. The trend towards infrastructural or constructional persistence during the course of functional succession emerges clearly.

In contrast to this, it is evident that during the course of the nineteenth century the old, much-adapted building stock could no longer satisfy the demands made upon it and was largely replaced in the inner and outer fringe belts, having failed to match modern requirements. The factors highlighted by Conzen regarding the penetration of city-centre functions into the inner fringe-belt is, with certain reservations, only identifiable in the twentieth century. In this century, Conzen's concepts apply only to the recognition and explanation of relict urban fringe-belts since the totality of urban life-styles has transformed the countryside into an all-encompassing urban region.

Acknowledgements

I am grateful to Professor Fehn for allowing me to use this paper which was first published in the Journal *Siedlungsforchung-Archäologie-Geschichte-Geographie, 1*, (1983). Professors Schich and Jäger drew my attention to details of the working party on *Ostsiedlung* in Berlin. Initial translations of the original text were provided by Mrs. M. Cottrell and Dr Padraig Patridge to whom I am grateful. The final text was devised by the editor.

References

Blaschke, K., 1970. 'Altstadt-Neustadt-Vorstadt', *Vierteljahresschrift für Sozial- und Wirtschaftsgerichte*, 57: 350–62.

Boustedt, O., 1952. 'Die Stadt and ihr Umland', in *Raum und Wirtschaft, Bremen* [Forschungs- und Sitzungsberichte der Akademie für Raumforschung und Landesplanung III] 142ff.

Boustedt, O., 1970. 'Stadtregionen', in *Handwörterbuch der Raumforschung und Raumordnung*, eds. v.d. Akademie für Raumforchung and Landesplanung, Hannover 2, 3207–37.

Carter, H., 1980. *Einführung in die Stadtgeographie*, translated and edited F. Vetter (Berlin/Stuttgart).

Conzen, M. R. G., 1960. 'Alnwick, Northumberland: a study in town-plan analysis', *Publications, Institute of British Geographers*, 27.

Conzen, M. R. G., 1978. 'Zur Morphologie der englischen Stadt', in *Probleme des Städtewesens im Industriezeitalter*, ed. H. Jäger (Köln/Wien) 1–48.

Czok, K., 1979. *Vorstädte, Berlin* [Sitzungsberichte der Sächsischen Akademie der Wissenschaften zu Leipzig, Phil-hist. Klasse, *121*].

Dietz, J., 1962–3. *Topographie der Stadt Bonn vom Mittelalter bis zum Ende der kurfürstlichen Zeit* (2 vols) [Bonner Geschichtsblätter *16*, *17*].

von der Dollen, B., 1978a. *Vorortbildung und Residenzfunction. Eine Studie zu den vorindustriellen Stadt-Umland-Beziehungen* [Veröffentlichungen des Stadtarchivs Bonn, *20*] (Bonn).

von der Dollen, B., 1978b. 'Massnahmen zur Sanierung und Verschönerung der Altstadt Koblenz in der frühen Neuzeit', *Landeskundliche Vierteljahresblätter*, *24*: 3–15.

von der Dollen, B., 1979. *Die Koblenzer Neustadt. Planung und Ausführung einer Stadterweiterung des 18 Jahrhunderts*, [Städteforschung, Series A, 6] (Köln/Wien).

Ennen, E., 1950. 'Die Stadtwerdung Bonns im Spiegel der Terminologie', *Bonner Geschichstoblätter.*, *4*: 14–26.

Ennen, E., 1953. 'Frühgeschichte der europäischen Stadt', *Bonn*, *1*: 3 ff.

Ennen, E., and Höroldt, D., 1976. 'Vom Römerkastell zue Bundeshamptstadt', in *Kleine Geschichte der Stadt Bonn* (Bonn).

Herzog, E., 1964. *Die ottonische Stadt. Die Anfänge der mittelalterlichen Stadtbaukunst in Deutschland* [Frankfurter Forschungen zur Architekturgeschichte, 2] (Berlin).

Hofmeister, B., 1980. *Stadtgeographie* (Braunschweig).

Hofmeister, B., 1981. 'Moabit: Durchgangsstation im Zuge der Randwanderung der Industrie?' in *Berlin. Von der Residenzstadt zur Industriemetropole*, *1* (Berlin) 183–90.

Kuhn, W., 1971. 'Die Stadtdörfer der mittelalterlichen Ostsiedlung', *Zeitschrift für Ostforschung*, *20*: 1–69.

Lichtenberger, E., 1970. *Wirtschaftsfunktion und Sozialstruktur der Wiener Ringstrasse* [Die Wiener Ringstrasse – Bild einer Epoche, 6] (Wien/Köln/Graz).

Louis, H., 1936. 'Die geographische Gliederung von Gross-Berlin', in *Länderkundliche Forschung (Krebs-Festschrift)*, eds. H. Louis and W. Panzer (Stuttgart).

Maschke, E., and Sydow, J. (eds.), 1969. 'Stadterweiterung und Vorstadt. Protokoll über die VI Arbeitstagung des Arbeitkreises für südwestdeutsche Stadtgeschichtsforschung', *Veröffentlichungen der Kommission für geschichtl. Landeskunde in Baden-Württemberg* (Series B), *51*.

Matzerath, H., 1978. 'Städtewachstum und Eingemeindungen in 19. Jahrhundert', in *Die deutsche Stadt in Industriezeitalter*, ed. J. Reulecke (Wuppertal) 67–89.

Michel, F., 1937. *Kirchliche: Die Kunstdenkmäler der Stadt Koblenz I* [Die Kunstdenkmäler der Rheinprovinz, 20] (Düsseldorf).

Michel, F., 1954. *Profane: Die Kunstdenkmäler der Stadt Koblenz* [Die Kunstdenkmäler von Rheinland-Pfalz, I.] (Düsseldorf).

Michel, F., 1963. *Die Geschichte der Stadt Koblenz in Mittelalter* (Trautheim).

Plantiz, H., 1954. *Die deutsche Stadt im Mittelalter. Von der Römerzeit bis zu den Zunftkämpfen* (Graz/Köln).

Raisch, H., 1969. 'Stadterweiterung und Vorstadt in historische-geographischer Sicht dargelegt am Beispiel einiger Kleinstädte', in Maschke, E. and Sydow, J. (eds.), *op. cit.*, 80–95.

Slater, T. R., 1978. 'Family, society and the ornamental villa on the fringes of English country towns'. *Journal of Historical Geography*, *4*: 129–44.

Stoob, H. (ed.), 1973. *Deutsche Städteatlas*, I (Dortmund).

Stoob, H. (ed.), 1979. *Deutsche Städteatlas*, II (Dortmund).

Sydow, J., 1969. 'Kirchen- und spitalgeschichtliche Bemerkungen zum Problem der Stadterweiterung und Vorstadt', in Maschke, E. and Sydow J. (eds.), *op. cit.*, 107–13.

Schlesinger, W., 1969. 'Stadt und Vorstadt', in Maschke, E., and Sydow, J. (eds.), *op. cit*, 1–20.

Schöller, P., 1953. 'Aufgaben und Probleme der Stadtgeographie', *Erdkunde*, *7*: 161–84.

Stübben, J., 1924. *Der Städtebau* (Leipzig, 3rd ed.).

Whitehand, J. W. R., 1967. 'Fringe belts: a neglected aspect of urban geography', *Transactions, Institute of British Geographers*, *41*: 223–33.

Whitehand, J. W. R., (ed.), 1981 *The urban landscape: historical development and management. Papers by* M. R. G. *Conzen* [Institute of British Geographers Special Publication No. 13].

Whitehand, J. W. R., 1981. 'Fluctuations in the land-use composition of urban development during the industrial era', *Erdkunde*, *35*: 129–40.

Part VI

Townscape conservation

16 Conservation and the management of historical townscapes

Peter J. Larkham

It is now widely realized that 'preservation', in English planning usage, has unfortunate connotations implying a total lack of change. Conservation, by contrast, is seen to be a more active process embracing various changes, particularly those enhancing the area in question (see Mynors 1984 on conservation area legislation; Department of the Environment 1987). A more useful concept is that of townscape management which, in the case of historical townscapes, embraces aspects of preservation and conservation (Conzen 1966: 61) and 'management' is now mentioned in official guidance (Department of the Environment 1987). Historical townscapes are significant because of the number of long-established 'old town' centres, particularly in western Europe, and because they offer very considerable continuity of site, historical dynamism and variety of formative processes (Conzen 1975: 76). Over time, the operation of these processes leads to the townscape at any time being a palimpsest of the achievements of successive generations; an accumulation of relict, residual and modern features, with earlier features undergoing metamorphosis or partial or total replacement by later developments (Cherry 1981; Conzen 1958: 78; Martin 1968). The processes and rates of change being different in each place lead to the uniqueness of townscapes, the 'spirit of place' or *genius loci*, enabling inhabitants to identify with their town. The immediate problems for consideration are first, why emphasize conservation in townscape management, and secondly, how can this management be achieved?

This chapter concentrates on the immediate visual aspects of townscape, principally the town plan and standing buildings. There are a number of other aspects that could be considered in a wider examination of conservation, including archaeological remains that may be as yet undiscovered, or be unknown to the general public. Such lines of evidence should certainly be considered when building up a detailed historical profile of an area, more so since continuing urban development is constantly eroding this unseen heritage (Heighway 1972). Nevertheless, it is the visual heritage that has attracted most public and official concern, and has formed the basis for much of Conzen's own work. The topics considered are illustrated by examples drawn from a wide variety of small towns in Britain.

Why conserve?

Conservation is a growing trend in current European planning (Dobby 1978; Smith D. L. 1974). This may be due to a growing awareness of basic reasons for conservation, and an examination of recent literature suggests that psychological and historical reasons are of greatest significance.

In his all-encompassing examination of civilization, Lord Clark (1969) suggested that civilization could be defined as 'a sense of permanence', and that a civilized man 'must feel that he belongs somewhere in space and time, that he consciously looks forward and looks back'. Various studies in environmental psychology, particularly those of P. F. Smith (1974a, b, 1975b, 1977), strongly suggest that this 'looking back' is a psychological necessity. There is a human need for visual stimuli to provide 'orientation' – the observer's awareness of his own location in a given environment – and 'variety' (Lozano 1974). These needs are met by historical areas that have survived relatively unchanged, providing symbols of stability: 'the visual confirmation of the past provides a fixed reference point of inestimable value' (Smith P. F. 1974a: 903). Historical areas act as cushions against Toffler's 'future shock' (Toffler 1970). In a wider context, Lowenthal (1985) uses a detailed presentation of minutiae and ephemera to support his relating of ordinary everyday experiences to the need for some tangible 'heritage'.

There is some empirical evidence to support this theoretical work. Taylor and Konrad (1980), for example, construct a scaling system to measure the dispositions of people towards the past, and find strong sentiments in favour of conservation and heritage. Morris (1978) analyses reactions towards slides of different types and ages of buildings, finding that contemporary buildings are dismissed as discordant intrusions, while medieval buildings in particular, and classical styles to a lesser extent, possess considerable historical and architectural interest. Holzner (1970) gives an interesting description of conservation in practice in post-war Germany. He notes that, after wartime destruction of over one million buildings, every effort was made to repair as many of the old buildings as possible and to reconstruct them in the inherited manner. Holzner concludes that this preservation is not rational, but that a popular social need overcame rational approaches to post-war reconstruction. This appears to be a practical and large-scale demonstration of the psychological argument for conservation, which may also be applicable in other countries, such as the case of the post-war rebuilding of Polish towns.

The notion that there is a moral duty to preserve and conserve our historic heritage, to remember and pass on the accomplishments of our ancestors (Tuan 1977: 197) is a common argument. The main reason underlying this moral duty appears to be pedagogic: the physical artifacts of history teach observers about landscapes, people, events and values of the past, giving substance to the 'cultural memory' (Lewis 1975). However,

Faulkner (1978) shows that the historical heritage can be divided into the heritage of objects and that of ideas, with the implication that one may be conserved without the other. 'This inevitably leads us to the question of architectural design and whether we can . . . separate the design from the building, and claim the design as a concept has a separate existence from the stones of which the building is built' (*ibid*: 456). If so, then the handing-down of the heritage could easily be achieved by the comprehensive recording of buildings or areas. Preservation of the actual fabric becomes no longer an absolute necessity in original or rebuilt form.

After 'the heritage' is defined, those parts of it worth saving must be identified. Conservation must be selective, or there would be little change in urban structures, which would then ossify: some change is a necessity. Further, if everything were to be conserved, '. . . then we would be faced with retaining in its original condition everything left to us by previous generations . . . warts and all' (Cantell 1975: 6). Yet the very acts of selection and designation for conservation imply assumptions about meaning and significance held by those making the selection, although such assumptions are rarely made explicit.

It could be argued that what is to be retained should be restored to its original state and use where possible: that is, 'preserved'. Alternatively, changes should be permitted to allow a new function to inject life into the building and its surroundings, even at the cost of some alterations. In the latter case, it is suggested that since the 'architectural morality' of both 'function equals form equals beauty' and 'the exterior should reflect the interior structure' (two of the principal tenets of Modern architecture) are unrelated to the manner in which buildings are perceived (Smith P. F. 1975a: 79), there should be little opposition to either facsimile reproduction if the original is unsalvageable, or 'facadism', the rebuilding in forms suitable for modern functions behind a retained and restored facade. Both of these suggestions seek to retain the visual appeal of a townscape – the 'aesthetic texture' (Lewis 1975), the 'aesthetic justification for preservation' (Tuan 1977), while permitting the necessary modern uses. Yet even this preservation of style destroys the 'patina of age', the 'aura of history', that is also of considerable importance.

The argument of conserving for posterity is not wholly convincing, except possibly in the case of undisturbed archaeological deposits. This is because modern urban functions require some change in the townscape, and the selection of what is to be preserved and/or conserved, together with differences over how such conservation should be effected, do interfere with the pure notion of preservation for posterity. More so than other arguments for conservation, the historicist arguments do highlight the fact that an overall philosophical framework for conservation is lacking. Faulkner, in particular, has attempted to formulate such a framework (Faulkner 1978), but his theory has not been translated into practical terms. Conzen has put forward more concrete suggestions on approaches to conservation and townscape management, which have met with a similar fate (Whitehand 1981), but which merit further discussion.

Conzen, conservation and townscape management

Conzen's ideas on conservation form an important part of his wider concept of townscape management. These ideas are derived from his detailed studies of a variety of towns in Britain during the 1940s and 1950s, and were first expressed in his contribution to the *Survey of Whitby and the surrounding area* (Conzen 1958). By this time, he had already made detailed, plot-by-plot surveys of a number of similar small towns, including Conway (Gwynedd), Frodsham (Cheshire), Ludlow (Shropshire), Newton Stewart (Dumfries and Galloway), Pickering (North Yorkshire), Whithorn and Wigtown (both Dumfries and Galloway). Notable throughout the first part of Conzen's contribution to the Whitby volume are numerous references to buildings of the period under consideration that still survived in the townscape, and the importance of their continued preservation. In the second part, he emphasizes the importance of the townscape as a composite historical monument. Conzen returned to conservation as a theme in his paper on historical townscapes (Conzen 1966), using as illustrations some of the material obtained in his earlier studies of small towns. Here the concept of 'management' is introduced, 'being less suggestive of restriction to physical preservation of particular and in a sense isolated landscape elements' (Conzen 1966: 61). The key attribute of a townscape that requires management was identified as its 'historicity'. It was noted that this quality was not a permanent attribute, but may be lost: the rate of loss increasing almost geometrically compared with the amount of destruction of traditional forms and the quality of the associated redevelopment. Conzen sees three major factors as making up a townscape's historicity, these being the town plan, building fabric and land utilization. The quality of historical townscapes – their historicity – rests largely upon the survival of their town plans and the remaining stock of traditional buildings. Land utilization is a more minor, indirect, aspect of historicity.

In the second major paper dealing with geography and townscape conservation (Conzen 1975), the concern has changed from a delimitation of aspects of historicity to a concern for how this historicity is shaped. It is noted that the three aspects of historicity possess differing degrees of persistence in the townscape. The town plan is the most durable element, reflecting past patterns of land ownership. Building form is somewhat less conservative, representing capital investment, and being subject to the natural processes of ageing, obsolescence and replacement (Cowan 1965). These two elements in particular form a morphological 'frame', constraining development to some degree. Land use patterns are rather more ephemeral.

If town plan, building type and land use are the components of townscape historicity, and if this historicity is the key to informed townscape management, then it must be asked whether there is any method of systematic examination of these components. Conzen has twice discussed the mapping of these elements (Conzen 1966; 1988) and has twice presented an amalgamation of all three elements to form a map of morphological regions for Ludlow (Conzen 1975; 1988). Being thus based on a combination of the three components of townscape historicity, these regions are a direct reflection of the town's historicity. They clearly show that this elusive quality is not spread evenly throughout the town, hence the hierarchy of regions. Nevertheless, despite the importance of this concept of morphological, or townscape, regions, there is no clear published explanation of precisely how these regions are constructed, and no attempt has been made to replicate this detailed study elsewhere.

However, Conzen has mentioned several other possible criteria for the assessment of historicity. First, are the time range and morphological periods represented within the townscape and within each of the three components. Secondly, there is the spatial distribution of historical forms within each component, including considerations of concentration and admixture. Thirdly, there is the degree of mutual conformability of the three components; for example, Georgian town houses may sit conformably upon medieval burgages, but the larger scale of recent buildings inevitably means plot amalgamation, a loss of historic plot patterns and new and very different building types within the townscape. Fourthly, obsolescence and structural decay inevitably affect historicity, as does unsympathetic or inappropriate 'restoration'. Lastly, historicity is affected by the circumstances of a site, including adjoining land uses and landscape settings (Conzen 1975: 82–3). The presence of archaeological deposits should be added to this list. Whether or not such deposits have been examined, their presence does add an element to the historicity and value of the area.

The current management of historical townscapes

Although Conzen's ideas have not yet been developed into a working theory of townscape management, a way forward has clearly been shown with his discussions of townscape historicity, suggestions for its assessment, and argument that a thorough understanding of the historical and spatial structure of these townscapes is a prerequisite for successful management. However, his ideas have not consciously been adopted by practising town planners in Britain. Fennell notes in a study of Chichester (West Sussex), for example, that 'perhaps the most disturbing conclusion that emerges from this case study is the failure to appreciate the significance of plan form. Little or no attention has been given to the contribution that street pattern, plot shape and building plan inevitably make to the character of the city' (Fennell 1982: 7). This omission may be because Conzen's concepts are still largely at the theoretical, rather than practical, stage and partly because his papers are little known outside a small circle of urban and historical geographers (Whitehand 1981; Samuels 1985: 7). Nevertheless, an examination of current planning practice in historical townscapes inevitably brings some of Conzen's ideas to mind, and these are worth exploring in detail.

(a) The concept of areas

The concept of the delimitation of areas of townscape is fundamental to Conzen's ideas, particularly in the mapping of the three 'systematic form complexes' of town plan, building type and land use leading to the construction of morphological regions. In terms of conservation management, the use of this type of analysis to give a visual presentation of the historicity of a town, especially in its spatial variability, has considerable potential. This is particularly the case when it is considered that much conservation management in Britain is currently carried out through the exercise of the development control system in designated conservation areas. The designation of such areas is not, however, carried out with the refinement of Conzen's mapping.

This problem is partly due to the manner in which the concept of conservation areas was introduced. No legislative guidance was given on the qualities distinguishing a conservation-worthy area beyond the official description as 'areas of special architectural or historic interest, the character or appearance of which it is desirable to preserve or enhance' (1971 Town and Country Planning Act, Section 277). Various Department of the Environment Circulars emphasized the duty of local planning authorities to designate areas, and indeed designation was rapid in most areas (*Civic Trust News* 1980). The mechanics of the designation process vary widely between, and even within, authorities (see Gamston 1975). Most area designations are initiated by planning officers, relatively few by councillors, and these may be for distinct political reasons. Public pressure groups are responsible for a number of suggestions, although in one case in Solihull (West Midlands), when presented with several alternative boundaries, a vociferous society opted for the largest possible area for its village, apparently regardless of the quality of parts of the area thus encompassed (Solihull planning officers, personal communications). Some authorities may carry out detailed evaluation processes (Gamston 1975; Robinson 1982), but many authorities depend on *ad hoc* approaches with no formal designation criteria (Staffordshire planning officers, personal communication). None of these methods begin to approach the detail apparent in Conzen's surveys.

This diversity of approaches naturally produces anomalies. Even a cursory examination of conservation area boundaries in the Midlands region shows a considerable number. Chipping Norton (Oxfordshire) is essentially a two-row planned town, with market-place and regular medieval plots, yet the area boundary cuts through the plots on the east side of the square, rather than following the back lane (Robinson 1982: 127) (Fig. 16.1). An obvious morphological feature of some antiquity is thus ignored. St John's Square, Wolverhampton (West Midlands), was a formal Georgian square surrounding

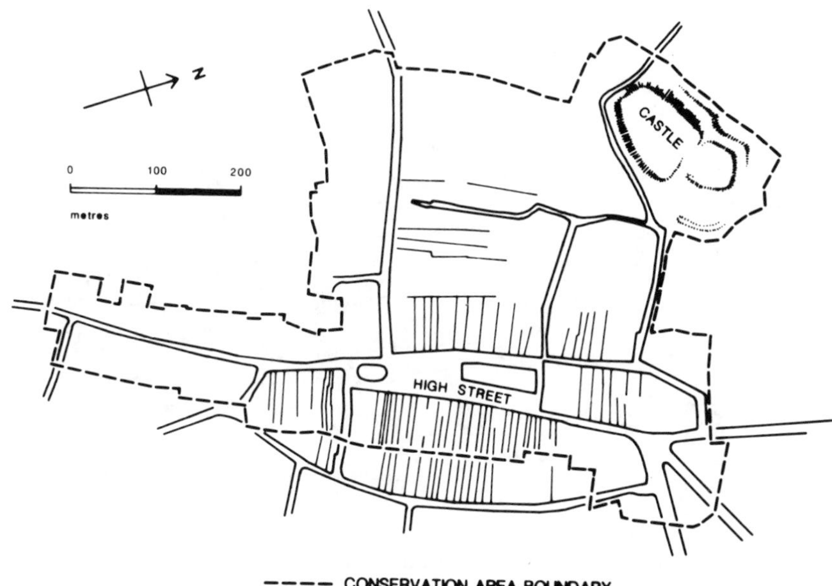

Figure 16.1 Chipping Norton Conservation Area (medieval plots cut by area boundary)

a church dating from 1750, yet the layout has been partially destroyed by a ring road that also exposes untidy modern rear additions to Georgian buildings, only one of the four approaches remains largely Georgian, and the conservation area boundary includes the large and obtrusive British Telecom building of 1982 (Fig. 16.2). Many designated areas contain a multiplicity of Conzen's townscape units, this being best shown for Ludlow. One official designated area covers the entire historical town (Fig. 16.3A), although this large area is subdivided into three zones, each with different management policies. Conzen himself, in contrast, shows five orders of morphological regions and some 115 regions in total, excluding part of Corve Street and some areas south of the town wall (Conzen 1988) (Fig. 16.3B). It is very rare for a designated conservation area to encompass only one townscape unit, unless it is a 'feature' area (Larkham 1986: 73–7). One of the few exceptions is the recent designation of Ashleigh Road in Solihull (West Midlands), a small homogenous area of large plots along a road, virtually all developed between 1902 and 1913. Unusually, in this instance the research carried out by the local authority prior to designation made considerable use of building plans, one of the few data sources suitable for detailed research on the urban fabric over the past 150 years (Solihull Metropolitan Borough Council 1985) (Fig. 16.4).

This is one obvious case where Conzen's concepts and methods could

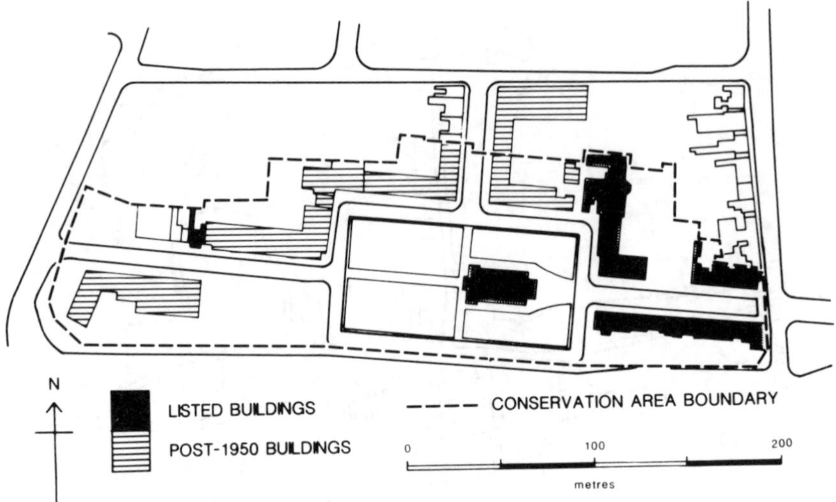

Figure 16.2 St John's Square Conservation Area, Wolverhampton

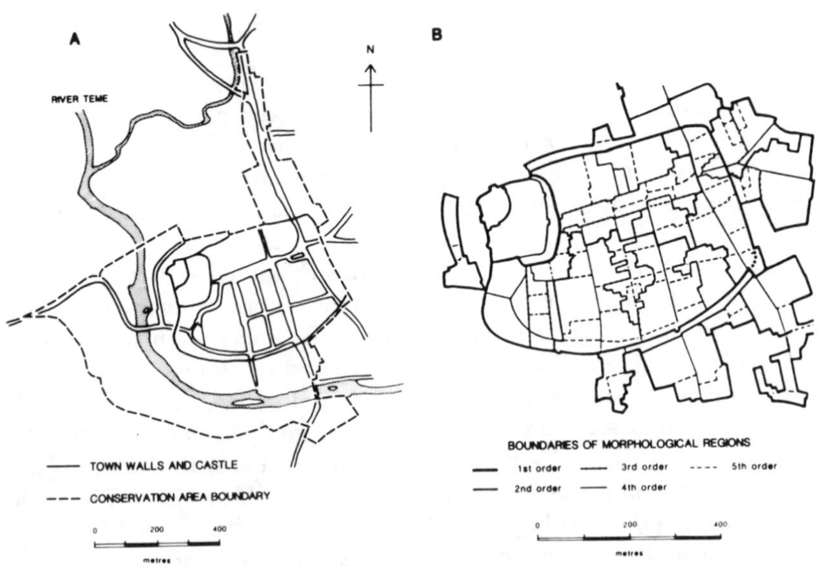

Figure 16.3 Area designation in Ludlow: (A) Ludlow Conservation Area; (B) Morphological regions (reproduced from Conzen, 1988, by permission of Cambridge University Press)

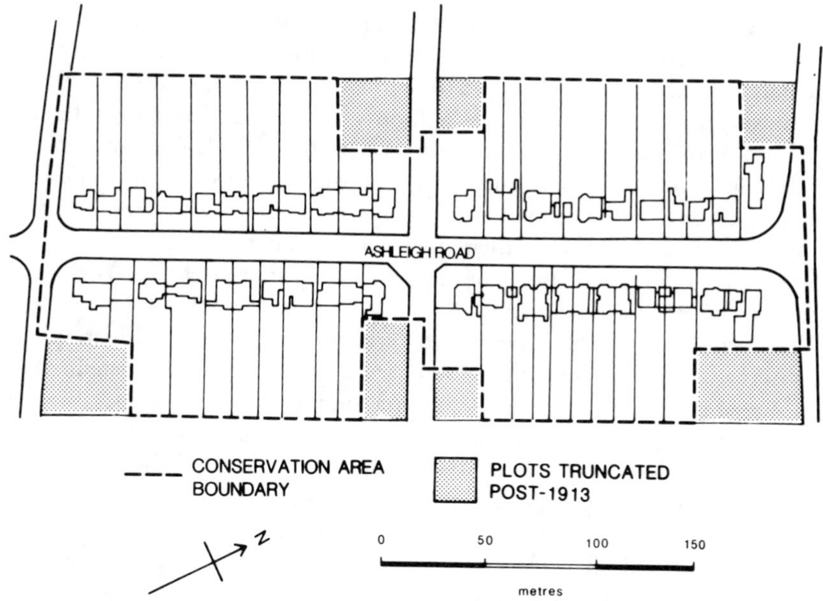

Figure 16.4 Ashleigh Road Conservation Area, Solihull

profitably be employed by planning departments for accurate and detailed surveys of historic areas. The notion of conservation areas, at the time a considerable advance on previous building- and monument-only legislation (Boulting 1976), could be considerably updated and placed on a rational footing in terms of survey, designation and management. Placing conservation area management on a firmer foundation of knowledge and concept may go some way to quietening those who, with Price (1981), fulminate against conservation. The concept of areas is given a wider treatment by Whitehand (this volume), and also overlaps with the following section.

(b) Sense of place and attitudes to place

(i) Views of the community. It is commonly assumed that the residents of an area have a common sense of identity, of place, or of neighbourhood. This notion is embodied in Conzen's concept of 'objectivation of the spirit', yet the validity of the idea is essentially unproven. Lee (1954) notes that neighbourhood, in terms of both the place and its occupants, is 'a really salient experience ... something that could be quickly and easily acknowledged and fairly readily described', although the actual delineations of neighbourhoods may vary widely. Lee also related 'local involvement' or 'community participation' to neighbourhood patterns. Local amenity groups are one manifestation of this involvement that have been both extensively studied and been incorporated into the planning system through a process of consultation. The rise of public participation in British planning seems to

have been rooted in the idea that such consultation would facilitate consensus, and it did not seem to be appreciated 'that citizens might seek to change planning policies, and that this might conflict with established political processes by which local authority policies are determined' (Healey 1983: 52). In the majority of cases it is not the individual member of the public who responds to consultation, but the organized amenity societies, many of whom become part of the planning system when the planning authority actively solicits their views or facilitates their activities by providing information (see the surveys in Gamston 1975 (Yorkshire), Larkham 1985 (West Midlands)).

Nevertheless, there have been many criticisms of public participation and amenity societies. Community groups are frequently undisciplined in their pursuit of goals. Lack of expertise, inertia, and fear of novel proposals impel citizens to oppose whatever is proposed: the goals pursued by citizen participation thus tend always toward the preservation of the status quo. The myopia of local groups may prevent or irretrievably delay the formulation of long-range plans (Porteous 1977: 366–7). Such groups are accused of élitism (Eversley 1974), and indeed their members have been shown by most surveys to have predominantly educated, middle-class occupations and values. This may be true for the types of group categorized by Short *et al.* as 'stoppers' (protectors, or preservationists), who in central Berkshire are overwhelmingly professional, seeking to protect their physical and social environments. The 'getters' (enhancers) are 'a more mixed bunch, reflecting the importance of council and lower-income private estates in this category . . . here the concerns are with not only protecting but also enhancing the local physical and resource environments' (Short *et al.* 1986: 227). In a wider context, however, this socio-cultural stopper/getter classification may not adequately represent the attitudes to place of these groups.

Thus, although some reference is implicitly made in current conservation planning to the sense of place possessed by residents (usually as represented by amenity groups), it appears that this is not only inadequate but probably unrepresentative. Little study is devoted to large-scale studies of place imagery (Goodey *et al.* 1971 being a rare example), and it would probably be difficult to incorporate such work into current planning practice (Goodey 1974). Yet planners and the public are only indirect agents of townscape change. A more problematic point is the extent to which the direct agents of change, those involved in initiating, designing and constructing new buildings, have consistent views on the area in which development is proposed.

(ii) Views of the agents of change. Recent work using detailed local authority data sources (Freeman, 1986; Larkham 1986; Whitehand 1984) has been able to identify the direct agents active in various areas of Britain, including town centres and conservation areas, with some precision. Examination of correspondence, questionnaires, interviews and the analysis of patterns of

development has enabled the rationale behind parts of the decision-making process to be deduced. An intensive study of several small and contrasting areas thus highlights the influences on individual townscapes of 'insiders' and 'outsiders'. 'It seems inescapable . . . that boardroom decisions taken in the metropolis against the background of national-scale operations . . . produced different results from those taken by local individuals with a field of vision ending abruptly at the edge of their town's sphere of influence' (Whitehand 1984: 4). 'Insiders', the local agents of change, seem to have greater knowledge of, and sympathy with, their local environment. The exceptions to this rule are occasional owner-occupiers building for themselves, who seek to create a new impression with an eye-catching novel style. By contrast, 'outsiders' in the post-war period imposed uniform house styles throughout the country and, having greater financial resources and desiring rapid returns on investment, were able to build at a considerably larger scale, leading to much plot amalgamation and buildings being intrusive by their very scale. Only in recent years has the nationwide concern for conservation and the rise of Post-Modern architectural styles led to both insiders and outsiders producing similar forms in the townscape. These themes are discussed by Freeman (this volume). Particularly from the end of the Second World War, townscapes have increasingly become the objectivation of the commercial spirit of national, profit-making concerns.

(iii) The views of those affected by changes. Lastly, the sense of place and attitudes of those affected by conservation planning (whether proposals for new development or otherwise) should be examined: how far do these attitudes reflect the interests, for example in the character and potentialities of their own property, of those involved? The example of several recent planning applications in Old Street, Ludlow (Shropshire) are instructive in this respect.

An application for ten dwellings, maisonette and shop at 18/20 Old Street entailed total demolition of the existing garage premises, followed by new construction. This provoked strong protests from property owners overlooking and overlooked by the proposed development, from others out of sight of the site, and from the local Member of Parliament, an acquaintance of one of the protesters (Fig. 16.5A). Interestingly, there was opposition to the removal of the garage use and its associated small sheds, incongruous in a part of the street otherwise largely in residential or antique retailing use. Although this was a new development on individual burgages, in a street of obvious burgages, there was an alleged 'violation of the historic pattern of building and space in the inner town', and 'such crowding in such a small site . . . opens up the possibility of site infilling along the length of the old gardens of Old Street, either by separate or group developers – thus changing forever the character of the centre of old Ludlow . . .', yet the infilling of burgages is an integral part of the burgage cycle (Conzen 1962). Furthermore, several protesters suggested that this new development would

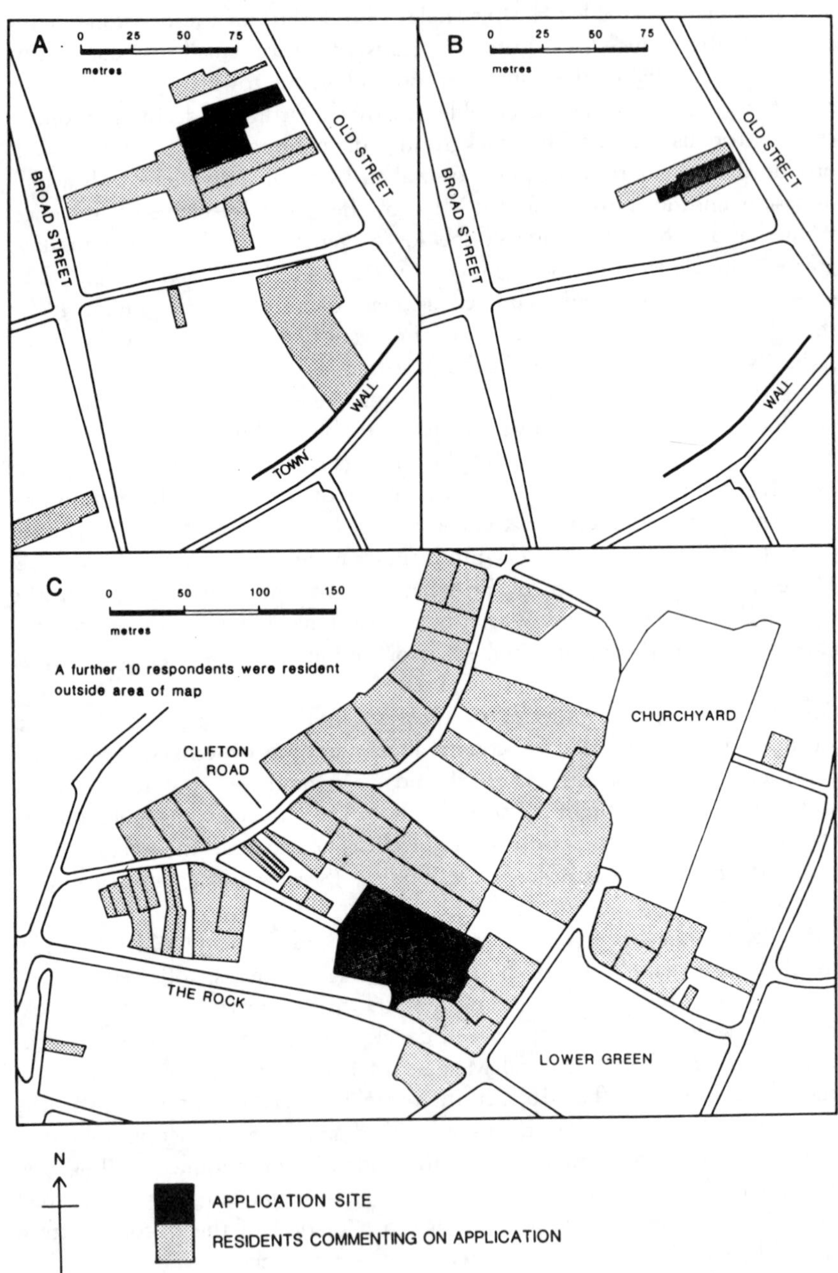

Figure 16.5 Comments on planning applications: (A) 18/20 Old Street, Ludlow; (B) 32 Old Street, Ludlow; (C) 26 Clifton Road, Tettenhall, Wolverhampton

devalue their own property, although there was no suggestion of how this devaluation would occur, or by how much. This proposal was refused, although a similar application with reduced housing density was later permitted (application 81/231, South Shropshire District Council planning records). By contrast, an application proposing four houses, a studio flat and frontage house at 32 Old Street entailed the conversion of a semi-derelict public house and outhouses; no new construction was proposed. Two letters were received as a result of public consultation, both from properties adjoining the site (Fig. 16.5B). Both had only minor criticisms concerning the maintenance of their privacy, which directly resulted in conditions to the grant of planning permission. Indeed, one correspondent felt 'sure [that] when completed the alterations would enhance the Old Green Dragon and surrounding area very much . . .' (application 84/327, South Shropshire District Council planning records).

An application to convert a large Victorian villa in Tettenhall, Wolverhampton into three flats, with a three-flat extension and a new block of nine flats produced a veritable storm of protest from neighbours (Fig. 16.5C). Many were worried about being overlooked, the possible devaluation of their properties, and increased traffic. The adjoining property owner to the west did not complain, as a similar proposal was contemplated for that site. Examination of the proposals suggests that much of the new construction would be hidden by the trees surrounding the site, and would not be visible from the main road (A41 'The Rock'), which is in a cutting at this point. It is also unlikely that residents of the north-eastern part of Clifton Road would suffer from any extra traffic. Some objectors cited the area's Conservation Area status as a reason for refusing permission for this development, without recognizing that the area's original characteristic of large villas in extensive grounds east of Clifton Road had been eroded by demolition and subdivisions throughout the previous decade. Indeed, many objectors themselves live in 1970s' houses built speculatively on such subdivided plots (application A/C/1551/78, Wolverhampton Metropolitan Borough Council planning records).

There are distinct similarities between this opposition to new building and misconceptions of area, and those seen in a study in Amersham (Whitehand 1990). In their reactions to proposed new development, the local residents appear preoccupied by considerations of privacy, property devaluation, and often incorrect local history. This is very much a self-centred sense of place. The cases cited here have parallels in rural development, when vociferous newcomers attempt to ensure that theirs is the last new house to be built in a village, thus preserving its character and halting the influx of outsiders (Cloke and Park 1985: 3). None of the residents appear to have considered that adjoining development may indeed enhance their own properties, in the Ludlow example by the removal of a non-conforming and nuisance-causing semi-industrial land use. Likewise, none of them appear to have been spurred by the adjoining development to partially or totally redevelop, or merely enhance, their own property.

(c) The morphological frame: control by antecedent conditions

Following much of Conzen's work, a number of recent studies have suggested that townscape change is constrained to a considerable degree by the existing built fabric (Conzen 1975; Freeman 1986; Whitehand 1984). These general studies are supported by specific examinations of change in historical areas (Larkham 1986). At any given time, the fabric of town plan and building form combine to create a morphological frame, within which further development usually lies. Although this is demonstrably not the case during periods of comprehensive redevelopment, such as *c.*1955–65 in many major British cities, and there are frequently examples where the morphological frame exerts relatively little control over development, particularly in the plot amalgamations of developments by large, external agents of change (Freeman, this volume; Whitehand 1984), the influence exerted by the morphological frame usually affects the layout of new buildings and the design of both new and modified buildings.

(i) Layout of new buildings The town plan exerts greatest control over the layout of new buildings. As Conzen noted, street layouts are rarely changed, and may persist for centuries. Even when they are blocked up, traces often remain in public footpaths and the alignment of surviving buildings. The progressive colonization of an area of terraced housing by Manchester University (Charlton 1951, especially Appendix VI) left relict features including the Arts Building (1919) facing the former Lime Grove, and a former chapel, successively a library extension and drama workshop, facing Wright Street (surviving in 1950 but totally built over by 1977). The plot pattern may exert a considerable influence, particularly when financial resources do not allow large-scale rebuilding, and small, individual developments result. In historic towns this often involves a simple replacement of the plot dominant with a new building sited conformably upon the plot. In the case of the development at 18/20 Old Street, Ludlow, referred to earlier, the new plot dominant (*c.* 1985) sits conformably on the burgage plot, and indeed is of similar style to its surviving Georgian neighbours. (The plot amalgamation behind the dominant occurred earlier in this century and, not having been built over, can be ignored for present purposes.)

(ii) Design and modification of buildings Modifications to existing buildings may similarly be influenced by the morphological frame. This is particularly noticeable in the case of additions to buildings which, in some cases, may be distinguished from the original only by minor features such as brick bonding and apparent age of materials. There are also cases where buildings are refronted. This is frequently undertaken for reasons of fashion; for

Figure 16.6 40 Broad Street, Ludlow: (A) before rebuilding; (B) after rebuilding (photographs reproduced by permission of Messrs Shrimpton and Salmon, Chartered Architects, Ludlow)

example, the re-fronting of medieval timber-frame buildings with Georgian brick (see the example of buildings in Broad Street, Ludlow, in Lloyd 1979: 37–63), or in order to produce a new corporate image, as when the Wolverhampton Freeholders Permanent Building Society re-fronted 37–9 Queen Square, Wolverhampton, in 1933, in the typical British commercial fusion of classical and Art Deco styles (Building Plan B478, Wolverhampton Reference Library). However, the recent example of 40 Broad Street, Ludlow is noteworthy. Here, a housing association was converting a small building with a totally undistinguished facade into maisonettes, and took the opportunity to make major changes to the style of the facade, necessitated only partly by the internal reorganization of the building. The resulting building conforms much better with its Georgian-fronted neighbours (Fig. 16.6).

Particularly during the past fifteen or so years, and paralleling the rise of public concern over conservation, a variety of devices have been used to minimize the visual intrusiveness of new buildings many of which, however, continue to be constructed on a large scale. Such devices include the subdivision of long facades to give the outward appearance of separate buildings on plots of traditional width, facadism, and the use of historicist and neo-vernacular veneer styles. In Solihull High Street, for example, seven planning applications involving facadism were made between 1970 and 1984.

Yet these are often mere gestures at sense of place, indeed one of the Solihull applications proposed the construction of a replica of the original facade instead of its retention. Facadism and similar devices have been severely criticized: recent Sainsbury's stores are mere 'gestures at traditional effects' (Gardiner 1985), facadism 'makes a complete nonsense of the concept of conservation . . . it is ridiculous to have a street made up of historic front walls' (Bearman 1982) and vernacular styling is 'the architectural equivalent of reproduction Chippendale' (cited by Aldous 1978).

(iii) Planning and management Conservation management has emphasized the significance of the morphological frame in guiding development. Representations to planning authorities made by amenity groups frequently stress the importance of the use of matching or, at least, conforming rather than sharply contrasting, materials (Larkham 1985). In this they are frequently supported by explicit conditions attached to grants of planning permission. The design of buildings continues to occupy the attention of planning authorities, despite official advice to leave detailed design considerations to the developer (Department of the Environment 1980). Together with changes in architectural fashion and a changing attitude to place on the part of large developers, this has led to the widespread use of techniques such as facadism and the use of historicist styles. Nevertheless, the significance of underlying morphological features such as plot patterns has frequently been ignored by both developers and planning authorities in the post-war trend of larger buildings and plot amalgamations. Although the trend towards comprehensive urban redevelopment has now ceased (Esher 1981), local planning authorities continue to encourage developers of both commercial and residential schemes to avoid piecemeal development in favour of comprehensive schemes involving several plots. The explicitly stated concern of the planning authority in Wellington (Somerset) for the retention of the remaining burgages, and the walls marking the boundaries of these medieval plots, is unusual in this respect (Taunton Deane Borough Council 1984: 17).

Recent work by the Italian architect Caniggia (1979, see also Samuels 1982 and this volume) is of interest due to his interpretations of constraints and morphological frames. His novel concept is the 'leading type' of building (*tipo portante*), where there is optimum relationship between the building type and the urban fabric at a given period and location, because both are constructed simultaneously. This occurs only in extensions to settlements built during periods of growth. At any given period, the leading type is thus found on the expanding fringes, while earlier buildings have been modified to incorporate features of the new leading type. Such modifications may be severely constrained by the existing morphological frame. Caniggia identifies historical leading types, and uses this information in new designs first for infilling, with a variation of contemporary leading types compatible with their surroundings; secondly for cleared areas in towns, using not copies of previous buildings but relating contemporary leading types to the first buildings of the area; and lastly in green-field sites, recognizing the usefulness of inherited forms rather than inventing new forms. This approach again requires a great knowledge of local urban development, but the existing morphological frame is used in conjunction with historical patterns and knowledge of contemporary developments to constrain new development.

Conclusions

Although the past two decades or so have seen a revolution of official and public attitudes towards conservation, it could be argued that this topic has reached the peak of Downs's issue-attention cycle. There may well be a 'decline in the intensity of public interest as the difficulties and costs of solving the problem become apparent and as new issues arise which exert more novel and powerful claims on public attention' (Downs 1972). Symptomatic of this is the low priority still accorded to conservation in the financial allocations of local and central government in Britain, despite the fact that overtly conservation-orientated actions may serve multiple roles including inner-city regeneration and building rehabilitation. This low priority frequently precludes 'active' conservation management, and management is commonly reduced to the provision of small 'pump-priming' grants and the more negative control exercised over proposed development. This control itself is becoming constrained by government guidance (Punter 1986) and the overturning of local authority planning decisions at appeal or in the courts.

Conservation has never been on firm foundations in terms either of theory or of methods. The very term may indeed be used pejoratively. 'Theory' is, in any case, almost certainly inappropriate in this context. It is itself a value-laden idea, particularly in positivistic terms, implying the ability to predict. In planning terms, theory is academic and divorced from practice, and it has been noted that 'planning theory' in general was only just beginning to emerge by the early 1970s (Goodey 1974: 111). Faulkner (1978) also shows the lack of a philosophical framework for marking decisions on what to conserve and how to do so. Oliver (1982) suggests that the manner in which conservation is currently practised is itself destroying individual place identity by promoting a form of nationwide anonymity and uniformity. The same may be said for the current spread of historicist architectural styles (see Larkham 1986: chapter 7), and indeed for the uniformity of suburban design and layout in general (Edwards 1982 *passim*).

Yet in his detailed approach to the study and mapping of urban form, Conzen has produced a method that may profitably be applied to conservation, despite the fact that the basis for delimitation of his townscape regions remains unpublished and, almost certainly, somewhat subjective and intuitive. Conzen doubts that a fully quantitative approach to these problems will be possible (Conzen 1975: 82) and indeed, despite Openshaw's (1982) suggestions, no such attempt has been made. Developments of Whitehand's postulated theory of urban form (Whitehand 1977) may be of greater use in providing the wide understanding of urban origins and development that Conzen suggests is necessary, and indeed shows in the Whitby paper (Conzen 1958).

However, Samuels (1985) notes that Conzen's analyses are time-consuming, and designers must weigh the effort expended in such a study against the practical benefit derived. He warns that these detailed studies may be ' . . . used as a ritual to be carried out in exorcism of the urban context before the designer takes a leap into the unknown to produce a proposal which bears no apparent relation to the analysis'. If used to assess the potential offered by a set of buildings, for example in terms of available space, morphological analysis may then usefully be compared to demand and demographic analyses, a procedure common in Italian practice (Comune di Venezia 1979: Samuels 1982; 1985: 13). British planning education is unfortunately deficient in such morphological concern (Samuels 1985: 13–15).

The future, therefore, will ideally see an amalgamation of Conzen's particularly detailed methods with ideas developed over some years of application abroad, especially in Italy. As Samuels (1985) suggests, changes to British planning education would be helpful. The present situation remains obscured by confused thinking, but in its presentation of a survey method and a variety of concepts for future elaboration, and in its emphasis on the absolute requirement for a wider understanding of the processes of past and present urban development, the value of Conzen's work remains evident.

References

Aldous, T., 1978. 'Defending vernacular', *Building*, 15 December 24–5.

Bearman, R., 1982. Cited in Beard, P., 'All the street's a stage . . .', *The Sunday Times*, 28 March: 14.

Boulting, N., 1976. 'The law's delays: conservationist legislation in the British Isles', in Fawcett, J. (ed.), *The future of the past*, 9–33.

Caniggia, G., 1979. *Dialettica tra Tipo e Tessuto* (unpublished paper, Académie de France, Rome).

Cantell, T. C., 1975. 'Why conserve?', *The Planner*, *61*: 6–10.

Charlton, H. B., 1951. *Portrait of a university 1851–1951*.

Cherry, G. E., 1981. 'An historical approach to urbanisation', *The Planner*, *67*: 146–7.

Civic Trust News, 1980. 'Legislating for enhancement: the Trust's greatest Act', *Civic Trust News*, 78: 4.

Clark, Lord K., 1969. *Civilisation*.

Cloke, P. J. and Park, C. C., 1985. *Rural resource management.*

Comune di Venezia, 1979. *I Piami di Coordinamento di Campo Ruga, Seco Marina, Paludo S. Antonio.*

Conzen, M. R. G., 1958. 'The growth and character of Whitby', in Daysh, G. H. J., (ed.), *A survey of Whitby and the surrounding area*, 49–89.

Conzen, M. R. G., 1962. 'The plan analysis of an English city centre', in Norborg, K. (ed.), 'Proceedings of the I. G. U. Symposium on urban geography, Lund 1960', *Lund Studies in Geography B, 24*: 383–414, reprinted in Whitehand, J. W. R., (ed.), 1981. *The urban landscape: historical development and management: papers by M. R. G. Conzen*, 25–54.

Conzen, M. R. G., 1966. 'Historical townscapes in Britain: a problem in applied geography', in House, J. W. (ed.), *Northern geographical essays in honour of G. H. J. Daysh*, 56–78.

Conzen, M. R. G., 1975. 'Geography and townscape conservation', in 'Anglo-German symposium in applied geography, Giessen Würzburg-München, 1973', *Giessener Geographische Schriften*: 95–102; reprinted in Whitehand, J. W. R. (ed.), 1981, *The urban landscape: historical development and management, papers by M. R. G. Conzen*, 75–86 (page numbers in text refer to reprint).

Conzen, M. R. G., 1988. 'Morphogenesis, morphological regions and secular human agency in the historic townscape, as exemplified by Ludlow', in Deneke, D. and Shaw, G. (eds.), *Urban historical geography: recent progress in Britain and Germany*, 258–72.

Cowan, P., 1965. 'Depreciation, obsolescence and ageing', *Architects Journal*, 141: 1395–1401.

Department of the Environment, 1980. Circular 22/80. *Development control – policy and procedures.*

Department of the Environment, 1987. Circular 8/87. *Historic buildings and conservation areas: policy and procedures.*

Dobby, A., 1978. *Conservation and planning.*

Downs, A., 1972. 'Up and down with ecology: the issue attention cycle', *Public Interest*, 28: 38–50.

Edwards, A. M., 1982. *The design of suburbia: a critical study in environmental history.*

Esher, Lord L., 1981. *A broken wave: the rebuilding of England, 1940–1980.*

Eversley, D., 1974. 'Conservation for the minority?', *Built Environment*, 3: 14–15.

Faulkner, P. A., 1978. 'Definition and evaluation of the historic heritage', 'Is preservation possible?', 'Preservation within a philosophy', Bossom Lectures, *Royal Society of Arts Journal*, *CXXVI*: 452–80.

Fennell, R. I., 1982. 'Theory into practice: the effect of planning on the urban form of Chichester', paper presented at Institute of British Geographers conference 'Urban morphology: research and practice in geography and urban design', Birmingham.

Freeman, M., 1986. 'The nature and agents of central-area change: a case study of Aylesbury and Wembley town centres, 1935–1983' (Ph.D. thesis, University of Birmingham).

Gamston, D., 1975. *The designation of conservation areas: a survey of the Yorkshire region* (Research paper 9, Institute of Advanced Architectural Studies, University of York).

Gardiner, S., 1985. 'Sainsbury's other sites', *The Observer*, 26 May.

Goodey, B., 1974. 'The sense of place in planning' in *Images of place: essays on environmental perception, communications and education* (Occasional paper 30, Centre for Urban and Regional Studies, University of Birmingham), 109–120.

Goodey, B, Duffett, A. W., Gold, J. R. and Spencer, D., 1971. *City-scene: an exploration into the image of central Birmingham as seen by area residents* (Research Memorandum 10, Centre for Urban and Regional Studies, University of Birmingham).

Healey, P., 1983. *Local plans in British land use planning.*

Heighway, C. M. (ed.), 1972. *The erosion of history: archaeology and planning in towns.*

Holzner, L., 1970. 'The role of history and tradition in the urban geography of West Germany', *Annals, Association of American Geographers*, 60: 315–39.

Larkham, P. J., 1985. *Voluntary amenity societies and conservation planning* (Working Paper 30, Department of Geography, University of Birmingham).

Larkham, P. J., 1986. 'Conservation, planning and morphology in West Midlands conservation areas, 1968–1984' (Ph.D. thesis, University of Birmingham).

Lee, T. R., 1954. 'A study of urban neighbourhood' (Ph. D. thesis, University of Cambridge).

Lewis, P. F., 1975. 'The future of the past: our clouded vision of historic preservation', *Pioneer America*, 7: 1–20.

Lloyd, D., 1979. *Broad Street: its houses and residents through eight centuries* (Ludlow Research Paper 3)

Lowenthal, D., 1985. *The past is a foreign country.*

Lozano, E. E., 1974. 'Visual needs in the urban environment', *Town Planning Review*, 45: 354–66.

Martin, G. H., 1968. 'The town as a palimpsest', in Dyos, H. J. (ed.), *The study of urban history*, 155–69.

Mynors, C., 1984. 'Conservation areas: protecting the familiar and cherished local scene', *Journal of Planning and Environment Law*, March: 144–57, April: 235–47.

Morris, C. J., 1978. 'Townscape images: studying meaning and classification' (Ph.D. thesis, University of Exeter).

Oliver, K. A., 1982. 'Places, conservation and the care of streets in Hartlepool', in Gold, J. R. and Burgess, J. (eds.). *Valued environments*, 145–60.

Openshaw, S., 1982. Review of Whitehand, J. W. R. (ed.), 1981. *The urban landscape: historical development and management: papers by* M. R. G. *Conzen, Environment and Planning A*, 14: 1416–17.

Price, C., 1981. 'The built environment – the case against conservation', *The Environmentalist*, 1: 39–41.

Porteous, J. D., 1977. *Environment and behaviour: planning and everyday urban life.*

Punter, J. V., 1986. 'The contradictions of aesthetic control under the Conservatives', *Planning Practice and Research*, 1: 8–13.

Robinson, A., 1982. 'The evaluation of conservation areas', in Grant. E. and Robinson, A. (eds.), *Landscape and industry: essays in memory of Geoffrey Gullett* (Occasional paper, Middlesex Polytechnic), 121–30.

Samuels, I., 1982. 'Towards an architectural analysis of urban form: conservation studies in Britain and Italy', paper presented at Institute of British Geographers conference 'Urban morphology: research and practice in geography and urban design', Birmingham.

Samuels, I., 1985. *Theorie des Mutations urbaines en pays developpes* (unpublished paper, Joint Centre for Urban Design, Oxford Polytechnic).

Short, J. R., Fleming, S. and Witt, S. J. G., 1986. *Housebuilding, Planning and community action: the production and negotiation of the built environment.*

Smith, D. L., 1974. *Amenity and urban planning.*

Smith, P. F., 1974a. 'Familiarity breeds contentment', *The Planner*, 60: 901–4.
Smith, P. F., 1974b. 'Human rights in architecture', *The Planner*, 60: 933–5.
Smith, P. F., 1975a. 'Facadism used to be a dirty word', *Built Environment Quarterly*, *1*: 77–80.
Smith, P. F., 1975b. 'The conservation syndrome', *Built Environment Quarterly*, *1*: 162–5.
Smith, P. F., 1977. *The Syntax of Cities*.
Solihull Metropolitan Borough Council, 1985. *Ashleigh Road Conservation Area*.
Taunton Deane Borough Council, 1984. *Wellington local plan: written statement and proposals maps*.
Taylor, S. M. and Konrad, V. A., 1980. 'Scaling dispositions toward the past', *Environment and Behaviour*, *12*: 283–307.
Toffler, A., 1970. *Future shock*.
Tuan, Y-F., 1977. *Space and place: the perspective of experience*.
Whitehand, J. W. R., 1977. 'The basis for an historico-geographical theory of urban form', *Transactions, Institute of British Geographers*, *NS 2*: 400–16.
Whitehand, J. W. R., 1981. 'Conzenian ideas: extensions and developments', in Whitehand, J. W. R. (ed.), *The urban landscape: historical development and management: papers by* M. R. G. *Conzen*, 127–52.
Whitehand, J. W. R., 1984. *Rebuilding town centres: developers, architects and styles*, (Occasional Publication 19, Department of Geography, University of Birmingham).
Whitehand, J. W. R., 1990. *Residential development under restraint: a case study in London's rural-urban fringe* (Occasional Publication, School of Geography, University of Birmingham).

17 Townscape management: ideal and reality

J. W. R. Whitehand

Preoccupied as most societies are with immediate practical problems, it is not surprising that Conzen's approach to townscape management, with its emphasis on the long-term relation between townscape and society, has been largely overlooked outside academe. Even among academic town planners who know of Conzen's work, there is scant knowledge of the basis that he has suggested for appraising proposals for change to the townscape. Essentially historico-geographical, this basis is derived to an important extent from morphogenetic ideas, especially Conzen's own ideas, about the nature of cultural landscape change. These ideas have undergone a revival of academic interest in the past decade owing in substantial part to the work of the Birmingham School. They stand apart from the perspectives of practising planners, which are heavily constrained by political pressures from both central and local government. The gulf between Conzen's perspective and the standpoints of those most directly involved in townscape change – developers and, in some circumstances, property owners – is probably larger still. This chapter is an exploration of these different perspectives by means of detailed case studies of individual developments.

Planning practice at the landscape level in Great Britain consists overwhelmingly of development control. Viewed simply, developers and property owners propose changes and local authority planning committees of elected councillors approve or disapprove. Between these two groups of decision makers are the activities of a sizeable proportion of the planning profession – local authority planning officers – advising their committees in the light of central government policies, local policies and a multitude of other considerations. The formal procedures of development control are well known, and Short *et al.* (1986) have recently uncovered many of the activities that accompany them. But the connection between these activities and the physical manifestation of change in the landscape has rarely been investigated, the work of Punter (1985) being a notable exception. Not surprisingly, therefore, a number of aspects of this connection remain poorly understood. Among the more important of these are the significance of property owners, about whom less would appear to be known than about their nineteenth-century predecessors, the extent to which and the way in which planning is influential, and the way in which townscape considerations enter into the complex and often protracted communications between interested parties.

Prime facie it would seem reasonable to suppose that the influences exerted by the various parties to development will vary both within and between urban areas. For example, a local authority seeking to attract development may well adopt a more flexible stance towards the townscape changes that developers propose than a local authority struggling to restrain development. Since attention devoted to the townscape may entail additional costs, it is likely to prove less attractive to developers where profit margins are low, as was the case during much of the 1980s in large parts of northern England and Scotland. Conversely it might be supposed that townscape considerations would be an important issue in high-class residential areas in south-east England. Here, profits for the more intensive development of existing urban areas, predominantly the gardens of large houses, have been relatively high for several decades and the upper-middle-class lobby seeking to preserve its amenities is articulate and well organized. Pressure on local planning committees to restrain further development and maintain exclusiveness is high. In such areas the parties to development would seem likely to be more concerned about the townscape. It is in this ostensibly favourable environment in south-east England that an attempt will be made to uncover the processes underlying townscape change, assessing the extent to which changes may be construed as 'planned', and comparing them with Conzenian ideals.

Conzen's ideas

Conzen's ideas about townscape management have been developed in the cores of historic towns. Bandini (1985), one of the few architects familiar with Conzen's work, believes that the successful promulgation of these ideas and the propositions that have stemmed from them will depend on their suitability for much wider application, including to the modern urban periphery. Before viewing low-density residential areas in south-east England in relation to these ideas, it is necessary to summarize Conzen's argument about townscape management.

Quintessentially, for Conzen, the past provides the key to the future. The idea of the townscape as the 'objectivation of the spirit of a society' is fundamental. The spirit of a society is objectivated in the historico-geographical character of the townscape and becomes the *genius loci*. In Conzen's view this is an important environmental experience for the individual even when it is received unconsciously. It enables individuals and groups to take root in an area. They acquire a sense of the historical dimension of human existence. This stimulates comparison, encourages less time-bound attitudes, and provides a basis for a more integrated approach to contemporary problems. The townscape becomes an educational experience, enriching the lives of those living in it now through its contact with previous generations. Townscapes with a high degree of expressiveness of past societies exert a particularly strong educative and regenerative influence (Conzen 1975: 101). The Conzenian townscape is a stage on which successive societies work out their lives, each society learning from, and working to some extent within, the framework provided by the experiments of its predecessors. Viewed in this way townscapes represent accumulated experience, historical townscapes especially so. A responsible society therefore acts as the custodian of the townscape for future generations.

Although the translation of this standpoint into a fully-fledged theory has scarcely begun, and the practical problems of its application in planning are likely to be great, Conzen has indicated the main elements to which consideration needs to be given (Conzen 1975: 98–102). It is on the historical expressiveness or historicity of the townscape that he places most emphasis. It is accordingly the nature and intensity of the historicity of the townscape that provides his main basis for devising proposals for future townscape management. This is articulated in practical terms by utilizing his division of the townscape into three basic form complexes – town plan, building forms and land use. These are regarded as to some extent a hierarchy in which building forms are contained within plots or land-use units, which are in turn set in the framework of the town plan. These three form complexes, together with site, combine at the most local level to produce the smallest, morphologically homogeneous areas that might be termed 'townscape cells'. These cells are grouped into townscape units, which in turn combine at different levels of integration to form a hierarchy of intra-urban regions. Since the three form complexes change at different speeds, their patterns frequently differ. Particularly in old towns, the delimitations of cells, units and regions are complex, although the commercial core, fringe belts and different types of residential accretion are recurrent features. The hierarchy of areal units is the geographical manifestation of the historical development of the townscape and encapsulates its historicity. It is the reference point for all proposals for townscape change. The approach, therefore, is essentially conservative. The accent is on the transformation, augmentation and conservation of what already exists.

It is not the intention here to consider the philosophical basis of this perspective or examine the technical problems of translating Conzen's accounts of the constituents of townscape regions into actual delimitations on the ground. Instead attention will be devoted to an examination of major issues in the actual development process in low-density residential areas in south-east England with a view to assessing them from Conzen's standpoint. The task is to compare ideal and reality.

Issues and study areas

Four interrelated questions will be addressed. First, how do agents who have a potential management role in the townscape become involved in specific developments and to what extent does this affect the townscape? Secondly, as a means of creating townscape change, how do the interactions between parties to development appear in the light of Conzen's philosophy? For example, does a local planning authority (LPA) have a coherent strategy and to what extent does it exercise a townscape management role, as distinct from reacting to pressures from other parties? Thirdly, given the fundamental importance of the *genius loci* to Conzen's viewpoint, to what extent do the different parties seeking change, especially owner-occupiers and developers, vary in their sense of place? Finally, how much awareness of townscape regions, a key feature of Conzen's perspective, is shown by the parties to change?

Discussion will be limited to four small study areas, ranging in size from about 0.1 ha. to about 1.5 ha., that have been the subject of proposals for substantial change since the 1950s and have been subject to the initiation of a second cycle of development clearly distinguishable from their original development. The four areas were chosen in particular for the quality of their development records. They are not a random sample in a statistical sense, but inspection of over 300 planning applications for second-cycle development in south-east England suggests that many of the key issues in these areas will be found to recur widely in those mature areas with large gardens in which pressures for more intensive development are strong. Information has been derived from the files of the main parties involved in the second-cycle development of these areas, especially the LPAs, and from correspondence and discussions with individuals who played a significant role.

In the 1950s each area consisted of predominantly large (0·1–0·5 ha.) residential plots within 400 m. of a town centre, and was thus particularly subject to pressures for more intensive development (Whitehand, 1988). Two of the areas, just to the south-west of the town centre of Epsom, some 20 km. south-west of the centre of London, were initially developed for residential purposes in Victorian times (Fig. 17.1C). The other two areas, located just to the west and east of the town centre of Amersham, some 40 km. north-west of the centre of London, mostly underwent their initial development as residential areas during the first thirty years of the twentieth century (Fig. 17.1A, B). The two Epsom areas had frontages on to minor roads whose alignments dated from the pre-railway era. They were set in a larger area that retained elements from Epsom's days as a medieval village and, later, spa town, and contained numerous, mid- to late-Victorian villas, often built of a yellowish brick which had weathered almost grey, and a scattering of pre-railway cottages faced in white weatherboard. Both the Amersham areas had frontages on to busy main roads leading out of a town centre that was entirely a creation of the period since the opening of the railway at the end of the nineteenth century. In one case, Hyrons, the surrounding mature 'Stockbroker's Tudor' landscape incorporated pre-urban hedgerows and buildings. These abutted on to a 'Metroland' of small detached and semi-detached houses (Fig. 17.1B). In the other area, Devonshire, similar houses faced small, Edwardian, detached and semi-detached dwellings, not unlike

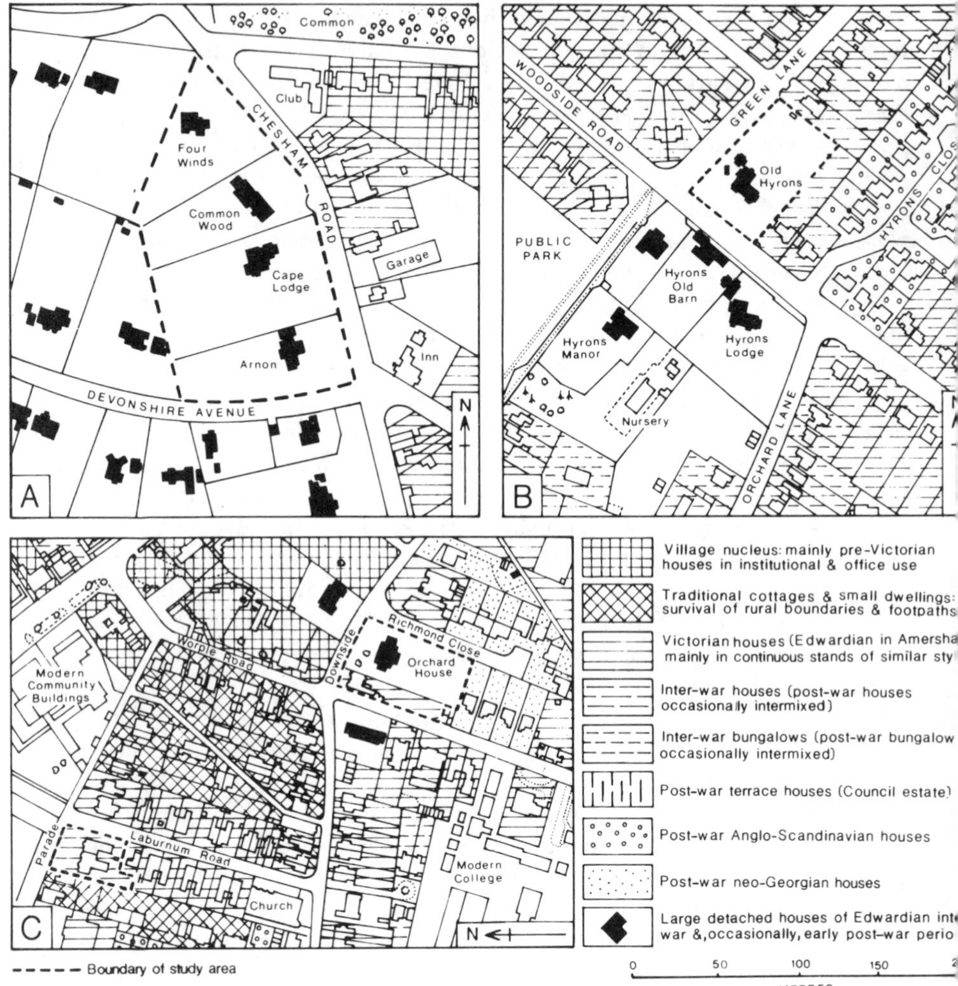

Figure 17.1 The four study areas before the main phase of second-cycle development: (A) Devonshire, Amersham *c.*1960; (B) Hyrons, Amersham *c.*1980; (C) Parade and Downside, Epsom *c.*1977. Compiled from field surveys, planning applications and Ordnance Survey plans

Figure 17.2 Devonshire and its environs in 1949. Photograph by Aerofilms Ltd

the somewhat older buildings in Epsom. All areas retained a 'rural' atmosphere, consciously and very successfully contrived in the case of the pseudo-vernacular residences of the Amersham areas. In Amersham especially, tree and hedgerow planting by initial owners had augmented existing trees to give, by the 1950s, an almost woodland landscape from the air (Fig. 17.2). There was little visually to suggest that these were townscapes requiring any more management than to be left to the ministrations of their generally high-income residents, concerned for the most part to enhance the existing character of their areas.

However, this picture belied, for a few years in the 1950s, underlying economic forces that were to lead to transformation of the townscape. The combination of a tight green belt around London, within which further housebuilding was largely precluded, and strong middle-class in-migration made attractive to developers the 'recycling' of existing residential areas for more intensive use. The low dwelling densities and large plots that had endowed the townscapes of the study areas with much of their character made them particularly susceptible to change. The scope they provided for a variety of types of more intensive use, ranging from the insertion of an additional dwelling in an existing garden at one extreme to complete redevelopment at the other, was much greater than in areas of higher density, where it is rarely practicable to achieve further density increases without acquiring numerous individually-owned sites and comprehensively redeveloping them.

The settings of the four study areas in terms of townscape regions are shown in Figure 17.1. Although a completely objective means of delineating Conzenian townscape regions has not been worked out, and may not be feasible in every respect, it is possible, using the guidance that Conzen (1966, 1975, 1988) provides, to produce a delineation consistent with Conzenian principles. Indeed, it is easier to do so in townscapes still retaining most of the features they acquired when first urbanized than in the medieval cores examined by Conzen. Whereas Conzen was dealing with townscapes that had in many parts been adapted and redeveloped several times over, the upper-middle-class residential areas of south-east England have mostly only entered a first phase of major redevelopment since the 1950s. In town plan, building form and land use, many of them until then closely resembled their original state.

The problem of managing change in low-density residential areas generally was, however, far from new in the 1950s. In areas of Victorian villas and mansions near major city centres, a wide variety of types of second-cycle development took place earlier in the century, some paying scant regard to the existing townscape, while others were Conzenian in their sympathy with the *genius loci*. Similarly, in each study area in the 1950s a variety of solutions can be recognized. Those in which the new grows out of the old, range from insertion of individual houses in existing gardens, to extensions of existing houses to form a number of dwellings. Dealing with the problem can be seen as much in Conzenian terms as the much longer-standing problems of adaptation and redevelopment in medieval cores on which Conzen has focused attention. The art in both cases is to graft sensitively the new on to the old. The actual processes by which more intensive development was brought about in the study areas will be examined in this light and obstacles to a Conzenian approach in practice will be discussed.

The initiation of change

By the 1960s, if not earlier, three of the areas to be examined – Devonshire, Hyrons and Downside – were 'ripe' for more intensive development. They had densities of less than five dwellings per ha., were adjacent to areas of much higher density, and had road frontages on two sides (Fig. 17.1). The fourth area – Parade – was more problematic. It was subsequently to be designated as part of a Conservation Area and had a much higher density – about fifteen dwellings per ha. But it too had the advantage for development of having road frontage on two sides. In the first three cases a formal proposal for more intensive development was triggered by the death of an owner-occupier, probably the most important single factor in the timing of major townscape change in low-density residential areas. At Parade it was the circumstances of a developer, rather than an owner-occupier, that were particularly important in the initiation of change. A firm of developers who had acquired much of the land in the vicinity of the town centre was seeking a site to which a church could be relocated from another potential redevelopment site. The owner-occupiers of one of two matching pairs of mid-Victorian semi-detached houses were bought out for this purpose. The project was, however, delayed and eventually abandoned owing to changes in a number of factors affecting its viability, including the putting forward of a proposal by the LPA for the construction of a ring road south of the town centre through large areas of the developer's land. The eventual proposal to redevelop the land for residential, rather than religious, purposes was thus a by-product of changes elsewhere.

At Devonshire the first planning application was submitted by the executors of a deceased owner-occupier; owner-occupiers of adjoining properties (in one case the trustees of the owner-occupier) then following suit. At Hyrons the widow of the owner-occupier submitted the first application. At Downside a prospective developer submitted an application after purchasing for his own occupation one of the two properties and in anticipation of purchasing the other.

Apart from the fact that the study areas were designated to continue in residential use, there is no evidence to suggest that the issue of their more intensive development had been considered by the LPAs, let alone the townscape form that such development might take, until they received a planning application or informal approach. The executors and the widow employed agents to prepare and submit outline planning applications on their behalf; the executors employed a local estate agent and, later, an architect from a nearby town; the widow employed a member of her family. They anticipated that obtaining outline planning permission would enable them to realize a development value that was appreciably greater than the existing use value of the properties. In the case of Downside, the initial development proposal, which was a detailed application, was submitted on behalf of the developer by a central London architect, whereas in the case of Parade, the initial application, also detailed, was prepared 'in-house' by the prospective developer.

Interactions between agents

It is important to appreciate, at least in outline, the interactions between the main parties with interests in the study areas. For it is these interactions that provided the framework within which an outcome in the townscape is to be understood.

At Devonshire an initial outline application, prepared in 1963, proposed the addition of three dwellings to one side of an existing detached house (Cape Lodge in Figure 17.3A) to provide a courtyard development. Although another application for this type of development near to Devonshire had been refused in 1961, precedents for courtyard development had been created by planning approvals on two sites closer to the town centre in 1960 and 1961

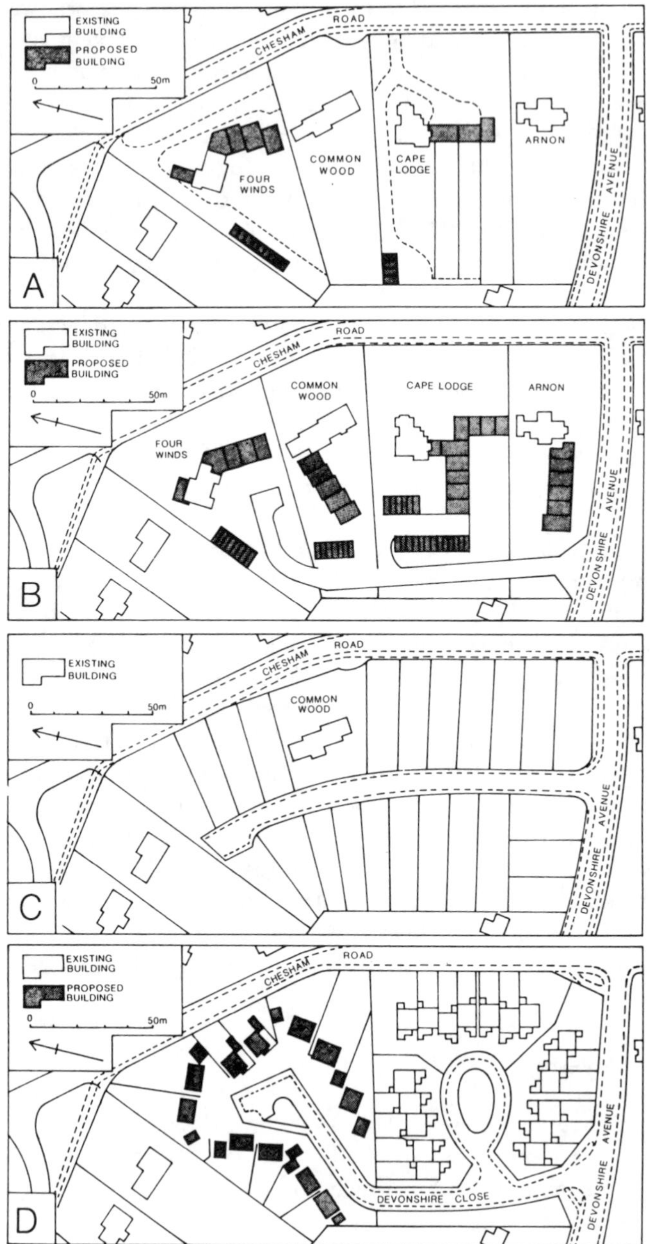

Figure 17.3 Proposed developments at Devonshire: (A) Individual courtyards at Cape Lodge, 1963 and Four Winds, 1965; (B) Co-ordinated courtyard scheme, 1966; (C) Comprehensive redevelopment, 1967; (D) Comprehensive redevelopment in stages (to south – stage 1, constructed 1968/9; to north – revised stage 2, disapproved 1970). Redrawn from planning applications

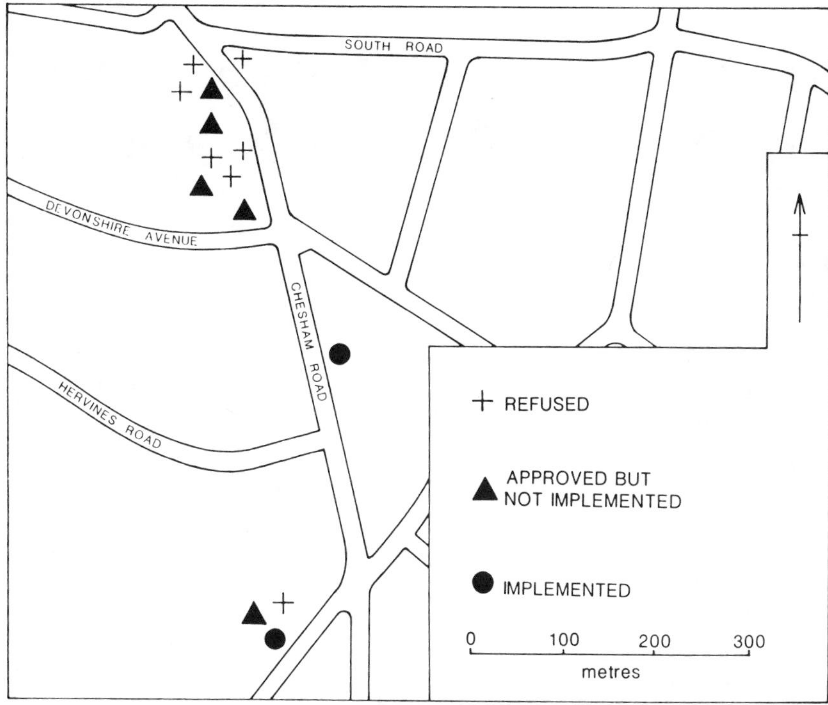

Figure 17.4 Formal proposals for courtyard developments incorporating an existing house in part of central Amersham, 1959–70. The number of proposals (fourteen) exceeds the number of planning applications (twelve) since in two cases a single application related to two separate sites

(near the southern edge of Figure 17.4). The first had been approved by the Planning Committee despite the view of their planning officers that the density was too high. The planning officers also pointed out that the site had not been programmed for further development. However, since this was true of practically all existing residential areas in the town, it hardly added weight to their argument for recommending that the application be disapproved.

The Planning Committee refused permission for the first application for a courtyard development at Devonshire on the formal grounds that it would increase traffic on the already busy main road and it was desirable that the site should either by part of a comprehensive redevelopment scheme or one dwelling only should be constructed adjoining the existing house. Since the planning files on comparable developments closer to the town centre make no mention of the desirability of comprehensive redevelopment, it is a reasonable inference that this notion reflected a belated realization of the wider implications of those earlier developments and of the development now proposed. There followed in 1965 and 1966 a flurry of seven outline applications on this site and adjacent Devonshire sites. All bar one owner engaged,

Figure 17.5 Terrace houses in an Anglo-Scandinavian style at Devonshire, approved 1968. Redrawn from a planning application

as an agent for planning application purposes, the same architect, from the nearby town of Rickmansworth, who had secured planning permission for the first two courtyard proposals. Appeals to the Minister of Housing and Local Government against the LPA's refusal of the first two of these applications were dismissed, but the Minister considered it unreasonable to delay development until all the plots of land became available that would be necessary for a comprehensive redevelopment with a single access to the main road. It became clear to the four owners that co-ordination of their proposals was likely to increase the chances of gaining permission, and eventually there were approved in quick succession, between August 1966 and March 1967, a number of schemes in which courtyards shared a single access road (see, for example, Fig. 17.3B). At this stage two developers (prospective purchasers), interested in the potentialities of the area, but not in the intricate scheme of interconnected courtyards that had evolved piecemeal, submitted applications for the comprehensive redevelopment of as much of all four sites as would be consistent with the desire of one or two owners to retain parts of their plots. Figure 17.3C shows one of the schemes put forward. The applications were refused. Ironically, in the light of the LPA's reaction to the first courtyard proposal at Devonshire, a major reason given was that a courtyard type development was considered to be most appropriate. However, after further proposals for 'estate' developments by several developers who had in turn purchased, or were prospective purchasers of, part or all of the site (for example, Fig. 17.3D), two similar estates of terrace houses in an Anglo-Scandinavian style were built in the late 1960s and early 1970s (Fig. 17.5). Thus a townscape was created that was quite out of character with both its predecessor and the surviving townscape surrounding it.

At Hyrons, where a large, neo-Tudor detached house existed (Fig. 17.6), there was a similar absence of consideration of the future of the area before informal discussions about development were initiated by the owner in 1983. The planning officer dealing with the matter apparently had virtually no previous knowledge of the site. Again, 'management' of the development consisted of a protracted and complex interaction between the owner (and the owner's agent), the LPA and central government. An initial draft outline proposal from the owner to the LPA was to demolish the existing house and

Figure 17.6 Old Hyrons in 1955. Photograph by Ronald E. Haddock

build a single block of twenty flats/maisonettes (Fig. 17.7A), retaining virtually all the surrounding tree screen. The LPA's response after some two months' delay was to recommend twelve flats in three small blocks (Fig 17.7B), but as a result of a misunderstanding between officers dealing with the matter it cited as an example of acceptable development an existing block of nearby flats upon which the owner's initial proposal had to a large extent been modelled both in density and appearance. Furthermore, the LPA communicated the view of the Highway Authority that the access way should be more centrally located on the longest frontage, rather than at one end of it as proposed by the owner, who was seeking to minimize damage to the tree screen. Although the owner's agent wrote seeking clarification, his points were ignored in the LPA's reply, which recommended the submission of a formal application. When such an application was duly lodged (Fig. 17.7A) it was rejected by the Planning Committee without discussion essentially on grounds of excessive density, inadequate car parking, and the precedent it was thought would be created. It was followed by an outline application for a lower density development, comprising four blocks, one of which was the existing house converted into two dwellings (Fig. 17.7C). But the LPA officers were in no hurry to expedite an approval. The rate of housebuilding in their area was greater than that specified by the County Planning Authority and they were only too aware that their Planning Committee was

Figure 17.7 Proposed developments at Hyrons: (A) Draft proposal by owner, August 1984, later submitted as first formal application by owner, February 1985; (B) Scheme envisaged by planning officer, October 1984; (C) Second application by owner, May 1985; (D) Second application by owner, revised, June 1985; (E) Third application by owner, August 1985; (F) Application by developer, March 1986; (G) Informal proposal by developer to modify scheme, November 1986; (H) Formal proposal by developer to modify scheme, March 1987

under great pressure from local residents to restrain further development. They therefore insisted on the submission of information on all five matters that the outline application specified as being reserved for subsequent approval. Having received this information and a revised layout (Fig. 17.7D), they eventually recommended rejection of the application, citing the same grounds for refusal as previously, but adding the further reason that an adjacent property would be overlooked. The Planning Committee having endorsed this recommendation without discussion, an appeal against the decision was lodged simultaneously with a third outline application (Fig. 17.7E), much the same as the second application although the density was somewhat lower. The third application was approved, although one of the conditions was that both vehicular accesses to the existing house should be blocked off, thereby virtually necessitating demolition of the main garage block in order for vehicular access to be gained to the existing house.

At this stage the site was sold to a developer and for a period of over a year, during the early part of which the appeal against refusal of the second application was dismissed, further interaction took place, this time most importantly between developer and LPA. The developer put forward a detailed proposal for an entirely new layout (Fig. 17.7F), including twelve essentially back-to-back houses (Fig. 17.8) – termed 'maisonettes' in the application – which was accepted with modifications. However, an attempt to get reinstated one of the vehicular accesses to the existing house proved fruitless. This was followed by an informal proposal to demolish the existing house and replace it with six back-to-back houses (Fig. 17.7G), it now being argued that it was not economic to convert the house into two dwellings. The LPA case officer was unwilling to recommend this to the Planning Committee. Finally, the substitution of two detached houses for the existing house, vandalized while standing empty for some seventeen months, was eventually approved and completed in 1987 (Fig. 17.7H). By this time the once secluded site had been divested of most of its trees and its ancient hedgerow had been devastated by the insertion of a road (to adoptable standards) about half way along its length. This was despite a barrage of protest from local residents and the stress placed on tree and hedgerow preservation by all major parties except the developer.

At Parade, there were significant differences in both interactions and townscape outcome. Having been brought to the threshold of change as part of the developer's activities elsewhere, it was, according to the developer, delays and uncertainties in these other activities that were responsible for Parade remaining unused for some three years. During this time it was included within a Conservation Area, a fact that strengthened the influence that the LPA could exercise. Eventually the developer submitted a detailed planning application to demolish the houses, which had by now been vandalized, and construct seven essentially neo-Georgian terrace houses in their place (Fig. 17.9A), arguing that it was not economic to renovate the

Figure 17.8 Neo-Tudor back-to-back houses at Hyrons, approved 1986. Reproduced from the sales brochure of A. C. Frost & Co. by permission of Martin Grant Homes Ltd

existing houses. After resistance from the LPA's case officer and considerable delay in dealing with the matter on the part of the LPA, the developer proposed to reduce the number of dwellings to five, comprising a terrace of three dwellings and a pair of semi-detached houses (Fig. 17.9B). This second application was submitted some nine months after the original one. After a further seven months of communications, few of them in writing on the part of the LPA, and much lobbying, including by various amenity bodies, there was a failure to achieve agreement. A further application was then submitted for the construction of five houses. This was recommended by the planning officers for approval but rejected by the Planning Committee on the grounds that it would constitute over-development and that the parking arrangements were unsatisfactory. An appeal against this decision was dismissed some thirteen months later, the Secretary of State supporting the view that the proposed scheme would result in 'over-development'. After a further interval of some seven months the developer received approval of a planning application to refurbish the existing houses.

As at Devonshire and Hyrons, the issuing of a planning permission was no guarantee that it would be implemented as long as more profitable alternatives remained unexplored. It would appear that little, if any, of the work of refurbishment was undertaken, and four months later an application was submitted to convert the houses into offices. This was refused for several reasons, notably the fact that the site was shown on the Development Plan to continue in

Figure 17.9 Proposed developments at Parade: (A) Application to construct seven dwellings, December 1975; (B) Application to construct five dwellings, August 1976; (C) Application to construct four dwellings, October 1979

residential use. It was followed within three months by an application to construct two pairs of semi-detached houses (Fig. 17.9C) in a style similar to those existing (Fig. 17.10). By this time the existing houses were in a very poor state of repair. Little effective pressure could be brought to bear on the developer to rectify this, and the planning officers again recommended approval, this time securing the acquiescence of the Planning Committee. The new dwellings harmonized with the mid-Victorian character of the area. Though not what had been wished initially by any of the principal parties, the resulting townscape was much more satisfactory in Conzenian terms than at Devonshire and Hyrons.

At Downside, a plumbing and heating engineer, having expanded his business into house refurbishment and proposing to expand further into small-scale development, purchased one of the two properties involved after the death of its elderly owner. He did so with the primary purpose of

Figure 17.10 Development at Parade: (A) Existing mid-Victorian dwellings; (B) Two of the four replacement dwellings, approved December 1979. Redrawn from planning applications

refurbishing the Victorian house, initially for his own occupation, but he was also aware of the possibility of acquiring the adjacent larger property, Orchard House, whose owner had also recently died, which would provide him with sufficient land to undertake a small rear-garden development. A much larger developer, who some twenty years earlier had developed as Richmond Close the site adjacent to Orchard House, had retained a narrow strip of land (a 'ransom strip') immediately west of Richmond Close (Fig. 17.11A). In this way he had secured access for himself on to Richmond Close, the obvious means of access, when Orchard House came on to the market and planning permission for the redevelopment of its site was eventually obtained. By the same token, any other developer bidding for the site would need to purchase the ransom strip from him to gain access to the site from Richmond Close.

In the event the small developer, already in possession of part of the site,

Figure 17.11 Development at Downside: (A) Existing; (B) Proposed. Redrawn from the planning application

managed to negotiate the purchase of Orchard House from the widow of the former owner on the basis of a proposed access to a rear-garden development from Worple Road, retaining both existing houses. Significant in this outcome were successful negotiations with LPA officers. They were opposed to a redevelopment for flats such as had been contemplated by the larger developer. The site was strategically placed just beyond a Conservation Area boundary, but there was a precedent for three-storey flats within 100 metres and within the Conservation Area boundary. The small developer consulted the LPA Highways Department and, through them, the County Council Highways Department. Provided the wall along the boundary with Worple Road was set back, it was felt by the LPA Officers that resistance to development on highway grounds would not be supported if there were an appeal. The success of a planning application was therefore likely to depend on other matters. On the matter of dwelling density, the LPA officers preferred no more than three dwellings, but eventually they seemed willing to accept four dwellings as a compromise. This provided the small developer with a potentially highly profitably development of appropriate scale for his first venture. Trying to obtain a higher density would have entailed a battle of attrition, almost certainly incurring the delays and uncertainties of an appeal. Furthermore, if attained it would have diminished the existing use value of the developer's refurbished house or entailed its demolition. He decided to concentrate on expediting the approval of a detailed planning application for four dwellings (Fig. 17.11B). He and his architect undertook discussions with several planning officers and others consulted by the LPA, especially about the preservation of the tree screen on the boundary of the site with Richmond Close, to ensure that objections that might arise at the meeting of the Planning Committee could be met. The viability of all existing buildings, including a Listed outbuilding to the rear of, but just outside, the site, was ensured and the pseudo-vernacular design was compatible with the styles of existing buildings.

From the planning officers' standpoint the proposal had the merit of reducing the likelihood of, if not pre-empting, further pressures for a high-density redevelopment on the site. They reported favourably to the Planning Committee, so much so that they reported the proposed density to be significantly lower than was actually the case. Receipt of the application by the LPA was notified by letter to four local residents only, all of whom had indicated that they wished to be informed in the event of an application being lodged. The objection by the one local resident who opposed the development outright was not mentioned in the written report to the Planning Committee, although the maintenance of the tree screen on one side, which had been the subject of representations by five local residents, was presented as a major issue. Within three months of it having been received, the application was approved by the Planning Committee without discussion. Construction was essentially complete, in the form approved, within a further year.

This remarkably smooth passage for a proposal on a site with considerable development potential just beyond the edge of a major Conservation Area, in contrast to the complex, protracted interactions in the other three study areas, can be attributed to a number of factors. First, unlike at Devonshire and Hyrons, the developer who was to undertake the development was able to make an integrated assessment of both the various aspects of the development and its likelihood of success well before lodging a formal planning application. He also went to great lengths to ensure that favourable evidence was presented to the Planning Committee. Secondly, the planning officers adopted an acquiescent, even flexible attitude, contrasting with that taken by the planning officers at Hyrons. Thirdly, the developer had a vested interest in the existing use value of the house that he now occupied. Furthermore, since he was embarking on his first development, he was content for it to be quite small in scale. Thus the circumstances of the developer were of major importance. If the other developer who had been in contention for the site had been successful a quite different scenario can be envisaged.

The issues reviewed

In the light of this brief and necessarily selective account of interactions underlying examples of townscape change, a number of findings that bear upon the questions raised earlier in this chapter require discussion.

First, the initiation process was largely determined by the domestic affairs of property owners at Devonshire, Hyrons and Downside. At Parade it was influenced to a considerable extent by a developer's plans for a larger area. Except perhaps at Parade, the way in which the process of change was embarked on had considerable influence upon the way in which other agents of change, such as estate agents, architects and developers, became involved. In three cases the way in which attempts were initially made to gain permission to develop sites appears to have influenced the outcome in the townscape. A lengthy train of cumulative causation was evident at Hyrons. At Devonshire, in contrast, the legacy of early attempts by owner-occupiers to gain planning permission ultimately had a negligible effect on the townscape.

Secondly, townscape change in the study areas was far from being the outcome of a coherent strategy. It was, furthermore, not at all the integrated process of the Conzenian ideal. There was no general underlying theory and seldom were views and reports on specific matters, such as highway considerations and trees, integrated in the light of the personality of the area. Among bodies and individuals officially consulted for their views on planning applications, for example the local plans section of the LPA, the town or parish council, and the highway authority, significant differences of view occurred. These views were frequently transmitted to applicants, either informally or on a formal decision notice, without integration by the officer responsible for handling the application. If to this are added the contributions of planning committees, local pressure groups and the DOE, all of which differed substantially on occasions, it is not surprising that even the most carefully considered application could prove to be only the first step in a protracted conflict between various parties that led ultimately to a townscape change utterly different from that initially envisaged. The dominant impression left by the events underlying townscape change at Devonshire, Hyrons and Parade is of a number of poorly co-ordinated activities. The LPA case officer was a collector and transmitter of views and instructions. He might, usually for his own purposes or those of colleagues, commit to paper a sketch layout, exceptionally a sketch elevation, but his creative role was minimal. Development control was an almost mechanical reaction using predominantly standardized responses. When, as was often the case, such aspects as tree screening and access were interrelated, the consequences of the independent treatment of each aspect in terms of mechanically applied rules could at worst create an absurd situation, as occurred at Hyrons, where the existing house was left without a means of vehicular access.

Thirdly, in terms of compatibility with the *genius loci*, proposals from owner-occupiers would appear to have been more sensitive to Conzenian precepts than those of developers. Out of twelve applications for new dwellings by owner-occupiers, or their representatives, spread among six different owners, all but one entailed retention of the existing house or houses.

Furthermore, as far as can be ascertained from the drawings available, all twelve applications seem to have entailed the retention of most of the existing trees and hedgerows. In contrast, of sixteen applications for new dwellings from seven developers, all but one proposed demolition of existing dwellings and substantial tree felling. The exception was the application from the developer who was refurbishing the existing house for his own occupation. The concern of developers to maximize dwelling densities and floor-space was apparent in their attempts to obtain permission for more dwellings and/or larger dwellings than had previously been obtained by owner-occupiers when outline permission had been granted. A common means proposed by owner-occupiers in Amersham to retain existing buildings was to incorporate them in a courtyard, a solution to which the LPA was inconsistent in its attitude. Among the reasons for the difference between the proposals of developers and those of owner-occupiers were the identification of owners with their property and the fact that they were primarily seeking approval for the principle of development, often for valuation purposes.

Finally, awareness of townscape regions was slight among all parties. It was strongest at Parade, where the designation of a Conservation Area served to focus attention on the townscape and virtually ensured the interest of various amenity bodies. Although in relation to the initial planning application only four out of ten local residents who wrote letters to the LPA actually objected to the demolition of the existing pair of houses, there was an awareness by the planning officers and, when an appeal was eventually lodged, by the DOE inspector, that the relation of the site to those around it, especially the matching pair of houses on the other side of Laburnum Road, was of major importance. Indeed this was one of two reasons – the other being 'over-development' – that were formally given for dismissing the appeal. Although the existing houses were eventually demolished, the replacements were to a considerable extent modelled on them, in contrast to the neo-Georgian design that had been suggested earlier by the Borough Planning Officer. In Downside, there was no explicit awareness of the fact that the area was astride a boundary between townscape regions. It is evident, however, that the planning officers and the occupier-developer were aware of the sensitivity of the site. The letters of all six residents that wrote to the LPA revealed a concern with hedgerows, but other townscape matters were not mentioned. At Devonshire, the owner-occupiers' schemes were consistent with existing townscape regions, but those of developers were not. The LPA vacillated. The DOE inspector had agreed that courtyard development, as proposed by the owner-occupiers, was architecturally satisfactory but felt that this was of lower priority than achieving a single access to the whole area. At Hyrons, again the owner-occupier's schemes were noteworthy for the consideration given to the character of the area, including the preservation of the rural hedgerow. The planning officers acknowledged the importance of the hedgerows and the existing house but were more concerned about restricting the density of dwellings. The DOE inspector gave the existing house only a glance on his site visit. His concern was about density, 'noise disturbance' (owing to the proximity of proposed dwellings to their garages) and the risk of undermining part of the tree screen to the site owing to the proximity to it of one of the proposed blocks of flats. Of the written observations on the proposed development, including letters from some twenty local residents, only two (both from owner-occupiers of neighbouring Hyrons houses) showed any awareness of the group of Hyrons houses as an entity. Of the several objectors to the demolition of the house, all stressed the character of the house itself; none viewed it as one of a distinctive group of houses. The concerns of objectors in fact changed as the perceived threats of successive planning applications changed, a concern with density being succeeded first by a concern over the loss of trees and hedgerows, and finally by a concern over demolition of the house.

Conclusion

The drawing of firm conclusions must await the extension of this investigation to cover many more cases. Work on this wider coverage is sufficiently far advanced, however, to suggest that the main findings that have emerged from the four study areas examined in this chapter are by no means aberrant within the context of low-density residential areas in south-east England. Furthermore, it is not too soon to be seeking in these findings lessons for planning practice.

In each of the study areas the motivation for change was unequivocally economic. In three cases the effect of the LPA's actions was to reduce the amount of floor space created to a level below that considered the most profitable by the developer. In the fourth case it suited the purposes of the developer to settle at an early stage for a density below what would have been most profitable. In terms of restraining development it could be argued, therefore, that the LPAs had achieved a measure of success. However, the process whereby it was achieved was highly inefficient and the outcome in the two Amersham cases was seriously damaging to the townscape. Although pressures for infill had been evident in Amersham in the 1950s, the LPA had no policy on the matter. Despite the almost invariably sensitive townscapes involved, planning applications in the study areas were approached mainly in terms of individual aspects of development, among which density and roads were foremost. There was little attempt to devise or encourage integrated solutions. In a weak position to prevent development, but with their local residents and Planning Committee clamouring for restraints on development, LPA officers resorted to delaying tactics and spurious reasons for refusing planning permission. The form of the development, particularly its architectural style, tended to be an afterthought, when battles over density and access had been concluded. In three out of four study areas the scheme ultimately implemented was inconsistent with that advocated by LPA officers at an earlier stage.

The gulf between Conzenian precept and planning practice is large. Not only was the integrated view of townscape development recommended by Conzen almost non-existent in the cases examined but, even if it had been adopted in the preparation of local plan documents, it is hard to see how it could have survived the crude interaction that characterized decision-making on individual proposals. The nature of this interaction and its consequences for the townscape need a thorough reappraisal. If an integrative role is to be played, then the place of the LPA case officer must surely be central, especially in ensuring that the total character of a development is not subordinated to technicalities. This is an important lesson for planning practice. Its application faces serious obstacles in an established context of conflict between the parties to development and its control. But the cost to the environment of its non-application is high.

Acknowledgements

The research on which this chapter is based was funded by the Leverhulme Trust. It has benefited from comments by Dr T. R. Slater, Dr P. J. Larkham, Mr N. D. Pompa, Mr P. N. Booth and Mr A. N. Jones. The author is indebted to the Planning Departments of Chiltern District Council and Epsom and Ewell Borough Council for granting access to their records and to individual officers in these departments for their observations on specific development proposals. Among the property owners and developers who kindly made information available were Mr P. V. Nesbitt of Fairbriar Homes Ltd, Mr R. Trendle of Courtney Builders Ltd, and Mr A. G. Wilson of Martin Grant Homes Ltd. The illustrations were prepared for publication by Mr K. Burkhill.

References

Bandini, M., 1985. 'Urban morphology: the British contribution', unpublished report for the French Ministry of Urbanism, Housing and Transport, commissioned by the Institute of Urbanism at the University of Paris VII, 39–40.

Conzen, M. R. G., 1966. 'Historical townscapes in Britain: a problem in applied geography', in House, J. W. (ed.), *Northern geographical essays in honour of* G. H. J. *Daysh*, 56–78.

Conzen, M. R. G., 1975. 'Geography and townscape conservation', in Uhlig, H. and Lienau, C. (eds.), *Anglo-German symposium in applied geography, Giessen-Würzburg-München, 1973*, 95–102.

Conzen, M. R. G., 1988. 'Morphogenesis, morphological regions and secular human agency in the historic townscape, as exemplified by Ludlow', in Denecke, D. and Shaw, G. (eds.), *Urban historical geography: recent progress in Britain and Germany*, 251–72.

Punter, J. V., 1985. *Office development in the borough of Reading 1954–1984: a case study of the role of aesthetic control within the planning process.* University of Reading Department of Land Management and Development, Working Papers in Land Management and Development Environmental Policy No. 6.

Short, J. R., Fleming, S. and Witt, S. J. G., 1986. *Housebuilding, planning and community action: the production and negotiation of the built environment.*

Whitehand, J. W. R., 1988. 'The changing urban landscape: the case of London's high-class residential fringe', *Geographical Journal, 154: 3*: 351–66.

18 Preservation planning in post-colonial cities

Aidan McQuillan

In a persuasive explanation of the need for preservation, M. R. G. Conzen explained that historic townscapes have an important educational and psychological function: they develop an awareness of community continuity, they give evidence of social progress, and they impart a sense of rootedness in a place.

> An urban environment of strong historicity is an important asset to any healthy and expanding form of social life at advanced levels of civilisation. It engenders a sense of continuity and diversity of human effort and achievement at different periods, and a 'tradition' in a wider rather than in a narrow sense. It enables the social mind as much as that of the individual to take root in an area through the depth of time perspective and the sense of group-supported continuity which it adds to the awareness of ones own social existence on the ground. (Conzen 1981: 84)

The educational function may also include strong impulses which can be used to reinforce national unity and political ideology.

In European cities the most painful episodes of the past are reflected in the historic townscape (whether of feudal subjugation, or of religious persecution), yet these experiences are sufficiently far in the past that their memory does not inflict pain. On the contrary, historic townscapes are in many ways comforting and reassuring of human progress. But what of new societies emerging from the recent shadows of a painful colonial past in which their cultural aspirations were often repressed, where imperial subjugation and economic exploitation stifled the national culture? If the historic townscape is the product of imperial rulers then justification for its preservation may be difficult. The townscape, reminiscent of this painful period in history, may well serve an educative function but it rarely provides the comforting psychological benefits normally associated with historic townscapes. In fact, it may arouse antithetical feelings demanding eradication of these symbols of shame and subjugation. With time, symbols may assume new significance for those who have overcome inequities from the past. The role which historic townscapes play in coming to terms with the past is complex and difficult as new nations struggle to attain a higher level of civilization.

Townscape preservation in the Third World proceeds with much greater difficulty than in the developed world for other reasons. On the one hand physical decay is rapid, especially in tropical climates, and on the other hand financial resources for preservation are often scarce. Governments are constantly faced with an avalanche of short-term crises which accompany rapid urbanization – the instant slums with high residential densities, limited employment opportunities, and inadequate sanitation and water supply. Few developing countries can afford the luxury of preserving their urban and architectural patrimony when the more pressing problems of hunger, disease, unemployment, and housing shortages seem insurmountable.

Proponents of townscape preservation face a very difficult task for they must sustain a long-term view in the face of demands to solve short-term crises. They must persuade their governments of the powerful cultural benefits to be derived from preservation, benefits which may not be realized for at least one and perhaps several generations. They must argue that to be cut off from one's past through decay of the urban patrimony is but another form of under-development. In turn, they must also demonstrate that preservation will not hinder economic development; given the pressure for space at the urban core, no-one can afford to maintain an historic centre as a museum piece. Consequently, two fundamental elements are necessary in any successful proposal for preservation: the cultural rationale must be strong and the economic feasibility must be clear. In this chapter I propose to examine two cities with a long colonial past, San Juan and Zanzibar, where the rationales for preservation were remarkably different. In both countries the preservation of national monuments was undertaken by the public sector, but the preservation of areas of vernacular housing was quite different. The economic systems within which revitalization occurred were also quite different; San Juan represents a mixed capitalist economy while Zanzibar has developed a markedly socialist economy. Puerto Rico's economy is more developed than that of Zanzibar. Both systems, however, have shown flexibility in dealing with problems such as housing which affect widespread preservation. But first let us look at the evolution of the townscapes and what they symbolize of the past.

Townscape evolution in San Juan

San Juan, Puerto Rico is a Spanish colonial city founded in 1521 when the initial Spanish settlement was moved to the islet that guarded the entrance to San Juan Bay (Coll y Cuchi 1947: 17). The site of the new settlement was a steeply-inclined slope which dropped southwards to the inner harbour and fell sharply in cliffs to the Atlantic Ocean along its northern and western edges. The cliffs along this western edge were broken be a small cove with a beach where ships could land (Fig. 18.1). It was here, according to some historians, that the nucleus of the city was established (Zeno 1959: 77).

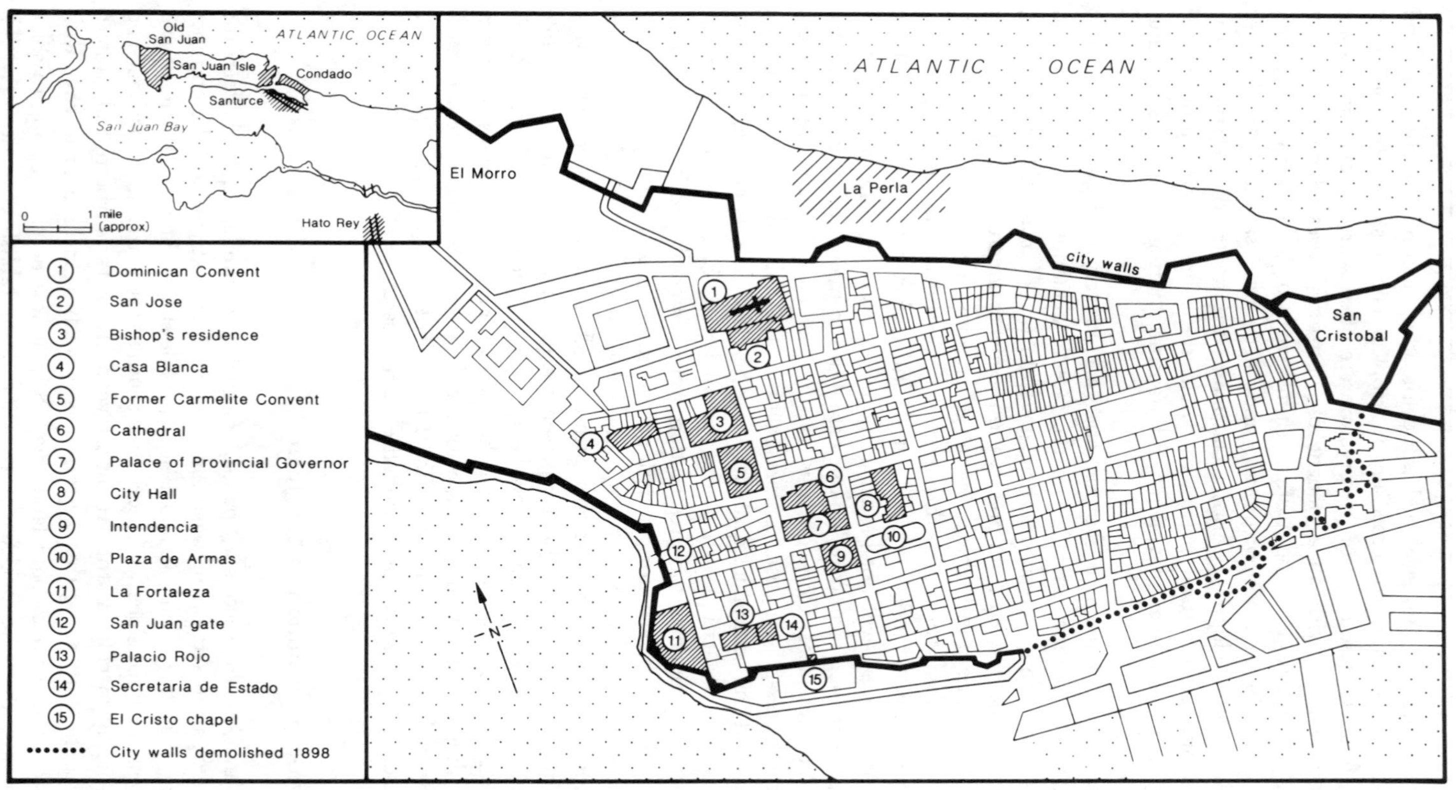

Figure 18.1 Plan and townscape dominants of Old San Juan

Travellers from Europe, on landing at the cove, would climb the short Caleta San Juan through the Plazuela de las Monjas to the Cathedral and give thanks for a safe journey (Dooley 1969: 99). Sepulveda, however, argues that the city grid was laid out around the Plaza de Armas which was located some distance from the waterfront (Sepulveda-Rivera 1986).

Although the city developed on a grid-iron plan laid out on this sloping site, the origins of the plan are in some doubt because San Juan does not conform to the typical pattern of a Spanish colonial town. The cathedral, for example, was not built on a large central plaza opening to the sea (Reps 1965: 30). The Plazuela de las Monjas was both too small and too steep to accommodate equestrian traffic and military exercises, and the Caleta San Juan was not properly aligned within the city grid, the origin of which was based on the intersections of San Cristo and Recinto Oeste with San Francisco and Fortaleza streets (Fig. 18.1). An explanation of these idiosyncrasies in the urban plan lies in the fact that the site was developed almost half a century before the Laws of the Indies were promulgated, standardizing the urban morphology of Spanish colonial towns (Caplow 1964: 26–9). The Plazuela and Caleta represent early planning adjustments to a difficult site and are important survivals of the original urban nucleus.

Few of the initial structures have survived however. The first houses were mostly wooden with thatched roofs so that none of them remain although a few substantial stone buildings have survived including the Casa Blanca, built in 1527 as a family home for the Conquistador Ponce de Leon, and the Dominican church known today as San Jose, completed in 1530, one of the oldest surviving churches in the western hemisphere. Soon thereafter the first primitive fort, La Fortaleza, was built in 1533, followed by a military stronghold at the entrance to the harbour, El Morro, in 1539. In the following year a new, more substantial cathedral was built but it was replaced in 1649 (Dooley 1969: 69–70). Walls were built around the city as a result of attacks by British (in the 1580s and 1590s) and the Dutch (in 1625). The first walls were built on the eastern and southern sides between 1630 and 1650 anchored on the new San Cristobal Fort, and later on the western and southern sides in the 1700s (United States Army 1943: 126). These early colonial structures form the townscape dominants in San Juan today (Fig. 18.1).

During the eighteenth century, peace and economic prosperity resulted in substantial growth within the city. New buildings were constructed in a simplified Baroque style and included the bishop's palace, the Palacia Rojo and Secretaria de Estado next to La Fortaleza, along with the Hospital de la Concepcion and a market place in the northern part of town. A substantial number of ordinary residential structures survive from the eighteenth century, many of them in the westernmost part of town. These single- and two-storey buildings are simple and elegant, built on elongated lots with a small garden patio at the rear. Construction continued apace during the nineteenth century when most of present-day structures were built. The neo-Classical style, then popular in Europe, was used in such landmark buildings as the Carmelite Church on the Plazuela de las Monjas, the Intendencia, or Treasury Building, on the Plaza de Armas, and the palace of the provincial government (Fig. 18.1).

By the end of the nineteenth century a compact city, enclosed by walls and dominated by the huge forts at the north-western and north-eastern end, was clearly the product for four centuries of Spanish control and development. The city was bursting at the seams. As congestion within the walled town increased, a shanty town sprang up beyond the northern walls creating the infamous slum of La Perla. To the south of the old walls the harbour was expanded by means of landfill and a dockland area with piers and warehouses was developed east of the swampy low-lying peninsula of La Puntilla. Then, in 1897, parts of the southern and eastern walls were demolished to permit easy access to the harbour and to allow the city's expansion eastwards (Capo 1929: 34).

The last years of the century were tumultuous years. in 1898 the United States attacked San Juan and 'liberated' Puerto Rico from Spanish colonial rule. For many inhabitants of the island a new master had simply taken control. United States military forces occupied the forts of El Morro and San Cristobal and set up their headquarters in the old Dominican Convent at the northern end of the town. For the next sixty years the US military occupation of these historic sites symbolized the relationship between the island and the mainland and, even when Puerto Rico gained its first measures of political self determination in the 1940s, the denial of access to these sites was a major irritant. The historic core of Old San Juan was a constant reminder of a distinctive Hispanic identity that had not been and would not be surrendered to the new political and economic masters.

Townscape evolution in Zanzibar

The city of Zanzibar, although of much more recent origin than San Juan, has an urban plan which is much more complex in terms of form and is of greater diversity in terms of the cultural origins that have contributed to the townscape.

The city of Zanzibar began as a collection of mud and thatch huts built on a triangular spit of land, a virtual island at high tide, which projected westward into the Zanzibar Channel (Fig. 18.2). Here traders had come for millenia, from the north and from the east across the Indian Ocean, sheltering their dhows on the leeward side of Shangani Point, depending on the prevailing monsoon. The Portuguese built a church in the seventeenth century, but with their expulsion the Omani Arabs appointed a governor and used the stones of the church to build a fort. When the British naval officer, Captain Smee, visited the island in 1811 he found a town that was large and populous, composed mostly of straw huts with sloping thatched

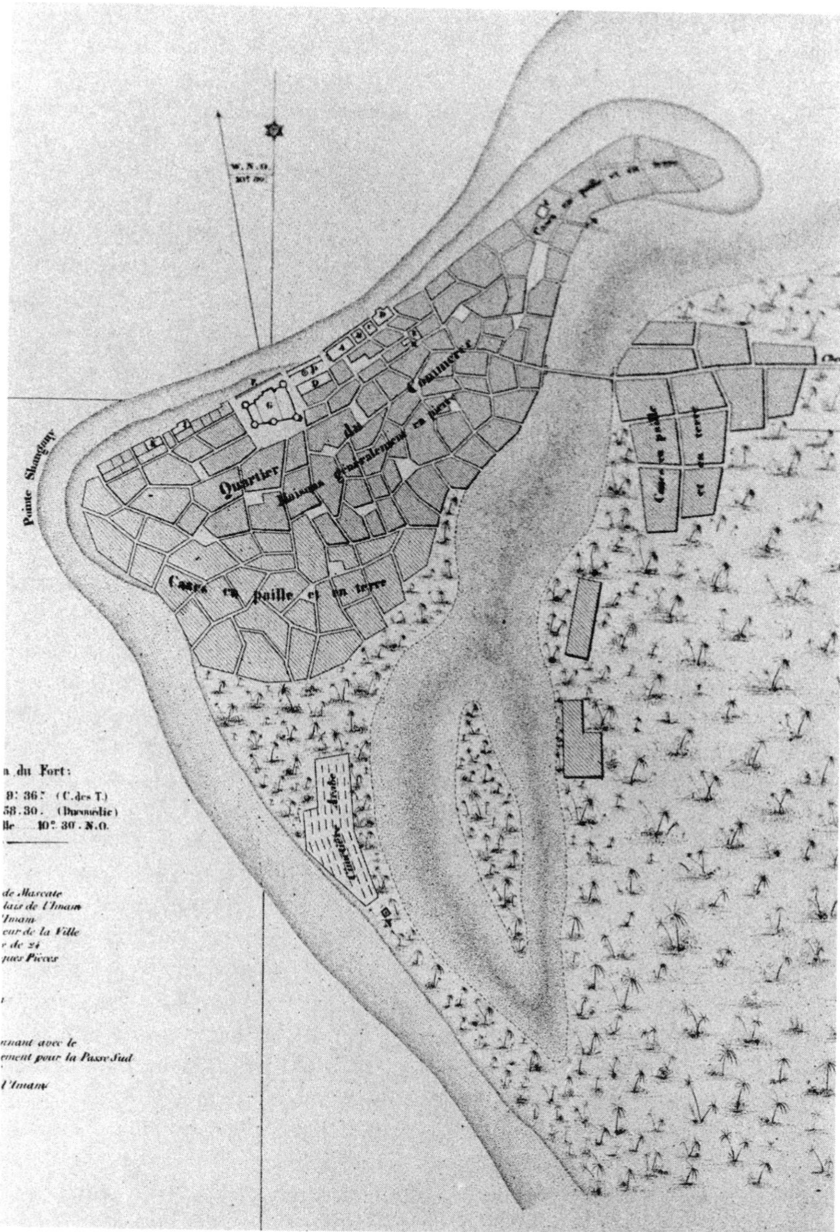

Figure 18.2 Zanzibar in 1846 (from Guillain 1857)

roofs and noted that there were also 'a good number of stone buildings in it belonging to the Arabs and merchants . . .' (Pearce 1967: 187). It was to this town that the Sultan Seyyid Said decided to move his headquarters from Oman in 1832, the better to control his possessions along the East African littoral.

The urban plan which developed consisted of an irregular labyrinth of narrow lanes and alleys. Local tradition attributes the morphology to an incremental pattern of growth and the traditional system of land distribution. Plots of irregular shape were assigned according to the size and needs of an extended family, and on these plots large Arab houses were built. The spaces between the houses became public rights-of-way and roads giving rise to the maze of narrow lanes and alleys created by the densely-packed housing. There are few maps showing Zanzibar in the early decades of the nineteenth century and none which record the development of the street system. However, one French map of 1846 shows that the town developed inland from the northern shore (Guillain 1851). The earliest rude shelters of wood and straw were replaced by stone houses as the proprietors improved their economic well-being.

The port developed along the northern shore where a series of impressive buildings were constructed. The Sultan's palace, which stood next to the Old Fort, overlooked a battery of guns which commanded the foreshore, the centre of maritime commerce. The British, French and Americans located their consulates nearby, together with the commercial houses of European and American traders. These three- and four-storey structures, built in the Arab style with flat roofs and crenellated roof-lines, dominated the seafront. At the northern end, in the Malindi district, the mud huts survived for a time continuing to house those seasonal residents, the dhow crews. The Malindi Mosque, probably the second oldest surviving building in Zanzibar, was built in this area in 1831. It is a small, plain, whitewashed structure made of coral limestone and incorporates a small courtyard for ablutions. The mosque, with its unique conical-shaped minaret, is similar only to the nineteenth-century mosque at Shela, on the island of Lamu north of Mombasa. The austere simplicity of the building, however, is typical of the majority of mosques in the old town built by the predominant Ibaadi Moslems (Aalund 1983: 132).

Beyond the port, the most impressive residential structures built in the old core of Zanzibar were large, three- and four-storey buildings, usually quadrangular in plan (LaNier and McQuillan 1985: 44–5). These houses have an introverted character; they present a blank facade to the street punctuated only by shuttered windows and the only decorative feature is the magnificently carved wooden door studded with large brass bosses. Family life revolved around the central courtyard where the womenfolk were screened from public life. Typical examples of these houses are found in the well-preserved home of Tippu Tip, an infamous slave trader of the mid-nineteenth century, and the Mambo Msiige, a large house on Shangani Point which became the residence of the British representative after 1874 (Fig. 18.3).

Figure 18.3 Plan and townscape dominants of Zanzibar

Although these large Arab houses tend to dominate the skyline of the town, many smaller, two-storey structures were also built; they combined residential and commercial functions. A series of hinged shutters could be opened across the entire front of the house to reveal a shop with a storeroom behind it. The living quarters were located at the rear of the house and on the second floor. These houses are quite common along the bazaar streets and were built by Indian craftsmen and traders who set up their shops in increasing numbers after the middle of the nineteenth century. Virtually all the buildings were made of local coral limestone, thereby giving the historic centre its name: the Old Stone Town.

The economy on which Zanzibar was developed was one of trade in gold, ivory, spices and, most important of all, slaves from the mainland (Coupland 1939). Slave caravans descended to selected points along the African coast and the slaves were carried on dhows to the market in Zanzibar. The slave market was virtually hidden at the back of the settlement along Creek Road where a tidal inlet separated the town from the mainland in the nineteenth century. Here slaves were sold to the Arab owners of plantations in Zanzibar and to slave dealers from Persia and Arabia. Britain sustained a continuous campaign to eradicate this infamous trade (Ayany 1970: 13–14), but met with resistance because so much of Zanzibar's and, indeed, the Sultan's, wealth derived from it. The major Arab structures in the town, the Sultan's palace, the Beit-el-Ajaib, the Hamamni Baths and the substantial Arab townhouses (Fig. 18.3), reflected the wealth generated not only by the trade in gold and ivory but more importantly, by the slave trade.

Indians had also been major players in the Zanzibar trade for centuries and when Seyyid Said established his home on the island he contracted major government functions to Indian merchants such as the collection of customs duties. Indians rather than Arabs were avid entrepreneurs and they were energetic in all aspects of trade including the slave trade, despite British prohibitions. With the wealth they generated they brought to Zanzibar Indian craftsmen and builders who added new variety to the townscape. Indian taste modified the austere Arab house facades with loggias and screened balconies of elaborate latticework; new arched doors, as elaborately carved as the Arab doors, bespoke the Indians' increasing wealth. Indian philanthropists also built striking new buildings such as the Khoja Ismail Caravanserai (1892), a temporary lodging place for newly-arrived Indian workers, and the elaborately carved Ithnasheri Dispensary (1899) located prominently along the main waterfront (Fig. 18.3). Indian wealth and success were now much in evidence in the townscape.

The European imprint also appeared with increased vigour in the last quarter of the nineteenth century and was concentrated in the eastern and southern parts of the town. British influence over the Sultan, though carefully veiled, was none the less powerful. When the Sultan finally agreed to close the slave market in 1873, an important Anglican abolitionist group, the Universities Mission to Central Africa, built a cathedral in a combined Gothic and Arab architectural style over the old market and symbolically placed the altar on the site of the whipping post where slaves had been auctioned. Other traces of British influence can be found along Creek Road where the creek was dredged and two new structures were built. The Baharmal Building was used as offices for senior officials and a market was built for merchandising locally-produced fish, meat, poultry, and produce at the turn of the century (Fig. 18.3). These buildings, redolent of colonial India, were designed by J. H. Sinclair, the British Resident, who had spent part of his career in India before coming to Zanzibar.

European residents now favoured this southern district in the town. After Britain declared a Protectorate over Zanzibar in 1893, a new home was built along the sea-front for the imperial representative and became known as the British Residency. Nearby, new French and German consulate buildings were opened. Here the houses were not as densely packed as elsewhere but were set back from the street and were surrounded by low-walled gardens and trees, giving the district the appearance of a garden suburb. The High Courts were located here and, farther south, a Peace Memorial was erected in 1925. The Residency, High Court, and Peace memorial were also designed by Sinclair (Fig. 18.3).

The Old Stone Town was largely an Arab town but with strong Indian and European elements among the townscape dominants. The architectural pattern reflected the population structure for the old city core; it was the exclusive preserve of the elite – the Arabs, the Indians and the Europeans. Descendants of the Swahili people, those of mixed Persian and African blood who had occupied the island for centuries, were scarcely represented among the town's residents. Instead, they, along with descendants of the African slave population from the mainland, occupied the ever-expanding Ngambo district to the east of the creek. The Ngambo was an area of poorly-built, single-storey, mud-and-thatch homes. But it continued to grow as poor rural people migrated to town in search of work. The temporary character of the Ngambo and its inadequate facilities contrasted sharply with the permanent structures of stone and the much higher standard of living in the Stone Town.

Development of preservation policies and initiatives

In Europe and North America preservation initiatives often began with a concern for national monuments and historic sites. In countries such a Britain, France, and the United States, national legislation was first introduced in the late-nineteenth and early-twentieth centuries to protect historic monuments; protection was later extended to the environs of the monuments. The rationale for preservation crystallized as preservation policy evolved over several decades and national governments were persuaded that an important national interest was served by heritage preservation. Gradually governments assumed responsibility for the sites and funds for their preservation were made available from the public sector.

In the last two decades preservation initiatives expanded beyond a concern for monuments to include entire districts of vernacular housing where individual structures are neither historically nor architecturally significant but which together form a complex that is unique. Creation of historic districts results in a much more comprehensive preservation effort than hitherto. Consequently, monuments survive as townscape dominants in their natural environment rather than as isolated structures without temporal context. But with the proliferation of historic districts the burden of funding preservation efforts has fallen on local governments and the private sector which sought to turn around a general deterioration in physical structures and decline in local economies. Economic decline was a major factor in the physical deterioration of historic areas in both Puerto Rico and Zanzibar.

Economic decline in the Stone Town began after the Revolution. When the African majority overthrew the Sultan in early 1964, the Arab and Indian population of the Old Stone Town fled. Many houses were abandoned, shops were closed, and the retail economy suffered a dramatic decline. The abandoned residential and commercial properties were confiscated by the new government and used to rehouse population from the overcrowded Ngambo area. Despite these changes the number of residents dropped from 18,179 in 1985 to 15,493 in 1978. As in the case of Old San Juan the drop in population coincided, paradoxically, with an increase in housing densities and the development of slum conditions. The new residents did not have the technical skills to maintain the solidly-built stone dwellings. Their landlord, the government, afforded scant attention to the repair of its confiscated properties and the tenants, many of them recent arrivals from the countryside, knew little about maintaining eaves troughs and down drains. The result was that rain water poured from the roofs, ran down the walls, seeped through the coral limestone into the ends of the mangrove poles which acted as joists, and eventually the ceilings and roofs collapsed and buildings folded inwards like a house of cards. Finally, after fifteen years of neglect the government became alarmed at the loss of solid housing with the accelerated rate of building collapse in the Stone Town.

Economic decline in Old San Juan began in the 1930s; several of the oldest streets in the western part of the town had become dilapidated and an infamous red light district developed during World War II associated with the increased American military presence. The middle-class flight to new suburbs in Santurce and a physical deterioration of buildings marked the changes in the old town as population densities increased. This paradoxical situation, a decline in total population accompanied by an increase in living densities among poorer people, continued in the post-war years. New retail strips developed in Santurce and beyond, and tourism moved to the new beachfront area of Condado in the 1950s. As the city expanded aggressively to the east and south in the 1960s, a new business district began to emerge in Rio Piedras. Although the physical and economic survival of Old San Juan was clearly threatened, the government had begun to take action.

Government policy evolved against this background of economic decline and physical decay. To begin, the rationale for preservation was easier and simpler in Puerto Rico than in Zanzibar. The townscape dominants of San Juan represented a proud Hispanic tradition which symbolized the Puerto

Rican heritage and affirmed a sense of nationhood, especially after the United States asserted sovereignty at the end of the nineteenth century. It was clearly in the national interest to preserve the symbols of Puerto Rico's heritage which demonstrated how deeply rooted Puerto Ricans were on the island. The old city core evinced a strong sense of community continuity over several centuries that long pre-dated American influence in the region. Here was a clear example of 'objectivation of the spirit'.

The patrimony of the Old Stone Town of Zanzibar, however, contained no symbols of the indigenous Swahili culture but represented the culture of Arabs, Indians and, to the lesser extent, Europeans. The landmark buildings in the Stone Town loudly proclaimed the wealth, power, and domination of the colonial era. But the theme of continuity had also been evident in Zanzibar after the Revolution where the newly-victorious socialist party seized the Sultan's Palace and the Beit el Ajaib as centres from which the new government would rule. Within twenty years this government demonstrated a remarkable political maturity when it decided to invest in a major effort, with some initial United Nations support, to halt the collapse of housing, revitalize the local economy and so preserve the urban patrimony of the Stone Town as a testament to the diverse origins of the population of Zanzibar, notwithstanding the recent painful memories which many of the structures evoked. The United Nations' interest sprang from a concern for the collapse of one of the most unique and most significant urban patrimonies to be found on the east coast of Africa.

The evolution of preservation planning in Puerto Rico and Zanzibar has followed a general pattern from the developed world although the evolution has been more rapid because concern for preservation is fairly recent in the Third World. Because both countries are small island communities the national governments continue to play a dominant role in the development of policies and programmes. The roles of the public and private sectors have also varied in each country because of differences in the system of government. In one respect both countries have shared a common experience; economic decline followed by physical decay in the old urban core finally jolted the national government into action.

(a) Puerto Rico

The first serious step here was taken during the late 1940s. A new wave of national pride swept the island with Munoz Marin's election as the first native Governor. His wife helped organize a group of private citizens to form the Society for the Development and Preservation of Old San Juan, which included leading intellectuals and professionals in San Juan (National Trust 1976: 32). The immediate aims of the group were to create a sense of urgency about the collapse of the old town and to develop a commitment to preservation in both the public and private sectors (Alegria 1985). First, a number of the major monuments were declared protected by law – the two forts of El Morro and San Cristobal, La Fortaleza, and the city walls – and were designated as San Juan National Historic Sites to be administered by the United States National Park Service. Soon thereafter, the group persuaded the Legislature to authorize the planning authorities to establish an historic zone for the preservation of the urban fabric. In March 1951 the historic zone was created by the Puerto Rican Planning Board, and preservation was placed in the hands of the city planning authority (National Trust 1976: 33).

In the meantime the private citizens group wanted to develop a commitment to preservation by showing the private sector how it could be done and the economic benefits which could be derived. They proposed to purchase five houses on Cristo Street, one of the oldest areas in the city which had become part of the red light district. They approached several private banks for financing but their application for funds was rejected. Eventually they obtained financing from the new Puerto Rican Industrial Development Agency; the houses were restored and then sold to the private sector. The demonstration was a success (Alegria 1985).

These initial efforts could not be sustained indefinitely by the voluntary efforts of a small group. So, in 1955, the government created the Institute de Culturo Puertorriquena which became responsible for protecting and furthering Puerto Rican culture (Alegria 1971). A most important charge to the Institute was the protection of historic sites and buildings. Thus the historic monuments in San Juan were to be preserved with public funds granted to the Institute. The Institute was also given authority over planning and construction in Old San Juan. This meant that any structural changes to buildings in the old town had to be approved by the Institute. But the Institute did not have funds to buy other residential buildings and continue the process begun on Cristo Street. It therefore had to draw the private sector into the preservation movement. The Institute promoted preservation in different ways. First, it made available the expertise of its staff in preservation techniques to private developers and renovators; secondly, it established norms for renovation and construction to which all owners carrying out changes to their properties had to adhere; and thirdly it supervised new programmes which drew the private sector more fully into the effort.

Although all property owners were bound by the strict guidelines laid down by the Institute, a new series of regulations were created for properties which would be granted tax exemptions. A property-owner who carried out a 'complete renovation' of his property according to the stringent guidelines of the Institute was eligible for a ten-year tax exemption on property taxes, and an income tax exemption from rental income. This exemption could be renewed at the end of each ten-year period if the owner maintained the property in good condition and in accordance with the guidelines of the Institute. Properties which had a 'partial renovation' – facade, vestibule, and main staircase at a minimum – were eligible for a five-year exemption from property taxes only, and the owner might apply for only one five-year extension if he continued the work with the intention of doing a 'complete renovation'. The Institute is closely involved at all stages of the programme: it must

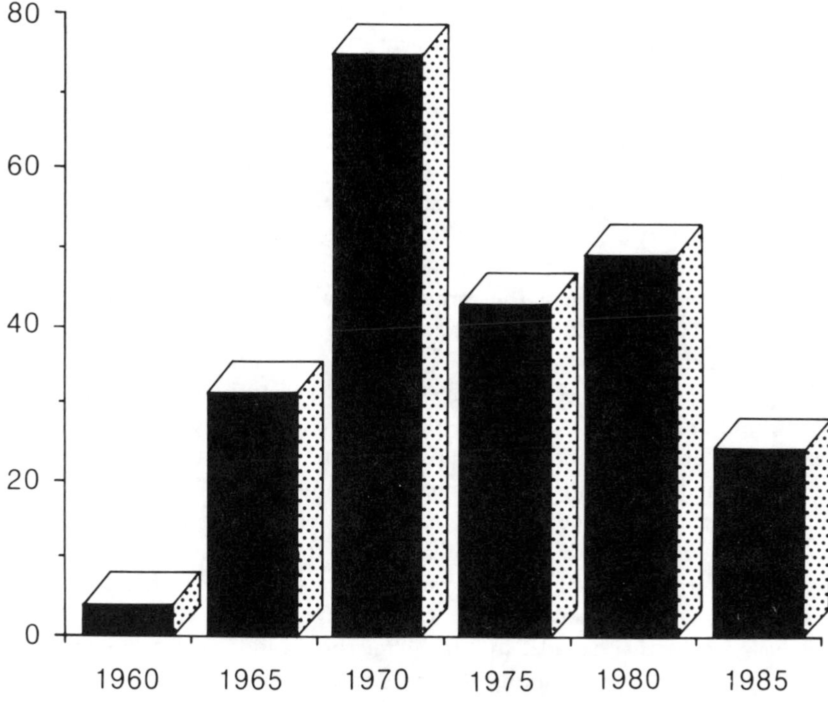

Figure 18.4 Tax-exemptions in Old San Juan, 1955–1985

approve applications, review and approve plans for renovation, and indicate whether the work has been satisfactorily completed.

A major feature of preservation in Old San Juan, therefore, has been the effort to draw the private sector into the process. The tax-exempt programme was the first initiative and was quite successful. The number of owners applying for tax exemptions got off to a slow start and the programme did not really get under way until after 1960 (Bellinger 1986: 145–56). The peak years were between 1965 and 1970 (Fig. 18.4). But since the early 1970s there has been a steady decline in the number of owners applying for the programme. Several reasons may explain this; the number of cases eligible for the programme was dropping as more and more applicants completed their restorations, and the decline in the local economy, reflecting the worldwide recession of the early seventies, may have had an impact.

A second surge in preservation rode the wave of government concern with increasing housing supply and stimulation of a depressed construction industry. The federal government's Department of Housing and Urban Development allocated funds for rehabilitation loans to be administered by the municipal government to developers who would otherwise have difficulty obtaining commercial loans because their projects were in a high-risk area. The loans were for rehabilitation only and could not be used for acquisition or refinancing existing mortgages. Rates were set at current levels in the banking industry. The municipal government supervised the project and the norms of the Institute of Puerto Rican Culture were to be adhered to in the renovations. Some fourteen projects were completed using the programme totalling $1.123 million. A supplementary programme was added which, later, set interest rates at three points below current levels at a time when interest rates were very high in a renewed effort to keep the construction industry buoyant. Only two projects were completed during the period totalling $101,000 in loans. Increase in housing and stimulation of the construction industry may have been the principal goal of these federally-funded programmes but preservation of vernacular housing in Old San Juan has been a major beneficiary.

The first signs of recovery and gentrification were apparent in Old San Juan by the mid 1960s. Middle-class professionals were doing more and more of the renovation and lower-income groups could not afford the rents of the renovated buildings. With median incomes of under $4,000 per year, a rent of $150 per month would take almost half of the family income. The municipal government therefore embarked on the ambitious programme to provide low-income housing which ran foul of rising construction costs and the project had to be sold to the private sector. Government did not get involved for another decade. In 1977, after the creation of the Puerto Rico Housing Finance Corporation, the public sector joined hands with the private sector in another effort to stimulate the construction and housing industry and create desperately needed housing for low-income groups. It did so by guaranteeing mortgages which developers could obtain for housing projects. Although the programme again extended across the island, developers were encouraged to use the funds in Old San Juan as well. Seven projects were completed under the programme in the urban core, creating 184 dwelling units for low-income families. The government supervised the allocation of housing so that only families who earned less than the median income were eligible and their rent was subsidized so that they paid no more than 25 per cent of their income.

The success of historic preservation in Old San Juan is due in some part to drawing the private sector into the process through tax exemptions, housing programmes and finance incentives. But the major portion of its success is due to the Institute of Puerto Rican Culture. As an independent body it has spearheaded the preservation movement in the old town. Some have argued in the past that its norms were too restrictive and demanding and thus represented an obstacle to rehabilitation of the fabric. In the final analysis the Institute refused to compromise the high standards which it set thirty years ago and so, in the short term, there may indeed have been some resistance to renovation by owners. But, in the long term, this uncompromising stand has yielded abundant results for, although there are still many properties to be rehabilitated, the old town no longer faces the danger of decay and destruction it once did and the quality of its renewal is high indeed.

(b) Zanzibar

The need for preservation in Zanzibar was apparent by the late 1970s when houses in the Old Stone Town began to collapse. Steps had already been taken to preserve some of the more important monuments; the Ancient Monuments Preservation Decree had been used to protect monuments around the island since 1941, but in 1979 the government gazetted six structures in the Stone Town (the Old Fort, Hamamni Baths, Malindi Minaret Mosque, the two cathedrals, and the Khoja Ismail Caravanserai). The buildings were placed under the authority of the Ministry of Sports and Culture and therefore became the concern of the public sector. But these measures applied to only a few buildings and did not address the problem of the numerous structures, representative of vernacular architecture, which were falling into disrepair or actually collapsing.

As in the case of San Juan, preservation in Zanzibar at first piggy-backed on solutions to the housing crisis. The rate of urban growth in the capital after the Revolution outpaced growth in the housing supply and, in the late 1970s, a crisis loomed. Serious decay of many older stone houses made them unsafe for habitation. The rate of collapse alarmed government officials who saw the destruction of highly-prized housing made of permanent materials as a needless waste and the government was roused to action to prevent further loss of life. Officials of the United Nations also became concerned because they saw the elimination of one of the most unique urban patrimonies in Africa south of the Sahara. Consequently, in 1982, a new plan for conservation of the Stone Town was undertaken with assistance from the United Nations and a comprehensive plan was laid out for renewal in the Stone Town (LaNier and McQuillan 1983).

The comprehensive redevelopment plan called for major policy changes, a revitalization of the local economy and the creation of an historic district with an independent authority which would become responsible for preservation and rehabilitation. Conditions of land tenure and property ownership were particularly confused after the Revolution and clarification was critical to any economic recovery. With unemployment around 25 per cent there was an evident need to create jobs through a rejuvenation of traditional handicraft industries such as wood carving, silver working, and embroidery production. Fisheries and tourism represented undeveloped potential for economic expansion. But immediate needs focused on housing issues.

Since the Revolution, the rate of tenancy had increased from less than 50 per cent to 74 per cent in 1982. With this increase came a rise in living densities as unrelated nuclear families shared facilities formerly occupied by extended families. Public spaces within the buildings were poorly maintained and few accepted responsibility for their maintenance (Fig. 18.5). Social surveys conducted in preparation of the comprehensive plan showed that most residents paid only minimal rents and these were totally inadequate to pay for the most basic costs of building maintenance. Government financial

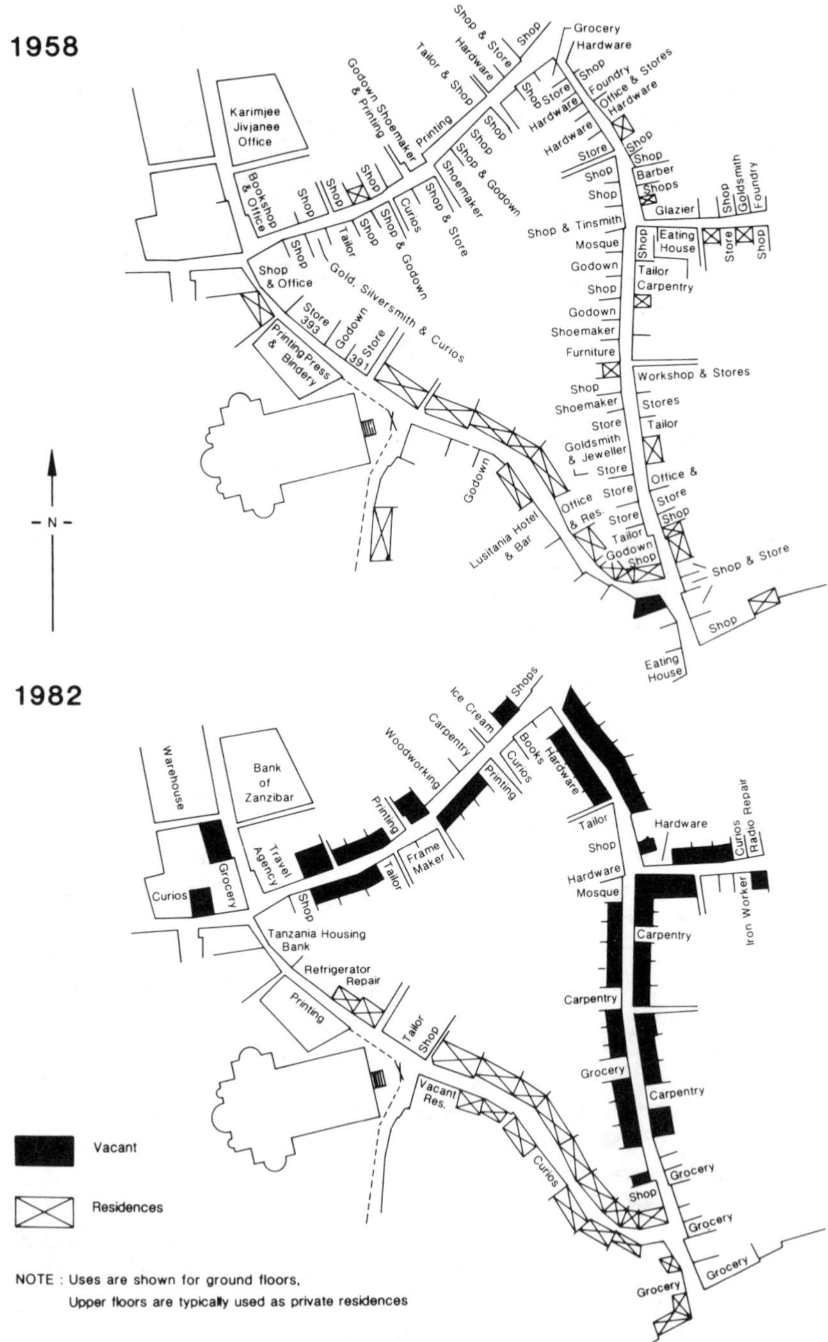

Figure 18.5 Land-use change in the centre of Zanzibar, 1958–1982

resources were so scarce that funds could only be found for emergency maintenance needs. The plan recommended that the government sell some of its buildings to the tenants and that responsibility for the programme be turned over to a new government institution.

In 1985, the government of Zanzibar established the Stone Town Conservation and Development Authority and adopted policy changes which gave the Authority the tools necessary to deal with problems in the old city core. Since its creation the Authority has acted decisively and adopted some remarkable free-enterprise innovations. The Authority's terms of reference included: development and implementation of an economic revitalization plan for the Stone Town, in particular stimulation of the small business sector; implementation of an emergency shelter assistance programme and a long-term rehabilitation programme; and promotion and co-ordination of a conservation programme for historic buildings in the Stone Town. Programmes for shelter upgrading and historic preservation would operate conjointly and were high on the agenda of the Authority.

An urban homestead programme was immediately instituted whereby residents of a government-owned building in danger of collapse could purchase it for a small sum (about 25 per cent of current market value) provided that they guaranteed to rehabilitate the property within two years of purchase according to specifications established for each house by the Authority. Participants in the programme were screened to ensure that they would have sufficient funds to carry the renovation to completion. Over one hundred buildings have already been transferred under the programme. A programme of this type addresses several of the problems of tenancy. The government is relieved of a drain on scarce financial resources in maintaining the most endangered buildings, which were also the most problematical. None of the properties sold are of individual significance architecturally or historically. All were in a very poor state of repair and within two years the downward slide in their physical condition has been reversed. The funds derived from the sale of the properties remains within the budget of the Authority and are therefore available for the repair and maintenance of other government-owned historic properties.

The problems of funding are of critical importance in the Stone Town, particularly where landmark buildings are concerned. Although six buildings were gazetted and placed under the protection of the Ministry of Sports and National Culture in 1979, none of the additional fourteen buildings recommended in the 1982 plan have been added to the list because of lack of funding for restoration in many instances. Present prospects for restoration depend on bilateral assistance – from the United Nations Development Programme, for example, which has granted $400,000 for the restoration of several landmark buildings in the Stone Town. Most recently the European Community has considered a grant of $600,000 for the restoration of several other landmark structures, including part of one of the major bazaar streets. As the local economy slowly improves adaptive re-uses are being found for the main structures which dominate the townscape so that those not supported by bilateral aid will pay their own way, continue to provide a strong sense of identity to the town, and not be a burden on the public treasury.

The historic preservation movement is still very young in Zanzibar but already, within three years, the Stone Town Conservation and Development Authority has begun to produce results. The rate of building collapse has dropped dramatically, residential upgrading and structural improvements have gone hand in hand, and as the local economy turns upward many of the vacant commercial properties of the bazaar streets are being reoccupied as wood craftsmen, silversmiths, and merchants take over abandoned shops (Fig. 18.5). On 23 March 1988, the Stone Town was officially declared a conservation area by the Government of Zanzibar. Gradually the Stone Town is being brought back from the edge of collapse.

Conclusion

The experience in both San Juan and Zanzibar in preservation planning are not directly comparable in that no two cities are alike and so the purposes and goals of preserving the urban patrimony vary from one city to another. This is particularly apparent in the symbolic nature of the townscape in the two cities: one represents a unique heritage, the other a diverse heritage; one reflects a proud tradition, the other contains reminders of colonial domination and exploitation. But in both cases the preservation of the patrimony serves an important educative need, reminding the nation of its predecessors' achievements and struggles. The townscape serves to remind each generation of the progress which has been accomplished and from which they are the direct beneficiaries. From a purely utilitarian point of view the townscape serves an important political function since it represents not only the focus of a national spirit but also the continuity of government and people. Preservation of the urban partrimony forges a strong bond of national unity notwithstanding the diverse origins of its citizens. In this regard the rationale for preservation is common to both Puerto Rico and Zanzibar.

The political and economic systems in both countries were also quite different and so the methods by which preservation of the townscape was achieved were poles apart. Certainly, in Puerto Rico and Zanzibar, government played an important direct role in preserving national monuments, but preservation of the vernacular townscape was quite another matter. Housing programmes were critical in both cases. In Puerto Rico's mixed capitalist economy the private sector would not have become involved in the work of preserving the urban heritage had it not been for continuous government programmes, marked by considerable ingenuity, which drew private sector capital into the process. In the case of Zanzibar the public sector, the major landowner, seemed incapable of halting the collapse and wastage of vernacular housing in the Old Stone Town until an imaginative programme was introduced which shifted responsibility to individual families by granting them ownership of their homes. The key to the success of the combined private and public sector participation in both Puerto Rico and Zanzibar was the creation of a local agency which was given responsibility for preservation efforts.

The Instituto de Culturo Puertorriquena and the Stone Town Conservation and Development Authority share a few features in common. Both are government bodies but they have some independence from other government agencies and pursue the goal of preservation as a specific responsibility. The Institute has a watchdog function over national culture which is not shared by the Authority; the Authority on the other hand, has a responsibility for housing and economic growth which is not shared by the Institute. Both agencies have played a key role in drawing the private sector into the preservation process and both have adopted an approach which emphasizes preservation of the entire structure and not simply the preservation of facades, which is so common in North American and British preservation. Because financial resources are much leaner in Zanzibar, adaptive re-use of buildings is given greater emphasis than in Puerto Rico, especially in the preservation of townscape dominants.

The implementation of a preservation programme has to have a clear economic viability and it needs to have clear direction. It cannot be left entirely to the bottom line of the private sector – that much is apparent. But neither can it be left entirely to government planning departments, for, whatever their good intentions, they are often swamped with conflicting pressures and demands, and planning is nothing if not the art of compromise. The experience in Puerto Rico and Zanzibar has shown that preservation succeeds when a separate agency is created with a good deal of independence. If the agency has a clear focus, understands its goals, and pursues them single-mindedly, avoiding short-term gains at the expense of long-term benefits, then of course it can work in co-operation with the private sector and with local planning officials. Therein lies the success in Puerto Rico and the hope of Zanzibar.

References

Aalund, F., 1983. 'Zanzibar Old Stone Town', *Monumentum*, 143–62.

Alegria, R., 1978. *El Instituto de Cultura Puertorriquena 1955–73* (San Juan).

Alegria, R., 1985. Personal communication, 27 February.

Ayany, S., 1970. *A History of Zanzibar: a study in constitutional development, 1934–1964* (Nairobi).

Bellinger, S., 1986. 'Historic preservation: a case study of Old San Juan, Puerto Rico' (MA thesis, University of Toronto).

Caplow, T., Stryker, S., and Wallace, S., 1964. *The urban ambience: a study of San Juan, Puerto Rico* (Totowa, NJ).

Capo, C., 1929. *The romantic capital of Porto Rico* (San Juan).
Coll y Cuchi, V., 1947. *Resena historica sobra la ciudad de San Juan de Puerto Rico* (San Juan).
Conzen, M. R. G., 1981. 'Geography and townscape preservation', in *The urban landscape: historical development and management, papers by* M. R. G. *Conzen*, ed. J. W. R. Whitehand, 75–86.
Coupland, R., 1939. *The exploitation of East Africa, 1856–90: the slave trade and the scramble* (Evanston, Ill.).
Dooley, E., 1969. *Old San Juan* (Williamsport, Penn).
Guillain, C., 1851. *Voyage a la cote orientale d'Afrique* (Paris).
Lanchester, H., 1923. *Zanzibar: a study in tropical town planning.*
LaNier, R., and McQuillan, D., 1983. *The Stone Town of Zanzibar: a strategy for integrated development* (Nairobi).
LaNier, R., and McQuillan, D., 1984. 'Urban upgrading and historic preservation', *Habitat International*, 8: 43–59.
National Trust for Historic Preservation, 1976. *A guide to delineating edges to historic districts* (Washington, D.C.)
Pearce, F., 1967 (reprint), *Zanzibar, the island metropolis of East Africa.*
Puerto Rico Urban Renewal and Housing Administration, 1963. *Old San Juan and Puerta De Tierra: a general neighbourhood renewal plan* (Rio Piedras).
Reps, J., 1965. *The making of urban America: a history of city planning in the United States* (Princeton, NJ).
United States Army Coast Artillery Command, 1943. *A history of the harbor defences of San Juan P.R. under Spain, 1509–1898* (San Juan).
Sepulveda-Rivera, A., 1986. 'San Juan de Puerto Rico: growth of a Caribbean capital city' (unpublished Ph.D. thesis, Cornell University, Ithaca, New York).
Sheriff, A., *Slaves, spices and ivory in Zanzibar* (Dar-es-Salaam).
Zeno, F., 1959 (2 vols.). *Historia de la capital de Puerto Rico* (San Juan).

19 Architectural practice and urban morphology

Ivor Samuels

Unlike their Continental counterparts, the notion of urban morphology would, even if recognized, be considered by most British architects to have little practical relevance to their work. Symptomatic of this attitude is the minority representation of the architect/planner with respect to the other contributors in this volume and the way this author, familiar only with the urban morphological work of Italian architects, was introduced for the first time by a geographer colleague, Brian Goodey, to the Conzenian oeuvre. There were many concepts which seemed to be common between the Italian and the British schools although they never cite one another, nor, indeed, do they seem to be aware of each others' existence (Choay and Merlin 1986). Although this mutual neglect can easily be attributed to a linguistic divide, it cannot be the justification for the striking neglect of Conzenian ideas by the architecture and planning professions in Britain. That the prolific output of conservation area plans which followed the Civic Amenities Act of 1967 should so completely ignore methods and concepts of urban morphological research can only be due to the gulf between normative and cognitive disciplines and their apparent inability to engage in a common discourse.

If urban morphology and building typology studies have become part of the everyday technical skills of Italian architects, then are British circumstances really so different as to render them irrelevant? If not, then how can the design professions use these notions in their work? This chapter examines these questions by critically considering first, Italian practice and its potential as a source of ideas for Britain and secondly, where urban morphology stands with respect to architectural practice.

Morphological concepts in Italian practice

Over the last twenty years architectural interest in the past as a source of inspiration has shifted in a way that is summed up by Venturi (1966). For him, the architectural paradigm is no longer the Greek temple, so admired by Le Corbusier for its pristine clarity and simplicity of form, but the Italian piazza with its indeterminate complexity and richness that results from a

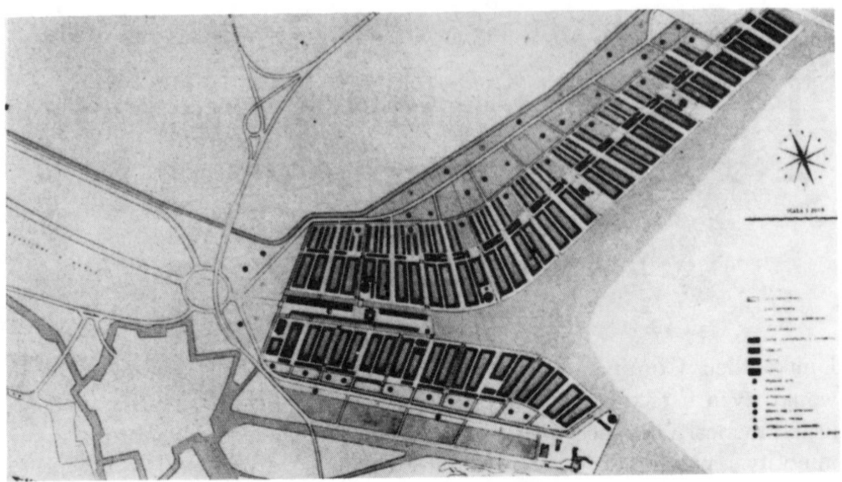

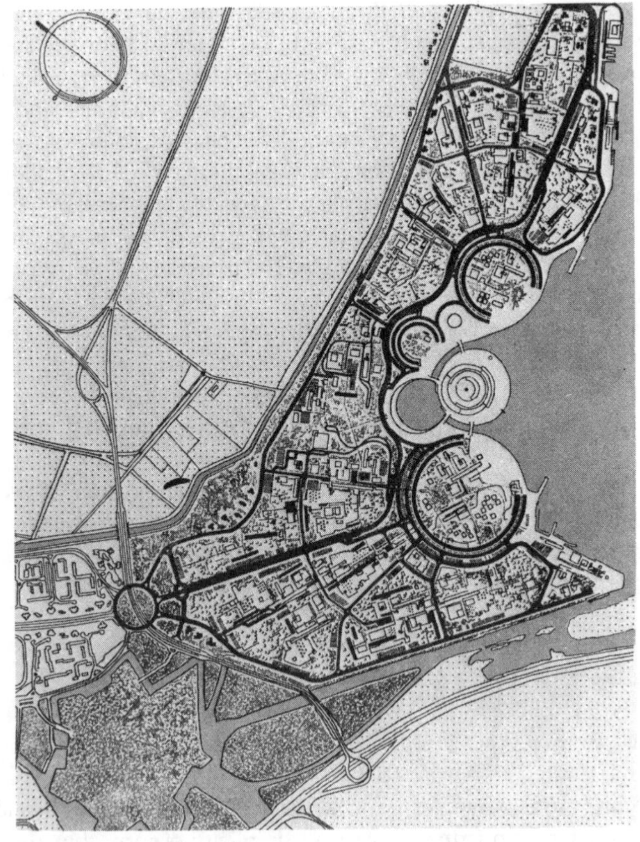

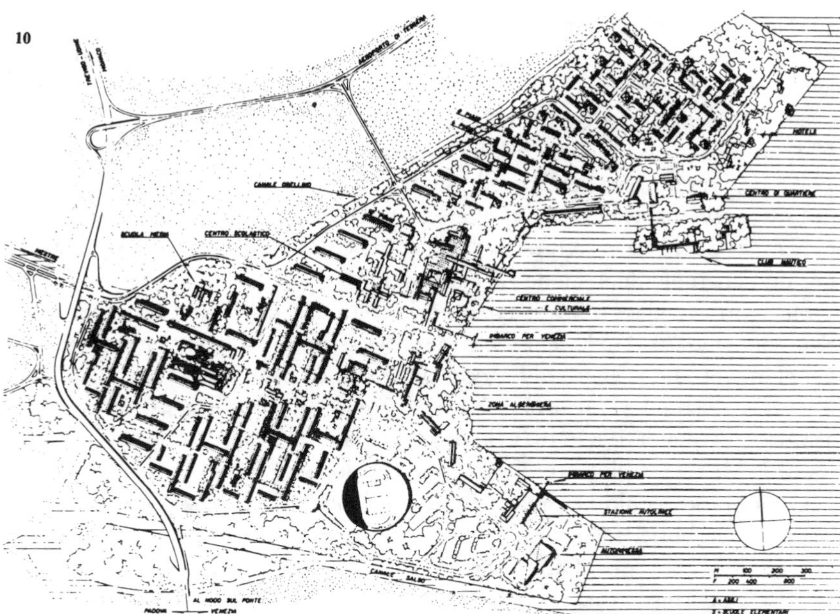

Figure 19.1 S. Guiliano Competition 1959. **a.** First prize, Muratori *et al.* **b.** Joint second prize, Quaroni, De Carlo *et al.* **c.** Joint second prize, Piccinato, Samona *et al.* Source: *Edilizia Popolare*, November–December 1983, No. 175: 39

layering over time as each (morphological?) period leaves its traces. Working in a context of such richness, and touched to a lesser extent by the Modern movement than their peers elsewhere (see below), it is understandable, perhaps, that Italian architects should have shown an earlier interest than their British colleagues in studying the urban fabric of their cities.

By common agreement (Choay and Merlin 1986), the architect Saverio Muratori (1910–1973) is the seminal figure in the development of systematic ways of investigating the evolution of the Italian city. it is therefore worth touching on his work and that of his followers, not least because they use concepts which approach those of Conzen. In 1950, Muratori was appointed to the Chair in the Istituto Universitario di Architettura of Venice where he embarked on a programme of urban analysis. He had, in his own words,

> to make the hardest effort to unburden myself of the platitudes I had acquired as a son of foolish Modern ambitions; I devoted all my experience from twenty to forty to identifying the unanswered problems of contemporary culture; from forty years on, with the study of the urban tissues of Venice and Rome, I was able to understand the laws of typology, of urban form, and of urban cycles . . . (Cataldi 1984: 8, author's translation).

Concerned to emphasize the continuity between historical knowledge and contemporary action, Muratori made his students undertake investigations of the evolution of Venice from direct observation and documentary evidence that were to be published as an 'operational history' (Muratori 1959). He sought, through these studies, to inculcate in his students a sense of their being 'technicians of the organisation of human space' (Caniggia 1979), interpreting societal needs in transforming inherited urban fabrics, just as previous epochs had altered them before. He thus rejected the prevalent idea of the architect as an artist, concerned above all with working out an individual mode of expression.

Muratori's Venetian work culminated with his prize-winning scheme for San Giuliano in 1959. This was a project for a new settlement on the mainland of the Venetian Lagoon where 'the inspiration . . . was drawn from the examples furnished by the Venetian town plans of previous centuries' (Cataldi 1984: 102). It demonstrated a certain scepticism in Italy towards Modern architecture that this scheme, with its traditional perimeter housing blocks, could be preferred to two rampant Modernist projects owing more to Corbusier's Algiers or Ville Radieuse than to Venice (Fig. 19.1).

It was his rejection of the Modern movement before the fashionable rise of Post-Modernism that led to Muratori being labelled as reactionary; in favour of retaining the status quo instead of searching for new forms. At Rome, where he moved in 1960, his lectures were boycotted and he found himself at odds with both students and other teachers whom he accused of being 'a school of puppeteers, whose only aim was to create stars from the tender shoots in their care' (Cataldi 1984: 116). Towards the end of his life Muratori seems to have moved away from a concern with the operational, as exemplified by his urban histories of Venice and Rome. His last lecture courses were on topics such as 'self consciousness and reality in the history of ecumenical civilizations' and it was left to the generation of his students and assistants to develop his ideas towards more specifically applicable conclusions.

Perhaps the most significant of these, both from the point of view of the development of techniques in general, and specific town studies, is Gianfranco Caniggia. Based in Rome from 1983, where he had a chair of architectural composition until his death in 1987, he previously taught at Genoa and Florence where he was able to develop concepts of urban form through work on these towns. He also undertook consultancy work ranging from Como, where Muratorian methods were applied to a city of Roman foundation (Caniggia 1963), to Naples where he was involved with earthquake reconstruction in the Spanish quarter.

The essentials of Caniggia's ideas have been outlined elsewhere (Samuels 1983). In summary, he is concerned with the maintenance of the continuity between each part of a city and the form of its 'first building' (Caniggia 1979). Dwellings form the 'basic type' of any 'urban tissue' (which, defined as the 'aggregation of a building type, surrounding space and access ways', corresponds to Conzen's plan unit). This 'basic type' is modified according

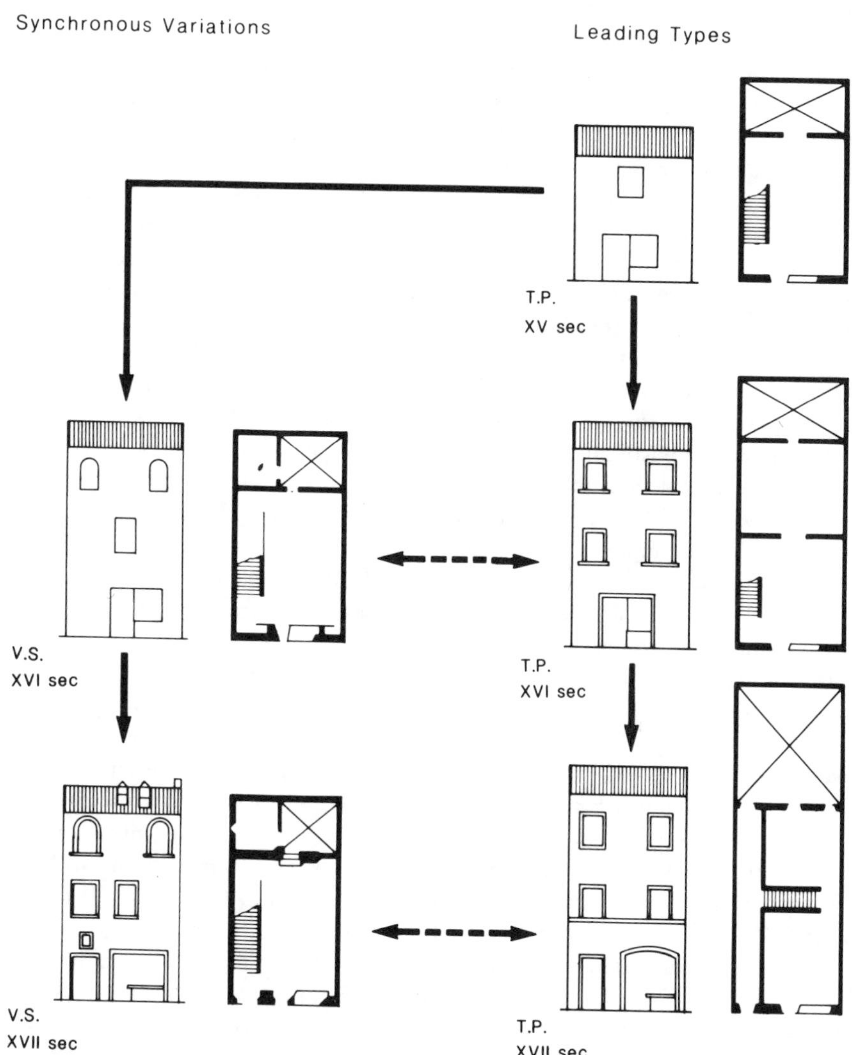

Figure 19.2 Caniggia's concept of the 'leading type'. Source: Caniggia 1979: 5

to changing social and economic conditions. In times of economic growth, buildings become more complex with the addition of rooms which are designated for more specialized activity, while during periods of economic decline the reverse is true. Thus, the medieval decline of Rome is expressed by a regression from the *domus* to a simple, single-cell dwelling.

The model according to which the mutation of the existing fabric takes place is the 'leading type' (*tipo portante*). This is represented by the form of a dwelling which is not restricted by the surrounding urban tissue – in other words it is built on a green-field site in a period of town expansion (although it could be agreed no site is without constraints). Figure 19.2 exemplifies this process whereby the simple two-storey, two-cell house with a yard is modified in the next period to accord with the 'leading type' which has three floors with two cells on each floor. In the subsequent cycle (morphological period?), increasing specialization has led to the division of the ground floor activities from the upper floor by the provision of a corridor and a separate entrance. This is an interesting idea and one only has to notice how Victorian and Edwardian houses in Britain are being converted to make large family living spaces similar to those offered by new houses, to realise that a *prima-facie* case exists for its confirmation as a model of change in the built environment.

While Caniggia has articulated these ideas most thoroughly, they do seem to be the implicit basis for most Italian practice concerned with conserving or rehabilitating historic towns. There are a number of text books setting up similar methods (Cairdini and Falini 1981: Baculo 1975), and numerous towns where analogous techniques have been used (Aymonino 1970; Salotti and Dell'Acqua 1981), besides the widely-quoted case of Bologna (Cervellati *et al.* 1977). Common to these examples is the notion that, because of continuous processes of accretion and transformation, it is most unusual to come across a structure recognizable as a first building. Only those alterations which are compatible with the original building type, or with the surrounding urban tissue, should be retained. In practice this is often a difficult intention to implement as the example of Venice, discussed below, will show and often requires decisions of a subjective and pragmatic nature which are difficult to reconcile with the theory. At the same time, it is recognized that any proposals must be compatible with housing conditions and social norms. The intention is to design a variation of a contemporary leading type that is compatible with the tissue both in formal terms and in terms of range and intensity of use. The widely-publicized work at Bologna (Cervellati *et al.* 1977), illustrated two contemporary narrow frontage dwellings (both foreign examples) which match the narrow medieval plots in the historic centre (Fig. 19.3). Since they were compatible with the urban tissue they could be used to reinstate the plot subdivisions where these had been eliminated.

Conservation in Venice

In order to explore the use of these theories in practice it is proposed to examine their application in Venice. Here the importance of maintaining the ordinary buildings of the city, as well as the recognized monuments, was acknowledged by the Italian state when it passed the Special Law (*Legge Speciale*) of 1973. This, in addition to providing for measures against pollution and high tides, proposed a framework for the conservation of areas of

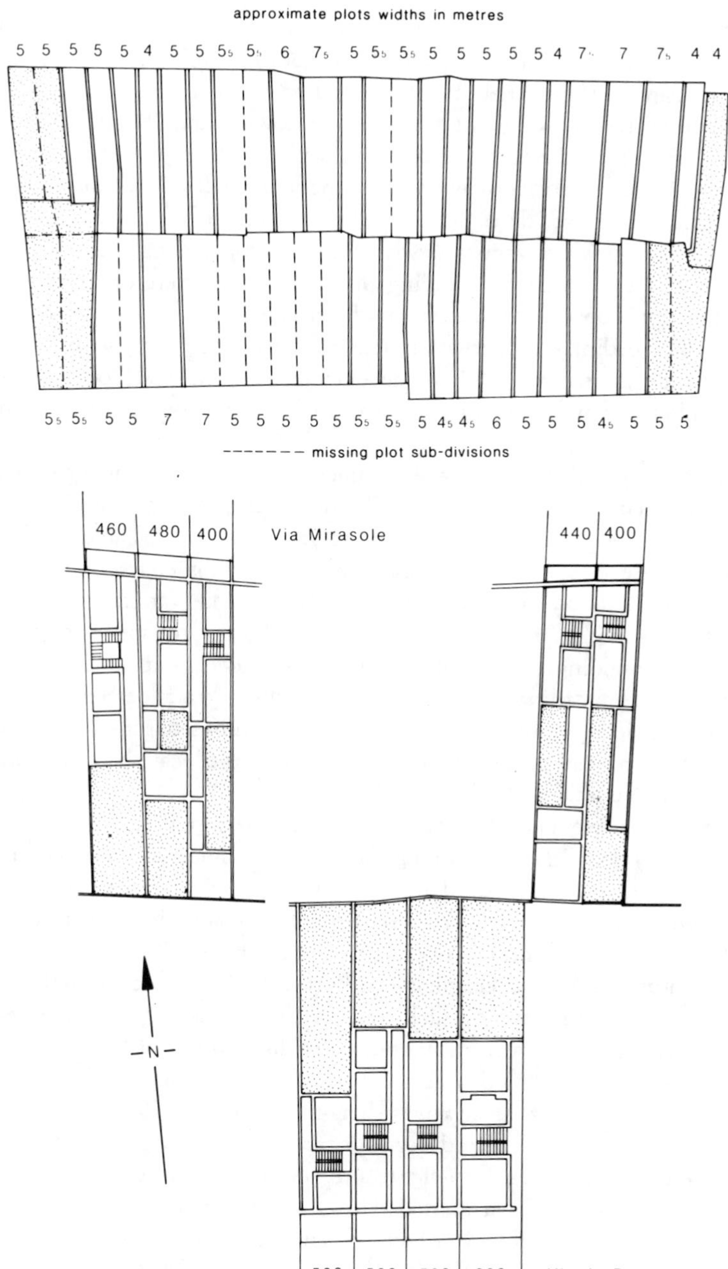

Figure 19.3 Bologna: narrow frontage house types used to reinstate plot sub-divisions. Source: Cervellati *et al.*, 1977: 142, 157

traditional housing. The *Comune* has tried to implement these procedures both to conserve the physical fabric and to retain the working population in the historic centre (the islands in the Lagoon) by offering them access to better housing without their being obliged to move to the mainland.

The Special Law lays down a rational 'top down' administrative procedure starting with *Piani Particolareggiati* (PP), within which are *Piani di Coordinamento* (PC), which in turn are implemented by *Piani di Comparto*. The instrument of the PP dates from 1942 (an example of the continuity in Italian legislation which contrasts with the numerous changes of the government), and was devised as a zoning plan for town extensions rather than for detailed proposals for densely built up areas. The PC was therefore devised to co-ordinate conservation action over a given area, with the *Piano di Comparto* adopted to facilitate development at the scale of a block or single building complex to solve problems of different ownerships (Comune di Venezia 1979: 27).

There are equivalent financial instruments provided by the Special Law which allocated funds according to whether a project is entirely public, or private (when 40 per cent of the cost of work is available in loans). Although these measures are beyond the scope of this chapter they are, of course, central to any operation involving the conservation of old urban areas. For example, in Venice it has proved easy to spend money on monumental buildings, the great palaces and churches, but more difficult to subsidize work on ordinary houses. Of 10·6 million lira allocated in the first five-year plan for private housing using the procedures outlined above, only 1·8 million lira were spent and the balance was reallocated to monuments (Comune di Venezia 1983: Tabella B1).

The first PP (Arsenale – Castello Est) was adopted in 1972 and within this the PC of Campo Ruga, a working-class area of under 500 inhabitants (29 per cent living in sub-standard housing) was approved in 1980 (Fig. 19.4). All the buildings in the PC area were broadly classified into pre-nineteenth century, nineteenth century, restructured pre-nineteenth century or nineteenth century, and non classifiable. Effort was then concentrated on the pre-nineteenth century types which were carefully classified according to five models depending on structural module, the distribution of habitable spaces and vertical and horizontal access (Comune di Venezia: 74) (Fig. 19.5).

A characteristic of Italian towns is their excellent historical documentation – in Bologna conventual land registers provided plans and elevations of buildings from the sixteenth to eighteenth centuries. Venice is no exception, and work at Campo Ruga started with the de Barbaro prospect of 1500 which shows a morphology which is confirmed by nineteenth-century Napoleonic and Austrian cadastral plans (Fig. 19.6). The detailed analysis confirmed the characteristic elements of each type and led to proposals which ranged from the conservation of walls, openings and staircases, to the demolition of extensions and extensive rebuilding. Examples of the former are retained staircases, while demolitions included internal partitions so as

Figure 19.4 Location of the first *Piani di Coordinamento* (P.C.). Source: Comune di Venezia, 1979:60

Classification of Building Units													
Area number	Building unit number	Type	Schematic plan	Frontage		Depth		Staircase	Schematic elevation	Number of floors		* End of row Variations ■ at front of plot
				No. of spaces	metres	No. of spaces	metres	a) single flight b) helical 'Leonardesque' c) separate space d) external		1808	1978	
16	18	B		2	7.2	1	5.0		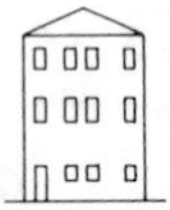	2	3	
19	19	A₁		1	6.7	1	5.5			3	4	
		A₁		1	6.2	1	5.5				4	
18	20	B	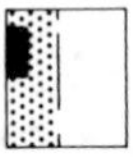	2	6.0	1	5.0		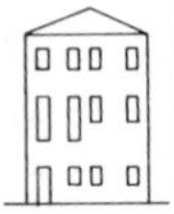		4	■
17	21	B	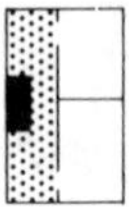	2	6.4	2	11.0	a	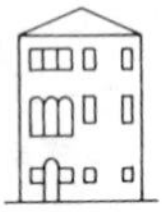		3	

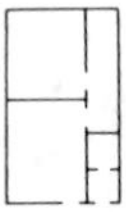

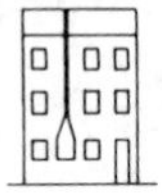

Figure 19.5 Campo Ruga: typological classification of buildings

to restore the central space into which all the other rooms opened, a characteristic of many Venetian dwelling types. Plans and elevations showing constraints of this sort were proposed for all the buildings in the area covered by the PC and these represented the supply of space available to accommodate the different uses in the area. Parallel studies were carried out into the economic and demographic characteristics of the population in Campo Ruga and their living conditions so that a forecast could be made of their space needs in terms of the number of dwellings of different sizes required. The project for Campo Ruga was then derived from an adjustment of this demand to match the supply dictated by the studies of the physical fabric. Within the area covered by the Campo Ruga PC a number of *comparti* were identified according to their degree of homogeneity with respect to use, ownership or building type. Those *comparti* where there was a high proportion of substandard housing for rent were selected for public intervention.

Comparto No. 9 was one of the first projects to be implemented in 1984–6. It consists of seven terrace houses running perpendicular to the Canale S. Pietro. This sixteenth-century block is a bourgeois version of the Venetian palace with separate dwellings on three floors, each with its own front door and staircase. The entrances were on opposite sides of the block to

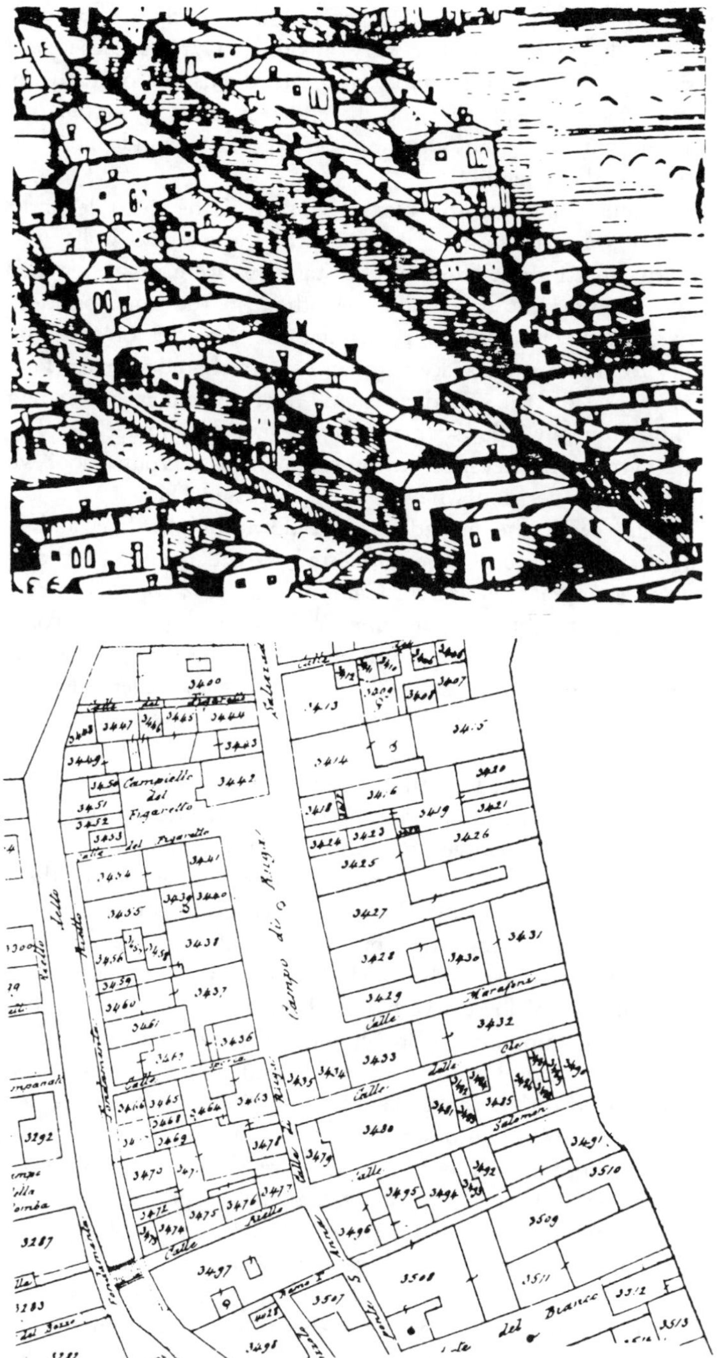

Figure 19.6 Campo Ruga: De Barbaro (1500) and Austrian cadastral plans (1842). Source: Comune di Venezia 1979: 53

give maximum privacy, resulting in an unusual building form with two public sides. The architects were very anxious to preserve the particular characteristics of this unusual type, and the discussion over the project between the time of PC of 1979 and the contract drawings of 1984 offer an interesting insight into the adoption of typological and morphological analysis as a working method.

The constraints plan for the block, between Calle del Ole and Calle Salomon, shows a restriction to alterations of the external walls and most of the internal partitions. Three of the staircases were to be retained and there was a requirement to rebuild the others in the same position (Fig. 19.7). Thus, in the interests of preserving the integrity of the type, the opportunity to obtain extra space through using a shared staircase had been given up. Most of the windows and door openings were retained, particularly the *bifore* windows which give the first floor its feeling of a *piano nobile*. The narrow end-elevation to the canal shows a ground-floor window to be retained – a decision which will be discussed below.

In accordance with the procedures laid down by the Special Law the proposals for Campo Ruga were submitted to the regional authority for comment and approval. The PC for Campo Ruga was approved in February 1979 by the Comune, but only in June 1980 by the region. The comments of the region's technical officers must be seen in the light of the different political complexions of the two authorities, but they nevertheless present an interesting perspective on the method of work (Regione del Veneto 1980).

The first criticism related to the neglect of visual linkages between the individual buildings which are the basis of both the analysis and the proposals. Relationships between buildings are only noted where there is an identifiable historical reason deriving from the characteristics of the single buildings. The region considered that it was necessary to take into account the relationship between the single building and its surrounding structures by some sort of townscape analysis, while at the same time acknowledging that it was difficult to do this with any degree of objectivity or precision. To a practitioner coming from a British context, the complete neglect of any analysis of the appearance of the area in the studies cited comes as a shock, given the importance that the Cullenesque tradition of townscape analysis has for the practice of urban design in Britain (Cullen 1961). This is all the more surprising since Cullen and his school drew a great deal of inspiration from the richness and variety of the Italian townscape.

The work was further criticized for the reduced number of types used in the analysis and for not taking into account the value of the historic layering which exists in Campo Ruga. Seen from Britain the analysis is very thorough, but it can be seen that problems might arise from the implicit attempt to return to a supposed period of initial building. The difficulty of doing this is illustrated by the attitude towards the staircases. Those staircases which are sometimes called 'Leonardesque' were introduced around

Figure 19.7 Campo Ruga: Comparto No. 9. Source: Comune di Venezia 1979: 183

Figure 19.8 Campo Ruga: canal elevation of Comparto No. 9. Source: author

1540; yet if it is likely that the origins of the buildings are earlier, why should there be such concern to maintain the form of a staircase which could be interpreted as a later addition? Clearly, the method is not as sternly objective as its practitioners would like to believe and, inevitably, value judgements intrude into decisions of retention or deletion.

The region noted that the nature of the *Piano di Coordinamento* as a 'constraints plan' was too negative since it did not make specific proposals for the planning of the dwelling but delegated this to a lower level in the planning process – the *Piano di Comparto*. The point was made that all the survey work had to be done again because, in spite of its apparent depth, the *Piano di Coordinamento* was not sufficiently detailed for contract drawing. It was only in undertaking this more detailed study that factors emerged which conflicted with decisions already taken.

An example of this, and also of the difficulty of being objective, is the discussions over the elevation of Comparto 9 facing the canal. Here there was considerable disagreement between Comune, region and the Superintendent of Monuments because of the ground floor windows. Evidence can be seen from the photograph (Fig. 19.8) of traces of two arched entrances – yet the plan proposed to retain one, more recent, rectangular opening. The outcome was an agreement to reinstate two openings.

The example of Campo Ruga does not show any major modification to the urban tissue and it would therefore be appropriate to consider another example from Venice to illustrate attempts at a more radical modification

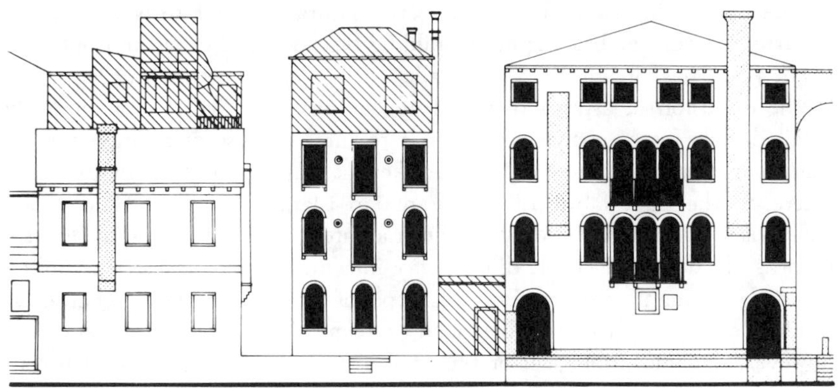

Figure 19.9 Calle Alberagno, showing single storey and rooftop extensions to be removed. Sources: author and Comune di Venezia 1979: 89

of streets and blocks. Calle Alberagno and the Campiello of the same name lie within the PC of Calle Caliari which, in turn, is part of the PP Cannaregio Nord. In this plan it was proposed to demolish a single-storey extension to a four-storey block in order to open up a public route which had been identified on nineteenth-century cadastral plans. At the same time the top-storey addition to two of the surrounding buildings were to be removed in order to reinstate them as identifiable types (Fig. 19.9). These alterations seem drastic and naturally were vigorously opposed by the property owners concerned. It has to be remembered, however, that since this is a Comparto for private intervention, the Comune has no power to enforce the proposals and only if one of the owners makes an application for alterations or major repairs can any changes be enforced.

Understanding Italian practice

The following observations attempt to link the cases described above to more general aspects of architecture and planning practice in Italy.

The first noteworthy aspect is the close relationship between morphological analysis and building typological studies, with most of the work described in Italy being of the latter category. For most Italian practitioners, these studies are part of one continuum and it is not surprising to find architects most involved in the building aspects, especially as this is where they are likely to have the greatest opportunity to effect change. It has also to be recognized that there is no equivalent of the town planning profession in Italy so that there is no division of responsibility for the urban fabric between architects and planners as in the Anglo-Saxon countries. Planning work is performed by architects, and planning forms part of every architect's training so that it is perfectly natural for architects to cover a spectrum of work embracing both building typology and urban morphology.

The point has already been made about the deep concern with plan forms to the exclusion of aspects of visual appearance. This work at a relatively detailed scale for extensive urban areas requires the use of a large team of trained manpower – the work undertaken at Burano in 1984 for example, where all the built fabric of this Venetian island was surveyed to 1/500 scale, used a team of twenty newly-graduated architects working for six months in the field. It is difficult to imagine a British district council investing so many resources in this type of work or, indeed, whether it would be possible to assemble such a team. It has to be remembered however, that morphological or typological analysis forms part of all Italian undergraduate architectural courses and, furthermore, that Italy, with around the same population and about the same level of material wealth, has around sixty thousand architecture students compared with seven thousand in Britain. There is thus a vast pool of labour anxious for any form of contact with the world of practice (the majority hardly ever work as architects) and willing to accept low rates of pay.

If the availability of trained labour is one aspect of the favourable context then a two-hundred-year-old system of publicly available cadastral maps is of inestimable value – as any British practitioner who has tried to discover the ownership of a site will testify. The importance of these pragmatic reasons must be examined in considering the transferability of practices and concepts from one context to another. Equally, the role of pragmatism within the apparent theoretical rigour of Italian practice should not be underestimated. At Campo Ruga the proposals for reinstating chimneys were dropped at the contract stage because they were too expensive. The rational but cumbersome top down system involved the checking and, if necessary, the modification of proposals with the increased availability of data at each level of plan.

Venice has now begun to question this approach. If the apparent detail of the PC can so easily be faulted (as in the case of the elevations described above), is it worth carrying out such labour-intensive work only to repeat it at the next level down? Currently, the city has embarked on more detailed surveys covering the whole of the historic centre with the intention of enabling plans to be produced with more confidence for the PC and so eliminate further survey work at the level of Comparto.

If the continuing professional responsibility for town planning directs Italian architects towards aspects of urban form, there is also a parallel cultural attitude towards the inherited urban fabric which, it is suggested, distinguishes the Italian profession from its British counterpart. In Italy the need for continuity in historic towns has been much more accepted. There is no conservation area legislation such as the British Civic Amenities Act or the French Loi Malraux which set aside defined zones of a town to be specially treated because of their visual, historical or architectural qualities. In Italy the historic fabric, probably because there is so much of it, is part of the normal field of operations and not regarded as something special.

It can be suggested, furthermore, that the Modern movement in urban design and architecture was absorbed and practised to much less a degree in Italy. We have seen how Muratori's S. Giuliano project won a competition and there were a number of contemporary buildings which rejected the canons of functionalism and the machine aesthetic. Among the most significant of these was the Torre Velasca built in 1952 where the architect Ernesto Rogers, in taking clues from the medieval skyline of the city of Milan for a skyscraper office block, provoked accusations from critics like Rayner Banham of having betrayed the Modern movement. It is arguable that there was in Italy a continuous interest and involvement in the form of the traditional city in contradiction to the Modern movement for which the traditional city held no lessons for designing projects for the future. For CIAM-style Modernists only small areas were to be preserved and, since we could not learn anything from them, there was no need to bother studying them – especially with the care that any typological or morphological analysis requires.

It may be that another reason for the relative lack of penetration of CIAM ideas in Italy was the weakness of the Italian planning system. There are few equivalents of the great comprehensive redevelopments of Britain and France made possible by powers to assemble land and intervene on a large scale. These schemes, the Roehamptons or the *Grandes Ensembles*, were the product of CIAM-indoctrinated architects. The same architects in Italy had much less opportunity and the large developments on the periphery of

Italian cities never had the same cultural importance, in that they were never held up to the same extent as models of the future.

The weak planning system is perhaps, paradoxically, the reason for so much of the old Italian city surviving. Unlike Britain there was neither the power nor the cultural concern to restrict the growth of urban areas by such devices as the Green Belt. In this way, most development pressure was accommodated on the edges of towns and there was neither the need nor, given the weak planning system, the possibility of achieving comprehensive redevelopment. In this way, too, architects in Italy are confronted with a relatively larger stock of historic urban fabric without the possibility of clearing it. They therefore have to devise means of understanding the form and operating within the constraints of the existing urban tissue – another reason for an interest in typological and morphological analysis.

Morphology and British practice

In the last twenty-five years British architects, in common with their colleagues elsewhere, have reacted against the tenets of CIAM and have returned to historical models as a source of ideas. One can interpret the work of such 'Team Ten' members as Peter and Alison Smithson in these terms. In 'Upper Case 3' (Crosby, undated) they describe projects including the Golden Lane (1952) and Berlin (1958) as searching for patterns of association and identity by reinterpreting the traditional elements of house, street and district. The consequences of this approach proved no less disastrous than the results of following the Charter of Athens, with the concept of 'streets in the air' producing such notorious estates of gallery-access flats as Park Hill, Sheffield or Broadwater Farm, Haringey where, to quote Hillier, 'the environments of the future now appear without a future' (Choay and Merlin 1986: 89).

More recent attempts to use the past have looked more closely at ancient towns. These towns, which are so admired today, are not the result of the presence of isolated significant monuments but depend on a continuity of scale and codes used by their developers and, on the other hand, a variety resulting from the craft building process. If we study the tissues of these towns perhaps we can evolve a similar set of rules so that a proposal can 'be teased out of the existing grain as if it were already there' (Walker 1984: 49). 'History is thus massaged a little, in order to yield a context of sufficient intensity and authority for the scale of work in hand' (Maitland 1984: 5). It is, however, a mystical process which never gets down to the hard, time-consuming task of a true morphological analysis – and one can understand how the attitude might seem less than serious to a historical geographer.

A major criticism can thus be levelled against the Anglo-Saxon Contextualist School (one of its most important exponents, Rowe, writes in the United States) in that it ignores the link between social and economic change and built form which is so important for the Italians in their theoretical work. This enables a critic like Krier (who has built very little) to propose the rebuilding of the city with streets, squares and blocks on a nineteenth-century pattern. It does not seem to worry Krier, in spite of his severely anti-capitalist views, that he adopts as a model the city of class exploitation *par excellence.*

The increased interest in traditional forms could also be due to rather more mundane economic realities. In the current climate, who is going to maintain the open, free-flowing parkland that surrounds the blocks of the Ville Radieuse? Much more sensible to reduce the amount of space that must be maintained at public expense and return to a city based on perimeter blocks, with private space located behind buildings where it cannot be seen. The fact that architects are once again recognizing the value of the past is to be welcomed since we are bound up with past experiences, and architects 'cannot innovate at the social level and only marginally at the technical level – but – within certain limits – at a formal level' (Choay and Merlin 1986: 125). If the past (and it starts with projects constructed last year) can be studied in a dispassionate and thorough way then perhaps we can avoid having to constantly reinvent the wheel.

Hayward (1987: 2–4) has described the use of urban tissues derived from Habraken's (1982) work as a way of exploring housing design solutions and investigating the way that factors such as car parking (the major problem in adapting traditional forms to current requirements), market needs and planning regulations can modify forms. This method does require detailed design work – it is not a question of looking for broad underlying principles – yet it does not require the slavish adoption of forms which may be socially or economically obsolete. Any method must be capable of responding to the different actors in the development process. The designer is only one, and at his most effective can only hope to act as medium between all the private and public interests inevitably concerned with even the simplest development.

Conclusion

If architects seem to use morphological terms loosely, without precision, then geographers must be tolerant. It is one of the attractions of the nexus of concepts, ideas and approaches that occupy the field of urban morphology that they are capable of being appropriated for use by different professions in different contexts who seek to use them for their own purpose. Choay and Merlin (1986), having invited twelve professionals from three countries and different disciplines to respond to a questionnaire on urban morphology (Samuels 1985), complain about this. Everyone seemed to be discussing something different and there was very little common ground or methodological base, quite apart from language problems. This, however, is one of the strengths of morphology. It is open to approach by various disciplines with their own methods and any attempt to restrict or strait-jacket the discourse could stifle it.

More disturbing are the very real language barriers. Not one of the four Italian experts contributing to the Choay and Merlin work seems to be aware of the German school of geographers. Although they do acknowledge some debt to French geographers it is very grudging, for only one of them quotes a foreign reference. The Americans are no better, with only one of three quoting a non-English reference. So that, seen from the other side, if Italy exercises 'a verbal hegemony in concerns of morphology' (Choay and Merlin: 113), can Anglo-Saxon geographers completely ignore that body of work? Aldo Rossi emerges from the study as the most widely quoted authority (there were no geographers among the respondents!), yet his first influential book took sixteen years between Italian and English publication.

Architects cannot, by virtue of their profession, be concerned solely with an elegant explanation – they must go on to make proposals even it they seem to study urban form with a lack of rigour and with apparent preconception. These 'character defects' must be accepted by geographers if we are to begin to bridge the gap between cognitive and normative activities.

The renewed concern with the past should be seen as a positive movement in the architect's professional awareness. As its intentions have shifted, the value of the inherited context has become recognised. The test of a building's success is no longer its capacity to fulfil a function or stand out from its neighbours by virtue of its originality. The polemic over Mansion House Square, London, with the proposal for a Mies van der Rohe block, shows that the ability of a building to contribute to the quality of its context is now important. So, the study of this context now becomes an acceptable activity. On the other hand, in some Italian work (Meneghetti 1987: Dal Co 1980) there often seems to be no link between analysis and proposal. There is therefore a suspicion that morphological analysis becomes a sort of ritual which, having been performed, discharges the architect's obligations to the past so that he can get on with the real business of design. Let Aldo Rossi, the most often-cited authority in Choay and Merlin have the last word:

> The study of the city is an important part in formation and practice of an architect but generally it cannot be a goal in itself . . . To think that typomorphological studies represent the main vehicle of architecture could be another way of narrowing down the freedom of training for the young architect . . . Teaching must help this training, or at least not hinder it by continually creating new myths, as functionalism did or as typomorphological analysis runs the risk of doing. (Rossi 1985: 100)

Acknowledgements

This case study was made possible by a fellowship from the Gladys Krieble Delmas foundation and the generous help of the *Assessorato all' Urbanistica* of Venice, in particular Arch. Edgarda Feletti.

References

Aymonino, C., 1970. *La cittá di Padova* (Rome).

Baculo, A. G., 1975. *Centri storici e progettazione* (Naples).

Cannigia, G., 1963. *Lettura di una cittá: Como* (Rome).

Cannigia, G., 1979. Dialettica tra tipo e tessuto, Paper given at the Academie de France, Rome.

Cataldi, G., 1984. *Saverio Muratori* (Florence).

Cervellati, R., Scannavini, P. and De Angelis, C., 1977. *La nuova cultura della cittá* (Milan).

Choay, F. and Merlin, P., 1986. *A propos de la morphologie urbaine.* (Noisy-le-Grand).

Ciardini, F. and Falini, P., 1981. *L'analisi dei centri storici* (Rome).

Comune di Venezia, 1979. *I piani di coordinamento di Campo Ruga, Seco Marina, Palude S. Antonio* (Venice).

Comune di Venezia, 1980. *P.P. Cannaregio Nord, Calle Caliari.*

Consiglio Comunale di Venezia, 1983. Minutes of Meeting 27 May.

Crosby, T., ed. (undated). *Uppercase 3.*

Cullen, G., 1961. *Townscape.*

Dal Co, F., 1980. *10 immagini per Venezia.* (Rome).

Habraken, J., 1982. *Transformations of the site* (Cambridge).

Hayward, R., 1987. 'The use of housing tissues in urban design', *Urban Design Quarterly*, 25, December: 2–4.

Maitland, B., 1984. 'The Uses of History', in Gosling and Maitland, *Urbanism.*

Meneghetti, L., 1987, *Quaderni 4*, (Milan).

Muratori, S., 1959. *Studi per uma operante storia urbana di Venezia.* (Rome).

Regione del Veneto, 1980. Deliberazioni della Giunta Regionale, 11 July 1980, Venice.

Rossi, A., 1985. 'Dieci opinioni sul tipo', *Casabella*: 509–10: 100–1.

Salotti, G. D. and Dell'Acqua, A., 1981. *Centri storici: analisi e progetto per il riuso. Verifica sul tessuto urbano di Vercelli* (Milan).

Samuels, I., 1983. 'Towards an architectural analysis of urban form: conservation studies in Britain and Italy', Research Note 14, Joint Centre for Urban Design, Oxford Polytechnic.

Samuels, I., 1985. 'Urban morphology in design', Research Note 19, Joint Centre for Urban Design, Oxford Polytechnic.

Venturi, R., 1966. *Complexity and Contradiction in Architecture* (New York).

Walker, D., 1984. 'Docklands, Rotterdam', in Gosling and Maitland, *Urbanism.*

Index

*Numbers in italic refer to figures